A MALDIVIAN DICTIONARY

The Maldive archipelago, a long string of small islands south-west of Sri Lanka in the Indian Ocean, has been settled and independently ruled for at least twelve centuries. The Maldivian language, also known as Divehi, is closely related to the Sinhalese language, but few scholars had studied it until the time of H.C.P. Bell (1851–1937) and Wilhelm Geiger (1856–1943).

Since the Maldive Islands were opened to tourism in 1972, tourist booklets have given some account of the language, but no dictionary has hitherto appeared and this publication is the first specifically Maldivian–English dictionary.

The language has its own script, known as *taana* and written from right to left. Although a system of transliteration is employed in this dictionary, the headwords are also given in their *taana* form.

Christopher Reynolds received his BA degree in 1948 from Oxford University. He was Lecturer in Sinhalese at the School of Oriental and African Studies, University of London, between 1953–87. After spending four months in the capital city of Male in 1967, he made a special study of the Maldivian language (Divehi), before the country was open to foreigners.

A MALDIVIAN DICTIONARY

Christopher Reynolds

RoutledgeCurzon
Taylor & Francis Group
LONDON AND NEW YORK

First published 2003
by RoutledgeCurzon
11 New Fetter Lane, London EC4P 4EE

Simultaneously published in the USA and Canada
by RoutledgeCurzon
29 West 35th Street, New York, NY 10001

RoutledgeCurzon is an imprint of the Taylor & Francis Group

Printed and bound in Great Britain by
TJ International Ltd, Padstow, Cornwall

British Library Cataloguing in Publication Data
A catalogue record for this book is available from the British Library

Library of Congress Cataloging in Publication Data
Reynolds, C. H. B. (Christopher Hanby Baillie)
A Maldivian dictionary/Christopher Reynolds.
p. cm.
1. Divehi language–Dictionaries–English. I. Title.

PK1836.4 .R49 2003
491.4′8–dc21
2002036790

ISBN 0–415–29808–3

INTRODUCTION

This dictionary is based on a vocabulary compiled during a four-month visit to Male in 1967. There were at that time three existing dictionaries: 1) An Arabic–Maldivian and Maldivian–Arabic dictionary (al-īqāẕ fī ta'līm al-alfāẕ and t'āsis al-adīb al-ẖurūf al-muhmal) by Musa Malim Kalegefanu, printed by Sitar-i-Hind Press, Calcutta, 1357H; 2) A compilation by the Maldivian Ministry of Education made in the time of the late President Amin Didi, of which parts 1–6 were published in 1378H, entitled *Divehi Bas Fot* (i.e. Maldivian Dictionary); 3) *Ran Tari* (i.e. Golden Star), by Malim Musa Kalegefanu, 1377H, which specifically excludes words of more than four 'letters' and gives examples of the uses of the words rather than definitions. The latter two are Maldivian–Maldivian, and produced in the Maldive Islands. Since then, the *Divehi Bas Fot* has been taken over by the National Council for Linguistic and Historical Research in Male and was completed in 1991 in sixteen parts.

Transliteration

Maldivian (Divehi) is an Indo-Iranian language, closely related to Sinhalese (although nowadays it uses a different script). This dictionary is therefore arranged according to the Indian order of letters, with necessary modifications, namely:

a ā i ī u ū e ē o ō
k g c j ñ ṭ ḍ t d n f p b m
y r l v s z h ř ḷ

There are no aspirated consonants in Maldivian, and final -**ṅ** (velar nasal) is not distinguished from -**n**. The Maldivian order is quite different, namely: H Ř N R B Ḷ K *alif* V M F D T L G Ñ S Ḍ Z Ṭ Y P J C (the order of the last six is variable). Maldivian dictionaries arrange their words in an Arabic order, i.e. according to the consonants without distinction of vowels, and include all initial vowels under *alif*. In this dictionary the transliteration uses the following system:

1 Long vowels are indicated by writing the vowel twice.
2 Retroflex ṭ and ḍ are written in the traditional manner with subscript dots (though I believe the system used by J.R. Firth in A.H. Harley, *Colloquial Hindustani* (London, 1944), with long tails for the retroflex consonants, would in that respect have been preferable had it been available).

3 In the alphabetical order, **c** and **j** are kept in their Indian place (although the great majority of words with initial **c** or **j** are loans). **ñ** is only distinguished from **n** when it is doubled (as in **kanñek**), and in the very few Maldivian words which begin with this letter.
4 The 'half-nasal' which Maldivian shares with Sinhalese is written as **n̆**; this half-nasal was formerly always omitted in Maldivian script, though nowadays it is usually inserted (usage appears to vary here) and accordingly **n̆g** is listed to follow **g**, **n̆ḍ** to follow **ḍ**, **n̆b** to follow **b**.
5 **f** is given in the place of Indian **p**, since it is in fact a relatively recent development under Arabic influence of the **p**-sound which still remained in Pyrard's day (1607). In modern Maldivian, **-p-** only occurs when doubled, i.e. **-pp-** instead of **-ff-** or **-tf-**. Initial **p-**, which occurs in a very few loan-words, is listed after **f**.
6 **ř**, though it usually represents Indian (non-initial) **ṭ**, and becomes **-ṭṭ-** when doubled, is here placed after **h**. (It is realized as an affricate.) The use of **sh** for the letter traditionally given as **ř** has been suggested in other publications, but we would prefer to retain **ř**.
7 **l** and **ḷ** are differentiated in pronunciation, but **ṇ**, which formerly had a separate symbol in the script, is no longer distinguished from **n** either in script or in speech. Here **ḷ** is placed after **ř**.
8 **ś**, though it can be distinguished from **s** in Maldivian script, is not usually so marked, and is not separated from **s** here. **z** is placed after **s**.

An official scheme of transliteration from the Divehi language was adopted by the Maldive government in the 1970s, but it suffers from certain drawbacks, notably the treatment of long vowels where, though **ā** appears as **aa**, **ē**, **ī**, **ō** and **ū** are represented by **ey**, **ee**, **oa** and **oo** respectively. Such a system obviously makes sense only against a background of English and of English spelling, and not always then (**oa** being particularly ambiguous). For retroflex and dental stops, the system adopted was that which is sometimes used in Sri Lanka of using **th** and **dh** for the dental letters (there being no aspirated consonants in Sinhalese or Maldivian), and on the other hand using **lh** for retroflex **ḷ**.

Final consonants are written here in a manner which deviates from Maldivian usage, where only *alif*, **s**, **n**, **t** and **ř** are allowed in final position.

1 A final **-n**, if it becomes **-m-** before a case-ending, is written as **-m** (this follows the system used in Sinhalese). Thus we write **ran** (gen. **ranuge**), 'gold', but **ḷem** (gen. **ḷemuge**), 'poetry', though in Maldivian script the latter is written **ḷen**.
2 A final *alif*, if it becomes **-k-** before a case-ending, is written as **-k**. (This again corresponds with Sinhalese pronunciation and usage.) Thus we write **buk** (gen. **bukuge**), 'breast', rather than ***buh*** which is the official transliteration. We have also followed this pattern in compound words such as **uk-dan̆ḍi**, **ek-bas**.
3 In Maldivian script the *alif* is sometimes also still used for final **-ř**, which usually has the same (glottal or nasal) realization. Here we keep **-ř**, and write **vař** (gen. **vařuge**), 'circle'.

The *alif* is also used in Maldivian script to indicate the first member of a doubled consonant (except **n**, which must be written twice). **-řC-** also sounds as a doubled consonant. Thus in **raajje**, 'country', the first **j** is written as *alif-sukun* in Maldivian script. We have preferred to transliterate as **raajje**, but a difficulty arises with **-tt-**. In Maldivian, a final written **-t** is pronounced **-y***, and this also applies where **t** is written before another consonant, e.g. **hattari** (as written), 'seventy', is pronounced **hayttari** (with doubled **-tt-**). On the other hand, a normal double t-sound also occurs intervocalically, and is written, according to rule,with an *alif-sukun*, e.g., **vattaru**, 'species'. Therefore, since we write the former as **hattari**, in words such as **va<u>tt</u>aru** we have underlined the **-<u>tt</u>-**.

4 Maldivian words ending in final **-n** may or may not be written with a final **-u (ain/ainu)**, **u** being the final vowel which is lost in declension (as against the Sinhalese final **-a**. Maldivian final **-a** is retained in declension). The same will apply to loanwords ending in other consonants, e.g., **rool/roolu**, 'roll'.

Script

Maldivian was formerly written in a script resembling Sinhalese script, but after the islands became exclusively Islamic it was found convenient to design a script reading from right to left, so that Arabic words could be accommodated in Divehi sentences. This script, known as *taana*, has been exclusively used for the last two centuries or so. It is as follows:

އަ **a** އާ **ā** އި **i** އީ **ī** އު **u** އޫ **ū** އެ **e** އޭ **ē** އޮ **o** އޯ **ō**

ކ **k** ގ **g** ޗ **c** ޖ **j** ޏ **ñ** ޓ **ṭ** ޑ **ḍ** ތ **t** ދ **d** ނ **n** ފ **f** ޕ **p** ބ **b** މ **m**

ޔ **y** ރ **r** ލ **l** ވ **v** ސ **s** (ށ **ś**) ޒ **z** ހ **h** ޜ **ř** ޅ **ḷ**

Vowel strokes (*fili*) are added as in the first line above (ކަ **ka** ކާ **kā** ކި **ki** ކީ **kī**, etc.) The sukun ް is used where no vowel follows, e.g., ކް **k**. The half-nasal or *hus nuunu* is written as **n** without any *fili* (އަނޑަ, **aňda**), and the same system may be used to transliterate the English soundless **r** (ރަބަރ, **rabar** = 'rubber').

Arabic loanwords are now increasingly being written in modified Maldivian script (*taana*), and a certain number of them are included here. Many such words, however – and they are very numerous – have traditionally been written in Arabic script amidst the *taana* (which fortunately reads in the same direction, right to left). The decision on which such words should be included here has been individualistic. Words which do not appear in the listing may appear in illustrative examples. Some Arabic sounds are used in speech by educated Maldivians, in particular **<u>kh</u>** in certain words such as **<u>kh</u>abar**. In such cases, **<u>kh</u>** is listed as a variety of **h**.

For the Divehi (*taana*) script I have used a font obtained from Ecological Linguistics in Washington, D.C. (in which the form of the letter **L (laamu)** is not entirely satisfactory, and the larger sizes of character are not very clear). Each headword is written also in *taana*, but the rest of the data is in transliteration. This dictionary will therefore be primarily of use to westerners who wish to study the Maldivian language. Though it is not very likely to be of actual use to Maldivians themselves, I hope that they may find it of interest, and that they will assist by reporting back on anything which seems erroneous; there are bound to be errors and omissions. I understand that Simon Fuller has compiled both a Maldivian–English and an English–Maldivian dictionary, but they are said to be still in manuscript, so that I have not been able to profit by them.

Verbs

Maldivians list their own verbs in the form of a verbal noun, e.g. **hedum**, 'making'. However, as these verbal nouns may involve 'umlaut' vowels, they do not in themselves make clear what the root vowel is, namely in the quoted case,whether it is **had-** or **hed-**. (Verbs with roots containing **-o-** and **-u-** are not subject to umlaut in Maldivian, though they are in Sinhalese.) We have therefore listed the quoted verb as **hadanii**, and all other verbs in a similar form, this being a form which approximately corresponds to the Sinhalese forms in **-navaa** under which Sinhalese verbs are often listed. (Some of these Maldivian forms in **-nii** will be used only in restricted contexts.) Where necessary, the verbal noun is added in brackets.

The Divehi language still possesses a large number of honorific forms, both of nouns and of verbs. These are used according to the rank of the person being addressed or spoken about (they are not used of oneself). Many verbal forms are therefore listed here with their honorific forms. Irregular forms of the past participle and of the absolutive are also listed, together with certain forms of the present indicative and imperative. Verbs are also compounded with forms of **lanii** (**lum**, basically 'putting'), especially as a politeness; such verbal forms when quoted here are described as 'enlarged'. Some very high honorific words appear to have developed without reference to any apparent original meaning (**avahaara**, **ituru**, **kiirti**).

Nouns

Nominal inflexion involves several regular changes (apart from the matter of the final consonant mentioned above). The following exemplify the indefinite ending **-ek**.

1 **-kiV-** becomes **-tkV-** (**boki**, **botkek**, 'lamp')
or **-kkV-** (**heki**, **hekkek**, 'proof')
2 **-giV-** becomes **-tgV-** (**agi**, **atgek**, 'weight of shells')
3 **-ňgiV-** becomes **-tňgV-** or **-ngV-** (**kuraňgi**, **kuratňgek**, **kurangek**, 'kind of bird')
4 **-tiV-** becomes **-ccV-** (**mati**, **maccek**, 'top')
5 **-diV-** becomes **-jjV-** (**kudi**, **kujjek**, 'child')
6 **-ňdiV-** becomes **-njV-** (**haňdi**, **hanjek**, 'trowel')
7 **-niV-** becomes **-ññV-** (**duuni**, **duunñek**, 'bird')
8 **-fiV-** becomes **-tpV-** (**gofi**, **gotpek**, 'branch')
9 **-biV-** becomes **-tbV-** (**obi**, **otbek**, 'oilpress')
10 **-ňbiV-** becomes **-tňbV-** or **-nbV-** (**aňbi**, **atňbek**, **anbek**, 'wife')
11 **-liV-** becomes **-yyV-** (**ali**, **ayyek**, 'light')
12 **-viV-** becomes **-tvV-** (**avi**, **atvek**, 'sunshine')
or **-vvV-** (**revi**, **revvek**, 'mustard seed')
13 **-sV-** becomes **-hV-** (**gas**, **gahek**, 'tree')
14 **-hiV-** becomes **-ssV-** (**Divehi**, **Divessek**, 'Maldivian')
15 **-řiV-** becomes **-ṭṭV-** (**foři**, **foṭṭek**, 'box' – alternative spelling, **fořṭek**)
(The internal **-tC-** in all such cases involves a pronounced **-yCC-**, as explained above, e.g., **atvek** sounds as **ayvve***, **otbek** as **oybbe***.)
16 Many nouns ending in **-aa** (formerly written **-au**) have stems in either **-al** or **-aal** (**hiyaa** or **hiyau**, **hiyalek**, 'shade'; **haa** or **hau**, **haalek**, 'cock')
17 Nouns ending in **-uu**, **-oo** and **-eu** or **-eyo** also have **l**-stems (**muu**, **mulek**, 'root'; **boo**, **bolek**, 'head'; **teu** or **teyo**, **telek**, 'oil'; **kanneyo**, **kanneelek**, 'pillow')
18 Nouns ending in **-aa** where the alternative spelling is with **-ai** do not have **l**-stems (**guraa** or **gurai**, **guraek**, 'parrot')

19 The euphonic final vowel, which is lost in inflection, is **-u** (as in Arabic), and not **-a** (as in Sinhalese): **bañḍu, bañḍek**, 'tummy', but **bada, badaek**, 'knuckle'
20 The changes under 13 and 16 above are applied also to European loanwords: **klaas, klaahek**, 'class'; **hoṭaa, hoṭalek**, 'hotel'.

Alternation between **-aa** and **-ai** is normal in regularly formed absolutives: **hadaa** or **hadai**, 'having made'. The orthography of Maldivian is not yet fixed. Besides the **aa/au** and **aa/ai** alternatives already mentioned, vocalization is variable in many cases, e.g., **dena/dene, heyo/heu, bee/bei, roo/roi**, as are some occurrences of the half-nasal. Transcriptions of foreign words may also give rise to differences of spelling, especially in the use of **-u-** or *sukun* (**tarjamaa/tarujamaa**) in Urdu-based words and of vowels in English loanwords (**krikaṭ/krikeṭ/kirikeṭ**). In oblique plural cases of nouns and pronouns **-n-** is usually doubled, but may also be written singly (**dariinnař/dariinař**). Intervocalic **-y-** is optional after **-i-** in Maldivian script, e.g., **kiyum** and **kium** are both found.

The recent completion of the *Divehi Bas Fot* referred to above will enable much further linguistic research to be done on this little-known language. But in the absence of any other published Maldivian–English dictionary (apart from brief wordlists given in some tourist guides due to the sudden opening up of the Maldives to tourism in 1972), it seems desirable to issue the present work as a 'First Maldivian–English Dictionary'. Maldivian (Divehi) is by origin closely connected to Sinhalese (Sinhala), with a large number of Urdu or Persian loanwords. Etymological references are therefore given to Sinhalese (together with Sanskrit equivalents) or to Urdu-Hindi, and occasionally to other languages. References to 'Turner' refer to the dictionary mentioned in the next paragraph. References to 'Geiger' refer to *An Etymological Glossary of the Sinhalese Language*, by W. Geiger, Royal Asiatic Society, Ceylon branch, Colombo, 1941. References to 'Helmer Smith' refer to 'Wilhelm Geiger et le vocabulaire du singalais classique' in *Journal Asiatique* ccxxxviii, 1950, pp. 177–223.

Sources

Since the original basis of this dictionary was *Ran Tari*, produced in 1957, a number of the entries refer to practices which are now outdated. The Maldives were opened to the outside world in 1972, and changes since then have been great. Nevertheless it would clearly be wrong to omit all words which have become outmoded – these are largely to do with religion, with royalty (the last King was deposed in 1968) or with sailing vessels – especially as many works written by the late Muhammad Amin Didi (1910–1954) are still likely to be read. But words which appear in *Ran Tari* have been omitted if my Maldivian advisers no longer recognize them. The vocabulary of *Ran Tari* has been supplemented from a) some literary works of the late Muhammad Amin Didi; b) newspapers, mostly of the 1970s; c) collections of ephemeral popular dramas of the same period; d) the literary periodical *Fattaru*. The language attested is the standard Maldivian, as spoken in the capital, Male; the language of the southern atolls, which is appreciably different, is not covered.

For a linguistic description of the Divehi language, see B.D. Cain and J.W. Gair: *Dhivehi (Maldivian)*, Lincom Europa, Munich, 2000. Though an excellent scholarly work, it is written in technical 'linguistic' language, which reduces its value to the ordinary student. The language has traditionally been referred to as Maldivian, and appears as such in R.L. Turner's *Comparative Dictionary of the Indo-Aryan Languages* (OUP, 1962–1985), and also in the works of H.C.P. Bell (1851–1937), to whom outside knowledge of the Maldives and their language was primarily due in the twentieth century. The Maldivian name for their own language is *Divehi bas*, and since the opening up of the Maldives to the general world in 1972 this name, usually written as 'Dhivehi', has been increasingly used. Since in English it is normal to refer to foreign languages in a familiar form such as 'Chinese', 'Japanese', 'Arabic', 'Russian', it has seemed preferable to retain the name 'Maldivian', which makes the geographical reference clear to those who might otherwise well be perplexed.

ACKNOWLEDGEMENTS

I offer my sincere thanks to my colleague David Matthews for checking Urdu references, and to Norman Robson of the Natural History Museum, London, and Professor R.N. de Fonseka of Colombo for assistance with botanical names. For names of fishes, I am greatly indebted to Mr Jaudullah Jameel of the Ministry of Fisheries and Agriculture in Male for their magnificently produced book *Fishes of the Maldives* (1997).

For the bulk of the dictionary my primary and unbounded thanks are due to Mr Mohamed Shareef of Male, who helped me to lay the foundations of the work during 1971–1974. I also express my grateful thanks to the many others who have assisted me during the intervening period, especially the late Dr Mohamed Jameel, Mrs Abida Ford, Mr M. Fahumy, Ms Annagrethe Ottovar, Mrs Naseema Mohamed Kalefaanu, Mr Hassan Ahmed Maniku, Mr A. Atif, Mr Shaheen Hameed, Mr Hassan Shaafeu, Mr Mohamed Latheef, Ms Aishath Khaleel and the Japan Overseas Corporation Volunteers office in Male.

Furthermore, I must acknowledge with sincere gratitude the generous financial help offered by the School of Oriental and African Studies, University of London, towards the publication of this dictionary.

Christopher Reynolds
Westerham, February 2001

Since writing the above I have received a copy of *A Concise Etymological Vocabulary of Dhivehi Language*, by Hassan Ahmed Maniku, published by the Royal Asiatic Society of Sri Lanka, Colombo 2000, issued in summer 2001. This is a substantial work of 261 pages, and I have pleasure in acknowledging assistance received from it.

Of those named in the preceding paragraph, I must now sadly record the deaths of Mr Hassan Ahmed Maniku and Mrs Abida Ford.

C.H.B.R.
April 2002

ABBREVIATIONS

A.	Arabic
abl.	ablative
abs.	absolutive
adj.	adjective
adv.	adverb
anc.	ancient
caus.	causative
cf.	compare
coll.	colloquial
conj.	conjunction
D.	Dutch
dat.	dative
dim.	diminutive
E.	English
esp.	especially
excl.	exclamation
f.	feminine
gen.	genitive
Gk.	Greek
gram.	grammatical
H.	Hindi
hon.	honorific
ibc.	as first member of a compound
ifc.	as final member of a compound
imp.	imperative
incompl.	incomplete
indef.	indefinite
inf.	infinitive
instr.	instrumental
interrog.	interrogative
intr.	intransitive
invol.	involitive
lit.	literally
lit.	literary
loc.	locative
m.	masculine
math.	mathematical
med.	medical
met.	metaphorical
mod.	modern
n.	noun
naut.	nautical
neg.	negative
num.	numeral
obs.	obsolete
onom.	onomatopoeic
P.	Pali
part.	participle
pej.	pejorative
pl.	plural
poet.	poetical
Port.	Portuguese
postp.	postposition
p.p.	past participle
pr.	pronoun
pres.	present
pron.	pronounce
prov.	proverb
q.v.	which see
resp.	respectful
s.	singular
S.	Sinhalese
sc.	understand
Skt.	Sanskrit
s.v.	under the word
T.	Tamil
tr.	transitive
U.	Urdu
usu.	usually
v.	verb
v.n.	verbal noun
voc.	vocative
vulg.	vulgar

بسم الله الرحمن الرحيم

އ ALIFU, the eighth letter of the Maldivian alphabet

Alifu atoḷu, Ari atoll, the eighth atoll from the north; in atoll numeration, alifu also stands for uturu, north: Haa Alifu, H atoll North (N. Tiladunmati).
This letter covers all words beginning with a vowel

1 AI އައި v. come (p.p. of annanii 1 : in sandhi, a-eve, a-ee, aya-tiive; incompl. aii) [S. ā, Skt. āgata]

2 AIN (AINU) އައިން (އައިނު) n.. 1. shoal of fish:
ainu fennan vaane keoḷaře̋e, the captain must see the shoal first (prov.); dahi ainu, a surfacing shoal: ainmatii gaaduuni, seagull on the shoal : ainu-miyaru, ainmatii miyaru, a kind of shark, carcharhinus falciformis [S. ainu]
2. See aim

3 AINI އައިނި See aani

4 AINU އައިނު n . 1. spectacles [U. ‘ain, eye; ‘ainak, ā’īna, spectacles]
2. See ain 1
3. For aanu, q.v.

5 AIBU އައިބު n . deformity; deformed, ugly : aibu miihek, an ugly man :
aibu-kam, perversion; criticism; critical: aibu kiyanii, makes personal remarks: aibu bas kiyanii, makes critical remarks [U. ‘aib]

6 AIM (AIMU) އައިމް (އައިމު) v. came (past tense of annanii 1): aim, I came: aimu, we came; Also 2nd p. interrogative, aim(u) ta? aimek nu? did you come?

7 AIS 1. (AAS) އައިސް (އާސް) v. having come (abs. of annanii 1): aḷugaňḍu mihirii aiheve, here I am. Enlargements: aisgen, aisfai, aissaa: ais-lii, enlargement of aii [cf. S. ävit, Pkt. āgacca or āvijjha]

8 AIS 2. އައިސް n . ice: ais alamaari, refrigerator : ais tarumoozu, thermos of ice [E.ice]

9 AISA އައިސަ n. Maldivian form for the name ‘Aiśaa: Aisaidi, for Aisha Diidii

10 AU އައު See aa

11 AUDA އައުދަ adj. mighty (title of kings) [for audaana]

12 AUDAANA އައުދާނަ adj. mighty (title of kings) [Skt. avadāna]

13 AUDE-EVE އައުދެއެވެ v. Old spelling for aadee, comes

14 AUNSU އައުންސު n. ounce [E. ounce]

15 AUM އައުން v. coming (v.n. of annanii 1.) [cf.S. ēm, īm]

16 AKA އަކަ n. crisscross pattern used for charms (often bad, as v. ana): aka kurahanii, aka jahanii, draws charm: rizquge akaek, a charm for getting wealth: ibc., square (geom.); aka fuuṭu, square foot: aka min, area measurement [Skt. aṃka]

17 AKAYAŇBOO (-ek) އަކަޔަނބޫ n. a. hadanii, boasts:
akayaňboo yamakuvaa mavaa moḷiimee (or doniimee) (children's rhyme, said to boasters)

18 -AKAS -އަކަސް suffix although... (see also -as) : eakas, though that be so: konmeakas, anyway

19 AKIRI އަކިރި n. small broken coral (from muraka : used for flooring, also burnt for lime): a. endum, burning coral for lime [S. akuru, Skt. śarkarā]

20 -AKII -އަކީ emphatic nominal suffix : e taalibunnakii, those pupils... ; vakkam kuriikii ahannek nuun, it is not I who was the thief

21 -AKU -އަކު suffix even, also: hama denmeaku, just now; see also kam(aku). Also in negative sentences: iiyeaku for iiye , maadama-aku for maadam

22 AKUḌI އަކުޑި n. competence: akuḍi nufilaa miihun, incompetent people

23 AKUNI-VAI އަކުނިވައި n. cramp: aḷugaňḍu akuniva-ař damaagenfi, I have got cramp: fai akuniva-ař damaagenfi, (my) leg has got cramp [S. akuṇu-vā, 'lightning rheumatics', U. akařbāī]

24 AKURU އަކުރު n. letter of the alphabet: Dives akuru, obsolete script formerly used in Maldives: hisaabu akuru, figure, numeral;
a. aḷanii, inscribes letters: a. damanii, prolongs letters [S. akuru , Skt. akṣara]

25 AGAḌU-BAGAḌU އަގަޑުބަގަޑު n. mixing up, jumbling up: a. kuranii, jumbles up [H. agař-bagař]

26 AGALU އަގަލު n. kindness (always with neg.): agalek kulunek nuhunna, unkind: agalu kuḍa, bullying (adj.)

27 AGI (atgek) އަގި n. a measure of five shells

28 AGINÑA އަގިންޏަ n. south- east [Skt. agni-, agnya]

29 AGIIDU އަގީދު n. a red-coloured precious stone; agate [U. ‘aqīq, cornelian]

30 AGU އަގު n. price; charges:

agu boḍu, expensive: agu huri,valuable: agu heyo, cheap: agu maat, majestic (of people, things, actions);
a. denii, pays price: a. kuranii, values; agu nukurevee, priceless: a. dař kuranii, a. heyo kuranii, reduces the price: agakaa nulaa, free of charge [S. aga, Skt. argha]

31 AGURABU އަގުރަބު n. name of two compass directions: a. astamaanu, south-west by south; a. iiraan, south-east by east [U. ‘aqrab, Scorpio]

32 AGUḶI އަގުޅި n. stopper at end of bamboo steamer; a. aḷanii, inserts stopper for cooking: circular cloth at end of bolster [S. aguḷu, bolt, Skt. argala]

33 AŇGA އަނގަ n. mouth: miihaage a., mouth of a man; fuḷiige a., mouth of a bottle:

aňgain damaalum, sucking (of babies): a. itaa vanii, is dumbfounded:
a. ori (angoori), facially deformed: angoori kuranii, makes funny faces:
a.-gada (angada) chattery: angada kuranii, gossips:
a.-doři vanii, speaks out of turn:
a.-faaru, sore on the mouth:
aňga-matii, uncovered (adv.): aňgamatiin bahaṭṭanii, leaves uncovered:
aňga maḍu, reticent: aňga maḍu kuraaře, be quiet!
aňga-haddu, beating for blasphemy ;
a. jehenii, only in phrase aňga nujehi kessum, coughing ceaselessly: kessaa varun aňga jehee varek nuunee, cannot keep (his) mouth shut for coughing:
a. taḷanii / taḷuvanii, chatters:
a. baananii, butts in (on, dat.) [? cf.S. aňgāranne, gapes]

34 AŇGUN އަނގުން n. limb (usu. in pl., aňgun-tak): aňguntakun bindaalaafai vaḷulum, breaking off limbs before burial (of Borahs) [cf.S. aňga, body]

35 AŇGUNU އަނގުނު n. projecting piece of wood to fasten the seat-rope of swings, etc.

36 AŇGURU އަނގުރު n. coconut-shell charcoal [S. aňguru, Skt. angāra]

37 AŇGUU (aňgulek) އަނގޫ n. inch (also hinci) [S. aňgal, Skt. angula]

38 AŇGOṬI އަނގޮޓި n. ring, usually containing a gem, worn by men on R.hand, by women on L. [H. angūṭhī, Skt. anguṣṭhya]

39 AŇGOḶI އަނގޮޅި n. junction: hataru a., crossroads [? Skt. samghāṭa]

40 AŇGOORI އަނގޯރި See aňga-ori (s.v. aňga)

41 ACCI އައްޗި n. acci lanii, defecates (used to children: hon., acci-koḷu laigen); acci kuranii, is naughty (of children): acci kor uḷum, naughty behaviour

42 ACCII އައްޗީ excl.. of disgust

43 AJALU އަޖަލު n. fate: magee ajalugai huri gotek, my destiny; aharenge ajalu jehunii, that's the end of me [U. ajal]

44 AJAABU(AJAIBU) އަޖާބު (އަޖައިބު) n. wonder: a. vanii, marvels (ekamaa deeteree / e fenifai, at that) [U.'ajāib]

45 AJUMA އަޖުމަ n. experiments: kamtakuge ajuma balanii, experiments with things [U. āzmā]

46 AṬṬA-MAS އައްޓަމަސް n. kind of fish, remora

47 AṬṬEK އައްޓެއް See aři

48 AḌAFI-KOḶU އަޑަފިކޮޅު n. chew of betel (hon.): aḍafikoḷu hippavanii, takes a chew (cf. bilet dussavanii)

49 AḌAA(-ek) އަޑާ n. a measure of rice (10 naali): aḍaa-fai, an adaa-sized scoop

50 AḌI އަޑި n. lower part, bottom portion (inside): kaňḍuge aḍi,bottom of the sea; vaḷuge aḍi, bottom of well; ruňbaage aḍi, internal bottom of jar; (met.) hituge aḍi, bottom of one's heart: aḍiyař danii / hiňganii, declines, sinks: aḍi-gaňḍu hoodanii, investigates the cause: aḍi aḷanii, declines (of profits): aḍi vanii, goes down, declines [S. aḍi, T. aṭi, foot]

51 AḌU އަޑު n. noise, sound; rumours: kaaruge aḍu, sound of a car; miihaage aḍu, voice of a person, news of the person; aḍuge veriyaa, vocalist: aḍu-gada, loud noise; kon beekaaru aḍugadaek, what a useless racket; aḍu-gadakuraa, loudspeaker: aḍu-fař(gaňḍu), noise from various sources; aḍufař gada kurum, increasing the noise: aḍu-foři, loudspeaker: tuuli aḍu, shrill voice; fala a., hoarse voice; bun a., bass voice: aḍu aruvanii, publicizes; hama aḍu aruvaalaa, idly boasting: aḍu-ahanii, listens (to): a. aḷanii, records:

a. gada kuranii, is noisy: a. govanii (of inanimates), a. govvanii (of animates), makes a noise: a. kiyanii, makes an unsatisfactory sound (e.g.creaking): a. bedum, losing one's voice; aharen aḍu bedijje, I have lost my voice: a. lanii, scolds (with dat.); mařar a. lanii, scolds me: aḍu-baḍu (doublet), sound: aḍek baḍek nuivi, soundlessly [S. (h)aňḍa]

52 AḌUBAA (AḌUBAI) އަޑުބާ (އަޑުބައި) n. a liquid measure (4 laahi, now 2 bottles) [S. aḍabaya, ? half]

53 AḌḌANA އަޑްޑަނަ n. shield [Skt. aḍḍana (lex.)]

54 AḌḌU ATOḶU އައްޑު އަތޮޅު See under ař-

55 AT އަތް n. hand, arm (hon., atpuḷu): turn (at a game): sleeve:

atun, with the hand; also postpositionally, from: Divehiin atun mas gatum, buying fish from Maldivians: atugai, in the hand, in the possession of; atugai de-ek, (in arithmetic) two to carry: de-atař, in both directions; deat deatař riyaa lanii, changes sail from side to side: ataa(a)taa jahanii, shakes hand; ataa ataa lanii, engages in contest with joined hands to make the opponent bend his wrist ;

at-kam, smithery: atkam kuraa miihaa, smith:

at-gaňḍu, arm of a chair or garment: handle (of drawer or jar):

at-guḷi, stretch of a man's arms (cf. elavaru):

at-tila, palm of hand, hand; attilabaḍi taḷanii, claps hands:

at-teri masakkat, handicraft, embroidery:

at-daňḍi, arm:

at-dařu, 1. near side of anchored ships, atdařu at (as v. geňburu at). Also addařu; 2. ibc. assistant: atdařu (also atdořu) miihek, an assistant; miihekge atdařu vum, being in the power of someone (usu.financially):

at-daani, short scoop (for watering graves):

at-doř, ovencloth, pair of cloths used for carrying hot things; atdoř lanii, puts ovencloth on:

at-bai, (at cards) hand; trick; atbai denii / bahanii, deals cards; atbai naganii, wins more than seven tricks:

at-buri,with short sleeves:

at-mati, possession; possessions; atmaccař arajje, fell into (his) hands; eenaage atmaccař duukořlanii, puts in his charge; atmati avas, quick with the hands; atmati tat, slow with the hands; atmati tanavas, comfortably off; atmati dati, badly off; atmati baraa anhenek,woman with too many children; atmati taraa,tambourine; atmatii fot, handbook:

at ellanii / ukanii, gesticulates: at oḷanii, rolls up sleeves:

at kaňḍanii, inoculates (the arm); kujjaage at kaňḍan vaane, the child must be inoculated:

at gaat kuranii, brings (things) near, to assist (usu. in kitchen or in boatbuilding):

at balanii, practises palmistry :

at-baaru aḷanii, gives help:

at lanii, touches (with -gai), gaigai at nulaa, don't touch me!; puts the hand in (with dat.):

at huuranii,waves;

atu angii, gloves: atu angii lanii, puts on gloves:

atu ura, mittens (for undertakers):

atu kuri (anc., at-kuri), cuff (of women): atukurii gaḍi, wristwatch:

atu masakkat, crafts, esp.carpentry:

atulahi (atulafi), support: atulahi kuranii, gives an arm as support; aharen eenaa atulafi kořgen, I supported myself on him:

atu jehenii, gets into the hands (lit. or met.); vagukaleege atu jehijje, the thief was caught; reelu ataku nujehunu, the train was missed; atu nujehigen uḷenii, is elusive:

atu lanii, captures; eenaa atulaa, catch him!; seizes (from..,..atun / gaatun); dooni atu lanii, salvages a drifting boat ; beats a boat in a race: atu vanii, arrives (atu vejje serves as past tense of aum) [S. at, Skt. hasta]

56 ATA 1. އަތަ n. asterism Hasta [S. hata]

57 ATA 2. އަތަ n. custard apple : Divehi a. (green colour), sweetsop, anona squamosa: vilaatu a. (red colour), anona reticulata; cf. anoonaa [S. ātā, T. attā]

58 ATARU އަތަރު n. scented oil: a. lanii, applies oil [U. ‘a̠tar]

59 ATIRI އަތިރި n. seashore: atiriyař danii, goes to defecate on the beach; enme atiriyař, nearest the shore; Atirii Maafannuge, name of house on, or formerly on, the coast in Male. Also atiri-mati: atirimatii, on the shore: atiri atiri matin, very close to the beach [cf.S. tera, shore, Skt. tīra]

60 ATU އަތު See at

61 ATURANII އަތުރަނީ v. arranges in order (v.n. eturum, see also eturenii) [S. aturanne, Skt. ā (or saṃ) √stṛ]

62 ATOḶU އަތޮޅު n. atoll: atoḷu-ge, official house of the atoll chief: atoḷu-veri, atoll chief

63 A<u>TT</u>AVAA އައްޓަވާ n. clear area round a paddy field

64 A<u>TT</u>AVAAḶI އައްޓަވާޅި n. pit in the game of ‘hat attavaaḷi’ (seven pits): a<u>tt</u>avaaḷi jahanii, scoops out coconut shell

65 A<u>TT</u>AARAFANI (pl., attaarafanin) އައްޓާރަފަނި n. a class of ancient functionaries

66 A<u>TT</u>ELI އައްޓެލި n. spar for adjusting lower part of square sail [S. atväla]

67 ADA އަދަ n. asterism Ārdrā [S. ada]

68 ADADU އަދަދު n. numbers, total numbers, quantity: gina adadekge taketi, large numbers of things: a. jahanii,writes down numbers: a. kuraniii, finds total, does sums [U. ‘adad]

69 ADABU އަދަބު n. 1. respect: a. kuranii, a. bahaṭṭanii, a. vanii (with dat. or -aa medu), respects: adabu-sadabu, manners (doublet): adabek sadabek net, without manners: adabu-verikam, respect; adabuverikam dakkanii, makes show of respect; adabuveri kořu (adv.),with

dignity:

2.punishment, torture: a. dakkanii, a. denii, punishes:
3.bahuge adabu, literature: adabiyyat, literature [U. adab]

70 ADARAN FARU އަދަރަން ފަރު n. name of a reef in H atoll, and of a much loved passenger transport vessel, now superseded

71 ADARAADA GOŇḌI އަދަރާދަ ގޮނޑި n. chair

72 ADAA 1 އަދާ n. completion: a. kuranii, renders, performs (duty), pays (debt) [U. adā]

73 ADAA 2. އަދާ See adu: adaa hama-ař, up till today [adu + -aa]

74 ADI އަދި adv. yet; again; furthermore:

With pres.tense verb of the past : adi ves naade, hasn't come yet: adiek neeňgee, is not yet known; adi aas bala, come back a moment: adi ves, once more: adiek net! no buts! adi aa, still uncommon: adi mi-ii Mee mas viimaa, since it is still only May; eenaage umurun adi vii saaḷiis fas ahareve, he was still only 45

75 ADU އަދު n. today : adun feřigen, from todaay: adaa hama-ař, up to today: adugai, nowadays: adakii..., today is... In mod. speech, usually mi-adu [S. ada, Skt. adya-]

76 ADDAŘU އައްދަރު See atdařu 1

77 ADDEE އައްދޭ excl. of surprise: adde-addee,what's the matter?

78 ADDOO އައްދޫ n. sound indicating pain (also ADDO އައްދޮ): addoo kiyanii, exclaims for pain: addoo govanii, shouts in pain: addoo govvanii, makes (someone) shout in pain [cf.S. ayyoo]

79 ADDOOI, ADDOOT އައްދޫއި - އައްދޫތް (In reported speech, addooyyee)
excl. The actual cry of pain [addoo]

80 AŇDA-GOŇḌI އަނދަގޮނޑި n. the stocks: a. jahanii, puts in the stocks (tr.)

81 AŇDA-VAḶU އަނދަވަޅު n. hidden pit (used for smoking fruit to ripen it)
[S. aňda, blind, Skt. andha]

82 AŇDANII އަނދަނީ v. burns (intr.) (v.n. eňdum, past tense eňdi, enjee): boki aňdaifi, the bulb has gone; see also andanii [S. danne (danavā), P. jhāyati (or saṃdahati)]

83 AŇDIRI އަނދިރި n. 1. darkness, dimness; dark, dim: loo aňdiri, shortsighted: voř a., pitch dark: a. vanii, gets clouded (of spectacles, lampbulbs); gets dark, overshadowed (of water; (met.) of the grave) [S. aňduru, äňdiri, Skt. andhakāra]
2. kind of dragonfly

84 AŇDUN އަނދުން n. kohl: a.- kuuru, lines of kohl: a.- davaadu, kind of ink: a.-hanu, grindstone for kohl; a. aḷanii, applies kohl [S. aňdun, Skt. añjana]

85 AŇDE އަނދެ v. having put on (abs. of annanii 2) [S. äňda]

86 AN 1. އަން excl.. here, take it! [S. anna]

87 AN 2. އަން v. (pron.. atň) put on (p.p. of annanii 2): an-boňḍi, sarong 'pocket'; anboňḍi jahanii, makes pocket

88 ANA އަނަ n. patterns on the ground (for good purposes, as v. aka) [cf. S. aṇa-ira, magic line, Skt. ājñā-]

89 ANA-GAŇḌU އަނަގަނޑު n. crosspiece of fruithook

90 ANARUUFA އަނަރޫފަ adj. thin, unhealthy: a.kujjek, a thin boy: a. bimek, parched earth: a. malek, a wilting flower: a. hitek, low spirits; [?for Skt.avarūpa]

91 ANAA އަނާ n. anna, former Indian coin: hataru a., four annas (quarter- rupee), also used for 25 Maldivian cents or laaris: baara a., 75 cents or laaris [H. ānā]

92 ANIYAA (aniyaaek) އަނިޔާ n. harm, injury: a. kuranii, does harm (to.., dat.): aniyaa-veri, cruel [Skt. anyāya]

93 ANUM އަނުން v. putting on (v.n. of annanii 2) [S. äňdum]

94 ANEK އަނެއް adj. the other (as v. ehen): anekaa / anekaku , the other chap (even if not previously mentioned, cf. coll. E. 'this'); one's neighbour : anekekge nubai vaahaka nudakkaa! don't speak ill of your neighbour: eege anek duvahu, on the following day: maadam nuun anek duvahu, the day after tomorrow [S. anek, cf.Skt. anya]

95 ANEKATI (anekaccek) އަނެކަތި n. the other thing, or animal [anek]

96 ANEKKAA (ANEKKAI) އަނެއްކާ (އަނެއްކައި) adv. again (usually anekkaa ves). Mostly used with past tense verb (cf. adi ves or den): anekkaa ves mi aii fini

duvahekeve, another cold day! anekkaa ves! (a threat) don’t do it again !
moreover,what is more (often with little meaning): anekkaa kaleař aniyaaek vi ta? but are you hurt? eii anekkaa kaaku baa, I wonder who it is <u>now</u> [anek]

97 ANOONAA އަނޫނާ n. soursop, anona muricata, cf. ata 2 [S. anōnā, Port. anona]

98 ANGADA އަނގަދަ See aňga-gada (s.v. aňga)

99 ANGANII (ANGAVANII) އަނގަނީ (އަނގަވަނީ) v. informs: orders (with inf. or dat. of v.n.): announces (that...,....kam) (v.n. engum, engevum, imp. angaa!) : ma atu vejje kam eenaa-ař angai dinum edem, please tell him I’ve come; sarukaaruge engevum-tak, Government orders (caus. of eňgenii) [S. aňgavanne, cf.P. saññāpeti]

100 ANGAARA އަނގާރަ n. Tuesday [S. aňgaharuvā(dā), Skt. angāra-]

101 ANGII އަނގީ n. cotton glove or mitten (for work on coral reef); (atu angii) : angii lanii, puts on gloves

102 ANḌAA-PUUL އަނޑާފޫލު n. a trumpet-shaped scented flower, ipomoea crassicaulis [H.]

103 ANTARIIS އަންތަރީސް n. puzzled: a. vanii, is puzzled; a. kuruvanii, puzzles (tr.)

104 ANDANII އަނދަނީ v. burns away (tr.) (v.n. endum): alifaan naandaaře, don’t have a fire! mee andaee, it burns the breast (of hot curries): ranakun endum, burning off blood poisoning with heated gold thread [S. davanne, cf. aňdanii]

105 ANDAAZAA އަންދާޒާ n. estimate: a. kuranii, estimates: andaazaa-akař, at a guess [U. andāza]

106 ANNANII 1. އަންނަނީ v. comes (v.n. aum: p.p. ai : abs.ais : imp. and 3s., aadee); the basic word, of which the honorifics are duruvanii and vaḍaigannavanii, q.v. See also atu vejje and aadevenii.
Maale ais, having come to Male: (met.) veriyakař ais hurii, had become leader; pres. part. anna, about to come: anna aharu, next year : anna-nivi, consequent [S. enne, P. ēti]

107 ANNANII 2. އަންނަނީ v. puts on clothing (v.n. anum : p.p. at : abs. aňde : hon. annavanii , high hon., aňde vaḍaigannavanii): anna eti, women’s garments : anna foti, men’s garments: anna fořaa, garment for Hajj: anna-unu, clothing; naaňdeveene, will not be wearable (invol.) [S. aňdinne, Skt. saṃ√dā or √dhā]

108 ANNAARU އަންނާރު n. pomegranate, punica granatum [U. anār]

109 ANBALAM އަންބަލަމް n. heap of sand decorated with fruit, used for wrestling games during Ramzan: corresponding to a public Christmas tree. Now obsolete. [T. ampalam, public place x T. amparam, heap of corn]

110 ANDAA އަންދާ n. antiphonal shanty, working song: e.g. hoolo malii yallaao! [S. ambā]

111 AN-BOŇḌI އަންބޮނޑި See an 2

112 ANHEN އަންހެން n. female: a. kujjaa, girl: a. gor̆, granny knot; anhenaa, woman (coll., anhen miihaa) : pl., anhenun, wife (= an̆bi-miihaa); magee anhenun, my wife : anhen-vanta, feminine [S. an̆gana, Skt. anganā]

113 AFA އަފަ pr. I, myself (used in South) [S. apa, * apphe]

114 AFIHUN އަފިހުން n. opium, papaver somniferum [U. afyūn, Gk.opion]

115 AFUNOOS-KAŘI އަފުނޫސްކަށި n. pin with a head: a. duuni, small kind of dragonfly [S. alpinetti, Port. alfinete]

116 AFUREN އަފުރެން pr. Southern form of aharen, I; pl., afuremen, we [S. api, * apphe]

117 APPAT އައްޕަތް n. flat wedge for caulking [See abu]

118 APPAA އައްޕާ n. father (local usage, for bappaa) [S. appā]

119 ABA NEERUM އަބަ ނޭރުން v.n. protracting endlessly

120 ABA-FILI އަބަފިލި n. sign for short a after a consonant

121 ABADU (ABADAKU) އަބަދު (އަބަދަކު) adj. always, eternally (abadu ves, abadu- me): abadař fehi, for ever green, always happy; Evergreen (Maldivian house in Colombo): abadaa abadu / abaduge abadař, for ever [U. abad]

122 ABAHADDA އަބަހައްދަ adj. very old

123 ABAAJJAVERI އަބާއްޖަވެރި adj. ill-starred [Skt. a-bhāgya]

124 ABU އަބު n. wedge, usu.of wood: a. jahanii, drives in a wedge; appat (q.v.), flat wedge (for abu- fat)

125 ABUI އަބުއި adj. serious, reserved; fussy, careful of one's public image; a. kiyanii, tells off, tells not to (with dat.of the person): bappaa abui kamek, an action forbidden by father

126 ABUNAA އަބުނާ n. pipes of a hookah: noḷiige a., bottom portion of pipe; a. bedigen, the pipe is clogged [U. āb-nai, water-tube]

127 ABURU އަބުރު n. self-respect: a. danii, self-respect is lost: aburaa behenii, defames; eenaa miihekge aburaa behijje / behefi, he has defamed someone : aburu-veri, respected, civilized [U. ab-rū]

128 ABUUNAA އަބޫނާ n. temporary deputy for head of state

129 AÑBI (atñbek, anbek; pl., añbin) އަނބި n. wife (grades: añbi- miihaa, añbi - kañbuleege (anc.), añbi - kañbalun): añbi-firikamu vanii, has sexual intercourse: añbi furaavaru vejje, has had her first period [S. añbu, Skt. ambā]

130 AÑBIHI އަނބިހި n. a medicinal fruit, garcinia cambogia

131 AÑBU އަނބު n. mango, mangifera indica (varieties: boḍu a., hut a., aavi a.): añbu aḷanii (tr.) picks mangoes (by shaking the tree) ; (intr.) mangoes grow (on the tree) [S. añba, Skt. āmra]

132 AÑBURANII އަނބުރަނީ v. twists (tr.); spins; changes round; translates: (v.n. eñburum, see also eñburenii):

magee boo añburanii, my head is swimming; añburaigen daane, one will feel giddy; boo añburaa kamek, what makes you dizzy; bolař eñburum araigen, feeling faint; oḍi añburan, to turn the boat round; eenaa dimaa-ař naguu añburaafaa, having called him a dog (viz. insulted him), lit. twisted a tail at him; fuk añburan, to set the teeth of a saw:

mendurun añburaa, in the afternoon; añburaa (adv.), back again: gellijje aburakii añburaa libee eccek nuunee, self-respect that is lost can not be got back again (prov.) [S. añbaranne, twists]

133 AÑBOFFUḶU އަނބޮއްފުޅު n. character in the fairy tale Añboffuḷaa Dañboffuḷu

134 AMAYYAAT އަމައްޔާތް excl. used to frighten children; excl. of horror or warning [cf. maali ?]

135 AMARAALI އަމަރާލި n. pennant

136 AMARUTA އަމަރުތަ Only in phrase amaruta ooga, auspicious time

137 AMALU އަމަލު n. 1. activities : a.kuranii, acts, deals with: adj., amalii, practical [U . ‘amal]

138 AMALU އަމަލު n. 2. liquor : amalu vanii, is drunk or intoxicated [U. amal]

139 AMAŘAKU އަމަޅަކު adv. extremely (with scornful implications, in negative or interrogative sentences): amařaku mii moyayek heyyeve! he is an unbelievable fool: fotaa hedi amařaku varek nuunee, he is simply crazy about the book

140 AMAA (amaek) އަމާ n. mother (not used in Male); kalee amaa! (an insult, cf. mayaa-inu) [amma]

141 AMAAN އަމާން adj. safe: amaan vejje hee? is the room safe to enter, i.e. have the ladies left? amaan-kam matiigai, at peace: amaan dida, flag of the Sultan or President of Maldives (with star as well as crescent) [U. amān]

142 AMAANA(A)T އަމާނަތް - އަމާނާތް n. safety : amaanaatugai / amaanatař, in trust; amaanaat-teri, trustworthy [U. amānat]

143 AMAAZU އަމާޒު n. aim: amaazař, amaazu koř , straight (adv.): a. fatgañḍu, target: a. kuranii, takes aim; amaazu-veri, good at aiming [U. āmāj]

144 AMILLA އަމިއްލަ adj. own,private: a. bali, characteristic (chronic) disease: amilla edum, ambitions; amilla edum boḍu, selfish: amilla-kam, personal independence, assertiveness; personal affairs; amilla-ař (adv.), independently, automatically: amilla-amilla-ař kořlan vegen, trying to do everything oneself: amilla-ař hadaa, artificial: amilla-verikam, independent outlook

145 AMUDUN (AMUDAKUN) އަމުދުން (އަމުދަކުން) adv. altogether: adi amudun, especially: Often in neg.sentences, (not) at all : amudun annaane ves kamek neeñge, I don’t know at all if he’ll come: amudun kamakaa nulai miihaku merum, killing someone without any reason [? U. ‘amd, intention]

146 AMUNANII އަމުނަނީ v. strings together (v.n. emunum, see also emunenii) [S. amunanne, Skt. āvṛṇāti]

147 AMURU އަމުރު n. command: a. kuranii, commands; eenaage amurař, at his command: amuru-verikam, superiority ; permission: a. denii, gives permission, a. naganii, gets permission [U. amar]

148 AMMA (ammaek) އަންމަ n. mother (low grade, as v. mamma) [S. ammā]

149 AM-MAS އަންމަސް n. kind of fish, surgeonfish, acanthurus

150 AMMAA އަންމާ Ammaa fot, the last book of the Qur'an, which is read first

151 AYA- އަޔަ- See ai : ayatiive, because one comes : ayatii ufaa kuram, you are welcome

152 AYYAA އައްޔާ n. oh Ali (voc. of Ali)

153 AYYUUGU އައްޔޫގު n. name of two compass directions: a. astamaan, North-west, a. iiraan, North-east [U. 'aiyūq, Capella]

154 ARAIRUM, ARAARUM އަރައިރުން - އަރާރުން n. quarrel (n.): a. vanii, quarrels; a. kuranii, causes quarrels: araarum-gaňḍu, big quarrel

155 ARAGU އަރަގު n. distilled rosewater or other medicinal liquid: davikgaňdu a., gripe water [U . 'araq, liquor]

156 ARAT އަރަތް n. problem, riddle: a. filuvanii, arat saafu kuranii, solves the problem

157 ARANI އަރަނި n. credit [cf. darani, debt]

158 ARANII އަރަނީ v. climbs, rises, arises (v.n. erum : hon. aruvvanii):

atař a., reaches up to the arms: aavi a., vapour arises: aahař a., rises to the sky: iru a., sun rises: isṭaakiinař a., gets into stockings: ekgamař a., goes inland: gahař / gahaa a., climbs tree: gaa-koḷakař a., treads on a stone: gaaduuni araa finoḷu, sandbank where seagulls perch: dum a., smoke rises: faivaanař a., puts on shoes: baiskalař a., gets on bicycle: bokkura-ař a., gets into the boat: miskitař aranii, enters the mosque: muudař a., goes into the sea: raa a., is a toddy-tapper: rehi a., fish come up: rooḷi a., blast arises: araa muriňgu, East ;

comes to land; dooni rařař a., dhoni comes ashore: fureeta mi rařař arajje, a spirit has come ashore: mi rařař araa kaa-boo taketi, provisions brought ashore here: farumaccař a., goes aground on reef (cf. farař erenii, s.v. erenii);

(met.) hini araafai, ants got in: majiliihař araa miihun, men appointed to a high post under the monarchy: araa huri miihun, prominent people: atmaccař arajje, got into (his) power: ekgalař a., ('climbs on to same rock') comes to a compromise: kasiyaaru a., slips off, slips aside: kuri a., prospers: kuriyař a., overtakes: kurimaccar a., steps forward: gayař a., touches another person, assaults: gaa a., keeps quiet as a stone, sulks: maguge anek faraatař araiganevi, crossed to the other side of the road: fař a., gets a stripe (of NCOs): faalař a., goes into gear (of bicycles, sewing-machines): furaavarař a., reaches puberty: hitař araee, (I) think, wonder;

In various special usages - eenaage faalař araifi, suited his description: magee faalakař e miihaa neeri, I couldn't get an answer from him;

Of diseases, arise ; araa bayyek, a contagious disease: naaraa duumi, kind of non-contagious disease: boo eňburum araigen, getting a feeling of dizziness : arikaṭṭař tadu a., pain arises in the ribs: duli a., cataract appears: karař naarek araifi, (I) have got a stiff neck:

similarly buruu a., tangles come (nanař, in the fishing line: (met.) kamtakař, affairs get complicated): eenaa uttara aranii, he gets angry (hon.): etifaharek araifi, received a blow: koři a., chokes (intr.): gugum araafai, a vibration arose: banḍugini a., gets hungry: eenaa boḍaa a., he gets sulky: eenaa / eenaa-ař malaru araifi, he got scolded: varu a., reaches climax: vaagi a., gets fits: eenaa habaek naaraee, he is never satisfied: heivari a., awakes: hee a., revives, (non-Male) awakes: aḷugaňḍaai araa, having approached me: vilaatař araigatii, invaded another country: hit furi araa,with heart full to overflowing ;

Caus., aruvanii, lifts, applies ; aavi a., inhales 'balm': ekgamar a., brings (coral) ashore: dum a., belches smoke: mudaa batteyyař a., loads goods on to batteli: munḍun aruvaa jehum, tucking up the sarong: deloo mudunař aruvaigen, opening both eyes very wide: havaa a., lets off rockets; (met.) ḷos uňdooyyař a. ('lifts on to a weak swing'), makes a fool of: ofu aruvanii, polishes: guḍum meezař a., shakes table: dila a., scorches: dum-buru a., gets very heated and voluble: duli a., operates for cataract: ruḷi a., provokes: rodi a., darns by machine (with dat.) : varu a., provokes anger: vaagi a., induces fits ;

aruvanii (resp.) gives, offers : atpuḷař a., presents : javaabu a., gives answer (hon.): fenfodu a., offers water (to wash, at meals): vedumař a., gives;

Enlargement: aruvaa-lanii ; huṭṭumek aruvaalum, putting a stop (to, dat.); aruvaalum, exile. See also erenii [S. arā (aranne), Skt. āruhati]

159 ARAFAATU KOTARU އަރަފާތު ކޮތަރު n. kind of pigeon originating from Mecca ['arafaat, a place-name]

160 ARAFOODI އަރަފޫދި adj. (lit.) of mature competence (of animates) [foodi]

161 ARABU އަރަބު n. 100 crores, a thousand million [U. arb, Skt. arbuda]

162 ARAHURI, ARAHUŘI އަރަހުރި - އަރަހުރި adj. almighty [araa- huri]

163 ARAA(aralek) އަރާ 1. n. wooden safety strip on sailing vessel
2. v. part. or imp. of aranii

164 ARAA-MATI އަރާމަތި n. far side of the bait net

165 ARAAMU އަރާމު n. rest; comfort: a. kuranii,takes rest; a. tanmati, comfy bed [U. ārām]

166 ARAARUṬ އަރާރުޓް n. arrowroot , canna edulis [E. arrowroot]

167 ARAARUM އަރާރުން See arairum

168 ARI އަރި n. 1. side: In particular, sidepiece of a dress; side of fish, half section (mas ari); single comb of bananas (keyo ari); section of banana leaf (keyofat ari); leaf of paper or of betel;

ari-kaři, rib; arikařii tadu, aching ribs:

ari-gaňḍu, portion of fish, half of mas ari (kaři-arigaňḍu, mula-arigaňḍu):

ari-mati, side, lengthways measurement: arimatii saraka, side-wheel of a drill; ari aḷanii, tilts over (of big things): ari kuranii, tilts (tr.) to one side: ari vanii, slants (of small things) [S. äla, side: ila, rib: ävari, comb of bananas]

2. name of A atoll

169 ARIDA-FUS (anc. ARIDAŘ-FUS; also ARUDOOS) އަރިދަފުސް - އަރިދަރުފުސް

n . a cold: a. aḷaifi, caught cold; mucus, a. foḷanii,blows nose: aridafus aḷaigen miirii kooccek? what is sweet with a cold? (a riddle or joke)
[perhaps aru - dař- fus, 'cloudy lower throat']

170 ARIS (arihu) އަރިސް n. nearness, presence (of people):

arıs mıhek, a close friend or servant: enme aris ehiiteriyaa, very close helper: arihu beekalun, former royal domestic servants: aris-tak, honourable gentlemen:

arihugai / ariahugai, in the presence of (hon.): beefuḷekge arihugai, in the presence of a nobleman

171 ARU އަރު n. throat : aru-tere, inner throat

172 ARUGA އަރުގަ n. an old measure of fish

173 ARUGOOLA އަރުގޯލަ n. hooked bolt, for swings or beds; a. jahanii, fixes the hook [Skt. argala]

174 ARUDOS , ARUDOOS (arudohu) އަރުދޯސް - އަރުދޮސް For aridafus, q.v.

175 ARUNU އަރުނު n. rhinoceros

176 ARUMAADU, ARUMAAZU (anc.) އަރުމާޒު - އަރުމާޑު n. fleet of ships; royal expedition [Port. armado]

177 AROḶI އަރޮޅި n. a medicinal nut, terminalia chebula (myrobalan)
[S. araḷu]

178 ALA އަލަ n. yam; taro: Various kinds: aadaige ala, ordinary yam; fen ala or goboḷi ala, kaṭṭala, hiṯṯala, oḷu ala, maa ala: alagoňḍi,tuber [S. ala, Skt. ālu]

179 ALA VANII އަލަ ވަނީ v. loves passionately (non-Male usage)

180 ALAKA އަލަކަ n. plover

181 ALATU އަލަތު adj. eldest

182 ALANAASI އަލަނާސި n. pineapple, ananas comosus [Port. ananas]

183 ALABAŇGU އަލަބަނގު n. crowbar [S. alavangu, Port. alavanca]

184 ALAMAARI އަލަމާރި n. cupboard; ais a., refrigerator [S. & U. almaari, Port. almario]

185 ALAŘ އަލަށް adv. newly [See aa]

186 ALAA އަލާ n. craving: a. keňḍenii, hope is lost; tiya kamtakun aharen alaa keňḍijje, I have had enough of that: eenaage matin aharen alaa keňḍijje, I have had enough of him: aḷugaňḍu mikamun alaa keňḍee gotek nuvee, I'm not satisfied with this: kobaa, alaa keňḍijje ta? well, I told you so [? Skt. ālaya]

187 ALI (ayyek) އަލި n. light ; adj., clear , bright ; ali gada, flooded with light: (met.) hit ali, intelligent, enlightened;
ali-ainu, clear spectacles:
ali-kam, light, (met.) information:
ali-kokaa, firefly:
ali-daňḍi, kind of firework, Roman candle: ali-naru, sparklers:
ali-faan, fire; alifaanuge kuḷivaru, firework display: alifaan-gaňḍu, a fire: alifaan-koḷu, 'a light' (alifaankoḷek dii bala! give us a light): alifaan kani, spark: alifaan foři, matchbox: alifaan daňḍi, matchstick: alifaan aavi, acid;
ali-ba<u>tt</u>i, bright lamp:
ali-bim, ground clear of trees:
ali-boki, bright bulb:
ali-haňḍuu, white rice:
ali-hoḷi, coloured rocket;
siluňbař a. aḷanii, puts fire into hookah burner: hilain ali aḷanii, strikes fire from flint: ali keňḍenii / eḷenii, fire bursts out: ali kořlanii, a. aḷuvaalanii, sheds light: ali dillee, fire is alight [S. eli ; alifaan= S.elipahan]

188 ALIFU އަލިފު n. a letter of the Arabic and Maldivian alphabets; in Maldivian it is used, with the appropriate fili, in all syllables without an initial consonant:
alifu-baa, Arabic alphabet: alifun yaa-ař, from A to Z: Alifu atoḷu, Ari atoll

189 ALIMANIKU އަލިމަނިކު n. almanac [E., adapted to Mald.nomenclature]

190 ALIMAS (alimahek) އަލިމަސް n. diamond [U. almās]

191 ALIILAAN އަލީލާން n. jingle forming part of the children's game elangalan; cf. baliilaan

192 ALUI އަލުއި See aluvi

193 ALUN އަލުން adv. all over again; alun balun (doublet) [See aa]

194 ALU(V)I އަލުވި - އަލުއި n. edible tuber; dańḍi a., manioc, manihot esculenta: vilaatu a., potato, solanum tuberosum [U. ālu]

195 AVA އަވަ n. influence, spell; eenaage avaagai jehifai, under his spell: ava-geri, bull pursuing a cow: ava lanii, haunts (a house, geyař ava laigen; a person, mařaa ava laigen)

196 AVAGURAANA އަވަގުރާނަ n. obscene language

197 AVADI (avajjek) އަވަދި n. 1. leisure (only in phrase avadi neti) [Skt. avadhi]
2. end: a. vanii, finishes (intr., used after abs. or with abl.): kai a. vum, finishing eating: kamakun a. nuvevigen, being unable to finish (with) a job; a. kuranii, (met.) does for: aharen mulin a. vejje, I am quite done for [cf. S. ivara]

198 AVARU އަވަރު n. squint, squinting [cf.S. vapara]

199 AVALI / AVELI (aveyyek) އަވަލި - އަވެލި n. imported parboiled beaten rice, used in Ramzan ceremonial meals [T. aval]

200 AVAS (avah-) އަވަސް n. speed:quick;
avas masakkatteriyek, a quick worker: atmati avas miihek, a deft worker: avas hini, kind of ant : avas las, ' fast-slow', regulator;
a. kuranii, hurry (it) up; avas kuree! be quick (politer, avas koř dii!): gaḍi avas vejje,the clock is fast; masakkat hińgaa- lek avaheve, how quickly the job is getting done!
adv., avahař, soon, early: avas avahař, very soon: vii hai avahakař, as quickly as possible: avahař feebee faseeha ge-ek, a house easy to get into, easily available

201 AVAHAARA އަވަހާރަ n. high honorific, used in the following:
a. vanii, dies: a. lappavanii, sleeps: a. gańḍuvaru, bathroom, W.C.: a. gońḍi, commode: avahaara-fuḷugai, asleep; a. kořlanii, kills a high nobleman
[?Skt. avahāra, putting aside; apahāra, taking away]

202 AVAŘ އަވަށް n. ward (of an island): avař-gańḍu,village (in stories): avař-ṭeriyaa, neighbour: avař-ṭehi, fairy: avařu miihun (anc.), labourers
[S. avaṭa, neighbourhood, Skt. āvarta]

203 AVAA-MENDURU އަވާމެންދުރު n. mirage [ava + menduru]

204 AVI (atvek) އަވި n. sunshine : avi -ainu, sunglasses;
avi dillanii, sun comes out: mitanař avi denii, the sun is shining here: avi gada vanii, sun gets hotter: avii lanii, keeps in the sun(tr.) [S. avu, Skt. ātapa]

205 AVIHI (avissek) އަވިހި n. 1. kind of dragonfly
2. a former intercalary asterism [Skt. Abhijit]

206 AVELI އަވެލި See avali

207 AS (ahek) އަސް n. 1. horse; knight (at chess) [S. as, Skt. aśva]
2. row of knots: a.jahanii, ties knots; as bai, double knot: fuḷi as, slipknot
3. See as-duuni

208 -AS -އަސް suffix although (cf. -akas):
gadayas, although strong: tuunas, although sharp: beefuḷakas, although a nobleman: diya-as, diya-akas, although (one) went : eakas, though that be so [S. -at]

209 ASARU އަސަރު n. emotion; implications, effect; symptoms: honuge asaru, the effects of lightning; a. gada, affecting (of things), attractive (of people); a. kuranii, has an effect (on, dat.): a. koř̃gen, receiving an impression: eenaage asarugai jehunu, under his spell [U. a<u>th</u>ar, impression]

210 ASAḶIYAA (-ek) އަސަޅިޔާ n. a medicinal substance, a kind of minaa bees

211 ASAA (-ek) އަސާ n. staff of office, stick: a . devvanii, presents staff (together with a title) [U. ‘a<u>s</u>ā]

212 ASAARA އަސާރަ n. pickle (to keep food): a. aḷanii, makes pickle [U. acār]

213 ASURU-MAA (-malek) އަސުރުމާ n. kind of flower, mirabilis jalapa, blooming in the afternoon, used for dyeing side-caps [U. ‘a<u>s</u>r, evening prayer]

214 ASEE KARA އަސޭކަރަ n. Indonesia [D. Atjeh]

215 ASEE MIRUS އަސޭމިރުސް n. pepper, piper nigrum
[= ‘Indonesian chillies’]

216 ASKAN(U) އަސްކަން (އަސްކަނު) n. a class of medicine (askanu bees)

217 ASKANI, ASKENI, ASGENI އަސްކަނި - އަސްކެނި - އަސްގެނި n. eaves ; a. vaḷu, hole made by drips from the eaves [S. agukon]

218 ASKARU (pl., askarun) އަސްކަރު n. a class of ancient functionaries, including Dořimeenaa, Hakuraa, Maafat, Velaanaa and Daharaa

219 ASTAMAANU އަސްތަމާނު n. the west (in compass directions) : galbu a., southwest (cf. iiraan) [Skt. astamana, astamayana]

220 ASTAA އަސްތާ excl. of surprise : astaa astaa-eve!

221 AS-DUUNI އަސްދޫނި n. goose (raada a.; Divehi a.; Sina a.): asduuni-mahugai deenii kilaa rahaek, goose-flesh tastes muddy (prov.)
[S. has, Skt. haṃsa]

222 ASRAFII އަސްރަފީ n. a gold coin [U. aśrafī]

223 ASLU އަސްލު n. origin [U. as̲l]

224 ASVAARU (pl., -un) އަސްވާރު n. horseman [as 1]

225 ASSANII އައްސަނީ v. ties (v.n. essum) : vaa rukugai assan, to tie rope to coconut tree [as 2]

226 ASSARI އައްސަރި n. Only in assari bas, words of praise

227 ASSAVANII އައްސަވަނީ v. asks, listens to (v.n. essevum) : assavamu dogek too, you hear, don't you? Enlarged: assavaa-lavvanii (hon. of ahanii)

228 ASSI އައްސި adj. gone to sleep, insensible (of limbs): assi tañburu, a plant, ipomoea pes caprae: assi bali, paralysis; a. kuranii, anaesthetizes

229 ASSIDA އައްސިދަ n. asterism Aśvayuj [S. asvida]

230 ASSUN އައްސުން adv. without good cause; usu.followed by kamakaa nulai: assun kamakaa nulai miihaku maraifi, he killed a man without any reason

231 ASSEERI އައްސޭރި n. bank, shore (seen from the sea, as v. atiri)

232 AHANII އަހަނީ v. listens, listens to; asks questions (v.n. ehum : hon. assavanii: imp. ahaañde: see also ehenii):

aḍu- a., listens to (tr.): mi dakkaa vaahaka aḍu-ehum, listening to what is said; bas a., obeys; innan a., proposes marriage; with kuren or kairiigai of a person questioned: Aisaa kairii ahaa bala, ask Aisha! ahaalafaanam, I might ask:

ahaañde! listen! ehin ta? do you hear? (response, ahaifim). Also ahaifin ta? ivunu ta? (v. ivenii), and response, ehijje [S. ahanne, Skt. āśṛṇoti]

233 AHANN- އަހަންނ- See aharen: ahannee, it's me; ahannek nudam, I'm not going

234 AHAMMADEE އަހަންމަދީ n . For the name Ahmad Maniku

235 AHARU އަހަރު n. year: aharu-mati, yearly remembrance: adj., aharii, yearly [?mod. for anc. averodu, cf.S. avurudda]

236 AHARUMEN އަހަރުމެން See aharen

237 AHAREN އަހަރެން pr. I, me (dat. ahannař, aharennař : pl. aharumen, (lit.) aharemen) aharen ataku net, I haven't got (it): aharen koppaalaifi, pushed me: aharen balaa boḍukuri bappa, I am (his) father who brought him up [afa]

238 AHAANAMA އަހާނަމަ (gram.) the letters aliph, h, n, m (before which alif sukun sounds as n)

239 AŇHAA އަނހާ excl. of surprise: look! fancy! aňhaa saharoo, oh alas!

240 AHI (assek) އަހި n. kind of tree, used for red dye, morinda citrifolia, Indian mulberry: ahi- vak, fruit of the tree [S. ahu]

241 AHUREN އަހުރެން pr. I, me (older form of aharen : pl., ahuremen)

242 AHULIHA އަހުލިހަ n. asterism Āśleṣā [S. Aslisa]

243 AHULU(VERI) އަހުލު(ވެރި) n. patron: instigator (of motion) : reader (of paper): inhabitant (of country) : ahulu-vahulu, people (doublet) [U. ahl, person]

244 AH(U)VAALU އަހުވާލު - އަހްވާލު in haalu-ahvaalu, general condition (doublet) [U. h̲āl (pl.)]

245 AŘ- (ařek) އަށް- num. eight(-): ař-kan, octagonal: ař-ḍuvas, ař-duvas, week: ař-mahek haa duvas, about eight months: Ař-ḍuu, name of S atoll (Addu): ař-nuva miihun, eight or nine men; ařaara, 18: ařaaviis, 28: ařaaḷiis, 48 (=saaḷiis ařek): ařaahi, 88 (= ařḍiha ařek): ařaanavai, 98 (= nuvadiha ařek);
ařutiriis (ař-tiriis), 38 (= tiriis ařek): ařuvanna, 58 (= fansaas ařek): ařuhaṭṭi, 68 (= fasdoḷas ařek): ařuhattiri, 78 (= hatdiha ařek); ařekka, about eight [ařek haa]; ař-ḍiha, 80: ař-sateeka, 800: ař-haas, 8000: ař-vana, eighth [S. aṭa, Skt. aṣṭa: higher numerals as Hindi, not as S., cf. H. aṭhārah (old S. aṭaḷos), aṭṭhāīs, ařtīs, ařtālīs, aṭṭhāvan, ařsaṭh, aṭhattar, aṭṭhāsī, aṭṭhānvē]

246 AŘAGANNANII އަށަގަންނަނީ v. is formed (v.n. ařagatum) (of roots, foetus, habits) ; caus., ařagannavanii (v.n. ařagennevum), inculcates [S. (h)aṭaganne]

247 AŘI (aṭṭek) އަރި n. solid seat or platform in the sittingroom of house (beeruge), for ceremonial reception or formal eating; reception room or guard room; kuḍa a., on the right as you enter, seat of honour: boḍu a., on the left, seating about 20 or to sleep on: boḍu ařii sañduvaa, canopy over boḍu ari: : tiri a., a low couch in ancient houses: ori a., seat of tied sticks: dañḍi a., slatted seat: namaadu a., seat for women's prayers: aři-mati, surface of the seat : ařii kiyevum, recitation of prayers in the former royal palace: aṭṭař diyum, going on duty in the palace [S. aṭu, platform, Skt. aṭṭaka]

248 AŘI-GAÑḌU އަރިގަނޑު n. trellis (for creepers): bier (where coffins are not available) [aři]

249 AḶANII އަޅަނީ v. (v.n. eḷum: hon., aḷuvvanii) Basic meaning, 'puts down'; used in a large number of disparate contexts.

1. drops, pours; spreads: at a., puts hand down flat: añbu a., picks mangoes: alifaan a., puts fire (into hookah), strikes fire (from flint): ustuñbař a., piles up: em diruvaan aḷaa lagari, box in which bait-fish are put to adapt them: karuna a., sheds tears: kaanaa a., puts out food(for birds): kaafuuru fenař a., puts camphor in water: kaaři a., picks coconuts: kuni a., scatters dirt: kiñbihi a., sneezes: kokoo a., mixes cocoa: tanmati a., makes bed: tarufaalu a., lays lino: taḷumgañḍu a., lays floor: daa a., casts net: dum a., gives off smoke: fiyavaḷu a., takes a step (high hon., fainpuḷu aḷuvvanii) : fen a., takes first bath after circumcision: fotigañḍu a., spreads tablecloth: bañḍu- aḷanii, swallows(tr.): bat a., serves rice: bilet a., stores betel: bis a., lays egg: bees a., applies medicine with a dressing: boñbi a., soaks coconut fibre: boo a., rests head: maḍisiila-ař aḷaigen, putting into the betel-bag: muudu-a., soaks in the sea: ruku a., picks (coconuts from) a tree: rodu a., lays fishing line: lee a., transfuses blood: vanař aḷaa, having put into the mortar : vaaree- fen aḷaa jaaḍi, pot to collect rainwater: saibooni a., spreads soap: hakuru aḷaafaa, putting sugar in (it): happuñḍu a., spits out end of a chew: haba a., takes mouthful of chew: (met.) aḍi a., declines(of profits): ari a., tilts (intr.): ali aḷuvanii (caus.), casts light: duniye a., leaves this world: namaadu a., misses prayers: bai a., distributes share: mahuge karu a., removes gills etc. from fish: hiyani a., casts shadow: hut a., is overbearing, constrains;

2. fixes, fixes on : aguḷi a., puts stopper in: akuru a., inscribes letters: añdun a., applies kohl: uigañḍu aḷaa kaali, rack on which thread is wound: galadun a., applies antimony: buḷiigai emgañḍu a., fixes bait on hook: oṭṭu a., fixes splint: kairi a., fixes hem: kañdu a., puts rollers (under boat): kañdugañḍu a., fixes fish-post: kappi aḷuvaane kusagañḍu, noose to hold a pulley: kastalu a., affixes handcuffs: kinaari a., affixes chevrons: keha a., fixes fencestick: goř aḷuvanii (caus.), does up button: tiñbi a., fixes roof-ridge: tun eḷi sigareṭ, cigarettes with filters: duḷa a., applies decorative patterns: bañḍavaru a., fixes thatch-ropes: bandu a., fixes straps: buḷi a., puts hook through: beri a., fixes beam: huunu boñḍi a., applies hot poultice: boovaḷu eḷi libaas, gown with a smocked collar: maḷu a., fixes plank: miya a., sets blade: muu a., grafts a root: rodigañḍu a., applies smocking: vaalu a., fixes crossbars: hungaanu a., fixes rudder: huras a., fixes crossbeams (met., places obstructions) ;

3. applies,uses: aḍu a., records sound: atbaaru a., gives help: etifaharu a., gives blows: esfiinaa a., applies the evil eye: obi a.,uses oilpress: kanḍa a., decides: kaḷi a., fixes the gaze, stares: kuuru a., scratches: furaana a., gives life: goñḍifoo a., uses tinderbox: goñḍi a., occupies seat: tammatu a., writes'finis': tunmaḷi a., applies nose-ring; controls (tr.): dat a.,bites (with -gai:): dunkaraas a., applies the jack: durumii a., uses binoculars or telescope: namuunaa a., uses pattern: faalu a., engages gear (of drill): filaa a., uses sextant: funaa a., uses comb: bai a., allots shares: barugonu a., uses the horn: baḍidañḍi a., exerts force: baaru a., gives encouragement: burus a., uses brush: biḍi a., applies leg-irons or clamps: boñḍi a., gives blows: min a., takes measurements: mařandati a., uses rake: maa fen a., uses 'flower-water': vaki a., scratches with claws (with -gai): viruvaa a., makes a mould

or copy (of something): vořifilaa a., uses sandboard: hanaa a., beckons: huunu uḷaa a., applies wrist-twisting;

Especially of putting on or wearing clothes, etc., e.g.with ainu, spectacles; aňgoṭi, ring; kamaru, belt; koori, sou'wester; gahanaa, jewellery; gaadii, a sack (on the head); guňguru, anklets; taakihaa, cap; tofi, hat; dahanaa, armour; doḷi, veil; doori, thimble; faguḍi, turban; fařṭaru, ornamental chain; fanvat, leaf worn as a charm; bolufoti, headdress; maafati, garland; minaafati, string of beads; mudi, ring; haaru, necklace; hedum, clothing;

4. makes, constructs: e.g.with ai̇ři, seat; asaara, pickle; iskuru, screw; istiri, an iron; uḷaali, kind of cake; kanvaaru, fishing line; koři, cage; ge, house; jooli, garden seat; davaadu, ink; dufaa taketi, a chew; gořfaḷi, splice on a rope; fallava, storehouse; fuk, twisted wick; nanu, twisted line; fuḷař, fence; bari, weights; bilet, sheaf of betel; bookibaa, kind of cake; maaru,thick plaited rope; miskit, mosque; mugooli, pit in the sand; loovaḷu, holes; (met.) gada a ., gives emphasis : buru a., draws a circle: roňgu a., draws a line: hama a., gets three in line(see tinhama) : with onomatopoeic words, e.g.kakakaka a., laughs: guḍuguḍu a., wobbles: ruuruu a., shivers: cakacaka a., laughs loudly;

5. In certain phrases, appears as an infestation or growth (intr.): aňgafaaru a., mouthsores appear: aňbu a., the mangoes are coming: aridafus a., a cold is coming: ukunu a., lice are appearing: kaňḍumati a., St.Elmo's fire appears: kavi a., fleas appear: kas a., a rash appears: fani a.,worms appear: fuḷa a., maggots appear (also met. of getting lazy): fuu a., mould appears: makunu a., bugs apppear: maa a., flowers appear: muḷa a., rot appears: meevaa a., fruit appears (on tree): reňdu a., cracks appear: himabihi a., measles breaks out: honu a.,thunderbolt falls;

6. keeps close (intr.) : ainugai duuni a., birds hover over the shoal: oḍi a., boats tie up, anchor: karugai kaṭṭek aḷaafaa, with fishbone stuck in throat: gooḷi(ař) a., turns into sidelane: aḷaafi atakař maru, wherever you turn there is death: goňḍiyekgai aḷaigenfai, stumbling over a chair: rařaa eḷi nivaa vefai, sheltering behind the island: magee fahatun aḷaiganegen, pursuing me closely : aḷaigatii, felt attracted: enme aḷaiganna kamek, a most interesting feature: aḷaa duvvaigatum, running away : aḷai balanii, compares;

7. Caus., aḷuvanii , hooks on; exchanges ; hangs up temporarily; kooṭ aḷuvaa koňḍu, coathanger: kappi aḷuvaane kusagaňḍu, noose to hold a pulley: goř aḷuvanii, does up button: (met.) mati aḷuvanii, puts the blame (on...,...-aa); mudalakaa aḷuvanii, exchanges for goods: vai aḷuvanii,wins the favours (of.. , ..-ař), flatters: vaahaka-ař aḷuvaa levum, getting into the conversation: aḷuvaa kiyanii, suggests liaisons (said of women);

8. Enlargement: aḷaa-lanii , cares for, bothers with: ekamaa aḷaa nulaa!never mind that!

See also eḷenii [S. (h)eḷanne, drops, pours x arinne, sends, * chāḍeti x Skt. √hṛ]

250 AḶAA އަޅާ 1. n. slave; myself (in addressing God) (pl., aḷamen : see also aḷu): mi aḷaa-ař,to me

2. abs. and part. of aḷanii

251 AḶI އަޅި n. ash ; ash-colour, grey: aḷi-boňḍi, hot fomentations: aḷi-fen, water boiled with ash (for bleaching): aḷi-ken[illegible]ḍi, ashtray [S. aḷu]

252 AḶU އަޅު n. slave (pl., aḷun, aḷu-takun) ; see also aḷaa. Respectfully, myself (usu. aḷu-gaňḍu, pl. aḷugaňḍumen):

aḷu-kam, any religious act; a. kuranii,worships (with dat.):

aḷu-daas, humble - only in a. vanii, is humble; aḷudaas-verikam, humility:

aḷu-veti, slavish; aḷuvetikam, slavery:

aḷu-veri, religious; aḷuveriyaa, religious man [?T. āḷ, person]

253 AḶUVANII އަޅުވަނީ v. caus. of aḷanii :

AḶUVVANII އަޅުއްވަނީ hon. of aḷanii (v.n. eḷuvvum): fainpuḷu aḷuvvanii, takes step (high hon.): furaana a., (of God) gives life: hedum aḷuvvanii, gets dressed (hon.)

254 AḶE އަޅެ excl. of assent or surprise [cf.S. arē, T. aṭē]

255 AḶOO (aḷolek) އަޅޯ n. aerial roots [S. araḷu]

256 -AA, -AAI -ާ -ާއި connecting suffix : riiňdun malaai nuu malun,with yellow flowers and blue flowers; geaa varař kairi, very near to the house

257 AA, AU (al-) އާ - އައު adj. new: adi aa, still uncommon:

adv., alun, alař, anew, again; (doublet) alun- balun: alun fařaa, begin again! aḷugaňḍumen hama alařee,we are quite new ; aa kuranii, renovates, renews; godaḍi aa k., recovers a mattress: gedoru aa k., modernizes a house: ummiidu aa vaa hai ve-eve, was enough to renew hope: enlarged, aa ves kořlevidaane kamugai, that it might be renewed.
See also aa-laa [S. alut]

258 AAŇ އާން excl. of assent: aaň, mi faharaku deraek nuvaane, he certainly won't lose this time: aaň, mi otii kaleege fot, look, here is your book: aaň, boḍu geri eba aade, careful, the bull is coming: aaň, mihaaru tiya bunaa eccek eňgijje, ah, now I see what you meant: aaň aaň, forsooth : aaň taa ee, oh yes? aaň-ekee, yes (in reported speech, or in repetitions); kiikee? aaň-ekee, what? I said Yes.

259 AAŇBAS އާނބަސް n. approval, word 'yes' : aaňbas bunanii / kiyanii, approves (esp. of marriage proposals); has the final word [aaň + bas]

260 AAŇHUUN އާނހޫން n. aaňhuun kiyanii, uses lower forms of address (cf. aade- vaḍaigennevum)

261 AAŇLEE އާނލޭ excl. of annoyance or surprise

262 AAILAA އާއިލާ n. family [A. ' āilat]

263 AA-GANNANII އާގަންނަނީ v. stammers (v.n. aagatum)
[? aa onom. + gatum, cf. aafurenii]

264 AAGAMA އާގަމަ n. a surprise: a. vanii, is flabbergasted

265 AAGU-BOOṬU އާގުބޯޓު n. steamship [H. āgbōṭ, 'fireboat']

266 AAŇGA, AAŇGU އާނގަ - އާނގު n. vent-holes in walls of houses

267 AAJUFAAJU އާޖުފާޖު n. the know-how, what's what: kamtakuge a. datum, knowing what's what [H. ājūbājū, around]

268 AAJENṬ އާޖެންޓް adj. urgent [E. urgent]

269 AAḌA އާޑަ n. mocking : aaḍa furassaara kuranii, mocks

270 AAḌATTOḌAA އާޑައްޓޮޑާ n. a tobacco-like leaf, 'Malabar nut', justicia adathoda (adhatoda) [Skt. āḍātōḍā, T. āṭṭātoṭai]

271 AAT އާތް excl. of surprise or horror, used by women

272 AAT VANII އާތް ވަނީ v. is shy, coy (of girls): aat vaane kamek net, don't be shy

273 AADA އާދަ n. custom; a. kuranii, accustoms (with inf.); aada koř, aada vegen (adv.), customarily: a. hifanii, adopts a custom: aadaige kuyyakař, cheaply: aadaige miihun, 'ordinary people' (a sociological term): varař aadaige gotekgai, very simply: aadaige irekgai ves, even in normal times; aada-kaada (doublet), customs dues ; aada negum, collecting dues: aadaa-ge, Customs House in Male [U. 'ādat]

274 AADANAA އާދަނާ n. oh Adam (voc. of Aadam)

275 AADIITTA އާދީއްތަ n. Sunday [Skt. āditya, sun]

276 AADE އާދެ excl. yes (high hon.); in repetitions, aadeehee : aade-vaḍaigennevum kiyanii, uses the highest forms of address (cf. aaňhuun; equivalent to S. eheyi)

277 AADEVENII އާދެވެނީ v. (v.n. aadevum) is able to reach, arrive (with dat. of person): Mufiidaa-ař aadevunii migeař, Mufida landed up at this house (invol. of annanii 1)

278 AADEE އާދޭ v. come! (imp. of annanii 1); also 3 s., comes (old spelling aude-eve): eenaa eba aade, he's coming

279 AADEES (aadeehek) އާދޭސް n. supplication: a. kuranii, supplicates, appeals

280 AADEEHEE އާދޭހޭ 1. aade+- eve; aade, yes, when repeated

2. aadees + -eve: aadeehee mi kurii, I do beseech you

281 AAN̆DOGEE އާނޑޮގޭ excl. of decided annoyance, you can't beat me; can't I just!

282 AANI (AINI) އާނި (އައިނި) n. small nails, tintacks: a. jahanii, fixes nails [S. äna, T. āṇi]

283 AANU(AINU) އާނު (އައިނު) n. very hard layer of coral (aanu-gan̆ḍu)

284 AAFALU އާފަލު n. apple: a. mařanii, peels apple [?E.apple]

285 AAFAAT އާފާތް n. severe misfortunes (aafaat-tak) [U. āfāt]

286 AAFURENII އާފުރެނީ v. yawns

287 AABAKURU އާބަކުރު n. Maldivian form of the name AbuuBakr

288 AABAA-FILI އާބާފިލި n. sign for long a after a consonant

289 AABAADU އާބާދު adj. inhabited; founded: prosperous, developed; a.kuranii, inhabits, reinhabits; makes prosperous [U. ābād]

290 AAMANAKA އާމަނަކަ n. a medicinal plant, castor oil, ricinus communis ; a. teo, castor oil [T. āmaṇakku]

291 AAMDANII އާމްދަނީ n. income [U. āmdanī]

292 AAMMU އާންމު adj. general, common: aammun (pl.), the generality, ordinary people: aammu koř (adv.), in general [U.'ām]

293 AARAASTAA, AARAASTU އާރާސްތާ - އާރާސްތު adj. prepared; cleared; equipped; settled, built on: a. kuranii, equips [U. ārāsta]

294 AARU އާރު n. 1. heartwood; strength, freshness:

aaru laa, strong, mature (of wood); worth doing (of actions); steady (of people): aaru-veriyaa, strong man: aaru nufilaa, half-cooked (of rice): aaru fili , properly cooked. Often with baaru: aaraai baaru, strength [cf. S. araṭu]

2. spring of water (fen aaru) [T. āṟu, river]

295 AARUKAATII އާރުކާޓީ n. pilot, guide [U. arkāṭī, man of Arcot]

296 AAROS (AARUS) އާރޮސް (އާރުސް) n. kind of sweetmeat popular in the

south

297 AALAT, AALAAT އާލަތް - އާލާތް n. apparatus, tool(s) [U. ālāt]

298 AA-LAA އާލާ adj. rejuvenated, revived(of customs), improved (of habits): a. vanii, gets better; starts bearing (of trees) [See aa]

299 AALAASKAM-FUḶU އާލާސްކަންފުޅު n. illness (high hon.): aalaaskamfuḷaa uḷuvvanii, is ill: aalaaskamfuḷek jehigen uḷuvvi, was ill [H. ālas, inactive]

300 AAVI އާވި n. vapour; steam, gas, spray; 'balm': boḍu a., eucalyptus: alifaan a., acid: baaroozu a., an acid used to clean jewellery: aavi aňbu, 'balm-mango' , Jaffna mango; a. aruvanii, inhales [T. āvi]

301 AAS އާސް 1. v. See ais 1.
2. n. See aahu

302 AASIINUTAŘI އާސީނުތަރި (gram.) the letters aliph, s, n, t, ř (which alone can take sukun)

303 AAŚOOKHU VANII އާޝޯޚު ވަނީ v. is bowled over [U. asokh, asoc]

304 AASMAANU އާސްމާނު n. the firmament: a. kula, sky-blue [U. āsmān]

305 AAH އާހް excl. of sympathy or sorrow

306 AAHI އާހި num. eighty (usu. aŕḍiha) [cf.S. asū, Skt. aśīti]

307 AAHU (AAS) އާހު (އާސް) n. (poet.) the sky [S. ahas, Skt. ākāśa]

308 AAŘU އާރު num. eight (in Navata tables: saatu aaŕu fanara, 7 = 8=15)

309 IULAAN އިޢުލާން n . notice, announcement [U. i'lān]

310 IGTISAADII އިޤްތިޞާދީ adj. economic [U. iqtiṣādī]

311 IŇGIREESI އިނގިރޭސި adj. English: n.., Iňgireesiin (pl.), the English (British) [S. Iňgiriisi]

312 IŇGILI (iňgiyyek) އިނގިލި n. finger, toe : i. dimaa kuranii, points the finger, leads : i. bindanii, counts on the fingers (by bending them): i.bonii, sucks the thumb: i. lonnanii, licks the finger (a rudeness); kuḍavai i., little finger : boḍuvai i., thumb

[S. äňgili, Skt. anguli]

313 IŇGURU އިނގުރު n. ginger, zingiber officinale: i. soḍaa, ginger beer (anc. jinjaru) [S. iňguru, Skt. śṙngavēra]

314 IŇGEE އިނގޭ particle representing ‘ you know; if you please’: Usually stands at the end : danii iňgee (too) / ma daanam iňgee (too), may I go? annaati iňgee, please come [? cf. eňgee, is understood]

315 IJAABA އިޖާބަ n. response: i. denii, gives response (to prayers, or to political petitions) [U. ijābat]

316 ITAA އިތާ n. oyster: i. mut, pearl: itaa-gaňḍu, small shovel (formerly made of oyster-shell); i. vanii, is dumbfounded (see aňga-itaa) [cf. Skt. śukti]

317 ITI އިތި adj. bent backwards; strained: iti miihek, a stiff proud man: iti-fuřař damaa bali, tetanus : iti kořfaa(adv.), pompously

318 ITUBAARU އިތުބާރު n. confidence : i. kuranii, trusts, relies on (with dat.): itubaaru hunna, reliable [U. i‘tibār]

319 ITURU އިތުރު adj. 1. extra (to..,.-ge): miige iturař, additionally; i. kuranii, increases, adds to (tr.), saves (money): fas guna-ař ituru vum,being multiplied by five: tinek ituru deek fahek, 3+2= 5 (or, as in Navata, tiin dui faas); nam ituru (gram.), pronoun

2. good, holy (esp. of deeds of the Prophet, see kau-ituru): ituru heu, revered

3. ituru-fuḷu (high hon.), a lie [S. itiri, Skt. uttari]

320 I<u>TT</u>IFAAGUN އިއްތިފާގުން adv. unanimously [U. ittifāq]

321 I<u>TT</u>IHAADII އިއްތިހާދީ n . ally [U. itti<u>h</u>ādī]

322 IDA-MATI އިދަމަތި n. windward side of an island (i. faraat)

323 IDI-KIILI(-kiiyyek) އިދިކީލި n. contrary grain (of timber) ; (met.) stubbornness: i. heree mitanař, the grain catches here (of the body, i.e.pricks the finger), i. heree mitanun (of the timber): idikiiyyař, where the grain slopes (in planing); (mus.) off-beat

324 IDI-KUKUḶU އިދިކުކުޅު / IDI-HAA އިދިހާ / IDI-FIYOK އިދިފިޔޮކް n. hen, cock, chicken with puffed-up feathers

325 IDI-KOḶU އިދިކޮޅު n. opposite end; opposite (to.., gen. or -aa): i. vanii, opposes: gina miihunaa idikoḷu nuvaařee, don’t oppose a lot of people! idikoḷu paaṭii, the opposition party: idikoḷař, in opposition [? cf.S. idiri]

326 IDI-FUŘ އިދިފުރު n. back end: idifuřun, (adv.) backwards

327 IŇDE އިނދެ v. having sat down; having got married (abs. of innanii) [S. iňda]

328 IŇDEVENII އިނދެވެނީ v. (v.n. iňdevum) gets married: e kaňbuleegeaai kaleař ıňdeveenii, you will get married to that lady (invol. of innanii)

329 IN އިން v. sat; married (p.p. of innanii): in-eve, was sitting [S. (h)un, Skt. sanna]

330 INAAMU އިނާމު n . prize [U. in'ām]

331 INUM އިނުން v. sitting, marrying (v.n. of innanii) [S. iňdum]

332 INJIINU އިންޖީނު n. engine: i. li eccek, a powered boat: injiinu uňdun, primus stove (Petromax) [E. engine]

333 INṬAVAL (INṬOOL) އިންޓަވަލް (އިންޓޯލް) n. interval : i.boifin ta? did you have a drink in the interval? [E. interval]

334 INTIZAAMU އިންތިޒާމު n . arrangements [U. intizām]

335 INTIZAARU އިންތިޒާރު n. awaiting: Husain Fuḷuge intizaarugai, while waiting for Husain Fulu; i. kuranii, awaits (sometimes pronounced intiḷoor) [U. intiźār]

336 INTIHAA އިންތިހާ adj. extreme [U. intihā]

337 INTIKHAAB އިންތިޚާބު n . election [U. intikhāb]

338 INDANII އިންދަނީ v. plants, sows ; sets into, esp. of handles: fixes a joint : gas indum, planting trees: oř indunii, seeds were planted (invol.): daani indum, fitting handle to well-scoop (caus. induvum, hon. indevum) [S. indanne, caus.of iňdinne]

339 INDAA އިންދާ v. while being [see innanii]

340 INNANII އިންނަނީ v. sits, is; marries (with -aa of the second party, miihakaai iňdegen, having married a woman) (v.n. inum : p.p. in : abs. iňde, iňdegen; niiňde, not having married: 3s. iňde-ee : imp. iňdee! hon. innavanii . See also iřiinnanii); indaa, while being (hon. innavai): iňdejje, sat: iňdevijje, found oneself married. Enlargements: iňde-laařee !(imp.), iňdefi (3s. past) [S. iňdinne, inne, Skt. sīdati]

341 INNA-KURAA އިންނަކުރާ n. washpot in latrine:

INNA- FAT އިންނަފަތް n. thwart (of boat, for sitting on) [innanii]

342 INSAAFU އިންސާފު n. justice, judgment:

eenaa-ař i. kuranii, eenaage khidmattakař i. kuranii, makes judicial enquiry about him, about his services: gives him justice: insaafun, insaafu koř (adv.), justly; insaafu-veri, judicious, legal: insaafu-vantaverikam, judiciality of God [U. inṣāf]

343 IFURIITU އިފުރީތު n. evil djinn [U. ʻifrīt]

344 IPIL IPIL އިޕިލް އިޕިލް n. a minty plant, leucaena leucocephala

345 IBA އިބަ pr. you (in religious contexts: pl., iburemen): iba-suvaamiin, Thee (used of God) [S. oba, Pkt. *yubbha]

346 IBAARAAT އިބާރާތް n. sentences, words [U. ʻibārat]

347 IBI-FILI އިބިފިލި n. sign for short i after a consonant

348 IBILIIS / IBULIIS (ibiliih-) އިބިލީސް - އިބުލީސް n. The Devil: ibiliihař govanii, calls for the devil, i.e.makes loud yawn: ibiliihu(ge) kaavani, the devil's wedding, i.e.the Greek calends (tiyaii ibiliihuge kaavanñek, that is a thing that will never happen): ibuliihuge vasvaahař nuhelleeřee, don't succumb to the temptings of the devil (prov.): faḷoo gahu ibiliis, kind of ugly humming insect found on papaw trees [U. iblīs]

349 IBRAAHIIMII RAN އިބްރާހީމީ ރަން n. pure gold coin

350 IBREE އިބްރޭ For the name Ibraahiim Maniku

351 IŇBA އިނބަ pr. you (anc. or dialectical: pl., iňbaremen) [S. uňba, cf. Skt. yuṣma-]

352 IM (IMU) އިމް (އިމު) n. 1. boundary (lit.): im vegen ot,being adjacent: faaraa im nukoř, not touching the wall: imař araafai, transgressing the boundary

2.kamtakař varař imu miihek, a man of principle [S. im, him, Skt. sīmā]

353 IMTIKHAAN އިމްތިޙާން n . examination [U. imtikhān]

354 IYAHUUDI / IYAFUUDI (iyahuuccek) އިޔަހޫދީ - އިޔަފޫދީ n. hypocrite ; Jew (mod. yahuudi) (pl., iyahuudin) [U. yahūdī]

355 IYAARU އިޔާރު n . helper (pl., iyaarun): vaarun iyaarun, helpers: vaalek iyaarek net, without a helper (doublets) [yaaru, friend]

356 IYYE އިއްޔެ n. yesterday; in the past: iyyein feřigen, from yesterday: iyyeakii..., yesterday is...: mi zamaanuge iyye, recently [S. īye, P. hiyyo, Skt. hyas]

357 IRA-MAA(-malek) އިރަމާ n. a scented white flower, clerodendrum sp.

358 IRANII އިރަނީ v. tears, rends: Enlarged invol., iriiri-lavanii, feels itchy, irritable: iriirilavaa tiya uḷenii, you are irritable [S. iranne, ?*śīrayati, *cīrayati]

359 IRAA-IRU އިރާއިރު n. 1. suns, see iru
2. early evening, see iraakoḷu

360 IRAA-KOḶU އިރާކޮޅު n. early part of the evening, 6.0-9.0 (also iraa-iru) : ree(ge) iraakoḷu, early evening

361 IRAA-DAM އިރާދަން n. (anc.) early watch of the night (iraa- damfaḷi)

362 IRAA-FOORI އިރާފޯރި n. early watch

363 IRAADA އިރާދަ n. God's will: iraada kurevviyyaa / iraadafuḷaa laigen, if God wills, D.V. [U. irāda, purpose]

364 IRU އިރު n. 1. sun; the east (iru-mati): i. aranii, sun rises: i. ossenii, sun sets; iru alikamaa laigen, by daylight: iru-dařu vai, east wind: iru-dekunu, southeast: iru-mas, solar month;
2. time: gaḍiin kihaa irek,what's the time? kihaa irek vaane, how long will it be? kihaa irakař ta, at what time? kihaa iraku(n) ta, how long does it take? hagaḍi iru, space of six hours: reaa duvaalu deiru, twice daily: tin iru iraku, thrice daily: irakař bai laahi magun, at the rate of half a laahi per mealtime; also in plural:, gina irutakek nuvaniis, before very long; irař irař, from time to time: irun irař, at (the right) times;
After participles : when ,while; nidaa iru, while sleeping [S. hiru, Skt. sūrya, and cf. S. vāra]

365 IRU-KOḶU އިރުކޮޅު n. time, piece of time: irukoḷaku, for a time: irukoḷakun, shortly: iruirukoḷaa, irukoḷakaa, repeatedly, intermittently: irukoḷek viyyaa irukoḷakař, from time to time

366 IRUDEE-MAA(-malek) އިރުދޭމާ n. a fragrant jasmine, jasminum sambac

367 IRU-VAI, IRUVAA އިރުވައި - އިރުވާ n. north-east monsoon: i. fureeta, kind of kite with long tail: iruvaa-hudu, kind of egret [iru+ vai, east wind]

368 IRU-VARU އިރުވަރު n. auspicious time: i. balanii, looks for personal auspicious moments [iru + Skt. vāra]

369 IRU-VIDI އިރުވިދި adj. preoccupied, motionless (of animates): iruvidifai in maakanaa, motionless heron [iru+ videnii]

370 IRUŚAADU އިރުޝާދު n . information [U. irśād]

371 ILAA (ilalek) އިލާ n. coconut spathe (used for straining: kiru felaane ilaa-gaňḍek, a spathe for pressing out milk)

372 ILI (iyyek) އިލި n. dowelling: i. jahanii, i. aruvanii, fixes a dowel

373 ILEKṬRIK އިލެކްޓްރިކް n. electricity : ilekṭrikge kaaru<u>kh</u>aanaa, Power House (in Male): i. lanii, installs electric light [E. electric]

374 ILOŘI (iloṭṭek) އިލޮށި n. eakel, mid-rib of palm leaflet (iloři-gaňḍu, often derogatory): iloři-fati, small broom of eakels: kiru iloři, eakel smeared with breadfruit sap, used as flypaper; iloři mařanii, cuts out a broom from eakel [S. iraṭu, and cf. ilapata, broom]

375 ILOḶI އިލޮޅި n. snipe, godwit [S. oley]

376 ILMU-VERI އިލްމުވެރި adj. studious, learned; ilmuveriyaa (pl., ilmuverin), learned people [U. ‘ilm, learning]

377 IVENII އިވެނީ v. is heard (hon. ivi-vaḍaigannavanii) : kanfatař aḍu ivenii, the ear perceives the sound: kanfatun aḍu-ehum, hearing: ivunu ta, did you manage to hear? [?Skt. √śrav]

378 IVVANII އިވްވަނީ v. announces, reads out (in person) (hon. ivvavanii, v.n. ivvevum) (caus. of ivenii)

379 IS (ih-) އިސް n. head (commonly met., =principal): enme is masakkat, the most impŏrtant job: is varu ǎri, seat in the old Palace for the principal section of the ha-varu ;

is kuranii, appoints (to, dat.): namaadař is kurum, appointing as imam: gives preference to; vaat is nukuraaře, don’t give preference to the left, always right before left! at is kuranii, prefers violence, is turbulent: ruḷi is kuranii, shows anger easily: is vanii, succeeds (to, dat.);ta<u>kh</u>tař isve vaḍaigati, succeeded to the throne (hon.); kamtakař amilla-ař isvegen, putting oneself in charge; koofaa isve vaḍaigati, anger was manifested (hon.); is fas vefai, jumbled up: is koř, isve (adv.), firstly; isve diya fatfuřtakugai, on previous pages: is naganii (hon., is nangavanii), raises head; gives a lead; kamtakař is negum, giving a lead in activities; is jahanii, drops the head; is jahaigen inum, keeping your head down. See also ihu [S. his, Skt. śīrṣa]

380 IS-KOḶU އިސްކޮޅު n. height (of a person): iskoḷu(n) digu,tall; i. keum / jehum, being able to stand (in water): magee iskoḷu kae / jehee, I can stand: iskoḷu

nukaa hisaabu, out of one's depth

381 IS-TAŘI (-taṭṭek, hon. istaři-fuḷu) އިސްތަރި n. hair (usually on the head): istaři-gaňḍu, the hair of a particular person: istaři turu kuranii, cuts hair (hon.)

382 ISABA އިސަބަ n. sign Taurus [Skt. vṛṣabha]

383 IŚAARAT އިޝާރާތް n . signal: i. kuranii, points out [U. iśāra]

384 ISAAHITU(N), ESAAHITU(N), ISAAHITAKU އިސާހިތު - އިސާހިތުން - އިސާހިތަކު - އެސާހިތުން - އެސާހިތު adv. within a short time (cf. mi-saahitu)

385 ISKURU އިސްކުރު n. screw; bolt: i. jahanii, puts in a screw: i. naganii, takes out a screw: i. aḷanii, makes a screw [E. screw]

386 ISKOOLU (anc.) އިސްކޯލު n. school (mod. iskuul) [S. iskoolee, P. escola (E.school)]

387 ISṬAAKIINU އިސްޓާކީނު n. socks: i. lanii, puts socks on: i. baalanii, takes socks off: isṭaakiinař araa, with socks on [E. stocking]

388 ISṬAAṬU އިސްޓާޓު n. start : i. kuranii(tr.), starts (car, race): isṭaaṭek nuvi, did not start (intr.) [E. start]

389 ISṬEEJU އިސްޓޭޖު n. stage, platform [E. stage]

390 ISṬEEM(P) އިސްޓޭމްޕު (އިސްޓޭމް) n. postage stamp: i. jahanii, affixes stamp [E. stamp]

391 ISṬOORU އިސްޓޯރު n. stores: Boḍu Isṭooru, old Government supply depot [E. store]

392 ISTAFAA އިސްތަފާ n. oakum (for caulking) [Port. estopa]

393 ISTIUFAA އިސްތިއުފާ n . resignation : i. devvanii, resigns (hon.) [U. isti'fā]

394 ISTIŇGI / ISTINGI އިސްތިންގި - އިސްތިނގި n. method of lowering sail on a schooner , clewing [H.]

395 ISTIRI އިސްތިރި n. 1. an iron: i. aḷanii, makes an iron: i. kuranii, irons (tr.) [S. istirikke, D. strijker]

2.woman:in phrase istiri (varitoḷi) hadanii, uses charms to get a woman [Skt. strī]

396 ISFIREENU އިސްފިރީނު n. a spring [E. spring]

397 ISPANJU އިސްޕަންޖު n. sponge: foam rubber [E. sponge]

398 ISBAGULU އިސްބަގުލު n. seed of plantago ispaghul, used for syrup
[U. isbag<u>h</u>ol, 'horse's ear']

399 ISMATI (ESMATI) އިސްމަތި (އެސްމަތި) n. mons veneris [?U. ' ismat, modesty]

400 ISMAALEE އިސްމާލޭ For the name Ismaiil Maniku

401 ISLAAMUN އިސްލާމުން n. (pl.) Muslims [islām]

402 ISLAAHU އިސްލާހު n . amendments [U. i<u>s</u>lā<u>h</u>]

403 IZZAT އިއްޒަތް n. honour, glory : izzatugai, in pomp; izzat-teri, honourable (esp. of foreigners) [U. 'izzat]

404 IHAVANDIPPOḶU އިހަވަންދިއްޕޮޅު / IHAVANDIFFUḶU އިހަވަންދިއްފުޅު n. name of the northern part of H atoll

405 IHAA (ihalek) އިހާ n. 1. bunch of coconuts or arecanuts: ihaa-goňḍi, main stem of a bunch of nuts: ihaa-vak, stalk of each nut in a bunch(used as toothbrush)
2. compassion: in phrase ihaa neti koř hitanii, treats badly

406 IHI (issek) އިހި n. 1. kind of lobster [S. issā, prawn, Skt. iñcaka]
2. a base thwart on a fishing vessel

407 IHU އިހު n. previous(ly): ihu zamaanu, old times: ihu miihun, men of old: ihugai, in the past: ihussure, since previously: ihekee ekfadain, just as before: ihu, ihař (adv.), previously; firstly: iha(ka)ř duvahu, in the past: ihař ree, yesterday evening, the previous night: ihakař ree, a previous night: iiye nuun ihař duvas, the day before yesterday: hama ihakař duvahu, very recently [is]

408 IHUTIRAAMU އިހުތިރާމު n . respect: i. ekugai, respectfully (in letters) [U. i<u>h</u>tirām]

409 IHURU އިހުރު n. 1. expert (for inaugurations)
2. name of an island in Male atoll [S. isuru, Skt. īśvara, lord]

410 I<u>KH</u>LAAS-TERI އިޚްލާސްތެރި adj. faithful, sincere [U. i<u>kh</u>lā<u>s</u>]

411 IŘIINNANII އިރީންނަނީ v. sits : is, esp. of women or goldsmiths (v.n.

iřiinum : p.p.iřiin : abs. iřiiňde : imp.iřiiňdee ! hon.iřiinnavanii : caus.iřiiňduvanii): iřiiniieve, sat down; See also innanii [cf.S. iňdinne]

412 II އީ adj. shy: ii vanii, is shy

413 IIṬU އީޓު n. roofing tile: geegai i. jahanii, puts tiles on house [U. īṭ, Skt. iṣṭakā, brick]

414 IIDU އީދު n. festival of Id (Eid): kuḍa I., Fitr Id : boḍu I., Azha Id: Iidu miilaadii, the Prophet's birthday: vaḷu I., day following the Eid [U. 'īd]

415 IIBII-FILI އީބީފިލި n . sign for long i after a consonant

416 IIRAAN(IIRAANU) އީރާން (އީރާނު) n. the east (in compass directions): galbu iiraan, south-east (cf. astamaanu)

417 IILI އީލި n. strands of rope (twisted on the knee; first stage in rope-making)

418 UI އުއި n. cotton yarn: ui-koḷu, bit of yarn: ui-gaňḍu, bundle of yarn: ui-boḷu, skein; ui jahanii, marks a line (for cutting or painting up to) : uigaňḍu aḷanii, spreads out yarn: ui guḷaa soru, character in stories who twists yarn [S. hū, Skt. sūtra]

419 UK- އުކް- n. sugar, only ibc.; uk-daňḍi, sugarcane, saccharum officinarum: uk-sakuru, ussakuru, molasses [S. uk, Skt. ikṣu]

420 UKANII އުކަނީ v. throws, throws away (hon. ukkavanii):

at u., waves hand, gesticulates: gaňḍu u., turns (several) pages: govaam u., sows corn: fen u., scatters water (on a fish-hook): boola u., bowls ball; mařař fentaři ukaa-levunii (enlarged invol.), my dish of water got upset. Cf.also ellanii, which is more specific [cf. S. ukanne, scoops, P. ukkaṃseti]

421 UKUḌI އުކުޑި n. fish-scales (word used in S. atolls, cf. huḷumbu)

422 UKUNḌI އުކުނޑި n. hiccups: u. koṭṭanii, has hiccups [cf. S. ikkā]

423 UKUŇḌI-BUKUŇḌI އުކުނޑިބުކުނޑި n. kind of jumping insect

424 UKUNU އުކުނު n. louse : u. bolugai aḷaifi, lice are in the hair; weevil: ukunu haňḍuugai aḷajje, weevils are in the rice [S. ukuṇu, Skt. utkuṇa]

425 UKURANII އުކުރަނީ v. scrapes out (esp. of scraping coconuts, kaaři ukurum)

[cf. S. ukanne, Skt. utkhanati; ?*utkṣurati]

426 UKUḶU އުކުޅު n. 1. hip, groin (ukuḷu-vaḷu): eenaage ukuḷun naṭṭaalii, his leg is dislocated [S. ukuḷu (ukuḷuvaṭa), Skt. utkaṭa]
2. skilful tricks: u. dannanii, u. hadanii, uses such tricks

427 UŇGANNAI DENII އުނގަންނައިދެނީ v. teaches, lectures (at high level) (with dat. of the pupil) [uňgenenii]

428 UŇGU އުނގު n. lap (uňgu-tere): uňgu matii baavvanii, puts on the lap: uňgu haavaalaafai, with opened sarong: u. viyafaari, street trading [S. iňga]

429 UŇGURI އުނގުރި n. stopper: fuḷiigai u.jahanii, puts stopper in bottle: u. lussanii, pulls out stopper; kanfatu u., earplugs: girisliinu u., glycerine suppository: fuḷimadu uňguri, (met.) one who turns up everywhere

430 UŇGURU އުނގުރު n . the top of the back: uňguru-vatař jahaaře, throw (him) on to his back! (in fights); u. jehunu mas, fish with broken backbone; uňguru biňdum, fracture of the neck

431 UŇGULI އުނގުލި n. a preparation of vermilion [S. iňgul, Skt. hiṃgula]

432 UŇGUḶANII އުނގުޅަނީ v. rubs; smears; rubs on: gai u., rubs the body: bees gaigai u., rubs ointment on the body: tabař u., polishes trays: dat u., cleans the teeth [? cf.S. uguḷanne, uproots]

433 UŇGENENII އުނގެނެނީ v. learns (v.n.uňgenum : caus. uňgannai denii)
[S. igena- (caus., ugannanne), Skt. udgṛhṇōti]

434 UJAALAA އުޖާލާ adj. shining, bright [H. ujālā, cf.S. udul]

435 UJUURAA އުޖޫރާ n. official payment for ad hoc jobs [U. ajūra, wages]

436 UJJEE އުއްޖޭ v. For udi + -ee, rose up: see udenii

437 UḌAFAIN އުޑަފައިން adv. squatting (uḍafain iřiiňde)

438 UḌI އުޑި n. grindstones, hand mill

439 UḌU އުޑު n. firmament, sky : hatvana uḍař erum, climbing to the seventh

heaven; uḍu-mati, the sky [S. uḍa, up, Skt. ūrdhva]

440 UḌU-TILA- އުޑުތިލަ- n. In adverbial phrases ; uḍutila matin otum, lying on one's back: dimaa uḍutilain, facing straight upwards

441 UḌUVILAA އުޑުވިލާ n. mica

442 UḌḌUN, UḌḌUM އުއްޑުން adv. face upwards: dimaa uḍḍun ove, lying right on one's back: uḍḍun veṭṭum, falling on one's back [cf.uḍutila-]

443 UŇḌALI އުނޑަލި n. brown layer round the developed coconut: u.kahanii, scrapes off this layer [S. aḍala]

444 UTURA އުތުރަ n. asterism Uttaraphālgunī [S. turupal]

445 UTURU އުތުރު n. north: uturu-gahaa, magnetic north: u. eňdu, northern or principal bed (for the lady) [S. uturu, Skt. uttara]

446 UTURUHAḶA އުތުރުހަޅަ n. asterism Uttarāṣāḍhā [S. turusala]

447 UTURENII އުތުރެނީ v. overflows (v.n. uturum): uturi aranii, boils over [S. itirenne, uturanne, Skt. uttarati]

448 UTUVANII އުތުވަނީ v. tears off

449 UTTANII އުއްތަނީ v. cleans jewellery in the fire: plates metals

450 UTTAMA އުއްތަމަ adj. excellent (title of the faňḍiyaaru) [Skt. uttama]

451 UTTARA އުއްތަރަ n. 1. north [Skt. uttara]

2. u. aranii, is irascible: rasgefaanu u. araa vaḍaigenfi,the king got annoyed

452 UDA އުދަ n. swell of the sea [S. oda, Skt. ōjas]

453 UDANII އުދަނީ v. puts on to the cooking fire: bat-teli udaaře, put the rice pot on!

454 UDARES (udarehek) އުދަރެސް n. horizon: iru udarehun arajje, the sun rose from the horizon

455 UDALI (udayyek) އުދަލި n. hoe, mammoty [S. udalu, Skt. kuddāla]

456 UDAAS (udaahek) އުދާސް n. enclosed heat, steaminess: u. kuranii, sweats in fever: u. kořgen kakkanii, steams food: u. aranii, steam arises

457 UDUSSANII އުދުއްސަނީ v. lets fly (caus. of uduhenii)

458 UDUHENII އުދުހެނީ v. flies: uduhee saalu, flying carpet: nuuduhevee (invol.), unable to fly

459 UDENII އުދެނީ v. rises up: fenun ujjee, rose from the water (of stars)

460 UDOI އުދޮއި n. current (of water) [uda + oi]

461 UŇDAGUU (uňdagulek) އުނދަގޫ n. difficulty; difficult: uňdagulun, with difficulty: maa uňdaguu boḍu, very difficult;
miihunnař u. kuranii, u. jassanii, disturbs people, makes disturbances: u. vaa kamek, a disturbance: u. kaňḍaalum, stopping the disturbance

462 UŇDUN އުނދުން n. fireplace; oven: injiinu u., Primus stove: faaroři u., baking oven; u. jahanii, constructs fireplace (with 3 supports in ash clay)
[S. udun, ?Skt. uddh(m)āna]

463 UŇDUḶI އުނދުޅި n. long wooden spoon : uňduḷi deefat, spoon and stirrer: torufi uňduḷi, ladle with holes in it; u.jehumakii badigeař gada vaa kamekeve, getting one's hand on the spoon means getting authority in the kitchen (prov.)

464 UŇDOOLI (uňdooyyek) އުނދޯލި n. swing: uňdoolii aňgun, wooden side-piece of swing : ḷos uňdooyyař aruvanii, praises falsely, makes a fool of ('puts on to a weak swing'): eňburee u., circus wheel; u. hallanii / hellanii, sets swing swinging: u. hellenii, swing is swinging [S. (h)idolu,Skt. hindōla(ka)]

465 UNA- އުނަ- n. waist (only ibc.); una-gaňḍu (unu-gaňḍu), waist, hips: una-fař, sarong string: una-faṭṭaru, waist chain [S. ina (inapaṭi)]

466 UNI އުނި 1. n. kind of tree, guettarda speciosa: uni-maa fen, scented water made from the flowers

467 UNI އުނި 2. adj. lacking: uni vanii, is lacking: tinek uni de-ek ekek, three less two is one [S. unu, Skt. ūna]

468 UNIYA އުނިޔަ n. slow kind of fish, 'silverbiddy' or bream: u. baananii, catches u.

469 UNU- އުނު- unu-gaňḍu, waist: cf. anna-unu, clothing [See una-]

470 UN-KAARU އުންކާރު n. u. denii, makes great efforts [onom., 'sound un']

471 UNḌA އުނޑަ n. cannonball [T. unṭai]

472 UFADDANII (UHADDANII) އުފައްދަނީ (އުހައްދަނީ) v. produces: aa taketi ufeddum, making new products: ufaddaa dogu, deliberate lies (caus. of ufedenii: S. upaddanne)

473 UFAN އުފަން adj. born: ufan vanii, is born; aharenge ufan duvas, my birthday [S. upan, Skt. utpanna]

474 UFAA (UHAA) (ufalek) އުފާ (އުހާ) n. happiness ; happy (ufaa-veri): ufaa kuranii, makes merry (intr.): miadu raňgaḷii-tii ufaa kuram, I'm glad that it was all right today: ufaa koř (adv.), happily; u. vanii, is happy

475 UFURANII އުފުރަނީ v. pulls up (individual plants; pej. if used of flowers, cf. binum); pulls out (teeth, hair) [S. upuṭanne, MInd.*uppaṭṭeti]

476 UFULANII (UHULANII) އުފުލަނީ (އުހުލަނީ) v. carries heavy things: ufulaa miihun, (harbour) porters; lifts: fen maccař ufulanii, raises to the surface of the water: ge ufulanii, builds house higher: nu-ufuligen (invol.), being unable to lift: (met.) mařař ufulee varuge mas'uuliyyatek nuun, not a responsibility I can undertake [ufullanii]

477 UFULLANII (UHULLANII) އުފުއްލަނީ (އުހުއްލަނީ) v. carries heavy things (= ufulanii; hon. ufullavanii) [S. upullanne, Skt. utplāvayati (or S. usulanne, Skt.*utcālayati)]

478 UFULI އުފުލި n. a float: u. lanii, fixes a float; floating grains in gruel [S. ipilla]

479 UFEDENII (UHEDENII) އުފެދެނީ (އުހެދެނީ) v. is conceived (as v. ufan vum); is produced, is founded (of a club) [S. upadinne, Skt. utpadyate]

480 UBU-FILI އުބުފިލި n. sign for short u after a consonant

481 UŇBU (unbek) އުނބު n. small-mouthed shell (cup), opened kurunba: : miidaa kee unbek, a shell gnawed by rats; (met.)the head of a fool: u. alun hovum, picking up the pieces: uňbař jehum, going back to pick up the pieces

482 UŇBU-GAŇḌU އުނބުގަނޑު n. bowl (of any material): lamp-bowl

483 UŇBUNANII އުނބުނަނީ v. (vulg.)kisses amorously (abs. uňbe suňbe, doublet) [S. iňbinne]

484 UM އުމް n. wart, mole (esp. on the face): u. jahanii, u. laḷanii, spots appear; protuberances on fruits such as pineapple, knobs: um jehi maravaḷi, sandals with knobs (as opposed to straps) - also written uř jehi

485 UMAGU އުމަގު n. central ulcer of a wound: u. vanii, goes septic

486 UMAT އުމަތް n. tightness: u. vanii, gets stuck (in carpentry)

487 UMURU އުމުރު n. age: magee umurun vihi aharu vejje, I am 20 [U.'umr]

488 UMMIIDU އުންމީދު n. hope: u. kuranii, hopes (that.., dat. or kamugai) [U. ummed, umīd]

489 URA އުރަ n. sheath : atu ura, mittens (for undertakers): onu ura, bamboo case (for storage or cooking): kaňḍi u., scabbard: kanneelu u., pillowcase: fai u., prayer stockings for women: siṭii u., envelope [T. uṟai]

490 URA-FAŘ އުރަފަށް n . outer edge of reef round island,where it falls away: urafařu gaa, stone to mark this point

491 URA-MATI އުރަމަތި n. female breast (technical term, cf. kiru) [Skt. uras]

492 URA-VAḶI އުރަވަޅި n. testicles; scrotum

493 URANII އުރަނީ v. carries (child) on hip: uraalan dii bala, let me carry (him) a bit : at uraalaigen, folding the arms (hon. uruvvavanii, and see uru-vaḍuvanii)

494 URANNA އުރަންނަ Imprecation used at end of koli proclamations: mikam nukuri miihaku uranna, cursed be he who does not comply!

495 URAHA އުރަހަ n. upper fin of shark (as v. kotari)

496 URAA (-ek) އުރާ n. millet, panicum miliaceum: bimař u. lanii, sows millet

497 URU އުރު n. hip, under the arm (where child is carried): uru-tere, bosom [S. ora, ura, Skt. uras]

498 URU-VAḌUVANII އުރުވަޑުވަނީ v. carries (used of servants carrying noble children; cf.uranii, uruvvavanii)

499 URUṬṬANII އުރުއްޓަނީ v. sways (intr., e.g. of boats) [T. uruṭṭu]

500 URUVANII އުރުވަނީ v. gets boat stuck in shallows, runs aground(tr.): enlargement, uruvaa-lanii (caus. of urenii)

501 UREDENII އުރެދެނީ v. defies God: Kalaaňgeaa uredijje, Kalaaňge kiba-ař uredijje, blasphemed

502 -UREN -އުރެން pl. termination, see e-uren

503 URENII އުރެނީ v. runs aground (intr.)

504 UL- -އުލް See uu

505 UVA އުވަ n. quicklime: uva-gaňḍu, lump of plaster: uva-dooni, mixing trough; u. davanii, makes lime by burning: uva-vaḷu davanii, sets fire to lime pit: uva jahanii, u. lanii, applies limewash or plaster

506 UVANII އުވަނީ v. abolishes, dissolves (e.g. assemblies, laws, promises, stamps etc.): uvi hiňgajje, are abrogated (invol.)

507 US (uh-) އުސް adj. high, tall (of man-made objects -- not used of people or trees, cf. digu): us-koḷun digu, tall: us-ge, a part of the old royal palace: us min, height: usminuge ruk = digu ruk, tall coconut tree : uhugai, above: (met.) us alitak, highlights [S. us, Skt. ucca]

508 USUULU އުޞޫލު n. principles [U. uṣūl]

509 USTAAZU އުސްތާޛު n. teacher (legal degree conferred by the Government) [U. ustāẕ]

510 USTUŇBAŘ އުސްތުނބަށް adv. heaped up, to the brim;

[Now taken as us+ tuňbu, high lip, but probably originally from ustuňbu, stupa (as formerly on Gan in Addu atoll)]

511 USSAKURU އުއްސަކުރު n. molasses [See uk-]

512 USSANII އުއްސަނީ v. steams food

513 UHADDANII އުހައްދަނީ v. produces [older form for ufaddanii]

514 UHAA, UHAU (uhalek) އުހާ - އުހައު n. happiness:

u. kuranii, rejoices; uhauveri, happy; uhaa-faa kam, happiness [older form for ufaa]

515 UHULANII, UHULLANII އުހުލަނީ - އުހުއްލަނީ v. lifts, carries [for ufulanii]

516 UHEDENII އުހެދެނީ v. See ufedenii

517 UŇHU އުނހު excl. of disagreement: oh no!

518 UŘ އުށް n. wax: uřteyo, wax oil: uř-batti, candle [S. iṭi]

519 UŘ JEHI އުށް ޖެހި See um

520 UḶA އުޅަ n. raised patterns on cloth: u. naganii, u. gannanii, makes such patterns

521 UḶAI އުޅައި n. See uḷaa

522 UḶAK އުޅައް n. handle (of jar or pan); cleat: u. jahaifi, fixed the handle

523 UḶAŇDU އުޅަނދު n. official vessel, ship [cf. S. vaḷaňda, pot ?]

524 UḶAŇBOŘI އުޅަނބޮށި n. elbow [S. välamiṭa]

525 UḶA-HARU އުޅަހަރު n. instrument for making raised patterns [uḷa]

526 UḶAA, UḶAI (uḷalek) އުޅާ - އުޅައި n. bangle: uḷaa-bai, set of bangles (usually 4 on each arm): huunu uḷaa, 'hot bangle', see huunu;

uḷaa-gaňḍu, hanging ring for fastening ropes or chains: kaňḍinmaa u., chains formerly at the harbour entrance in Male; (met.) a chatterbox [S. vaḷalu]

527 UḶAALI އުޅާލި n. kind of circular fried cake: u. aḷanii, prepares u.

528 UḶAAS (uḷaahek) އުޅާސް n. warping: uḷaahař demum / diyum, getting warped

529 UḶI އުޅި n. strand of rope; deuḷiek nuvaa miihek, a man who can't put two and two together

530 UḶUŇBU އުޅުނބު n. kind of dye (uḷuňbu diya): u. jahanii, applies u.

531 UḶENII އުޅެނީ v. lives, exists (used of animates, of diseases and sometimes of ships) (abs.uḷe : impv. uḷee ! hon. uḷuvvanii):

eba uḷee ta? is (he) in? geegai uḷee miihun, domestic servants: uḷenii daan vegen, have to be going; uḷum (v.n.), habits: uḷum goos miihek, an illbehaved man;
After inf., tries to, begins to, wants to: kamtaktak oḷum filuvan uḷee huśiyaaru miihek, a competent man who tries to sort things out: mi annaan uḷee matindaa booṭutak, these aeroplanes which are due: adives hifaakař nuuḷee hee? is (it) still not going to stick? bunaan uḷee eccek bunaan uḷee-lek avaskamun, as he said so quickly what he had to say: Mufiidaa ves annaakař nuuḷunu viyyaa doo, I suppose M. won't be coming: salaamat vaan uḷeeřee, try to escape! ekamaai(gen) uḷuvvum, taking trouble about that (hon.): mi kam kurevee too uḷenii, (is) trying to get this done: daan uḷee, get out! damaa uḷe, let's go
After abs., is used to: ginain mi bas bune uḷenii, this word is frequently used...: kakkaalaa uḷeene kujjek, a boy who will do the cooking : liyegen uḷee banḍaara rukek, an officially registered coconut tree: vegen mi uḷee gotakii, what has happened is.. : kamakaai gen uḷum, having a problem; (invol.) ekugai nuuḷevuniimaa, when unable to live together: aḷugaňḍumennař uḷevi-daane, we will be able to live [T.√uḷ-]

532 UU (ulek) އޫ n. spit, cooking fork: velaa bis vaḷař uu jahaařee, poke the fork into the turtle's egg-hole! ulun furoḷaa varu vefai, being lazy enough to need poking; sharp-pointed : uu-gaňḍu, sharp stick [S. ul, spike, Skt. śūla]

533 UUŇ އޫން excl. indicating assent: yes I can:

eenaa uuň ves neeḷi, he didn't say anything, took no notice: uuň-ee bunaa bas, words indicating assent

534 UUH އޫހް excl. of surprise etc.

uuh miotii, look, here it is! uuh miok kamek, what a nuisance!

535 UUBUU-FILI އޫބޫފިލި n. sign for long u after a consonant

536 UURU އޫރު n. pig (not found in Maldives): eenaa dimaa-ař uurař govum, calling him a pig (a dreadful insult) [S. ūru, Skt. sūkara]

537 E އެ adj. (as n., eige, eege) that (before nouns); there (before verbs);

e miihaa, that man: e gas, those trees: e annanii, is coming over there: eyoo anekkaa? what do we mean? eii? why that? eii too ee? is that so? shall I tell you what I mean? eii, that is, that is because..: eyyeve, it is that: hama eaa eku, at that same moment ; eiti, see eeti: einii, see eenii: eiru, see eeru: e-uren, those people (obs.): eok (coll., eokgen, cf.miok, tiok), look there; eok annanii, there they come: eok aii Yahya, that was Yahya: e gas eokgen ari vamun danii, look, those trees are leaning over; eoomen (pl.), they, them: eyoo anekkaa! what's all this? e-eccek, any given object:

e-kamaku, but, however; e-kamaku naee, but he hasn't come: e-kaňbuleege, she: E-kalaaňge, He (of God) : e-kahala, of that sort : e-koi, my child, our child; you, child! e-koi mihaaru vii raajjeen beerugai, my son is abroad just now: ekoi Zaahir! young Z.! e-koi dariful̩aa! my child! e-kol̩ukol̩u, upside down, on the wrong end; hikiige ekol̩ukol̩u, the opposite of dry: ekol̩ukol̩u naganii, stands upside down(tr.): ekol̩ařaai mikol̩ař hiňgum, walking up and down: (adv.) ekol̩ukol̩un ; ekol̩ukol̩un ellanii, turns somersault,throws on (its) back; ekol̩ukol̩un jahanii,turns upside down:

e-gee, of that house; egee Hasanful̩u, H. of that address: e-gotakii, that is because...: egot-migotař, in this direction and that: e-goyye, my daughter: e-tak, so many (followed by indef. ending); etak miihunek, etakek miihun, so many people: etak etak maidaanekgai, on many a field: saal̩iis etak aharu, 40 years or so: derufiyaa etak laariyakař, at 2 rupees odd: etakek taaňgai, etak tanekgai, in very many places: etakek faharu matin, several times: etak etak haas meelekge durugai, many thousands of miles away: e-taa, there; etan-mitaagai, here and there: etaa huri, etaaňgai huri, who was there: etoo-mitoo, state of indecision; etoomitooek ovegen nuvaane, there shouldn't be any doubt: etoomitoogai huri miihek, a man who havers:

e-Diidii,that noble lady: e-nuun, other (followed by indef. ending); enuun kamek nukuree! don't do anything else: enuun ves kamek kořfi, he did other things as well: enuun gotakař, otherwise: enuunas, even otherwise:

e-fada, of that sort: e-ful̩u, the child (non-Male usage): e-bai, that portion, that team; ebai miihun, they: e-varu, that amount; evarař, evarun, repeatedly: evarun kuri daturek, a journey over which so much trouble was taken: e-veni, a certain (followed by indef. ending); eveni miihek, a certain person : vaki eveni miihek, anyone particular: e-verin, those people: e-veelaa, of antique times; eveela akuru, ancient script: e-haa 1., that much; ehaa boḍu, so big: ehaa varu, so much: ehaa varař fen naal̩aa! don't pour so much water: ehaa tanař, ehaa tanaai jehen den, till then, up to there: de-ek jahaa ehaa iru, at about 2.0: ehaakař haa iru, at about that time: e-haaru (eha-iru), at that time: ehecceti,those things (for e+ ecceti): e-hen 1., thus; mařař ehen hiivanii, I think so: ehen ves vedaane, it may be so: ehen nu? isn't it so? ehen kamun, ehen vegen, ehen vaa tii, ehen viimaa, therefore: ehen nudee! don't go that way: ehen laigen, passing that way: ehen viyyaa, if so: ehen nuun too, isn't that so? ehen nuuniyyaa, if not: ehen nama ves, ehenas, though it be so, nevertheless: hama ehen, just the same: ehenii 1.,because in fact..: e-hera,that there; ehera annanii, there he comes: ehera kuḍa ge, that little house: also eheragen (cf. eokgen), ruňbaa eheragen utureniiee, look, the jar is overflowing: e-herii, stood there (for e-hurii)

[S. ē, cf.Skt. ayam]

538 EK އެއް num. one : ek aharu, one year: ek gaḍi, one hour; one o'clock: ekves fotek net, ekme fotek ves net, there is not a single book: ekek jehiieve, it is one o'clock: ek duvahu, on the first of the month: ek duvahun, within a single day: ekaku ves net, there is nobody (here):

ek-kauvanta, single,unique(of God): ek-kaři, of solid bone structure (see viiru): ek-kahala, of the same sort, similar; don amaekee niaňdurekee ekkahalaee, a stepmother is as sour as a citron (prov.): kaleyaa haada ek-kahalaee, is very like you: ek-kibai / ek-kibaa vanii, keeps apart from, avoids; faafain ekkibaa vaaře, avoid evil: efada miistakunge kibain ekkibaa vaaře, keep away from such people! ek-kuranii, unites (tr.), collects, adds together; ekakař ekek ekkuriimaa de-ek, ekakaa ekakaa ek- kuriimaa de-ek, one and one is two: ek-kol̩u,the same direction; ekkol̩u daturek, a single journey: (adv.) ek-kol̩ař, in favour of; veriinnaai ekkoḷař, in agreement with the authorities: hufahelumaai ekkoḷař, in favour of the proposal: ek-gam(u), the inland part of an island; ekgamař danii, ekgamař aranii, goes inland: ekgamu muraka, a plant, euphorbia tirucalli: ek-gaa, ('one rock', met.) ekgalař aranii, comes to a compromise agreement: ek-gaani, see nuekgaani: ek-got, of the same kind, resembling; miaa ekgot eccek, something similar to this: e-gee Don Kamanaaekee naasi anhenekee ekgotee, D.K. of that address is like a slut: (adv.) ekgotař, in accordance (with); miaa ekgotař, in accordance with this; ekgotakař ves, not at all (with neg.verb): ek-fada, like (adj.): miaa ekfada eccek, a thing like this: (adv.) iyye-ekee ekfadain, just like it was yesterday; ek-faharu, once; ekfaharaa, all at once : ek-fuḷař vanii, has a common fence; ekfuḷař vegen huri ge, the house next door: ek-bai, one part, half, one party; debai kuḷa ekbai, one half: ekbai kuranii, accepts into a team: eenaa uḷenii mi miihunaa ekbai vegennee, he has become one of their people: ek-baňḍu, of the same mother: ek-bas, in agreement; ekbas vanii, comes to an agreement (with.., -aa:: that...,...kamugai), ekbahek nuveve-eve , (they) couldn't agree : ek-baaru lanii, cooperates: ek-maabaňḍu, at a single birth; ekmaabaňḍu debeen, twin brothers: ek-me, a single (with indef. nouns), the most (esp.before adjectival words): ekme gahek, a single tree: ekme miihek, a single man: ekme riiti, the most beautiful: ekme doři, the eldest: ekme fahu, the last: ekme furihama, the most perfect: hituge (hama) ekme aḍiin, from the very bottom of the heart: ekme atiriyař, right on the shore: ekme gellum libunii.., .. had the greatest losses: ekme vissaara muusum, the stormiest season: ekme bitdařun, in the far background: mařař ekme vattarii..,..is the most like me: ekme hai.., every..: ekmen, enmen (pl.), all: ekmenař-me, to absolutely everyone: hurihaa ekmen, everybody: ek-medu, 'in the middle', used of shared property (ekmedu mudaa): ek-vattaru, identical; eii varař ekvattarakař hiňgaa demiihekeve, those two men walk very similarly: ek-vana, first (in order), ekvana-ař aum, coming first: ek-vanii, unites (intr.), collects together; havaru ekvegen, the whole people were gathered together: ek-varu, equal; mi dekudin ekvaree, these two children are equal: ekvarař (adv.), equally; ekvarař bahaa, distributing equally [S. ek, Pkt. ekka, Skt. ēka]

539 -EK -އެކް indefinite nominal suffix : fotek, a book: miihek, a person; necessary also in negative statements : mi boḍek nuun, this is not big: mii mage-ek nuun, this is not mine: aharen danii-ek nuun, I am not going

540 EKATA އެކަތަ n. steel [T. eku]

541 EKATI (ekaccek) އެކަތި n. one thing (also used of animals): deetin ekaccař hifum, putting all one's energy into something: ekati-gaňḍa(ka)ř vum, sticking together, (met.) e miihun uḷenii ekatigaňḍakař vegennee, they are a united group: hama ekaccek, only one, the same [ek + eti]

542 EKANI (ekaňňek) އެކަނި adj. only, alone: aḷugaňḍuge ekani koňḍugai, on my sole shoulders: hama ekani, hus ekani, quite alone: ekani maa ekanin, very alone: miadu ekani ves, only today: ekani kaa taři, individual plate: (adv.) aḷugaňḍař ekaňňee, (it is) only to me:

as n.., loneliness: aharen ekani filuvum, removing my loneliness, keeping company with me; ekani-veri, unaided

543 EKA-HERI އެކަހެރި adj. alone; (gram.) singular [For -heri, cf. duru-heli]

544 EKAŘA AḶANII އެކަށަ އަޅަނީ v. drafts, declares, resolves

545 EKAŘIIGEN VAA އެކަޅީގެންވާ, EKAŘEENA އެކަޅޭނަ adj. suitable: ekařiigen ve-eve, (it) is possible

546 EKAA- -އެކާ num. ibc., plus one (in compound numbers): ekaanavai, 91 (= nuvadiha ekek): ekaavanna, 5l (= fansaas ekek): ekaaviis, 21: ekaahaṭṭi, 6l (= fasdoḷas ekek): ekaahattari, 71 (=hatdiha ekek): ekaahi, 81 (= ařḍiha ekek): ekaaḷiis, 4l (= saḷiis ekek) [cf. H. ikānvē, ikāvan, ikkīs, iksaṭh, ik-hattar, ikāsī, iktālīs]

547 EKI އެކި adj. various, separate: eki miihunař vakivakiin engum, informing each person separately: eki gee-ge, various houses: eki koḷař, in various directions

548 EKII, EKIIGAI އެކީ - އެކީގައި adv. together, altogether : tiya filaavaḷu ekii hitun daskuraařeve, learn the whole of that lesson by heart! ekii ekgotař, entirely alike: ekii-ekař halaaku ve, completely destroyed: eki-ekiigai, all together, at the same time: eenayaa ekii, with him (see also ekkaku)

549 EKU އެކު adv. with (after -aa): ahannaai eku,with me: eku eku hen, almost simultaneously; Also ekugai, eku-ekiigai:: ekugaek nuun, not together ; bat-tařì ekugai hus kořlaifi, completely emptied the plate of rice: eku vegen, eku laigen, getting on together: fenaa telaa eku nuve-ee, oil and water do not mix:

eku-lavanii, compiles, composes: ekulevigen vii sateeka fansaahakař miihunge maccařee, was composed of about l50 people;

eku-veri, friendly: ekuveri davlat-tak, United Nations: ekuverikam, peacefulness: ekuveriyaa, friend

550 EKUN އެކުން adv. so much, too much (in neg. sentences); ekun aḍu gada-nukuree, don’t make such a noise! ekun baarař nuduvee, don’t run so fast! ekun riiti nuunek kamaku, though it isn’t all that beautiful

551 EKETI އެކެތި n. For ekati

552 EKOḶAS (obs.) އެކޮޅަސް num. eleven (= egaara) [S. ekoḷos, Skt. ēkādaśa]

553 EKKAKU އެއްކަކު adv. indefinite form of ekii, in neg.sentences : ekkaku e beenumek nukurameve, I don’t want that at all: ekkaku beerakař nudee, don’t go out together!

554 EKKALA އެއްކަލަ adj. the aforesaid: ekkala gotař, as before: ekkala kamtak, the matter we mentioned

555 EGAARA އެގާރަ num. eleven [H. igārah]

556 EŇGA އެނގަ n. lower ropes for adjusting square sails

557 EŇGENII އެނގެނީ v . is realized, is understood, known (hon. eňgi vaḍai-gannavanii) ; mařakař neeňge, I don't know, don't understand: kam neeňge, perhaps: eenaa annaane kam neeňgee, I daresay he will come: eenaa annaanee kamek neeňgee, I don't suppose he'll come: tiyayek ves eňgidaane taa! we shall see: eňgevigen, having come to realize: fun min eňgumek nuvaa, of incalculable depth ; aharen eňgijje ta, can you recognize me? (hon., aḷugaňḍu eňgi-lavvaifi too?)
(invol. of aňganii) [S. (h)äňgenne]

558 ECCEK އެއްޗެއް See eti: ecces, anything (for eccek ves)

559 ECCITI, ECCIHI, ECCETI, ECCEHI (eccissek) އެއްޗިތި - އެއްޗިހި - އެއްޗެތި - އެއްޗެހި n. things (hon., ecceti- koḷu, perquisites; mahu eccetikoḷu, monthly stipend: pl., ecceti-tak); also used of animals. eccehi kiyanii, makes insulting remarks: ecceti govanii, scolds: ecceti govum gaňḍek, a host of jibes [For eti-eti]

560 EḌRES އެޑްރެސް n. address [E. address]

561 ET އެތް n. elephant: spray of coconut flowers (etu-maa); etu-madu, a medicinal plant, gynura pseudochina [S. ät, Skt. hastin]

562 ET-TEḶI އެތްތެޅި n. instrument used by toddy tappers

563 E-TAK އެތަކް See e

564 ETI (eccek) އެތި n. thing,unit :

fen eti, water container (wooden bath for the aged): roří fihaa eti, frying pan: anna eti, woman's undergarment; mii eccakař nuvee, this is no good: eccakař vaa kahala eccek, a thing of use: ivee ta ma kiyaa eccek? do you hear what I say? rufiyaa-akař diha eti, ten for a rupee: dunidaňḍiyekge ha eti, six bows; hedumek eccek, a garment or the like.

Used of animals: muḍuhaalakii varař us eccek , the Chittagong fowl is a very big creature; and of ships : manavarek eccek, a man-of-war or the like.

Also frequently ifc., e.g. eeti, miiti, ecceti, taketi, anekati, boḍeti; eti-koḷu, piece, bit (esp. of food): libee e., income: etietikoḷu, various pieces: eti-gaňḍu, larger piece, object: fen dee etigaňḍu, watering can; liyaa etigaňḍu, object being turned: eti-faharu, blows, strokes; etifaharek jahaifi, gave a blow; etifaharek araifi, received a blow; kitak etifaharu eḷi hee, how many strokes did he give you? eti-fodu, drop of liquid: eena-ař etifodek nubovee, he can't drink a drop

565 ETURENII އެތުރެނީ v. is arranged in order : safař etureeře, stand in line!
(Enlargement: eturi-lanii) (invol. of aturanii) [S. ätirenne]

566 ETERI-GE (anc. ETERE-GE) އެތެރިގެ - އެތެރެގެ n. innermost room, principal bedroom

567 ETERE އެތެރެ n. the inside : jooḍuge etere,the inside of the cup:

Often ifc., e.g. deetere, geetere (and see tere); etere kuranii, imports;
etere-koilu, inner part of the former royal palace:
etere-ge, see eterige:
etere-fuř, inner surface (e.g.of clothing):
etere-vari, 1. inner lagoon of an atoll 2. South-East Asia (irumatii eterevari):
etere-haři (eterehaṭṭek), the inner body
[S. ätulu (aturu, atara), Skt. antara]

568 ETTIRIIS އެއްތިރީސް num. 31 (= tiriis ekek) [cf. H. iktīs]

569 ETTEYO (ettelek) އެއްތެޔޮ n. cane plant, calamus: goňḍiyekgai etteyo furanii, canes a chair

570 EDURU އެދުރު n. religious teacher: eduru bee, teacher: eduru daita, teacher's wife; great expert: raazuvaage e., chess expert (also used sarcastically, of poor teachers) [S. äduru, teacher, Skt. ācārya]

571 EDENII އެދެނީ v. asks, requests (abs. ede : hon. edi vaḍaigannanii) :

often with dat., kaleař edunii, asked you, ehiiař edijje, asked for help: eenaa kibain / faraatun / ariahun (hon.) edum, personally requesting him: mu'aaf edi-daanu heyyeve, will you apologize? ma atuvejje kam eenaa-ař angai dinum edem, please tell him I've come; aharen adi ekfaharu kalee duřum / duřumař / deken edemee, I should like to see you once more: varař edunu, asked pressingly
edevee, edevigen vaa, suitable (invol. part.); edumtak, desires (v.n.);
edum-veri, desirous [S. ayadinne, Skt. āyācate]

572 EŇDU އެނދު n. bed (hon., eňdu(daan)koḷu): eňdek jahaalum, constructing a bed; dimaa e., bed facing the entrance(belonging to the owner): uturu e. / boḍu e., principal lady's bed: fat jehi e., folding bed: eňdu- fat, two edges of bed: eňdu-foti, sheets [S. äňda, cf.Skt. śayyā]

573 EŇDUM އެނދުން v. burning (intr.) (v.n. of aňdanii) [S. dām]

574 ENI-GAŇḌU އެނިގަނޑު n. mucus: enienigaňḍu, drops of mucus

575 ENGUM އެންގުން v. announcement (v.n. of anganii, hon. engevum)

576 ENJEE އެންޖީ For eňdi + -ee, burnt: see aňdanii

577 ENDUM އެންދުން v. burning (tr.) (v.n. of andanii)

578 ENDERI އެންދެރި n. a black coral, sea ebony: enderi-sabaa, a Hindu play

579 ENNEVUM އެންނެވުން v. putting on (hon.) (v.n. of annavanii) [S.ändavīm]

580 EN-MULI އެންމުލި n. a plant, hedyotis umbellata (called 'kotaru kaa vina', pigeon-grass)

581 ENMEN އެންމެން See ekmen (s.v. ek)

582 EBA އެބަ particle of present continuity , used before verbs:

eba uḷee ta, is (he) at home? eba uḷuvvaa (hon.), he is: sarukaarun eba masakkat kuravvaeve, the government is taking action: fotek eba ot, there is a book: miihaku eba huri, there is a man (but miihaku hunnaniiee, a man is staying (here)): gahek eba hedee, a tree is growing: eenaa eba aade, he's just coming: aharen eba annam, I'm just coming: eba bolugai rissaa, my head aches: fonuvan eba uḷem, I'm going to send [H. ab, now]

583 EBE-FILI އެބެފިލި n. sign for short e after a consonant

584 EBOT އެބޮތް v. is [= eba+ ot]

585 EŇBURENII އެނބުރެނީ v. twists, revolves (intr.); is sprained: duniye eňburenii irun huḷangařeve, the earth revolves from east to west:

(adv.) eňburi, back again; eňburemun seňburemun, revolving (doublet) (invol. of aňburanii) [S. äňbarenne]

586 EŇBUU (eňbulek) އެނބު n. kind of tree, ximenia americana or glochidion [S. äňbul (phyllanthus emblica), P. ambila, Skt. āmalaka]

587 EM އެން n. bait-fish (of various kinds) : em damanii, catches bait in net: em hifanii, catches bait; em (boo) maḍi, kind of sting ray, manta: em-gaňḍu, shoal of bait; chopped up piece of bait: em-beeru, shallow part of open sea: em-vat, compartment for bait on fishing boat; emvatu-fali, pair of oars by the bait compartment: em-vaři, basket for bait on the boat [S. äm, Skt. āmiṣa]

588 EMUNENII އެމުނެނީ v. gets spiked: ořtak varař faseehain emununu, the seeds were threaded very easily (on the rosary); (met.) mitanař neemuneeřee, don't barge in! (invol. of amunanii) [S. äminenne]

589 ERAHAṬṬANII އެރަހައްޓަނީ v. (anc.) sends off on a journey (v.n. ereheṭṭum): daturu / daturař ereheṭṭum (mod., daturař eruvum)

[Enlargement of aranii (cf. hifahaṭṭanii, obahaṭṭanii)]

590 ERENII އެރެނީ v. is lifted; climbs in (as v. climbs up), enters (hon., eri--vaḍaigannanii): goňḍudořař erifai, after going to the beach (as a latrine): farař erenii, walks on the reef (as v. farumaccař aranii, of a shipwreck):bokakař erijje, trod on a frog: ruňba-ař kaňḍaa eruni, ants have got into the pot: vevař neereeřee, don't go into the tank! (invol.

of aranii)

591 ELAKUNIYYAA އެލަކުނިއްޔާ adv. if so (dialectical)

592 ELANGALAN އެލަންގަލަން n. a children's game, involving recital of a jingle beginning aliilaan baliilaan. Doublet, elangalan - milangalan.

593 ELAVARU އެލަވަރު n. the stretch of a man (used with keum, 'eating'): mi gas magee elavaru nukai, I can't reach round this tree: tin miihun elavaru kaa varuge gahek, a tree it takes three men to reach round (cf. at-guḷi)

594 ELUVANII އެލުވަނީ v. hangs(tr.) -- of objects: karu e., bows the head: eluvaa taḷu, padlock (caus. of elenii)

595 ELENII އެލެނީ v. hangs down (intr.): rukuge fantak elijje,the coconut foliage hangs down: (met.) magee hitvaru elijje, I have lost heart: hit nueleeřee, don't despair! [S. ellenne]

596 ELMENIYAM (ELMINIYAA) އެލްމެނިޔަމް (އެލްމިނިޔާ) n. aluminium [E. aluminium]

597 ELLANII އެއްލަނީ v . throws, throws away (hon. ellavanii): at e., waves hand: gañḍu e., turns page: guḍi e., flies kite: nanu e., casts fishingline; booḷa e., throws ball; Enlargement: daḷigañḍu ellaa-lanii, throws the stem away.
The word is more specific or individual than ukanii.

598 -EVE -އެވެ suffix marking a quotation (cf.Skt. iti); ending added to literary verb-forms (see -ee) [S. -yi]

599 ES (ehu) އެސް n. decorative gem in a ring; bicycle reflector; ibc., eye: es-fiya, eyelash: esfiya jahanii, blinks: es-fiinaa, evil eye, evil influence; esfiinaa lanii, esfiinaa aḷanii, exerts evil influence: es-bari, row of gems: es jehi, adorned with gems [S. äs, eye, Skt. akṣi]

600 ES-MAA(-malek) އެސްމާ n. a tough medicinal seed, strychnos potatorum

601 E-SAAHITU އެސާހިތު adv. See isaahitu

602 ESMATI އެސްމަތި n. See ismati

603 ES-VAḶU, ESU-VAḶU އެސްވަޅު - އެސުވަޅު n. a deep wart

604 ESSI-GANNANII އެއްސިގަންނަނީ v. attacks verbally (slang), with -aa of the person attacked (invol. of assanii, ties= clings)

605 ESSUM (hon. essevum) އެއްސުން v. tying (v.n. of assanii)

606 EHAŇḌA އެހަނޑަ n. hawk, eagle

607 E-HAA އެހާ 1. See e

608 EHAA އެހާ 2. onom. sound of a child crying: ehaa ehaa kiyanii, is sobbing

609 EHII އެހީ 1. n. help (esp. financial): e. denii, gives help in kind (to, dat. or -aai); ehii vanii, ehii ve denii, gives help in action: ekamaai ehii ve, helping in that matter: ehiiek sarukaarun ve dinii, help was given by the government: daulatuge ehiigai, with state assistance:

ehii-teri(yaa), helpful (person) : aḷugaňḍař ehiiteri ve devvi, gave me help

610 EHII އެހީ 2. v. heard, asked: 2p. ehin ta, did you hear? [ahanii]

611 E-HEN އެހެން 1. See e

612 EHEN އެހެން 2. adj. other, different: mařař ehen gotakař hiivanii, I think otherwise: ehen miihek, a different man: ehenehen, ehenihen, several other: ehennaa, ehenñaa, in different circumstances, formerly: in isolation, indicates assent

613 E-HENII އެހެނީ 1. See e

614 EHENII އެހެނީ 2. v. is heard, is listened to: ehijje, (I) heard (invol. of ahanii) [S. ähenne]

615 EHELANII އެހެލަނީ v. drags (boat) ashore

616 EḶENII އެޅެނީ v. is spread, is poured: au furaanaek eḷuneve, a new life was given: miihakaa e., engages in intercourse (esp.homosexual) : libaahař sai eḷijje, tea was spilt on the tunic: vai eḷenii, has to do with ('gets the smell'), eenaa-aa vaek neeḷeenam, I won't have anything to do with him: hiyani eḷifai, a shadow fell ;

keňḍi neeḷi (adv.),without ceasing (cf. keňḍenii)

Caus., ali eḷuvee too, (to see) if light be thrown (invol. of aḷanii)

617 -EE (-EVE) -އީ (-އެވެ) suffix added to verbal forms, or to complete literary sentences [S. -yi]

618 EE (EI) އޭ (އެއި) excl . look here! (Also written een, eet):

ee ee! ahoy! ee too eve! is that so?

619 EE- -އޭ ibc. for e- in compound words or before case-endings:

eege (eige) , eegai, of that, in that: eege anek duvas, the following day;
eeccek (e+ eccek), that thing: eeccekee miiccekee bunefai, spoke of this and that:
eeti (eiti), that thing, it; also of animals or spirits (pl. eetimen):
eetikoḷu (e+ etikoḷu), that piece:
eeti-miiti, this and that:
eeňda (e + iňda), that sitting: eeňdagen annanii, is coming (e.g.in a car)
eenii (e+ inii), is sitting there:
eeru (eiru), at that time, then: eerunnoo, what then?

620 EEKU އޭކު num. one (in Navata tables: eeku eeku dui, 1 + 1 = 2)

621 EEḌI-FEEḌI އޭޑިފޭޑި n. (anc.) skill: eeḍi-feeḍi nuhunna, not having good taste, unskilful : kamtakugai eeḍifeeḍi net miihun, those who are unskilful (doublet; also heeḍi-feeḍi [feeḍi]

622 EET އޭތް excl. See ee : sometimes answered by oot

623 EEN އޭން excl. See ee

624 EENAA އޭނާ pr. he, she (used of all grades in the singular)

625 EEBEE-FILI އޭބޭފިލި n. sign for long e after a consonant

626 OI އޮއި n. current (oi-gaňḍu): udoi, rising tide: fuloi, falling tide:beeru oi, seaward current: vavoi, landward current: oi matii, on the current: oyaa danii, oyaa lanii, drifts; oyaa daa kaaṭṭakun rukek nufaḷaane, a palm tree will not arise from a drifting coconut, i.e. a rolling stone gathers no moss (prov.): oi vanii, rots in the sea;

oi-kaḷu, dark clouds without rain:
oi-kaaři, coconut that has rotted in the sea:
oi-kuni, floating rubbish,flotsam:
oi-naaři, floating coconut shell:
oi-fař, place where two currents meet:
oi-varu, current, tide: (met.) state of things, storminess:
oi-vaali, flotsam [S. oya, river, Skt. srōtas]

627 OGARU އޮގަރު n. ancient type of perquisite for royal service

628 OṬṬARU އޮއްޓަރު (އޮށްޓަރު) See oř

629 OṬṬU އޮއްޓު n. splint : o .aḷanii, fixes splint

630 OḌAA (oḍalek) ޮއޑާ n. adze: o. lanii, uses adze, planes wood, (met.)gesticulates insultingly (at..,..-aa dimaa-aṙ): oḍaa-vaḷu, instep

631 OḌI ޮއޑި n. large sailing boat, now obsolete, with two masts and a square sail: also used for any type of vessel; o. aḷanii, keeps o. anchored;
gaa oḍi, coral- loading dhoni: mas oḍi (anc.), fishing dhoni: vatu o., lower spool of sewing machine: oḍii kuňbu, mast of an odi:

oḍi-keňḍi, the last sail to be raised:
oḍi-kee (-kee-ek), kind of woodworm:
oḍi-koḷu, nobleman's odi:
oḍi-faharu, (collective pl.) odis:
oḍi-mati, deck of an odi:
oḍi-vaḷu, pit serving as dry dock for an odi:
oḍi-veri, owner of an odi (or doni):
oḍi-hanu, mixing bowl for medicines:
oḍi-haruge, boatyard (in general) [cf. S. oru, ? T. ōṭam]

632 OḌUVANII ޮއޑުވަނީ v. Used in phrase deba oḍuvaa (debooḍuvaa), backbiting (as adj.)

633 OT ޮއތް v. lying, lain (p.p. of onnanii): mi otii, here it is: otiyyee = otii+ -eve: ot gotaṙ ovvai, being as it is: mihaaru otii ot gotakaṙ nuunee, is not now as it was: dooni tayyaaraṙ oteve, the dhoni was ready: rayyitunnaṙ ot kamek, action incumbent on citizens: eenaa-aṙ ot raṙek, an island in his charge [S. (h)ot, Skt. supta]

634 OTUM ޮއތުމް v. lying (v.n. of onnanii): ota nudii, not letting be

635 ONA- -ޮއނަ num. ibc., one less than: ona-vihi, 19: ona-tiriis, 29 (= navaaviis): ona-saaḷiis, 39: ona-fansaas, 49: ona-haṭṭi, 59: ona-hattari, 69: ona-aahi, 79: onavai, 89 (for ona-navai): ona-satta, 99 [S. unu, Skt. ūna]

636 ONI (onñek) ޮއނި n. skeleton, frame (e.g. of drum, picture, kite, building) (oni-gaňḍu)

637 ONU ޮއނު n. bamboo, bambusa vulgaris:

onu-ura, bamboo case (for steaming food, or keeping documents):
onu-galam, pen with bamboo handle:
onu-gaňḍu, blowpipe (as bellows, fumee onugaňḍu) :
onu- hiri, kind of coral limestone with holes in it:
onu-hui, a plant, panicum maximum [S. uṇa, Skt. vēṇu]

638 ONNANII ޮއންނަނީ v. lies, remains, is (v.n. otum: abs. ove , ovegen: p.p. ot: 3s. ove-eve) : fotek eba otee, there is a book: booṭ baňdarugai otee, the steamship is in harbour: bagiicaaek ove-eve, there is a garden:
ovvai, while being; mihen kam ovvai, things being so: ove ove, by remaining:

ovejje,was: ovevenii (invol.), finds itself to be: bunan onnaane kam, that (I) have to say: geneveekař noonnaane-ee, it won't be possible to import : Enlargement: ove-laafai, having waited. Both onnanii and hunnanii frequently correspond to E. 'is', the distinction being one of idiom [S. hovinne, Skt. svapiti]

639 OFI އޮފި n. branch: ofi-koḷu, twig: ofi-gaňḍu,branch [cf. gofi]

640 OFIIS (ofiihek) އޮފީސް n. office: ofiis otii ta, do you have 'office' (this morning)? [E. office]

641 OFU އޮފު n. sheen: o. aruvanii, polishes [S. opa, Pkt. oppa]

642 OBANII އޮބަނީ v. presses down: (invol.) settles down (of liquids); aḍiyař obenii, settles to the bottom; fai hilavaḷu obenii, all sounds die away; obee diyavaru, ebb tide:

disappears from sight: (enlarged) loo matiin obaa-laifieve, went out of sight: rař obaa hisaabun, when the island was no longer visible;

Caus., obbanii : enlargement (invol.), obbaa-levenii [S. obanne]

643 OBAHAṬṬANII އޮބަހައްޓަނީ v. maintains (habit): controls (child), keeps quiet (v.n. obaheṭṭum, obeheṭṭum) [Enlargement of obanii (cf. erahaṭṭanii, hifahaṭṭanii)]

644 OBI (otbek) އޮބި n. oilpress; shuttle presser:

o. aḷanii, uses the oilpress: (met.) o. onnanii, is under control: eenaa obi nootiiyaa, if he is not under control: obi onna varakař kamtak gendee, keep things under control! aḷugaňḍař obi onna varek nuun, I can't cope:

obi-gaňḍu, shuttle presser: splint

645 OBO-FILI އޮބޮފިލި n. sign for short o after a consonant

646 OMAA, OMAAN އޮމާ - އޮމާން adj. smooth: o. kuranii, makes smooth; omaa-mas, glans penis

647 ORI އޮރި 1. n. kind of fish with a distinctive smell (galu o.)

2. adj. warped, lopsided (cf. aňga-ori); (doublet) ori-bori: o. damanii, is warped: o. vanii, is lopsided [cf.S. ora-kopu venne, slants]

648 ORIYAAM އޮރިޔާމް n. nakedness: naked

o. nivaa kuranii, hides nakedness: oriyaamun vanii, oriyaamun hunnanii, is naked: oriyaam kaaḍu, filthy postcard [U. 'uryān]

649 ORUDAA އޮރުދާ n. In case-form orudaa-ař, in streams (e.g.of blood, sweat)

650 OLA އޮލަ adj. thick (of liquids): ola koř geenum, grinding till thick: (met.) absorbing, o. vaahaka, absorbing conversation

651 OLA-FUŘ އޮލަފުށް n. fine flour of hi<u>tt</u>ala

652 OLAŇBU އޮލަނބު n. plumbline: o. baalanii, o. jahanii, drops plumbline [S. olaṅbu, P. olambaka]]

653 OLI އޮލި n. thatched hut (oli-fatigaňḍu)

654 OVE އޮވެ v. having lain (abs. of onnanii): ove ove, by lying in storage [S. heva]

655 OVVAI އޮއްވައި v. while being [onnanii]

656 OSSANII އޮއްސަނީ v. pours out (tr.): invol., sets (of heavenly bodies): iru ossunii, the sun set: (met.) ossen daa tariigai vidum kuḍa vaane-eve, a star which is going to set will give little light (prov., referring to old age) [caus. of ohenii]

657 OHI-VARU އޮހިވަރު n. solidified spill-over (of a chew) [ohenii]

658 OHENII އޮހެނީ v. pours out (intr.), overflows: fengaňḍu ohigenfi, the water overflowed: fen eti ohijje, the water container overflowed [S. ihinne, Skt. siñcati]

659 OHORANII, OHORENII އޮހޮރަނީ - އޮހޮރެނީ v. is shed (e.g. tears or blood); caus., ohoruvanii , sheds [S. ihiranne, Skt. utsārayati]

660 OŘ އޮށް n . 1. seed (ořu madu, kernel: toḷi oř, bean in pod): eyeball (loluge oř): testicle (slang, or of animals): marbles (fas oř, a girl's game) : oř kuranii, chews the cud;

oř-kafa, bush cotton (as v. fuř- kafa, hanaa-kafa):

oř-guḍuvaa, a swelling on cats' tails, used medicinally, and (met.) as an insult;

oř-goňḍi, board for playing ořvaḷu:

ořṭaru, grains (kanjař aḷaa ořṭaru): ořṭaru kuri, ořṭaru kurevvi, consisting of grains (also written oṭṭaru):

oř-dautak, drops of sweat:

oř-vaḷu, a board game (esp. for women) =S.oliňda [S. äṭa, Skt. asthi]

2. camel (anc., mod. jamalu) [S. oṭu, Skt. uṣṭra]

661 OŘANI އޮށަނި n. a medicinal plant, datura [cf.S. attana]

662 OŘAAḶA n. pimples on the face, acne: o. naganii, pimples arise

663 OŘI n. central rib of coconut frond: o. aři(-gañḍu), a seat made of tied sticks (instead of planks)

664 OŘU n. See oř

665 OŘOONNANII v. lies down (v.n. ořootum : p.p. ořoot : abs. ořoove : imp. ořoovee!) See also onnanii [cf. iřiinnanii and innanii]

666 OḶANII v. rolls up (at o., atukuri o., rolls up sleeves; kunaa o., rolls up mat):

winds up,winds on (nanu o., winds up twine: with enlargement, dañḍigañḍakař barani oḷaa-lanii, winds up line on reel: fořaa oḷanii,winds on a headdress : faguḍi o., winds a turban on):

oḷenii (invol.), gets mixed up: nanu oḷijje, the line is tangled; (met.) kamtak oḷenii, things get mixed up: buddi oḷenii, senses get confused: mařař magu oḷijje, I lost the way; oḷumek nufilaa, unintelligible: oḷum- boḷum vejje, got all confused (doublet)

Caus., oḷuvanii: (with enlargement) mii oḷuvaa-lumek nuun, this is no deception: oḷum filuvanii, makes clear, solves problem [S. veḷanne, Skt. √vēṣṭ]

667 OḶI n. threshold (tiri o.): mati oḷi, lintel: kañḍu oḷi, straits, narrow entrance: oḷi-gañḍu (met.), housewife: migee oḷigañḍu vařař rañgaḷu, your wife is excellent: oḷi-medu, a former class of royal officials and their duties; tin oḷimedu, the functionaries known as varuhagu, attaarafani and askaru [S. eḷi-pata, uḷu-vasu]

668 OḶU 1. adj. tame [S. hīlä]

2. n . shallow pool for husking coconuts, or planting yams (oḷu- ala): natural gap in a reef (oḷu-tere):

3. oḷu añbaranii, oḷu aḷanii, applies 'Spanish windlass' : oḷu lanii, wrestles; cuddles

669 OḶU-DUU n. Ceylon, Lanka [S. Eḷu (=Sinhala) + dū (Skt. dvīpa)]

670 OḶU-FAŘ n. non-heartwood, growing portion of tree

671 OḶUM - BOḶUM v. confusion, misunderstanding (doublet, v.n. of oḷanii)

672 OOKAŘ n. In phrase ookař damanii, retches [S. okkāra, P. uggāra]

673 OOKIḌU އޯކިޑު n. ground orchid (pen name of M. Amin Didi; name of a main road in Male) [E. orchid]

674 OOGA އޯގަ n. auspicious moment (in phrase amaruta ooga) [Skt. yōga]

675 OOGAA-TERI, OOGAA-VERI (hon. OOGAA-VANTA) އޯގާތެރި - އޯގާވެރި - އޯގާވަންތަ adj. kindly

676 OOT އޯތް excl. to shout assent (answering to eet!), or to attract attention: miihakoot! anyone there?

677 OOBAT އޯބަތް n. medicinal plant, fenugreek, also used in cooking: oobatu haluvaa, a medicinal sweetmeat

678 OOBU އޯބު n. an ancient measure, quarter of a laahi

679 OOBOO-FILI އޯބޯފިލި n. sign for long o after a consonant

680 -OOLA(-eve), -YOOLA(-eve) -އޯލަ(އެވެ) -ޔޯލަ(އެވެ) suffix indicating 'they say', e.g. netoola, it is not, they say: eccekoola, it is such a thing, I hear: aiiyoolaeve, they came, I hear ; oola kořlanii, throws doubt [S. -lu]

ކ KAAFU, the 7th letter of the Maldivian alphabet

Kaafu atoḷu, Male atoll (North and South), the seventh atoll from the north

681 KAI, KAA ކައި - ކާ v. having eaten (abs. of kanii): kai boi hadaigen, after food and drink [S. kā, Skt. khāditvā]

682 KAITUVAK-BAḌI ކައިތުވަކްބަޑި n. (anc.) musket [T. kaittuvakku, pistol: S. kālatuvakku, cannon]

683 KAIRI (KAARI) ކައިރި (ކާރި) n. edge: vicinity, near: magee kairiigai, near me, beside me: aharenge geaa varař kairieve, it is very near our house: eenaa kairiigai bune, having spoken to him:

k . aḷanii, hems a garment: k. kuranii, brings near (to..,..-aa); mas nimeen varař kairi vefai vani kоř, when the month was nearly finished;

kairi-fař, edge (e.g. of table, kerchief: not of wells, bowls) [S. karā]

684 KAIRU ކައިރު n. a chewing substance, acacia catechu
[H. khair, Skt. khadira]

685 KAIVAT ކައިވަތް n. a span, 9 inches, a third of a riyan
[T. kai, hand + S. viyat, P. vidatthi]

686 KAIVANI, KAIVENI (KAAVENI) (kaiveññek) ކައިވަނި - ކައިވެނި (ކާވެނި) n. marriage: k. kuranii (high hon., k. ballavaigannanii), enters into marriage: k. koř denii, k. laa denii, solemnizes marriage: k. denii, gives in marriage: [U. kābin, marriage portion]

687 KAU ކައު adj . holy (kau ituru), used of God or the Prophet (cf. ekkauvanta) ; also in firi-kau-kalun, husband (high hon.)

688 KAUNI ކައުނި n. See kaani

689 KAUḶU ކައުޅު n. See kaaḷu

690 KAK ކައް n. armpit gusset : kak nulai kaňḍaa libaahek, a libaas cut without gusset [H. kākh, Skt. kakṣa]

691 KAKAKAKA ކަކަކަކަ onom. kakakaka aḷanii, laughs loudly

692 KAKAA ކަކާ n. kakaa beekalun, a class of former royal officials

693 KAKAARA ކަކާރަ n. a feat of games in shieldsmanship: k. naganii, performs the feat

694 KAKUNI ކަކުނި n. crab (k.-haru, crab burrow) : pincers (mohoru nagaa k.)
[S. käkuḷu, Skt. karkaṭa]

695 KAKUU (kakulek) ކަކޫ n. knee: k. huḷu, knee-joint: k. jahanii, kneels
[S. kakul, leg: P. -kankala (aṭṭhikankala, skeleton)]

696 KAKKAKAAKOO ކައްކަކާކޯ onom. k. govanii, crows as a cock (cf.kaakaa)

697 KAKKANII ކައްކަނީ v. cooks (v.n. kekkum : imp. kakkaa! Enlargement, kakkaa-lanii: see also kekenii): fen k., boils water: fenu kekki, boiled in water: bat k., cooks rice: bařiigai kakkaa riha, curry cooked with brinjals: sai kuraa kakkaalum, boiling the kettle; Caus.(met.), lee kakkuvaalum, making the blood boil

[? cf. S. kakiyanne, aches, or Skt. kvathate, boils]

698 KACAVARU, KACOORU ކަޗަވަރު - ކަޗޯރު n. artificial slipway or jetty

699 KACCALA, KACCELA ކައްޗަލަ - ކައްޗެލަ n. a creature found on seaweed

700 KACCAA ކައްޗާ 1. adj. inferior
2. adv. sideways, see kati

701 KACCEE ކައްޗޭ 1. n. a cap worn by the former hangubeekalun
2. v. an imp. of kanii, will you eat!

702 KAṬAKARAA ކަޓަކަރާ n. part of the old royal palace

703 KAṬAARII ކަޓާރީ n. dagger [H. kaṭārī, Skt. kaṭṭāra]

704 KAṬU ކަޓު adj. old-fashioned (pej.): kaṭu mullaa, ignorant mullah

705 KAṬUURAA (-aek) ކަޓޫރާ n. a small metal storage container [H. kaṭōrā]

706 KAṬṬAFUḶI ކައްޓަފުޅި n. kind of fish, easily adaptable to fresh water, flagtail, kuhlia

707 KAṬṬALA ކައްޓަލަ n. kind of edible tuber, dioscorea pentaphylla: bilet k., kind of kaṭṭala, dioscorea purpurea [kaři + ala, 'thorn-yam']

708 KAṬṬAA ކައްޓާ n. 1. huge scales, weighbridge (for fish)
2. = kaři + -aa, bones and..

709 KAṬṬI -BALI ކައްޓިބަލި n. malingering, unexplainable illness

710 KAṬṬEK ކައްޓެއް See kaři

711 KAḌA ކަޑަ 1. n. wooden peg : k.jahanii, drives peg in
2. adj. of unseemly levity (usu. of girls): hiiňganegen kaḍa vejje, became choked with laughter; kaḍabok, in phrase kaḍabok jahaafai, going very fast (? making a noise like a frog): kaḍa-hini, giggling (n.): kaḍahini(-tak) hunum, giggling (v.); kaḍa-kam, levity

712 KAḌI ކަޑި n. red powder applied to boats or trees: k. lanii, applies k.

[H. khaȓī, chalk]

713 KAŇḌA- AḶANII ކަނޑައަޅަނީ v. decides (to, infin.; that..,..kamugai) adv., kaňḍa eḷigen, intentionally; decidedly : kaňḍa neeḷi, keňḍi neeḷi, unceasingly [kaňḍanii]

714 KAŇḌAT̲T̲U KURANII ކަނޑައްތު ކުރަނީ v. passes a point (of space or time) [Malayalam]

715 KAŇḌANII ކަނޑަނީ (v.n. keňḍum : hon. keňḍuvvum) v. breaks off, cuts away:
at k. cuts off hand; inoculates: fotun kuȓ k., corrects proofs of a book: gas k., ruk k., cuts down trees: of certain fruits, baňbukeyo k., picks breadfruit (cf.also eḷum, binum): mas k., cuts up fish: godan k., husks rice: person: taas k., shuffles cards: dat k., levels children's front teeth with a grindstone: faȓ k., breaks the (illegal) succession of marriages to the same person: riyaa kaňḍaa foti, sailcloth: haňḍuu k., husks rice: hedum k., cuts out clothes; (met.) musaarain rufiyaaek k., cuts one rupee from salary: subtracts, fansaviihun egaara k., subtracts 11 from 25; kaňḍaa fas nambaru, five subtraction sums; dismisses (with enlargement), madrasaain kaňḍaa-lanii, expels from school : booṭun kaňḍaalii, dismissed from ship; medu kaňḍanii, interrupts: vaahakaige medu kaňḍuvvaalevvii (hon.), interrupted (my) words; kaňḍaalanii, (I'm) ringing off (cf. baavvanii): kaňḍaa naganii, cuts out; engraves: kurehumgaňḍu kaňḍaa naganii, engraves a picture: oḍi kaňḍaigen furanii, stealing the odi from the harbour; viduvaru kaňḍaigen nude-eve, the lightning never ceases (cf. keňḍenii, invol.).

In some cases this word is used with a singular object, as v. koȓanii of plural objects , see huňguli.

Caus., miihun doonin kaňḍuvanii, signs the men off from the dhoni: miihun jassaa keňḍuvum, employing and dismissing men ; see also keňḍenii
[S. kaḍanne, Skt. khaṇḍayati]

716 KAŇḌAA (kaňdaek) ކަނޑާ 1. n. large ant [S. kaḍi]
2. v. cutting (pres. part. of kaňḍanii)

717 KAŇḌI ކަނޑި n. sword; (anc.) 300 naaḷi of rice [S. kaḍu, Skt. khaḍga]

718 KAŇḌIKI (kaňḍikkek) ކަނޑިކި n. traditional black woman's underskirt: k. foti, gingham

719 KAŇḌINMA ކަނޑިންމަ n. principal entrance to a harbour: kaňḍinmaa uḷaagaňḍu, chains formerly at the entrance to Male inner harbour

720 KAŇḌU ކަނޑު n. ocean, deep sea (maa kaňḍu) ; the crease (in game of manḍi): eenaa mihaaru kaňḍu kaňbanii, he is punting in the deep, i.e.trying to do the impossible: k. duvanii, sails the sea; k.-fat̲t̲anii, sinks (tr.) in the sea; k. beeru vejje, got into the open sea: k. vanii, is shipwrecked; kaňḍek kam faḷek kam neeňge, don't know if it is deep water or shallow, (met.) don't know what is going on;

k.-oḷi, straits, narrow entrance to shallow water:

k.-kukuḷu, a fish curry:
k.-kos, partially exposed flotsam: (met.) a useless man:
k.-toři, exposed reef:
kaňḍu-mati, St.Elmo's fire(appearing at night in calm weather): kaňḍumati aḷanii, phosphorescence appears: kaṇḍumatii duuni, bird of the deep sea
kaňḍu-mas, deep sea fish (esp. bonito): kaňḍumahu garudiya, oil from deepsea fish:
k.-labari, copycat : kaňḍulabari hadanii, repeats someone's words:
k.-hoḷi, coral encrustations (used medicinally)

721 KAŇḌUU (kaňḍulek) ކަނޑޫ n. fruit or timber of mangrove, Bruguiera sp.: fařan kaňḍuu-gaňḍu, piece of mangrove timber for a keel ; kaňḍuu-faa, mangrove swamp [S. kaňḍol]

722 KATAA (pl., katun) ކަތާ n. (anc.) person

723 KATI (kaccek) ކަތި adj. not straight; not vertical; sideways; crooked; (of roof) steep: kati kani, diagonal wall timber: kati-kam kuḍa, katikam maḍi, gently sloped; katikam boḍu, steeply sloped: kati riyaa, lateen sail; kati lolakun, askance: kati vadu, diagonal straps (of shoes); kati vaḷi, pruning sickle; (adv.) kaccař, sideways ; kaccaa duvanii (of kites), is easy to manoeuvre [? back formation from S. käti, sickle: T. katti]

724 KATILANII ކަތިލަނީ v. slaughters (religiously) [U. qatl, cf. gaatilu]

725 KATIIBU ކަތީބު n. administrator of an island; Friday preacher [U. khaṯīb]

726 KATURAAN ކަތުރާން n. tar : katuraanun dum aḷanii, makes smoke from tar [U. qaṯrān]

727 KATURU ކަތުރު n. scissors (katurek, pair of scissors): k.- kařigaňḍu, jawbone: k.- mas, saw- fish, pristis [S. katuru, Skt. kartari]

728 KATTIRI ކައްތިރި n. 1. sloping supports, esp. of a swing [S. kattirikā, tripod]
2. in royal titles, kṣatriya

729 KATDAA ކަތްދާ n. Maldivian form of the female name Khadiija: Katdaidi = Khadija Didi: Safaru Katdaa, a mythical being who gives capricious favours

730 KADARAATU ކަދަރާތު n. k. keňḍum, a system of arithmetical division [? ' quadratic']

731 KADAA (kadaek) ކަދާ n. metal drinking pot with splayed base

732 KADURU ކަދުރު n. dates (fruit) : k.ruk, date palm
[S. kaduru (mod. iňdi), Skt. kharjūra]

733 KADUU (kadulek) ކަދޫ n. bottle gourd, lagenaria vulgaris

734 KAŇDI (kañjek) ކަނޑި n. gruel, porridge (of various types: bat k., fufuu k., faḷoo k., kař̌ikeelu k.): kaňdi duvas, 9th and l0th Muharram,when rice pudding is eaten and children weighed against it: k. mas, the month Muharram
[S. käňda, T. kanji]

735 KAŇDILI ކަނޑިލި n. 1. paper lantern: lampshade: bright light
2. kinds of creeper: also a kind of banana (kaňdili- keyo)

736 KAŇDU ކަނޑު n. kind of tree, hernandia sp. (varieties: varu-kaňdu, mas-kaňdu; see also keňdi): k. aḷanii, puts rollers under boat ; k. demum, boys' indoor game, where a boy acts as a roller; k. vanii (anc.), gets exhausted (kaňdu-gaňḍakař vum);
mas kaňdugaňḍu, wooden post on dhoni for stunning fish when caught:
kaňdu-fati, raft: (met.) a go-between:
kaňdu- valuduuni, white tern (which nests in k .tree)

737 KAŇDURAA ކަނޑުރާ n. nape of the neck (of people) - considered a beauty spot

738 KAŇDOḶU ކަނޑޮޅު n. kind of plant , crinum asiaticum (rat k., boňḍi k.)

739 KAN ކަން n. 1. corner , point: hatareskan, square, a square; kankoḷu, utmost corners: kan matiigai, on the corner, near by; kankuti, slanting: (adv.) kankuccař, diagonally, across the corners ; kan-gaňḍu, projecting corners of the bolu-rumaa headdress [S. kan, Skt. kōṇa]

2. ear: kan dii ehum, kanu laa ehum, listening attentively: usually ibc. ; kan-kaři, corner of jaw, top of cheek; bows of ship: kan-neyo (kanneelek), bolster [S. kanvayin]: kan-fat, ear; kanfatu mudi, earring; kanfatu fuuḷu, ear lobe; kanfatu bagiicaa, a plant, acalypha sp.; dik-kanfat(i), a plant, commelina sp.: kanfati, toddy- tapper's sickle: kanfati vanii, see s.v. ; kan-huḷi, sideburns, hair beside the ear (also of women)
[S. kan (kanpata), Skt. karṇa]

740 KANA ކަނަ n. fruits of the midili tree (kana-madu, don kana, don madu)

741 KANA-KURI ކަނަކުރި n. dry fleshy coconut leaf tips (used medicinally)

742 KANA-MADU ކަނަމަދު n. ripe fruit or seed of midili tree

743 KANA-HAŇDUN ކަނަހަނދުން n. a medicinal timber, sandalwood [S. haňdun, Skt. candana]

744 KANAA ކަނާ n. (anc.) heron (mod. maa-kanaa) [S. kana-kokā, Skt. kaṃka]

745 KANAAT ކަނާތް n. right hand: right ; kanaatu fai, right leg ['eating hand', kana (mod. kaa) + at]

746 KANI (kanñek) ކަނި n. 1. spark (alifaan- kanı, dila-kani): kani(kani) lanii, becomes faintly visible: ran kani buraigen diya hen, like golden sparks flying

2. drizzle (vaaree k.): kani lanii, is drizzling

3. blackened upper portion of wick (kani-gaňḍu): batti kani kuranii, turns down the lamp: kani kaňḍanii,trims the wick: (met.) alifaangaňḍu kani vanii, the fire is going out

4. forked stick, prop (esp. for roof) : kuru k., short prop; medu k., medium prop; as- kani, eaves (q.v.): also kani-gaňḍu:

kani-fař, barb on harpoon, or on foreign fish-hooks:

kani-vaa, rope to hold a prop: kanivaa aḷanii, fastens the rope:

5. doorpost (dorukani: dekani, both doorposts): top or bottom edge of garment (munḍuge kani) [S. kaṇu, P. khāṇuka, post]

adj. 6. stale, bad (of liquids): kani hakuru, stale juggery; hakuru kani vejje, the juggery has gone off

747 KANII ކަނީ v. eats (v.n. keum : p.p. kei, kee : inf. kaan : abs. kai, kaa: 3s. ke- ee: imp. kai! caus. kavvanii : as hons. keem ballavanii and farikkuḷuvvanii, q.v.): masguḷa kanii, gets stiff muscles: iskoḷu keum, being able to stand: kai uḷenii, earns a living (by...); Enlargement, kai-lii, ate with pleasure, ate up; kamaa hiňgaa, let's eat ! See also kevenii [S. kanne, Skt. khādati]

748 KANIIRU ކަނީރު n. a flowering bush, oleander [S. kaṇēru, P. kaṇavīra]

749 KANU ކަނު adj. blind (pej.; polite, lolař neeňgee or nufenna):

loo kanu, ekloo kanu, blind in one eye: deloo kanu, blind in both eyes: loo aňdiri, short sighted: kanař govanii, accuses of blindness (a criminal action); kanu bannanii, blindfolds (tr.) [S. kaṇa, Skt. kāṇa]

750 KAN - ILI ކަންއިލި n. harpoon, spear [? for kani-ili]

751 KANKUN ކަންކުން n. a plant, ipomaea aquatica [S. kankun]

752 KAN-GATI ކަންގަތި n. an old class of officials: k. koli, appointment of such officials [? for kam-gat]

753 KANNELI (kanneyyek) ކަންނެލި n. a deep sea fish, yellowfin tuna, thunnus [cf. S. kaḷuvāllā]

754 KAN-FATI VANII ކަންފަތިވަނީ v. gets worn away (esp. of cooking vessels)

755 KANBAḶI ކަންބަޅި n. blanket (as clothing; not found in Male); stuffing for bicycle saddles; sheep (not found in Maldives) [T. kampaḷi, Skt. kambala]

756 KANBAA ކަންބާ n. kanbaa munḍu, a sarong woven in one piece, but cut and resewn [S. kambāya, E. 'comboy' (from Cambay)]

757 KANVAARU ކަންވާރު n. 1. old-fashioned metal cooking pot:
2. fishing line : karaa k., nylon fishing line; k. aḷanii, makes (twists) fishing line

758 KANZU ކަންޒު n. moat (formerly round the royal palace): k. kahaňbu, tortoise [U. khandaq, Persian, kanda, dug]

759 KANZUURI ކަންޒޫރި n. ceremonial food consumed at certain shrines at certain times [U. kandūrī]

760 KAFA ކަފަ n. cotton (varieties: oř k., fuř k., hanaa k.): kafa-gaňḍu, poultice (esp. for headlice): kafa-roolu, roll of cotton-wool [S. kapu, Skt. karpāsa]

761 KAFANII ކަފަނީ v. cuts up (v.n. kefum : hon. kappavanii) [S.kapanne, Skt. kalpayati]

762 KAFAAḶA ކަފާޅަ n. soft head of small children: kafaaḷa kekenii, (his) head is boiling, i.e. he is being troublesome [U. kapāl, Skt. kapāla, skull]

763 KAFI (katpek) ކަފި n. mast-crutch: fork of tree: kafi vanii, branches out, forks (of roots or trees)

764 KAFIHI ކަފިހި n. k. boli, a small striped cowrie

765 KAFU ކަފު n. towing; tow-rope; towing portion: k. jahanii, tows: batteli aii doonñek kafu jahaigen, the batteli towed a dhoni in; dooni genaii batteli kafugaee, the dhoni was brought in under tow from the batteli

766 KAFUN ކަފުން n. winding sheet, shroud: k. kuranii, k. lanii, puts shroud on (usu. 3 layers, or 7 layers if it can be afforded) [U. kafan]

767 KAFURU-TOḶI ކަފުރުތޮޅި n. cardamoms (see kaafuurutoḷi)

768 KAFU-LOO ކަފުލޯ n. a metal alloy (used for trumpets), bronze [for kahu-, S.kas, Skt. kaṃsa]

769 KAFEERAA ކަފޭރާ n. poultry cage (esp. on board ship)

770 KAPPI ކައްޕި n. pulley [T. kappi]

771 KAPPITAANU ކައްޕިޓާނު n. captain of a steamer (pl. kappitaanun (tak)) [Port. capitão]

772 KABI ކަބި adj. stupid

773 KABIILAA ކަބީލާ n. large metal rivet : k. jahanii, inserts rivet

774 KABBAABU ކައްބާބު n. cubeb (piper cubeba), kind of matikaraa bees [H. kabāb (kabāba)]

775 KAŇBAIDI ކަނބައިދި See kaňbaadi

776 KAŇBANII ކަނބަނީ v. punts (imp. kaňbaa!): eenaa mihaaru kaňḍu kaňbaniiee, he is punting in the deep, i.e. attempting the impossible [T. kampam, pole]

777 KAŇBALU(N) ކަނބަލު(ން) n. lady, wife (hon.): aňbi-kaňbalun, wife: de-kaňbalun, married couple: rani-kaňbalek, queen

778 KAŇBAA(-aaek) ކަނބާ n. name formerly applied to princesses (kaňbaa-faanu, famous lady)

779 KAŇBAADI, KAŇBAIDI ކަނބައިދި - ކަނބާދި n. a female title (=kaňbaa Diidii)

780 KAŇBILI (kaňbiyyek) ކަނބިލި n. a swift-flying bird, water-hen

781 KAŇBURU ކަނބުރު n. smith (mod. daganḍu taḷaa miihaa): kaňbu-verikam, smithery (on a larger scale than the finer tileerukam): k. maruteyo, smith's hammer [S. kaňburu, P. kammāra]

782 KAŇBULEEGE ކަނބުލޭގެ n. woman,wife (mid-grade) (hon., kaňbuleege-faanu): aňbi-kaňbuleege,wife: e kaňbuleege, she

783 KAŇBULOO(-oek) ކަނބުލޯ n. (my) daughter (all ranks); also as part of a name

784 KAŇBOO(-ooek) ކަނބޫ n . fruit pod of hittala

785 KAM ކަން n. deed, action:

ek ves kamek nukuram, I am not doing anything, I have nothing to do: kamtak boḍu vejje, (he) has a lot to do: eenaa-akař e kamek nuviee, he couldn't manage to do it: e miihaage kamtak fennanii varař nubai kořee, he is not shaping well (of an employee) or he is dangerously ill : e kamtakun najaa vaan, to be rid of that bother: tiya kamtakgaňḍun salaamat vaan, to be rid of that bother: kamek netiyyaa dee! if you don't want anything, go away: kam neeňge, perhaps: mihen kamun, by virtue of this: (ek ves) kamakaa nulai, without cause: maadamaa annaane kamek net, there is no need to come tomorrow, don't come tomorrow: kamek nuvee, no matter: tiyaii ek ves kamek nuun, that's no problem; kam-taktak, kam-kam, various actions:

This word is much used in reported speech, after nouns or participles, indicating 'the fact that' ; aḷugaňḍu dekenii eii varař ves raňgaḷu fotek kamařeve, I regard that as a very good book : ahannakař neeňge tii kaaku(ge) eccek kamek, I don't know whose it is: taalibun śukru namgannaanee kam yagiineve, it is certain that pupils will thank him: mi-ii ekařiigen vaa kamek kamugai hiivaa miihun, people who realize that this is a natural thing: beenum huri kamek kamakař ves nuhadateve, they don't even pretend that it is a necessary thing: vevidaane kamek kamakařek nufenee, doesn't seem possible: daa huri kamee, you must go

With the verb vum, this word is used to soften a previous verb; libunu kamař viyas, though (they) obtained(= libunas): nuvi kamugai viyas, though (it) was not (= nuviyas): kuḷenii kamugai nuvanii nama, if (it) doesn't play (tricks) (= nukuḷee nama).

This word may also represent 'in the function of'; ekme muhimmu badalek kamugai vii.., the most important change was..: gaaimagaam kamugai is kurum, appointing as deputy: e vaanii ehen kamař, it may be so.

kamaku may be used in a concessive sense, 'although' : irukoḷu kuḍaek kamaku, though the time was short: e miihaa boḍek kamaku, though he is an important person: beebe-ek kamaku, though (he) is a brother: e kamaku, nevertheless.

Grammatically, kam corresponds to 'tense': nimunu kam, past tense.

It also forms a nominal abstract termination, '-ness': madu-kam, fewness: ehiiteri-kam, helpfulness:

kamaakemi: all the actions, the full business:

kam-net, lazy: aḷugaňḍumen kamnetek nuvamueve,we are not lazy:

kam-faseeha, slack, careless: k. kořlanii, takes things easy:

kam-fuḷu, small amount (usu. in neg.sentences):

kam-boḍu, worried : k. kuranii, exaggerates:

kam-verikam, magic: kamveriyaa, magician:

kamu danii, is useful: gina miihunnař hiivii kamaku daakař net kamařeve, many people thought it was hopeless: aḷugaňḍakař maakamakař nudiyaee, it wasn't very satisfactory:

kamu voři, important (of people):

kamee hitanii, helps, respects (with dat.): mainbafainnař kamee hitaan vaane, you must honour your father and your mother [S. kam, Skt. karma]

786 KAMANA ކަމަނަ n. nickname for women

787 KAMANAA ކަމަނާ n. lady, princess (in stories, or in some islands)

788 KAMARAA ކަމަރާ n. cabin on a ship (kamaraa-tere) [H. kamarā, Port. camara]

789 KAMARU ކަމަރު n. strap, belt [U. kamar, belt]

790 KAMAḶI ކަމަޅި n. 1. chopping block 2. k. feḷenii, has a haemorrhage

791 KAMAA ކަމާ v. See kanii

792 KAMAALU ކަމާލު n. completion: k. kuranii, stacks and sorts cargo: hoards: appropriates [U. kamāl]

793 KAMIINAA ކަމީނާ adj. delicate, thin, undernourished [U. kamīna, ignoble, base]

794 KAMIIRU ކަމީރު n. leaven k. kuranii, makes dough with yeast [U. khamīr]

795 KARA ކަރަ n. The Coast, esp. of south India; foreign: Siinu k., China: Śaamu k., Syria: Oḷuduu k., Ceylon; karaa miihun, foreigners: karaa eňdu, imported bed (without railings): karaa duňburi, yellow oleander, thevetia sp. [T. karai]

796 KARANII ކަރަނީ v. burns, stings(intr.) (v.n. kerum): mii-ii varař karaa beehekeve, this medicine stings a lot

797 KARANKAA ކަރަންކާ n. kind of lily, hedychium coronarium

798 KARANṬIINU ކަރަންޓީނު n. quarantine [E. quarantine]

799 KARANṬU ކަރަންޓު n. electricity : k.burumaa, electric drill [E. current]

800 KARANFUU (-fulek) ކަރަންފޫ n. cloves [S. karābu, Port. cravo]

801 KARABU ކަރަބު n. a hundred thousand million (100 arabu)

802 KARA-MATI ކަރަމަތި n. wind blowing from India (karamatii vai) [kara]

803 KARAVERI ކަރަވެރި n. kind of fish (vehi-mas) , Indian mackerel, rastrelliger

804 KARAA (karaek) ކަރާ n. 1. watermelon, citrullus lanatus

2. See kara

805 KARAA ކަރާ v. 3. stinging (part. of karanii)

806 KARAANII ކަރާނީ n. clerk [H. k(i)rānī]

807 KARAAMAAT-TERI ކަރާމާތްތެރި adj. miraculous, holy (esp. of places) [U. karāmāt, miracles]

808 KARAASIINU ކަރާސީނު n. kerosine [E. kerosine]

809 KARU ކަރު n. 1. neck, throat:

mahuge k. aḷanii, removes gills etc. from fish: k. kahanii, clears the throat : k. hikkanii, dries up the throat, makes thirsty; aharen / magee karu hikkaee, I feel thirsty: karu hikkaa eccek, something that makes you thirsty :

karu-kuru bee, 'Short-neck' (a name in stories): karu-gohoru, fish entrails: karu-taafat, inner gill of fish (cf. kootaafat): karu-dan jehenii, gets besotted; eena-aa uḷenii karudan jehigen, (he) is besotted about her: karudan jehee varař moya vegen, being foolish to the point of imbecility: kamtakaa gen karudan jehijje, was madly keen on the matter: kamek kuran vegen karudan jehum, swotting something up; karu-fařṭaru, chain round the neck: karu-foḷu, dangerous swelling on the neck: karu-vaḷu, neck opening of the libaas : karu-viha, a disease of the throat [S. kara, shoulder, cf.Skt. kaṇṭha,throat]

2. core of certain fruits or flowers : karu-gaňḍu, pistil

3. staleness, of oil or oily food: karu-teo, rancid oil: karu-hakuru, thick white juggery: karu lanii, oozes sugar

810 KARUKAŘA ކަރުކަޑަ n. the sign Cancer [Skt. karkaṭa]

811 KARUDAAS ކަރުދާސް n. paper (karudaahek, a piece of paper):

guḍi hippaa k., tissue paper: deli k., blue- prints: faranjii k., newsprint: foti k., soft paper for decorations: paarusal k., brown paper: billuuri k., cellophane: boo k., cardboard: luuṭu k., glossy coloured paper: varaňgu k., silver paper: zinku k., silver paper: hila k., sandpaper [S. kaḍadāsi, Port. cartaz]

812 KARUNA ކަރުނަ (anc. KARUNU ކަރުނު) n. tears: lee k., 'bloody' tears [S. kaňdulu, cf.Skt. krandati, weeps]

813 KARUVANII ކަރުވަނީ v. gathers together haphazardly (v.n. keruvum):

miihungaňḍu keruviganegen, people gathering in a bunch: fuuhi k., bores: ruu k., crushes, wrinkles (tr.): hii k., shivers: hiili k., tickles (tr.)

814 KARENṬ ކަރެންޓް n. karenṭ hatiyaarek, a power tool (cf.karanṭu) [E. current]

815 KALA ކަލަ n. k. govanii, talks of own's own generosity (For -kala ifc., see e-, kon-, mi-)

816 KALANḌARU ކަލަންޑަރު n. a calendar [E. calendar]

817 KALAMIDI ކަލަމިދި adj. of very good (royal) family

818 KALAMINJAA ކަލަމިންޖާ n. person of kalamidi descent

819 KALARU ކަލަރު n. ancient large detachable collar for women [H. kālar, E. collar]

820 KALAA (KALAI) KURANII ކަލާ (ކަލައި) ކުރަނީ v. metal-plates, galvanizes [U. qala'ī]

821 KALAA ކަލާ 1. pr. you (more respectful than kalee)

2. n. God (when followed by -koo, in religious oaths): kalaa- koo(ee), maat kalaa- koo, for God's sake; kalaa- kooee, aharen duu kořlaifiyyaa, I wish to God you'ld let me go: mi-ii nudakkaa vaahaka-akař vejjiyyaa kalaa- kooee, I wish (you) hadn't said that (see also kalek, kalaañge)

822 KALAAŇGE ކަލާނގެ n. God: K. minvarufuḷu, the will of God

823 KALAAMU-FUḶU ކަލާމުފުޅު n. the word of God, the Qur'an [U. kalām, word, sentence]

824 KALAASIIN ކަލާސީން n. (pl.) former naval crews (who distributed Government allowances) [U. khalāsī, sailor]

825 KALIMA ކަލިމަ n. word (esp. the Islamic confession of faith) [U. kalima]

826 KALIYAA ކަލިޔާ n. a sweet dry curry of chicken entrails [U. qaliya]

827 KALIYAA-BIRINJII ކަލިޔާބިރިންޖީ n. a kind of cooked rice [U. birinj, rice]

828 KALUN ކަލުން n. (pl.) ifc., male people: de-kalun, two people: debafaa-kalun, father and child (hon.): dari-kalun, children(hon.): ras-kalun, Kings; also in meaning gods (pl. of kalek)

829 KALEK ކަލެކް n. a god (pl.kalun): kalek net miihun, godless people; also used as indefinite form of kaleege: eduru bee kalek, a religious teacher [cf.S. kenek]

830 KALEE ކަލޭ pr. you (pl. kaleemen): Enlarged form: kalee- vaa , now you.. (vaa (7)) [cf. S. kallu, Maldivians]

831 KALEEGE ކަލޭގެ n. ifc., a male suffix:

mudim-kaleege, the mosque official: bafaa-kaleege, father in law; used with other words, often somewhat offensively: kaňburu k., smith: Bumbaa k., Bombay man (Borah): raaveri k., toddy drawer; vagu k., thief; vaḍi k., carpenter: Singaḷa k., Sinhalese man: Sooḷiyaa k., 'Moor': Husain kaleege, Hussein (respectful)

832 KALEEGE-FAANU, KALEEFAANU ކަލޭގެފާނު - ކަލޭފާނު n.

a title, now used as a name

833 KALOO ކަލޯ n . hi you!(masc.) ; used to known children, e.g.Kuḍa kaloo! Otherwise impolite. In stories, used of animals, e.g.boňḍana kaloo (a bird)

834 KALOOGE ކަލޯގެ n. an ancient title, corresponding to kaleegefaanu

835 KALLI ކައްލި n. a children's game, played with stick and ball (also killii, kulli)

836 KAVANII ކަވަނީ v. moves aside (tr.), drives (a shoal of small fish) ; fastens a rope; muř kavanii / kavaa-lanii, closes the fist

837 KAVARU ކަވަރު n. harpoon

838 KAVAA ކަވާ n. cupping (bleeding): k. jahanii, practises cupping; kavaa-fuḷi, cupping bottle

839 KAVAABU ކަވާބު n. kind of fishcake

840 KAVI ކަވި 1. n. fleas: k.aḷaifi, is infested with fleas

2. adj. fiddly and troublesome: k. masakkat, k. kamek, a delicate job (e.g. watchmaking, needlework, cleaning rice)

841 KAVVANII ކައްވަނީ v. gives to eat, feeds (=kaan denii) (caus. of kanii)

842 KAS (kahek) ކަސް n. skin disease [S. kas, itch, Skt. kacchū]

843 KASABU ކަސަބު n. gold or silver thread in clothing: k. kinaari, ornamental stripes on cuffs etc.: k. boovaḷu, old type of fixed collar

844 KASAARII ކަސާރީ n. ancient type of metal kettle

845 KASIYAARU ކަސިޔާރު n. going aside: magun k. vanii, goes off the road; also k. aranii: siidaa magun k. araigen, departing from the direct route: fot-takař ves k. araifi, even made the books slide off

846 KASIIDAA ކަސީދާ n. silver thread embroidery on a libaas: k. kuranii, does such embroidery [U. kaśīda]

847 KASIIRAA ކަސީރާ n. sap of a tree, used medicinally

848 KASṬAM ކަސްޓަމް n. Customs house [E. customs]

849 KASTAḶU, KASTOḶU ކަސްތޮޅު - ކަސްތަޅު n. handcuffs; leg-irons: k. aḷanii, applies handcuffs

850 KASTUURI ކަސްތޫރި n. perfume from the musk mallow, hibiscus abelmoschus muscatus [S. & U. kastūrī, Skt. kastūrikā]

851 KASBII (pl.kasbiin) ކަސްބީ n. a classy prostitute (cf. naasi) [U. kasbī]

852 KASMATI ކަސްމަތި n. edge (esp. back edge of hair on the head): k. jahanii, shaves the back of the neck

853 KASRATU ކަސްރަތު n. exercise: k. kuranii, takes exercise: k. mubaaraat, sports- meet [U. kasrat]

854 KASRU ކަސްރު n. fractions (one of the 5 branches of arithmetic) [U. kasr]

855 KASSAÑDU-VAANI ކައްސަނދުވާނި n. medicinal sulphur (used as oil)

856 KASSAALANII ކައްސާލަނީ v. slips, slides [H. khisalnā]

857 KAHANALA ކަހަނަލަ n. kind of yam liable to cause itching : miinaa hiivanii kahanala kaigen uḷee henee, he seems to have eaten k., i.e. he talks too much

(prov.) [kaha- + ala]

858 KAHANII ކަހަނީ v. (v.n.kehum) 1. itches, causes to itch: gai kahanñaa, if your body itches; scratches; scrapes off, peels: toři kahaafai, having scraped off the bark or rind, e.g. of mangrove; duli k., e.g. of kañdoḷu ; uñḍali k., e.g. of coconuts; scrapes fish (Enlargement, kahaa-lanii; see also kehenii) [S. kahanne, Skt. kaṣati]
2. drags; pulls open (curtains) ; pulls up (anchor); sweeps: kuni kahanii, sweeps up rubbish; atař k.,winds up a skein (Enlargement, kahaa-lanii) [Skt. karṣati]

859 KAHAFATI (-faccek) ކަހަފަތި n. bony growth on mouth of fishes

860 KAHAŇBU ކަހަނބު n. turtle: k. fat, tortoiseshell; k. taři, ordinary ricebowl (with lid and handles) [S. käsubu, Skt. kacchapa, AMg.*kacchabhi]

861 KAHALA ކަހަލަ adj. like (following the object of comparison, or after a verbal participle): hama ajaibek kahala kujjek, a real wonder child: mi-kahala, of this sort: e-kahala, of that sort: tiya kahala taakař, to such places: eki kahala, various kinds of: keumakař vaa kahala eccek netee,there is nothing suitable to eat: kon kahala, of what sort? romun kahala gotakař, as if crying, almost crying: Naazim dakkaa kahala vaahakaek nuun, not the sort of thing N. says: hit-takun kehigen gosfai vaa kahalaeve, seemed to have disappeared from their minds

862 KAHAA ކަހާ n. a substance made from leaves, ground up for washing corpses

863 KAHIINU, KAHIINAA ކަހީނު - ކަހީނާ n. one who speaks with angels (mostly in stories) [U. kāhin]

864 KAHURABU ކަހުރަބު n. amber [U. kah-rubā]

865 KAŘ ކަށް n. corpse: kař-gaa, tombstone: kař-ḍevi, a jinni who haunts graveyards: kař-bim, graveyard: kař-vaḷu, grave; dogu bunumakii kařvaḷu añdiri vaa kamekee, telling lies darkens the after-life (prov.); kařu kamaakemi, funeral rites: kařu vat, a funeral fund [old S. kaṭa, P. kaḷēbara]

866 KAŘA ކަށަ n. 1. peg for clothes line; stilts for fishing from
2. ifc., certainty: in kařa-kuḷadunvanta, kařa-kuḷadaana, omni-competent (of God) [See kařavaru]

867 KAŘA-VARU ކަށަވަރު n. 1. certainty: kařavareve, kařavaru vi-eve, is certain; kařavaru koř denii, assures someone ; (adv.) kařavarun, certainly
2. carpenter's instrument for marking lines: k. aḷanii, uses the instrument (cf. kaḷihi) [cf.S. kañdakaṭu]

868 KAŘI (kaṭṭek) ކަށި n. thorn; bone; used of other pointed objects, e.g. hand of a clock (gaḍiige k.), spur of a cock: ek-kaři viiru, strong man without individual bones: torufaa kaři, awl: fahaa k., needle: fuk k., cold chisel: burumaa k., drilling bit: mahu k., fishbone; k. govvanii, cracks the knuckles; k. jahanii (of insects), stings;

k.- ari, bony side of bonito fish(as v. mula-ari): k.- iňgili, fourth finger: k.-uuru, porcupine: kaři-kuňḍi, fishbone meal fertilizer: kaři-kuňburu, a prickly plant, caesalpinia bonducella [S. kuňburu-väl, and see laaguḷa]: kaři-keyo (kařikeelek), screwpine, pandanus sp., or fruit of screwpine (varieties: maa-kařikeyo, medu-k., boo-k.), used in making sweets (kařikeelu meṭaa, kařikeelu haluvaa); kařikeyo liyanii, slices screwpine fruits; kařikeyo liyaa vaḷi, slicing knife with long handle: kařikeyo-gaňḍu,bunch of screwpine fruits: kařikeyo-foti, part of the crest of a cock [cf.S. väṭa-kē, screwpine]: kaři-kotan, a shrub, lantana: kaři-koli, a prickly fish:

kaři-gaňḍu, a particular bone (katuru k., jawbone: hiili k., funny bone); can be used of various prickly or bony objects, e.g.whistle, hooter: screwdriver: smokers' pipe: stethoscope: thermometer: lamp pricker: table fork: skeleton;

kaři-gooˇbili, a medicinal fruit,tribulus sp.: kaři-fati, spine of fish (also kařifoti); dark horizontal stripe at top and bottom of sarong: kaři-buroḷi, gall nut (oak apple), quercus infectoria: kaři-maḍi, stingray: kaři-mati (-maccek), shin: kaři-mas, a small bony reef fish; kařimasgaňḍu, a collection of such fish (smaller than ainu): kaři-maa(-malek), a scented flower (used in wardrobes): kaři-miyaru, kind of shark: kaři-viduri, smallpox: kaři-veli, rough sand: kaři-ḷeeňbuu, a variety of ḷeeňbuu (q.v.), achyranthes aspera

[S. kaṭu, Skt. kaṇṭaka]

869 KAḶAŇGAARI ކަޅަނގާރި n. a medicinal timber, imported from Chittagong

870 KAḶI ކަޅި 1. n. section of the eye (kaḷu k., coloured portion: hudu k., the white): k. aḷanii, stares, glares - in love, anger or supplication (at.., .. dimaa-ař); vař-kaḷiin, askance ; kaḷi-mati, glance, direction of gaze; kaḷimati balanii, watches the eyes; kaḷimati tuunu,with a sharp gaze: kaḷi-rava,whole shape of the eye:

2. adj. wet and woebegone, stained with tears, blood, dirt etc. (k. vanii)

871 KAḶIMAS ކަޅިމަސް n. dark flesh near the bone of a fish [? for kaḷu-mas]

872 KAḶIHI (kaḷissek) ކަޅިހި n. 1. kind of fish, emperor fish: kaḷissař danii, goes to catch k.

2. a carpenter's instrument for marking lines (cf. kařavaru 2)

873 KAḶU ކަޅު adj. black: kaḷek nuvee, is not black: kaḷař danii,goes out in the dark (after girls);

kaḷu-oř, kind of reef fish, goatfish, parupeneus; Kaḷuoř-fummi, name of Boḍu Takurufaanu's ship: k.-kaňdili, a plant whose leaves are used to blacken writing on palm-leaves, ?eclipta alba or hedyotis auricularia: k.-kaḷḷa, a plant, pedilanthus sp.: k.-tila, a black mark below the skin: k.- dati, hairpin (originally black): kaḷu-diri, 'black cummin', a medicinal plant (minaa bees), nigella sativa, also used in cooking [S. kaḷuduru]: kaḷu- mugu, black gram, phaseolus sp.: kaḷu- vakaru, ebony [S. kaḷuvara]: kaḷuhuṯṯu meevaa, a fruit, anona glabra [perhaps named after a certain Kaḷu Huṯṯu?]

[S. kaḷu, Skt. kāla]

874 KAḶUBILA ކަޅުބިލަ n. kaḷubila-mas, bonito, the Maldive fish par excellence, skipjack tuna, katsuwonus pelamis [S. kaḷu + bala-]

875 KAḶUVAA(-aaek) ކަޅުވާ n. kaḷuvaa-mas, flesh of the leg: kuḍa k., calf: maa k., thigh [S. kaḷavā, thigh]

876 KAḶḶI ކަޅްޅި n. hold or storage hatch on small ships (as v. falukaa)

877 KAA ކާ 1. n. section of larger sailing ships (between kavarunaa and booruduu) (kaa-gaňḍu),

kind of rhyming ḷem poem or baňdi

2. v. eating (pres.part. of kanii): kaa kahala mahek, an edible fish; kaa- ge, dining room [S. kana]; having eaten (abs. of kanii, also written kai) [S. kaa]

878 KAAITUVAK ކާއިތުވަކް n. For kaituvak, q.v.

879 KAAKAŘ ކާކަށް 1. pr. to whom? (dat. of kaaku)

2. v. to eat, neg.inf. of kanii: kaakař nukeveene, can't really be eaten

880 KAAKAA ކާކާ 1. onom. kaakaa lanii, makes croaking noise as of hens (cf.kakka- kaakoo), or babbling old people)

2. = kaaku + -aa , with whom?

881 KAAKII ކާކީ adj. khaki colour : hudu k., pale khaki [E. from U. khākī]

882 KAAKU ކާކު pr. who? (gen. kaage / kaakuge, whose?): kaakaa vaahaka dakkan beenumii, whom do you want to speak to? kaakař netee, no one has [S. kavu, kā, Skt. ka-]

883 KAAJAA(-aaek) ކާޖާ n. kind of fudgy cake [H. khājā]

884 KAAṬṬEK ކާޓްޓެއް n. See kaaři

885 KAAḌU ކާޑު n. card (Iid k., Eid card); certificate, esp.ration card (anc.); rations: hama kaaḍu, full rations (as v. bai kaaḍu) : kaaḍu-ge, former rationcard office: k. nambaru, ration-card: k. fořı, ration box: k. booṭu, supply ship: kaaḍuge taketi, rationed food [E. card]

886 KAATIBU ކާތިބު n. clerk [U. kātib]

887 KAATTANII ކާއްޓަނީ v. strokes, rubs, touches (v.n. keettum); with -gai: eccetiigai at k., rubs the hand in or on something: gaigai k., strokes the body; caus., kaňḍugai kaattuvaan, to make to skim the water

888 KAADA ކާދަ n. In aada-kaada (doublet), customs; see aada

889 KAADU ކާދު n. manure [H. khād]

890 KAAN ކާން v. to eat (inf. of kanii): kaan hadanii, lays the table, serves food: e tibii kaařee, they are eating

891 KAANAA(-aaek) ކާނާ n. foods (usu. for animals), dishes of food; k. aḷanii, puts out food (for birds) [H. khānā]

892 KAANI (KAUNI) ކާނި (ކައުނި) n. a tree, cordia subcordata (rehan dye can be obtained from the leaves)

893 KAANIVAL ކާނިވަލް n. carnival fair (introduced by Amin Didi, later held in Boḍu-galu Maafatge): k. hadanii, holds carnival [E. carnival]

894 KAANNAA ކާންނާ n. a kangati title (kaannaa kaleefaanu)

895 KAANÑA ކާންޏަ n. the sign Virgo [Skt. kanyā]

896 KAAFA ކާފަ n. grandfather (see also munikaafa, huurukaafa) : kaafa dirifuḷu, grandchild: vaḷu kaafa, a jumping insect: bolu kaafa, crown of the head: de-kaafa, having hair which springs from two places: de-kaafain, grandfather and grandchild; kaafaa-maamaa vanii, goes off, gets old (used of rihaakuru)

897 KAAFARU ކާފަރު n. infidel: immoral (also kaafiru): kiyevi-kiyevi hen kaafaru vee, much learning is bad for you (prov.) [U. kāfir]

898 KAAFIYAA ކާފިޔާ n. rhyme (in ḷem poetry) : k. hama kuranii, keeps the rhyme [U.qāfiya]

899 KAAFIRU (pl.,kaafirun) ކާފިރު n. infidel (see kaafaru) [U. kāfir]

900 KAAFU ކާފު n. the letter K in the Arabic and Maldivian alphabets: Kaafu atoḷu, Male atoll

901 KAAFUURU ކާފޫރު n. camphor, cinnamomum camphora [S. kapuru, Skt. karpūra]

902 KAAFUURU-TOḶI ކާފޫރުތޮޅި n. cardamoms, elettaria cardamomum (also written kaafuru-toḷi, kafuru-toḷi); fonitoři-kaafuurutoḷi lanii, exaggerates

903 KAA-BAFAIN ކާބަފައިން n . (pl.) ancestors [cf. kaafa, bafa]

904 KAAMARAŇGA ކާމަރަނގަ n. a fruit, averrhoa carambola [S. kāmarañgā]

905 KAAMINII-PUUL ކާމިނީޕޫލް n. kind of jasmine, murraya paniculata [H.]

906 KAAMIYAABU ކާމިޔާބު adj. successful : k. vanii, succeeds (of people): kaamiyaabii, success [U. kāmyāb, kāmyābī]

907 KAARI ކާރި n. See kairi

908 KAARU ކާރު n. motor-car (hon., kaar-koḷu): kulii k., taxi: kaar duvvanii, drives car [E. car]

909 KAARU-KHAANAA ކާރުޚާނާ n. workplace: ilekṭrikge k., power house (in Male) [U. kārkhāna]

910 KAARUDA ކާރުދަ n. a tax: kaarudaveri, tax-collector

911 KAARUBAARU/ KAARUUBAARU ކާރުބާރު - ކާރޫބާރު n. happenings, affairs [U. kār-o-bār]

912 KAARUVANII ކާރުވަނީ v. rubs noisily together (of hard things); scratches (v.n. keeruvum): dat kaaruvanii, gnashes teeth [S. kūrukanne]

913 KAARUSAANAA ކާރުސާނާ adj. very active

914 KAALAŇGA ކާލަނގަ n. slipway; rollers

915 KAALAA ކާލާ n. spades (at cards): k. rañga, suit of spades: kaalaain ekek, one spades!

916 KAALI (kaayyek) ކާލި n. a cross: crosspiece: the Southern Cross: cross-shaped rack for winding thread (ui vařaa k., uigañḍu aḷaa k.) or making rope (uḷi añburaa k., vaa añburaa k.): a swinging rack for holding the Quran: dum k., rack for drying or scenting

clothes: Hiṭlaruge kaali-gaňḍu, swastika; kaaligaňḍu miyaru, hammerhead shark, sphyrna lewini: de-atař kaali kaňḍanii / aḷanii, sways from side to side: e-koḷař kaali kaňḍanii / aḷanii,wanders up and down

917 KAAVANI (KAAVENI, KAIVANI) (ކައިވަނި - ކާވެނި) ކާވަނި n.
See kaivani

918 KAAVIYAA ކާވިޔާ n. float on stone anchor (kaaviyaa-gaňḍu)

919 KAASINJII ކާސިންޖީ n. wild citronella, cymbopogon nardus

920 KAASI-MAJAA(-majalek) ކާސިމަޖާ n. musical party

921 KAAHI (kaassek) ކާހި n. a scented substance

922 KAAŘI (kaaṭṭek) ކާރި n. fully developed coconut, or dried kernel of same:
kaaři-huni, squeezed white of coconut: k.- teo, coconut oil; taavak-kaaři, double coconut: mas k., a fish dish (mas k. is also used for maskaaři- duuni, q.v.): mudi k., seed coconut : hutmas k., a side dish: (met.) a mature man; a knot or tangle

923 KAAḶIVAK ކާޅިވަކް n. kind of lamp used for magical purposes

924 KAAḶU (KAUḶU) (ކައުޅު) ކާޅު n. crow: (met.) person of easy morals; kaaḷu kujjek, an immoral girl: kaaḷu vanii, acts immorally: kaaḷu-ge, brothel: kaaḷu-luňboo, a plant, phyllanthus urinaria: kaaḷu-dadu, a scurvy rash on the head
[S. kapuṭu, kavuḍu, Skt.*katpuṣṭa,*kadvřddhaka]

925 KIUM ކިއުން v. For kiyum (see kiyanii): so also kiuvvanii (anc. kiavvanii) [S. kīm]

926 KIEK ކިއެކް pr. See kiik

927 KIEVENI ކިއެވެނި n. See kiyeveni

928 KIEVELI ކިއެވެލި n. See kiyeveli

929 KIḌIKII ކިޑިކި n. window, usu. with bars (k. doru) [H. khiřkī]

930 KITAK ކިތައް interrog. how many? (of countable things);
kitak fot (ta), how many books? kitak gaḍi iru, how long? kitakař, approximately how many?

kitak muř foti, how many cubits of cloth? kalee atugai kitak, how many are you left with now ? diha diha kitakek, what is ten tens? mii mahun kitakek, what day of the month is it? kitak(ek) miihun, how many people? kitak-vana, adj., 'how- many-eth',which in order?

kitak-me, several (with indef.noun) : miige kitakme vattarek hure-eve, there are several kinds of this: kitakme getakek etaagai ve-eve, there are many houses there; with concessive verb or with ves, however (many): kitakme bayaku ayas, however many people come: kitakme duras, however far it be: kitakme kuḍa nama ves, however small [cf. e-tak]

931 KITTAANI ކިއްޓާނި n. For kiittaani

932 KIŇDU ކިނޑު n. filmy layer over newborn baby : k.filuvanii, removes k.

933 KINAARI(I) ކިނާރި (ކިނާރީ) n. ornamental ribbon as 'stripe' or chevron (k.- fař) on libaas [U. kinārī]

934 KIFUḶI ކިފުޅި n. coconut fibres near the stem, soft fibre : k. roonu, fluffy fibre

935 KIBA ކިބަ n. half section ; kanaat kiba, righthand side: kaaři k., half-coconut (viz. loo k. or fuu k.): dař k., lower sail: fook k., one arecanut: mati k., upper sail; windward side (of vessel): mas k., half of a cooked fish (= 2 gaňḍu): luňboo k., half-lime; kibaa fook, double or half-developed arecanut: mi kibaa(gai), this side:

Kalaaňge kibafuḷu, the side of God (= God): furagaskibaa(doru), rectum; abl. used postpositionally, from: eenaage kibain, from him: buḷaluge kibain, from the cat

936 KIBAA(kibalek) ކިބާ n. smith's stove (dum k.) : Boḍu Kibaa (Kibai), part of the old royal palace

937 KIBAAVARU ކިބާވަރު n. pastry board

938 KIBURU ކިބުރު n. pride (as a vice) : kiburu-veri, proud (man) [U.kibr]

939 KIŇBI ކިނބި n. kind of tree, barringtonia asiatica

940 KIŇBIHI(kiňbissek) ކިނބިހި n. sneezing: kiňbihi aḷanii, sneezes [S. kiňbihinne, sneezes = kiňbi + isinne, Skt. √kṣīv or khipitaka]

941 KIŇBI-HINI ކިނބިހިނި n. small ant

942 KIŇBUU (kiňbulek) ކިނބޫ n. crocodile [S. kiňbul, Skt. kumbhīra]

943 KIMERU(pl.kimerun) ކިމެރު n. royal prince [? H. kumār]

944 KIYANII ކިޔަނީ v. makes a public cry; recites aloud; reads (v.n.kiyum, kium:: hon. kiyuvvanii, high hon. kiyavaa vidaaḷu vanii : p.p.kii : impv. kiyaa!): sateeka miihunge listakař k., delivers invitations to 100 people: ecceti k., makes insulting remarks: das k., completes the Quran test: bappa-ař bappa kiyanii, addresses father as 'father': maibafaa k., makes abusive remarks (about parentage): ran kiyanii, agrees on the bride- price: vaahaka k., recites story: nagaa kiyanii, leads the chanting or reciting; Haajii kiyunii, was called 'Haji' (invol.): eenaa-ař Iñgireesi kiyenii, he can speak English (invol.): kiyee kamugai vefai vaa, readable;

Caus., kiyavanii (v.n.kiyevum), recites (Faatiha k.): studies (fot k.) ; kiyavaa kujjek, a student; kiyevumuge kamtak, syllabuses: invites : masverikamař kiyavanii, recites fishing charms: kiyavaa- ge, place built for recitation of charms: fen kiyavanii, charms a dish of water: ařii kiyevum, recitation of prayers in former royal palace: olii kiyevum, recital at funerals [S. kiyanne, Skt. kathēti]

945 KIYAMAN ކިޔަމަން adj. obedient: kiyaman vanii, is obedient: kiyaman-teri, obedient

946 KIYUM-TERI ކިޔުންތެރި n. person good at recitation [kiyanii]

947 KIYEVENI (KIEVENI) (pl., kiyevenin) ކިޔެވެނި (ކިއެވެނި) n. former officials of the Jumma mosque: kiyeveniinge veriyaa, the former Malim

948 KIYEVELI (KIEVELI, KIEVILI) (kiyeveyyek) ކިޔެވެލި (ކިއެވެލި - ކިއެވިލި) n. a good charm or group prayer

949 KIYOFOTI ކިޔޮފޮތި n. For keyofoti

950 KIRANII ކިރަނީ v. weighs (tr.): kiraa mas, dried fish weighed for export; deatař kirenii (invol.), is undecided: kirikiri, just balanced; foni kiri- kiri, only just sweet enough: mi saitařiigai denii foni kirikiri rahaee, there is not quite enough sweetener in this tea: kirikiri hurum, being evenly balanced [S. kiranne]

951 KIRIKEṬ ކިރިކެޓް n. cricket : k. kuḷenii, plays cricket [E. cricket]

952 KIRIM / KIRIIM ކިރިމް (ކިރީމް) n. ointment : kirim keekar, cream cracker [E. cream]

953 KIRIYAA ކިރިޔާ adv. scarcely; (with neg.) almost (kiriya-kiriyaa, kiriya-ee): kiriyaa at jehee, just touches: kiriyaa fenee, is hardly visible: kiriyaa maru nuvii, almost died: kiriyaa nuveṭṭuni, almost fell: kaan kiriyaa keree varuge, hardly edible: kiriyaa fudee varakař, barely enough: kiriyaa foodunu, hardly mature: adi kiriyaa, only now: hama kiriyaa, only just: kiriyaa ves vaan ot faharaku, at any possible time

954 KIRIYYAA(-aaek) ކިރިއްޔާ n. formal rent: kiriyyaa-ař denii, hires out: kiriyyaa-ař hifaigen, taking for rent [U. kirāya]

955 KIRILI ކިރިލި n. fishing line

956 KIRIS ކިރިސް n. dagger [Malay, kris]

957 KIRU ކިރު n. breast milk; (coll.)breast (technical, uramati: childish, buk); white sap: mini kiru / boo kiru, breast milk: kaaři k., coconut milk (for cooking): godan k., wheat gum: murañga k., sap from drumstick (used as glue); kiru denii, gives the breast: kiru felanii, squeezes out milk; gerin k. felanii, milks a cow;

k.-iloři, kind of flypaper (made from bañbukeyo kiru):kiru-keyo, a kind of porridge: kiru-garudiya, a milky curry: k.-tina/ k.-tona, a milky grass, euphorbia spp.(rat kirutina, hudu kirutina): kiru-duuni, a white seabird, blacknaped tern: kiru-bis, soft roe: kiru-sai, tea with milk: kiru-hakuru, milk and honey: kiru- hippi, bra [S. kiri, Skt. kṣīra, milk]

958 KIRUNU ކިރުނު n. anvil [S. kinīra]

959 KIRUḶI ކިރުޅި n. a colour of birds, mixed grey and white : karu-kuru-kaḷu-kiruḷi- kukuḷu (a traditional tongue-twister)

960 KIRUḶIYA ކިރުޅިޔަ n. kind of reef fish, 'pinjalo' and rudderfish

961 KILAU ކިލައު n. See kilaa

962 KILAGE (KILEGE) ކިލަގެ (ކިލެގެ) n. highest Maldivian title: kilage-faanu, holder of such title: kilage-kam, office of the same

963 KILAŇBU ކިލަނބު adj. dirtied, muddy (of liquids): k. naganii, churns up mud: k. vanii, gets muddy: (met.) hituge kilañbukam, a muddied heart (poet.)

964 KILAA (KILAU) (kilalek) ކިލާ (ކިލައު) n. adhesive dust and mud:

geař k. lanii, scatters dirt in the house: k. vanii, gets dirty; kilaa-gañḍu, muddy place: kilaa-fani, long earthworm; kilaafani batpen, chopped up worms in porridge (used medicinally against seasickness): kilaa- fas(-fahek), black dust: kilaa raha, muddy taste (attributed to geese, see asduuni) [S. kalal]

965 KILAAS(kilaahek) ކިލާސް n. (anc.) school class (mod. kulaas) [E. class]

966 KILEGE ކިލެގެ n. See kilage

967 KILLAA ކިއްލާ n. fort, palace (in stories) [U. qil'a]

968 KILLII ކިއްލީ n. 1. a 'chew', areca and clove wrapped in betel : k. taḷanii, grinds up areca for a chew for the aged: k. dufanii, chews a 'chew' [H. khīlī]
2. a children's game (also kalli, kulli)

969 KISAḌU ކިސަޑު n mud: kisadu-gañdu, muddy place [H. kīcař]

970 KISUḌI ކިސުޑި n. threadbareness: k. vanii, k. hilenii, gets threadbare

971 KISSARU ކިއްސަރު n. curvature, shaped quality; esp. kissaru vaḍaam, curved carpentry (as used in boatbuilding - cf.tedui vaḍaam for houses)

972 KIHAK(kihaakek) ކިހަކް n. edible white of coconut (used for chutney, or for hutmas-kaaři, eaten with batpen for Ramzan)

973 KIHAS ކިހަސް n. coconut milk, squeezed from kihak: aňga k. vanii, mouth gets dry (as after eating unripe areca or guava)

974 KIHAA ކިހާ interrog. approximately how much / how many? (cf.kitak).With indefinite ending of following noun: kihaa varakař ta, how much are (they)? kihaa irakař ta, at what time? kihaa irakun ta,within how long, i.e. how long does it take? gaḍiin kihaa irek, what's the time? kihaa varakař hakuru, what price is the juggery? kihaa hakurek,what quantity of juggery? kihaa irek vaane, how long will (you) be? dihakaa hatakaa kihaa varek, what is 10 + 7?

In rhetorical questions or exclamations : kihaa riiti bagiicaaek hee, what a beautiful garden! kobaa, kihaa varek vi hee, well, how much is that, i.e. I told you so: kihaa rañgaḷu, how excellent! [cf.e-haa]

975 KIHAAK- ކިހާކ- n. See kihak

976 KIHINEK(KIHINET) ކިހިނެއް (ކިހިނެތް) interrog. how? how much? (optionally followed by ta); also in case-form kihinakun :
beebe kihinek, how are you, brother? kihinek too vii, what's the matter? vikkanii kihinek, how are (you) selling it? [S. kesē]

977 KIHILI ކިހިލި n. hip: k. jahanii, carries on hip: kihilifati, armpit
[S. kihili, armpit, Skt. kaccha + -lla]

978 KIHUNU ކިހުނު n. a dangerous disease (gonorrhea?)

979 KII ކީ v. recited (p.p. of kiyanii) [S. kī, Skt. kathita]

980 KIIK (KIEK) ކީއް (ކިއެއް) interrog. what? kiik kuraanii, what is to be done? kiik kuran ta tiya uḷenii,what are you trying to do? kiik vii ta / kiik ta vii, what has happened? kiik vefai (tiya hurii), kiik-ta tiya vanii, what has happened to you? kiik ve (ta) naii, why didn't you come?

kiik ve(gen), why? kiik kuran (ta), what for? kiik kuraa miihek ta,what do you want? kiik kuran mi aii, why have you come? kaleař kiik hee/ kaleakaa kiikii hee, what is it to you? adi kiik tooee, nay rather: kiik kuran tooee, not only that but.. [cf.S. kim]

981 KIIKEE ކީކޭ interrog. what? kiikee tiya bunanii, what do you say (about it?) kiikee tiya bunii, what did you say? kiikee too, what? (resp.): kiikee hee, I still didn't hear: kiikee hitaa, why? kiikee hiivanii, so don't you realize? mi mahař kiyanii kiikee, what is this fish called? [kiik]

982 KIITU ކީތު n. central area of sailing boat

983 KIITTAANI (KITTAANI) ކީއްތާނި (ކިއްތާނި) n. canvas, sailcloth [T. kittān, U. katān, linen]

984 KIIMA(-KOḶU) ކީމަ (ކޮޅު) n. a covering formerly held over aristocratic ladies as they walked [U. khīma, tent]

985 KIIMIYAA ކީމިޔާ n. kiimiyaa roři, kind of fish roll

986 KIIRAN-MAA(-malek) ކީރަންމާ n. a plant, ixora coccinea

987 KIIRITI ކީރިތި n. 1. an epithet of great honour: kiiriti rasuulaa,the Prophet: kiiriti guruaan, the Qur'an; also used as part of former royal titles: kiiriti-kam, kiiriti-muuriti-kam, grace

2. kiiriti kuravvanii (hon.), weeps

[Skt. kīrti, fame]

988 KIIRU ކީރު n. strip (non-Male usage): kiiru-fař, strip

989 KIILI (kiiyyek) ކީލި n. splinter (kiili-gaňḍu): mařař k.hedijje/ vadejje, I have got a splinter; grain of timber (see idikiili): k. fala, rough-grained: k. himun, smooth-grained [S. kīri]

990 KIIS (kiihek) ކީސް n. carpenter's saw: fuk gaat k., small-toothed saw: fuk duru k., large-toothed saw: himun kuraa kiis, fine saw (not set): duni kiis, metal hack- saw: kiis filaa, a creeper, nephrolepis sp. (also called nirili) [S. kiyata, Skt. krakaca]

991 KIISAA ކީސާ n. money-bag (in stories) [U. kīsa]

992 KIIHANII ކީހަނީ v. saws, saws up : loo kiihanii, operates on the eye (southern usage; in Male usage loo faḷanii)

993 KUKUM ކުކުމް n. a medicinal powder, true saffron: k.fen, saffron water [S. kokum, Skt. ku˘kuma]

994 KUKURANII ކުކުރަނީ v. gasps, moans, grunts (of animates)

995 KUKUḶU ކުކުޅު n. hen; poultry in general: kukuḷu niyafati, ugly long nails: kukuḷu-fai, kind of medicinal leaf: k. fiyok, female chick: fiyok kukuḷu, hen and chickens: kukuḷu-fai, kind of medicinal leaf: k. mas, chicken meat: kukuḷuvahi, gable end [cf.S. baḷalvāya] [S. kukuḷu, cock, Skt. kukkuṭa]

996 KUJJAA(-aaek) ކުއްޖާ n. child: anhen kujjaa, young girl [kudi, small]

997 KUṬUNI ކުޓުނި n. witch (in stories): kuṭuni daita [U. kuṭnī, bawd]

998 KUṬUVANII ކުޓުވަނީ v. slanders: deba kuṭuvum, backbiting

999 KUḌA ކުޑަ 1. n. umbrella [S. kuḍa, T. kuṭai]

2. adj. small (of single objects, cf. kudi): kuḍa kudin, small children: kuḍa miihun koḷek, a small group of men: vii haa ves kuḍa, as small as possible: faruvaa kuḍa kořlanii, is careless: kamek kuḍa ta, are you getting disrespectful?

adv., kuḍa koř, kuḍai koř, a little;

kuḍa-ař̌i,traditional seat of honour on the right of the entrance:

kuḍaimis, insulting(k.bas); kuḍaimis koř hitanii, behaves insultingly:

kuḍa-kam, pissing; kuḍakamu danii, goes to piss:kuḍakamu daa ecceti,urine:

kuḍa-kaḷuvaa, calf of the leg:

kuḍa-tan vanii, draws near; maru k. vanii, death approaches: dooni k. vanii,the dhony is approaching: eenaa kuḍatan vegen, he is taken short (Kuḍatan is also used as a proper name);

kuḍa-duu, uvula: kuḍaduu digukamun,because of a long uvula, i.e.because (he) talks nonsense:

kuḍa-doru,window:

kuḍa-fuuḷu, a spirit with a long navelstring:

kuḍa-rumaa (-rumaalek), handkerchief:

kuḍa-huḷu, wrist: faige kuḍahuḷu, ankle joint [S. kuḍā, Skt. kṣudraka]

1000 KUḌAA ކުޑާ when small: kuḍaa iru, when (one) was small: tiya kam kuran katiibu kuḍaa hee, is it beneath you to do that, katiib? [for kuḍa + vaa]

1001 KUḌEE ކުޑީ n. For Kuḍa beebe (as a name)

1002 KUŇḌI ކުނޑި n. little bits: kiis k., kiihu k., sawdust: teyo k., oily deposit (e.g.on coconut milk): dagaňḍu k., iron filings: dat k. vikanii, gnashes the teeth : mas k., fish 'chips': haňḍuu k., haňḍulu k., chaff; kuňḍi kuňḍi kuranii, crushes

1003 KUTTAN ކުއްތަން n. nearness; used of God in phrase kuttan ve voḍigen vaa, immanent [for kuḍatan]

1004 KUTTAA (-aaek) ކުއްތާ n. dog [H. kuttā]

1005 KUDI ކުދި adj. small (usu. of more than one object, cf. kuḍa): kudi doru,windows (pl. of kuḍa-doru); but also kudi ořek, a small kind of seed: kudi mahek, a small kind of fish; kudi kudi vanii, gets broken to pieces;

as n.. (pl., kudin), children, youths, chaps (esp. students and athletes): (voc., kudiinnee! kudiinneeve!) kuḍa kudin, small children:

k. guḷa, small type of fishcakes: kudi dati, safety pins: kudi-bat, kind of millet, setaria italica: kudi maguu, kind of plant: kudi maa (-malek), kind of jasmine: kudi ratmaa (-malek), a plant, ixora coccinea: kudi ruvaali, a plant, dodonea viscosa: kudi luňboo, ' citron', citrus limonum, triphasia trifolia: kudi hiti (-hiccek), a medicinal plant, indigofera [P. khudda]

1006 KUDIINAA(-aaek) ކުދީނާ n. mint (Also pudiinaa) [for pudiinaa]

1007 KUDEHI ކުދެހި n. kind of tree, ficus retusa

1008 KUNA-MEHI ކުނަމެހި n. kind of very small fly

1009 KUNA-HAŇGAALI (-haňgaayyek) ކުނަހަނގާލި n. a medicinal plant, dipteracanthus ringens; see also nitabaḍi and rukureni: maa-kunahaňgaali, a fern, nephrolepis sp.

1010 KUNAA (kunalek) ކުނާ n. mat : boḍufatafoḷi kunaa, tuňḍu kunaa, decorative kinds of mat; huras kunaa, the imam's mat on the ař̌i: : kunaa-hui, mat sedge, fimbristylis sp. ; loo kunaa kuranii, screws up the eyes, blinks

1011 KUNI ކުނި 1. n. dirt, rubbish: k. aḷanii, scatters dirt: k. ukanii, throws rubbish away: kuni kahaa miihun / kuni miihun, dustmen;

kuni-gaňḍu, pus: kuni-buni, rubbish (doublet): kuni-mila, dirt on the body (of animates): kuni-vas, nasty smell

2. adj. stale, gone bad (of meat, cakes, fishsoup etc.): kuni vanii, goes bad [S. kuṇu, ?Skt. kuṇapa, carcase]

1012 KUNIYAN ކުނިޔަން n. quinine [E. quinine]

1013 KUNḌU ކުނޑު n. See kunnu

1014 KUNTA ކުންތަ n. an ancient form of grain tax

1015 KUNDAAN ކުންދާން n. extra sail for naakoḷu (royal yacht)

1016 KUNNAARU ކުންނާރު n. a fruit, zizyphus jujuba, stone apple: Viláatu k., a sour variety [? U. ‘unnāb]

1017 KUNNU (KUNḌU) ކުންނު (ކުނޑު) n. cliff (in stories): side spur of a reef [T. kunnu, hill]

1018 KUNFUNI (kunfunñek) ކުންފުނި n. trading company [E. company]

1019 KUNBAḶA ކުންބަޅަ n. a bait fish (vehimas), anchovy, cetengraulis: kunbaḷa-gaňḍu, shoal of k.

1020 KUFI ކުފި n. small type of cowrie : (met.) kufi dat, undeveloped or distorted tooth

1021 KUFIIRU ކުފީރު n. kind of brush used for sweeping difficult places

1022 KUFURAA ކުފުރާ n. copra (booḷa k., ball copra: faḷi k., cut copra); anc. kofuraa [S. kopparā, T. kopparai, H. khōprā]

1023 KUFURU ކުފުރު n. blasphemousness [U. kufr]

1024 KUFUU ކުފޫ adj. of equal status; kufuu hama nuvum, not being of equal status [U. kufū, class]

1025 KUŇBU ކުނބު n. mast : k. kafi, mast crutch [S. kuˇba, Skt. kūpa, T. kūmpu]

1026 KUŇBURAAN ކުނބުރާން n. firewood: kuňburaan-govikaleege, woodcutter

1027 KUŇBURU ކުނބުރު n. seed or fruit of a creeper, entada pusaetha (cf.also fenkuˇburu- vaani)

1028 KUŇBULI ކުނބުލި n. 1. local name for koveli (cuckoo)
2. local form for kuňboo, q.v.

1029 KUŇBOO ކުނބޫ n. 1. speckled colour (used of fowls)
2. For guňboo, q.v.

1030 KUMUNZAANI ކުމުނޒާނި n. incense

1031 KURA ކުރަ n. spot of hardened skin, a callous: k. laifi, k. jahaifi, a callous developed; (met.) kamek kořkoř kura laifi, got hardened to doing something; kura-foḷu, kind of hard boil: kura-magaali, scab [S. kara, Skt. khara]

1032 KURAKI (kuratkek) ކުރަކި adj. rough (usu. of skin)

1033 KURAŇGI (kuratňgek, kurangek) (KUREŇGI) ކުރަނގި (ކުރެނގި) n. kind of bird

1034 KURAŇḌI ކުރަނޑި n. 1.bowl with lid; casket: maa k.,bowl of flowers
2.kidney of birds [S. karaňḍu, Skt. karaṇḍaka]

1035 KURADI (kuratjek, kurajjek) ކުރަދި n. See kuredi

1036 KURAŇDU ކުރަނދު n. hard red sandstone,used for grindstones

1037 KURANII ކުރަނީ v. does (imp.kuree ! enlarged kořlaa ! abs.koř : p.p.kuri : caus.kuruvanii : hon. kuravvanii : invol. kurevenii, q.v.; hon.kurevvenii).Much used in compound verbs, with invol. counterpart with vanii. (See also kerenii)
[S. karanne, Skt. karōti]

1038 KURA-FAT ކުރަފަތް n. long razor : k. jahanii, circumcises; bow railings of dhonies [S. kara, Skt. kṣura]

1039 KURAFI (kuratpek) ކުރަފި n . cockroach [S. kärapotu]

1040 KURAHANII ކުރަހަނީ v. draws(pictures) (v.n.kurehum) : kurehum-gaňḍu, large picture; carved or painted planks: kurehum-teriyaa, artist

1041 KURAA ކުރާ n. 1. container for water or other liquid; 'kettle': fen boo k., water jug: inna k., washpot in latrine: at donna k., fingerkettle: loo k., brass fingerkettle: sai k., tea kettle, teapot [S. koraha]
2. flower of grain or grass (kuraa-gaňḍu)

v. 3. doing (pres.part. of kuranii) [S. karana]

1042 KURI ކުރި 1. n. shoots of trees etc.; ḷa-kuri faḷajje, the young shoots are coming: ruk- kuri, edible shoots of coconut palm: atu kuri, wrist: tip, end; bilet- kuri, betel tips: (met.) filmuge kuri numaraa, don't spoil the end of the film [S. kuru, shoots]
2. n. front; kuriyař aranii, comes forward, comes to the front: reehekgai fahatun ais kuriyař erum, overtaking in a race: kuriyař tibbevi, prominent (of people): kuri-aranii, gets-ahead (met.), masakkatugai kuri- erum, getting on in your job: kuri-baddanii, blocks passage, obstructs(tr.); (adv.) kuriyař / kuriigai, before (of time): ekme kurin, first of all, principally: furumuge kurin,before setting out: kuriyakun nudevuneve, didn't get there first: miige kuriigai, before this: eige ařekka duvahuge kuriin, about a week earlier: kurii.., the former (kurii rei,the previous night: kurii aharu, last year: kurii zamaanugai, in former times); kuri kihaak filaa, kind of creeper : kuri-booři, decorative spire on house or flagpole; similar way of cutting ceremonial betel leaves for weddings; kuri-mati (-maccek), front, in front of (hon., kurifuḷumati): gee(ge) kurimatiigai, in front of the house: kurimati huri ge, the house opposite: kurimati faraat, the private parts: kamakaa kurimati lanii, faces up to a problem: kamek / kamakaa kurimati vanii, encounters an obstacle: kurimaccař erum, coming at you: kuri- ruk, a valuable kind of coconut
3. v. done (p.p. of kuranii)

1043 KURIKIILA ކުރިކީލަ n. frosted glass

1044 KURU ކުރު adj. short : kuru miihek, a short man: kuru fali, short type of oar, paddle; kurufali jahanii, paddles: kuru gaḷuvanii, cuts short [T. kuṟu, ?S. koṭa]

1045 KURUKAALI ކުރުކާލި n. kurukaali kańḍanii, loafs around ['cuts a short cross'?]

1046 KURUKURU ކުރުކުރު n. kind of yam, dioscorea

1047 KURUNIIS (kuruniihek) ކުރުނީސް n. k. kuranii, salutes humbly (with dat.)

1048 KURUPPAT ކުރުއްޕަތް n. young banana foliage [T. kuruttu + fat]

1049 KURUŇBAA (KURUŇBAI) ކުރުނބާ (ކުރުނބައި) n. young coconut (at drinkable stage): k. baananii, picks young coconuts [S. kurumbā, T. kurumpai]

1050 KURU-MAS ކުރުމަސް n. kind of long fish, shearfish, 'wahoo', acanthocybium

1051 KURUVELI(-veyyek) ކުރުވެލި n. woven betel basket (used esp. in Minicoy)

1052 KURE, KUREN ކުރެ - ކުރެން postp. from: magee kuren vaahaka naahaa, don't ask me! vakiilun kure de-suvaalu kuravvai, asking two questions of the deputies [S.

keren]

1053 KUREŇGI ކުރެނގި n. See kurañgi

1054 KUREDI (kurajjek) / (KURADI) ކުރެދި (ކުރަދި) n. kind of hard red wood, pemphis acidula: kuredi-gañḍu, piece or stick of k.wood

1055 KUREVI (kurevvek) ކުރެވި n. sewn edge of cloth or net with rope attached

1056 KUREVENII ކުރެވެނީ v. is able to be done: ahannař ekamtak kerevidaane, I can do that: ahannař ekamek nukureveene, I can't do that: kurevveen ot hai masakkatek, all possible efforts (hon.) (invol. of kuranii)

1057 KUREHUM ކުރެހުމް v. patterns, pictures: kurehum riiti (of wood), prettily grained (v.n. of kurahanii)

1058 KUROḶI ކުރޮޅި n. ball of hardened copra in a dried coconut: kaařitak k. vefai, the coconuts have dried solid: mas- kuroḷi, a kind of sambol, eaten during Ramzan

1059 KUROOḌU ކުރޯޑު n. ten million, a crore [H. karōř, Skt. kōṭi]

1060 KULA ކުލަ n. colour, colouring: mood, atmosphere; rat kulaige eccek, something red-coloured: fansurutak hunnanii rat kulaagaa, the pencils are red-coloured: k. gada, colourful: kula riiti, gaily coloured: baek foṭoo kula, some pictures are in colour: kaa kula, dye used in food: fenna hai kula-akař hellumakii gellumekeve, it is no good being deceived by what colours you see (prov.);
k. jassanii, applies colour, dyes: k. danii, colours fade

1061 KULABU / KLAB ކުލަބު (ކްލަބް) n. social club [E. club]

1062 KULAAS (kulaahek) / KLAAS ކުލާސް (ކްލާސް) n. school class (anc. kilaas) [E. class]

1063 KULI (kuyyek) ކުލި n. hire, rent: kulii miihun, hired labourers: kuli-kaaru, taxi: aadaige kuyyakař, cheaply [T. kūli]

1064 KULUNU ކުލުނު n. compassion (towards, dat.); k. jahanii, develops a liking; kulunu kuranii, kulunu hunnanii, is affectionate [S. kuluṇu, Skt. karuṇā]

1065 KULLAABU-GE ކުއްލާބުގެ n. a pavilion in the old royal palace

1066 KULLI ކުއްލި n. 1. sudden jerk: k.taḷanii, pulls with a jerk; kulliyakař (adv.), suddenly

2. See kalli

1067 KUVAA ކުވާ n. discolorations on the face, or on fruit

1068 KUS ކުސް n. whining noises: k. taḷanii (of children), whines: k. jahanii (of chickens), chirps [onom.]

1069 KUSA ކުސަ n. 1. complaints: k.kiyanii, complains: kusakam boḍu, fussy

2. loop (kusa-gaňḍu): kusa(gaňḍu) furanii, loops together

1070 KUŘ ކުށް n. error : k. aḷanii, makes mistakes (esp. in writing): k. kuranii, makes mistakes (in general): k. jahanii, makes mistakes (esp. in arithmetic): k. hadanii, makes slight errors;

kuř-kam, erroneousness: kuř madu, almost perfect: kuř-veri, guilty party; kuřveri kuranii, holds to blame [?H. khōṭ]

1071 KUḶA ކުޅަ v. done (alternative p.p. of kuranii, from which v.n. kuḷaum (cf. diyaum from diya): kuḷayyaa, if you do [S. kaḷa, Skt. kṛta]

1072 KUḶADAANA, KUḶADUNVANTA ކުޅަދާނަ - ކުޅަދުންވަންތަ

See kuḷedenii

1073 KUḶAŇDILI ކުޅަނދިލި n. female pudenda: k. maa, a flower, clitoria ternatea

1074 KUḶAŇDU ކުޅަނދު n. a unit of weight : fas kuḷaňdu madu, (met.) not 'top drawer' [S. kaḷaňda, T. kaḻancu]

1075 KUḶAŇDURU ކުޅަނދުރު n. kind of wasp: goř k., a plant, cyperus; (met.) kuḷaňdurakař vefai, getting very angry [S. kaḷāňduru]

1076 KUḶI ކުޅި 1. adj. pungent (of taste): kuḷi-tuḷaa, a minty herb, ocimum sanctum: k. bisgaňḍu, spicy omelette: kuḷi-miiru, pros and cons: k. roří, spicy cakes [S. kuḷu, Skt. kaṭuka]

2. n. games: k. jahanii, performs ceremonial games: k. balaa ge, private platform for women to watch ceremonies from (surviving in Māfannuge, Irumatī Āge, Mūnimāge): kuḷifas libenii, gets chance to begin ('wins the toss') at game of ořvaḷu : kuḷi-gaňḍu, a single game, esp. of chess, ořvaḷu, tinhama ; method of playing (fas fukař vaa kuḷigaňḍu, etc.): kuḷi-varu, formal games (alifaanuge kuḷivaru, anc. baḍi k., fireworks): makunu kuḷi, buggery;

a chessman(kuḷiyek): kuḷi-bai, set of chessmen [S. keḷa, Skt. krīḍā]

3. n. muddy inland pond [T. kuḷi]

1077 KUḶU ކުޅު n. spittle, saliva: eenaa kuḷu diyaa vejje, his mouth is watering: k. jahanii, spits: k. talanii (slang), constantly spits: kuḷu-gańḍu, lump of spittle [S. keḷa, Skt. khēṭa]

1078 KUḶUGAŇDU ކުޅުގަނޑު n. a medicinal root, withania somnifera

1079 KUḶEDENII ކުޅެދެނީ v. is able (invol.form, with dat. of the person); usu. in form kuḷedigen (vaa), tolerable, able: kamař nukuḷedee kamuge, of (his) practical incapacity. From v.n. kuḷedum is also formed an active form kuḷadaana, able: kamtakař kuḷadaana, practical (anc. kuḷakařadaana); dekeekař aḷugańḍuge lolakař kuḷadaanaek nuun, I can't bear to see..: noořaa nukuḷadaana kunivas, nasty smell unpleasant to the nose: fiyokkukuḷu haavaa varun nukuḷadaanaee, (I) can't bear the way that chicken scratches around

kuḷadun-vanta, omnicompetent (usu. of God), kuḷadunvanta-verikam, omnicompetence (for kuḷedumvanta)

1080 KUḶENII ކުޅެނީ v. plays (game, or as actor) (hon.kuḷuvvanii : caus. kuḷuvanii : invol. kuḷevenii : v.n. kuḷum : abs. kuḷe). kuḷum-teri (pl.-in), player, good player: kuḷe denii, plays for (a club) : kuḷee-kuḷee (as adj.), as a game, pretending: rufiyaatakaa kuḷe hedii, played about with rupees : kuḷemaa, let's play [S. keḷinne, Skt. krīḍati]

1081 KUḶḶA-FILAA ކުޅްޅަފިލާ n. a small edible plant, launaea sarmentosa

1082 KUḶḶA-VAK ކުޅްޅަވަކް n. a sour milky fruit, sonneratia alba (mangrove): kuḷḷavakfalu rani hedigen, pretending to be a queen from a k. swamp, i.e. pretending to be what one isn't

1083 KUUḌI ކޫޑި n. infestation of black organisms found under leaves, or on coral: gahugai k. aḷaafai, infestation has occurred on the tree

1084 KUUDU ކޫދު n. old type of earthernware container: eenaa hiivanii kilaa kuudek hen, he looks like a pot made of mud, he looks dusty or muddy. (Also kuuzu) [U. kūza]

1085 KUURU ކޫރު n. scratch, line: gaigai kuuru aḷanii, scratches the body: lolugai k. damanii, applies lines on the eye; ańdun kuuru, lines of collyrium (make-up for children)

1086 KUUS ކޫސް n. groans of pain: k. kiyanii, groans: kuus ves kiyaa nulii, did not even groan [onom.]

1087 KUUSANI ކޫސަނި n. nasty smell (k. vas), nasty taste (k. raha): kuusani tak, smelly rubbish: kuusani miihun, collectors of rubbish: (met.) kuusani vaahaka dekkum, talking rot ;   moody, fussy

1088 KUUZU ކޫޒު n. old type of earthernware pot (for drinking water).See also kuudu [U. kūza]

1089 KEI ކެއި v. See kee

1090 KEIM / KEEM ކެއިން - ކޭން n. a special garnished dish of food (now obsolete), providedby rota by a keem matii miihaa in a public haruge on occasions such as boḍu mauluud [S. kā̃m, food]

1091 KEU ކެއު n. See keyo

1092 KEUM ކެއުން v. eating (v.n. of kanii) [S. kā̃m]

1093 KEUḶAM ކެއުޅަން n. setting for gems

1094 KEUḶU / KEOḶU (KEYOḶU) ކެއުޅު - ކެއޮޅު (ކެޔޮޅު) n. captain of fishing boat: ainu fennan vaane keoḷaře̋e, the skipper must see the shoal first (prov.); keoḷukam, a method of fishing, usu.at night, with line but no rod, stationary near the reef: keoḷukamu diyum, going fishing in this way (as v. mahař diyum, deepsea fishing by day; vadaa diyum, fly-fishing): maa keoḷukam, fishing involving longer journey and more risk from evil spirits: ekgamu keoḷukam, hunting on land

Also a kind of fish maggot, like fori [S. kevuḷu, Skt. kaivarta]

1095 KEO ކެއޮ n. See keyo

1096 KEKURI ކެކުރި n. small kind of cucumber: boḍu k., large cucumber: hiti k., a bitter variety [S. käkiri, Skt. karkaṭa]

1097 KEKUḶUM ކެކުޅުން n. discomfort: rihumuge k., pain

1098 KEKENII ކެކެނީ v. gets cooked: viri kekenii, melts (intr.) in fire: (met.) hit-tak fooriakun kekiganna aḍek, a sound of enthusiasm, lit.. of cooking hearts (invol. of kakkanii)

1099 KEKKUM ކެކްކުން v. cooking (v.n. of kakkanii)

1100 KEṬṬU-BAARU ކެއްޓުބާރު n. difficulties [?S. keṭṭu, thin , bāra- , difficulties]

1101 KEŇḌI ކެނޑި n. cutting, cutting short (in compounds): aḷi-keňḍi, ashtray: oḍi-keňḍi, last sail to be raised before departure of an oḍi: koňḍu-keňḍi, 'banyan' : daḷu-keňḍi, tin-opener: naru-keňḍi, pliers: ruk-keňḍiyaa, tree-feller

1102 KEŇḌENII ކެނޑެނީ v. gets cut, subtracted, etc. (see kaňḍanii): defatař k., havers; kujjakař madarusaain keňḍeveenii, a pupil will be removed from school (invol. caus.); daturu kurumun keňḍijje, was dismissed from the ship: daturu kurum keňḍijje, left the ship;

disappears, stops (of rain, lightning): nuva-ree fenun keňḍum, ceasing from sprinkling water on visitors on the 9th night after a birth: keňḍi neeḷi (adv.), unceasingly (cf. kaňḍa aḷanii) (invol. of kaňḍanii)

1103 KET ކެތް n. patience: ket-teri, ket gada, patient: ket kuranii, is patient: k. levenii,waits patiently: lagoˇḍiyař ket vaane too, can I bear it? ket net miihaa, impatient man: ket kuri miihaa faaru buḍugai maru viiee, the man who waited (too long) died at the foot of the wall (i.e. never got there) (prov.): huunu boňḍibat libeenii ket levi miihakařeve, the man who waits patiently will get the hot porridge (prov.)
[old S. kät, Skt. kṣānti]

1104 KETI ކެތި n. asterism Kṛttikā [S. käti]

1105 KEŇDI (kenjek) ކެނދި n. fruit of kaňdu tree

1106 KEŇDENII ކެނދެނީ v. is importunate (pej.) : eenaa gaatugai / kairiigai keňdi-keňdigen, importuning him [?Skt. krandati]

1107 KENI ކެނި n. (of eggs) hudu keni, the white: riiňduu keni, the yolk

1108 KENERII ކެނެރީ n. canary [E. canary]

1109 KEFUM ކެފުން v. cutting up (v.n. of kafanii) [S. käpīm]

1110 KEŇBU ކެނބު n. main rope of a ship, mainstay : k. aḷanii, spreads out the rope (to splice it): k. hus vi, the rope has run out; oḍiyař kuraa baaru eňgeenii keňbařee, it is the rope that knows best the forces against the ship (prov.);
Also mainspring of a clock (gaḍii k.) [S. kaňba]

1111 KEŇBUM ކެނބުން v. punting (v.n. of kaňbanii)

1112 KEMERAA ކެމެރާ n. camera (mod., anc. foṭoo-foři, kurahaa foři)
[E. camera]

1113 KEYO (keelek) (also written keu, keo) ކެޔޮ n. bananas (often called 'plantains'), usu. ifc.: don-keyo, fat- keyo ; Varieties: (bonti)rat keyo (commonest and best), fus k., boḍu k., maaḷos k., kaňdili k., sampaa k., goř-sampaa k.;
keyo-ari, 'comb' of bananas: keyo-gaňḍu,whole bunch of bananas:

keyo- daḷi, banana stem (used as brush for non-stick saucepans); keyodaḷi diya,water from the succulent stem used medicinally: keyo-foti (kiyofoti), cock's comb: keyo-vak, single banana fruit: keyo-vaḷu, pit for ripening bananas: keyo don kuranii, ripens bananas artificially: keyo baananii, picks bananas.

This word is also applied to certain other fruits: bañbu-keyo, breadfruit; keyo-foti, slices of breadfruit: telu li keyo, fried breadfruit: kaři-keyo, screw- pine; boo- (kaři) keyo, variety of screwpine: sak-keyo, jakfruit [S. kehel, Skt. kadalī, in latter senses x T. kai, fruit]

1114 KEYOḶU ކެޔޮޅު n. See keuḷu

1115 KERAM ކެރަމް n. the game of carrom

1116 KERAVAḶU ކެރަވަޅު n. kind of fish, small taavaḷa ; deceitful man

1117 KERI ކެރި 1. n. rain (esp. in fishermen's language): keri-koḷu, drops of rain
2. v. daring (abs. of kerenii)

1118 KERUM ކެރުން v. stinging,burning (v.n. of karanii);
daring (v.n. of kerenii)

1119 KERUVUM ކެރުވުން v. bunching together (tr.) (v.n. of karuvanii)

1120 KERENII ކެރެނީ v. 1. dares: kamtak kuraan kerum, daring to act: keree miihunař kaamiyaabu vaanee, fortune favours the bold: keri huregen, confidently

2. Also serves as additional invol. of kuranii; tedu vaan keree varek nuunee, can't get up: mi otii helilaan ves nukerifaee, I can't even move: kaakař nukereene, can't really be eaten: nukereene! you mustn't! keri foorum, ability, capability

1121 KELAA (-aek) ކެލާ n. sandalwood, santalum sp.: Varieties: huvañdu k., agali k.(agalu k.), ratbaburu k. (white, yellow and red respectively);

Also name of the northernmost Maldivian island (also written Kelai)

1122 KEVENII ކެވެނީ v. 1. is eaten: rañgaḷař kevijje ta, have you eaten enough? kevee fada eccek, something edible (invol. of kanii) [S. kävenne]

2. is driven, moved aside (usu. of fish): masgañḍu kevigen diyum, group of fish changing direction: masgañḍu kevi erenii, fish get moved aside (invol. of kavanii)

1123 KEVELI ކެވެލި n. jewelled chain on wrist or ankles, usu. of children (k.-fař)

1124 KES ކެސް n. hair, usu. pubic hair [S. kes, hair, Skt. kēśa]

1125 KESSANII ކެއްސަނީ v. coughs: kessum bali, tuberculosis: hook govaa kessum, whooping cough: kessamun looganḍu ukaalevenii varař madu miihakařeve, few can empty the spittoon as they cough, i.e. do two things at once (prov.). Enlarged: kessai-genje, coughed [S. kasinne, Skt. kāsatē]

1126 KEHA ކެހަ n. cross-stick in cadjan fence: k. aḷanii, fixes the cross-stick

1127 KEHI (kessek) ކެހި n. trap, trick: k. denii, acts cheatingly (towards someone, dat.): k. libijje,was cheated: kehi-veri, cunning

1128 KEHENI ކެހެނި n. itchiness (not commonly used in Male): aňga-keheni, garrulous: aňga- keheni lanii, gets an 'itchy mouth': keheni laiganegen, feeling inclined to scratch [cf. kehenii]

1129 KEHENII ކެހެނީ v. slips out, slips away: hańdaanun muḷin kehigen hiňgajje-eve, quite slipped my memory: furoḷu kehigen, the wheel slipped: loo matin kehijje, slipped out of sight: farudaa kehigen diyaii, the curtain was raised: karu kehenii, clears the throat (invol. of kahanii)

1130 KEHERI ކެހެރި n. animal hair, fur, wool: keheri rajaa, woollen blanket: k. foti, woollen cloth: keheri ganna taketi, fruits which have down on them [Skt. kēsara]

1131 KEE (KEI) ކޭ (ކެއި) v. eaten (p.p.of kanii): kee-lek ginakamun, by the great amount eaten : keemaa, when eaten: oḍi-kee,woodworm in ships' timbers: boli-kee, kind of fish [S. kā̃, Skt. khādita]

1132 KEEKAR ކޭކަރ n. kirim keekar, cream cracker [E. cracker]

1133 KEEKU ކޭކު n. cake [E. cake]

1134 KEEKULI (keekuyyek) ކޭކުޅި n. (of birds) crop, gizzard (used by children as a balloon)

1135 KEETA ކޭތަ n. eclipse: iru keeta hifaifi, eclipse of the sun began: hańdu keeta viillaifi, eclipse of the moon ended: k. namaadu, special prayer for times of eclipse [Skt. kētu, 'descending node']

1136 KEETTUM ކޭއްޓުން v. rubbing (v.n.of kaattanii)

1137 KEEN BALLAVANII ކޭން ބައްލަވަނީ v. (v.n. keen bellevum) : eats and drinks (mid-grade)

1138 KEEM ކީމް n. See keim

1139 KEERUVUM ކީރުވުން v. grating together (v.n. of kaaruvanii)

1140 KEELA ކީލަ n. 1. a whiskered baitfish, polydactylus
2. For keeli

1141 KEELI (KEELA) ކީލި (ކީލަ) n. kaaři(-takuge) keeli jahanii, ties up coconuts in pairs with husk-fibre: keeli hama vanii, pairs are formed; is an even number

1142 KEELU- ކީލު- n. See keyo : keelu-booři, banana flower

1143 KEEHUSEENU ކީހުސީނު n. capstan [For E. capstan]

1144 KO ކޮ vocative enclitic raskalaa ko! O God

1145 KOI (koyek) ކޮއި n. (pron. koe) 1. child; son: aharenge kuḍa koi, my younger son: boḍu koi, elder son: e-koi, mi-koi, my child (m. or f.). Also used as a name, or part of a name: Koimalaa, founder (Islamic) king of the Maldives [Malayalam]

2. pupil of the eye (loluge koi) [U. koyā]

1146 KOILU / KOOLU ކޮއިލު - ކޯލު n. royal enclosure: koilu-tere, royal palace: budu-koolu, heathen temple: etere-koilu, palace interior [T. kōyil, palace]

1147 KOKAṬAARU ކޮކަޓާރު n. squawks of a hen: k. govanii, squawks (v.) [onom., cf. kakkakaakoo]

1148 KOKAḌI ކޮކަޑި n. red arsenic: kokaḍi kee miidaa gada vum, the rat who has eaten arsenic getting better (prov., of an unexpected recovery)

1149 KOKAA(kokaalek) ކޮކާ n. butterfly : alifaan- k., firefly: lee -k., red butterfly: k.-fani, caterpillar: kokaa- mas, angelfish: kokaa avitak, flickering sunlight; kokaa-aranii, flickers

1150 KOKIN ކޮކިން n. cocaine [E. cocaine]

1151 KOKOO ކޮކޯ n. cocoa, chocolate [E. cocoa]

1152 KOKKO (pl., kokkomen) ކޮކްކޮ n. younger sibling; commonly used also for son- or daughter-in-law, or for any younger friend (ifc. also -hokko; hon. kokkoofuḷu)

1153 KOCCEE ކޮޗްޗޭ n. Cochin: koccee fat, a scented medicinal leaf, ageratum conyzoides

1154 KOṬARI ކޮޓަރި n. room of a building [H. koṭhrī, Skt. kōṣṭha]

1155 KOṬIKURAA ކޮޓިކުރާ n. cosmetic powder [E. 'cuticura']

1156 KOṬṬANII ކޮއްޓަނީ v. scratches: ukuňḍi k., has hiccups: gaigai k., scratches the body: giligili k. (childish), tickles: foḷu koṭṭaa-lanii (enlarged), squeezes boils: bihi k., scratches blisters: hiili k., tickles; koṭṭaa foři, squeeze-box, Indian banjo

1157 KOṬṬAVANII / KOŘṬAVANII ކޮއްޓަވަނީ - ކޮރްޓަވަނީ v. See kořanii

1158 KOṬṬEK ކޮއްޓެއް See koři

1159 KOṬṬEE (koṭṭee-ek) ކޮއްޓޭ n. 12,000 cowries (12 faa)

1160 KOḌI ކޮޑި n. body of a carpenter's plane: koḍi-gaňḍu, frame; koḍi-fuuṭu, cubic foot

1161 KOŇḌU ކޮނޑު n. shoulder: gamiis aḷuvaa k., coathanger: koňḍu-keňḍi, vest, 'banyan'; koňḍukeňḍiek laigen,wearing a vest: koňḍu-maa, 'pips' on shoulder, k. libenii, gets pips; (met.)boḍuvegen koňḍumaa jahaa, got too big for his boots [old S. koňḍa, ?Skt. krōḍa]

1162 KOŇḌELI (koňḍeyyek) ކޮނޑެލި n. attachment for the at-teli of a square sail

1163 KOTAN ކޮތަން n. kind of medicinal herb, plectranthus zeylanicus: kaři k., lantana: mas k., anisomeles malabarica: huvaňdu k., crotalaria laburnifolia

1164 KOTANBIRI / KOTAŇBIRI ކޮތަންބިރި - ކޮތަނބިރި n. coriander [old S. kotaňburu, lex. Skt. kustumbarī]

1165 KOTARI ކޮތަރި n. top fin of fish: kotari vilaa, spiral cloud formation

1166 KOTARU ކޮތަރު n. pigeon: Arafaatu k., a kind of pigeon; see also enmuli [U. kabūtar]

1167 KOTAḶU ކޮޓަޅު n. bag; plastic bag: k. lai dinum, putting a protective bag on fruit trees

1168 KO<u>TT</u>U ކޮއްޓު n. rations of food: lower class food; k. noḷi,servants' hookah

1169 KON ކޮން 1. adj. which? (followed by indef. noun ending)

kon baek,which ones, who? kon iraku, at what time? kon eccek, which one? kon taakař, where to? kon taakař too? hullo! (lit.., where are you going): mii kontaaku miihek, this useless fellow! kon varu- bayyek, why so het up? (lit., what a lot of weakness!) kon-kala, which? (aggressive);

kon-me, some, every: konme kamekme, every single task: konme gahek ves, every tree: bunuvvi konme gotakař, exactly as you say: konme duvahaku (ves), every day: konme ves zamaanakun, some day or other: konme ves gahek, some old tree: konme gotek viyas, whatever happens: konme hen beenum kamek net, there is no need at all: hama konme hen ves, somehow or other, in any case: konme hen nais heyo, anyway it doesn't matter if you don't come: konme ves nukaati, please don't eat: konmeakas, anyway: konmes = konme ves [cf.S. koyi, Skt. kaḥ punar]

1170 KON ކޮން 2. v. For absolutive koř̌ in contexts where the ř sounds as n, esp. in sentences ending -konneve (kor̆ + -eve)

1171 KONUM ކޮނުން v. digging (v.n. of konnanii)

1172 KONTI ކޮންޓި n. (anc.) lance (mod. lonsi): measurement of the height of the sun (iru kontiakař aranii) one hour after sunrise, used to determine the time of Id prayer [old S. kot, Skt. kunta]

1173 KONNANII ކޮންނަނީ v. digs, gouges (abs.kone : v.n.konum : p.p. konunu); (met.) searches out: bas hoodan konum, searching out clues, cross-examination: tihen konnaane kamek net, no need to be so inquisitive [S. kaninne, Skt. khanati]

1174 KONNEVE ކޮންނެވެ See kon 2.

1175 KOFANII ކޮފަނީ v. eats (low slang): (invol.) kofenii, is disturbing: mitanař nukofeeřee, don't butt in here!

1176 KOFII ކޮފީ n. coffee (cf. gahuva, bun): kiru aḷaafaa kofii,white coffee [E. coffee]

1177 KOFURAA ކޮފުރާ n. (anc.) copra (mod. kufuraa) [S. copparā,

T. kopparai, H. khōprā]

1178 KOPII ކޮޕީ n. 1. kinds of vegetable, brassica: boňḍi-kopii, cabbage: aadaige k., lettuce: puul- k., cauliflower: baňdaa k. [H. kōbī, gōbhī]
2. copy: k. kuranii, copies: k. naganii, reproduces: kopii karudaas, carbon paper [E. copy]

1179 KOPPANII ކޮއްޕަނީ v. shoves, pokes in: tantanař ecceti koppanii, pokes things in: miihun koppaa hedum, jostling people; (met.)kamtakař at koppanii, meddles in affairs [cf. kofenii; ? H. khubhnā]

1180 KOBAI / KOBAA ކޮބާ - ކޮބައި interrog. where? what? masvaḷi kobaa hee, where is the fish knife? namakii kobaa, what is your name? kobaa ta tiya kiyevi eccakii, what about your education? kobai too kamek netifai, (hon.) how can there be no work? aumuge beenumakii kobaa, what is the reason for your coming?
Initially, see! do you know? kobaa, dii bala! look, just give (it) me: kobaa, ma buniimek nu, well, didn't I tell you: kobaa, kihaavarek vi (hee), there you are, I told you so [S. koba, where?]

1181 KOBAḌI ކޮބަޑި n. yellowness of the teeth: dat-takugai k. jahaifi, teeth are discoloured

1182 KOMAA ކޮމާ n. comma; inverted commas: komaa-kooḷi, inverted commas [E. comma]

1183 KOMIṬII ކޮމިޓީ n. committee [E. committee]

1184 KOYYA(A) ކޮއްޔަ - ކޮއްޔާ n. child (local usage); also a name (Koyyaa) [koi]

1185 KORAKALI ކޮރަކަލި n. kind of reef fish, smaller version of fanihaňdi or muḍahaňdi

1186 KORANII ކޮރަނީ v. hops: korum, hopscotch: koraa ge, hopscotch ground; koree ta (invol.), can (you) hop? [cf.koru]

1187 KORU ކޮރު adj. lame: koru jahanii, limps [S. kora, Skt. khōra]

1188 KORU-KOKAA ކޮރުކޮކާ n. small kind of butterfly: korukokaa-hui, kind of grass where they settle

1189 KORUDAN ކޮރުދަން n. fuse for firing guns (also styptic for cauterizing 'white skin')

1190 KORU-VAḶU ކޮރުވަޅު n. ear-hole: socket for doorposts

1191 KOLI (koyyek) ކޮޅި n. 1. ceremonial procession with gong for official proclamations, esp. of kilegekam etc., or for hiti (now discontinued) : kolii nam, title so announced: koli kaleege, official gong-beater for the ceremony: koli lanii, holds such a procession, appoints to a post, e.g.raskamař koli lum, confirmation of election of a king, held after about five years (the last king never received one): koli hiňgaa magu, circular route round Male taken by the procession

2. kind of fish that can puff itself up; kaři-koli, porcupine fish, diodon: puffed-up portion of stomach, or of a pot

1192 KOLIZAAN ކޮޅިޒާން n. a valuable scented root (imported), alpinia galanga , galingale [U. kulījan]

1193 KOLU- ކޮޅު- n. See koo

1194 KOLLAVAANI ކޮއްޅަވާނި n. irregular indentations

1195 KOVI ކޮވި n. a rotted coconut

1196 KOVELI (KOOLI) ކޮވެޅި (ކޯޅި) n. cuckoo, 'kohoo' bird: kaḷu k., male cuckoo: ḍinḍin k., female cuckoo [S. kovul, Skt. kōkila]

1197 KOS (kohek) ކޮސް adj. stupid: kos kamtak, stupid actions: kos miihaa, stupid man: maru kos, very silly man: kaňḍu kos, silly man; partially submerged floating timber

1198 KOŘ ކޮށް v. 1. having done (abs. of kuranii). Pronounced, and often written, as n before a vowel, konneve = kořeve. Serves as an adverbial termination, e.g. avas koř, quickly;

After an incomplete verbal form, used as a particle introducing temporal clauses, e.g. kanii koř, while eating [S. koṭa, cf.Skt. kṛtvā]

2. koř jahanii, pecks (at, dat.) [kořanii 2.]

1199 KOŘANII ކޮށަނީ v. 1. chops off, cuts, slices up (hon. koṭṭavanii): karudaas k., cuts up paper: daňḍu k., clears a field: daru k., chops firewood: fotigaňḍu k., cuts cloth: fook k., slices areca: boo k., cuts hair: magu k., clears a path: mas k., chops fish: mirus k., slices chillies: riyaa k., unties sail: vaa k., clears jungle (but vaa kaňḍanii, cuts rope): vina k., mows grass: sometimes of cutting or trimming plural objects, as v. kaňḍanii of single objects; gas k., prunes trees (gas kaňḍanii, cuts trees down): huňguli k., trims bottoms of thatching strip (h.kaňḍanii, of a single strip); kořaa vaḷi, carpenter's knife

2. pecks: aharenge ataku kořaek nugannaane-eve, will not peck at my hand: (met.) kořakořaigen, haltingly [S. koṭanne, P. koṭṭēti]

1200 KOŘAARU ކޮށާރު n. small store,barn [S. koṭāra, Skt. kōṣṭhāgāra]

1201 KOŘI(koṭṭek) ކޮށި 1. n. enclosure; a) cage: duuni k. aḷanii, makes birdcage: k. vanii, gets encaged(of animates): k. kuranii, closes up (fishing nets): k. fattaafai, sinking lobsterpots:
b) vegetable plot: mirus k., bed of chillies:
c) walking frame, play pen (hiňgaa koři):
d) ancient teams for military exercises, e.g. Banḍaara koři, Turukii k.: korii miihun, members of the team [S. koṭu, Skt. kōṣṭhaka]

2. n. choking: koři aranii, chokes, gets choking fit: fen-koři a., chokes while drinking: fook-koři a., chokes on arecanut; hum koři, swollen tummy

3. adj. blunt: koři vanii, gets blunt: loo koři, shortsighted: loo-boo koři vanii, loses all senses with age: koři billuuri, frosted glass
4. v. trimmed (p.p. of kořanii)

1202 KOŘI-FILAA ކޮށިފިލާ n. part of hull of fishing boat [koři 4]

1203 KOĻANII ކޮޅަނީ v. caulks; (met.) gaňḍutak koḷanii, rummages through the pages [?cf. S. galappatti, H. kālāpattī, caulking]

1204 KOĻAAKOĻU ކޮޅާކޮޅު n. See koḷu

1205 KOĻI-GAŇḌU ކޮޅިގަނޑު n. storm cloud, downpour: k. naganii, storm arises

1206 KOĻU ކޮޅު n. end; diruňbaa k., bows of boat: boo laa k., head of bed: fai laa k., foot of bed: anek koḷun, on the other hand: koḷu net koḷu, limitless: dekoḷu, both ends: koḷukoḷař, corner to corner: koḷu fali, front oars: dekoḷu-dekoḷař hiňgum, walking up and down: dekoḷu nujehee, nonsensical: dekoḷu jessum, managing to get along: kamuge dekoḷu nubalaa, without considering the pros and cons: furatama koḷu, at first: koḷun lanii, reaches the limit: koḷaakoḷu nufenna, the two ends being out of sight;
ifc. 1.small piece of, some; alifaan koḷek, a small fire: uva-k., pile of lime: eti-koḷu, piece,bit: duvas-koḷu, some days: miihun koḷek, miis koḷek, some people: haňḍuu- koḷu, some rice: hiňdu-koḷu, a little time: hurihaa ruk-koḷu, all the coconut trees;
2. honorific termination for inanimates; kuḍa-k., nobleman's umbrella: guḍaguḍaa-k., nobleman's hookah: dooni-k., nobleman's boat: haalu-koḷu, nobleman's health;
koḷu-daali, bits left over, esp. of timber; koḷudaalikoḷu, pile of shavings: koḷudaalifoti,bits of cloth, remnants: koḷudaalikarudaas, odd bits of paper: koḷu-fai, foot, in certain phrases ; koḷufain jahanii, kicks: koḷufai lanii, touches with the foot (necessitating an apology): koḷufas-koḷu, stern of boat: koḷu-filaa-goňḍi, three piece stool: Koḷu-maḍulu, name of T atoll, the 13th atoll from the north: deeti deeccař koḷu-bit vanii, two things collide: koḷu-mati, black stripe down edges of sarong (in front for men, behind for women); (met.) signs, tokens (e.g. of disease, news): koḷuvan, unwoven thatch with chopped ends [?for koḷufan]: koḷu- veṭṭi, landing craft ('opening at the end') [S. keḷa(vara), Skt. kōṭi]

As adj., upright: koḷu vanii,becomes erect: koḷař hunna, standing upright: koḷař jahanii, puts upright (see also koḷḷař). (koḷuvanii is also caus. of koḷanii) [S.

keḷin]

1207 KOḶUŇBU ކޮޅުނބު n. Colombo; Ceylon, Lanka [S. Koḷaňba]

1208 KOḶḶAŘ ކޮއްޅަރް adv. Alternative form of koḷař, upright: koḷḷařgaa fasee, stand at ease! koḷḷař fasee, easy! (orders to cadet force founded by Amin Didi)

1209 KOO (kolek) ކޯ n. cheek: koo donnanii, rinses the mouth (esp. by gargling when breaking the Ramzan fast): koo donna loogaňḍu, gargling basin: koo donnan diyum, going outside to gargle before breaking fast: koo-taafat, outer cheek (of men), outer gill (of fish): koo fuppi, mumps: koo-varu, mouthful (of liquid): Gaaduu kolu-, principal entrance to Male lagoon [S. kopul, Skt. kapōla]

1210 KOOCCEK(KOOCEK) ކޯއްޗެއް (ކޯޗެއް) n. what thing? (for kon eccek): kooccek beenumii, what do you want? (Also kooncek)

1211 KOOṬU ކޯޓު n. coat: kooṭ faṭluunu lanii, puts on a suit [E. coat]

1212 KOOṬṬEE (kooṭṭee-ek) ކޯއްޓޭ n. flagpost, esp. that formerly in the inner fort at Male: kooṭṭee-koḷu, area of flagpost and former Customs: kooṭṭee-tere, barracks: k. negum, raising the flagpost, a ceremony formerly performed at hiti [T. kōṭṭai, fort]

1213 KOOḌI ކޯޑި n. an ancient game, in particular the woven article hung up in the game: kooḍi kaňḍanii, puts said article on women's heads

1214 KOOḌU ކޯޑު n. (obs.) loop in a rope

1215 KOODU ކޯދު n. (obs.) sending out shoots from seeds (ořtakun k. lanii)

1216 KOONARU ކޯނަރު n. corner-kick (in football): k. naganii,takes the kick [E. corner]

1217 KOONI ކޯނި n. bunch (also kooḷi)

1218 KOONCEK ކޯންޗެއް n. what thing? (Also kooccek) [kon + eccek]

1219 KOOFAA ކޯފާ n. anger (hon.): mařař koofaa vejje, he (hon.) was angry with me: of God, koofaa is vanii, koofaa lavvanii, is angry; cf. ruḷi duruvum for mid-grade [Skt. kōpa]

1220 KOO-MAS ކޯމަސް n. porpoise, dolphin

1221 KOOMAAŘI ކޯމާރި n. bowsprit

1222 KOORAA-HANḌUU ކޯރާހަނޑޫ n. best quality rice [?H. kora, new]

1223 KOORAAḌI ކޯރާޑި n. large kind of axe used for coral breaking

1224 KOORI ކޯރި n. kind of souwester worn by fishermen: k. aḷanii,wears souwester

1225 KOORU ކޯރު n. water channel; river, lake

1226 KOOLAA ކޯލާ n. coal (=booṭu deli) [E. coal]

1227 KOOLAA-GE ކޯލާގެ n. look-out on bastions

1228 KOOLAA-VAAṬAR ކޯލާވާޓަރ n. eau de Cologne [E. water, koo laa = to put on the cheeks]

1229 KOOLI ކޯލި n. See koveli

1230 KOOLU ކޯލު n. See koilu

1231 KOOS (koohek) ކޯސް n. course of study [E. course]

1232 KOOḶI ކޯޅި n. 1. finger span, digit (shorter than kaivat)

2. bunch (of flowers, or of certain fruits) (Also kooni): maa- kooḷi, bunch of flowers: komaa- kooḷi, inverted commas: fili-kooḷi, double rhyme

1233 KOOḶENII ކޯޅެނީ v. fights like cats (slang when used of people)

1234 KLAAS (klaahek) ކްލާސް n. See kulaas

ގ GAAFU, the 15th letter of the Maldivian alphabet

(More correctly called ga-viyani: cf. U.qāf)

Gaafu atoḷu, Huvaduu atoll (North and South),the fifteenth atoll from the north.
In loanwords, this letter may represent U. q

1235 -GA -ގަ suffix, used in the south as imperative ending: balaga, look out!
[old S. imp. suffix -ga]

1236 GAI ގައި n. surface of the body (hon., gai-koḷu): gai uňguḷanii, anoints the body: bees gaigai u˘guḷum, anointing the body: gayař aranii, assaults: gayin gayař araa bali, contagious diseases: gai gooḷi vanii,becomes very close (to..,-aa): gai- keheňbuḷi (gaa-keheňbuḷi), a stinging plant, tragia involucrata, flourya interrupta
[S. kahaňbiḷiyā] [S. gat, Skt. gātra]

1237 -GAI / -GAA -ގައި - -ގާ suffix of locative sense: geegai, in the house: kamtakugai baiveri vanii, shares in the activities: anhenungai huri, among women: of cooking; bařiigai kakkaa rihaek, a brinjal curry (cooked in brinjal, i.e.with brinjal): in reported speech after kam, nufenna kamugai hii vamun, thinking it wouldn't appear: used before connecting -aai in forms -gayaai or -gayyaai

1238 GAIGAA ގައިގާ excl. watch it! mind out! vulgarly, indicating disbelief : acci gaigaa! oh no it won't: gaigaa, tiyotii moḷu vefai, you've won, forsooth: gaigaa duru, look out!

1239 GAIDU ގައިދު n. prison: g. kuranii, arrests [U. qaid]

1240 GAIMU ގައިމު n. certainty : gaimu ta, are you sure? hama gaimu, quite certainly: gaimun (adv.), certainly : gaimu kuranii, makes sure: hit-gaimu, pleasing, comforting [U. qaim]

1241 GAU ގައު n. See gaa

1242 GAUMU ގައުމު n. nation: gaumii salaam, national anthem : gaumii ruuhu, patriotism [U. qaum]

1243 GAŇGU ގަނގު (obs.?) adj. g. vanii, becomes deaf
[also given as gugu vanii]

1244 GAṬARI ގަޓަރި n. very large bundle or bale [H. gaṭhrī, Skt. granthikā]

1245 GAṬAA (gaṭaek) ގަޓާ n. wooden stopper-joint of hookah
[H. gaṭṭhā, cork, cf.Skt. granthaka]

1246 GAḌAGAḌA ގަޑަގަޑަ onom. gaḍagaḍa lanii, g.aḷanii, makes a bubbling sound

1247 GAḌI ގަޑި n. hour; clock,watch: atukurii g.,wristwatch: boḍu g. / eluvaa g., wall clock: soonaa g., alarm clock [H.sōnā, sleep]: gaḍii keňbu, mainspring:

g. jahanii, clock strikes; nuvagaḍi jahaa iru, at 9.0: ekgaḍi bai vejje, it is 1.30: degaḍin degaḍin, every two hours: tin gaḍi iru, for the space of 3 hours: Divehi gaḍiyek naganii, takes a Divehi period (in school): gaḍi jehigen, being late; aharen gaḍi jehijje, I am late: g. nujehecce, don't be late: ehera madrasaa-ař daa gaḍi jehenii, it is high time to go to school: gaḍi jassanii, clocks in: gaḍi balaalum, checking the time: gaḍiař balaalum, looking for the watch: gaḍiek netee, there is no time [H. ghaṛī, Skt. ghaṭikā]

1248 GAḌUBAḌU ގަޑުބަޑު n. hostilities: g. kuranii, fights [H. gaṛbaṛ, disorder]

1249 GAḌḌAAMI ގަޑްޑާމި adj. arrogant: gaḍḍaami-kam boḍu, of a bullying nature

1250 GAŇḌU ގަނޑު n. 1. piece: g. lanii, g. fattanii, fits a new patch of wood: page, leaf of book (fotuge g.), g. kaṇḍaa fot, note pad: kamtak gaňḍu, various matters: keyo-gaňḍu, bunch of bananas: miihun gaňḍu, group of people; used in enumeration: de-gaňḍu foti, two bits of cloth, fas-gaňḍu gaňḍu-fan, five pieces of cadjan: gaňḍu- vaa, bits of rope;

Much used ifc., sometimes with pejorative effect; e.g. gas-gaňḍu, treetrunk, log: taas-g., playing card; taasgaňḍu jahanii, plays a card: fati-gaňḍu, ruler: fan-gaňḍu, piece of cadjan: fas-gaňḍu, plot of earth, arena: fun-gaňḍu, deep place: fus-gaňḍu, raincloud: fuřgaňḍu, lump of dough: fen-gaňḍu, pool: foti-g., piece of cloth: mas-gaňḍu, quarter section of fish: ruk-gaňḍu, grove; log: loo-gaňḍu, brass pot; mirror; pejorative, e.g. ge-gaňḍu, miserable house: fořaa-gaňḍu, ancient turban: aḷu-gaňḍu, I (dim., 'miserable slave'): kam-tak gaňḍu, a great nuisance: ecceti govum-gaňḍu, a host of jibes; sometimes after verbal nouns : vehum-gaňḍu, a woven cover;

gaňḍu-fan, kind of cadjan used for roofing: g.- fen, ice: gaňḍu-fillaa, a Maldivian game, in which gaňḍu aḷanii = sets up the Home, g. fillanii = hides under the blankets, g. govanii = identifies oneself, gaňḍu helee= move! gaňḍu-mauluud, a festival on 11th Rajab; g. vanii, becomes frozen; becomes a taciturn recluse: gaňḍu kořَ (adv.),wholesale [S. kaňḍa, Skt. khaṇḍa]

2. blister, boil : gaňḍu naganii, boil arises: g. jahaigen, developing a boil [S. geḍi, Skt. gaṇḍa]

1251 GAŇḌUVARU ގަނޑުވަރު n. palace of the nobility (no longer so named)

1252 GAŇḌETI ގަނޑެތި n. piece, unit, usually of clothing: tin gaňḍeti, three pieces of clothing given to a bride: also of boats, de-gaṇḍeti , two vessels [gaňḍu + eti]

1253 GAT ގަތް v. bought, taken (p.p. of gannanii) [S. gat, *ghṛpta]

1254 GATANII ގަތަނީ v. plaits: makes lace (v.n. getum : past tense geti, geccee): kinaari g., makes chevřons: jooli g., makes hammock: bit gatanii, fills up gaps in walls of houses: gataa fai, instrument for making lace on [S. gotanne, Skt. granthayati]

1255 GATUM ގަތުން v. buying: saifat gatum varař madee, sales of tea are very low (v.n. of gannanii) [S. gatum]

1256 GADA ގަދަ adj. strong: g. aḍek, a loud sound: g. nidi, deep sleep: g. muři kula, dark brown: g. valek, a strong rope: g. haalek, a stout cock: aňga g., garrulous: kaňḍu g. duvahek, a day when the sea is rough: fenař g., stable in water (of boats): ruḷi g., irritable: vas g., scented: varu gada, strong; fanvaru gada, out of control (of children): hitvaru g., brave: gadakamun devii, gave by force, forced to marry: g. aḷanii, strains, insists; ekme gada aḷuvvaa bunuvvaafai vanii, he (hon.) spoke most emphatically: gada-bayyař hifanii, fights ('strong-versus-weak'): gada kuranii, increases; aḍufař g. kuranii, increases the noise: etanař at gada kořuḷenii, has influence there: g. vanii, gets strong; (of the sea) is rough; (of the sick) recovers; gada ve hunnevi, in good health (hon.); (in games) wins, is the strongest: badigeař gada vaane, will rule the kitchen (see uňduḷi), ge-haa gada vaane, the home team (lit. domestic cock) will win: gadayyaa = gada viyyaa: vai gadayyaa, if the wind is strong: nukuḷadaana gadaige boḍeti raaḷu, unbearably strong waves: gadaigai jehum, running into stormy weather: gada dakkanii, struggles; gada-ař (adv.), strongly: gada- fada (doublet), strong: gadabim-faaḷa, a creeper, scindapsus aureus

1257 GADARU ގަދަރު n. dignity: gadaru-veri, dignified [U. qadar]

1258 GADAHA ގަދަހަ n. (obs.) drinking pot [U. qadaḫ]

1259 GAŇDA-KOOḶI ގަނޑަކޫޅި n. a scented plant, basil, ocimum basilicum: Misuru g., angelonia salicariifolia

1260 GAŇDU-RAHA ގަނޑުރަހަ n. kind of askanu medicament, balsam

1261 GAN DII ގަން ދީ v. calling to witness (in oaths): Maat Allaahu gan dii, swearing by God

1262 GANA ގަނަ n. struggling, difficulties: g. teḷenii, is destitute

1263 GANE ގަނެ v. having bought, taken (abs. of gannanii) [S. gena, P. gaṇhiya]

1264 GANJAA ގަންޖާ n. cannabis, hashish: g. bonii, smokes cannabis [S. ganjā, H. gānjhā]

1265 GANJU ގަންޖު n. razorbox [U. ganj]

1266 GANJU-FARAAS(-hek) ގަންޖުފަރާސް n. undervest with sleeves, T-shirt; sometimes written ganjifaraas [H. ganjī, E. Guernsey]

1267 GANNANII ގަންނަނީ v. buys (abs. gane , ganfai : p.p.gat : v.n. gatum : imp. ganee ! past tenses ganefi, gatfi, gati, ganejje, ganijje, genje : caus. ganuvanii : invol. ganevenii : hon. ballavai-gannanii): daulatar̃ gane, buying for the Government: gannan buni miihek, a man who offers to buy: gannan libeenii,will be able to buy:
takes (in restricted contexts): buḷiigai gannanii, bites the hook: mas ganna tanek, a place where the fish take the bait: dum gatfi, gets a burnt taste: sooḷa an̆diri ganna ree, during the darkness of the 16th day of the moon (an inauspicious time): huhi ganna rukek, a coconut which bears undeveloped fruit: gat gatiinun, by constantly taking: (met.) nidi gannanii, feels sleepy: biru g., feels frightened: ladu g., feels embarrassed;
ifc. abs. -gen after another absolutive has little meaning (kan̆ḍaigen for kan̆ḍaa): ibc. gen-, having taken, see gennanii, gendanii [S. ganne, P. gaṇhāti]

1268 GANNAVANII ގަންނަވަނީ v. shoves into, stuffs into (v.n. gennevum): eccessar̃ taketi gennevum, shoving things into other things (caus. of gannanii)

1269 GANBANII ގަންބަނީ v. sinks (tr.) (caus. of gan̆banii)

1270 GAFARU ގަފަރު n. fifth sail of the former royal yacht

1271 GABARAA ގަބަރާ n. confusion: g. vanii (poet.), is perplexed [H. gar̃bar̃ā]

1272 GABIYAA ގަބިޔާ adj. stupid [U. ghabī]

1273 GABIILAA ގަބީލާ n. tribe [U. qabīla]

1274 GABU ގަބު adj. silly [U. ghabū]

1275 GABURU ގަބުރު n. dead body; grave: g. konnanii, digs grave: gaburustaanu, public cemetery [U. qabr, grave]

1276 GABUḶA ގަބުޅަ interjection of encouragement to physical effort: also hin-gabuḷa, hun-gabuḷa

1277 GABUḶI ގަބުޅި n. coconut in final stage before the water dries inside: g. aḷanii, picks such coconuts (used in cooking): g. taana, crude or old taana (Maldivian script)

1278 GABUULU ގަބޫލު n. consent: consenting: eenaage g. hoodanii, seeks his permission: g. kuranii, approves: g. vanii, agrees: aḷugan̆ḍu gabuulu, I agree: bappage gabuulugai ta, with father's consent? e kaaveni gabuulek nukuram, I didn't agree to that marriage: gabuuliyyaa (for g. viyyaa), if (you) agree [U. qabūl]

1279 GAŇBANII ގަނބަނީ v. dips, sinks (intr.), e.g.in a swamp (gañbaa tanek); usu. in form gañbaigatum, or geňbenii (invol.); used of people, not ships (cf. fetum)

1280 GAM ގަން n. In phrase gam hinganii, takes (criminals) round the town (an ancient punishment); gama-tere, gamu-tere, interior centre of an island (in Male called ekgamu); gamatereař aranii, goes inland.

Also used as proper name of certain islands, e.g. Gan in Aḍḍu atoll [S. gam, village, Skt. grāma]

1281 GAMAARU ގަމާރު adj. stupid, 'simple' [P. gāmadāraka]

1282 GAMIIS (gamiihek) ގަމީސް n. modern-type shirt: gamiis-gañḍu, rotten old shirt: buri g., bush shirt [U. qamīs, Port. camisa]

1283 GAYAA VANII ގަޔާ ވަނީ v. is interested (in,..-aa): gayaa vaa kamek, an enjoyable activity: aharen kaleaa gayaa vee, I like you [cf. gai ?]

1284 GARAḌA-MAA(malek) ގަރަޑަ މާ n. a stinking flower, abroma augusta

1285 GARAŇBU ގަރަނބު adj. cloudy (of water)

1286 GARAHITA ގަރަހިޓަ n. skink

1287 GARU ގަރު n. scum on cooking water: garudiya, fish-water, fish soup: g. fen, salty rice-water : g. raha, scummy taste

1288 GARUNU ގަރުނު n. century [U. qarn]

1289 GARUBA ގަރުބަ n. conception: g. gannanii, evolves in the womb: (met.) g. laigen uḷenii, is heavy-hearted [Skt. garbha, womb]

1290 GALAGADI ގަލަގަޑި n. kind of putty or paste used for caulking

1291 GALADUN ގަލަދުން n. antimony: g. aḷanii, applies antimony (to the eye) [galu- + añdun]

1292 GALAM ގަލަމް n. pen: g. jahanii, makes a pen: galan-daanu, pen-case: galamu doori, pen cap [U. qalam, Latin calamus]

1293 GALU- ގަލު- See gaa: galu-ori, kind of fish, siganus stellatus: galu-faḷu, Male quarantine harbour in the lagoon: Galoḷu, one of the four wards of Male: galaa veyyaa, rock and sand

1294 GALBU ގަލްބު n. name of two compass directions: g. astamaanu, south-west; g. iiraan, south-east [U. qalb, heart (of the Scorpion), Antares]

1295 GAVAAIDU ގަވާއިދު n. rules: fas gavaaidu,the five basic arithmeticaal operations (addition, subtraction, multiplication, division, fractions) [U. qavā'id]

1296 GAVI (gatvek) ގަވި n. 'gaw', distance of a league [S. gav, P. gāvuta]

1297 GA-VIYANI ގަވިޔަނި n. the letter G in the Maldivian alphabet (also called gaafu)

1298 GAS (gahek) ގަސް n. tree; plant: gas dořař nerenii, (anc.) hands over to be beaten (near the Gasdořu Miskit): boḍu gas, raintree, samanea: riiti gas, flamboyant tree, delonix regia: vina gas, clumps of grass: gas-gahaa-gehi (-gessek), vegetation: gas-kara, (view of) wooded shore: gas-gaňḍu, tree-trunk, log: gas-muři, flowerpot: gas-vakaru,timber [S. gas, P. gaccha]

1299 GASTU (GASDU) ގަސްތު (ގަސްދު) n. decision: g. kuranii, decides, plans: hama gastugai, quite deliberately [U. qas̱d, intention]

1300 GAZU ގަޒު n. measure of a yard (in trade), two muř [U. gaz]

1301 GAHAḌU ގަހަޑު n. harbour [H. ghāṭ]

1302 GAHANAA(-ek) ގަހަނާ n. jewellery [H. gahnā]

1303 GAHAA(gahaaek) ގަހާ n. magnetic north : gahaa-tari, pole star [A. jāh]

1304 -GAHAAGEHI, GAHU- -ގަހާގެހި / -ގަހު See gas; kaani gahu uňdooli, a swing of kani wood

1305 GAHUVA ގަހުވަ n. (lit.) Turkish coffee (only drunk by nursing mothers) [U. qahva]

1306 GAŘANII ގަރަނީ v. stirs up with water, mixes two liquids (v.n. geřum): uva g., mixes lime: davaadu g., mixes paint or ink: bat tavaa geřijje (invol.), the rice pan is over-watery: gaŕaa bat, kind of rice porridge

1307 GAḶANII ގަޅަނީ v. pushes (v.n. geḷum): koppaa gaḷanii, shoves in: munḍun fuu g., tucks up sarong; caus., kuru- gaḷuvanii, cuts short: gik- gaḷuvanii, shoves around; see also geḷenii

1308 GAḶI ގަޅި n. pieces of wood used esp to throw up for fruit picking (gaḷi-gaňḍu): gaḷi keňḍi, striped (of animals)

1309 GAA (GAU) (galek) ގާ (ގައު) n. 1. hard coral from the sea: iruvaru gaa, nakat gaa, foundation stone: roo gaa-tak, undried coral: vaan gaa, stone weight as partial anchor; gaa oḍi, coral-loading dhoni, also its load when stacked ashore: gaa-oḍi lava, coral-loading shanties: gaa-duuni, seagull (boḍu gaaduuni, large crested tern: ainmatii gaaduuni, lesser crested tern): gaafoḷu, gaafuḷu, base, podium; small wall round flowerbeds: gaa-bis, 'stone egg', infertile egg laid first: gaa-viha, gaa-viya, kind of poisonous fish: gaa-haka, large kind of clam; mekunu fumunas, gaahaka-aŕ nufumeveene-ee (prov.), though a flying fish can leap a clam can't, i.e.don't be over-ambitious: gaa-huli (-huyyek), kind of strong beetle: gaa aranii, keeps quiet as a stone, sulks; eenaa gaa araafai, he is sulking [cf.S. gal gähenne]: gaa vanii, gets shrivelled up; also of people, gaa kujjek, a stunted child: hit-gaa kujjek, a mentally dull child

2. quarter pound weight: gaa-gaňḍu, weights on a scale (even when of metal); also stony area [S. gal, stone: T. kal]

1310 -GAA / -GAI -ގާ / -ގައި suffix of locative sense, see -gai

1311 GAAIMU ގާއިމު n. establishment; in g. kuranii, establishes: gaaim-magaam, acting official (for.., -ge) [U. qā'im, fixed]

1312 GAA-KEHEŇBUḶI ގާކެހެނބުޅި See gai-

1313 GAAḌIYAA (gaaḍiyalek) ގާޑިޔާ n. trolley, cart; bicycle: at g., hand trolley: damaa g., bigger trolley: as g., horse coach [H. gāṙī, Skt. gantrī]

1314 GAAT ގާތް n. vicinity: bappage gaataŕ, towards father: aharenge gaatugai bunuvvaeve, tells us: aḷugaňḍu gaatu bunanii, speaks to me (dat. case not used in these contexts): eenaage gaatugai, in his presence: at gaat kuranii,brings a helping hand; eenaa-aa at gaat koŕla dii, helping him: gaat timaage, closely related: gaat bee, disciple; gaat gaňḍakaŕ (adv.) approximately: libum gaatii, what you are likely to get: enme gaatkam boḍii, the most likely [cf. S. gāvā, near]

1315 GAATULU / GAATILU KURANII ގާތުލު ކުރަނީ - ގާތިލު ކުރަނީ v. kills [U. qātil, qatl, killing; cf. katilanii]

1316 GAADII ގާދީ n. sack worn on the head when carrying loads: g. aḷanii, puts the sack on [H. gādī, cushion]

1317 GAANANII ގާނަނީ v. scrapes, rubs away (v.n. geenum): huni g., scrapes coconut; grinds medicines by hand in liquid: aňdun g., grinds kohl: kelaakoḷu g., grinds up some sandalwood: geenifai (of shoes), worn out (invol.) [S.gānne, Skt. gharṣati]

1318 GAANU ގާނު n. handful (esp. of medicinal leaves)

1319 GAANUUNU ގާނޫނު n. legal act: gaanuunu asaasii, constitution [U. qānūn]

1320 GAAFILAA ގާފިލާ n. 'caravan', body of travellers [U. qāfila]

1321 GAAFU ގާފު n. the letter G (better, ga-viyani): Gaafu atoḷu, Huvadu atoll (divided into North and South, Gaafu alifu and Gaafu daalu) [cf.U. qāf]

1322 GAABILIYYATU ގާބިލިއްޔަތު n. competence [U. qābilīyat]

1323 GAARII-VERI ގާރީވެރި n. qualified reciter of the Qur'an (the Maldives have a unique style) [U. qārī, reader]

1324 GAALI (Gaayyek) ގާލި n. Galle (Lankan city) [S. Gālu]

1325 GAAVIYAA (gaaviyalek) / GAAVII ގާވިޔާ / ގާވީ n. topsail on a schooner [H.]

1326 GAASILU ގާސިލު n. name of two compass directions: g. astamaanu, north-west by west; g. iiraan, north-east by east [cf. U. wāqi', Vega]

1327 GIU-GAŇḌU ގިއުގަނޑު n. small frame, picture frame

1328 GIUḶI-LAAŘI ގިއުޅިލާރި n. gum arabic : giuḷilaaři teras, gum arabic glue [S. divul-lāṭu]

1329 GIUḶU ގިއުޅު n. kind of reef fish, aprion

1330 GIK-GAḶUVANII ގިއްގަޅުވަނީ v. shoves around

1331 GIGUNI ގިގުނި n. little bells, dancers' anklets, tambourine jingles: viha g., a plant shaped like an anklet, crotalaria sp. (also called giguni maa) [S. gigiri]

1332 GIḌIGE ގިޑިގެ n. 'pandal', ornamental arch [S. geḍigē]

1333 GITAA(-ek) ގިތާ n. plaiting: g. kuranii, plaits together (of rope)

1334 GITI ގިތި adj. half-ripe (of coconuts or areca)

1335 GITEU, GITEO (gitelek) ގިތެއު - ގިތެއޮ n. 1. clarified butter, ghee: g.mirus, kind of chillies [S. gitel, Skt. ghṛta-taila]
2. he-goat

1336 GINA ގިނަ adj. many: haada miihun gina ra̋rek, an island with many people: gina guna vaa, manifold: mitaa derufiyaa gina, Rs.2 extra here: gina kuri akurutak, extra letters: gina kořlanii, gina vefaa uḷenii, hangs around, frequents a place: adv., ginain, gina koř, gina vegen : ekun ginain nukaařee, don't eat so much! nuhanu ginain e geař de-ee, goes to that house extremely frequently: tiya devvii derufiyaa ginain, you have given me two rupees too much; ekme gina vegen, at the most

1337 GINAFATI ގިނަފަތި n. For ginifati

1338 GINAVELI (GINIVELI) ގިނަވެލި (ގިނިވެލި) n. a plant, premna (same as dakaňdaa)

1339 GINI (ginñek) ގިނި n. tangible heat (not of weather): uňdunuge gini gada kurum, increasing the heat of the oven: maḍu giniigai kekkum, simmering: gini kaa maaduuni, ostrich (believed to eat fire):
gini-kaňdu, large shooting star: gini-fati (ginafati), tongs: gini-mas, a reef fish, snapper, lutjanus: gini-raahi (-raassek), [the sign Aries: giniveli, see ginaveli: gini-hila, shooting star; firestone [S. gini, Skt. agni]

1340 GINIKANÑAA ގިނިކަންޏާ adv. alone (hon.)

1341 GINTI ގިންތި n. category [H. gintī]

1342 GIFILI (gifiyyek) ގިފިލި n. Maldivian latrine [For ge-fili]

1343 GIYAAMAT ގިޔާމަތް n. Last Judgment, end of the world [U. qiyāmat]

1344 GIRANII ގިރަނީ v. dissolves in liquid by stirring (e.g.stirring tea, mixing medicines): sifts rice: washes away islands in the sea (rař-rař girum): (invol.) karaa tiyotii muḷin giri halaaku vefai, the watermelon is all shaken up inside: hiru girenii, toothgums dissolve away: Giraa-varu, name of a historic island near Male [S. garanne, sifts]

1345 GIRAA KURANII ގިރާ ކުރަނީ v. steps across (tr.)

1346 GIRAAVARU SIRRU ގިރާވަރު ސިއްރު n. secret which is no secret [Giraavaru island near Male formerly had a primeval population]

1347 GIRI ގިރި 1. n. large rocks in the sea: giriitere, rocky area [S. & Skt. giri, mountain]
2. v. being stirred: adi rañgaḷaŕ nugiri, not stirred properly yet (of tea) (invol. abs. of giranii)

1348 GIRIṬII ގިރިޓީ n. gilding: g. kuranii, gilds [E. gilt]

1349 GIRIS ގިރިސް n. grease [E. grease]

1350 GIRISLIINU ގިރިސްލީނު n. glycerine: g. uñguri, kind of enema [E. glycerine]

1351 GIRUÑBAA(-aek or -alek) ގިރުނބާ n. bellows: g. aḷanii, uses bellows: g.-filaa, kind of creeper, euphorbia sp. [A. qirba, waterskin]

1352 GIRUVAANU ގިރުވާނު n. collar of libaas [U. girībān]

1353 GILA ގިލަ n. part of bows of dhoni

1354 GILA-FATI ގިލަފަތި n. necklace (for children up to the age of 10) [S. gela, neck + fati, row]

1355 GILAN ގިލަން n. sad plight: gilanek jassanii, brings about a sad plight

1356 GILIGILI ގިލިގިލި n. tickling: g. koṭṭanii, tickles (childish, cf. hiili)

1357 GILUVANII ގިލުވަނީ v. gulps down (coll.) [S. gilinne, Skt. gilati]

1358 GILEE ގިލޭ n. necklace (mod. gilafati)

1359 GIS ގިސް n. gulping with sobs: gis lanii, gulps [onom.]

1360 GII-FATI (giifaccek) ގީފަތި n. nonsense: g. amunanii, talks a lot of nonsense

1361 GUI ގުއި n. dung, excreta (usu. of animals): g.- tafaa, turd: gui-buraňda, a troublesome kind of fish; gui renii, excretes (of animals): da-gui, metal dross [S. gū, Skt. gūtha]

1362 GUK ގުކް onom. g. kiyanii, makes a forcible noise (as of punching, or while eating)

1363 GUGUM ގުގުމް n. vibratory noise: g.araafai, a vibration has arisen [old S. gigum]

1364 GUGUMANII ގުގުމަނީ v. reverberates, booms [gugum]

1365 GURURANII ގުގުރަނީ v. (it) thunders [S. guguranne, Skt. ghuraghurāyati]

1366 GUGURI ގުގުރި n. thunder: g. jahaafai,with thunder: g. damanii, snores: g. tasbiiha, a prayer against thunder: guguri-filaa, kind of creeper [guguranii]

1367 GUŇGURU ގުނގުރު n. musical rattle, jingle bells: g. aḷanii, wears bells (on the feet, and sometimes on the arm) [S. gigiri]

1368 GUṬṬU ގުއްޓު n. a blow: gaigai g. aḷanii, deals blows to the body [S. guṭi, Skt. ghřṣṭi]

1369 GUḌANII ގުޑަނީ v. quivers and shakes, moves (caus.guḍuvanii : hon. guḍaa-lavvanii): mee guḍum-tak, heart throbbings: rař guḍum, earthquake: guḍum aranii, gets shaken, shocked; rař guḍaa, a kind of drum-beat: (enlarged) Maalein guḍaa-lanii, leaves Male: (invol.) guḍaa nulevee, immovable (of animates): guḍuvaa nulevee, immovable (of inanimates): guḍi laifi, moved

1370 GUḌAAKU ގުޑާކު n. mixture of tobacco and sugar for smoking in hookah [H. guřākū]

1371 GUḌI ގުޑި n. 1. kite (of all sizes): g. aruvanii, g. ellanii, sends up kite: g. atař damanii, brings kite down: g. hippaa karudaas, tissue-paper: fuř-guḍi, flying fluff, 'soft feathers' (childish for duuni-fuř) [H. guḍḍī]
2. cup used by toddy tappers
v. 3. invol. abs. of guḍanii

1372 GUḌUGUḌAA (-aaek) ގުޑުގުޑާ n. hookah [H. gařgařā, Skt. gargaraka]

1373 GUḌUGUḌU ގުޑުގުޑު n. wobbling: g. aḷanii,wobbles: furifai huri eccek guḍuguḍek naaḷaane-ee (prov.), a full vessel will not wobble, i.e.the competent may be confident [onom.]

1374 GUDAN ގުދަން n. godown,warehouse [S. gudan, Malay gadong]

1375 GUDAARU ގުދާރު n. shoulder-blades: g. matii baavvaigen, putting (a load) across the shoulderblades

1376 GUDU ގުދު n. a bend; bent: arm of a gramophone; eenaage gudu nukutiiee, he is hunchbacked: gudu kuranii, bends (tr.): gudugudu lanii, goes zigzag [S. kudu, Skt. kubja]

1377 GUDURAT ގުދުރަތް n. nature: Maatkalaañge gudurat-terikam, the incomprehensibility of God [U. qudrat]

1378 GUN ގުން onom. g. kiyanii, makes a swallowing noise

1379 GUNA ގުނަ n. multiplication: eege fas guna deeṙee, give (me) five times that! fas guna-aṙ ituru vanii, is multiplied fivefold, by five: libee guna, the answer to a multiplication sum: g. kuranii, multiplies; deekaa hayakaa guna kuraaṙee, multiply two by six: guna kurevee (kurevee-ek), the multiplicand: guna kuraa faahaga, the sign 'x': guna-gellum, multiplication and division: guna-haru, the multiplier: gina guna vaa, manifold [S. & Skt. guṇa]

1380 GUNAN ގުނަން n. See gunavan

1381 GUNANII ގުނަނީ v. counts [S. gaṇinne, Skt. gaṇayati]

1382 GUNAVAN, GUNAN ގުނަވަން - ގުނަން n. limb, bodily organ

1383 GUNAA (gunaaek) ގުނާ n. offence [U. gunāh]

1384 GUNḌAA (gunḍaaek) ގުނޑާ n. foolish and ignorant man (pej.) [H. guṇḍā, rascal]

1385 GUNḌOḶI ގުނޑޮޅި n. wall of sand, at sea or at sides of a pit

1386 GUNTURA ގުންތުރަ n. (hon.) digging pole in nobleman's latrine

1387 GUNBAḶA ގުންބަޅަ n. kind of fish, herklotsichthys quadrimaculatus

1388 GUNBAA ގުންބާ n. pump: boḍu g. kuranii, gives an enema

1389 GUBBU ގުއްބު n. dome: top of stupa [U. qubba]

1390 GUŇBU HILANII ގުނބު ހިލަނީ v. is asthmatic

1391 GUŇBOO (guňboolek) ގުނބޫ n. a sandbug which dances to music: kiyaa haa lava-ař nařanii guňboolee (prov.), only a g. dances to any tune (does whatever he's told); one recites to him the rhyme - 'guňbooloo guňbooloo, fuppi hakuru boon teduvee, aa libaas laan teduvee!'

1392 GURAI ގުރައި See guraa

1393 GURAŇDA, GURAŇDU ގުރަނދަ - ގުރަނދު n. state eulogy recited on great occasions by the abuunaa

1394 GURAHA ގުރަހަ n. bright constellation [Skt. graha, planet]

1395 GURAA (GURAI) (guraek) ގުރާ (ގުރައި) n. parrot: guraa-fehi, parrot-green [S. girā, ?Skt. kīraka]

1396 GURAABU ގުރާބު n. 1. lime-case (huni guraabu)
2. ancient battleship: vai g., toy ship [U. ghurāb]

1397 GURU ގުރު adj. 1. very small and undeveloped; used of coconuts (guru kaaři) and children [S. uguḍu]
2. guru vegen, curled up [for guḷa vegen]

1398 GURUATU ގުރުއަތު n. lot: g. lanii, casts lots, tosses up (mod. ṭos kuranii) [U. qur 'a]

1399 GURUAAN ގުރުއާން n. The Qur'an [Qur'ān]

1400 GURUḌU, GURUŇḌU ގުރުޑު - ގުރުނޑު adj. undeveloped, deformed (of fruits) [cf.S. uguḍu]

1401 GURUDAA (-aaek) ގުރުދާ n. kidney [U. gurda]

1402 GURUBAAN ގުރުބާން n. sacrifice: g. kuranii, g. vanii, sacrifices [U. qurbān]

1403 GURUVA ގުރުވަ n. kind of fish, said to be the favourite food of the maakanaa heron, 'sweetlips', plectorhynchus; also terapon: kaňḍu g., a large kind of g.

1404 GURUS (guruhek) ގުރުސް . n. 1. a gross, 12 dozen [E .gross]
2. disc of sun or moon: g. fenmati vum, appearance of the disc at sea level,which marks an auspicious moment [U. qurs̱]

1405 GURUZU ގުރުޒު n. spiked club (as used by Rustum) [U. gurz]

1406 GURRAAS (gurraahek) ގުއްރާސް n. 'form' of paper

1407 GULAAMU ގުލާމު n. jack, knave (at cards) [U. g͟hulām]

1408 GULIKAŇDU, GULUKAŇDU ގުލިކަނޑު - ގުލުކަނޑު n. rose-petal syrup [U. gulqand]

1409 GULEE NUURAN-maa(malek) ގުލީ ނޫރަން n. a scented jasmine [U. gul-e- + Maldivian]

1410 GULKOOZU ގުލްކޯޒު n. glucose [E. glucose]

1411 GUL- ގުލް- n. ibc., flowers: gul-dastaa, bouquet, garland [U. guldasta]: gul-śan, garden [U. gulṣan]: gul-zaaru, garden [U.gul-zār]: gul-haaru, garland of flowers [U. gul-hār]

1412 GULLA ގުއްލަ n. a religious measurement of water (usu. de-gulla, two g.) [U. qulla]

1413 GULL-ALAA ގުލްއަލާ n. a plant

1414 GUL-SANPAA (GUL-CANPAA) ގުލްސަންޕާ (ގުލްޗަންޕާ) n. frangipani, 'temple tree', plumeria sp. [U. gul +Skt. campaka]

1415 GUḶA ގުޅަ n. ball of something; tablet; fishcake, 'cutlet' (varieties: boḍu g., medu g., kudi g.): guḷa bees, pill; g. karuvanii, collects in a ball, scrumples up: g. jehenii, piles up (intr.): g. vanii, gets curled up, crowded up (also guru vegen for guḷa vegen): g. vaŕanii, makes a ball of something: masguḷa kanii, gets stiff muscles: guḷa kuḷee fasgaňḍu, former name of open space in front of the royal palace where ceremonies took place; (adv.) guḷa-akaŕ, curled up [S. guḷi, Skt. guḍikā]

1416 GUḶANII ގުޅަނީ v. joins (tr.) (with...,-aa): (invol.) ahannaa varař guḷee miihek, a man who gets on with me very well: ui guḷanii, twists thread together ; Ui guḷaa soru, character in an old story: guḷum, (an) Association; siyaasii guḷum, diplomatic relations: (on telephone) fahun guḷaalan vii nu, please ring later: kon nambarakaa ti-guḷanii, what number are you calling? [cf.S. gaḷapanne; Skt. ghaṭayati]

1417 GUḶAMATI ގުޅަމަތި n. formal wrestling (esp. practised on island of Maḍuvvari): g. hifanii, practises this wrestling

1418 GUḶI ގުޅި n. 1. wide squat jar (for oil) [Skt. ghaṭa]
2. large log: ruk-guḷi, log of coconut:bařbukeyo g., log of breadfruit
3. name of an island, known for its music
v. 4. being joined (invol.abs. of guḷanii)

1419 GUU ގޫ n. burnt tobacco left in hookah: g. taḷanii,breaks up the residue (for re-smoking): dumgařḍu guu vejje, the hookah has burnt too quickly, is spoilt [U. gul]

1420 GUUḌU-HAKURU ގޫޑުހަކުރު n. unrefined juggery in lumps [S. guḍa, U. guř, treacle]

1421 GE (pl., gee-ge, geige) ގެ n. house: g. aḷanii,builds a house (politer, binaa kuranii): g. hadanii, repairs house: gee tere, inner part of house: ge-koḷu, nobleman's house: ge-gařḍu, rotten old house: ge-doru, own house and belongings, home [S. gedara]: ge-fuḷu, House of God at Mecca: ge-mati 1., roof space of a house (used as wood store): ge-veri miihaa, owner of house: ge-vehi (adj.), domestic; gevehi-kanvaaru, domestic furniture; gevehikam huri miihek, good housekeeper, home-lover: ge-haa, domestic fowl. See also gee [S. gē, Skt. gṛha]

1422 GECCEE ގެއްޗޭ For geti + -ee, plaited: see gatanii

1423 GETUM ގެތުން v. plaiting (v.n.of gatanii) [S. getum]

1424 GEDABUḶI ގެދަބުޅި n. soot, smuts: faarugai g. jahaafai, soot has collected on the wall: g. heekeene-ee, soot will rub off (on to you) [ge + duřbuḷi]

1425 GEDA ގެދަ n. a creeper used in inferior curries, portulaca oleracea: geřdafatugai kekki riha, curry made with these leaves [S. geřda]

1426 -GEN -ގެން v. ifc. for gane, abs. of gannanii: e.g. hadai-gen, kařḍai-gen, cf.hadaa, kařḍaa, and also eok-gen, ehera-gen, mihira-gen: after nouns with ending -aai is equivalent to 'concerning': miihakaai gen dan jehum,being very much in love with someone: kamakaai gen uḷum,trying to do something, 'having a problem': ninjaai gen, sleepily: sakaraat nugen, not joking: aḷugařḍumennaai gen kurimati lii, faced us: masakkataai gen helifeli vaan, to be dedicated to work: bařḍuhai gen haanti vefai, exhausted with starvation [S. gäna, concerning]

ibc., taking; see gennanii, gendanii

1427 GENAI ގެނައި v. brought (p.p. of gennanii) [S. genā]

1428 GENAUM ގެނައުން v. bringing (v.n.of gennanii) [S. genaīm]

1429 GENES / GENAS ގެނެސް - ގެނަސް v. having brought (abs. of gennanii); enlarged, genessaa [S. genat]

1430 GENGUḶENII ގެންގުޅެނީ v. uses, keeps for use: looks after, brings up (child): keeps (birds, fish): employs (servants) (abs. genguḷe : hon.genguḷuvvanii): genguḷee miihun, servants employed in the house: sṭeemp genguḷee vatgaňḍu, drawer one keeps stamps in [?ge + guḷanii]

1431 GENGOS ގެންގޮސް v. having taken (abs. of gendanii)

1432 GENḌAA(-aaek) ގެނޑާ n. rhinoceros [H. gēnḍā]

1433 GENDANII ގެންދަނީ v. takes away (abs.gengos : imp.gendee ! invol. gendevenii : v.n. gendiyum : caus. genduvanii : :hon. gendavanii, see also devvanii 2.): aharen gengos diifaanan ta, can you take me with you? gendevee varuge, buyable: genduvaigen, having imported: kaaḷu gengossaane (for gengosfaane), the crow might take;

After a pres. absolutive, this word indicates 'continue to': rayyitunnař ekbaaru lamun nugendevunu kam, inability of the people to go on cooperating: daulatun leveen ot hai baarek lamun gendiya kam, the persistence of the Government in exerting all possible influence: uḷemun gendanii, continues to live

[gen- + danii; S. geni-yanne (which is also used in sense of continuity)]

1434 GENNANII ގެންނަނީ v. brings (abs. genes, genas, enlarged genessaa : imp. genee ! p.p genai: : v.n. genaum : 3s. gene-ee : hon.gennavanii : invol. genevenii : caus. genuvanii : past tense genaii, genesfi, genessi): juus taṭṭek gennaařee, bring a cup of juice! hitař gennanii, visualizes: samaa gennanii, announces a special festival: geneveekař noonnaane-ee, it won't be possible to import: raňgaḷu asarutak genneviee, brought about good effects [gen- + annanii, and so S. genenne]

1435 GENNEVUM ގެންނެވުން v. 1. bringing (hon.) 2. shoving into (v.n.of gennavanii, or of gannavanii)

1436 GENBUM ގެންބުން v. sinking (tr.), dipping into water (v.n.of ganbanii)

1437 GEFAANU ގެފާނު n. honorific title, used ifc.: rasgefaanu, King: kilegefaanu, holder of rank of kilege : Muhammad-gefaanu,the Prophet: Iisaa-gefaanu, Jesus [for -ge faanu, S. pāṇan, sacred foot of..]

1438 GE-FILI ގެފިލި n. See gifili

1439 GE-BAINDANII ގެބައިންދަނީ v. performs circumcision ['keeps in the house']

1440 GEŇBURU ގެނބުރު n. outer side of anchored ships: g. at, outer side: g. vaa, rope on outer side (as v. atdařu at, near side, fuřu vaa, nearside rope)
[S. gäňburu, deep, Skt. gambhīra]

1441 GEŇBUM ގެނބުން n. sinking (intr.) (v.n. of gaňbanii)

1442 GEMA ގެމަ n. (obs.) dues formerly paid to persons of honour

1443 GEMAŘ ގެމަށް n. (in dat. case) (obs.) gemař diyum, emigration

1444 GEMATI ގެމަތި n. 1. See ge-
2. extra sail at stern of an oḍi

1445 GERI ގެރި n. cow: geri gui, khaki colour: geri mas, beef: Boḍugeri, name of a bogey: geri-gaňḍu,three-legged support for boats in dry dock
[S. geri, Skt. gaura]

1446 GERIVARU ގެރިވަރު n. (obs.) ropes for tying someone up

1447 GEREVI (gerevvek) ގެރެވި n. woodworm droppings [?ge-revi, 'house mustard']

1448 GELA ގެލަ n. nukut gela, the answer to a division sum: gela-haru, the divisor

1449 GELLANII ގެއްލަނީ v. divides; gellenii (invol.), is lost: gellum (v.n.), loss: gellevee, dividend (in a sum)

1450 GEHERI ގެހެރި n. pieces of wood providing temporary covering for boats

1451 GEŘUM ގެޑުން v. mixing, stirring up (v.n. of gařanii)

1452 GEḶENII ގެޅެނީ v. pushes: mitanař nugeḷeeřee, don't push! (slang) (invol. of gaḷanii)

1453 GEE ގޭ n. For gee-ge, esp.in names, e.g.Hilihilaagee Muusaa Diidii, M.Didi who lived in Hilihilaage: gee tere, inside of house: gee-geege, of various houses: geen, from the house (for gein) [ge]

1454 GEENUM ގީނުން v. scraping: grinding (v.n. of gaananii)

1455 GEES (geehek) ގޭސް n. gas (for lamps, or balloons) [E. gas]

1456 GOI ގޮއި n. Government-owned area of planted inhabitable land: goi-veri, lessee of a goi

1457 GOIDURUVAAN ގޮއިދުރުވާން n. sextant (mod. filaa)

1458 GOṬI ގޮޓި n. an old game: goṭi-bai, set of men to play it with

1459 GOŇḌI ގޮނޑި n. 1. seat; board for playing games such as chess, tinhama, oř̌vaḷu :

adaraada g., chair: ihaa g., stem of a bunch of nuts: koḷufilaa g., kind of stool: digu g., bench: mas g., chopping board: saranfii g., reclining chair: soofaa g., sofa: huni g., coconut scraper; g. aḷanii , occupies a seat: g. jahanii, makes chair; arranges room: goňḍi-gaa, detachable base of a tombstone: goňḍi-foo (- foi), two sticks serving as tinderbox for lighting fire; goňḍifoo aḷanii, uses the tinderbox:

2. hard central part of a boil: dik g., boil in the armpit: tuberous root of a plant: faḷoo g., papaw root; ala goňḍi, yam tuber: g. faibanii, tubers form, roots develop; g. jahanii, hits the udder when milking

1460 GOŇḌU ގޮނޑު n. heap of rubbish : goňḍu-mati, rubbish heap: Boḍu goňḍu, a former feature of Male,the town rubbish-heap: goňḍu-doř, the beach (used as a latrine); aharen mi aii goňḍudořař erifaee, I'm returning from the beach: rař-goňḍu, the coast of an island, the shelter of an island; goňḍu kuranii,brings to shore

[S. goḍa, heap; dry land]

1461 GOT ގޮތް n. manner; manners: got gotun, in various ways: vii hai gotakun, in every possible way: egot- migotař, in various ways: mi gotuge matin, in this way: eaai ekgot vaa gotuge matin, in a similar way to that: mi vaa got, what is happening here: kam dimaa vi gotun, as things turned out: varař kuru gotakař, very briefly: varař aadaige gotekgai, very simply: varař nugotakař, very surprisingly: degotek nuvaa, unalterable: mi-ii abaduves mařař huri got baavaee, of course this is what always happens to me: huri net got, how it was (and wasn't): huri gotař, all of a sudden [S.hiṭi häṭiye]: hama ekgotek ves nuviee, had no success at all: (of something undesirable) injiinař gotek vegen, something happened to the engine: ekme fahu got vii, the last straw was..: got hus vii, all is lost: onnaane got hus vefaa, he will be at his wits' end: got kuḍa ve, conditions improve: got hadaa datgaňḍu, sewing machine attachment for making unusual (zigzag) patterns: got kuḍa, rude: got boḍu, fussy: got huri, polite: gotek fotek net miihaku, a man with no manners: gotek gotek neti, senseless: got-gaňḍu, behaviour; gotun, gotugai, in function of: izzatteri mehmaanuge gotugai, as guest of honour: Vaziir-ud-daakhiliyyaage gotun, in capacity of Home Minister;

After a participle, 'the way in which': eenaa-ař śakkuveri vaa got meduveri nukuraati, don't let him become suspicious: bappa ruḷi duruvaanee gotek aḷugaňḍu beenumek net, I don't want father to get angry: dee gotař otum, keeping on giving: daa gotař daane, will go very quickly: Gamugai Iňgireesin tibee gotař otum, the continued presence of the English on Gan: hoodaa gotař onna kamakař nuvaa, not being something that should be sought after: e-gotakii..., that is because.. : e kam vaa got viee, that happened to be possible: got kiyanii, makes comments: got balanii, examines the situation: got hadaalanii, does harm

1462 GODAḌI ގޮދަޑި n. mattress; stuffed seat [S. gudiri, U. gudṛī (Port. godrím?)]

1463 GODAN (godanuge) ގޮދަން n. wheat: g. kiru, wheat gum: g. fuř, wheat flour: g. boňḍibat,wheaten pudding; g. kaňḍanii, husks wheat, threshes [Skt. gōdhūma]

1464 GODAA (-aek) ގޮދާ n. large type of bonito fish

1465 GON ގޮން n. 1. a game played at Eid (gon kuḷenii): gon jahanii, challenges (in the game) by touching someone's head, saying 'Gon' and running away

2. wooden plate used in ropemaking to separate the strands: g. duvvanii, pulls the plate through

3. gon-gaňḍu, hump of cattle

1466 GONI ގޮނި n. hollow, concavity: goni kořlaafaa, hollowed out; gonii-fuu (-fulek), back point of semicircle in game of baibalaa: goniifulař lanii, sucks up to

1467 GONU ގޮނު n. 1. small basket

2. kind of fish, boxfish, ostracion

1468 GOFAḶU ގޮފަޅު n. raw recruit, tyro

1469 GOFI (gotpek) ގޮފި n. branch (lit. or met., e.g.branch of mathematics): gofi-koḷu, leaf-stalks, (math.) 'compound rules'; gofi kurevee gas, trees from which cuttings can be taken

1470 GOBU ގޮބު n. knob, knob handle: gobu-taḷu, lock with a knob; young kanamadu fruit

1471 GOBOḶI ގޮބޮޅި n. 1.young coconut in second stage of development; g. ala, type of yam

2. egg yolk (bihu g.); eyeball [S. gobolu, young coconut]

1472 GOŇBI ގޮނބި n.. a swelling: g. naganii, swelling arises

1473 GOMA ގޮމަ n. ambergris (=maa-vaharu): goma-kastuuri, a similar substance found in kinds of deer

1474 GOMAŘI ގޮމަޑި n. a plant resembling lime

1475 GOMAA ގޮމާ n. a royal lady (gomaa-fuḷu)

1476 GOYYE ގޮއްޔެ n. girl, country girl (non-Male usage): e-goyye, my child (fem. of e-koi): ḷii-goyye(obs.), daughter in law (mod. ḷii-darifuḷu)

1477 GORU ގޮރު n. (coll.) urine, esp. of animals: g. hañḍanii, pisses

1478 GOLA ގޮޅަ n. thing (vulg.)

1479 GOLAA ގޮޅާ n. lad, bloke (non-Male usage)

1480 GOVATI (govaccek) ގޮވަތި See gooti

1481 GOVANII v. ގޮވަނީ calls (to, dat.): eenaa-ař kaan govaan, to call him to eat: miihakař vagař govanii, calls someone a thief: kanař govanii, lolař govanii, insults the ears / eyes, viz. calls disrespectful attention to deafness or blindness: masakkatu g., summons to work: aḍu g., makes a sound or noise (usu.of inanimates, or of certain animals or birds), goes off (of a gun): ecceti govanii, is abusive: goos g., is delirious or raving: maibafaa govanii, makes insulting remarks about someone's parentage; govaigen (abs.), bringing (people),with..; eenaa govaigen aum, bringing him,with him: aharen govaigen diyum, taking me,with me; Enlarged: govaa-lanii; govaalan diyum, going to visit the sick: Iidu govaalum denii, makes a distribution of food at Eid: Bismillaahi govaalanii, says grace at a banquet (cf. B. kiyanii in a house): (invol.) eenaa-ař govaalevunii eenaage darifuḷařeve, he managed to speak to his son

Caus., govvanii, shouts (aḍu g., of animates); explodes (tr.);blows an instrument (sangu govvanii, blows a conchshell): miihun govvanii, teases people [perhaps old S. gohanne, Skt. ghōṣati]

1482 GOVAAM ގޮވާމް n. corn, grain (in general): g. toři, husk of grain; g. kañḍanii, reaps; threshes: g. kuranii, farms, grows grain : g. haddanii, produces food [S. govikam, Skt. gōpakakarma]

1483 GOVI (govvek) ގޮވި 1. n. ifc., -herd: bakari-govi, goatherd: by extension, kuñburaan-govikaleege, woodcutter: govvař baavvanii, leaves unhatched (of eggs) [S. govi, Skt. gōpaka]

2. v. called (p.p. of govanii)

1484 GOS ގޮސް v. having gone (abs. of danii: enlargements, gosfai, gossaa, gosgen): eenaa mihaaru vii vadaa gohee, he has gone fly-fishing: gos ais vum, going and coming: mi gos-lanii, I'm going (enlargement): gosgenek nuvaane, mustn't go [S. gos, Skt. -gatya]

1485 GOHORU ގޮހޮރު n. intestines (specifiable as kuḍa g., fala g., hima g.)

1486 GOHOḶU ގޮހޮޅު adj. foolish, stupid

1487 GOŘ ގޮށް n. knot (in string etc.; also knot in wood); button or hook: anhen g., mariyaňbu g., granny knot: ṭaii g., 'lace knot': damaa g., slip-knot: daṁmaanu g., sheet bend: fiṯṯaa g., press stud: buḷi-g., hook and eye; buḷigoř aḷuvanii, does up hook: libaahu g., button on libaas : g. aḷuvanii, does up button: g. jahanii, g. lanii, ties knot: g. naṭṭanii, undoes button: g. mohanii, undoes knot; goř-kuḷaňduru, a plant, cyperus sp. [S.kaḷāňduru]: g.-jooḍu, pair of shirtstuds or of cufflinks (libaahu atukuriigai laa gořjooḍu): goř-fati, (in dressmaking) strip for buttons: g.-faḷi, one half of a press stud; gořfaḷi aḷanii, splices end of a rope: goř-fuḷaňgi (-fuḷatňgek), locust: goř-muř, clenched fist; gořmuřu-baaru, inhuman behaviour: goř-vaḷu, buttonhole: goř-sampaa, kind of banana ; swelling on the neck: karugai g. naganii, swelling arises: g. lanii, develops such a swelling [S. gäṭa, Skt. granthi]

1488 GOŘI (goṭṭek) ގޮށި n. conical container or basket, usu. of paper; covering for food: gořì-jooḍu, food-cover with lid: g. batpoḷi, conical winnowing fan: saifat goṭṭek, a packet of tea [S. goṭu]

1489 GOḶAA(-aek) ގޮޅާ n.. mussels

1490 GOḶI ގޮޅި n. square, rectangle: g. jehi fot, exercise book of squared paper: goḷi goḷi jehi foti, chequered cloth; plot of land: gaa g., stony plot: hiki g., dry plot; market stall: Maccangoḷi, one of the four wards of Male

1491 GOOTI (gooccek) (GOVATI) ގޯތި (ގޮވަތި) n. house- compound (in Male): elsewhere, house; gooti-tere, inside of compound (or of house): gooti raivaru, nursery rhymes [S. ge-vatu]

1492 GOODI (goojjek) ގޯދި n. dry dock [H. gūdī, ?Skt. guptikā]

1493 GOONAA(-aek) ގޯނާ n. annoyance: g. kuranii, annoys(with dat. or -aa)

1494 GOONI (goonňek) ގޯނި n. jute sacking, sack: g.kotaḷu, jute bag ('gunny bag'): g. farudaa, jute curtain [S. & H. gōṇī]

1495 GOOŇBILI (gooňbiyyek) ގޯނބިލި n. a large tree with sour fruit, phyllanthus acidus: bees- g., a medicinal fruit, emblica : kaři- g., small caltrops, tribulus terrestris: g. ala, kind of yam, colocasia esculenta

1496 GOOS (goohek) ގޯސް adj. undesirable, useless: (maru)goos govanii, talks rubbish, is delirious: goos vanii, is corrupted; buddi g. vanii, is mentally backward: (maru)goos hadanii, makes stupid mistakes, does silly things

1497 GOOSII ގޯސީ n. a lateen sail

1498 GOOḶANII ގޯޅަނީ v. pokes (into): (enlarged) lolaȓ iňgili gooḷaa-laaȓee, poke a finger in (his) eye: (met.) mikamuge tereaȓ gooḷigatum, getting involved in this affair

1499 GOOḶI ގޯޅި n. 1. alley, blind alley: de-gooḷi, a through lane; defai degooḷi, space between the legs: gooḷiaȓ aḷanii, turns into a side-lane, (met.) goes out of line. gai-gooḷi vanii, becomes very close [H. gallī]
2. tool for drilling iron

v. 3. gooḷi-gatum, see gooḷanii (invol. abs.)

ޗ CA-VIYANI, the 24th letter of the Maldivian alphabet

1500 CAKA ޗަކަ adj. muddy, damp: caka vaḷugaňḍu, drain pit [cf. cas]

1501 CAKACAKA ޗަކަޗަކަ onom. cakacaka aḷanii, laughs vulgarly

1502 CANDAA ޗަންދާ n. subscription: c. denii, pays sub [U. candā]

1503 CARUKEES ޗަރުކޭސް n. circus ; c. kuḷum, doing stunts [E. circus]

1504 CA-VIYANI ޗަވިޔަނި n. the letter C in the Maldivian alphabet

1505 CAS ޗަސް adj. muddy and damp (cf. caka): cas jahanii, cas taḷanii, makes unpleasant noises, e.g.while eating [onom.]

1506 CAAKU ޗާކު n. pocket-knife (caaku fiyohi) [U. cāqū]

1507 CAAṬU ޗާޓު n. map, chart [E. chart]

1508 CAAŇDANII (also CAANDANII) ޗާދަނީ (ޗާންދަނީ) n. kind of white flower, tabernaemontana divaricata: C. magu, name of the principal shopping street of Male [H. cāndnī]

1509 CAAPU ޗާޕު n. printing, stamping: c. kuranii, c. jahanii, prints:

hila c., litho (as v. rooniyoo c., roneo) [H. chāp, Skt. √kṣamp]

1510 CAABII ޗާބީ n. winder; key of clock, handle of gramophone: gaḍiyař c. denii, winds up clock: c. hus vii, clock has run down [H. cābī, Port. chave]

1511 CAABUUKU ޗާބޫކު n. horsewhip (in stories) [U. cābuk]

1512 CAARAA-KAM ޗާރާކަމް n. alertness: caaraakam gada, alert [? for U. cālā]

1513 CAALAAKU ޗާލާކު n. smart alec; smart at business [U. cālāk]

1514 CAALU ޗާލު adj. beautiful: c. koř, beautifully (adv.) [H. cāl, deportment]

1515 CICANḌAA(-aaek) ޗިޗަންޑާ n. snake-gourd, tricosanthes [H. cicinḍā]

1516 CIṬU ޗިޓު n. chit, document [E. chit (from Hindi)]

1517 CIS ޗިސް onom. cis kuranii, crushes

1518 CIḶIYAA ޗިޅިޔާ n. clubs (at cards): ciḷiyaage nuvayek jahanii, plays the nine of clubs [H. ciřiyā]

1519 CIIS ޗީސް onom. ciis lanii, makes a rushing or spurting sound [cf. coos]

1520 CUKU ޗުކު adj. tiny (childish) [cf. cuppu]

1521 CUṬṬII ޗުއްޓީ n. holiday, leave: cuṭṭiiyek libigen, getting leave of absence [H. chuṭṭhī]

1522 CUPPU ޗުއްޕު adj. little (childish): cuppu ves nubunee, don't say a word! [cf. cuku]

1523 CUS ޗުސް onom. cus lanii, makes plopping sound (as of bursting blister, or spitting)

1524 CUUS ޗޫސް onom. cuus damanii, draws in breath with a gasp [cf. coos]

1525 CENCEENU ޗެންޗޭނު n. railings (of metal or rope): c. damanii, puts up railings [cf.ceenu]

1526 CEENU ޗޭނު n. small chain: c. buri, bicycle chain: karugaa laa c., necklace chain [E. chain]

1527 COK ޗޮކް onom. cokek jahaafai, giving an exclamation of annoyance

1528 COS ޗޮސް onom. cos jahanii, cos kaňḍanii, makes sound of disgust (tsk tsk)

1529 COOKU ޗޯކު n. 1. chalk (for writing) [E. chalk]
2. cooku batti, electric torch [by error for E. torch]

1530 COOS ޗޯސް onom. coos lanii, makes sound as of rushing water (cf.ciis) or by sucking with the lips: coos damanii, makes unpleasant gulping sound; smacks the lips

1531 -CCEE -އްޗޭ suffix, of polite verbal command: kaccee, will you eat?

ޖ JA-VIYANI, the 23rd letter of the Maldivian alphabet

1532 JAUZAA ޖައުޒާ n. name of two compass directions: j. astamaanu,West by South; j. iiraan, East by South [U. jauzā, Gemini or Orion]

1533 JAGAḌAA (JAGAḶAA) ޖަގަޑާ (ޖަގަޅާ) n. trouble, bother: j. kuranii(slang), stirs up trouble (against someone,...-aa): j. hadanii, riots [H. jhagṛā]

1534 JAGU (anc. JOGU) ޖަގު (ޖޮގު) n. jug; mug [E. jug]

1535 JAŇGIYAA (-aaek) ޖަނޑިޔާ n. (pair of) short underpants [H. jānghiyā, Skt. jānghika]

1536 JAḌAA (jaḍaek) ޖަޑާ n. kind of dragonfly

1537 JAḌIBU ޖަޑިބު n. standard-bearer heading a royal procession; chief of the former haňgubeekalun [? U. jarīb, measuring staff]

1538 JADALU ޖަދަލު n. dispute: j. kuranii, disputes, argues [H. jadal]

1539 JADU ޖަދު n. ancestry [U. jad]

1540 JANAVARII ޖަނަވަރީ n. January : janavarii maa, a flowering creeper [E. January]

1541 JANAVAARU ޖަނަވާރު n. (large) animal [U. jānvar]

1542 JANGALI (jangayyek) ޖަންގަލި n. jungle [H. jangalī]

1543 JANBUURA ޖަންބޫރަ n. 1. large pliers [U. zambūr]
2. a method of firing cannons (j. jahanii)

1544 JAPANU ޖަޕަނު n. Japanese: j. miidaa, mouse; j. haa, small variety of poultry

1545 JABBAARU ޖައްބާރު n. In pl.., jabbaarun (pej.), powerful people; jabbaaru-vanta (of God), Omnipotent [U. jabbār, omnipotent]

1546 JAŇBUROOLU ޖަނބުރޯލު n. a fruit, 'wax jambu', jambola, eugenia javanica [H. jambūl, but confounded with jambu]

1547 JAMALU ޖަމަލު n. camel (mod. ; anc. oř) [U. jamal]

1548 JAMALU-KOṬAA ޖަމަލުކޮޓާ n. kind of purgative, croton tiglium [H. jamāl-goṭā]

1549 JAMAA KURANII ޖަމާ ކުރަނީ v. keeps, preserves: deposits (money) [U. jama']

1550 JAMAA-AT ޖަމާއަތް n. congregation, group: jamaa(a)t-terin, members of a group, esp. undertakers [U. jamā'at]

1551 JAMMIIYAT ޖަމުއިއްޔާ n. a registered society [U. jam'īyat]

1552 JAMBU ޖަންބު n. a fruit, 'Malay apple', eugenia sp.: finifen j., a particular kind of jambu [H. jambu; cf. jaňburoolu]

1553 JARAASIIMU ޖަރާސީމު n. germs [U. jarāthīm]

1554 JARII KURANII ޖަރީ ކުރަނީ v. makes to glitter: applies sequins [U. zarī]

1555 JARRAAFU, JARRAAFAA ޖައްރާފު - ޖައްރާފާ n. dredger [A. jar'āfa, harrow]

1556 JALIYAA ޖަލިޔާ n. former royal barge (jaliyaa-koḷu - also called ba<u>tt</u>elikoḷu): jaliyaakoḷu jahanii, takes out the royal barge [H. jal-yān]

1557 JALU ޖަލު n. jail: jalař lanii, jalař aḷaalanii, puts in jail [E. jail]

1558 JALSAA ޖަލްސާ n. assembly: j. kořlanii, summons an assembly [U. jalsa]

1559 JAVAABU ޖަވާބު n. answer: j. denii, answers [U. javāb]

1560 JAVAAHIRU ޖަވާހިރު n. turquoise: j. maa, 'Rose of India', lagerstroemia speciosa [U. javāhir, jewels]

1561 JA-VIYANI ޖަވިޔަނި n.. the letter J in the Maldivian alphabet

1562 JASTU ޖަސްތު n. zinc, tin: jastuge saamaanu, zinc goods: jastu baddaa hatiyaaru, soldering iron: kuni nagaa jastu-gañḍu, dustpan [H. jast]

1563 JASSANII ޖައްސަނީ v. causes to touch; applies (tr.): (v.n. jessum): kula j., applies colouring; gamiihugai nuukula j., dyes shirt blue: dila j., scorches, smokes (fish): fuḷitoři j., applies broken glass (to kite strings): buraki j., applies brake: maa j., heats grain till it opens ('causes to flower'): ruu j., makes pleats: laki j., rocks a boat: vai j., takes the air, enjoys the breeze: va<u>tt</u>aru j., makes faces: svic j., turns switch on: hama j., arranges, settles; hit hama j., satisfies oneself, acquiesces:

of ships or aircraft, causes to stop: Nuumaraagai jessiimeve, we called at Nūmarā; beerař jassaalanii, goes outside; muudař jassaa matindaa booṭu, seaplanes ('aerial boats which are landed on the sea'); mařař kamtak j., puts (much) work on me; magee fahatugai jassaafai, following after me; gaḍi jassaifi, clocked in: maḍu j., causes to hesitate: miihun jassanii, employs men: mesejek jassanii, sends a cable: employs men: jessum, hostile behaviour: jessum kuranii, makes difficulties: jassajassaigen, consecutively (caus. of jahanii; see also jessenii)
[S. gassanne]

1564 JAZAA ޖަޒާ n. fruits of action: requital [U. jazā]

1565 JAHAḌUU ޖަހަޑޫ n. brush (anc., mod. burusu): j. aḷanii, uses brush [H. jhāřū,besom]

1566 JAHANII ޖަހަނީ v. (v.n.jehum:: past tenses, jehiyee, jessee, jahatpe: p.p. jehi, jihi)

1. strikes: ataa(a)taa jahan, to shake hands: etifaharu j., gives blows: kaři j. (of insects), stings: gaigai j., strikes the body: gaigai boňḍi j., strikes blows on the body: goňḍi j., hits the udder when milking: ˋ gaḍi jahaifi, the clock struck: saitaři tuňbugai jahan, to put the cup to the lips: baňḍu jahaigen duvaa, crawling, reptilian: baňdaru j., enters harbour: misraabu j., follows a compass point: raňgabiilu j., strikes bell; of clocks, ekek jahaifi, it struck one; gaḍi jahaifi, the clock struck; haddu jahanii, gives official legal beating; also with dat.., matindaa booṭař jahaanee baḍi, anti aircraft guns: cavalař jahanii, pulls on the mast-rope; jehi jehiinun, by constantly beating

Also used in various more general senses (cf. also aḷanii):

2. fixes, applies (uses): ili j., fixes dowelling: ui j., inks a line for painting up to: kakuu j., kneels: kaḍa j., fixes peg: kan-ili j., uses harpoon: kafu j., fixes tow-rope: kabiilaa j., fixes rivet: kavaa j., applies ‘cupping’: kihili j., carries on hip (tr.): kurafat j., circumcises: gaňḍufan j., fixes cadjan: goř j., ties knot: goḷi jehi (p.p.), checkered, squared: takgaňḍu j., applies stamp: taan j., applies starch (also taan lanii): taasgaňḍu j., plays a card: tilagaňḍu j., raises the winner’s flag: bolugai jahaa dati, hairpins: dantura j., sets a trap: didadaňḍi j., fixes a flagpole: dumdaňḍiek jahaa-lanii, fixes up a joss stick: doḷi j., adjusts veil: nakatgaa j., lays foundation stone: naařidila j., applies coconut oil-black: fai j., sets foot: faṭaas j., sets off fireworks: fat j., folds: fanvatu j., ties a palm leaflet on (as registration): fali j., rows (boat): fiyan j., puts lid on: filaa j., fixes shelf: fili j., applies vowel-signs to consonants: fistoola j., shoots pistol: fuugoḷi j., wears sanitary towel: fen j., splashes water: feelige j., pitches tent: fotigaňḍu j., fixes curtains: bain j., fixes a sling (atugai, on the arm): bagiyaa j., applies lacework: banbuḍi j., applies lamp pricker: baraa j., fixes outrigger: bumaru j., spins tops: beju jahaigen, putting on a badge: bees j., applies medicines: bonti j., bonti jahaa fumenii, does pole-vault: boosaa j., fixes anchor rope: mati j., puts lid on: marukaa j., stamps a mark: malaru j., puts a stop (to.., ..-gai:): maḷifati j., sets trap: muḍi j., fixes props: mohoru j., fixes nails; makes nails: ran jehi (p.p.), gilt: rehan j., applies dye: lavahoḷiyek j., puts gramophone record on: laňburaan j., fixes rope to mast: laa j., applies lacquer: vaan j., sets trap: sikka j., applies seal, mints coin: faarugai simenti j., applies rendering to wall: hak j., haka j., fixes pulley: hamarodi j., applies loose stitching

3. makes: alamaari j., makes cupboard: galam j., makes pen: fasgaňḍu j., repares arena: fallava j., makes a storeroom or larder: funi j., piles up (tr.): baňḍaha j., sets up temporary fishing quarters: buḷi j., makes a hook: mas j., puts on fat: mohoru j., makes nails: va-goř j., makes a reef knot: vaḷubari j., makes row of holes: sandook j., makes coffin: ḷiya j., cuts in strips;

does (of various activities): kuḷu j., spits: koru j., limps: gon j., challenges at game of ‘gon’: cas j., cos j., etc., makes various kinds of noise: faaḍu j., gives the appearance: fuřṭaki j., snaps the fingers: foḍi j., farts: baḍi j., shoots: baňḍiyaa j., does the pot dance: burraas j., squawks and runs: boki j., bubbles: boḍuberu j., performs drum dance: kamakař makaru j., shirks something: laki j., has a dancing motion (e.g. of kites): laňgiri j., performs the sitting dance: vakvak j., barks and snaps: saka j., larks about: sakaraat j., jokes; flirts: salaam j., begs alms (‘greets’ - used as a euphemism): ham j., raises distress signal, sends SOS

Special usages:

4. writes down: adadu j.,writes figures: kuř j., makes errors in arithmetic: jumla j., enters the total: taari<u>kh</u> j., writes a history: nambaru j., writes sums (on the board): raahi j., casts horoscope: viya j., solves mathematical problems: hisaabu j., does calculus

5. lets sink, drops: is jahaigen, bowing the head: esfiya j., blinks: kasmati j., shaves back of neck: dorufat j., (anc.) slams door: falukaa j., closes hatch: boo jahaa-

lanii, nods: vaḷu j., (met.) digs oneself into the ground, goes to ground

6. arranges: daara j., bevels edge, smoothes edge: fansuru j., sharpens pencil; fansuru jahaa eti, pencil sharpener: mas fallava j., stores fish: munḍu aruvaa j., tucks up sarong: libaas j., takes shirt in, tightens shirt

7. develops, forms (intr.): um jahanii, spots appear: kura(foḷu) j., boil develops: dat-takugai kobaḍi j., discoloration of the teeth develops: gañḍu jahaigen, blisters appeared: gedabuḷi j., soot collects: dabaru j., rust develops: dikgoñḍiek j., a boil develops: duumi j., white spots appear: bolugai nura j., white hairs come: faaḍu j., a tendency develops, looks like being: fii j., black spots appear (on cloth): fuu j., white spots appear (on fish): fehi j., green moss grows (on walls); mas j., fat is deposited: mila j., turns brown (in cooking): mulihi j.,blisters develop; aharen mi uḷenii m. jahaigen, I have developed blisters: bilet vak j., betel twigs develop: vaagi j., develops strength: sarubii j., fat is deposited; see also jehenii

Abs. jahaa is used adverbially in sense of 'violently': jahaa ellaifi,threw violently: jahaa kañḍaalaifi, violently broke: jahaa ganegen, snatching away: jahaa giluvaifi, gulped down: jahaa dumburu aruvailaifi, suddenly hotted up: jahaa duvvaigenfi, drove furiously: jahaa nindaalafaanam, I will knock you senseless: jahaa nimuni, went out bang: jahaa veṭṭuni, suddenly fell down [S. gahanne, strikes: P. ghaṃsati]

1567 JAHALAA ޖަހަލާ n. huge jar

1568 JAHAA MUGURI ޖަހާ މުގުރި n. wood apple, feronia elephantum (Sour and sweet varieties : hut jahaa muguri, foni jahaa muguri)

1569 JAAGA ޖާގަ n. vacant space, accommodation (esp. on board ship) [H. jagah, jāgā]

1570 JAAḌI ޖާޑި n. big waterpot [T. cāṭi]

1571 JAADUU ޖާދޫ n. magic: jaaduugaru, magician: jaaduuvii, magical [U. jādū]

1572 JAANU ޖާނު n. life, bodily life [U. jān]

1573 JAAFAT ޖާފަތް n. feast, treat [U. źiyāfat]

1574 JAAFAANU RUK ޖާފާނުރުއް n. short variety of coconut palm [for Japanu, Japanese]

1575 JAAMALAA ޖާމަލާ n. (obs.) lighter, barge for goods

1576 JAARIYAA ޖާރިޔާ n. a presented female slave, concubine [U. jāriya]

1577 JAASUUSU ޖާސޫސު n. a spy : j. kuranii, spies [U. jāsūs]

1578 JAAHILU ޖާހިލު adj. ignorant, barbarous: ignorant man [U. jāhil]

1579 JINJARU ޖިންޖަރު n. ginger-beer (anc., mod. iňguru soḍaa) [E. ginger]

1580 JINNI ޖިންނި n. djinn: jinni vasvaas jehitai, possessed by a djinn. jinni moya, moderately mad (as v. duniye moya) [U. jinnī]

1581 JINSU ޖިންސު n . 1. jeans [E. jeans]

1582 JINSU ޖިންސު n. 2. sex : jins-ul-latiif, womankind; jinsii, sexual [U. jins]

1583 JIFUṬI ޖިފުޓި n. hut

1584 JILAABI ޖިލާބި n . See zileebi

1585 JIZII ޖިޒީ n. tribute [U. jizī]

1586 JIHI ޖިހި v. For jehi, p.p. of jahanii

1587 JIIBU ޖީބު n. 1. pocket [U. jēb]
2. jibsail [E. jib]

1588 JIIMU ޖީމު n. the Arabic letter J

1589 JUMMA [ޖުމްމަ] n. Friday prayers [U. jum'a]

1590 JUMLA ޖުމްލަ n. total; sentence: j. kuranii, adds up: j. koř balaa iru, on the whole, all in all: j. jahanii, enters the total; jumla-koḷek, some sentences [U. jumla]

1591 JUMHUURII ޖުމްހޫރީ n. Republic, republican: j. duvas, Republic Day: j. meevaa, passionfruit, passiflora edulis [U. jumhūrī]

1592 JURUMAANAA ޖުރުމާނާ n. a fine: diha rufiyaain j. kuranii, fines (someone) Rs.10 [U. jurmāna]

1593 JULAI, JULAAII ޖުލައި - ޖުލާއި n. month of July [E. July]

1594 JULLAABU ޖުއްލާބު n. purgative [U. jullāb]

1595 JUVAA ޖުވާ n. gambling: j. kuḷenii, gambles [H. jūā, Skt. dyūtaka]

1596 JUZAAM- BALI (-bayyek) ޖުޒާމްބަލި n. leprosy [U. juẕām]

1597 JUUN ޖޫން n. month of June [E. June]

1598 JUURIMANAA ޖޫރިމަނާ n. For jurumaanaa

1599 JUUS ޖޫސް n. juice, cool fruit drink [E. juice]

1600 JESSENII ޖެއްސެނީ v. gets struck : lolugai jessenñaa, if you get something in your eye (invol. of jassanii) [S. gässenne]

1601 JEHENII ޖެހެނީ v. is struck; is stuck; disagrees; touches; hesitates; occurs; fits:

uňguru jehunu,with backbone broken (of fish): veṭṭi jehifai, fell and struck the ground: karugai kaři jehifai, bone being stuck in the throat: fulugoř jehijjeyyaa, if the bottom knot stays firm: defaraat jehuneve,the two parties disagree: aharen miigaa jehiliyyaa, if I touch this: kiru ilořiigai duuni jehum, birds getting caught on the local flypaper: tunfatu jehen den, up to the brim: kairiaa jehen den, till it got nearer: fenu jehifai, where the sea meets the horizon: jehigen huri geegai, in the house next door: jehigen anna fatfuřtak, the following pages: dekoḷu jehifai, having made both ends meet: fahakaai jehen den, till recently: jehilum vaa miihek, a hesitant man: fahař nujehi (adv.),unhesitatingly: emiihun jehilumek nuve-ee, they do not hesitate: maḍu jehilanii, hesitates: konme kamek jehuniimaa, when something happens: jehifai vaa uňdagulek, a disaster which has come upon you: boḍu kamek jehigen, when trouble has arisen: massaru jehenii, monthly 'period' occurs: faifala bali jehifai vaa miihun, people who have got filariasis: vasvaas (bali) jehifai, suffering mental breakdown: vagutu jehenii, the time comes: muunuaňdirikam j., it gets twilight: matigaňḍu nujehee, the lid doesn't fit : (ekves) taakun taaku nujehee, unplaceable, useless: dekoḷu nujehee miihek, an unintelligible person;

In various other contexts -

esfiinaa jehenii, the evil eye is cast: eena-aa karudan jehigen, being besotted with her : kaaři jehenii, is knotted: gaḍi jehigen, being late: taayyař jehenii, taayyaa jehenii, nods sleepily: dan jehigen, hanging oneself; (met.) miihakaaigen dan jehigen, being very much in love with a girl (cf. karudan jehigen): furitan jehenii, gets back to where one was (naut.); (met.) avoids bankruptcy: buruu j., gets into a tangle: aharen matinbai nujeheenam, I won't make the first move; matinbain jehigen, on one's own initiative:
iru medu j., the sun is at the zenith: ruu j., wrinkles appear: ruufa j., puts on weight: lak jehifai, stained: loobi jehenii, falls in love: vai jehenii, the wind blows: vaḷu j., goes to ground, buries itself: hama j., is arranged; works properly; (of time) is up: erařař daa hit jehigen, developing a liking for visiting that island; mikamaa dekoḷuveri hitek jehijje, showed a dislike for doing that: kai kai ḷis jehenii, gets full up, overeats; fahatař jehilamun, stepping back; beerař jehilaafaa, stepping outside; gaatař jehila! come closer!

With dat. case, lacks: karudaahař jehenii, is short of paper: kaaḍař j., baňḍař j., is short of food, starves.

After an infinitive, has to (hon., jehi vaḍaigatum): kooṭek deen jeheene-eve, will have to give (me) a coat: aḷugañḍu mikam kuran jehuneve, I had to do this (invol. of jahanii) [S. gähenne]

1602 JEEMU ޖީމު n. 1. a small fruit, 'jam tree', muntingia calabura [S. jā̃m]
2. jam [E. jam]

1603 JOGU ޖޮގު n. jug; mug (mod. jagu) [E. jug]

1604 JOOḌU ޖޯޑު n. pair (of animals or birds: not of people); pair of hinges; cup and saucer, cup (for sai-jooḍu); j. vanii, mates (of animals): at jooḍu koř, holding hands; jooḍu-bijooḍu, a game [H. jōř, junction]

1605 JOOLI (jooyyek) ޖޯލި n. string seat, commonly found in front of houses: jooli-fati, row of string seats: hellaa jooli, swinging hammock [H. jhūlī]

1606 JOOS (JOOŚ) (joohek) ޖޯސް (ޖޯށް) n. great energy [U. jōś]

ޏ ÑA-VIYANI, the 16th letter of the Maldivian alphabet

Ñaviyani atoḷu, Fook Mulaku (Fua Mulaku)

1607 ÑAMÑAM ޏަމްޏަމް n. kind of sour fruit, cynometra cauliflora [Malay]

1608 ÑA-VIYANI ޏަވިޔަނި n . the letter Ñ in the Maldivian alphabet

1609 ÑAKAS ޏަކަސް n. In ñakas taḷanii, talks nonsense

1610 ÑOKI ޏޮކި n. In ñoki taḷanii, has sexual intercourse

1611 -(N)ÑAA -(ން)ޏާ suffix: in conditional verb-forms: kuḷenñaa, if one plays: vanñaa, if it be

ޓ ṬA-VIYANI, the 20th letter of the Maldivian alphabet

1612 ṬAIPU JAHANII ޓައިޕު ޖަހަނީ v. types [E. type]

1613 ṬAII ޓައީ n. tie (neckwear): ṭaii goř, 'lace knot' [E. tic]

1614 -ṬAKAI, -ṬAKAA -ޓަކައި / -ޓަކާ suffix, following dative case-form: for the sake of: aḷugaňḍařṭakai, for my sake [For takaa, cf.S. takanne, Skt. tarkayati]

1615 ṬAKI (ṭatkek) ޓަކި n. tap, knock: bolugai ṭ. taḷanii, ṭ. jahanii, knocks on the head: dorugai ṭ. denii, ṭ. jahanii, knocks on the door: fuř-ṭaki jahanii, snaps the fingers; ṭ. kaňḍaa maḍi, kind of beetle. ṭ. aranii, sudden pain arises [S. ṭoku, H. ṭhōk]

1616 ṬAGU ޓަގު n. tugboat [E. tug]

1617 ṬANU ޓަނު n. ton (of 20 handaru): registration documents of a vessel; ṭanu naganii, levies customs clearance [E. ton]

1618 ṬAFARU ޓަފަރު n. top sail on the mainmast [E. topper?]

1619 ṬAFU ޓަފު 1. n. knot-line (ṭafu-nanu): ṭ. taḷanii, uses knot-line(to measure speed of vessel): ṭafu-fuḷi, sandclock used with this line [H. ṭab]
2. Go! (word used to start a race)

1620 ṬAPPU ޓައްޕު n. large round tin [T. ṭappai]

1621 ṬARUMOOZU ޓަރުމޯޒު n. See tarumoozu

1622 ṬA-VIYANI ޓަވިޔަނި n. the letter Ṭ in the Maldivian alphabet

1623 ṬAS ޓަސް onom. ṭas lanii, makes cracking sound: raas ṭas kiyaafai,very quickly

1624 ṬAAM ޓާމް n. school term [E. term]

1625 ṬIKIṬII (anc.), ṬIKEṬU (mod.) ޓިކެޓު -ޓިކިޓީ n. ticket: ṭ. naganii, ṭ. gannanii, buys a ticket, books a ticket [E. ticket]

1626 ṬINU(ṬIINU) ޓިނު (ޓީނު) n. corrugated iron: ṭinu-tak, bits of corrugated: ṭ. jahanii, puts a corrugated iron roof on: ṭinu-gaňḍu, sheet of corrugated [E. tin]

1627 ṬIŇBULI ޓިނބުލި n. curtain ring: ṭ. lanii, fits curtain ring

1628 ṬIINU ޓީނު n. For ṭinu

1629 ṬIIM ޓީމް n. team [E. team]

1630 ṬIICAR ޓީޗަރ n. teacher [E. teacher]

1631 ṬUKUNI ޓުކުނި adj. old(esp. of women): ṭukuni daita, old woman

1632 ṬUKURI ޓުކުރި n. kind of basket used as a shovel [H. ṭōkrī]

1633 ṬEKUM ޓެކުން v. (p.p.ṭekunu) cheating (v.n.) [* √ṭhakk]

1634 ṬEKUS ޓެކުސް n. tax [E. tax]

1635 ṬENIS (ṭenihek) ޓެނިސް n. tennis [E .tennis]

1636 ṬENṬU ޓެންޓު n. temporary cricket pavilion [E. tent]

1637 ṬEEṬARU ޓޭޓަރު n. (anc.) theatre show [E. theatre]

1638 ṬEEBALU ޓޭބަލު n. mathematical tables [E. table]

1639 ṬONIKU ޓޮނިކު n. tonic water [E. tonic]

1640 ṬOS ޓޮސް n. 1. ṭos kuranii, tosses (before a game) [E. toss]
2. tourist (pl., tohun) [E. tourist?]

1641 ṬOOCU ޓޯޗު n. electric torch (also cooku) [E. torch]

1642 ṬOOṬOO ޓޯޓޯ adj. See ham-ṭooṭoo

ޑ ḌA-VIYANI, the 18th letter of the Maldivian alphabet

1643 ḌAINU ޑައިނު n. old woman, witch (ḍainu daita) [H. ḍāyin, Skt. ḍākinī]

1644 ḌAINUMOO ޑައިނުމޯ n. bicycle or car headlamp (cf. fuḷi, dynamo) [E. dynamo]

1645 ḌAKAITU (pl., ḍakaitun) ޑަކައިތު n. witch [H. ḍakaut, ?Skt. dakṣaputra]

1646 ḌAKUTARU ޑަކުޓަރު n. (anc.) doctor (mod. ḍokṭaru) [E. doctor]

1647 ḌAGANAA(-aaek) ޑަގަނާ n. lampshade; metal lid of firebox of hookah; gramophone turntable [H. ḍhaknā, lid]

1648 ḌAŇḌUURAA, ḌANḌUURAA ޑަނޑޫރާ - ޑަންޑޫރާ n. chiming doorbell [H. ḍhanḍhōrā]

1649 ḌAN ޑަން onom. dull thud: ḍan lanii, makes thud

1650 ḌABALU ޑަބަލު adj. double: ḍabalu atukuri, double cuff [E. double]

1651 ḌABIYAA (ḍabiyalek, ḍabiyaaek) ޑަބިޔާ n. large square tin : ḍ. jahanii, drums on a tin [H. ḍabiyā, small box]

1652 ḌARUJANU ޑަރުޖަނު n. (anc.) dozen (mod. ḍazan) [E. dozen]

1653 ḌAROOGAA ޑަރޯގާ n. gardener (in stories): ḍ.- kaleege [cf.U. dārōgha, inspector]

1654 ḌA-VIYANI ޑަވިޔަނި n. the letter Ḍ in the Maldivian alphabet

1655 ḌAZANU ޑަޒަނު n. dozen (anc. ḍarujanu) [E. dozen]

1656 ḌIGU ޑިގު n. a card game, rummy

1657 ḌIŇGAA(-aaek) ޑިނގާ n. shrimps [H. jhīngā]

1658 ḌINḌIN ޑިންޑިން n. ḍinḍin koveli, the female cuckoo

1659 ḌEREGI ޑެރެގި n. crane, derrick [E. derrick]

1660 ḌESKU ޑެސްކު n. desk [E. desk]

1661 ḌOKṬARU (pl. ḍokṭarun) ޑޮކްޓަރު n. doctor (anc. ḍakutaru) : ḍokṭaru-ge, hospital: ḍokṭaru- siṭii, prescription [E. doctor]

1662 ḌONḌON ޑޮންޑޮން n. aerated waters [a trade name, originally made at Atirii Fañḍiyaaruge; cf. soḍaa]

ތ TAA, the 13th letter of the Maldivian alphabet

Taa atoḷu, Koḷumaḍulu atoll, the 13th atoll from the north

1663 TA ތަ 1. interrogative particle, ordinary grade (sometimes omitted): ivee-ta ma kiyaa eccek?do you hear what I say? kiikee-ta bunanii? what do (you) say? (hon. too, not omitted) [S. -da]

2. thou (local and colloquial: dat.case tař, tayař, pl. tamen) [S. tō, cf. Skt. tava]

1664 TA-AARUF KURANII ތަޢާރުފު ކުރަނީ v. introduces [U. ta'āruf]

1665 TAUBAA ތައުބާ n. repentance and confession: Maatkalaañge kiba-ař taubaa vanii, confesses to God [U. tauba]

1666 TAULIIMU ތައުލީމު n. education [U. ta'līm]

1667 TAUZIYAA ތައުޒިޔާ n. condolences [U. ta'ziyat]

1668 -TAK -ތައް suffix used as nominal plural ending: kamtak, affairs: basfuḷutak, words of a nobleman: miihuntak, people: ruktak, coconut trees: kañḍutaku terein, among the seas: hittakugai, in (their) hearts:
also -takun: miistakun, people

1669 TAK ތައް n. metal stamp (tak-gañḍu) : tak jahanii, tak-gañḍu jahanii, applies stamp (esp. on trees, to mark ownership); tak-kaři, metal stamper: takkaři jahaa miihun, men who stamp trees: tak-gañḍu, (also) mould for brass processing

1670 TAKA ތަކަ n. a tool used in net-making

1671 TAKATUVAA (takatuvaaek) ތަކަތުވާ n. cockatoo [H. kākātūā, from Malay]

1672 TAKAFATI (takafaccek) ތަކަފަތި n. kind of tree, used medicinally

1673 TAKARALAA (takaralaaek) ތަކަރަލާ n . kind of medicinal stick, Indian madder, rubia cordifolia

1674 TAKAHOḶI ތަކަހޮޅި n. woman's anklet

1675 TAKUBIIRU ތަކުބީރު n. recital of 'Allaahu akbar' : t. laigannanii, makes celebration of takubiiru tere, the 9th to the 13th of the month Zuulhijja [U. takbīr]

1676 TAKURAARU KURANII ތަކުރާރު ކުރަނީ v. repeats: takuraaru koř (adv.), repeatedly [U. takrār]

1677 TAKURU ތަކުރު n. a name, or nominal suffix for any male: muskuḷi takuru, former chief faqiir of the Hukuru Miskit in Male

1678 TAKURU-FAANU ތަކުރުފާނު n. (In the North) a Maldivian title: Boḍu Takurufaanu, the great Maldivian hero who expelled the Portuguese in the 16th century,and founded a new royal dynasty; (in the South) a proper name

1679 TAKUVVAK (anc. TAKUUVAK) ތަކުއްވަކް (ތަކޫވަކް) n. nutmeg, myristica fragrans

1680 TAKETI (takeccek) ތަކެތި n. thing(s) (including animals) : kaa boo taketi, food stuffs: muḷa taketi, dead animals [-tak + eti]

1681 TAKKATU ތައްކަތު adj. quiet, quietened

1682 TAGARI (anc. TAGAŘI) ތަގަރި (ތަގަރި) n. oblong wooden bowl [U. taghārī]

1683 TAGUḌI ތަގުޑި n. kind of drumming, acting as a postlude : damberař vure taguḍi digu vaane, the epilogue will be longer than the main drumming: you can't see the wood for the trees (prov.)

1684 TAGUDIIRU ތަގުދީރު n. predestination, fate [U. taqdīr]

1685 TAGURIIRU ތަގުރީރު n. lecture, talk [U. taqrīr]

1686 TAJURIBAA ތަޖުރިބާ n. experience : t. libenii, gets experience:

tajuribaa-kaarun, experienced folk [U. tajriba]

1687 TAJUVIIDU ތަޖުވީދު n. correct ecclesiastical intonation : t. magun hiňgum, observing moral correctness [U. tajvīd, improvement]

1688 TAṬṬU ތައްޓު n. deck of vessel; t. aḷanii, lays the deck [T. taṭṭu]

1689 TAŇḌI (also TAŇḌU) ތަނޑި (ތަނޑު) n. stalk of plant (taňḍi-gaňḍu): taňḍirat maa, kind of flowering tree: taňḍi-gaňḍu, (also) small spring bracelet [T. taṇṭu]

1690 TAT ތަތް adj. sticky : tatkam, viscosity: (met.) slow; atmati tat, slow with his hands: tat miihek, a slow fellow: tat-muḍu, sticky and damp (also tanmuḍu; cf. muḍu-daaru): t. kuranii, sticks together (tr.), (met., used colloquially of go-betweens) demiihun tat k., fixes two people up: t. vanii, sticks together (intr.), is sticky: feeraam daa ve tat vanii, clothes get dirty and sticky: tat teḷenii, sticks to the body (of clothing): tat laifi, stuck together (intr.), tat laa, tat lavaa, sticky

1691 TATUN ތަތުން n. 1.instrument used by weavers
2. kind of knot (t. jahanii, t. baddanii, ties this knot)

1692 TADU ތަދު n. 1. pain, ache: arikaṭṭař t. aranii, pain is felt in the back (lumbago): eenaa-ař t. vanii, he is in pain: mi dimaa-ař tadek vii, it hurts here: fiňdař t. vanii, pain is felt in the bottom: tadu vi taa bees, medicine for aches; (of fruits) is bruised
2. scarcity, shortage: tadu eccek, a rarity: t. duvasvarek, a time of shortages (Boḍu Tadu, the great famine): baazaaruge tadu-kam, tightness of the market: tadu-maḍu, economic distress; tadumaḍukam fillavai, relieving destitution: tadu-verikam, famine

1693 TADUBIIRU ތަދުބީރު n. plans [U. tadbīr]

1694 TAN ތަން n. place (with loc. suffix, tanugaa, taaňgaa, taagaa; before case-endings usu. contracted to taa-): tan tan hoodanii, searches here and there, everywhere: etan-mitanař, hither and thither; (met.) aḷugaňḍuge liyaaqat tan din ekme raňgaḷakař, as well as my capabilities allow: tan diifi, gave place, gave opportunity;

also of time : ehaa tanaa jehen den, till that time: tan ot taa goňḍi eḷum, taking a seat in good time: mahuge medek haa taagai, about the middle of the month: ve diya tanugai, in the past: aharen Maale ai tanun, when I got to Male; tanaa after a past part. is equivalent to 'when': baara jahaa baaviis miniṭ hiňgi tanaa, when 22 minutes had elapsed since 12.00: ali vii tanaa hen, about dawn;

At the end of a clause, tan is also equivalent to 'that' or 'how': badalu ai tan duṭṭee, saw how changes had occurred: Aḍḍuu dimaa-ař misraabu jassavaa tan fennan fařaifieve, began to appear that (they) were heading for Addu;

tan-koḷu, bit of space: mařař tankoḷek dii, give me a bit of room; esp. in adverbial expressions: tankoḷek avahař, tankoḷek baarař, a bit faster: tankoḷek fahun, a bit later: tankoḷek lahun, a bit slower

tan-gañḍu, locality; tangañḍu miihun, neighbours:

tan-doru, mental understanding: eenaa-ař tandoru filanii, tandoru eñgenii, he knows what is going on: tandoru vaki nuvaa, having no clear understanding: tandoru vakikoř datum, i.e.age of responsibility: hisaabakař tandoru danna, fairly intelligent: eenaa tandoru kuḍa vanii, he is going mad:

tan-doř,the space underneath: eñdu t., under the bed: meezu t., under the table:

tan-fuhi, tan-foḷi, duster on a stick:

tan-makunu, bed bug; tan-mati (tanmaccek), bedding (eñduge tanmati): tanmati aḷanii, makes bed : tanmati faturanii, spreads out bedding (on board): foři tanmati, travelling baggage:

tan-muḍu, dirty and damp: t. tan, damp dirty place: t. vas, damp dirty smell (also tat-muḍu):

tan-vaḷu, point in time; at point of time: e tanvaḷu, at that time

[S. tän, -tan, Skt. sthāna]

1695 TANAVAS (tanavah-) ތަނަވަސް adj. comfortable; spacious; comfortably off: tanavas-kam, facilities: tanavas koř devvum, facilitating: tanavahugai uḷum, dwelling in comfort: atmati tanavas, comfortably off: tanavas khiyaaluge miihek, a man of open mind

1696 TANU EḶI ތަނު އެޅި p.p. spread out: eenaaekee, egee tanu eḷi kunalekee ekgotee, he is just like the mats in that house (i.e. always around there) [tan + eḷenii]

1697 TANḌIYAA (tanḍiyalek) ތަނޑިޔާ n. long pole borne by two people for carrying fish or rubbish [S. taḍi, anc. taḍa]

1698 TANḌU ތަނޑު n. bolt (of door): t. naṭṭanii, unlocks

1699 TANBUURA ތަނބޫރަ n. large drum or tambourine [H. tambūrā]

1700 TAFAA (tafalek) ތަފާ n. 1. blow, knock: t. jahanii, gives blows

2. lump or heap of liquid dung: sii t. (of humans), gui t. (of animals)

1701 TAFAATU ތަފާތު n. difference; different, various, special: tafaatu miihek, an unusual man: mi deetiige ekves tafaatek net, there is no difference between these two things; adv., tafaatu koř, differently [U. tafāvut]

1702 TAFAAS ތަފާސް n. tafaas hisaabu, statistics

1703 TAFSIILU ތަފްސީލު n. details: tafsiilu koř, in detail (adv.) [U. tafsīl]

1704 TAPPAAS (tappaahek) ތައްޕާސް n. patronage (pej.): eenaage tappaahun, under his coat-tails

1705 TABAK ތަބަކް n. small tray [U. tabaq]

1706 TABAA VANII ތަބާ ވަނީ v. obeys; acquiesces (in..,-aa) [U. taba‘a]

1707 TABULAA ތަބުލާ n. small drum, tabla [U. ṯabla]

1708 TAŇBI (tatbek) ތަނބި n. ankle

1709 TAŇBI-VAK ތަނބިވަކް n. a nutty medicament, strychnos nuxvomica

1710 TAŇBU ތަނބު n. pillar (usu. of veranda) [S. ṭaňba, Skt. stambha]

1711 TAŇBURU ތަނބުރު n. kind of creeper, ipomaea sp.

1712 TAMMATU ތަމްމަތު n. finis (word written at end of chapter): t. aḷanii, writes ‘finis’ [U. tammat]

1713 TAMSIILU KURANII ތަމްސީލު ކުރަނީ v. stages (a show) [U. tamṯẖīl]

1714 TAYAŘ ތަޔަށް pr. See ta 2: to thee (dat.) [S. taṭa]

1715 TAYYAARU ތައްޔާރު adj. ready (for, dat.) : t. vanii, gets ready: t. vee! get ready! tayyaarař hunnanii, is ready: tayyaarař vee, be prepared! tayyaaru? dee! ready? go! tayyaarugai, in readiness: tayyaarii bees, readymade medicines [U. taiyār]

1716 TARAGGII ތަރައްގީ n. improvement [U. taraqqī]

1717 TARATARA ތަރަތަރަ onom. taratara lanii, sizzles: blinks at a light; t. jahanii, is glaring

1718 TARAFANA ތަރަފަނަ n. kind of cake, casual cake

1719 TARAFAALU ތަރަފާލު n. (anc. tarufaalu) tarpaulin covering: t. aḷanii, spreads a tarpaulin; plastic table-covering [E. tarpaulin]

1720 TARAA ތަރާ n. a soft metal alloy, kind of brass

1721 TARAADU ތަރާދު n. small scales [S. tarādi, U. tarāzū]

1722 TARAANAA(-aaek) ތަރާނާ n. popular tune [U. tarāna]

1723 TARAAFAT ތަރާފަތް n. cooking pot used for making toddy sugar

1724 TARAAVIIS (-hek) ތަރާވީސް n. a long prayer used during Ramzan: t. kuranii, recites this prayer; the meal eaten after this prayer: t. kanii, eats the meal; taraaviis dam / taraaviihu dam, time for eating such a meal (8 or 9 p.m.): taraaviis dam kanii, eats this meal [U. tarāvīh̲]

1725 TARI ތަރި n. star : tari baalaa denii, gives impossible promises (to a girl): dum tari, comet [S. taru, Skt. tārakā]

1726 TARUKAARII ތަރުކާރީ n. vegetables [U. tarkārī]

1727 TARUJAMAA ތަރުޖަމާ n. translation: t. kuranii, translates; tarjamaanun, interpreters (pl.) [U. tarjuma]

1728 TARUTIIBU ތަރުތީބު n. proper order : varař t. miihek, a very orderly man: t. koř bahaṭṭanii, arranges in order: Boḍu Ṭ., a book of religious rules [U. tartīb]

1729 TARUFAALU ތަރުފާލު n. (anc.) See tarafaalu

1730 TARUMOOZU ތަރުމޯޒު n. thermos (used for ice) [E. thermos]

1731 TARUHIIBU ތަރުހީބު n. applause

1732 TALA ތަލަ n. crown of the head: tala boo, bald head

1733 TALAKAN-FEN ތަލަކަންފެން n. water scattered on graves: talakan fen jahanii, scatters this water

1734 TALI (tayyek) ތަލި n. 1. palate of mouth (matii tali): dařu tali, lower portion of inner mouth 2. pick-up cartridge of a gramophone [S. talu, Skt. tālu]

1735 TALII-VAI ތަލީވައި n. prolapsus uteri

1736 TALUTERE ތަލުތެރެ n. certain timbers of the (former) oḍi

1737 TAVAA (tavaaek) ތަވާ n. flat clay pot formerly used for frying [U. tavā, Skt. tāpaka]

1738 TAVIIDU ތަވީދު n. amulet; transistor set [U. ta'vīz̲]

1739 TASDIIGU KURANII ތަސްދީގު ކުރަނީ v. ratifies [U. tas̲dīq]

1740 TASBIIHA, TASBIIHU ތަސްބީހަ - ތަސްބީހު n. rosary: t. ruk, small kind of palm tree, used only for fans and for rosary beads [U. tasbīh̲]

1741 TASVIIRU ތަސްވީރު n. picture (commonly foṭoo) [U. tas̲vīr]

1742 TAHUGIIGU ތަހުގީގު n. investigation [U. tah̲qīq]

1743 TAHUZIIBU ތަހުޒީބު n. culture [U. tahzīb]

1744 TAHHAAN (TA<u>KHKH</u>AAN) ތައްހާން n. a Maldivian name or title

1745 TAŘ ތަށް pr. to thee (dat.): tařakař neeňge, you don't realize [ta 2]

1746 TAŘI (taṭṭek) ތަށި n. dish, plate, bowl : ekani kaa t., individual plate: kahaňbu t., normal small ricebowl: dolaňgu t., side plate or dish: fen t., container of water: boo tař̌i, serving bowl (cup-shaped): matii t., saucer put on top of food: muři t., earthenware dish: muunu donna t., washbasin: liyaa t., plate for writing charms on: loo t., metal plate with rim: vatu t., saucer: salavaatu t., large sized serving bowl; taři-bari, pile of metal dishes for transport of food: taři- muři, glazed china in general: glazed tiles [S. taṭu, Skt. taṭṭaka]

1747 TAḶANII ތަޅަނީ v. knocks, beats, pounds (v.n. teḷum): aňga taḷanii, taḷuvanii, chatters uselessly: taři t., breaks dishes: taali t., lets the head nod sleepily: fen tiki t., tet t., water drips: boḍu t., boasts: mas t., pounds fish (for mas-kuroḷi): miihek t., beats a man (officially): meezugai t., knocks on the table: laki t., shakes excessively (tr.): vayaa t., flaps in the wind: haka t., gossips; of making certain articles- daani taḷaa miihun, makers of waterscoops, tinkers: mohoru t., makes nails: hanu t., makes grindstones; teḷi teḷiinun, by constantly beating. Doublet, taḷai-foḷum, noisily fighting; Caus., de-haa teḷuvum, causing two cocks to fight: fuḷi taḷuvanii, shakes the bottle: bolirava taḷuvaalan, to shake the rattle: meezu taḷuvanii, shakes the table; see also teḷenii [S. taḷanne, Skt. tāḍayati]

1748 TAḶAM, TAḶAM-MATI ތަޅަން - ތަޅަންމަތި n. women's living room

1749 TAḶU ތަޅު n. lock: gobu t., lock with knob: dorufatu t., lock with handle: yeel t., Yale lock: eluvaa t., fořiigai laa t., padlock: taḷu lanii, locks (v.): taḷu-kehi, old key of the Hukuru Miskit mihraabu-ge: taḷu-daňḍi, key: taḷudaňḍifati, bunch of keys: taḷu-fatgaňḍu, 'leaf' into which padlock goes: taḷu-maḷu(-gaňḍu), locking board (on a ship, an aři, a drawer, a storeroom): taḷu-vaḷu, keyhole: taḷu-hiri, keystone of ancient mosques (for dismantling) [H. tālā, Skt. tālaka]

1750 TAḶUM(GAŇḌU) ތަޅުން(ގަނޑު) n. hard floor (in house or round well): t. aḷanii, lays the floor

1751 TAA ތާ 1. Exclamatory particle at end of sentence, 'so you see' : kobaa, kamtak vii ma buni gotař taa, so things turned out as I said: ehen taa, doo, is it so, eh? den eňgidaane taa! you'll see: aaň taa ee, oh yes? kaleege kamakii abadu ves bolugai rihum taa ee, the fact is you always have a headache: kalee varař gina bañditak dannamu taa ee, you do know a lot of poetry

2. n. the letter T in the Arabic and Maldivian alphabets: Taa atoḷu, Koḷumaḍulu atoll

3. particle : after verbal participles, representing E. 'since': e kamtak vii taa kitakme duvahakee, what a long time since that happened; after nouns, representing 'as far as','up to','down to': karu taa fen, water up to the neck [S. tāk, Skt. tāvatka]

4. n. for tan, place: tan-taagai, in various places: mitaagai, here: ekves taakun taaku nujehee, lit. not touching anywhere, i.e. unplaceable, useless: mahuge ektiriis haa taagai, about the 31st of the month: tingañḍeti nudee taa, when (they) don't give the three marriage requisites: eenaa nai taagai, not only didn't he come, but..

5. n. certain thwarts on an oḍi

6. taa abadu (adv.) always, without a break: taa abaduge vaahaka, endless speech: taa duniye umuru, all its worldly life [U. tā, up to]

1752 TAA-RUK ތާރުކް n. palmyra tree, borassus flabellifer [S. tal, Skt. tāla]

1753 TAA-VAKARU ތާވަކަރު n. principal beam in roof of houses

1754 TAA-VAK-KAAŘI ތާވަކްކާޅި n. Seychelles double coconut (used for best kind of well- scoop)

1755 TAAKIHAA (taakihalek) ތާކިހާ n. cap, praying hat; Turukii t.,Turkey cap, fez (with tassel): boḍu t., ordinary lined cap: taakihaa-gañḍu, an old cap: hajju t., white cap (as worn for Hajj) [U. ṯāqiya]

1756 TAAŇGI(I) (taaňgiiek , taatňgek) ތާނގި n. closed water tank [Port. tanque]

1757 TAAJARU ތާޖަރު n. shopkeeper (in stories) [U. tājir]

1758 TAAJU ތާޖު n. crown [U. tāj]

1759 TAAṬṬEK See taaři

1760 TAAḌU ތާޑު n. creamy filling of coconut honey in faniyaaram cakes

1761 TAAN ތާން n. 1. small bundle of uncut sarongs

2. starch: taan lanii, applies starch: taan-kam, starchiness

1762 TAANA ތާނަ n. present-day Maldivian script : miinaage taana liyum, his hand-writing: tiki teḷi taana, 'drip-writing', a hieroglyphic script invented by Amin Didi

1763 TAANIYAA ތާނިޔާ n . a prayer against infidels (no longer in use) : 'ekme haa balaahatooin Divehi davlataai raiyyek rakkau kuravvai, nuniyat lii miihaku nikameti kuravvai' etc. [U. ṯa'na, curse]

1764 TAAFAT ތާފަތް n. 1. gill cover : koo-taafat, outer cheek (of man or fish); karu-taafat, inner gill

2. top section of goboḷi coconut

1765 TAAFATAA ތާފަތާ n. satin, taffeta (for linings) [U. tāfta]

1766 TAAFANAA KURANII ތާފަނާ ކުރަނީ v. heats gently (usually of water) [H. tapna, Skt. tapayati]

1767 TAABUUTU ތާބޫތު n. coffin (mod. sandook) [U. tābūt]

1768 TAARA ތާރަ n. large tambourine or similar drum (atmati taara); music on the tambourine: t. jahanii, plays the t.: vajji taara, music for ecstasies

1769 TAARAFINI ތާރަފިނި n. turpentine (used medicinally) [?E. turpentine, Gk. terebinthos]

1770 TAARIIFU ތާރީފު n. praise [U. ta'rīf]

1771 TAARIIKHU ތާރީޚު n. annals, history [U. tārīkh]

1772 TAARU ތާރު n. tar [S. tāra, ? D. tēr x E.tar]

1773 TAALI (taayyek) ތާލި n. sleepy nodding of the head: t. taḷanii, lets head drop sleepily: t. teḷenii, head nods sleepily; taayyař jehenii, taayyaa jehenii, nods sleepily

1774 TAALIBU ތާލިބު n. (pl., taalibun) student (fem., taalibaa) [U. ṯālib]

1775 TAAVALU ތާވަލު n. timetable [? E.]

1776 TAAVAḶA ތާވަޅަ n. kind of bait fish, hypoatherina temminckii

1777 TAAS (taahek) ތާސް n. 1. metal pan, wok (esp. for making coconut oil): taas dagaňḍu, cast iron [S. tācci, D. taatsje]

2. playing cards: taas kuḷenii, plays cards, plays a particular card game ('trumps'): t. kaňḍanii, shuffles cards: t. bahanii, deals cards; taas-gaňḍu, a single card: taasgaňḍu jahanii, plays a card; taas-bai, pack of cards [U. tāś, tās]

1778 TAAZAA ތާޒާ adj. fresh (of food, flowers etc.) [U. tāza]

1779 TAAHIRU ޠާހިރު adj. clean (in general): t. kuranii, cleans; esp. in a religious sense, fenuge taahiru kam, rules for ablution [U. ṯāhir]

1780 TAAŘI (taaṭṭek) ޓާރި n. tightness: boḍu taaṭṭekgai, in financial trouble; taaři vanii, gets stuck: dalugai boo t. vefai, with head stuck in the net

1781 TAAĻAFILI (-fiyyek) ޓާޅަފިލި n. horn, tuba; speaker of gramophone: beru-dummaari-taaḷafiliigai vaḍaigatum, processing to the threefold royal music: taaḷafiyyaa danii, goes round blowing at dawn (obsolete custom in Male)

1782 -TI ތި- suffix for imperative (less polite: -cce is politer): kuraati, kořlaati, do! balaigen uḷeeti, careful!

1783 TI- ތި- prefix of 2nd person: kontaakař ti-danii, where are you going? kalee ořoove ti-otii, you are lying down: ti-ge, your house: ti-baa, you: ti-varu, your price: ti rañgaḷu ta, are you all right? ti-ok, that over there (also written tiyok): ti-taa, there: ti-hira, that there: ti-hen, like that [tiya]

1784 TIA ތިއަ See tiya

1785 TIKI (tikkek) ތިކި n. dot; droplet : tiki teḷi taana, 'drop-writing', a hieroglyphic script used by Amin Didi

1786 TIJAARAA ތިޖާރާ n. trade : maẖkamat ul tijaaraa, Dept. of Trade [U. tijārat]

1787 TIJUURII ތިޖޫރީ n. a safe

1788 TIṮṮI ތިއްތި adj. pretty, nice (of children); also as part of a female name: tiṯṯaṯṯaa, pretty sister: Tiṯṯi gomaa, pretty princess

1789 TIN ތިން num. three (in Navata tables, tiin): tin munḍu, three sarongs: mařař libunii tinek, I got three (marks): tineti, three objects: diha laariyař tineti, three for 10 laris: tin gañḍeti, three pieces of clothing given to a bride (libaas, feeli, burugaa): hus gooniige tin gooni, three empty sacks: tin-kan, tineskan, triangle: tindoḷas, three dozen: tin fař, row of three (of marriages: tin fař vanii, marries the same man three times in succession): tin foi rooda, three fast days in every month : tin-vana, third [S. tun, cf.Skt. trīṇi]

1790 TIN-MUGOOLI ތިންމުގޮޅި n. kind of game (resembling baseball) ['three-pits']

1791 TIN-VAḶUGAŇḌU ތިންވަޅުގަނޑު n. kind of game ['three-pits']

1792 TIN-HAMA ތިންހަމަ n. 'three in a row', a kind of game for two, played with seeds: Varieties: baburu t., vagu t. (corresponds to S. nerenci , similar to ořvaḷu for women)

1793 TINA ތިނަ n. 1. a milky grass (mod. kirutina) [S. taṇa, Skt. tṛṇa; cf. also vina]

2. (anc.) bosom. tina-kiru, breast milk [S. tana, Skt. stana]

1794 TINES-KAN ތިނެސްކަން n. triangle [tin]

1795 TINOOS (tinoohek) ތިނޫސް n. needle: tinoohař rodi lavvanii, threads needle

1796 TIBA ތިބަ v. having been (abs. of tibenii)

1797 TIBAA ތިބާ pr. you, your (formal and obs.): tibaa rařu, in your island [ti+bai]

1798 TIBENII ތިބެނީ v. is (of more than one animate), sits, waits; also used of boats (abs. tibe, tiba : p.p. tibi : past tense tibi-eve, tibbee, tibijje : hon. tibbavanii): mi tibbevii nuun, here they are (hon.): tibba dii, allowing to be: tibbaa, while being; (invol.) diri duniyeegai tibevee minvarař, enough to support life [S. tibenne, cf. Skt. sthāpayati, places]

1799 TIBBANII ތިއްބަނީ v. fixes, clamps: dati t., sets trap: fixes vice to bench; datiigai t., fixes in a clamp (caus. of tibenii)

1800 TIBBAA ތިއްބާ v. while being (See tibenii)

1801 TIŇBI ތިނބި n. roof ridge (over the tiles): furaaḷuge t. aḷanii, fixes the roof ridge

1802 TIMAN, TIMANNAA, TIMAAŇ ތިމަން - ތިމަންނާ - ތިމާ pr. self; I (pl., timanmen, timannaamen, timaamen, (anc.) timauren) [S. taman , tamā, cf. Skt. ātmān ?]

1803 TIMARA ތިމަރަ n. 1. lead (kaḷu timara) ; hudu t., solder, tin : buḷi t. laan, to coat fish-hooks: timara fat, tinfoil

2. a skin disease: t. aḷaigen, having contracted the disease [cīmara, Turner 14496]

1804 TIMAAŇ ތިމާ See timan

1805 TIMAAGE ތިމާގޭ adj. related: aharenge gaat timaage miihun, my close relatives: timaage-kam, ralationship (gen. of timan)

1806 TIYA (TIA) ތިޔަ (ތިއަ) adj. that (relative to you): tiya kujjaku ahuren nudekemeve, I haven't seen such a boy as you mention: tiya kamek mařakař nuvaane-ee, I can't do such a thing: tiya gee, belonging to your house: kalee tiyaii..., you are..: tiya otii vaa, kamek kurevifaa! what a big deal, forsooth! tiyahara, that there (also tihira): tiyahen, in that way (also tihen, tiin); tiyahennek nuunee, not like that: tiyahennaa, tiyaheñaa, if you think so ;

as n.., tiyain, among those things [cf. S. oya]

1807 TIYARA ތިޔަރަ n. a plant, cassia sp.: Varieties, digu t., vař t. [S. tuvara, tōra]

1808 TIYAAGI, TIYAAGE ތިޔާގި - ތިޔާގޭ adj. prosperous, abundant : t. zamaanek, a prosperous period, t. rařek, a prosperous island: atmati t., prosperous (of people) [Skt. tyāgi]

1809 TIYOK (TIOK) ތިޔޮކް (ތިއޮކް) adj. that over there [See ti-]

1810 TIRAA VANII ތިރާ ވަނީ v. collapses (of a building, or an unconscious man) [tiri]

1811 TIRI ތިރި adj. low (not met., cf. dař); down: tiri-ař̌i, low couch in ancient houses or in royal palace: tiri-keetu, lowest sail of a schooner: tiri-goňḍi, low seat for visitors: tiri- diggaa, kind of tree, sida sp.: tiri-faaḷa, a medicinal creeper; tiriyař faibanii, goes downstairs: tiri kuranii, brings down (flag, sail, curtain), lands an aircraft; tirii buri, lower floor: tirii boňḍi, part below the eye: tirii riyaa, lowest sail

1812 TIRIKKU ތިރިއްކު num. times three (in Navata multiplication tables: saari tirikku baara, 4 x 3 = 12)

1813 TIRIIS (tiriihek) ތިރީސް num. thirty: the 30 sections of the Quran ; tiriis rufiyaa, 30 rupees: tiriis naganii, recites the Quran after the teacher [S. tis, Skt. triṃśat]

1814 TILA ތިލަ 1. n. cutting blade: tila-gaňḍu jahanii, raises a flag or other object on mast after catching six hiya of fish [S. tala, Skt. tala]

2. adj. shallow; shallow place: tila-ař diyum, going for fish in shallows at night with a line: (met.) tila koř vaahaka dekkum, speaking simply: tila vanii, gets shallow, viz. a) of fish, comes to surface b) of the sea, turns shallow c) of wounds, heals up [S. tala, flat?]

1815 TILADUNMATI ތިލަދުންމަތި n. Name of H atoll, North and South

1816 TILA-FAT ތިލަފަތް n. scales [S. tulā + pātra]

1817 TILAFIHI ތިލަފިހި n. smithy

1818 TILAVAT-GAA ތިލަވަތްގާ n. bottom stone of well

1819 TILAAFIYAA ތިލާފިޔާ n. a bait fish, tilapia, oreochromis [tila 2]

1820 TILAA-MAS ތިލާމަސް n. kind of lagoon fish [tila 2]

1821 TILEO, TILEYO ތިލެއޮ - ތިލެޔޮ n. gingelly oil : t. gas, sesamum indicum [S. tala (sesame) x teyo]

1822 TILEO-FILAA ތިލެއޮފިލާ n. a creeper, ipomoea litoralis

1823 TILEERU (pl., tileerun) ތިލޭރު n. smiths: tileeru atkam, tileeru-kam, fine craftsmanship (esp. of men of D atoll, south Nilande)

1824 TILOOŘI ތިލޯޑި n. bollard, stake

1825 TI-HIRA, TI-HEN ތިހިރަ - ތިހެން See ti-

1826 -TII, -TIIVE -ތީ / -ތީވެ suffix (literary) used after verbal forms, representing E. 'because..' : vaa tii, vee tii, vii tii, because it is/ was: nunimee tiive, because it was unfinished: otii tiive, hurii tiive, because (he) was: kairi vejje-a-tiive, because it was near: miadu rañgaḷii tiive,because it was all right today (for rañgaḷu vii tiive): mi uḷenii rissaa tii, because I have a pain; (lit.) also used like kam to mark reported facts: bunaa tii ehiimee, I heard it said: annaa tii fenijje, (were) seen coming: gellumek libifai vaa tii-ek nufenee, there doesn't seem to have been any loss: bunaa tii-eve gotugai, as I have heard it said

1827 TII (TI-II) ތީ (ތިއީ) adj. that: tii aharenge, it's mine
[For tiyaii, emphatic form of tiya]

1828 TIITI, TIINAA ތީތި - ތީނާ pr . those things, that man
[For tiya eti, ti- +eenaa]

TIIN ތީން thus [For tihen, see ti-]

1829 TIIRU ތީރު n. arrow; name of two compass directions: tiiru astamaanu, west- south-west; t. iiraan, east-south -east [U. tīr, Sirius]

1830 TUI ތުއި 1. excl.., what a bore!

2. tui vanii v. (of girls) gets excited and shows off

1831 TUKI ތުކި excl. sorry! (used in girls' games)

1832 TUKKO ތުއްކޮ n. For tuttu kokko, small brother

1833 TUŇḌI ތުނޑި n. treeless sandy spit: tuňḍii koḷu, end of such spit [cf. tuňḍu]

1834 TUŇḌU ތުނޑު n. point (of star: needle: knife: pen(nib): Arabic letters) [S. tuňḍu, Skt. tuṇḍa]

1835 TUŇḌU-KUNAA (-kunalek) ތުނޑުކުނާ n. ornamental mat (with pointy designs)

1836 TUŇḌULU ތުނޑުލު n. proximity (pej.): amaage tuňḍulugai, near (his) mother

1837 TUTIMAS ތުތިމަސް n. thin diamond shape: a sweet made in this shape for boḍu keem at mauluud festivities

1838 TUTIYAA (tutiyalek) ތުތިޔާ n. galvanizing zinc (for batteries etc.)

1839 TUTTU ތުއްތު adj. younger (childish, or in proper names):

Tuttaaniku, for Tuttu Maniku
Tuttiidi, for Tuttu Diidii (m. or f.)
Tuttee, for Tuttu Bee
Tutton, for Tuttu Don (f.)
See also -huttu (ifc.)

1840 TUN (tuňtbek) ތުން n. beak; lip of pot; baby's dummy : tun-tun matin, by word of mouth; tuňbun fumenii, whistles; tun digu toḷi, kind of fish; tun eḷi sigareṭ, filtertip cigarettes; tun-gaňḍu, beak of bird, protruding lip of fish: tungaňḍu miyaru, kind of shark: tungaňḍu hibaru, kind of swordfish, xiphias; tun-fat, lip (of people, cups, pans): tunfatu jehen den, to the brim: tun-fuhi, face towel; (met.) havaru tunfuhi, notorious courtesan: tun-bihi, pimples on the mouth; tunmati (riyaa), extra (jib) sail; tun-maḷi, ring in the nose of bulls: (met.) tunmaḷi aḷanii, aḷuvanii, keeps under control; tun fittamun ai, tight-lipped (See also ustuňbař) [S. tuḍu, Skt. tuṇḍa]

1841 TUNI (tuñee) ތުނި adj. thin and flat (of paper, planks, knives, cakes, cloth, skin): (met.) scarce [S. tunu, Skt. tanu]

1842 TUNIYA ތުނިޔަ n. kind of thin seashell: t. niyafati, nice square-cut fingernails

1843 TUNḌIYAA ތުނޑިޔާ n. kind of bowsprit

1844 TUFUREN ތުފުރެން pr. (anc.) you [S. topi, *tupphe]

1845 TUPPUḶU ތުއްޕުޅު adj. small (hon.) [tu<u>tt</u>u + fuḷu]

1846 TUŇBI ތުނބި n. kind of fish, unicorn fish, naso (See also buḷituňbi)

1847 TUŇBU ތުނބު See tun: tuňbu jahaalaafaa, having stuck (it) in his lips

1848 TUŇBUḶI ތުނބުޅި n. beard (tuňbuḷi-gaňḍu: hon., tuňbuḷi-fuḷu): t. baalanii, shaves: t. turu kuranii, t. hadanii, trims beard: tuňbuḷiek laafai, with a beard; tuňbuḷi hui, a grass, eragrostis tenella

1849 TURA VANII ތުރަ ވަނީ v. (used of the afterbirth) comes away

1850 TURAA (turaalek) ތުރާ n. trouble; troublesome: t. kuranii, disturbs (with dat.)

1851 TURAA-TAN ތުރާތަން n. private parts (esp. of men)

1852 TURIYYAANU ތުރިއްޔާނު n. name of two compass directions: t. astamaanu, west by north: t. iiraan, east by north [U. <u>th</u>uraiyā, Pleiades]

1853 TURU KURANII / KURAVVANII ތުރު ކުރަނީ - ތުރު ކުރައްވަނީ
v. (hon.) 1. wears (clothes, medicaments)
2. cuts, trims (someone's beard or hair)

1854 TURUTURU ތުރުތުރު onom. turuturu aḷanii, shakes (intr., usu. of animates): aḍu t. aḷanii, (his) voice shakes (for fear) [H. thar thar]

1855 TURRA-VAAS ތުއްރަވާސް n. plume of golden feathers (on royal crown) [U. <u>t</u>urra]

1856 TULA ތުލަ n. Libra, the Scales: t. laigannanii, Libra season arrives [Skt. Tulā]

1857 TUVAALI (tuvaayyek), TUVAALU ތުވާލު - ތުވާލި n. towel

[S. tuvāya, Port. toalha]

1858 TUVVANII ތުއްވަނީ v. pricks (a blister: an egg)

1859 TUHUMATU ތުހުމަތު n. suspicion : t. kuranii, suspects (with dat. or -aa medu): t. vanii eenaa maccaře, is suspicious of him [U. tuhmat]

1860 TUḶAA (tuḷalek) ތުޅާ n. 1. small water ladle
2. ifc., herb (see kuḷi-, foni-, fus-)

1861 TUḶU ތުޅު n. a weight, 2 stone; a spring balance

1862 TUUTU ތޫތު n. 1. kind of tree with edible berries, morus alba
2. insect (word used to children)

1863 TUUNU ތޫނު adj. sharp; of boats, manoeuvrable (mahař t., for fishing: vayař t., in the wind): of eyes, beautiful (kaḷirava tuunu): of lime, bad for the skin: vaḷi tuunu kuranii, sharpens knife (cf. fansuru jahanii, sharpens pencil): tuuniyyaa, if it is sharp ; raaḷu tuunu, serrated, rough: omaan tuunu, non-serrated [S. tiyuṇu, Skt. tīkṣṇa]

1864 TUUNU-FILI ތޫނުފިލި adj. sharpwitted

1865 TUUFAAN ތޫފާން n. storm: floods : vissaaraige t., typhoon: Nuugefaanuge t., Noah's Flood [U. t̠ūfān]

1866 TUURI ތޫރި n. 1. ear-drum
2. leaf-case of betel and breadfruit (used as sandpaper)

1867 TUULI ތޫލި adj. shrill: aḍu tuuli, shrill-voiced

1868 TE- ތެ- num. ibc., plus three (in compound numbers): teyaaḷiis, 43 (= saaḷiis tinek): teaahi, 83 (= ařḍiha tinek): teyaanavai, 93 (= nuvadiha tinek) [cf. H. tētālīs, tirāsī, tirānvē]

1869 -TE -ތެ suffix (anc.) for 3 pl. verbal forms: hadate, they make [S. -ti]

1870 TEU ތެއު n. See teyo

1871 TET ތެތް adj. wet ;wetness: tet fini, damp (wet and cold); tet taḷanii, drips; miihaa hurii tetaa-ee, the man was wet; tetař kaňḍaa, reducing the price because of the wetness: (met.) taking with a grain of salt: tet-kam, wetness: (met.) sikuňḍiige tetkam, sharpness of brain [S. tet, P. tinta]

1872 TE<u>TT</u>IRIIS ތެއްތިރީސް num. 33 (=tiriis tinek) [cf. H. teṃtīs]

1873 TEDU ތެދު adj. upright; straight: true, truth; flat (of roof) or gently sloping; tedu magu, (met.) straight road (of conduct): tedu tedař dannavanii nama, if I tell the real truth: hama tedek! it really is so: t. kuranii, straightens; agrees, accepts: tedu vanii, stands up (low hon., tedu vannavanii, tedu ve lavvanii): t. bunanii, speaks the truth; tedu-veri, trustworthy, teduveriyaa, trustworthy person

1874 TEDUI VAḌAAM ތެދުއި ވަޑާން n. straight carpentry (as v. kissaru v.) [tedu+ui]

1875 TEMENII ތެމެނީ v. gets wet [S. temenne, Skt. timyati, stimyati]

1876 TEMMANII ތެއްމަނީ v. wettens (caus. of temenii)

1877 TEYO (TEU) (telek) ތެޔޮ (ތެއު) n. oil: kakkaa teyo, cooking oil: kaaři t., coconut oil: faan teyo, oil evaporated by sunlight, very clear oil: velaa t., turtle oil (for boat polish): teyo felanii, squeezes out coconut oil: t. haananii, makes oil by boiling coconut milk: teyo-kuňḍi, oily deposit left on heeni tel after boiling: teyo- guḷaa saadaa kuranii, builds castles in the air: teyo-naaři, (slang) fiancee, girlfriend; teyonaaři kaaḷu gendiyum, another man (lit.. the crow) taking away one's girlfriend: teyo-filaa, kind of creeper: teyo-hanu, hone [S. tel, Skt. taila]

1878 TERAS (anc.. TERES) ތެރަސް (ތެރެސް) n. glue

1879 -TERI -ތެރި adjectival suffix : masakkat-teri, hardworking: masakkatteriyaa, hardworking man: beenum-teri, needful,useful [cf. -veri]

1880 TERE ތެރެ n. inside (used ifc., esp. in forms tereegai, terein (tereen)): medu-tere, the middle: medugooti-tere, centre courtyard: detin miniṭekge tereegai, within 2 or 3 minutes [See etere]

1881 TELA ތެލަ n. kind of tree

1882 TELAKAŇDI ތެލަކަނޑި n. large variety of kaḷuoř fish

1883 TELAŇGA ތެލަނގަ n . kind of kite, with raaraa rattle

1884 TELA-BAGUḌI ތެލަބަގުޑި n. tug of war (t. kuḷum)

1885 TELABAḌI ތެލަބަޑި n. kind of cake

1886 TELAARU ތެލާރު n. small variety of kaḷuoř fish

1887 TELAAHI ތެލާހި n. shoal of bait-worms

1888 TELI (teyyek) ތެލި n. large metal ccoking pot,with lid but no handle: fuu hama t., pan with flat round base: teli-buri, small pan: teli-seṭu, set of pans [S. täli, Skt. sthāli]

1889 TELIFOONU ތެލިފޯނު n. telephone [cf. E. telephone]

1890 TELU LANII, TELLANII ތެއްލަނި - ތެލުލަނި v. deep-fries: telu li mas, fried fish [teyo + lanii]

1891 TEḶENII ތެޅެނި v. is beaten, is broken (e.g. of china); breaks into bits (intr.): quivers, struggles (teḷi lanii): knocks around (intr.): gana teḷenii, struggles uselessly: taali t., nods head sleepily: teḷi mirus, powdered chillies: mi gotař abadu teḷiteḷi, knocking around like this: vaḷek nuteḷeene, teḷeene daani (prov.), the well will not break, the scoop will, i.e. the big boys will get away ; teḷum-teriyaa, boxer (invol. of taḷanii)

1892 TEE- ތޭ- num. ibc., plus three (in compound numbers): teeviis, 23: teevanna, 53 (= fansaas tinek): teehaṭṭi, 63 (= fasdoḷas tinek): teehattari,73 (= hatdiha tinek) [H. tēīs, and cf. tirpan, tirsaṭh, tihattar]

1893 TEERA ތޭރަ num. thirteen: mi mahu teera duvahun, on the 13th of this month [H. terah, cf. old S. teḷes]

1894 TEERAVAI, TEERAVAA ތޭރަވައި - ތޭރަވާ n. kind of sea-bird

1895 TEERI ތޭރި n. 1. window bars: wooden reinforcing bars in boats; t. lanii, fixes bars: teeri-doru, window with bars
2. lower spool of sewing machine: weaving shuttle
[S. tasara, H. tasar]

1896 TOI ތޯއި n. toi-koḷu, treble end of drum (as v. bum-koḷu)

1897 TOK ތޯއް n. mouth-string of fish: t. kaňḍanii, cuts the string (to prevent struggling): (met.) t. keňḍifai vaa miihek, a man without hope

1898 TOK JEHENII ތޯއްޖެހެނި v. is crowded

1899 TOK-FILAA ތޮއްފިލާ n. safety plank on boats

1900 TOŇGI (totňgek) ތޮނގި n. hinge of gatepost : t. naṭṭaalanii, unhooks hinge

1901 TOṬṬEK ތޮއްޓެއް See toři

1902 TOḌḌU ތޮއްޑު n. lower edge of fish net : t. dařun/ dořun danii, goes below the net, (met..) becomes a failure

1903 TOḌḌUU ތޮއްޑޫ n. name of an island in Ari atoll [For Toṭaduu]

1904 TONA ތޮނަ n. 1. builders' kingpost
2. weed: t. naganii, removes weeds [S. taṇa, Skt. tṛ̆ṇa, grass]

1905 TOFAḶA ތޮފަޅަ n. diseased hole in a tree: t. fen, water collected in such a hole

1906 TOFI (totpek) ތޮފި n. hat with a brim : t. aḷanii, wears hat [S. toppi, H. ṭōpī]

1907 TORAA (toraek) ތޮރާ n. ridge-gourd, luffa acutangula: t. naru(-gaňḍu), loofah

1908 TORAA-BOOṬU ތޮރާބޯޓު n. airship

1909 TORUFANII ތޮރުފަނީ v. bores, drills: torufaa kaři, awl: torufi uňduḷi, ladle with holes, (met..) nuisance: torufi-gannanii (met.), worms one's way in [S. torapana, gimlet]

1910 TOŘALI ތޮރަލި n. ordinary cadjan thatch (as v. fangi)

1911 TOŘI (toṭṭek) ތޮރި n. 1. rind, peel, skin; outer bark; eggshell: govaam t., husk: toḷitoři, bean-pod; t. kahanii, scrapes off the bark (after heating); fuḷitoři jahanii, applies powdered glass to string of kite: toři-gaňḍu, pen casing; skin of fruit; shell of nautilus
2. breakwater, causeway: beeru t., outer breakwater: etere t., inner breakwater; toři lanii, builds breakwater [? cf. S. toṭa, ferry]

1912 TOḶI ތޮޅި 1. n. kinds of bean (himeri toḷi); digu t., cowpea, vigna sinensis, or long bean, phaseolus vulgaris: toḷi-oř, beans (or peas) within the pod: toḷi-veyo, bean-creeper: bañbukeyo t., inflorescence of breadfruit tree; toḷiigai riha, bean curry

2. n. ifc., kinds of fish (farutoḷi: maatoḷi: tun-digu t.): toḷiař danii, goes fishing for toḷi fish: (met.) goes flop, kaput

3. v. fighting (abs. of toḷenii)

1913 TOḶUVANII ތޮޅުވަނި v. caus. of toḷenii (mod. tooḷuvanii, q.v.)

1914 TOḶENII ތޮޅެނި v. fights (against.., -aa), disturbs (used by children, or by adults of animals) (abs. toḷe,toḷi) : eenaa ahannaa toḷunii, he disturbed me: ek kujjaku anek kujjakaa toḷum, one child fighting with another; toḷee faaru, the half-step on the old Male city walls:

Enlarged: toḷi-lanii, quivers (also toḷenii in this sense), twitches, drips; aharenge kanaatu loo varař boḍař toḷe-eve, my right eye is quivering badly: fen toḷi- liimaa, when the water drips (out ofwet clothes); rises out of the water: iru fenun toḷi-li tanaa hen, soon after the sun rose out of the sea;

Caus. toḷuvanii, see tooḷuvanii

1915 TOO ތޯ 1. interrogative particle used to the two higher grades, and not omitted, cf. ta): kiik too vii, what has happened? hama tedek too, is that the truth? aḷugañḍu kihinek too hadaanii, what shall I do? nuun too, isn't it so?

2. conjunctive particle, to see if..(until, in order that), used after indicative verb, to all grades : lonu heyovaru too balaa balaařee, see if there is enough salt; bayaan kurevee tooek aḷugañḍu masakkatek nukuraanameve, I won't try to describe;

too kuranii, doubts: too-too kiyanii, speaks doubtfully; too-too kam, doubtful matter; tooccek, a possibility: mikahala eccek toocce, it might be so: tooccee! perhaps!

1916 TOOḌUVANII ތޯޑުވަނި n. sews up ends (of sarong) roughly

1917 TOOT ތޯތް excl. used to attract attention: t. govanii (of hawkers), calls out [cf.yoot]

1918 TOOTAA(tootaaek) ތޯތާ n. kind of bird

1919 TOOFAA (toofaaek) ތޯފާ adj. old and useless

1920 TOORAA-FANI ތޯރާފަނި n. kind of worm used as bait for catching fish

1921 TOOLAA (toolaaek) ތޯލާ n. a weight, two kuḷañdu [H. tōlā]

1922 TOOḶUVANII ތޯޅުވަނި v. (of kites) causes to fight, crosses their lines [For toḷuvanii]

ދ DAALU, the 12th letter of the Maldivian alphabet

Daalu atoḷu, South Nilande, the 12th atoll from the north;
in atoll enumeration daalu also stands for dekunu, south;
Haa Daalu, H atoll South (South Tiladunmati)

1923 DA- ދަ- n. iron; used ibc. da-gañḍu, iron, instrument of iron (such as pricker-pole, latrine shovel, spear): taas d., cast iron: fat hovaa d., implement for picking up leaves: reelu d., railway lines: honu d., lightning conductor: dagañḍukoḷu, piece of iron: dagañḍugañḍu, bits of iron: dagañḍu taḷaa miihaa, blacksmith: dagatfaanu, magnet: da-gui, metal dross: da-fat, mudguard: da-baru 1. rust; d.jahanii, gets rusty (of iron), d. jehenii, gets rusty marks (of clothes) [S. yabora]; (for dabaru 2., see s.v.): da-mila, tarnish, stain [S. ya(kaḍa), Skt. ayas]

1924 DAI (daek, daaek) ދައި n. flat grinding board (for grinding dry chillies, fuñḍaa d.) [S. dā-gal]

1925 DAI-GANNANII (DAAGANNANII) ދައިގަންނަނީ (ދާގަންނަނީ) v. bites (with -gai, usu. of animals), v.n. daigatum , see also deenum
[S. dähäganne, cf. Skt. daśati]

1926 DAITA ދައިތަ n. For da<u>tt</u>aa, elder sister, but used in Male for unrelated elderly women : ṭukuni d., old woman: ḍainu d., witch: muskuḷi d., old woman

1927 DAIVETI ދައިވެތި adj. For dahiveti

1928 DAU ދައު n. See daa

1929 DAURU ދައުރު n. revolving: period, age: fehi d., zuvaan d., period of youth: ran d., golden age ; dauru kuranii, dauru vanii, revolves (tr. and intr.): enmennař d. kuraa gotař, so as to give everybody a turn: daurek kuḷum, playing the lead [U. daur]

1930 DAULATU ދައުލަތު n. the State [U. daulat]

1931 DAUVATU ދައުވަތު n. invitation: d. denii, invites [U.da'vat]

1932 DAUVAA ދައުވާ n. charge: claim; d. kuranii, charges; claims
[U. da'vā]

1933 DAKAŇDAA ދަކަނޑާ n. kind of plant, premna obtusifolia (used for handle of well-scoop)

1934 DAKU ދަކު adj. miserly [Persian]

1935 DAKKANII ދައްކަނީ v. shows: pays a due (v.n. dekkum : caus. dakkuvanii): adi ves rañgaḷař dakkaa! let’s have another good look (lit. show!): gaigaa jahaa got dakkaaliee, made as if to hit him: Naazimař dakkaalan, to introduce (you) to Nazim: vaahaka d., speaks: eena-aai vaahaka dekkidaane ta, (invol.) may I speak to him? dekkee hitun uḷee miihek, a man who likes to be noticed; dekki varuvaa, rent paid: hama vii iru nudakkaa huri, unpaid when due; Enlarged: dakkaa-lanii, appears, turns up; see also dekenii [S. dakvanne]

1936 DAGAŇḌU ދަގަނޑު See da-

1937 DAGATFAANU ދަގަތްފާނު See da-

1938 DAGIIGU ދަގީގު n. minute of latitude [U. daqīqa]

1939 DA-GUI ދަގުއި See da-

1940 DAŇGA-TERE ދަނގަތެރެ n. front opening of underpants

1941 DAŇGU-HARU ދަނގުހަރު n. strengthening strip on boats

1942 DAŇGETI ދަނގެތި n. name of an island in A atoll

1943 DAJJAALU ދައްޖާލު n. a demon, The Deceiver [U. dajjāl]

1944 DANÑAA ދަންޏާ v. if one goes [conditional of danii]

1945 DAŇḌI ދަނޑި n. stick ; handle of broom, etc. : daaniige dañḍi lanii, fits handle on waterscoop; barani d., (empty) cottonreel: dañḍi barani, cotton on a reel: samugaage d., point on the compass: medu dañḍi, (of heavenly bodies) mid-course: dañḍi-gañḍu, rolling pin or similar tool (roři damaa d., for pastry: godaḍi taḷaa d., for mattresses), or club as used in games such as manḍi : digu dañḍi, kind of ancient ceremonial game;

d.-alui, manioc, manihot esculenta: dañḍi-duuni, a high gliding bird: dañḍi-fai, stilts: dañḍi-fan, lath and cadjan: dañḍi-faa, woody swamp: dañḍi-fuḷu duuni, a seabird, tropic bird: dañḍi-buri, bits of stick: dañḍi-beru, drumming with a stick: dañḍi-masfuḷu, the royal share of the daily catch (carried on a pole): d.-laa, stick of sealing wax: dañḍi-vaḷu, moment [S. dañḍu, Skt. daṇḍaka]

1946 DAŇḌU ދަނޑު n. field; playground: boola d., football pitch; d. kořanii, clears a field for agriculture: d. hedenii, (of crops) grow in a field; dañḍu-fañgu, grassy space (doublet): dañḍu-bim, space without trees: dañḍu-buḷi, long-handled sickle or scythe; dañḍubuḷi aḷanii, uses scythe: dañḍu-mati, lawn

1947 DAT ދަތް 1. n. tooth (hon., datpuḷu): hedi dat, false teeth; datugai rihenii, tooth aches: dat aḷanii (with -gai), bites, bites on : d. kaňḍanii, levels (children's) front teeth with grindstone: d. kaaruvanii, gnashes the teeth: dat jahanii, fits dentures: dat faḷanii, teeth are growing, coming through: d. vikanii, gnashes teeth: dat uňguḷaa bees, toothpaste: dat-kuňḍi vikanii, gnashes the teeth, sneers: dat-kuraňdu, a plant, barleria prionitis: dat-gaňḍu, jaw of animals; teeth of a saw; attachments for sewing machines (maḷaa d., for hemming: got hadaa d., for zigzags): dat-doḷi, chin and jawbone: datpilaa, complete set of teeth [S. dat, Skt. danta]

2. v. known (p.p. of dannanii) [S. dat]

1948 DATI (daccek) ދަތި n. 1. clip (paperclip: penclip: niyafati kaňḍaa d., nail-clippers: bolugai jahaa d., hairclip: boo kořaa d., hair-clippers: meegai jahaa d., brooch): kaḷu d., hairpin: kudi d., safety pins: viyaa d., loom: dati tibbanii, datiigai tibbanii, clips(v.):

2. trap: boḍu d., vice: (haňḍuu) muguraa d., rice-mill, mincer : Siinu d., 'Chinese trap' for rats; dati aḷuvanii, trips up (tr.): dati vanii, is squashed;

3. (met.) trouble; difficult : dati haalugai jehenii, is put in a tricky position; atmati dati, poor; bayaan kuran dati kekuḷum, indescribable discomfort; dati-kam, difficulties, trouble: fenuge datikam,water shortage [S. yatu, Skt. yantra]

1949 DATUM ދަތުން v. knowing (v.n. of dannanii) [S. datum]

1950 DATURU ދަތުރު n. journey: d. kuranii, travels; daturaku nukutum, going on an outing: daturu kuraa miihaa, sailor: mi daturu, on this trip, (met.) this occasion: daturu matii, on the voyage: daturu-faturu, journeys (doublet): daturu- foři, suitcase: daturu-varu, journeys (pl.): daturu-verin, travellers (pl.) : daturuveriyaa, tourist: [S. yaturu, Skt. yātrā]

1951 DATTAA (dattaek: pl., dattamen) ދައްތާ n. elder sister : boḍu d., aunt: mai d., mother- in-law [See also daita]

1952 DADU ދަދު n. ringworm [old S. dada, Skt. dadru]

1953 DANA ދަނަ n. Sagittarius [Skt. Dhanu]

1954 DANAARU ދަނާރު n. mosque

1955 DANII ދަނީ v. goes , goes away (v.n. diyum, dium : p.p. diya : inf. daan:: imp. and 3s., dee : abs. gos : hons. duruvanii and vaḍaigannavanii, q.v.): diyayas heyo, you may go: dannaa, if one goes: hataru aharař daa kujjek, a child approaching four years: aburu danii, self-respect disappears: daan dee, go away! daan fařaařee, get away! (rude), daan hada, get away!(non-Male usage), daan uḷee, get away! hiňgaa damaa, let's go ! varař agugai daa eccek, something which sells at a high price: kaḷař danii, goes after girls (in the dark) : kaḷissař danii, goes after kaḷihi fish: danii (iňgee too), good- bye (I am going);

After a present absolutive, indicates continuity: meduveri vamun diya datitak, difficulties which continued to occur: kuramun diya (hon., kuravvamun vaḍaigat) masakkat, work which was continually being done: mastak aharutakakař vamun diya diya hen, as the months turned into years. After a past absolutive , indicates a politeness: baddalu ve-daane ta, may I see (him)? [S. yanne, Skt. yāti]

1956 DANE ދަނެ v. having known (abs. of dannanii: also dena, dene) [S. däna]

1957 DANḌA-FILAA ދަނޑަ ފިލާ n. a creeper, emilia sonchifolia

1958 DANḌEHEḶU ދަނޑެ ހެޅު n. old title for chief fisherman

1959 DANTURA ދަންތުރަ n. trap : d.jahanii, sets trap [? cf.U.dām, trap]

1960 DANNA ދަންނަ adj. knowing, learned,. esp. in religious matters: danna beekalun, learned men (pres. part. of dannanii) [S. dannā]

1961 DANNAEE ދަންނައީ v. know ye! (used in proclamations) [dannanii]

1962 DANNANII ދަންނަނީ v. knows (v.n. datum, detum : p.p. dat : abs. dane, dene, dena : 3s. dane : hon., dene vaḍaigannanii): beelaa jahan dane-ee, knows how to play the violin;

Caus., dannavanii , causes to know, used as diminutive honorific , declares, announces, invites, tells, asks: farikkoḷař beefuḷunnař dennevii, invited noblemen to the meal (used with dat. or arihugai of person, and with kam, kamař, kamugai of facts)
[S. danne, Skt. jānāti]

1963 DANMARU ދަންމަރު n. torch (non-electric)

1964 DAFAT ދަފަތް See da-

1965 DAFARAA (DAAFARAA) ދަފަރާ (ދާފަރާ) n . buffer-pad; fender; washer; lining (of clothes); sheathing (of wire); d. kuranii,wards off [U. dafrā]

1966 DAFI (datpek) ދަފި n. brass pan with lid for storing betel: bilet dafi hadanii, arranges betel in the box: bilet dafi naganii, performs a kind of dance with the betel box

1967 DABARU ދަބަރު n. 1.See da-

2. in khabaru-dabaru, news (doublet)

1968 DABAS (dabahek) ދަބަސް n. satchel,bag: at d., handbag: kamaru d., pouch in belt: jiibu d., wallet: laari daa d., purse

1969 DABU ދަބު n. long stirrer (esp. for cooking sweets) ; hockey stick [old S. däi, Skt. darv ī]

1970 DAŇBAA (dañbaek) ދަނބާ n. kind of small fish, demoiselle, chrysiptera

1971 DAŇBI- ދަނބި- n. Used ibc., dañbi-koi, son-in-law : dañbi-dari, dañbi-darifuḷu, son-in-law, daughter-in-law (but in normal usage called kokko) [Skt. jāmātṛ]

1972 DAŇBU ދަނބު n. kind of fruiting tree, syzygium cumini; the colour of its fruits, purple [S. dañba, Skt. jambu, rose-apple]

1973 DAŇBU-RUK ދަނބުރުކް n. king-coconut tree: (ras)dañburuku kaaři, don dañbu, king coconuts [cf. S. täñbili]

1974 DAŇBOFFUĻU ދަނބޮއްފުޅު n. character in a fairy tale [cf. Añboffuḷu]

1975 DAM ދަމް 1. v. I go, 1st person sing. of danii, go: damaa, let us go!

2. n. period of three hours, a watch:

damakař duvefai, sailing for three hours: damakař iru araafai, the sun has been up for three hours: hataru dam(u), 12 hours: ree hataru damu, all night: haada damakun, very late: damu hiñganii, acts as night watchman; goes around praying (in times of crisis): damař tibi miihun, men on watch duty;

damu aři, clock guardroom in old royal palace: damu namaadu, optional night prayer : damu ree, (one's) watch night : damu haruge, police headquarters;

dam- iru, time of a watch, three hours; late hours: dam-faḷi, period of a watch: iraa-dam(faḷi), early watch; damfaḷi bahanii, allocates the watches: dam-fuḷi, sandclock: dam-beru, the evening curfew drum (formerly beaten at 11 p.m.): damvaru, very late at night, after midnight; dam vanii, it gets late [S. jāme, Skt. yāma]

3. dam jehenii, hangs oneself: dam jassanii, hangs someone: (met.), miihakaai gen dam jehenii, falls wildly in love with a girl [S. dam, chain; Skt. dāma]

1976 DAMANII ދަމަނީ v. drags, draws, pulls(imp. damaa : p. p. demi : v.n. demum 0: caus. dammanii (v.n. demmum): hon. dammavanii_): akuru d., prolongs a sound: at damaagenfai, pulling one's hand away; guḍi atař d., brings down a kite: ihaavak d., removes stalks of nuts: em d., catches bait in large net: lolugai kuuru d., applies lines on the eye: didafati d., strings up rows of flags: fař d., draws a line: feelifati d., spreads out cloths: riyaa d., spreads out sail (to dry): roñgu d., draws lines: roři d., rolls out roři on pastryboard: vaa d., pulls rope: ham d., skins (tr.); damaa gpř, slip-knot: damaa doru, sliding doors: damaa foti (-gañḍu), curtains; akunivayař damanii, gets cramp: (enlarged) añgain damaa-lanii, sucks in (of babies): guḍaguḍaa damaa-lanii, draws at a hookah: neefatun damanii, inhales: hin damanii, straightens the back; relaxes:

dorukanu damaafai otii, the doorframe is warped: demun hunna eccek, a thing which will warp;

With dat.., dařmaanař demum avas kuraařee, hurry up and pull on (i.e. tighten) the sail-rope! See also demenii [? cf. S. damanii, places, puts]

1977 DAMAHAṬṬANII ދަމަހައްޓަނީ v. prolongs (v.n. demeheṭṭum_) [Enlargement of damanii, cf. erahaṭṭanii]

1978 DAMAA ދަމާ v. See danii

1979 DA-MILA ދަމިލަ See da-

1980 DA-MUI ދަމުއި n. kind of spice used medicinally: two varieties, hiti d., carum copticum ; faḷi d, anethum graveolens (dill)

1981 DAYYUUSU ދައްޔޫސު n. willing cuckold, pimp [U. daiyūth]

1982 DARA ދަރަ n. name of a spirit bringing disease and death : dara hilenii, heavy mortality appears

1983 DARAJA ދަރަޖަ n. amount; status: d. huri beekalek, a man of status; geographical degree: tin daraja matiigai, on the 3-degree line [U. darja]

1984 DARANA ދަރަނަ adj. necessary, essential

1985 DARANI ދަރަނި n. debt : d. adaa kuranii, pays off a debt: d. naganii, raises a loan: darannar̃ denii, lends; darani kaaḍu, relief supplies; darani-veri, indebted, debtor [old S. daradi]

1986 DARANII (v.n. derum) ދަރަނީ v. is in debt (to.., dat.): kunfunñar̃ daraa ot miihun, those indebted to the company: varuvaa-ar̃ daranii, owes for rent: aḷugañḍu duisatta rufiyaa-ar̃ daraifi, I owed Rs.200: deri darani, a debt which is owed [H. dhārnā]

1987 DARAA ދަރާ 1. n. a lower reinforcement in boatbuilding

2. v. owing (part. of daranii)

1988 DARI (pl., darin) ދަރި n. child (impolite if used uncompounded, except in meaning ' citizen': Divehi darin, Maldivian citizens), normally used in form darifuḷu (not honorific: pl., darifuḷumen): darifuḷaa(ee)! child! dañbi-darifuḷu, son-in-law; Aadamuge darin, children of Adam, mankind;

Honorifics: darikalun (sing.), daridarikalun (pl.), dari-kañbalun (fem.); dari-koḷu, generation; ancestry: fasvana darikoḷuge timaage miihek, a man related to you five generations back; dari nu-vaa bis, unfertilized eggs; dari- vantakam, sonship: dari-varu, student [S. daru, Skt. dāraka]

1989 DARU ދަރު n. 1. firewood: daru-tak, items of firewood: darar̃ danii, goes out for firewood, goes for a picnic to a neighbouring island: daru-gañḍu, bundle of firewood: dari kor̃anii, cuts firewood: daru-maaru, packet of firewood [S. dara, Skt. dāru]

2. reef in a sail: riyalar̃ de-daru jassaalum, taking two reefs

in sail

1990 DARUBAARU ދަރުބާރު n. royal audience, durbar : darubaaruge, Conference Hall in Male [U. darbār]

1991 DARUMA ދަރުމަ n. helpfulness, charity: eenaa-aŕ varaŕ daruma hunnaane, blessings on him! daruma-aŕ, free, gratis: d.kuravvanii, is so good as to; adj., daruma-vanta, righteous [Skt. dharma]

1992 DALIILU ދަލީލު n. proof : d. dakkanii, provides proof [U. dalīl]

1993 DALU- ދަލު- n. See daa 1.(net); dalu-dańḍi, poles at the four corners of a fishing net: dalu-beerun jehenii, meddles in what doesn't concern one, gate-crashes; falls hopelessly in love (daa 1)

1994 DALEEKA ދަލޭކަ n. Maldivian form of the name Zulaikhaa

1995 DALLAALU ދައްލާލު n. salesman, broker (dallaalu- kaleege, in stories) [U. dallāl]

1996 DAVA ދަވަ n. saliva

1997 DAVANII (v.n. devum) ދަވަނީ v. heats: uva d., makes lime by burning coral: havaadu d., heats currystuffs before grinding: (slang) davaa-lanii, uses unlawfully, mudaakoḷu davaalaifi, pinched some goods [S. davanne, burns; P. jhāpeti]

1998 DAVAADU ދަވާދު n. paint; artificial ink (as v. deli): eccekgai d. lanii, paints something (for maintenance) : d. teo, paint-thinning oil, homemade ink (ańdun d.): davaadu eti, pot of ink: davaadek eḷum, the preparation of ink [U. davāt]

1999 DAVIGGAŃDU ދަވިއްގަނޑު n. fennel seed, foeniculum vulgare (locally called boḍu diri): d. aragu, gripewater

2000 DAS ދަސް num. ten (in Navata tables: saatu tiin das, 7 = 3= 10)

2001 DAS (dahek) KURANII ދަސް ދެ ކުރަނީ v. learns (hon., das vidaaḷu vanii:: hon. invol., dasfuḷu vanii) : das koŕ denii, teaches: das kiyanii, recites the Quran (as a test): hitu das kuranii, learns by heart: ahannakaŕ dahek nuvaanẹ, I cannot learn (it); aharennaŕ e-fot kiyaakaŕ dahek nuviee, I could not learn that book

2002 DASTUURA (anc. DASTUURU) ދަސްތޫރަ (ދަސްތޫރު) n. custom, habit; adj., dastuurii, according to law, democratic [U. dastūr]

2003 DASSUURA (anc. DASSUURU) ދަސްސޫރަ (ދަސްސޫރު) n. short detachable brass bowsprit: d. riyaa, jib sail (=tunmati riyaa)

2004 DAHAŇGU VANII ދަހަނގު ވަނީ v. becomes very calm (of weather)

2005 DAHANAA ދަހަނާ n. armour (in stories): d. aḷanii, puts armour on [Skt. daṃśana]

2006 DAHARAA ދަހަރާ n. a Maldivian title, Daharaa kilegefaanu: Daharaa kamař koll lavvaifi, inaugurated (him) as Daharaa

2007 DAHAREE (anc. form, still in use; mod. local form, DAHAŘEE, DAAŘEE) ދަހަރޭ (ދާޅޭ - ދަހަޅޭ) v. go! (imp. of danii): mi bunii nuun hee daharee? didn't I tell you to go?

2008 DAHI (dassek) ދަހި adj. greedy (for.., dat.); zealous: mudalař dahi miihek, a man greedy for possessions: miidaa dahi eccek, a thing rats like: mas dahi emek, a bait which fish like : dahi ainu, a surfacing shoal: dahi lanii, is greedy; eccakař dahi nulavaařee, do not covet : d. lavvanii, raises false expectations, tantalizes; dahi-veti, greedy

2009 DAHII ދަހީ n. curd [S. dī, Skt. dadhi]

2010 DAŘ, DAŘU ދަށް - ދަށު n. below, the place below:

daturugai dař vanii, gets off course(‘below the wind’, vai dař): kuḷivarugai dař vanii, loses at games: kiyevumugai dař vanii, fails at exams : faarekge dařu vejje, got under a wall: dařař vanii, declines in standard: dař kuranii, reduces:

dař miihun, the lower orders; tiya haa aharen dařek nuun, I am not so low: varař dařu darajaekge, of very low status;

dařugai (loc.), used postpositionally, usu. after gen.: eige dařugai, below that; so also dařu lai ;

adv., dařun, underneath : dařun damaa, ‘pulling from underneath’, a card game (resembling ‘snap’); ehiiterikamuge dařun, with the help of; dařun is often confounded with dořun, near;

dař-kiba, back of sail: dař-ṭanu, underfelt: dař(u)-tali, lower portion of inner mouth: dař-fai, sole of foot: dař-fuř, the underside: dař-bańḍu, lower belly: dař-maḷu, lower central thwarts: dař-maanu, sail-rope (to adjust billowing); dařmaanař demum, pulling on this rope, tightening it [S. yaṭa, cf.P. heṭṭhā, Skt. adhastāt]

2011 DAḶA ދަޅަ n. glare , esp. of the setting sun (iru ossee daḷa) : iru ossee daḷa-mati, the half-hour before and after sunset,when ghosts may appear

2012 DAḶI ދަޅި n. succulent leaf-stem (of banana, yam, fen-gas) , used medicinally or as a coffin for babies: keyo-daḷi, banana stem used as a brush for non-stick saucepans; keyodaḷi-diya, medicinal liquid squeezed from banana stem: daḷi-gaňḍu, empty 'comb' of banana after the fruits are eaten

2013 DAḶU ދަޅު n. 1. horn of an animal

2. round box or tin: daḷu-keňḍi, tin-opener: fantoři daḷu, imported sets of concentric cane boxes (for women): muři daḷu, tin for ointment (nowadays usually plastic)

2014 DAA, DAU (dalek) ދާ - ދައު n. 1. net : daa aḷanii, casts net: daa bannanii, makes net: daa hadanii, mends net: ree-dalaa danii, goes fishing with net by night; daa bai, set of nets: maa daa, digu daa, faḷi daa, varying sizes of net: daa-gaňḍu, esp. used for (imported) women's hairnets, drawstring for underpants, cotton sieve for straining lime: daa-muu, creeper stems which have suckers (such as betel)
[S. däl, Skt. jāla]

2. sweat (dalek): daa-tak, beads of sweat: aharen daa hillaa, I am sweating: daa vanii, (of clothes) gets sweaty, gets dirty: daa-bihi, 'sweat pimples', prickly heat [S. dā, P. dāha]

2015 DAA ދާ v. going (pres. part. of danii): mi daa duvahu, recently : daa den (or daan den), till (he) came back, while he was away: daa diyum, the course of going: daa gotař daane, will go very quickly [S. yana]

2016 DAAIMII ދާއިމީ adj. perpetual [U. dā'imī]

2017 DAAIRAA ދާއިރާ n. circles of people; influence; kasṭamuge daairaage tereegai, in the sphere of the Customs [U. dā'ira]

2018 DAA-GANNANII ދާގަންނަނީ v. See dai-gannanii

2019 DAAGIINAA (-aaek) ދާގީނާ n. unmanifested items of cargo , travelling equipment

2020 DAAŇḌU ދާނޑު n. an ancient kind of military exercise (daaňḍař demum)

2021 DAADI ދާދި adv. very closely (of time or place): daadi avahař, pretty soon: daadi ehaakař haa iru, just about that time: daadi kairiigai, very near: daadi madu, very rare: daadi gaat miihek, someone closely related: daadi denme, just now: daadi fahun, very recently: daadi fahakaa jehen den, until very recently

2022 DAAN ދާން v. to go (inf. of danii): daan uḷee, get out! daan annaařee, come for a visit! [S. yanna]

2023 DAAN ދާން n. bed (honorific): eňdu-daan: daan-koḷu, royal seat:

daan-mati(koḷu), bed and mattress (hon.); daanmati aḷanii, makes the noble bed: daanmatii vaḷukoḷu, nobleman's bathroom [S. yahan, Skt. śayana]

2024 DAANI ދާނި n. well- scoop for bathing: at-daani, scoop for watering graves; d. indanii, fixes handle to scoop

2025 DAANII ދާނީ v. will go (future of danii)

2026 -DAANU -ދާނު n. See fas-daanu [= daan]

2027 DAANNAA ދާންނާ n. an old Maldivian title: d. kaleefaanu, d. manikufaanu

2028 DAAFARAA ދާފަރާ See dafaraa

2029 DAAYAA ދާޔާ n. nurse, ayah [cf. H. dāī]

2030 DAARA ދާރަ n. edge: d. jahanii, smoothes, rounds, bevels an edge: d. aḷanii, d. naganii, adds decorations (to old furniture); ar̆-daara, octagonal : miskit-daara, wall of mosque yard [Skt. dhārā]

2031 DAARU ދާރު n.. a medicinal ointment [U. dārū, medicine]

2032 DAALA ދާލަ n. seats in porch of mosques

2033 DAALI (daayyek) ދާލި n. shavings (of wood or metal)

2034 DAALU ދާލު n. the letter D in the Arabic and Maldivian alphabets: Daalu atoḷu, the southern part of Nilande atoll

2035 DAAVANI ދާވަނި n . 1. train of a garment: radunge daavani-koḷu, the King's train [S. dāvalu]

2. very large fish-hook

2036 DAAVANII (v.n. deevum) ދާވަނީ v. grips (with a tool): han̆ḍahun d., grips with pliers: datiigai d., grips in a vice: of ants, bites fiercely; (met.), picks on: mar̆aa daavaigen uḷenii, keeps picking on me;

Enlargement: daavaa-lanii (of sailing craft), touches, scrapes: matikan fenugai daavaalaafai, with the gunwale under water

2037 -DAAS -ދާސް n. ifc., only in aḷu-daas, humble (See aḷu)

[Skt. dāsa, slave]

2038 DAAKHILIYYAA ދާޚިލިއްޔާ n. interior; Home Ministry building (Arabic terms for Government departments have now been replaced by English terms); daakhiliyyaa maa, bougainvillea [U.dākhilī, internal]

2039 DAAŘEE ދާށޭ v. go! (imp. of danii)

2040 DAAĻI ދާޅި n. (anc.) top portion of thatch

2041 DI ދި n. (In names) son , daughter : Hasange di Muhammad, M. son of H.: also used as a proper name [For diya, q.v., and for Diidii]

2042 DIUM (DIYUM) ދިއުން (ދިޔުން) v. going (v.n. of danii: also diyaum) [cf. S. yām]

2043 DIUĻI ދިއުޅި n. rope or belt for turning of tools: d. lavvanii, applies the rope; (met.) diuļi digu miihek, a slow man

2044 DIK- ދިއް- In dik kuranii, v. hands over; stretches out: at dik kuranii, iňgili dik kuranii, points (towards.., .. dimaa-ař): dik vanii, juts out; See also dippat [For digu, but cf. digu kuranii, lengthens]

2045 DIG- ދިއް- ibc. for digu: dig-gaa, a tree, hibiscus tiliaceus: tiri- diggaa, sida humilis: dig-guļa (anc.), a team for wrestling exercises: dig-goňḍi, boil or swelling under the armpit: d. naganii, a boil develops; d. jahaafai, a boil has developed

2046 DIGU ދިގު adj. long; tall (used of humans, and of coconut trees): iskoļun digu, tall : tun digu, long-mouthed (of a kind of fish): baara hinci digu, 12 inches (too) long; digu kuranii, lengthens;

digu kanfati (dik-kanfati), a medicinal plant, commelina diffusa (aneilena giganteum): digu tiyara, a plant, cassia sophera: digu toļi, cowpea, vigna sinensis: digu daňḍi, long stick used in certain ancient games: digu daa, kind of long net for fish: digu faļoo, kind of papaw: digu haru, lathe; diguharu liyanii, turns (on a lathe) [S. diga, Skt. dīrgha]

2047 DIJJE ދިއްޖެ n. (obs.) chief lady- in -waiting

2048 DIDA ދިދަ n. flag: dida-kuri, top of fence-stick: dida-daňḍi, flagpole; didadaňḍi jahanii, plants a flagpole: dida-fati, line of flags (for semaphore) [S. dada, Skt. dhvaja]

2049 DIN ދިން v. given (p.p. of denii) [S. dun, P. dinna]

2050 DINAŘA ދިނަޓަ n. asterism Dhaniṣṭhā [S. denaṭa]

2051 DINUM ދިނުން v. giving, allowing (v.n. of denii) [cf. S. dīm]

2052 DINNAVANII ދިންނަވަނީ v. pardons, esp. used of God (v.n. dinnevum)

2053 DIFAA ދިފާޢު n. defence [U. dif'a]

2054 DIPPAT ދިއްފަތް n. a plank on a doni [for dik-fat]

2055 DIMAA ދިމާ n. direction (instr. dimaain, vulg. dimaalun):

eki dima-dimaa-ař, in various directions ; eenaa-aa dimaa-ař, towards him: ehen dimaa-dimaalugai, in other directions: jamalaai dimaa-ař hiyaḷu buññeve, the jackal said to the camel: Hitaduaai dimaain, over towards Hitadu: eňdu dimaa matiigai, above the (place of the) bed;

open, unprotected: eenaa inii muḷin dimaa-ařee, he is quite in the open: dimaa-ař fennan otum, appearing clearly and openly;

straight (adv.): dimaa idikoḷu, the direct opposite: uḍutilain, facing straight upwards: dimaa mati, straight overhead: dimaa maccař, straight up: dimaa dekunu, due south: dimaa banḍun, facing straight downwards; dimaa eňdu, 'facing bed', the householder's bed in the beeruge ;

dimaa kuranii, confronts, argues with, attacks : mařaa d. kuranii, picks on me: dimaa kořfai hunnanii, is insistent, is determined: iňgili d. kuranii, points; dimaa vanii, tallies with; confronts one; happens: dimaa vi sababutakun hure, because of (unforeseen) circumstances: kam dimaa vi gotun, as things turned out [cf.S. disa, dihā, Skt. diśā]

2056 DIYA ދިޔަ 1. n. daughter (Southern usage); also used as a proper name, m. or f. See also di [cf. S. diyaṇi-, Skt. duhitṛ]

2. v. gone, went (p.p. of danii, also past tense): diya aharu, last year: diyaka nudinum, not letting go: ve diya tan, the past [S. giya, Skt. gata]

3. n. water , juice ; tide: diya hikkanii, bales dry (dooni diya hikkaařee, bale out the dhoni); diya hikkaa fai, wooden baler: diya hilenii, leaks (dooni diya hilijje, the dhoni is leaking): dooni diya vejje, the dhoni is full of water: diya-gaňḍu, water to be baled from a vessel; boḍu diyaagai, at high tide: hiki diyaagai, at low tide; fatu-diya felanii, squeezes out leaf juice (for medicinal purposes);

diya-dovi (-dotvek), horizontal gutter; diyadoviige hoḷi, down-pipe: diya-muḍoḷi, a plant, commelina sp.: diya-vat, (of a vessel) bilge: diya-varu, tide, tidal water; diyavaru hikeeneyee, the tide will be very low [S. diya, Skt. udaka]

4. maruge diya, compensation for death

2057 DIYAUM ދިޔައުން v. going (v.n. of danii; also diyum) [Cf. S. yām]

2058 DIYAA (diyalek) ދިޔާ adj. watery: diyaa kuranii, makes watery (diyaa koř kakkanii), melts in the sun: eenaa kuḷu diyaa vejje, his mouth is watering : diyaa-hakuru, liquid coconut honey ; fonu gina diyaahakurek, a foamy pot of honey

[cf.S. diyāru]

2059 DIYUM (DIUM) ދިޔުން (ދިއުން) v. going (v.n. of danii; also diyaum)

2060 DIRAASAA KURANII ދިރާސާ ކުރަނީ v. enquires, analyses

2061 DIRI ދިރި 1. n. cummin, cuminum cyminum: diri fiyaa li bat, a kind of pilau rice with saffron: boḍu diri , fennel (local usage, for daviggaňdu) : kaḷu diri, a medicinal herb [S. duru, Skt. jīraka]

2. v. lived (abs. of direnii)

2062 DIRUŇBAA (diruňbalek) ދިރުނބާ n. bows of a boat (diruňbaa-koḷu)

2063 DIRUVANII ދިރުވަނީ v. swallows; causes to adapt, keeps alive : mas d., em d., keeps fish or bait in store; Enlarged: miistakun diruvaa-laafaane-eve, the men may be revived (caus. of direnii)

2064 DIRUHAM(U) ދިރުހަމު - ދިރުހަމް n. (in stories) dirham (said to be 4 annas weight, drachm) [U. dirham, cf. Gk. drachmē]

2065 DIRENII ދިރެނީ v. is digested: lives; survives; gets adapted: fenař diree, gets adapted to fresh water (of fish); haada diree rařek, a very livable, i.e.very fertile, island: dirum raňgaḷu, fertile: dirumek neti, there is no livelihood: diri uḷum, diri tibum, life (of animates): diri hurum, life, living [S. direnne, decays, Skt. jīryati]

2066 DIREE RAHA ދިރޭރަހަ n. quicksilver (used in sextants): diree raha koḷek, a piece of mercury [S. raha-diya]

2067 DIREE LAALU ދިރޭލާލު n. a precious stone, ruby [laaalu]

2068 DILA ދިލަ n. burning; burning pain, smart:

bitař dila aranii, the wall gets scorched: ekves dilaek milaek naaraa, without any trouble : fiyaa- dila aranii, vapour arises from onions: vaḷoomastakugai dila jehenii, the turtlemeat is scorched, smoked: d. naganii (hon., nangavanii), throbs (of a burn or graze): dumgaňḍu dila vanii, the hookah tastes burnt, is finished; Caus., dila aruvanii, gives out smoke when cooked: mas dila jassaafai, having smoked the fish;

dila-kani, spark: naaři-dila, oily soot from burning coconuts

2069 DILAFUŘI, DILAFOŘI ދިލަފުރި - ދިލަފޮރި n.. cuttlefish (used for moulds) [S. dällā]

2070 DILUVANII ދިލުވަނީ v. opens with difficulty: dat diluvanii, shows the teeth:

Enlargement: loo diluvaa-lum, opening the eyes [old S. dalvanne, Skt. dālayati]

2071 DIL-BAHAARU ދިލްބަހާރު n. a scented tree

2072 DILLANII ދިއްލަނީ v. lights (of lamps, as v. roo kuranii of cigarettes, ovens), switches on (of electric lights) : dillenii (invol.), is alight: (met.), looks cheerful; miadu kalaa haada dillifaa huri duvahekee, (you) are looking very cheerful today [S. dalvanne, Skt. jvalayati]

2073 DIVARU ދިވަރު n. a rope on an oḍi

2074 DIVAANAA VANII ދިވާނާ ވަނީ v. is astonished (at.., ..-un or ..fenifai) [U. dīvāna, frenzied]

2075 DIVEHI (Divessek, pl. Divehin) ދިވެހި n. Maldivian ; Maldivian language (D. bas): Divehi ata, sweetsop: D. bilet, kind of betel: Divehi Raajje, the Maldive Islands: D. ruk, Maldivian coconut : D. libaas, Maldivian man's garment (boḍu libaas): D. hakuru, juggery sugar made from Maldive coconuts: D. haa, medium-size poultry ; Dives akuru, the script formerly used to write Maldivian ['island folk', cf. old S. div, Skt. dvīpa, island]

2076 DISSANII ދިއްސަނީ v. tantalizes

2077 DIHA ދިހަ num. ten: diha raataa, ten pounds weight; mi mahuge diha duvahun, on the tenth day of this month: diha diha kitakek, how much is ten tens? dihayakaa fahakaa kiha varek, what is 10 plus 5?
diha-vana, tenth: dihavana-ař faas vum, passing out tenth [S. daha-, Skt. daśa]

2078 DIHARE ދިހަރެ n. (anc.) seashore

2079 DIHI ދިހި n. sail tie-ropes

2080 DIHUN ދިހުން n. shining black colour (dihun kula): istařigaňḍař haada dihun kulaek araee, the hair is growing very dark

2081 DII ދީ v. give! (impv. of denii) [S. diya]
having given (abs. of denii) [S.dī]

2082 DIIDII (pl., Diidiin) ދީދީ n. a surname, in Male specific to beefuḷu noblemen, but also found in the South : Ḷa-Diidii, e Diidii, are used of noble women

2083 DIIN ދީން n. religion: diinii, of religion: diin-veri, religious [U. dīn]

2084 DIINAARU ދީނާރު n. dinar, an Arabic coin : fas diinaaruge ranař, for the value of five dinars [U. dīnār, Latin dēnārius]

2085 DIILATI ދީލަތި adj. generous: diilati-vanta, generous (of God)

2086 DIILANII ދީލަނީ v. gives head, lets run before the wind; Enlarged: dooni diilai-laařee, let the dhoni run with the wind; oḍi diileniiee (invol.), i.e. the wind is changing

2087 DIIVAALAA VANII ދީވާލާވަނީ v. (anc.) goes bankrupt (mod., baňguruuṭ vanii) [H. divālā]

2088 DUAA KURANII ދުޢާ ކުރަނީ v. prays (Maatkalaaňge kiba-ař, to God) [U. du'ā]

2089 DUAA-VERI (pl., duaaverin) ދުޢާވެރި n. committee of official imams, who used to pray daily at 9 p.m. in Medu Miskit: duaaverikam kiyavanii, recites official prayers [du'aa]

2090 DUISATTA ދުއިސައްތަ num. 200 [cf. S. desīya, Skt. dviśatam]

2091 DUKU ދުކު n. (anc.) distress: duku haalugai, in a distressing condition [S. duk, Skt. duḥkha]

2092 DUKUN ދުކުން n. a kind of small grain, pearl millet [A. dukhn]

2093 DUKUĻU ދުކުޅު n. (anc.) handle, esp. the detachable handle of a drill

2094 DUGI ދުގި n. junk, useless stuff

2095 DUŇGETI ދުނގެތި n. a plant, clerodendron inerme: duňgeti-vaa, duňgeti-gaňḍu, thicket of d. (with unpleasant smell)

2096 DUTTURAA, DUTTURAU (dutturaalek) ދުއްތުރާ - ދުއްތުރައު n. great difficulty: d. kuranii, makes great trouble (for.., dat.) [cf. turaa : Skt. dustara]

2097 DUDDANII ދުއްދަނީ v. 1. prepares (tr.): baḍi duddaafai huṭṭee,the gun is ready

2. follows close: miinaa hunnanii abaduves magee

fahatugai duddaafaeve, he is always close behind me

2098 DUNI (dunñek) ދުނި n. arrow (probably originally bow & arrow): vissaara-duni, rainbow: duni-kiis, hacksaw: duni-daňḍi, bow [S. dunu, bow, Skt. dhanu]

2099 DUNIYE ދުނިޔެ n. the world: d. aḷanii, leaves this world: duniye moya, mad & violent: deduniye, the two worlds (this and the next): duniye-mati, the atmosphere [U. dunyā]

2100 DUNKARAAS ދުންކަރާސް n. jack (for lifting): d. aḷanii, applies the jack

2101 DUNKUNI ދުންކުނި n. lance whirled round in ancient games

2102 DUNYAVII ދުންޔަވީ adj. of the world [U. dunyavī]

2103 DUFANII ދުފަނީ v. chews (low class or provincial duhanii, whence hon. dussavanii):

dufum hedum, chewing: dufum-gaňḍu, a chew; dufumgaňḍu varu vanii, the chew is nicely mixed, is comfortable [cf.S. hapanne, P. cappēti]

2104 DUPPAAN ދުއްޕާން n. storm; stormy: (met.) problem, nuisance: d.kuranii, disturbs (with dat.) [? tuufaan]

2105 DUŇBU ދުނބު n. kind of tree, ficus infectoria

2106 DUŇBURI ދުނބުރި n. kind of tree, neisosperma oppositifolia : karaa d., cascobela thevetia : boḍu d., cerbera manghas [S. duňbul, P. udumbara]

2107 DUŇBUḶI ދުނބުޅި n. soot (in Male usage, gedabuḷi) [S. duňbuḷu]

2108 DUM ދުން n. smoke; incense: d. aruvanii, belches smoke; dum aruvaa mas, right whale (dum= spray): dum gatum (of rice), getting a burnt taste; tavaa dum gatfi, the pan tasted burnt: d. taḷanii, makes incense from powder: d. bahanii, distributes presents of incense to the ziyāre when making vows: d. bahaṭṭanii, prepares incense for salvāt recitations: d. buruvanii, lets incense circulate (in wardrobes or mosques): d. bonii, smokes; dum boo fat, tobacco prepared for smoking: keyovaḷař dum lanii, smokes bananas in a pit;

dumař̃i, structure for smoking or drying fish: dum-kaali, smoke-rack for drying or scenting clothes; taḷaa dumkaali aruvanii, beats senseless: dum-kibaa(-kibalek), incense-holder: dum-gaňḍu, mass of smoke, esp. from a lit hookah; dumgaňḍu guu vejje,the hookah has burnt too quickly: d. kevijjeyyaa / bovijjiyyaa, if (you) have finished the hookah: dumgaňḍu huli vejje, the hookah has burnt low; dum-tari, comet: dum-daňḍi, joss sticks: dum-nika, a tree, vitex negundo: dum-fat, tobacco leaves (kudi d., Bengal tobacco, used for biḍi:: digu d., Pakistaanu d., used for cigars); dumfat aḷanii, prepares hookah: dumfat lanii, uses tobacco for chewing: dum boo fat, mixed tobacco for the hookah: dum-fini, mist: dum-buru aruvaalanii, (met.) gets very hot , is in full swing, makes a hullabaloo [S. dum, Skt. dhūma]

2109 DUMMAARI ދުންމާރި n. a musical wind instrument, forming part of the threefold royal music beru-dummaari- taaḷafili

2110 DURA ދުރަ n. (anc.) hole (mod. horu)

2111 DURAN ދުރަން n. coir ring for standing pans on, hob

2112 DURAA-LAI (DURAA-LAA) ދުރާލައި (ދުރާލާ) adv. in good time: duraalaa kaḍa-eḷum, deciding in advance: d. visnum, thinking ahead: d. hama-jessum, arranging in advance [duru]

2113 DURU ދުރު n. distance; far (from..,..-aa): Maaleaai 417 meelu durugai, 417 miles from Male: eege tankoḷek durun, a little way from it: varař duru rařek, a very distant island: durař faliitaa laafai, having set a fuse at a distance: duru-min, distance;
duru vanii 1.separates by consent (intr.): kamun duru vanii, resigns from a job
2.word used as middle grade equivalent for 'go', 'come'; sometimes with further honorific, duru vannavanii (v.n. duruvennevum): duruvefai duruve, having gone away and returned; ruḷi duruvanii, gets angry (mid-grade equivalent of ruḷi annanii) ; duru visnanii, has foresight: duru visnevee, forethoughtful (hon.) [S. duru, Skt. dūra]

2114 DURUMII ދުރުމީ n. binoculars (deloo durumii); telescope (ekloo durumii): d. aḷanii, uses binoculars, telescope [cf. H. dūrbīn]

2115 DURUHELI VANII ދުރުހެލިވަނީ v. keeps far away (from..,..-aai), keeps apart (intr., in metaphorical sense) : duruheli kořlevenii, becomes withdrawn [For -heli, cf. eka-heri, baru-heli]

2116 DUROO ދުރޯ n. fines formerly exacted for slandering title-holders: d. naganii, exacts such a fine

2117 DURRA(-aek) ދުއްރަ n. the judicial whip [U. durra]

2118 DULI (duyyek) ދުލި n. layer of thin skin found on eggs, oranges, leaves, liquids, or eyes (cataract): d. naganii, removes this layer: d. aranii, cataract develops: d. lanii, a skin forms (kiru tařiigai, on bowl of milk);
The skin of certain leaves, or of deer-horn (fullaa-duli), is used medicinally, or for writing charms: duli hippanii, ties a poultice

2119 DULU- ދުލު- See duu

2120 DULLISAA (-aaek) ދުއްލިސާ n. old kind of standing lamp, standard lamp

2121 DUVANI VANII ދުވަނި ވަނީ v. (of babies) goes blue

2122 DUVANII ދުވަނީ v. runs (abs. duve : imp. duvee!) ; is wafted (of scents): kaňḍu duvanii, sails the sea: duve filanii, runs away; (invol.) duvenii (with dat.), can run; Caus., duvvanii, drives: galam duvvanii, drives the pen: (invol.) fahatař duvvee too, to see if it could reverse; aḷaa duvvaigatee, ran away, started to run
[S. duvanne, Skt. dravati]

2123 DUVAS (duvahek) ދުވަސް n. day : duvahek viyyaa duvahakař, from day to day: duvas-duvahu, on various days: duvahakař fahu duvahek, day after day: konme duvahaku, every day: ekduvahaa / ekduvahun, within a day: duvas-koḷu, a few days: duvasduvaskoḷun, from time to time: duvas-varu, days; in (those) days: ekduvahu, on the 1st.; in one day : mi ot haa duvahussure, since about this time; mi daakař duvahu, recently; duvas vanii, gets old [S. davas, Skt. divasa]

2124 DUVAHAṬṬANII ދުވަހައްޓަނީ v. continues to run, keeps up speed
[Enlargement of duvanii; cf. erahaṭṭanii, obahaṭṭanii]

2125 DUVAA 1., DUVAALU (duvaalek) ދުވާ - ދުވާލު n. daytime; in the daytime: reakaai duvaa, day and night: reaa duvaalu, day and night: duvaalu deiru, twice a day: re-ek duvaalek neti, both day and night [S. daval, Skt. divasakāla]

2126 DUVAA 2. ދުވާ v. pres. part. of duvanii: duvaa-lek maḍiiee, it runs too slow [S. duvana]

2127 DUVELI (duveyyek) ދުވެލި n. speed: madu duveliigai, at low speed: baaru duveyyekgai, at a fast speed; (met.) tauliimge duveli, speedy spread of education
[duvanii]

2128 DUVEEDAARU ދުވޭދާރު n. kind of taall tree, deodar [S. devduru, Skt. dēvadāru]

2129 DUVVANII ދުއްވަނީ v. drives, steers ; aḷaa duvvaigatee, started to run away : vas duvvanii, gives off scent (caus. of duvanii)

2130 DUSSAVANII ދުއްސަވަނީ v. chews, takes a chew (mid-grade) (caus. of dufanii (duhanii))

2131 DUHANII ދުހަނީ v. chews (In Male, the educated form is dufanii)

2132 DUHU ދުހު n. variant form for duvahu: eki duhu, on certain days

2133 DUŘ ދުށް v. seen (p.p. from duřum:: tense- forms, 1st s. duřim, 3s. duṭṭee for duři-eve) [S. duṭu, Skt. dṛṣṭa]

2134 DUŘIM ދުށިން 1. n. kind of bird, golden plover
2. v. I saw (see duř)

2135 DUŘUM ދުށުން v. seeing (used as v.n. of dekenii) [See duř]

2136 DUḶA ދުޅަ n. swelling, swollen: pattern in relief; faitila haada duḷaee, the foot is much swollen:
d. aḷanii, applies relief patterns (on cloth or cadjan): d. vanii, becomes swollen; fai d. vanii, the foot swells: gañḍu d. vanii, boil swells up: miihaa d. vanii, the woman is swelling (with pregnancy); eenaa kujjakař duḷa-heyo vejje, she is safely delivered
[S. daḷa, Skt. dṛḍha]

2137 DUḶA-HEI ދުޅަހެޔި adj. (anc.) very good (of health): duḷahei haalugai, in excellent health [for duḷa-heyo]

2138 -DUḶAA -ދުޅާ adj. ifc., tending to, like: anhen-duḷaa vum, acting like a woman (a legal misdemeanour): firihen-duḷaa vum, acting like a man

2139 DUU (dulek) ދޫ n. 1. tongue: tongue of a lock, or of fountain pen: blade of an oar; buḷaa fen varanii dulunnee, a cat washes with its tongue : nubai duu, foul mouth; duu nubai anhenek, a foul-mouthed woman: vaṯṯarekge duu, unlucky tongue: duu faseeha kujjek, an eloquent child: duu furoḷi bas, tongue-twisting words (such as ' furaaḷař buḷaa araa'): duu-himeri, a straggling plant; duu lanii, licks (with -gai of the object) [S. diva, Skt. jihvā]

2140 -DUU (-duvek) -ދޫ n. 2. ifc., island (only used in proper names, the ordinary word for 'island' being rař), e.g. Hitaduu, Duuniduu, Ařḍuu (Addu)
[S. dū, Skt. dvīpa]

2141 DUU (dulek) ދޫ adj. 3. loose: duu kuranii, loosens: valař d. kuranii, slackens rope: libaas / libaahun d. kuranii, loosens shirt; leaves a place or thing, gives up a habit: duu nukuraa, got duu nukuraa, obstinate, tenacious; defers to: kuḍa kudin boḍeti miihunař duu kuraan vaane-eve, small children should defer to grown-ups; gives out, issues: kaaḍu d. kuranii, issues rations (but not used of stamps, newspapers); releases: jalun duu kurum, releasing from jail: booṭu duu kurum, releasing vessel from quarantine; Enlarged: duu kořlanii, abandons; d. denii, loosens: valař dulek denii, slackens rope

2142 DUUNI (duuñek) ދޫނި n. flying bird (including some insects, e.g. don duuni rafiigu, but excluding hens): hungaanu duuni, tiller: duuni-fat, bird feathers: ledge around interior of ancient tanks: duuni-fuř, flying fluff, ' soft feathers': duuni-bai, flock of birds; duuni hifaa bee, bird-catcher (viz. W.W.A.Phillips in 1957)

2143 DUUMI (duutmek) ދޫމި n. white spots on the skin (don duumi): d. jahaafa, white spots have come: araa duumi, contagious spots; naaraa d., non-contagious spots

2144 DUULA ދޫލަ n. prayer mat: carpet (in general): d. aḷanii, spreads carpet [? S. duhul, Skt. dukūla]

2145 DE ދެ num. two: de-atař, in both directions; deatař kirenii, is not balanced: deat deatař riyaa lum, changing sail from side to side: de-iru, twice: eena-aa de-anbař iňdefaanam, I could take her as second wife: de-kakuu, both knees: de-kena (anc.), two people: de-koḷu, 1.both ends: dekoḷu dekoḷař sossaalum, going up and down (the street): dekoḷu jehee vaahaka, intelligible speech: dekoḷu nujehee miihek, an unintelligible man: ..-un dekoḷu jassanii, makes do with...; dekoḷu jeheekař noonnaane, it won't be possible to make ends meet 2.hostile (to..,-aa): adv. dekoḷař, in hostility: dekoḷu-veri (adj.), hostile: de-gooḷi, a through lane: de-taňḍi maa, a dehiscent plant: de-diha (obs.), 20; dediha-nuvayek, 29: de-duniye,the two worlds, this and the next: de-fatař keňḍenii, havers: de-fař kuranii, repeats; defař vanii, marries one person twice consecutively (of women); defař laa jehum, applying two coats of lac: deba, two states of affairs; deba deeteree vanii, is half asleep; deba nufenna hisaabu, out of sight; deba fenna hisaabu, within sight; deba oḍuvanii, deba kuṭuvanii, is backbiting: de-bai, two parties, two shares; debai kuranii, divides into two; rař debai magu, the road dividing (Male) into two; debai nuvaniis, before the halfway mark; debai miihun, both parties: de-Baňḍos, the two Baňḍos islands : debandihaaru vanii, gets all confused, off one's head: de-bafaakalun, King and Prince: de-bas vanii, disagrees, quarrels: debaheli vanii, is undecided: de-baaskiilin, crisscross, over both shoulders: de-main, mother and child (m. or f.): demafiriin, demafirikalun, demafiri kaňbalun, de-kaňbalun, married couple: de-mammain, mother and child: de-medu, the part between; geaa rukaa demedugai, between the house and the coconut tree; hatarakaa fahakaa demedu, between four and five; degeege demedugai,between the two houses; manavaraai Maaleaai demedek haa hisaabun, about halfway between Male and the man-of-war; ařek jehumaai nuvayek jehumaai demedeve, it was between 8 and 9: de-verin, two people: de-samusaa, two spoonfuls: de-haa, two cocks; de-vana, second [S. deveni]; devana-ař, secondly : de-varu vum, being different [S. de-, deka, P. dvē]

2146 DE-EE ދެއޭ v. See dee 2

2147 DEKUNU ދެކުނު n. south: vai dekunu duvahek, a day when there was a south wind: dekunu faraat, kitchen area, (met.)wife [S. dakuṇu, Skt. dakṣiṇa]

2148 DEKENII ދެކެނީ v. sees, watches, regards (abs. deke, deki- : for v.n. uses duřum : hon. deki-vaḍaigannanii : enlarged, deki-lanii): Abs. deke is used as equivalent to 'in the presence of' : buḷaa deke birek nugane-eve, is not afraid of cats: musaḷu deke aharen varař loobi ve-eve, I am very fond of hares: tedu deke loobi vaa, truth-loving: e-tan dekefai mavaa gat birun, from the fear that I experienced on seeing that: aharen deke bappaa ruḷi atu vejje, father got angry with me; deke farita, known by sight [P. dakkhati, Skt. √drakṣ]

2149 DEKKUM ދެއްކުން v. showing (v.n. of dakkanii, hon. dekkevum): dekkumteriyaa, one who shows off: hama dekkum, proof: vaahaka dekkum, speaking [S. däkvīm]

2150 DETUM ދެތުން v. knowing (v.n. of dannanii; also datum) [S. datum]

2151 DEN ދެން adv. 1. then, afterwards, next : den fahu, thereafter: den anna, forthcoming: den kaaku, who else? den huri, den tibi, remaining: den heyo, enough! denoo, what now? den nudee! oh don’t go

with negative, any more: den naannaati, don’t come again! denek naannaanam, I won’t come again: denek nuhedeene-eve, won’t grow any more (of tree); den-me, just now: daadi denmeaku, just now: hama denmege <u>kh</u>abaru, the very latest news: den ehaa hisaabun, from then on, from that point [S. dän, now; Skt. idānīm]

2. particle, after infinitive or present participle, until, while : daadi fahakaa jehen den, until very recently: baazaarař daa den, while (he) went shopping

2152 DENA / DENE ދެނަ / ދެނެ v. having known (abs. of dannanii): dena hurii, knew: dene vaḍaigannanii, knows (hon.) [S. däna]

2153 DENI ދެނި v. in feniyek deniyek nuve, not appearing (doublet)

2154 DENII ދެނީ v. gives (v.n. dinum:: abs. dii:: 3s. dee : imp. dii:: p.p.din: : hon. devvanii : inf. deen): diifaanan ta? please give: diibala, give! mitanař avi denii, the sun is shining here: eegai foni raha denii, it tastes sweet: mi batugai denii garu rahaee, this rice has a scummy taste: ais dinii-tii ufaa kuram, you are welcome, I’m glad you have come; salaam dee miihun, beggars;

With infinitival forms, tries to, allows to : bañḍuhai viyaka nudemeve, I didn’t let (them) go hungry: feturuna nudii, not allowing to spread; after abs., does something for someone else: mi geegai hure deeřeve, stay here for me, please stay here: aas deeřee, please come. See also devenii , devanii [S. denne, P. dēti]

2155 DENNEVUM ދެންނެވުން v. telling, announcing, inviting (v.n. of dannavanii) [S. dänvīm]

2156 DEBA ދެބަ See de-

2157 DEBUDAARU ދެބުދާރު n. kind of juniper [Persian, dubūdār]

2158 DEBOOḌUVAA ދެބޫޑުވާ backbiting [deba + oḍuvaa, see de-]

2159 DEMENII ދެމެނީ v. is dragged, stretched: mooḷiař demenii, stretches out sleepily: demee filitak, long vowel-signs: daañḍař demenii, engages in an old kind of military exercise: demi hunna, demi onna, lasting, long-lasting; demi otumuge ‘aalam, the realms of eternity: demi onna-nivi ‘aalamař daturu kurevvum, travelling to the world of eternity, dying: hañdaantakař demihunna-nivi davuru, unforgettable period (invol. of damanii)

2160 DEMEHEṬṬUM ދެމެހެއްޓުން v. prolonging (v.n. of damahaṭṭanii)

2161 DEYOO ދެޔޯ n. a horned monster (in stories) [S. deviyo, Skt. dēvatā]

2162 DERA ދެރަ adj. inferior; weak; not clever: mee dera, timid: dera bas, slang: dera-kamek, a pity; weakness (of objects): also as n.., gellumaai dera, losses: varař dera, very sorry! dera kuranii, conquers: dera vanii, lоses (a fight); is sorry: Naadiyaa-ař dera vaa gotek, how N. should be upset

2163 DERUM ދެރުން v. owing, indebtedness (v.n. of daranii)

2164 DELI (deyyek) ދެލި n. lampblack; black charcoal from ruvaa gas (as v. aňguru); imported ink (deli-tak), as v. homemade davaadu : booṭu deli, coal: ruvaa deli, charcoal for gunpowder: deli hikkaa karudaas, blotting- paper; deli-uňbu, wooden inkpot (for carpentry): deli- fuḷi, bottle of ink: deli lanii, applies blacking (to the exterior of boats, before launching) [S. däli]

2165 DEVANII ދެވަނީ v. gives in marriage (of the parents): demiihun devum, giving a couple in marriage: iniikii nuunee, gadakamun devii, they didn't just marry, they were forced to (caus. of denii)

2166 DEVAA ދެވާ 1. v. giving in marriage (pres. part. of devanii)

2. (DE-VAU) (ދެވައު) n. two ropes

2167 DEVI (detvek, devvek) ދެވި 1. n. a mythical creature, godling (and see muḷa); an addiction: d. hifanii, becomes addicted: tiya kamugai tiya varař devi hifaifii viyyaa, if you get so addicted to that: sigareṭ buimař devi hifaafi, has got addicted to smoking [S. devi, Skt. dēvatā]

2168 DEVI ދެވި 2. v. given in marriage (p.p. of devanii): gone (abs. of devenii)

2169 DEVENII ދެވެނީ v. 1. is given, is able to give (with dat. of the agent) : aharemennař deveen noonnaane-ee, we shan't be able to pay: aḷugaňḍař javaabu nudevigen uḷeni koř, when I couldn't reply: hurelaan deveenee got meduveri ve, getting the chance to stay (invol. of denii) [S. devenne]

2. is gone: aḷugaňḍumennař Manaduař devunii, we managed to reach Manaduu : baiveri ve vaḍaigen- devum, continuing to share (hon.) (invol. of danii) [S. yävenne]

3. is heated: uva devum, heating coral into lime: havaadu devum, heating currystuffs (invol. of davanii) [S. dävenne]

2170 DEVVANII ދެއްވަނީ v. gives (hon.): fot gannan devvi ta, did he give money (i.e. ask you) to buy books? (hon. of denii)

2171 DESSA ދެއްސަ num. dessaek haa, about 200 [de+hiya]

2172 DEHAREE / DEHEREE ދެހަރޭ / ދެހެރޭ v. give! (imp. of denii; mod. deeřee)

2173 DEE ދޭ v. 1. gives (3s. of denii)
2. goes (3s. of danii, for de-ee)

2174 DEEK ދޭއް num. two: ekek deek, one two (in counting): deek jahaifi, it struck two: deek vii, on the 2nd day (in dating documents): deekge kurin, before 2.0 [de + -ek]

2175 DEETI ދޭތި n. two things or animals: deetin ekaccař hifan, to take one of two courses, to put all your energy into one thing: jekeţge deeti, two jackets [de+eti]

2176 DEETERE ދޭތެރެ n. the part between : eaa miaa deetereegai, between this and that: degas / degahuge deetereegai, between the two trees: deetere deeterein, from time to time: mi deeterein, recently: deetere-tak, the intervals ; deba deeteree vanii, is half asleep [de+ etere]

2177 DEEDARU ދޭދަރު n. kind of tree of coral, growing on the edge of the reef precipice [Differentiated form of debudaaru, q.v.]

2178 DEEDE ދޭދެ n. ornamentation on the eyes of children (childish word for aňdun): d. aļanii, applies this ornamentation (saying 'deede-kuureyoo!')

2179 DEEN ދޭން v. to give (inf. of denii)

2180 DEENUM ދޭނުން v. biting (of insects) (v.n. for daigatum)

2181 DEEFAT ދޭފަތް n. flat stirrer, used in cooking rice

2182 DEERII ދޭރީ adj. inferior (of intangible objects): eenaa masakkat deerii kamun, because his work is inferior [Differentiated form of dera]

2183 DEEVAANI (deevaanñek) ދޭވާނި n. an official of the administration of justice (deevaani- kaleege) [U. dīvānī]

2184 DEEVUM ދޭވުން v. gripping (v.n. of daavanii)

2185 DEESII ދޭސީ adj. inefficient, inferior [H. dēśī, provincial]

2186 DEESIIN ދޭސީން n. (pl.) local inhabitants [H. dēśī]

2187 DEEHA ދޭހަ n. understanding: d. kuranii, explains: deeha vanii, is understood

2188 DOEK ދޮއެއް n. a lie [For dogek, see dogu]

2189 DOGU ދޮގު n. lies: d. bunanii, d. hadanii, tells lies: ufaddaa dogu, deliberate lies; dogek too, doek too, is it not so? dogu nuhaddavaa, don't tell lies: dogu kuranii, denies, doubts something

2190 DOṬṬEK ދޮޓްޓެއް See doři

2191 DON ދޮން 1. adj. pale in colour ('pink'); ripe (of fruit); good (of children); don kuranii, ripens fruits artificially : keyo d. kurum, burying bananas in sand to ripen; don keyo, ripe bananas; donkeyo-bat, a kind of pudding: haada don kujjek, a very good child: don dagañḍu, white-hot metal: don dañbu, a kind of coconut: don duuni, kind of dragonfly: dondon, don-do (childish), ripe bananas; dondo vakek, a banana: don-fat-bagiicaa, a plant, codiaeum variegatum: don fas, builders' sand: don-fuuḍu, looking pale and unwell: don fehi, light green: don bis, fish eggs, hard roe: don beri, temporary outer support of a boatshed: don bees, a special medicine: don madu, ripe fruit or seed of midili tree: don muusa, a kind of tree, allophylus cobbe; don muusa duuni, kind of ladybird: don veli, building sand (as v. kaři-veli): don hasanu, pale- coloured jar used for diyaa-hakuru :

In relationships, step- : don mamma, don amaa, stepmother: don bappa, step-father: don dari, stepchild: don datta, step-sister, eldest sister

2. n.. prefix in personal names, e.g. Don Maniku

3. n. kiss (on cheek, or by smelling): donek dinum, giving a kiss

2192 DONAMATI ދޮނަމަތި n. (anc.) coffin cloth (mod. saalu)

2193 DONAĻA ދޮނަޅަ n. kind of grain, sorghum [T. connal, maize]

2194 DONNANII ދޮންނަނީ v. washes (v.n. dovum : abs. dove : imp. and 3s. dovee: invol. dovevenii : past tense, dovunii): donna miihun, washermen
[old S. dovinne, P. dhōvati]

2195 DORAA (doraage, doraluge) ދޮރާ n. kind of grain, similar to donaļa

2196 DORAAŘI (doraaṭṭek) ދޮރާށި See dorooři

2197 DORU دޮރު n. doorway; window: uturu faraatu d., front door: dekunu faraatu d., huḷañgu faraatu d., back door: kuḍa d., kiḍikii d., window : furagas faraatu d./ furagas kibaa d., rectum: anhenaage kurimatii d., vagina: doru-fat, door; dorufatu taḷu, door lock and handle: doru-foti(-gañḍu), curtain for door or window: doru-mati, front courtyard [S. dora, Skt. dvāra]

2198 DORUVAANU ދޮރުވާނު n. doorkeeper (doruvaanu- kaleege)
[U. darvān]

2199 DOROOŘI (dorooṭṭek) (DORAAŘI) ދޮރޯޅި (ދޮރާޅި) n. gatehouse, gateway [doru + aři, S. doraṭu, cf.Skt. dvārakoṣṭhaka]

2200 DOLAŇGU ދޮލަނގު n. large metal tray for food

2201 DOVI ދޮވި n. 1.(anc.) washerman (dovi- kaleege, mod. donna miihaa)
2. ifc. in diya-dovi (-dotvek), horizontal gutter

2202 DOVUM ދޮވުން v. washing (v.n. of donnanii) [old S. devīm]

2203 DOVE ދޮވެ v. having washed (abs. of donnanii) [old S. deva]

2204 DOS ދޮސް n. pus: dos-tak, effluxion of pus: dos- mohoru, a disease of the eyes

2205 DOHOKKO ދޮހޮއްކޮ n. For don kokko, fair sister

2206 DOHOTTIIDI ދޮހޮއްޓީދި n. For Don Tuttu Diidi, a proper name

2207 DOHOTTU ދޮހޮއްޓު n. For Don Tuttu, a proper name(voc., Dohottuu !)

2208 DOŘ / DOŘU ދޮޅް / ދޮޅު n. surrounding area; near by : e gee doř, near that house: meezu dořugai innevii, sat at the table: tandoř, the space underneath: dooňgi doř, area at the back of the knee: bañḍu doř, the stomach area; this word has become confounded with dařu,the space below, e.g. gas dořun, near the trees or below the trees

2209 DOŘA ދޮޅަ n. asterism Jyēṣṭhā [S. deṭa]

2210 DOŘI (doṭṭek) ދޮޅި 1. adj. older : mařař vure deaharu doři vaane, must be two years older than me: 'umuru doři kořlum, exaggerating one's age
[S. deṭu, Skt. jyēṣṭha]

2211 DOŘI (doṭṭek) ދޮރި 2. n. fishing rod (mas baana doři): doři-boňḍi, bundle of rods [S. yaṭa, Skt. yaṣṭi]

2212 DOŘI-MEENAA ދޮރިމީނާ n. 1. a former Maldivian title: d.- kamař koli lum, formal declaration of assumption of the title: Dořimeenaa kilegefaanu, one of the highest of Maldivian titles
2. kind of creeper with edible leaves

2213 DOŘUN ދޮރުން n. (pl.) 1. (obs.) a class of former royal functionaries: dořunge miihek, one of the functionaries
2. instr. of doř, near by

2214 DOŘ-DAŇḌI ދޮރްދަނޑި n. detachable handle for a harpoon

2215 DOḶAS (doḷahek) ދޮޅަސް num. twelve - used esp. in the form doḷahakař, 'about 12'; in weights and measures baara is more common [S. doḷos,Skt. dvādaśa]

2216 DOḶAHAGI (doḷahatgek) ދޮޅަހަގި n. an old measure for sugar or rihaakuru, half a bolihi [doḷas + agi]

2217 DOḶI ދޮޅި n. 1. woman's long prayer veil : d. aḷanii, puts veil on: d. jahanii, adjusts veil (to leave the face free); doḷi-daan(-koḷu), royal veiled palanquin: doḷi-feeli burugaa, short woman's veil
2. ifc. in dat-doḷi, jaw: vilu-doḷi, submarine ridge

2218 DOḶISSA ދޮޅިއްސަ n. a gross, one and a half hiya (used of fish catches): doḷissa godaa, 144 godaa -fish [doḷu]

2219 DOḶU ދޮޅު n. one and a half: doḷek, Rs.1 1/2: doḷu-bai, one and a half shares of the fish catch [S. yeḷa, ?P. diyaḍḍha]

2220 DOO (often pronounced DO) ދޯ (ދޮ) interrogative particle, expecting the answer 'yes' (equivalent to nuun too? ; when addressing aristocrats, dogek too? is used instead):

tii kihaa derakamek doo, I say how awful! diyaii tarukaarii ganna doo, (he) went to buy vegetables, didn't he? baddalu vaane doo, we'll meet then, O.K.? genai kujjek doo mii, so is this the servant-girl he brought? mii haada majaa miihekee doo, he's a funny chap, isn't he? doo, Mufiidaa? isn't that right, Mufiidaa? doo kuranii, is in doubt [S. dō, perhaps for da+ hotu, Skt. ca+ uta]

2221 DOOGI ދޯގި n. magic for protection of ships: d. hadanii, practises d.

2222 DOOŇGI ދޯނގި n. the back of the thigh (faige dooňgi-doř)

2223 DOODI ދޫދި n. ray of light [P. jōti, Skt. jyōti-]

2224 DOODIYAA ދޫދިޔާ adj. immature; vacillating (of people): doodiya vaahakatak, worthless words

2225 DOODO ދޫދޮ n. (childish) toy boat

2226 DOONI (dooñek) ދޯނި n. dhony, fishing boat (mas dooni): uva dooni, mixing trough: ba<u>tt</u>eli d., Male fishing boat, boat for personal travel: vadu d., smaller kind of fishing boat; dooni-koḷu, nobleman's boat: dooni-faharu, collective pl. of dooni [T. tōṇi]

2227 DOOBURAALI ދޫބުރާލި n. (also pronounced' doburaali') d. hakuru, cane sugar

2228 DOO-RAA ދޫރާ n. the morning toddy-flow (heňdunu (baalaa) raa)

2229 DOORI ދޫރި n. funnel for pouring (teo doori); thimble: d. aḷanii, puts thimble on; cap of a pen (galamu doori); finger guard, used for cutting fruits

2230 DOORU ދޫރު n. long-necked earthenware waterpot, carafe

2231 DOOLI(dooyek) ދޫލި n. privy on a boat (viz. packing-case suspended over the side): d. kuranii, uses this privy

2232 DOOHAḶI ދޫހަޅި adj. of inferior weave (of mats etc.)

2233 DOOḶAŇBU ދޫޅަނބު n. lemon

2234 DOOḶU ދޫޅު 1. n. sweet oil of seed coconuts

2. adj. fond of, friendly towards (with -aa): bafayaa dooḷu kujjek, a child who is fond of his father

ނ NUUNU, the 3rd letter of the Maldivian alphabet

Nuunu atoḷu, Miladunmaḍulu atoll South, the 3rd atoll from the north

2235 NA- ނަ- negative particle, used ibc. for nu-; see also ne- ; naeve, has not come: naii, did not come: nais, not having come; nais nudaane, which will not fail to come:

nayas, though one does not come: nahadaa, not having made: na-hama, improper; timaayaai nahama, unsuitable for oneself: (of people) not all there: na-halaalu, illegitimate; nahalaalař balive iňde, becoming illicitly pregnant: in sandhi, naangai, not having announced: naanna, not coming: naaňdeveene, will be unable to come [S. na-, Skt. na]

2236 NAI ނައި 1. n. kind of stinging prawn, 'sea-worm' (muudu- nai) : nai-haru, prawn-hole

2. v. not come (negated p.p. of annanii) : nai nama ves, even if (you) don't come [S. nā]

2237 NAI-BOLI ނައިބޮލި n. cone, deep sea shellfish, 'nautilus' (used for spoons)

2238 NAIKA ނައިކަ n. appliqué decorations on curtains: n. lanii, applies n.

2239 NAIBU ނައިބު n. 1. local judge (naibu- kaleege: in pl., naibu beekalun): naibukamaa hiňgum, ancient religious ceremony held on 6th Rajab involving procession of judges: banḍaara naibu, the attorney-general [For U. nāib, deputy]

2. kind of cake

2240 NAIRU / NAARU ނައިރު / ނާރު n. irritable person

2241 NAIS, NAII ނައިސް - ނައީ See na-

2242 NAU (navek) ނައު See naa

2243 NAULU ނައުލު See naalu

2244 NAEVE, NAEE ނައެވެ - ނައޭ See na-

2245 NAKAT ނަކަތް n. asterism: Mula nakatu, during the asterism Mūla: nakat balanii, selects auspicious seasons: nakat-gaa, foundation stone; nakat-gaa jahanii, lays foundation stone: nakat-ge lavanii, circumcises: nakatcaa(-aaek), (anc.) expert on the auspicious time for building: nakat-terikam, astrology [S. näkat, Skt. nakṣatra]

2246 NAKALU ނަކަލު n. copy: n. kuranii, copies: n. naganii, takes a copy [U. naqal]

2247 NAKUVAA (pl., nakuvaain) ނަކުވާ n. Borah captain [cf. U. nākhudā, pilot]

2248 NAKKAARA ނަކްކާރަ n. supper drum, formerly sounded at 2 a.m. during Ramzan [U. naqqāra]

2249 NAGANII ނަގަނީ v. lifts; takes, removes (v.n. negum:: imp. nagaa ! hon. nangavanii):
fen nagaa jaaḍi, pot for getting water; amuru naganii, gets permission: ṭikeṭ n., buys ticket: hurihaa Divehi gaḍiek n., (coll..) takes every Divehi period (in school): tiriis n., repeats part of the Quran after the teacher: teyo n., extracts oil: tooraafani n., collects worms (as bait): (bilet-) dafi n., performs a dance with betel-box: nagili n., weighs anchor: faḷurařek nunagaane-ee, they won't discontinue (your lease of) the island: filaavaḷu n., repeats lesson after the teacher; filaavaḷu nagaa denii, gives out a lesson: foṭoo n., takes a photograph: biiku n., collects alms: boodi n., collects baitfish: masaarii n., opens bed-curtains: musaara nangavanii, receives salary (hon.): riyaa n., hoists sail: radunnař varuvaa n., levies polltax for the king: vaziifaa n., gets job: vagař n., steals; kidnaps (persons): havaadu n., measures out curry-stuffs: haasilu n., charges the dues ; nagaa denii, gets for someone;
Technical usages; subtracts: tinakun deek negiimaa ekek, 3-2=1:
sails into the wind: dooni vayař nagaafai beheṭṭum, keeping the dhoni into the wind:
nagaa kiyanii, leads (esp. in singing): nagaa kiyaa miihaa, leader of the assembled people (ha-varu) who speaks for them;
(Intr.) arises; ořaaḷa n., pimples arise: koḷigaňḍu n., stormcloud arises: goř n., swelling arises: dikgoňḍi n., boil arises: dila n., throbbing arises: fusgaňḍu n., stormcloud arises: vilaagaňḍu n., stormcloud arises: harubihi gaṇḍek nagaafaa, a rash of hard patches has arisen;
Enlargement: nagaa-lanii (nagailanii), removes, gets rid of, loses: konmes nagaa nulaati, be sure not to lose (it): nagaek nulaanam, I won't lose it : vagututakek aḷugaňḍu nagaek nulameve, I didn't lose any time: fursat nagaalum, losing the chance (hon., nangavaa-levvum) ; see also negenii [S. naganne, Skt. √langh]

2250 NAGAHAṬṬANII ނަގަހައްޓަނީ v. changes course of vessel (v.n. negeheṭṭum) : oḍi nagahaṭṭaařee, change course on the oḍi!
[Enlargement of naganii, cf. erahaṭṭanii]

2251 NAGILI (nagiyyek) ނަގިލި n. anchor: n. lanii, n. vaṭṭailanii, n. duu kořlanii, drops anchor; n. naganii, weighs anchor [cf.S. näṇguram]

2252 NAGULANDAAŘI ނަގުލަންދާރި n. scorpion [naguu + ?]

2253 NAGUU (nagulek) ނަގޫ n. 1. tail (also niguu): naguu-baḷu, dog; boo jehi taa n. jahaafai, tail hitting head, i.e. (running) very fast
2. tornado (naguu-rooḷi, vai-naguu, nagulekge vai): naguu-seesaru, sea dragon; (met.) unreliable person
[S. nagula, Skt. lāngula]

2254 NAJAA KURANII ނަޖާކުރަނީ v. releases (lit.); e kamtakun najaa vum, getting free of such things [U. najāt, deliverance]

2255 NAJIS (najihek) ނަޖިސް n. dirt, dung; pollution: najis taketi, pollutants; najis vanii, is polluted [U. najis, dirty]

2256 NAṬṬANII ނަޓްޓަނީ v. 1. unclips, undoes, removes (v.n. neṭṭum); avoids: goř n., undoes button.

Enlargement: naṭṭaa-lanii, slips off (intr.): farun n., floats off the reef: bandarun jassaafai n., leaves a harbour: baiskalakun n., avoiding a bicycle: huḷaňgu faraatun n., avoiding the west: matiiburin naṭṭaalaigen veṭṭum, falling from the upper storey: farumatin naṭṭaalevee varu vii, was able to float off the reef: hamain naṭṭaalaafaa, going beyond the limit : Caus., maqsadun naṭṭuvailum, diverting (someone) from his purpose; see also neṭṭenii

2. causes to dance (for naṫuvanii, caus. of naṫanii)

[S. naṭavanne]

2257 NATIIJAA(-aaek) n. ނަތީޖާ results : natiijaaekge gotun, as a result : natiijaaek kamař vii.., the result was.. [U. natīja]

2258 NA<u>TT</u>AA-LANII ނައްތާލަނީ v. destroys, abolishes: hařdaanek na<u>tt</u>aalanii, destroys the memory: hee na<u>tt</u>aalanii, anaesthetizes [See also ne<u>tt</u>aalanii]

2259 NADURU ނަދުރު n. vow (made to saints): n.bunanii, makes vow [U. na<u>z</u>r]

2260 NANU ނަނު n. thick twine: fishing line: n.aḷanii, twists twine: n. ellanii, casts fishing line; nanu-gaňḍu-koḷu, end of the fishing line: nanu-bai, sections of line: nanu-buri, section of line: nanu-beddi, a plant, corchorus aestuans

2261 NANUKATI ނަނުކަތި See nannugati

2262 NANGANII ނަންގަނީ v. caus. of naganii (also naguvanii: v.n. nengum, neguvum):

NANGAVANII ނަންގަވަނީ hon. of naganii (v.n. nengevum)

2263 NANNAARI ނަންނާރި n. a creeper, hemidesmus indicus (used to purify the blood)

2264 NANNUGATI (nannugaccek) ނަންނުގަތި n. kind of tree snake(also called nanukati)

2265 NAFARATU, NAFURATU ނަފަރަތު - ނަފުރަތު n. detestation : n. kuranii, n. vanii, abhors [U. nafrat]

2266 NAFAA (nafaek) ނަފާ n. profit [U. naf'a]

2267 NAFII KURANII ނަފީ ކުރަނީ v. (lit.) forbids; negates [U. nafī]

2268 NAPPI ނަޕްޕި n. tasteless food

2269 NABAAZU HAKURU ނަބާޒު ހަކުރު n. medicinal lump sugar: barley sugar [U. nabāt]

2270 NABII ނަބީ n. prophet [U. nabī]

2271 NAM ނަން n. name: namakař, nominally: diumuge namugai, under pretext of going: nam ituru (gram.), pronoun : kon namek kiyanii miinaa-ař, what name do you call him? [S. nam, Skt. nāman]

2272 NAMA (namaka) ނަމަ Conditional particle, usually after participial or incomplete verb forms , if: aharen etanař daa nama / daane nama kaleař eňgeene, if I go there you will know: aharen danii nama kaleař govaalaanam, if I am going I will tell you: aharen diya nama e dooni atu liimuhee, if I had gone we would have beaten that dhoni (in the race) or have salvaged that dhoni : kalee ai nama aharen diyaimus, if you had come I would have gone: kaři jahaifi nama varař dila nagaane, if (it) actually stung you it will be very painful; nama ves, even if; when initial, but: nama nama, now now! (be careful): vagutii gotun nama ves, even if temporarily: mi kamaa kalee nuruhee nama ves, even if you don't approve of this: kitakme kuḍa nama ves, however small (it be): avahař nama ves lahun nama ves, sooner or later [S. nam]

2273 NAMAADU ނަމާދު n. formal prayers : n. kuranii, prays: n. aḷanii, omits to pray: namaadař govanii, calls to prayer: de-namaadu deetere, between dusk and dark (viz. between Maghrib and 'ishā prayers) ; namaadu-ge, mosque for women [U. namāz]

2274 NAMURU ނަމުރު n. leopard; (met.) man who does not bathe [U. namir]

2275 NAMUUNAA (-aaek) ނަމޫނާ n. sample, pattern [U. namūna]

2276 NAM-GANNANII ނަންގަންނަނީ v. tells, asks (used to middle grade, cf. bunanii , vidaaḷu vanii); specifies, mentions (all grades) (v.n. nam-gatum : p.p. nam-gat: invol. p.p. nam- genevunu, -ganevunu): tiriigai mi nam-ganna taketi, items specified below [nam + gannanii]

2277 NAMBARU ނަންބަރު n . number (in enumeration); sums: ek nambaru libum, coming first (= ekvana-ař aum): nambarutak jahanii, does sums: hisaabu nambaru-tak, sums: kaňḍaa fas nambaru, five subtraction sums: kaaḍu nambaru, ration card: nambaru hedum, approved long dress for women (= faas kuri hedum): nambaru-ge, Indian brothel

[E. number]

2278 NAYAS ނަޔަސް See na-

2279 NAYAA ނަޔާ adj. lovely, new : n. vairooḷi, fresh breeze [H. nayā, Skt. navaka]

2280 NARAKA ނަރަކަ n. hell [S. naraka, Skt. naraka]

2281 NARAVAA(-aaek) ނަރަވާ n. See naruvaa

2282 NARU ނަރު n. a thin round strip: wire (loo- naru), ratu loonaru, copper wire: ranvan loonaru, brass wire: hudu loonaru, white brass wire : vayiru n., steel wire, steel cable (for fishing); tendrils, suckers of a creeper (veyoveluge n.); fibre : boňbi-naru, coir yarn, toraa- naru(-gaňḍu), kind of 'loofah'; haa- naru, left-over bits of fibre: naru-gaňḍu, spring ring, spring bracelet: piece of wire; naru-keňḍi, pliers, wirecutters: naru-damaa (-aaek), drain; narudamaa hoḷi, drainpipe: naru-filaa(-gaňḍu), goldsmith's wire sizer: naru-maadaa, hook and eye fixings for rudder of a boat: naru-hiru, junction of tooth and gum [T. nār, fibre]

2283 NARUGIS ނަރުގިސް n. a plant, zephyranthes rosea [U. nargis, Gk. nárkissos]

2284 NARUVAA (anc. NARAVAA) (-aaek) ނަރުވާ (ނަރަވާ) n. whiskers (of cats, mice); antennae (of insects); ends of moustache (of men)

2285 NARUS (naruhek: pl., naruhun) ނަރުސް n. nurse [E. nurse]

2286 NARUSIŇGU ނަރުސިނގު n. an unpleasant mythical animal [cf.Skt. narasiṃha, hero]

2287 NALA ނަލަ adj. pretty, prettily dressed: n. hedee duvahek, a day when one dresses up nicely: n. haddanii, dresses (someone) up nicely; nala-nala, very pretty

2288 NAVAI ނަވައި num. (anc.) 90 (mod. nuvadiha) [cf.H. navvē]

2289 NAVATA ނަވަތަ n. special mathematical tables for addition and multiplication

2290 NAVAA- ނަވާ- num. plus nine (in compound numbers): navaaviis, 29 (= onatiriis): navaatiriis, 39 (= tiriis nuvaek): navaaḷiis, 49 (=saaḷiis nuvaek): navaanavai, 99 (=nuvadiha nuvaek)

2291 NAVAAN ނަވާން num. times nine (in Navata multiplication tables: nava navaan, 9 x 9)

2292 NAVAARA ނަވާރަ num. nineteen (= onavihi)

2293 NA-VIYANI ނަވިޔަނި n. name of the Maldivian retroflex ṇ as still preserved in Addu

2294 NAVU- (NAU) ނަވު- n. See naa: navaa = navu + -aa, ships and..

2295 NAVU-RUMAA (-rumaalek) ނަވުރުމާ n. Obsolete kind of formal kerchief

2296 NASABU ނަސަބު n. lineage: nasabu- naamaa, family tree [U. nasab]

2297 NASAARAA ނަސާރާ n. Christian (Nazarene) [U. na_sārā]

2298 NASIIBU ނަސީބު n. luck: nasiibu nura, white hair on the young: nasiibu-teri, lucky [U. na_sīb]

2299 NASURU ނަސުރު n. help; victory: n. denii, gives help [U. na_sr]

2300 NASEEHAT ނަސޭހަތް n. advice: n. denii, gives advice: main bafainge naseehat gabuul kuraařee, accept your parents' advice (prov.); naseehat-teri, advisory [U. na_sī_hat]

2301 NAZARU ނަޒަރު n. glance; n. hinganii, casts glance (at.., dat..) : opinion; aḷugaňḍuge nazarugai, in my opinion [U. naźar]

2302 NA-HADAA ނަހަދާ See na-

2303 NAHANAA (-aaek) ނަހަނާ n. a skin disease

2304 NAHII KURANII ނަހީ ކުރަނީ v. forbids (in religious contexts): diinugai nahii kurevvi kamtak, activities forbidden by religion [U. nahī]

2305 NAŘANII ނަޑަނީ v. dances (v.n. neřum:: past tense neṭṭee, for neři-eve : caus. nařuvanii:: hon. naṭṭavanii): baburu lava-ař neřum, dancing a loud and energetic kind of dance [S. naṭanii, Skt. nřtyati]

2306 NAA 1., NAU (nav-) ނާ - ނައު n. schooner, ship with many sails (pl., naa

(-naa)-faharu, naa- zooňgu, nau-zooňgu: hon., naa-koḷu, the former royal schooner)
[S. näv, Skt. nau, n āvā]

2307 NAA 2. ނާ Polite exclamation of contradiction, no! (after a refusal) please! naa naa, no indeed: kalee nukaanu ta? naa, won't you eat? yes I will: naa naa, now then, come now [See na-]

2308 NAAIBU ނާއިބު n. deputy, esp. deputy judge in islands (n.- kaleege, pl. naaibu-beekalun: coll., naibu, q.v.): naaibu-ge, law courts [U. nāib]

2309 NAA-KAAMIYAABU ނާކާމިޔާބު adj. unsuccessful: naakaamyaabii, lack of success [kaamiyaabu]

2310 NAAGA ނާގަ n. cobra (naaga harufaa) [Skt. nāga]

2311 NAAGAA ނާގާ n. name of two compass directions: n. astamaanu, north-west by north; n. iiraan, north-east by north [U. nāqa, she-camel, Cassiopeia]

2312 NAACARANGII ނާޗަރަންގީ n. dancing entertainment [H.nāc-rang]

2313 NAAṬṬEK ނާއްޓެއް See naaři

2314 NAAḌUVAA (naaḍuvalek) ނާޑުވާ n. ornamental tassel (n. fař) on flags, uniforms, shoes, circumcision 'shawls'

2315 NAADIRU ނާދިރު adj. unusual, rare [U. nādir]

2316 NAADII ނާދީ n. social club: N. al Tamaddun, 'Civilization Club', a former institution in Male [A.]

2317 NAADEE ނާދޭ v. doesn't come; naaňdeveene, will be unable to come
[na + aadee, na + aadeveene]

2318 NAANAA ނާނާ n. 1. lullaby [onom.]
2. naanaa-fuḷu fillavanii, takes bath (of royalty): naanaa beru, drum for the (former) king's bath (at 9 a.m. on Fridays) ; also naanee [cf.S. nānavā, bathe]

2319 NAANU (NAAN) ނާނު (ނާން) n. Indian bread: naan(u)-kaṭaa(-aaek), kind of sweetmeat [U. nān, nānkhaṭāī]

2320 NAANEE ނާނީ n. naanee fillavanii (high hon.), takes bath [naanaa-fuḷu]

2321 NAANGAI (NAANGAA) ނާންގައި (ނާންގާ), v. not having told [nu+ angaa, see anganii]

2322 NAANNA ނާންނަ v. not coming (neg. part. of annanii) [nu + anna , S. nēna]

2323 NAABA ނާބަ n. sunset drumming: n. jahanii, plays the sunset drum ; naaba-baḍi, the sunset drum during Ramzan [U. naubat]

2324 NAABUS - KHAANAA ނާބުސްޚާނާ n. drumming hall in the old royal palace

2325 NAAMAAN ނާމާން adj. out of bounds; dangerous; haunted (of places): naamaan beefuḷun, exclusive aristocracy; amaan too naamaan too, is it permissible to come in or not? [U. nā + amān]

2326 NAARAA ނާރާ v. non-contagious (of diseases) [nu + araa, see aranii]

2327 NAARIŇGU ނާރިނގު n. local orange, citrus aurantium (hiti naariňgu): hut n., citrus medica,'citron' [U. nāringī, nārang]

2328 NAARU ނާރު n. 1. veins, arteries; 'nerves', tendons: nuu n., veins: mai n., heel tendon: eenaage naaru-tak, his 'nerves', i.e. his general condition: karař naarek araifi, (I) have a stiff neck; lines on the hand: veins on the back of leaves: lee naaru, redness of the eyes [S. nahara, cf. Skt. snāyu]
2. See nairu

2329 NAARUKU (NAAROKU) / NAARUVAK ނާރުކު (ނާރޮކު) / ނާރުވަކް n. ind of berry used in making falida cakes in the South; also called muraaki

2330 NAARES ނާރެސް n. pivot or bearing, esp. of a mill

2331 NAAROKU ނާރޮކު See naaruku

2332 NAALIIS (naaliihek) ނާލީސް n. (anc.) court case [U. nāliṣ]

2333 NAALU (NAULU) ނާލު (ނައުލު) n. freight charges: n. negum, charging for freight; n. batteli, inter-atoll freight boat [U. naul, Gk. naulon]

2334 NAASI 1. ނާސި adj. like a prostitute, of abandoned morals [?U. nāz]

2335 NAASI 2. ނާސި n. name of two compass directions: n. astamaanu, north-north- west: n. iiraan, north-north-east [U. na'ś, stars of the Bear]

2336 NAASTAA ނާސްތާ n. breakfast; a snack: n. kuranii, takes breakfast [U. nāśtā]

2337 NAAZIRU ނާޒިރު n. Principal of a school [U. nāźir]

2338 NAA-ZOOŇGU ނާޒޯނގު See naa

2339 NAAHAA ނާހާ v. not obedient (neg. part. of ahanii) [nu + ahaa]

2340 NAAŘI (naaṭṭek) ނާރި n. coconut shell or husk : naaři- kiba, half-shell (distinguished as loo-kiba or loo-naaři,with the 'eyes', and fuu-kiba or fuu-naaři): naaři-gañḍu, shell or half-shell when in use, e.g.for winnowing; coconut bowl; skull: naaři-dila, smoke from burning coconut shells; naaridila jahanii, applies this medicinally: naaři lanii, puts coconut shells round fruit for protection; develops a shell: (met.) lagoṇḍiigai n. laafai huri miihek, a man who has grown a shell round his heart, viz. has got hardened to something [? cf. H. nāriyal, coconut or T. nāri, fibre]

2341 NAAḶAI, NAAḶAA ނާޅައި - ނާޅާ v. not having spread [nu+ aḷaa, see aḷanii]

2342 NAAḶI ނާޅި n. a 'measure' of rice, equal to four laahi, approximately 2 lbs.; hataru naaḷi hañḍuu, four measures of rice [S. näḷi, P. nāḷī, Skt. nāḍī, pipe]

2343 NAAḶU ނާޅު n . howitzer, mortar

2344 NIA- ނިއަ - See also niya-

2345 NIAŇDURU (NIYAŇDURU) ނިއަނދުރު (ނިޔަނދުރު) n. citron, shaddock, pomelo: don amaekee niañduruekee ekkahalaee, a stepmother is as sour as a citron (prov.)

2346 NIANETI (NIYANETI) ނިއަނެތި (ނިޔަނެތި) adj. kind, civilized

2347 NIAMI (NIYAMI) ނިއަމި See niyami

2348 NIAA ނިއާ See niyaa

2349 NIAAMA ނިއާމަ See niyaama

2350 NIUḶANII (NIYUḶANII) ނިއުޅަނީ (ނިޔުޅަނީ) v. unravels, undoes (invol., niuḷenii); removes a spell

2351 NIKA ނިކަ n. banyan tree, ficus bengalensis: nika-bilissa, a variety of banyan: dum-nika, another tree, vitex negundo [S. nuga, Skt. nyagrōdha]

2352 NIKAM ނިކަން adv. 1. fairly; a lot (cf.English 'quite'): nikam baarař, nikam avahař, fairly quickly: nikam miiru, nikam rañgaḷu, very sweet, very good
2. in commands, please: nikam dii bala, please give
[S. nikam appears to be different]

2353 NIKAMETI (nikameccek) ނިކަމެތި adj. weak, destitute, poor, lonely

2354 NIKUT, NIKUNNANII, NIKUME ނިކުތް - ނިކުންނަނީ - ނިކުމެ v.
See nukunnanii

2355 NIGAARAM ނިގާރަން n. ballast: n. laigen, having loaded ballast: (met.) stamina

2356 NIGUḶANII ނިގުޅަނީ v. takes away: rescinds; lagabu niguḷaigenfai, having cancelled the honour

2357 NIGUU (nigulek) ނިގޫ n. See naguu

2358 NIT ނިތް n. forehead: n. aruvanii, raises the eyebrows; nit-kuri, mid-forehead: nit-gañḍu, peak of a cap; front lock of ladies' hair

2359 NITUBAḌI (NITABAḌI) ނިތުބަޑި (ނިތަބަޑި) n. a dehiscent medicinal plant, ruellia ringens: also kunahañgaali , q.v.

2360 NIDANI ނިދަނި n. thick mattress [nidi]

2361 NIDANII ނިދަނީ v. sleeps (imp. nidaa ! hons., nidi kuravvanii, avahaara(fuḷu) lappavanii) : nidenii, falls asleep (invol.,with dat. of person)
[S. nidanne, Skt. nidrāyati]

2362 NIDAN-MIYARU ނިދަންމިޔަރު n. basking shark, nebrius ferrugineus [nidi]

2363 NIDI (niñjek) ނިދި n. sleep, sleepiness: nidi aisfi, I am sleepy: eenaa nidi annanii, he's getting sleepy: mi uḷenii nidi filaigennee, I can't get to sleep: nidi filaifi, I've really woken up: nidi kuravvanii, mid-grade hon. of nidanii : nidi gannanii, falls asleep: nidi baru kanii, is full of sleep; nidiige tereegai, sleepily: niñjaaigen, sleepily: nidi-kuḷu, spittle which oozes during sleep: nidi-mooḷa, sleepy state after waking up (nidimooḷa vanii, nidimooḷaigai uḷenii, is in this state) [S. nidi, Skt. nidrā]

2364 NINDA(VA)NII ނިންދަނީ (ނިންދަވަނީ) v. puts to sleep (v.n.nindum, nindevum); knocks senseless (caus. of nidanii)

2365 NIFAAS ނިފާސް n. the forty days after childbirth: nifaaskam matiigai inum, being ceremonially impure during this time [U. nifās]

2366 NIFIYYEVE ނިފިއްޔެވެ v. was not concealed (neg. past tense of filanii) [nu + fili-eve]

2367 NIBUU (nibulek) ނިބޫ n. twin: n. kudiin, twins (coll., ekmaabaňḍu kudiin) [S. niˇmbul]

2368 NIMA ނިމަ n. (obs.) tribute of juggery formerly given to official travellers by toddy-tappers

2369 NIMENII ނިމެނީ v. finishes (intr.): nunimee, to be continued: nimunii, finis: aharen nimijje, I've finished: nunimee ta, haven't you finished? eerun nimunii ta, is that the lot? madrasaain nimigen, after school: majliihun nimigen, after assembly: enme fahuge nimumakař vii.., it ended up with...; (gram.)nimunu kam, past tense: nimi nimunu kam, remote past tense; used after absolutives, hama jassaa nimigen, having finished adjusting [S. nimenne, Skt. nirmāpayati x nirvāpayati]

2370 NIMERI-DUUNI (also NEMERI-DUUNI) ނިމެރިދޫނި (ނެމެރިދޫނި) n. peacock [?cf. S. monaru]

2371 NIMMANII ނިންމަނީ v. finishes(tr.); finalizes, decides to (hon., nimmavanii): alamaari jahaa nimmum, finishing making the cupboard : nimmi nimumekge matin, as a result of a decision made (caus. of nimenii)

2372 NIYAU ނިޔައު See niyaa

2373 NIYAT ނިޔަތް n. resolve: n. gannanii, makes a resolve: n. kiyanii, recites a resolve (in Arabic) [U. niyat]

2374 NIYAŇDURU ނިޔަނޑުރު See niaňduru

2375 NIYANETI ނިޔަނެތި See nianeti

2376 NIYA-FATI (-faccek) (NIAFATI) ނިޔަފަތި (ނިއަފަތި) n. nail (of finger or toe); tuniya n., nicely cut nails: kukuḷu n., ugly long nails, n. kaňḍaa dati, nail- clippers: n. kaňḍaa vaḷi, pocket knife [S. niyapotu, Skt. nakha + ? pankti]

2377 NIYAMI, NIYEMI (NIAMI) ނިޔަމި - ނިޔެމި (ނިއަމި) n. navigator [S. niyamu, Skt. niyāmaka]

2378 NIYA-RODI (NIARODI) ނިޔަރޮދި (ނިއަރޮދި) n. cuticle, skin round the nails [old S. niya-rada]

2379 NIYAA / NIYAU (NIAA) (niyalek) ނިޔާ / ނިޔައު (ނިއާ) n. end: e mahuge niyalař, up to that month ; n. kuranii, completes (tr.); n. kuramun daa got, the way it was working out: n. kaňḍa- aḷanii, completes judgment, announces sentence: niyaa vanii, finishes (intr.), esp. finishes reading Qur'an (kiyavaa niyaa vum): dies; niyaa kam, judgment: niyaa-veri, judicial [H. nyāv, Skt. nyāya]

2380 NIYAAMA (-aige) (NIAAMA) ނިޔާމަ (ނިއާމަ) adj. easy, calm (of sea voyages): safety; n. baňdaru, safe haven [U. ni'mat]

2381 NIYUḶANII ނިޔުޅަނި See niuḷanii

2382 NIRILI ނިރިލި n. kind of creeper, nephrolepis (also called kiis filaa)

2383 NIRU ނިރު n. shoots from the root, suckers: n. faḷanii, n. lanii, suckers develop

2384 NIROḶU ނިރޮޅު n. coconut timber (carpenters' term, cf. vakaru) [S. neraḷu, Skt. nālikēra]

2385 NILA ނިލަ n. strip from trunk of screwpine or areca, used in thatching

2386 NILANDE ނިލަންދެ n. name of F and D atolls

2387 NILAMEHI ނިލަމެހި n. a bait fish, chromis [S. nalamas]

2388 NIVAI نިވައި See nivaa

2389 NIVAṮṮANII نިވައްޓަނީ v. is on point of starvation (v.n. niveṯṯum)

2390 NIVANII ނިވަނީ v. extinguishes: alifaan nivaa eti, box for collecting charred wood from the fire; (mod.)fire extinguisher [S. nivanne, Skt. nirvāti]

2391 NIVAA / NIVAI (nivalek) ނިވާ / ނިވައި n. sheltered side: n. kuranii, covers, shelters; oriyaam n. kuraaree, cover your nakedness: n. vanii, is hidden: gahakaa nivaa ve, sheltering behind a tree; iru udarehaai nivaa vum, the sun sinking below the horizon; nivaa-fatgaňḍu, screen, awning: nivaa magu, private parts, pubic hair (to be covered while praying): nivai- rooḷi, unexpected gust from different directions [Skt. nivāta]

2392 NIVAA-BOŇḌI ނިވާބޮނޑި See niivaaboňḍi

2393 NIVAALI ނިވާލި n. stuffing for guns to fire without ammunition

2394 -NIVI -ނިވި suffix added to present participles: annanivi, coming: onnanivi, lying: denivi, giving: kuruvanivi, causing

2395 NIVENII ނިވެނީ v. goes out (of flame) (invol. of nivanii)

2396 NIVVANII ނިއްވަނީ v. extinguishes (caus. form of nivanii)

2397 NIŚAAN ނިޝާން n. sign, token [U. niśān]

2398 NISBAT ނިސްބަތް n. comparison: n. kuranii, compares (with.., ..-aa); nisbatun, proportionately: raajjeegai miihun tibi nisbatekge matiin, proportionately to the population of the Maldives: lisṭu nisbat vaa faraat,the man the list is attributed to: konme ves bayakaai nisbat kořgen, with reference to any person [U. nisbat]

2399 NIHAAYAT ނިހާޔަތް n. excess: nihaayatař (adv.), exceedingly: nihaayatuge daraja-akař, exceedingly [U. nihāyat]

2400 NIHAALI (nihaayyek) ނިހާލި n. official silk apron or sash for men

2401 NII ނީ n. 1. smallest grains of broken rice (used for poultry feed), nii haňḍuu (cf. buri haňḍuu): nii kuňḍi, tabby colour (of cats or birds)
2. joint on mast of vessel

2402 NIIŇDE ނީނދެ v. not having sat (neg. abs. of innanii) [nu + iňde]

2403 NIIRANII ނީރަނީ v. leaks slowly, trickles out

2404 NIIRI ނީރި n. fibrous edge of coconut leaf

2405 NIILA-KAŘI ނީލަކަށި n. prickly roots of kurukuru yam

2406 NIILAM ނީލަމް 1. n. auction: n.kiyanii, niilamař lanii, auctions (tr.); n. kuḷenii, plays auction bridge [H. nīlām, Port. leilām]

2407 NIILAM ނީލަމް 2. n. sapphire in a ring [H. nīlam, for nīlmaṇi]

2408 NIILUUFARU / NIILOOFARU ނީލޫފަރު / ނީލޯފަރު n. blue waterlily [U. nīlōfar, Skt. nīlōtpala]

2409 NIIVAA-BAT ނީވާބަތް n. kind of thin-rolled rice pudding [nii 1.]

2410 NIIVAA-BOŇḌI (NIVAABOŇḌI) ނީވާބޮނޑި (ނިވާބޮނޑި) n. sole of the foot (faige niivaaboňḍi)

2411 NIIVEE ނީވޭ v. is not heard (neg.pres. tense of ivenii) [nu + ivee]

2412 NIISTAŘI ނީސްތަށި n. In niistaṭṭař aranii, is bothered, is fussed

2413 NIIHA ނީހަ n. (anc.) envy; n. lanii, envies

2414 NU- ނު- negative prefix, not.. (ibc.): nudee, don't go! nudaanam, I won't go: nunimee, 'to be continued'; nu-ekgaani (neeggaani), insubordinate, aggressive: nu-guḷum, disagreement: nu-gen, without: nu-tanavas, crowded; busy; inappropriate (nutanavas daňḍivaḷu, inappropriate moment; atmati nutanavas, poor): nu-tanvaḷu vanii, is in a hurry (aḷugaňḍu nutanvaḷu vejje, I was in a hurry): nu-niyat, evil wishes (nuniyat lanii, wishes evil (upon someone, dat. or ..-ge maccař); nuniyat lii miihaku, our enemies): nu-me, not (in verbal alternatives: nume keeme-ee nume diyame-ee, he has neither eaten nor departed(cf. nu-ves), i.e. is just sitting at table; nume nuunme, not at all; nume netme-eve, is not at all): nu-rakkaa (-rakkau; nurakkalek), danger; unsafe (nurakkaa kamek, a risky undertaking; nurakkaa-teri, unsafe): nu-lai (hon., nu-lavvai), without (following -aa); kamakaa nulai, without cause; miaa nulai, without this: nu-lafaa, unreliable, bad (of people): nu-laahiku, unbearably (adv.); nulaahiku kairikairiigai, uncomfortably close; nulaahiku ginaeve, are very numerous; nulaahiku nulafaa kujjek, a very unreliable chap: nu-ves, not even: nu-sahalu, unreliable, intolerable
[S. na-, Skt. na: see also na-, ne-]

2415 NU (NUŇ) ނު (ނުން) intensive suffix , you know; isn't it so? ehen nu? isn't that right? eňgijje-ek nu, do you hear? kalee beerakař nudaanamek nu? aren't you going out? ehaa boḍukamek nuunek nu, it's not so serious, you know: avahař feřiimaek nu avahař nimeenii, of course the sooner you begin the sooner you will finish [S. ne]

2416 NUI-BEES ނުއިބޭސް n. a black dye, used medicinally

2417 NUKUTAA (NUGUTAA) ނުކުތާ (ނުގުތާ) n. dot (in Arabic writing); full stop; (met.) points to be noticed [U. nukta]

2418 NUKUTUM ނުކުތުން v. going out (v.n. of nukunnanii)

2419 NUKUNNANII (NIKUNNANII) ނުކުންނަނީ (ނިކުންނަނީ) v. goes out, comes out (abs. nukume, nikume : p.p. nukut, nikut: : v.n. nukutum:: imp. nukumee ! hon. nukunnavanii): mařař nukumevunii (invol.), I was able to get out; nu-nikumevee fada haalugai tibi, being unable to go out: eenage gudu nukutii, he is hunchbacked: nukunnamaa hee, shall we go out? nukumeyoolaee, went out, we hear: fat nukutum, leaves coming out: natiijaa nukutum, results coming out: nukunna! exit
[S. nikmenne (p.p. nikut), Skt. niṣkramati (niṣkrānta)]

2420 NUKUME (NIKUME) ނުކުމެ (ނިކުމެ) v. having gone out (abs. of nukunnanii) [S. nikma]

NUKUMEE! ނުކުމޭ go out! (imp.)

2421 NUGUTAA ނުގުތާ See nukutaa

2422 NUJUUMII (pl., nujuumiin) ނުޖޫމީ n. astrologer [U. nujūmī]

2423 NUTVEVE / NUTVEE ނުއްވެވެ / ނުއްވޭ v. was not [For nu-vieve]

2424 NUFUUZU ނުފޫޒު n. influence [U. nufūẕ]

2425 NUBAI ނުބައި adj. bad, wrong: nubai nambarek, wrong number: nubai vii tantaagai, in wrong places: nubai fuř, wrong side of cloth (i.e.inside): mařař enme nubaii, it is worst for me: nubai vanii, (of liquids, curries) goes off, goes bad; miirek ves nuun nubaek ves nuun, neither sweet nor foul: mee nubai kuranii, makes one feel like vomiting: nubain nubayař, from bad to worse; nubaimis kor̃, insultingly (cf. kuḍai mis); nubai vejje, was out (at cricket)

2426 NURA ނުރަ n. grey hairs: bolugai n. jahaifi, grey hairs appeared on the head: nasiibu nura, grey hairs on the young [S. nara]

2427 NURABOḶU ނުރަބޮޅު n. kind of small fish

2428 NULU- ނުލު- See nuu

2429 NUVA ނުވަ num. nine: umurakii nuva aharu, umurun nuva aharu vejje, is nine years old: nuva-ree fenun keňḍum, see keňḍenii: nuvaree fenu tereegai, in its infancy: nuvayek jahaifi, it struck nine: nuvadiha, 90; nuva-vana, ninth
[S. nama, nava, Skt. nava]

2430 NUVATA ނުވަތަ conj. or (cf. nuun nama, ehennaa) [nu + vata, if it be not, S. nohot, P. na- hontam (Helmer Smith, Journal asiatique 1950, p.209)]

2431 NU-SIYAANU ނުސިޔާނު adj. naughty, unreliable, unpredictable
[nu + H. seyān]

2432 NUHANU ނުހަނު adv. (lit..) very (coll. varař)

2433 NUU(nul-) ނޫ adj. blue:
nuu-faa, weal, bruise; nuufaa genfai,with a weal: nuu-madaraka(nuu-mazaraka), a chemical powder: nuu-mas, kind of fish(don nuumas), blue snapper, paracaesio: nuumaa-filaa, a plant, clitoria ternatea: nuu-mugu, green dhal, phaseolus aureus: nuu-ruk, nulu-ruk, kind of fruiting green coconut [S. nil, Skt. nīla]

2434 NUUKAAŘEE ނޫކާޅޭ v. don't spit out (neg. imp. of ukanii) [nu + ukaařee]

2435 NUU-GEFAANU ނޫގެފާނު n. the patriarch Noah [U. Nūẖ]

2436 NUUṬ ނޫޓް n. currency note [E. note]

2437 NUUDUHEVEE ނޫދުހެވޭ v. unable to fly (neg. invol. part. of uduhenii)

2438 NUUN ނޫން neg. particle , not (after indefinite nominal forms): kurii hama ekani mi kamek nuun, what (he) did was not only this: tiya nuun galamek, any other pen than that: iyye bunuvviimek nuun too, didn't you say yesterday? tiya engevi got nuun gotakař, otherwise than as you told me: ahannakař beenumek nuun, I don't need (it): ehaa boḍukamek nuunek nu, it's not so serious, you know: nuun nama, if not: nuunas, although not: nuunii, except; kalee nuunii, except for you: aharen kaanii bat nuunii kudibateve, I will eat millet, not rice: mi faraatugaa ta nuunii anek faraatugaa ta, on this side or the other? nuuniyyaa, if not [for nuunii viyyaa]: nuunoola, they say not; sababek netek nuunee, it is not without reason: ehen viyyek nuun, not so!
(as excl.) No! nuunee nuunee, no no! nuunekee (in repetitions), I said ' no'
[cf.S. nā̆, nähä, H. nahīn]

2439 NUUNU ނޫނު n. the letter N in the Arabic and Maldivian alphabets: hus nuunu, nasality (N optionally written without fili, transliterated as ň): Nuunu atoḷu, the southern part of Miladunmaḍulu atoll

2440 NUUBII ނޫބީ n. Nubian, African: nuubii baburu, negro [Nubian]

2441 NUURII ނޫރީ n. 1. kind of parrot, lory [H. nūrī]
2. nautical almanac [? an English proper name]

2442 NUURU ނޫރު n. light (poet.): loluge nuuru keňḍenii, goes blind [U. nūr]

2443 NUUS (nuuhek) ނޫސް n. newspaper: nuus nerum, issuing a newspaper : nuus-verin, newspaper editors [E. news]

2444 NUUḶEE ނޫޅޭ v. is not here (neg. pres. tense of uḷenii) [nu+ uḷee]

2445 NE- ނެ- negative particle, used ibc.; see also na-, nu- : ne-hedee, does not grow: ahannakař nuhedeene, I can't make (this) [S. na-, Skt. na]

2446 NEGEṬIV (NEGṬIV) ނެގެޓިވް (ނެގްޓިވް) n. negative film [E. negative]

2447 NEGENII ނެގެނީ v. rises (invol. of naganii) [S. nägenne]

2448 NEGEHEṬṬUM ނެގެހެއްޓުން v. changing course of vessel (v.n. of nagahaṭṭanii)

2449 NEṬṬI ނެއްޓި n. kind of drum dance (baburu neṭṭi): n. jahanii, n. jassanii, n. kiyanii, n. nařanii, performs this dance [Skt. nṛtti]

2450 NEṬṬUM ނެއްޓުން v. 1. causing to dance (v.n. of naṭṭanii 2)
2. unclipping (v.n. of naṭṭanii 1)

2451 NEṬṬENII ނެއްޓެނީ v. breaks away (intr.), slips out : hayyarun neṭṭijje-ee, had a miscarriage: hamain neṭṭi, irregular (invol. of naṭṭanii 1)

2452 NET (NETI) ނެތް (ނެތި) v. is not (netii, netee, netiiee) : magee ataku galamek net, there is no pen in my hand, I haven't got a pen: hama netiiee, is not there at all: aharen beenumek net, I don't want (it): netiyyakii nuun, is: netii viyyaaeve, not at all! netas, net kamaku,though not: netoola, netiyoola, they say not: netiyyaa, if not: net nama, if not; neti nuvaane, can't be omitted: daakař netiimu, we won't go; aḷugaňḍu dannavaakař netimeve, I'm not going to say (hon.); neti kořlanii, exterminates; neti (nubai) mořenii, slanders a man in his absence: neti nudaane, will not be absent.

Also used as abs. or participle : deraek moḷek neti, doṭṭek hagaek neti, without distinction of class or age: re-ek duvaalek neti, both day and night: heňdunek haviirek neti, both morning and evening; kamtak huri net got, how things were [and weren't]
[S. näta, Skt. nāsti]

2453 NETAMA ނެތަމަ v. (poet.) if there is not

2454 NETENII ނެތެނީ v. is not present, is absent: nu-netee, is not absent: netigen danii, disappears; muḷin netijje-eve, have completely disappeared; netijjaum, disappearance: haňdaan netenii, may forget: khabaru netum, being unconscious: hee netenii, loses consciousness: vaḍaigen netum, being absent (high hon.)
[Back formation from net]

2455 NETTAA-LANII ނެއްތާލަނީ v. cancels: ekam haňdaan nettaalai, having forgotten it [Enlarged caus. related to netenii; better in form nattaalanii]

2456 NENGUM, NENGEVUM ނެންގުން - ނެންގެވުން v. lifting (v.n. of nanganii) [S. nängīm]

2457 NERU ނެރު n. artificial channel through reef [U. nahr, canal]

2458 NERENII ނެރެނީ v. pushes out, lets out: publishes, issues (abs. nere : past tense nerunii : :hon. neruvvanii, nere-lavvanii): eenaa e gein neregen nuvaane-ee, do not turn him out of that house! anhenun nerum, calling out the women: gas dořař nerenii, hands over to be beaten (obs.): alifaan nerum, producing a fire (from a tinderbox): goňḍi nerenii, squeezes a boil: got nerum, inventing methods: vagař mas nere, having stolen (some) fish [S. neranne, P. nīharati]

2459 NEVI (nevvek) ނެވި n. captain of small cargo-boat, professional pilot: banḍaara nevi-kaleege, government pilot: nevikamu annanii, acts as pilot [S. nävi, Skt. nāvika]

2460 NEŘUM ނެޅުން v. dancing : neři neřumtak, all kinds of dancing (v.n. of nařanii) [S. näṭum]

2461 NEE- ނޭ- n. See s.vv. neefat, neevaa

2462 NEEKA VANII ނޭކަ ވަނީ v. gets weak

2463 NEEGGAANI ނޭއްގާނި adj. insubordinate; stubbornly opposed
[nu+ *ekgaani]

2464 NEEŇGE ނޭނެގޭ v. is not understood; kam neeňge, perhaps
[nu + eňgee]

2465 NEEDEVEE ނޭދެވޭ v. undesirable (invol.neg. pres. part.of edenii)
[nu + edevee]
NEEDEE ނޭދޭ which one does not like (neg.pres. part. of edenii)
[nu + edee]

2466 NEEDDAARU ނޭއްދާރު adj. aggressive [nu +* ekdaaru ?]

2467 NEENGEVI ނޭނގެވި v. did not announce (neg. past tense of anganii)
[nu + engevi]

2468 NEE-FAT ނޭފަތް n. nose: neefat foḷanii, blows nose: neefatun damanii, inhales; neefatu vaskaři, bridge of nose [S. nähä, Skt. nāsikā + patra]

2469 NEEŇBURE-EE v. ނޭނބުރޭ doesn't revolve (neg. pres.tense of eňburenii)
[nu + eňburee]

2470 NEERII ނޭރި v. did not rise; neereeřee, do not enter! (neg. past tense and neg. imp. of erenii) [nu + erii, nu + ereeřee]

2471 NEE-VAA (NEEVAI) ނޭވާ (ނޭވައި) n. breath: n. lanii, breathes: n.hillanii, is asthmatic; pants: hama neevaa lanii, recovers one's breath: aḷugaňḍař neevaa(-tak) levilevi hurii, I was just breathing: maa neevaa levifai, panting; neevaa-hoḷi, windpipe: neevaahoḷiař eḷenii, has the death rattle [S. nähä, Skt. nāsikā + vāta,'nose-wind']

2472 NEEZAA(-aaek) ނޭޒާ n. daggger (in stories, or as used by ascetics)
[U. nēza]

2473 NEEHUM ނޭހުން v. not hearing (neg. v.n. of ahanii) [nu + ehum]

2474 NEEḶUM ނޭޅުން v. not putting (neg.v.n. of aḷanii) [nu + eḷum]

2475 NORA ނޮރަ n. asterism Anurādhā [S. anura]

2476 NORINMA ނޮރިންމަ n. a compass direction, south-west (= galbu astamaanu)

2477 NOḶANII ނޮޅަނި v. peels (by hand alone): don keyo n., peels bananas: naariňgu n., peels oranges (as v. aafalu mařanii): kukuḷu n., plucks a fowl: gas n., pulls up clumps of grass: fat n., pulls off leaves (e.g. of murаňga): ham n., skins
[S. neḷanne]

2478 NOḶI ނޮޅި n. hollow pipe: guḍaguḍaa n., pipes of a hookah: noḷi-buri, mouthpiece of hookah: kottu n., servant's pipe: vaagaňḍu n., coiled mouthpiece: binaatu n., ornamented mouth piece [H. nalī, nālī, Skt. nāḍikā]

2479 NOOKARII ނޯކަރީ n. work [U. naukarī]

2480 NOOKARU (pl., nookarun) ނޯކަރު n. domestic servant [U. naukar]

2481 NOOṬ n. ނޯޓް note, chit : nam nooṭu kuranii, puts name down [E. note]

2482 NOONNA ނޯންނަ v. not being (neg. part. of onnanii): obi noonna, uncontrollable [nu + onna]

2483 NOOVE ނޯވެ v. not having been (neg. abs. of onnanii) [nu + ove]

NOOVEVUNEVE ނޯވެވުނެވެ did not find itself to be (neg. invol. past) [nu + ovevunu-eve]

2484 NOOSSUNIIS ނޯއްސުނީސް v. before setting [nu + ossuniis]

2485 NOOŘ ނޯރް n. inside of nose, nostrils: nooř-mati, tip of nose; noořař damaalaafaa, inhaling: noořaa nukuḷadaana, unpleasant to the nose

2486 NOOḶEE ނޯޅޭ v. is not confused (invol. neg. of oḷanii) [nu + oḷee]

ފ FAAFU, the llth letter of the Maldivian alphabet

Faafu atoḷu, Nilande atoll North, the llth atoll from the north

2487 FAI ފައި n. leg (foot): hatares fai, hands and feet: fai digu makunu, long-legged spider: fai digu madiri, kind of humming insect: diya hikkaa fai, baler (shaped like a foot): fai laa koḷu (faa laa koḷu), foot of bed: fai vař koř iřiinum, sitting crosslegged: fai jahanii, sets foot: fai hilaavaḷu obum, cessation of all sounds: fai ellanii, kicks at (as an insult), aims (at.., dat.): diya hikkaa fai, wooden baler; de-fain, both feet; fai-ura, prayer stockings (for women): defai-kaři, two straight legs; the two wings of the Male breakwater: fai-kur, ankle; bottom leg of trousers: fai-taḷaa, antipodes: fai-tila, foot: fai-dańḍi, 1.shin 2. kind of fish: fai-dařfuř, solc of foot: fai doř 1. area round the feet; faidořugai, in the way; faidoř balaigen uḷee! look where you're going; faidořu fureeta, squib (also faidař-fureeta) 2. rafter: fainpuḷu, feet (hon.); fainpuḷu deken diyum, going to visit a nobleman; f. fenee too, is the gentleman available? f. dakkavanii, receives (hon.) a guest: f. aḷuvvanii, goes to visit (of the king): f. biissavanii, comes, goes (of the Prophet); fai fala bali, filariasis: fai-fuhi, doormat: fai-booḷa, obs. term for football (mod. fuṭbooḷa): fai-vak, one of the thwarts on a boat: fai-vaḷu, groin (coll., ukuḷuvaḷu): fai-vaagi, strength of leg: fai-vaan(u), footwear [S.pāvahan]; faivaanař aranii, puts on shoes: faivaanun faibanii, takes off shoes: faivaan-gańḍu lanii, has feathered legs (of birds): buuṭ faivaan, leather shoes: foti faivaan, canvas shoes: faivaanuge dařfuř, sole of shoe [S. pā, paya, Skt. pāda]

2488 -FAI (-FAA) -ފައި (-ފާ) verbal suffix used after absolutives: gosfai, having gone; see also -faane, -fi [old S.-pā, Skt. pidhāya]

2489 FAIDAA (-aaek) ފައިދާ n. material profit: f. aranii, makes a profit [U. fā'ida]

2490 FAIBANII ފައިބަނީ v. descends (v.n. feebum, feibum: : hon. feebannavanii): gahun f., descends from a tree: Maale f., lands in Male: geyakař f., settles in to a house: rařař f., settles in an island: fen f., water trickles out: hukurun f., comes out from Friday service: gońḍi f., roots develop, tubers form: naguu f., whirlwind forms (and descends): rooḷi f., blast dies away : (invol.) faibee aharu (coll.), in the past year [?S. pāvanne, floats]

2491 FAILABBA ފައިލައްބަ See faalabba

2492 FAILU ފައިލު n. file (of documents) : f. kuranii, files (documents) [E. file]

2493 FAISAA(faisaek) ފައިސާ n. money : faisaa jehijje, helped himself to money: faisa-aa jehuniimaa, when it comes to money: faisaa-veri, rich [H. paisā,Skt. ?pādikāṃsaka]

2494 FAU ފައު See faa

2495 FAUNU ފައުނު n. gold sovereign: as jehi f., i.e. with image of a horse on it [E. pound]

2496 FAURU ފައުރު See faaru

2497 FAU-ROŘI ފައުރޮޑި See faa-roři

2498 FAULAA(-aaek) ފައުލާ n. 28 lbs. weight: hakuru faulaaek, 28 lbs. of sugar

2499 FAUĻU ފައުޅު See faaļu

2500 FAKIIRAA (-aaek) ފަކީރާ n. shovel or poker for the oven

2501 FAKIIRU ފަކީރު adj. poor (coll., fagiiru): miskitu fakiiru, holder of an office or post in the Friday mosque (cf. muskuļi takuru) [U. faqīr]

2502 FAKURU ފަކުރު n. disgust, shrinking : f. gannanii, feels disgust: rihaakuru deke fakuru ganna miihek, one who is disgusted by rihaakuru

2503 FAKUSA ފަކުސަ n.. worms

2504 FAKUSAMA ފަކުސަމަ n.. the west [H. paccham, Skt. paścima]

2505 FAKKAA ފައްކާ adj. quite ripe (of fruit); (met.) clever : fakkaa kujjek, a clever fellow: fakka vagek, a proper thief: fakkaa Nuubii baburek, a real African negro (slave): fakkaa ge, a fine modern (brick) house, 'bungalow' [H. pakkā, Skt. pakva]

2506 FAGA (anc. FAŇGA) ފަގަ (ފަނގަ) n. eye of needle

2507 FAGIIRU ފަގީރު adj. poor [coll. for fakiiru]

2508 FAGUḌI ފަގުޑި n. made-up turban (worn on cap, cf. fořaa) [H. pagṛī, Skt. prāk or parikara]

2509 FAŇGU ފަނގު n. In daňḍu-faňgu, grassy space [doublet]

2510 FACIS (PACIS) ފަޗިސް (ޕަޗިސް) n. a traditional game [H. pacīsī, from pacīs, 25]

2511 FAJRU ފަޖްރު n. first dawn: f. lum, f. laigatum, dawn appearing [U. fajr]

2512 FAṬAANII ފަޓާނީ n. gipsy traveller (in stories) [H. paṭhān]

2513 FAṬAAS ފަޓާސް n. fire-crackers [cf. H. paṭākā]

2514 FAṬṬA(VA)NII ފައްޓާނީ (ފައްޓަވާނީ) v. causes to begin (v.n. feṭṭum, feṭṭevum) (caus. or hon. of fařanii, also written fařṭavanii)

2515 FAṬṬARU ފައްޓަރު n. metal belt, chain worn round the waist with pendants (silver for boys, gold for girls): karu f., neckchain: faṭṭaru-bai, ladies' large neck chain (formal dress); f. aḷanii, wears chain [fař]

2516 FAṬṬAA (-aaek) ފައްޓާ n. official sash [fař]

2517 FAṬLUUNU ފަޓްލޫނު n. trousers: f. buri, shorts [H. pāṭlūn, E. pantaloon]

2518 FAḌA ފަޑަ n. moisture from the vagina

2519 FAḌI ފަޑި n. wooden railings (on boat or bed)

2520 FAḌIT ފަޑިތް n. one of the old kangati officials

2521 FAḌUKKA ފަޑުއްކަ n. In f. hañḍuu, rice spilt on the floor

2522 FAŇḌIYAARU ފަނޑިޔާރު n. judge: Uttama f., chief justice of the Maldives: f. manikufaanu, the chief justice: Fañḍiyaaru-ge, Ministry of Justice [?Skt. paṇḍitakāra]

2523 FAŇḌIHI (fañḍissek) ފަނޑިހި n. coconut tree which cannot be classified

2524 FAŇḌU ފަނޑު adj. pale, faded, faint (in colour): f. duvahek, a grey day; f. vanii, burns low, fades [S. pañḍu, Skt. pāṇḍu]

2525 FAT ފަތް n. leaf : naaibu f., credentials: gootigootiige f., land registration: fat liyaa manikufaanu,the royal scribe: fat jahanii, folds (tr.); fat jihi goñḍi, deckchair; fat jehi eňdu, folding bed, cot: defatař keňḍenii, havers: fat-keyo (-keelek), ripe bananas: fat-koḷu, official document (also handful of leaves): fat-tuura, royal writ ; fattuura hinganii, sends a royal writ; fattuura fooraa hisaabu, area affected by writ: fat-fuř, page, one side of leaf: fat-foři, central beams: fat-pilaa-veli(-veyyek), medicinal leaves; greens: fat-vaḷu, place where leaf is attached to tree: amaazu fat-gaňḍu, target; fatun fat faḷaa, fatun gas faḷaa, a plant, kalanchoe pinnata: fatu fehi, dark green [S. pat, Skt. patra]

2526 FATAŇGU ފަތަނގު n. a medicinal shrub, caesalpinia pulcherrima [S. patangi]

2527 FATANII ފަތަނީ v. swims (v.n. fetum): fataařai fiinan danna kujjek, a lad who can swim and dive; see also fetenii

2528 FATAFOḶI ފަތަފޮޅި n. 1. kind of pancake (mas f., bis f.): (met.)havaru boḍu fatafoḷi, 'people's pancake', i.e. notorious courtesan

2. kind of mat (boḍu fatafoḷi kunaa)

2529 FATARAASII ފަތަރާސީ adj. fussy, 'wet' : at f. kuranii, waves arms about

2530 FATAVERI ފަތަވެރި n. a particular plank in a dhoni

2531 FATAHA KURANII ފަތަހަ ކުރަނީ v. is victorious, succeeds [U. fath]

2532 FATAA (fataaek) ފަތާ 1. n. kind of bait fish, cardinal fish, archamia

2. adj. flat [S. pätali, ?Skt. patrala]

2533 FATI (faccek) ފަތި n. strip, row: jooli-fati, row of string seats: dida-fati damanii, strings up rows of flags: niya-fati, finger nails: fuuṭu-fati, footrule: feeli-fati damanii, spreads out rows of feeli:: bok-fati, frogspawn: mas-fati, bunch of caught fish; row of fish spitted on an eakel: maa-fati, garland: ruk-fati, row of coconut trees: ruku fati, strip of cadjan: libaahu fati, seam of libaas : vaḍi-fati, setsquare; faccakař, in line :

fati kuranii, (of metals) flattens: fatii lanii, ties together in a row;

fati-koḷu, ornamental strip of wood: fati-gaňḍu, strip (raha f., spirit level: fati-varu amunanii, makes constant criticisms; fuuṭu f., ruler): fatigaňḍu nagaa munḍu, oldfashioned sarong with pleat in front: fatigaňḍu jahanii, plays kind of castanet: fati-fuř, wrong side (inside) of cloth; fatifuřun, inside out; (met.) miihunge fatifuř kiyum, telling the inside story: fati-roňḍu, file-fish [S. pet, Skt. pankti]

2534 FATIS (fatihu) ފަތިސް n. early morning, before dawn: (ree) fatihu, fatihaa, in the early morning: fatihu-fatihaa, before dawn [P. paccūsa, Skt. pratyūṣa-]

2535 FATURANII ފަތުރަނީ v. spreads(tr.) (v.n. feturum); spreads a mat : tanmati f., spreads bedding (on a boat); see also feturenii [S. patur(uv)anne, P. pattharati]

2536 FATURU ފަތުރު n. in daturu- faturu, journeys (doublet)

2537 FATUVAA ފަތުވާ n. religious decisions : f. denii, expounds decisions [U. fatvā]

2538 FATOḶU ފަތޮޅު n. joints in timber

2539 FATTANII ފައްތަނީ v. sinks (tr.) (v.n. fettum) : kaňḍu fattanii, sinks in the sea; makes to fit (in carpentry): gaňdu f., fixes a patch; (met.) implicates, involves (tr.): aharen fattaan nuuḷeeřee, don't try to involve me! fattaala, fattaala, sit down, do! (on a mat) : nufetteene, it can't be got to fit (invol.) (caus. of fatanii)

2540 FATTARU ފައްތަރު n. overlap: naazuku fattaru, a delicate balance

2541 FATTIYAA (fattiyalek) ފައްތިޔާ n. permanent mooring in harbour (also hattiyaa, non-Male usage)

2542 FATTU ފައްތު n. (anc.) stern of boat

2543 FATPILAAVELI(-veyyek) ފަތްޕިލާވެލި n. See fat-

2544 FAT-MINI ފަތްމިނި n. 1. kind of dragonfly 2. magic woman, siren [Skt. padminī]

2545 FADA ފަދަ n. manner: e-fada miihek, that sort of person: mi-fada kamek, this kind of activity: hama mifadain, in this same manner: miok fada, of this kind: ehen kamtakuge-ekee ekfadain, as in other matters; after participles : haňdumafuḷu hunnaanee fadain, as you will remember (hon.): hit hama jehee fada gotekgai, in a consoling manner: duniye nudekee fada haňguraamaek, a war such as the world had never seen before; ifc. in doublet gada-fada, strong

2546 FAN ފަން n. 1. coconut foliage; cadjan: fanek, section of cadjan: gaňḍu-fan, kind of cadjan used for roofing; fanaai daňḍi, cadjan and sticks: fanun aḷaafaa, using thatch; fan-gaňḍu, woven section of cadjan (with three ropes) for roofing or fencing: fan-ge, thatched house (as v. fakkaa ge): fan-toři, stem of whole coconut leaf (used for fencing); fantoři-daḷu, set of imported decorated cane boxes: fan-buḍu, fantoři-buḍu, base of stem of coconut branch (used as fuel): fan-boňḍi, bundle of sections (usually four) of cadjan: fan bolek, (a head of) straight hair: fan-vat, coconut palm leaflet; fanvat aḷanii, wears strip of fanvat as a charm; fanvatu jahanii, ties a leaf on, registers (of trees: also of people): fan-haa mas, kind of fighting fish, lionfish, scorpionfish: fan-hibaru (fangaňḍu hibaru), kind of swordfish, sailfish, istiophorus
[S. pan-, Skt. parṇa]
2. an old game usually played by women (fan kuḷenii)

2547 FANAI ފަނައި See fanaa

2548 FANARA ފަނަރަ num. fifteen: f. vilee ree, the eve of the 15th day of the moon; fanara-vanarakař, about fifteen [old S. paṇara, Pkt. paṇṇaraha, H. pandrah]

2549 FANAS ފަނަސް num. (anc.) 48 (mod. saaḷiis-ař-) [S. panas,

P. paññāsa, 50]

2550 FANAA (FANAI) ފަނާ (ފަނައި) n. stone anchor (fanaa gaa): f. jassanii, casts anchor

2551 FANAA VANII ފަނާވަނީ v. crumbles away: fanaa ve danii, perishes (in a disaster) [U. fanā, decay]

2552 FANI ފަނި n. 1. worms; larvae: fani-fakusa, all kinds of worms: lee boo f., leech: katuru f., white ant: eenaa fani vefai, he has got worms; fanii bees, medicine against worms ; fani-hañdi, kind of lagoon fish or 'jack', caranx [S. paṇu, Skt. prāṇaka]

2553 FANI (fanñek) ފަނި n. 2. syrup (often ifc., luñboo- f., kařikeelu-f., faḷoo-f., feeru-f., donkeyo-f., syrup of lime, screwpine, papaw, guava, banana): fani hevaa, white of young coconuts); f. aḷanii, produces juice (of decaying vegetable matter); fani(y)aaram, kind of sweet cake [S. päṇi, Skt. phāṇita]

2554 FANKAA ފަންކާ n. fan : boḍu f., punkah: eñburee f., revolving fan: fankaa ruk, fan palm, palmyrah; fankaa kuranii, fans (v.) [H. pankhā, ?Skt. pakṣaka]

2555 FANGI ފަންގި n. specially woven palm-thatch or cadjan (as v. tořali)

2556 FANGI-FILAA ފަންގިފިލާ n. ceiling

2557 FANḌITA ފަންޑިތަ n. good magic (as v. sihuru): f. hadaa miihun, those who practise magic [Skt. paṇḍita, learned man]

2558 FANTI ފަންތި n. class [S. panti, Skt. Paṅkti]

2559 FANNU ފަންނު n. arts and crafts: kurehumuge fannugai moḷu, skilled at drawing [U. fann]

2560 FANVARU ފަންވަރު n. level of strength, tension, temperedness; f. gada (of children), out of control [S. pannara]

2561 FANSA- ފަންސަ- num. ibc., plus five (in compound numbers): fansatiriis, 35 (= tiriis fahek): fansayaaḷiis, 45 (= saaḷiis fahek): fansayaanavai, 95 (=nuvadiha fahek): fansayaahi, 85 (= ar̃ḍiha fahek): fansavanna, 55 (= fansaas fahek): fansaviis, 25: fansahaṭṭi, 65 (= fasdoḷas fahek): fansahattari,75 (= hatdiha fahek)
[cf. H. paiṅtīs, paiṅtālīs, pañcānve, pañcāsī, pañcāvan, paccīs, paiṅsaṭh, pac-hattar]

2562 FANSAAN ފަންސާން num. times five (in Navata multiplication tables: tin fansaan, 3 x 5)

2563 FANSAAS ފަންސާސް num. 50: fansaahakar̃, about 5O
[H. pacās, cf. S. panas]

2564 FANSURU ފަންސުރު n. pencil: f. jahaa eti, pencil-sharpener [E. pencil]

2565 FAN-HAA ފަންހާ See fan

2566 FARAGU ފަރަގު n. measurable difference (as v. tafaatu) [U. farq]

2567 FARANJII (pl., Faranjiin) ފަރަންޖީ n. white foreigner : faranjii karudaas, foreign (i.e. old) newspapers [S. Parangi,'Portuguese', U. Farangī, E.'Frank']

2568 FARANSAA ފަރަންސާ n. plank projecting over side of boat

2569 FARANSEESI (vilaatu) ފަރަންސޭސި n. France; French [U. Frānsīsī]

2570 FARAA (-aayek) ފަރާ n. 25 'measures' [T. paṟai]

2571 FARAAT (hon., faraatpuḷu) ފަރާތް n . side; (met., of people), party: hingaa faraat, those in charge: anek f.,the other end,the back: bitdor̃u f., side (of bed) nearest the wall: magatu f., side (of bed) away from wall: faraatfaraat(ar̃) nubalaa, not looking from side to side: furagas faraatu bali, piles: e-faraatar̃ danii, goes out of sight: ha-faraat, all (lit. six) directions: e-miihunge faraatun, on the part of those people, by them
[? cf. S. pätta and Skt. pārśva]

2572 FARI ފަރި adj. young and beautiful; blooming:
f. kuranii, preens oneself (esp. of cocks before hens); fari haalek, a cock when puffed up; fari (kuraa) miihek, one who dresses for effect:
fari malek, a flower about to open; foḷeen fari vefai, just about to open; fari ve foḷenii, is just in bloom; (met., of people), looks cheerful [? U. parī, fairylike]

2573 FARI(I)KKUḶUVANII ފަރިއްކުޅުވަނީ (ފަރިއްކުޅުވަނީ) v. eats (grade 1 honorific)

2574 FARI(I)KKOḶU ފަރިއްކޮޅު (ފަރިއްކޮޅު) n. dinner (grade 1 honorific): f. bahaṭṭaa miihaa, servant who lays the table for grade 1 meals

2575 FARITA ފަރިތަ adj. fluent, clever (at.., dat. or inf.): f. kuranii, trains, practises at; rukař araalek farita kamee! how cleverly (he) climbs the tree; f. vanii, is close friends (with.., ..-aa): deke farita, known by sight [cf. S. purudu, accustomed]

2576 FARIVAḶU ފަރިވަޅު n. feast given on special occasions

2577 FARIHI (farissek) ފަރިހި n. popular song, love song: kii hai ḷem vii farissařee, every recited poem changed to a croon, i.e. everything went flop

2578 FARIIK- ފަރީއް- See farik-

2579 FARU ފަރު 1. n. reef : farumaccař aranii, goes aground on reef: farař erenii, farař danii, climbs on to reef: faru hilanii, collects cowries from reef at low tide: faru matin danii / araniii, gets round end of reef ; faru dařun danii, gets through reef to windward;

faru-toḷi, saw-fish: faru-foi diya(varu), times of low tides: faru-mas, 'reef fish', a class of fish (generally thought too smelly for eating except on Fridays): faru-vas, smell of the reef or of reef-fish: faru-veri (pl., faruverin), 'reef-man', i.e. collector of cowries: faru-haki, scallop (on undried coral) [S. (gal)para]

2580 FARU ފަރު 2. In faru jehenii, v. just manages: nuhiňgaa faru jehidaane, will manage to avoid walking: miaa nulai faraku nujeheene, can't do without this: mi faisain faru jehee too balaa, try to manage on this money

2581 FARUGADI ފަރުގަދި n. name of two compass directions: f. astamaanu, north by west: f. iiraan, north by east [U. farqadān]

2582 FARUGAALU ފަރުގާލު n. compasses [U. parkāl]

2583 FARUJU ފަރުޖު n. vagina [U. farj]

2584 FARUDAA ފަރުދާ n. curtain [U. parda]

2585 FARUDAA-BAGIICAA ފަރުދާބަގީޗާ n . kind of (curtain-like) tree, polyscias guilfoylei

2586 FARUBADA ފަރުބަދަ n. hills, mountains [S. paruvata, Skt. parvata]

2587 FARUMAA ފަރުމާ n. paper pattern [U. farmā, proofsheet, cf. E. pro forma]

2588 FARUMAANU ފަރުމާނު n. yard-arm [U. parvān]

2589 FARUMEEṬU ފަރުމީޓު n. (anc.) Permit Office, Customs [E. permit]

2590 FARUVAA (faruvaalek) ފަރުވާ n. care : f. kuḍa, careless: faruvaa netee, I don't care: faruvaa-teri, attentive: f. kuranii, gives care [U. parvā]

2591 FALA ފަލަ adj. fat, plump (also of trees): fala loki, very fat: fala masgaňḍu, thigh: f. roonu, thick grade of rope

2592 FALAKU ފަލަކު n. the firmament, solar system [U. falak]

2593 FALAŇGU ފަލަނގު n. bedding: f. feeli, bedspread [?Skt. palyanka]

2594 FALA-MAḌI ފަލަމަޑި n. root crops (tubers, yams, etc.)

2595 FALI (fayyek) ފަލި n. oar : f.-tanḍu, handle of oar: fali-duu, blade of oar: f. anbaa, rowing shanties: f. jahanii, rows (tr.): f. baalanii, uses the oars [S. palu-pat, ? P. phala, blade]

2596 FALIDA ފަލިދަ n. kind of sweetmeat (see naaruku)

2597 FALIITAA ފަލީތާ n . fuse(for guns):touchpaper : f. lanii, sets fuse; (met.) leaves something in a house as an excuse for calling again [U. falīta]

2598 FALUKAA ފަލުކާ n. hatch of a ship: f. jahanii, closes hatch [U. fālke]

2599 FALUUDAA ފަލޫދާ n. kind of sweetmeat [Persian, falūdāj]

2600 FALLAVA ފަލްލަވަ n. store-room: mas f. (for drying fish), uva f. (for storing lime); mas fallava-ař aḷanii, puts fish into store: mas fallava jahanii, stacks fish (in store), salts fish: f. kuranii, works in fish-store: f. jahanii, builds a store

2601 FALSAFAA ފަލްސަފާ n. philosophy: falsafaa-veri, philosopher [U. falsafa, Gk. philosoph-]

2602 FAVANII ފަވަނީ v. touches up, darkens (a line), colours (a drawing, kurehumgaňḍu f.), goes over a tracing; dyes in a vat (v.n.fevum)

2603 FAVVAARAA(-aaek) ފައްވާރާ n. fountain (formerly in Maizaange) [U. favvāra]

2604 FAS (fahek) ފަސް 1. num. five (in Navata tables also faas): fas iha, five bunches: fas oř, game of marbles: fas gaḍi bai, 5.30: fas tan(un) banum, tying up a corpse in five places: fas-doḷas, 60: fas-fiya maa (fassiya-maa), five- pointed star, the Seal of Solomon: fas maamugulu fas vagun, captains of teams in old games: fas mudim beekalun, the five former mosque officials in Male ('virgers'): fas rukun, the five pillars of Islam: fas qavaaidu, fas maigaňḍu viya, the five basic arithmetical operations (see viya): fas vagutu, the five times for prayer: fas-vana, fifth: fas-saňgu, the five medicinal parts of a tree: fas- sateeka, 500: fassiya-maa, see fas-fiya maa (above): fassihi (fassissek), 24 (anc..) [S. pasvisi, 25],used in selling duodecimally; fassissakař aňbu, about two dozen mangoes: fas-haas, 5000 [S. pas, Skt. pañca]

2605 FAS (fahek) ފަސް 2. n. earth, soil: f. aḷanii, f. jahanii, scatters earth: kaḷu fas, dark soil: kilaa fas, dust: don fas, builder's sand; fas-gaňḍu, earth; arena, public area: fasgaňḍu jahanii, prepares arena: guḷa kuḷee fasgaňḍu, ceremonial open space in front of the former royal palace: fas-daanu, grave; fasdaanu lanii, buries (hon., cf. vaḷu lanii): fasdaanu(gai) vaḍuvanii, buries (high hon.) : fas baaḍi jahanii, mucks up the ground, makes a mess; (met.) haňdaantakař fas eḷemun, memories being buried
[S. pas, Skt. pāṃśu]

2606 FAS (fahek) ފަސް 3. n. back end, behind: enme fahaa hama-ař, to the very end; duvaskoḷekge fas, after some time, some time after; fahakař ais, recently: fas kuranii, postpones; transmits: fas vanii, is postponed; is late: buddi fas vanii, loses one's head (met.): fas balanii, looks back (also met.): fas jehenii, is hesitant ; fas-kani, portion of a sail or a particular rope: dari fas-koḷu, generation: fas-bai, bottom hem, skirts (of coat or shirt); fasbai maḷanii, turns up the hem: Fas-baduruva, asterism Uttarabhadrapadā; lahek fahek, delay [doublet];

fahat(u), behind, the place behind: fahat balanii, looks back: fahatař jehenii, steps back: reehun / reehugai fahatař danii, comes last in the race: eenaa(ge) fahatun (hon., fahat-puḷun) diyum, following behind him;

fahu, after: eař fahu, after that: enme fahu, the last: fahu haftaa, previous week: fahu vagutu, last hours: daadi fahakaa jehen den, until very recently: miige fahař, ever after; fahu-koḷu, last part (e.g. of life, of month): fahun (adv.), afterwards; enme fahun, at the last: varař fahun, very recently: fahun aadee, come afterwards! [S. pasu, Skt. paścāt]

2607 FASAADA ފަސާދަ n. rebellion, rebelliousness, underhandedness: fasaada vanii, is rebellious: fituna- fasaada, riots: fasaadaveri, rebellious [U. fasād]

2608 FASINJARUN ފަސިންޖަރުން n. (pl.) passengers [E. passenger]

2609 FASULU ފަސުލު n. chapter of a book; standard(in school) [U. fasl, section]

2610 FASEEHA ފަސީހަ adj. easy, comfortable; recovering, better : kam kuran faseeha vagutek, a good time for taking action; bali faseeha vanii, the disease is getting better: miinaa balin f. vanii, he is recovering from the disease: faseeha nukurevee bayyek, an incurable disease; miinaage kibain faseehaek vee, help is received from him; kam faseeha, careless, slapdash: hit faseeha, convenient (of house, island); hit faseeha vaa kamek, something which gives one pleasure

adv., faseehain, faseeha(ek) koř, easily [cf. S. pahasu, Skt. phāsu-]

2611 FASSANII ފައްސަނީ v. 1. chases away, scares away (v.n. fessum:: hon. fassavanii): eeňda kaaḷu fassaala balaařeve, chase that crow away ! See also fessenii (caus. of fahanii 1)

2. causes to sew (caus. of fahanii 2)

2612 FASSIHA (FASSIA) ފައްސިހަ (ފައްސިއަ) n. following or favourable wind: fassiha-ař danii, runs before the wind: fassia kuranii, turns (boat) into the wind

2613 FAHAIRI ފަހައިރި See fahaveri

2614 FAHANA AḶANII, FAHANAḶANII ފަހަނަ އަޅަނީ - ފަހަނަޅަނީ v. passes by: Aarař fahanaḷaa hiňgajje, (he) has passed by Aarař island: namaadu vagutu fahanaḷaa hiňgajje, has passed over prayer-time; fahanaḷaa daa (gram.), transitive [fas 3; perhaps old S. pahaneḷu-]

2615 FAHANII ފަހަނީ v. 1. chases away, runs after (v.n.fehum): buḷaa miidaa fahaiganegen gos, the cat chasing the rat [old S. √paha]

2. sews (v.n. fehum): fahaa foři, sewing machine: fahaa miihaa, tailor [cf.S. mahanne]

2616 FAHARI ފަހަރި n. See fahaveri

2617 FAHARU ފަހަރު n. 1. time (fois); turn; ek faharu, once: devana faharař, for the second time: baek faharař, sometimes: faharugai, faharekgai, perhaps: defaharekge matiin, twice [S. pāra, Skt. prahara]

2. ifc., pl. suffix used of seagoing vessels: dooni-faharu, dhonies: manavaru-faharu, men-of-war: ṭagu-faharu, tugs [S. pāru, boat]

3. eti-faharu, blows [S. pahara, Skt. prahāra]

2618 FAHARUVA ފަހަރުވަ n. urine (vulg.): f. lanii, urinates: tanmaccař faharuva levee kujjek, a child who wets his bed

2619 FAHAVERI (FAHAIRI, FAHARI) ފަހަވެރި (ފަހައިރި - ފަހަރި) n. sister- in-law: fahaveri daita, fahaveri kokko, wife of elder / younger brother (usually called just daita)

2620 FAHI (fassek) ފަހި adj. easy, desirable: kam fahi, efficient, successful: hit fahi, contented; fahi kuranii, clears the way, makes things easy

2621 FAHUMU ފަހުމު n. comprehension: f. vanii, is understood [U. fahm]

2622 FAHURU-VERI ފަހުރުވެރި adj. proud (of) [U. fakhr]

2623 FAHULAVAANU (pl., -un) ފަހުލަވާނު n . warrior hero

2624 FAHE ފަހެ exclamation of certainty or of indignation: aañ fahe, yes indeed! den fahe, but then, but don’t you realize

2625 FAŘ ފަށް n. strip; layer : aḍu- fař, babel of sounds: aḍu ivee fařugai, within earshot ; una- fař, sarong string; cloth belt (for bathing): ran fař, thin gold necklace, or strand of same: vaa -fař, bit of rope: rooli- fař, a bit of a breeze; stripe (military); fař huri miihun, NCOs: fař aranii, gets a stripe; tin fař vanii (of women), marries the same man three times in succession: fař kañḍanii, breaks the said succession (through medufiri); fař kuranii, repeats: (adv.) fařfařun, repeatedly ;

fař-gañḍu, high detachable side for boats: aḍu fařgañḍu, babel of sounds: fařṭaru, see faṭṭaru: fař-varu, medallion on neck- chain: fařu fuu (fulek), pendant below the medallion: fařu risseyo, kind of medicament [S. paṭi, Skt. paṭṭaka]

2626 FAŘAN ފަށަން n. keel : f. lanii, lays keel

2627 FAŘANII ފަށަނީ v. begins (tr.) (v.n. feřum : imp. fařaa! caus. faṭṭanii : hon. faṭṭavanii): aḷugañḍař fařaiganevunii, I began (invol.); see also feřenii [S. paṭan(gannavā), Skt. prasthāna]

2628 FAŘALA ފަށަލަ n. layer [S. paṭala]

2629 FAŘAVAAḶU ފަށަވާޅު n. royal tailor (fařavaalu koi)

2630 FAŘUI / FAŘUVI ފަށުއި / ފަށުވި n. silk (fařui foti): fařui-kam, (met.) ‘silkiness’ of language [S. paṭa, Skt. paṭṭa + ui, yarn]

2631 FAḶA-GAŇḌU ފަޅަގަނޑު n. nursery for young coconut trees

2632 FAḶANII ފަޅަނީ v. (v.n. feḷum) 1. chops, rips; (med.) operates: gas f., chops trees: daru f., chops firewood; loo f., operates on eyes: bañḍu f., operates on stomach 2. shoots up (intr.): of plants (gas faḷajje), children’s teeth (dat faḷaifi), hair (datdoḷin faḷaa istaři), warts (um f.); (met.) baḍi faḷaigen diyum, explosion of a gun: faḷaa aranii, secrets are revealed (eenaage sirrutak faḷaa araifi, his secrets were revealed: faḷaa eri ree, the night when the cat is out of the bag, when it all blows up);

Caus., ruk feḷuvum, propagating coconut trees ; see also feḷenii [S. paḷanne, Skt. sphaṭati, sphāḷayati]

2633 FAḶA-RUK ފަޅަރުކް n. very young coconut trees

2634 FAḶI ފަޅި n. sector, segment :

tirii f., nether part, matii f.,upper part (of millstones): rumaa- faḷi, woman's 'peak' (half-cap): hañdu- faḷi, crescent moon: faḷi as, slipknot: f. kufuraa, cut copra: faḷi daa, half-size net; de-faḷi kuranii, cuts in half [S. paḷu]

2635 FAḶU ފަޅު 1. n. shallow water : hudufaḷu, sandy shallows: faḷu-tere, inner harbour at Male: faḷu-matii, in the inner harbour: faḷu oḍifaharu, ships in harbour: faḷu-verin (pl.), naval crew

2. adj. unoccupied, bare: faḷu-rař, uninhabited island: Dañgetii faḷu, jungle on island of Dañgeti ; (met.) faḷu filanii, removes the bareness, occupies: ge faḷu filajje, the house was occupied: jalsaa faḷu filuvai devvanii, graces the occasion (hon.): enme faḷu filuvaigen diya sababek, cause of creating a nice atmosphere (lit., occupying empty place)

2636 FAḶEE ފަޅީ n. in haḷee faḷee, confused noise (doublet) [haḷee]

2637 FAḶOO (faḷolek) ފަޅޯ n. papaw fruit, carica papaya:

veyo f., kind of papaw with long stalk: faḷolu asaara, papaw pickle: faḷoo- gahu ibiliis, kind of ugly humming insect found on papaw trees: faḷoo-faḷa, papaws and the like: faḷoo-faḷi, slice of papaw; faḷoo boo kuranii, thickens papaw by cooking in sugar [S. päpol]

2638 FAḶḶI ފަޅްޅި n. temple, church [S. & T. paḷḷi]

2639 FAA, FAU (falek) ފާ - ފައު n. 1. swampy place where mangroves etc. grow (kañḍuu f., kuḷḷavak f.): dañḍi f., pond for seasoning wood: boñbi f., husking pond

2. (in counting cowries) 8 hiya (=768)

3. For fai in faa laa koḷu, foot of bed

adj. 4. very ripe (more than fakkaa, less than fii): faa kuranii, lets get soft (e.g.of coconut fibre, or buried breadfruit); (met.) delays, sits idle, waits; unloads onto someone (kamek mařař f. kuranii, unloads a job on to me), (hon.) faa kuravvanii, (of God) sends upon mortals; faa vanii, (pej.) pops up, arrives;

faa-roři, fauroři (-roṭṭek), kind of rusk: madu faaroři, rolls: haru f., rusks baked twice: faaroři-ge, bakery: faaroři uñdun, baking oven

2640 -FAA -ފާ suffix See -fai

2641 FAAITU ފާއިތު See veatu (veitu, veeti) [U. faut]

2642 FAAGA ފާގަ n. bitter gourd (momordica charantia)

2643 FAAGATI ފާގަތި adj. (literary) enterprising, prosperous

2644 FAAṬAA (-aaek) ފާޓާ n. small barrel or tin (used domestically for oil)

2645 FAAṬU ފާޓު n. woven width of cloth: fanara faaṭuge riyaa, sail of 15 strips: faaṭu fuḷaa foti, cloth of wide strips: faaṭu hani foti, cloth of narrow strips [H. pāṭ]

2646 FAAḌAVAARI ފާޑަވާރި adj. f. vanii, is frustrated and idle

2647 FAAḌU ފާޑު n. type, character : maḍumaitiri faaḍu jahaa, who looks like being a quiet person; eii eenaage mammage ves faaḍu, that is her mother's character too: faaḍekge miihek, an odd chap: faaḍu faaḍun javaabu kuranii, (pej.)talks a lot of nonsense: faaḍakař iňdefai, acting strangely: miihakař faaḍakař hit kiyaafai, rather fancied a girl: meař ves faaḍekge gotek vefaa, and I have something wrong with my chest; f. kiyanii, criticizes (with dat. of object); faaḍu-veriyaa, artistic person; planner, designer

2648 FAATIHA ފާތިހަ n. prayers for the dead: f. kiyavanii, recites fatiha [U. fāṯiha]

2649 FAATUN ފާތުން n. Maldivian form of the name Faaṯima

2650 FAATURAA ފާތުރާ n. presence (high hon.): radunge (hiriyaa) faaturaa(ge) dařař, into the King's presence

2651 FAADIPPOḶU, FAADIFFUḶU ފާދިއްޕޮޅު - ފާދިއްފުޅު n. name of Ḷ atoll

2652 FAADIRII (pl.-iin) ފާދިރީ n. priest (f.- kaleege) [S. pādiri, Port. padre]

2653 FAADDANII ފާއްދަނީ v. penetrates, seeps through (of liquids, or light) (v.n. feeddum): furaaḷun fen faadaeve, the roof leaks ; see also feedenii)

2654 FAAN ފާން adj. crystal clear: faan-teyo, clarified oil [S. pahan, Skt. prasanna]

2655 FAANA ފާނަ n. kinds of reef fish, tripletail (lobotes) and grouper

2656 FAANABASAŇDU, FAANABASANDU ފާނަބަސަނދު - ފާނަބަސަންދު n. chickenpox

2657 FAANAVELAA ފާނަވެލާ n. iron used as a medicament

2658 -FAANU (pl., -faanun) -ފާނު nominal honorific suffix : rasge-faanu, King:

kilege-faanu, high rank of nobleman; also used after proper names in form -gefaanu: : Nuu-gefaanu, Noah [S. pāṇan, Skt. pāda-]

2659 FAANUUZU ފާނޫޒު n. hurricane lamp [U. fānūs, Gk. pharos]

2660 -FAANE ފާނެ - Verbal suffixes used after absolutives to denote future possibility: ma ves gosfaanam, I might go too [see - fai]

2661 FAANTILA ފާންތިލަ n . heavy shovel

2662 FAAFA ފާފަ n. sin: faafa-veriin, sinners: faafaveri-kam, sinfulness: budu hedi faafa, the sin of making an image [S. & Skt. pāpa]

2663 FAAFU ފާފު n. the letter F in the Arabic and Maldivian alphabets: Faafu atoḷu, the northern part of Nilande atoll

2664 FAAMUDEERI ފާމުދޭރި For faamuladeeri

2665 FAAMULADEERI ފާމުލަދޭރި n. an old Maldivian title : F. kilegefaanu (pl., F. beekalun), one of the highest Maldivian titles [S. pāmul-]

2666 FAARA ފާރަ n. spying, watching: f. lanii, keeps a watch (on.., dat.): faara-aŕ iňdefai, sitting down to watch: faara-veri, a spy

2667 FAARISII ފާރިސީ adj. Persian : Faaris kara, Iran

2668 FAARU, FAURU ފާރު - ފައުރު n. 1. wall (external): mai-faaru, the old town wall of Male: loo-faaru, the wall round the universe: faaru-gaňḍu, an old wall; faaraa laa, against the wall [S. pavuru, Skt. prākāra]

2. wound: faaru-koḷu, slight wound: faaru-gaňḍu, larger wound; faaru vanii, is wounded

2669 FAALABBA, FAILABBA ފާލަބްބަ - ފައިލަބްބަ n. glebe (goi faalabba): raŕekge f. liyuvvanii, rents a glebe island from the government: liye deven huri faalabbaek, a glebe to let

2670 FAALAM ފާލަމް n. jetty; bridge(in foreign countries) [S . & T. pālam, bridge]

2671 FAALIKII ފާލިކީ n. palanquin (in stories) [H. pālkī, Skt. paryaṁkikā]

2672 FAALIIS ފާލީސް n. varnish (made of meths and lacquer): f. kuranii, varnishes [E. polish]

2673 FAALU ފާލު n. 1. divination, magic; kamtakař f. balanii, practises clairvoyance: hurihaa sirrek eenaage faalař araifiyoolaeve, I believe he knew all the secrets [U. fāl]

2. freewheel (on bịcycle or drill); faalař aruvanii, gets into gear again: faalun neṭṭijje, got into freewheel: (met.) magee faalakař e miihaa neeři, I couldn't get an answer from him: gaḍi faalun neṭṭijje, the clock has gone all haywire: miihaa eenaage faalař araifi, he suits the man's description : faalu aḷanii, stops something working [A. fallu, notch]

2674 FAAS (faahek) ފާސް n. pass; permission : imtiẖaanakun faas vanii, passes an exam.: faas kuranii, passes someone (e.g.at Customs), approves: faas kuri hedum, officially approved dress for women (also called nambaru hedum) [E. pass]

2675 FAASIDU ފާސިދު adj. sinful, corrupt [U. fāsid]

2676 FAAZIL ފާޟިލް n. Mr (al- faazil, also pronounced faaḷil) [U. faaźil]

2677 FAAHAGA ފާހަގަ n . marker: f. kuranii, points out, marks, keeps an eye on: (enlarged, invol.) faahaga koř-leveene, should be noticed

2678 FAAKHAANAA ފާޚާނާ n. the privy [U. pā- khāna]

2679 FAAHI ފާހި n. loop: f. lanii, makes a loop

2680 FAAHITI ފާހިތި num. 72 (used in counting fish) [cf. old S.pas-hättä, 75]

2681 FAAŘANAA ފާރަނާ n . an old Maldivian title: F. kilegefaanu, one of the highest Maldivian titles

2682 FAAḶA ފާޅަ n. 1. areca-palm spathe (used as lining for storage bowls)

2. ifc., creeper (tiri-faaḷa, maa-faaḷa, gadabim-faaḷa)

2683 FAAḶU, FAUḶU ފާޅު - ފައުޅު adj. publicized: fauḷaai sirrugai,in public and in private; f. kuranii, publishes, declares [S. pahaḷa, Skt. prakaṭa]

2684 -FI ފި - verbal suffix, used after absolutives in past tenses: gosfi, went [S. -pi; see -fai]

2685 FIAFAAḶI ފިއަފާޅި See fiyafaaḷi

2686 FIKURAA VANII ފިކުރާ ވަނީ v. likes, yearns for (usu. of people, with -aa): eena-aa ma varař fikuraa ve-ee, I am much in love with her (coll., hitaa vanii) [fikuru]

2687 FIKURU ފިކުރު n.. thought: worry : tiya kamaa fikuru kuranii, thinks or worries about that: f. boḍu vanii, is panic-stricken [U. fikr]

2688 FIŇḌI ފިނޑި adj. timid

2689 FIT ފިތް n. 1. gall-bladder : fit-diya, bile; (met.) section of orange('pig'); bladder of football; fit kaňḍaigen danii, is very frightened: birun fit keňḍijje, was very frightened
2. large red pustule (fit-gaňḍu) [S. pit, Skt. pitta, bile]

2690 FIT-DAALI ފިތްދާލި n. a medicinal wood, pterocarpus santalinus

2691 FITANII ފިތަނީ v. squeezes : (invol.) fiti baaru vegen, being squeezed tight, jammed

2692 FITUNA ފިތުނަ n. hatred and malice, dissension; fituna fasaada, riots: fituna-veri, riotous [U. fitna]

2693 FITURU ފިތުރު n. Fituru Iidu, the festival of 'Īdu'l fitr : f. zakaat, obligatory alms given on this occasion: f. denii, gives the obligatory alms [U. fitr, breaking fast]

2694 FITUROONU ފިތުރޫނު n. kind of tree, casuarina equisetifolia

2695 FITTANII ފިއްތަނީ v. squeezes, pushes, jostles: fittaa goř, press-studs: fittum (v.n.), pressure; (met.) iqtisaadii gotun fitti kamugaa viyas, although they were economically oppressed (caus. of fitanii)

2696 FIŇDANA (FIŇDANU) ފިނދަނަ - ފިނދަނު n. kind of small bird, dipper

2697 FIŇDANII ފިނދަނީ v. fluffs up (mattresses etc.)

2698 FIŇDANU ފިނދަނު See fiňdana

2699 FIŇDU ފިނދު n. anus (fiňdu-mati): fiňdu-masgaňḍu, buttocks [H. pendā]

2700 FIŇDU-FAT ފިނޑުފަތް n. tail (of bird, or areroplane) [S. peňda]

2701 FINI (fiññek) ފިނި adj. cool, cold: fini eccek, cool drink: as noun, dew: eenaage meegai fini hifanii, he is catching a chest cold: aharen fini vejje, I feel cold: haviiru finňař, for a cool evening stroll: fini faibanii, dew descends: f. kořlanii, gets cool: (met.) hitař finikam libijje, felt relieved [S. pini, dew]

2702 FINI-FEN ފިނިފެން n. rosewater (for cooking): finifen-maa, rose: finifen jambu, a particular kind of jambu fruit

2703 FINI-HAK ފިނިހަކް n. snail: raajje f., Divehi f., local variety of snail: boḍu f., a larger variety, introduced from Ceylon

2704 FINOĻU ފިނޮޅު n. sandbank with vegetation

2705 FIN-DAŇḌI ފިންދަނޑި n. tool for cleaning toddy-pots

2706 FIYA ފިޔަ n. wing; petal: fiya-fat, wing; propeller blade; fan blade: fiya jahanii, twinkles: es-fiya, eyelash; esfiya jahanii, blinks; fas fiya malař koři fook, a chew cut like a 5-pointed star [S. piyā(pat), Skt. patatra]

2707 FIYAN ފިޔަން n. lid for pans (usually wooden): f. jahanii, puts the lid on [S. piyan, Skt. pidhāna]

2708 FIYAFAAĻI (FIAFAAĻI) ފިޔަފާޅި (ފިއަފާޅި) n. small temporary hut or shed: beru f., hut for practising drumming in

2709 FIYARI ފިޔަރި n. board used in rope-making

2710 FIYALA ފިޔަލަ n. kind of fish, dolphinfish, coryphaena

2711 FIYAVAI ފިޔަވައި v. except, besides (used postpositionally, like nuunii) [cf. S. piyā, having closed]

2712 FIYAVAĻU ފިޔަވަޅު n. footstep: halui fiyavaḷu matiigai, with quick footsteps: f. aḷanii, takes a step [cf. S. piya-vara]

2713 FIYAA (fiyalek, fiyaek) ފިޔާ n. onion, allium cepa: kudi f., small red onions: boḍu f., Bombay onions: hudu f.,white onions [U. piyāz]

2714 FIYAA-TOŘI ފިޔާތޮށި adj. pink colour ['onion peel']

2715 FIYAA-DAA ފިޔާދާ n. decorative bag of netted paper [‘onion net’]

2716 FIYOK ފިޔޮކް n. chicken: haa f., young cock: kukuḷu f., young hen: fiyok-kukuḷu, hen with chicks

2717 FIYOHI (fiyossek) ފިޔޮހި n. small knife: caaku f., pocket knife: tuni f., table knife: masdat f., sharks- tooth knife [S. pihiya]

2718 FIRI ފިރި n. male; husband (firi-miihaa): firi-kalun, husband (hon., grades 1 and 2: firi-kaukalun, husband (high hon.): vagu firi, paramour : demafirin, married couple [S. pirimi]

2719 FIRI-FURAA VANII ފިރިފުރާވަނީ v. reaches maturity (of both sexes) [cf. furaa-varu]

2720 FIRIHEN (pl., firihenun) ފިރިހެން n. male person: firihen hař̌i, penis [firi, adapted to anhen, woman]

2721 FIRUAUNU ފިރުއައުނު n. Pharaoh: firuaunuge mudaa, jellyfish [U. fir‘aun]

2722 FIRUKENII ފިރުކެނީ v. creeps, crawls : slips through: (enlarged, tr.) firukaa-lanii, passes rope etc. through something

2723 FIRUMANII ފިރުމަނީ v. strokes (lovingly): burikaři firumaan, to stroke the back: bolugai firumaalieve, stroked the head [S. pirimadinne, Skt. parimardatē]

2724 FIROOŘI (firooṭṭek) ފިރޯޅި n. spool for winding thread

2725 FILANII ފިލަނީ v. 1. lies hid (of animates), from.., dat. (imp. filaa ! hon. fillavanii, v.n. fillevum): aharen miotii eenaa-ař filaee, I am hidden from him; with abl., escapes: datitakun filum, escaping from troubles : filaigenek nude-ee, doesn’t vanish: (invol.) filenii, is able to hide, is forgotten: naanaafuḷu fillavanii, takes bath (high hon.): (caus.) filuvanii, fillanii, helps to hide or escape, hides people (tr.); erases (hon., filuvvanii): aḷugaňḍu hanḍi fillaifi, I lost my way (lit., a spirit concealed me): kuř filuvanii, erases errors: varubali f., rests: fuuhi f., whiles away the time;

2) is clear: filaifi too, is that clear? filaifi, I understand: oḷum filanii, gets cleared up; mi massalaa oḷum filum beenumee, this question must be solved: (caus.) clears up (tr.): oḷum filuvaa denii, explains the difficulty: dabaru filuvanii, clears away rust: toři filuvanii, rubs the skin off (of nuts or grain, as v. toři noḷanii) : boňbi filuvanii, husks coconuts: lakgaňḍu filuvaa bees, bleach; tuunu fili, sharpwitted

2726 FILAA ފިލާ n. 1. plank, board, esp. classroom sandboard (liyaa filaa): bitugai f. jahanii, fixes a shelf on the wall; filaa aḷanii, uses a sextant: mi eḷi filaa, the data on this sextant; filaa-gaňḍu, plank, board, esp. standing place for the keoḷu of a fishing boat (fen filaagaňḍu): coconut scraper: pastryboard (kuroḷi f.): mas liyaa f., board for slicing fish: viya f., arithmetical slate: bees filaagaňḍu, splint; bees filaagaňḍu aḷanii, prepares a splint: voŕu-filaa, voŕi-filaa, sandboard: mahaana- filaa, temporary headboard for a grave [Skt. phalaka]

2. ifo., ground stragglers (teyo-filaa, hunigoňdi-filaa, danda-filaa, fat-pilaa-veli) [S. palā, greens]

2727 FILAAVAḶU ފިލާވަޅު n. lesson: f. nagaa denii, gives out a lesson: f. naganii, repeats lesson after the teacher

2728 FILI (fiyyek) ފިލި n. 1. vowel-sign : akurugai f. jahanii, adds vowel signs to consonants: fili fot, alphabetical chart: fili kooḷi, rhyming syllable: ibi-fili, the sign for -i [S. pili]

2. metal band round hatchets, knives etc.

3. kind of tree; also its fruit (filigahugai aḷaa fili)

4.fili mas, fish prepared as bait

v. 5. concealed (p.p. of filanii): fiyyeve, 3rd s. (fili-eve)

2729 FILITU ފިލިތު n. flattened upper end of fishhook

2730 FILUŇDU ފިލުނދު adj. stale, 'off' (of rice or fish) [S. pilunu]

2731 FILOḶU ފިލޮޅު n. kinds of fish, snapper and emperor

2732 FILṬARU ފިލްޓަރު n. water filtering apparatus [E. filter]

2733 FILMU ފިލްމު n. film [E. film]

2734 FILLANII ފިއްލަނީ v. See filanii: naanee fillavanii (high hon.), takes bath

2735 FILLEYO, FILLEU ފިއްލެޔޮ - ފިއްލެއު n. oily fish scum

2736 FIS KURANII ފިސް ކުރަނީ v. crushes; fis (fis) vanii, is crushed [H. pīsnā]

2737 FISAARI ފިސާރި adv. very (in limited contexts): hama fisaari tedek mii, this is perfectly true: fisaari keri huregen, very confidently

2738 FISTOOLA ފިސްތޯލަ n. pistol: gayaŕ fistoola jahanii, shoots a pistol at (his) body [S. pistōla, Port. pistola]

2739 FISSAVANII ފިއްސަވަނީ v. scorches (hon. of fihanii)

2740 FIHAŇḌA ފިހަނޑަ n. a plant, ipomoea pescaprae

2741 FIHANII ފިހަނީ v. scorches, bakes (abs.fihe : impv. fihee ! hon.fissavanii): foḷi f., makes pancakes, goboḷi f., bakes eggs: mas f., barbecues fish; roři fihaa eti, pan for cooking crispcakes; (invol.) fihenii, gets burnt (of parts of the body, such as iňgili (fingers), duu (tongue), tala (mouth)); is grilled: nufihevigen, not getting properly cooked [S. pihanne, P. paccati]

2742 FIHAARA ފިހާރަ n. shop

2743 FIHI ފިހި n. 1. small brush: davaadu laa f., paintbrush: kurahaa f., paintbrush; fihi lanii, brushes: fihi-gaňḍu, brush, broom (for sweeping, or for cats to play with, or for cleaning guns)

2. stub (e.g. of chewing sugar, ukdaňḍi fihi): kuruňbaa f., cut-off portion of coconut husk

v. 3. being scorched (abs. of fihenii)

2744 FII ފީ n. 1. fee, rent, charge: f. dakkanii, pays fee: f. balaigannanii, accepts fee [E. fee]

2. rot: fii vanii, rots (intr.), goes bad (of solid inanimates, e.g. fruit, rice, flour, wood: cf. kuni vanii of meat, nubai vanii of liquids): fii jahanii, gets black spots, e.g. of faaroři , rice (handulugai fii jahaa) or clothing (fotiigai fii jahaa, gamiihugai fii jahaa): fii kuranii, gets eggs to hatch: fii hovanii, sorts out the rotten ones; fii kukulu, broody hen: fii fan, rotting thatch

2745 FIIKAḶAA ފީކަޅާ adj. funny, silly

2746 FIIKIRILI ފީކިރިލި n. a sea bird

2747 FIIKUDAANU ފީކުދާނު n. spittoon [H. pīkdān]

2748 FIIKOI, FIIKOOT ފީކޯޓް - ފީކޮއި n. hide and seek: f. kuḷenii, plays hide and seek [excl. shouted when you have hidden]

2749 FIITAA (-aaek) ފީތާ n. tape; wick of lamp; roll of film: fuuṭu fiitaa, tape-measure: fiitaa-fař, ribbon [Port. fita, cf.S. pītta]

2750 FIINANII ފީނަނީ v. dives [S. pīnanne, swims]

2751 -FIINAA (fiinaek) -ފީނާ n. See es-

2752 FIINI (fiinñek) ފީނި n. cluster (esp. of trees)

2753 FIIFAA (-aaek) ފީފާ n. cask [H. pīpā (S. pīppa), Port. pipa]

2754 FIIRU ފީރު n. file (instrument) : tin aři f., tinaři f., 3-sided file (for saws): faḷi f., semi-spherical file: miidaa naguu f., circular file: ham-fiiru, rasp : hoḷi f., semicircular file; fiiru-muraňga, a vegetable, sesbania grandiflora [S.pīra]

2755 FIIROOZU ފީރޫޒު n. turquoise [U. fīrōza]

2756 FUI ފުއި n. female pudenda [? cf. S. puk, anus]

2757 FUK ފުއް n. 1.floating wick: f. alanii, makes such a wick

2. tooth of a saw : f. aňburanii, sets saw; fuk gaat, small-toothed: fuk duru, large-toothed: fuk-kaři, small cold chisel

3. grain (in this sense confounded with fuř): fukufukun, in little bits; single cowrie (when playing ořvaḷu): fas fukař vaa kuḷigaňḍu, five-cowrie gambit: fasfuk boli, five cowries; fuk boḍu, lumpy (of rice, salt): fuk hima, fuk kudi, small-grained: fuk-lonu, imported rock salt

2758 FUṬUNI ފުޓުނި n . putty: f. aḷanii, spreads putty [E. putty]

2759 FUṬUBOOḶA ފުޓުބޯޅަ n. football (anc. faibooḷa) [E. football]

2760 FUṬṬARU ފުއްޓަރު See fuř-

2761 FUŇḌANII ފުނޑަނީ v. grinds up (wet on a board with rollingpin, as v. muguranii); (caus. fuňḍuvanii)

2762 FUŇḌUFUŇḌU KURANII ފުނޑުފުނޑު ކުރަނީ v. smashes: fuňḍufuňḍu vanii, is smashed up, crumbles away

2763 FUTU ފުތު n. son (mostly used in the South): ma-futu, my son (=ekoi) [S. put, putā, Skt. putra]

2764 FUDENII ފުދެނީ v. suffices; (of vows) is fulfilled, paid: hekkek kamugai nufudee too, isn't it evidence enough? edum nufudunii, wishes were not fulfilled: fudee varař, sufficiently

2765 FUDDANII ފުއްދަނީ v. satisfies (tr.); fulfils (vows, promises); pays (debts): edum fuddavai devvum, fulfilling (our) desires (hon., of God); Enlarged: den fuddaa-laanii, we'll make it do (caus. of fudenii)

2766 FUN ފުން adj. deep; as n.., deep place : fun min, depth; draught: adv. funař, deeply: (met.) f. maanaa, deep meaning; f. kuranii, refloats (tr.): fun-gaňḍu, deep part of the water; Boḍu Fungaňḍu, a deep place off the east side of Male

2767 FUNA ފުނަ n. 1. kind of tree, calophyllum inophyllum: also its nut (funa-oř); funa (gahu) oňu madu, string of these seeds on wire, used as a candle when camping [T. pu<u>nn</u>aı]

2. a kind of drum beat: funa-beru, drum used for this: funa jahanii, plays this drum-beat

2768 FUNAI ފުނައި See funaa

2769 FUNA-FATI ފުނަފަތި n. substance used as a chew on Minicoy

2770 FUNAFOŘI ފުނަފޮށި n. (obs.) outer skin of coconut flower, used as kindling

2771 FUNARU ފުނަރު n. anc. form for mod. hunaru, q.v.

2772 FUNAA, FUNAI (funalek, funaek) ފުނައި - ފުނާ n. comb: f. alanii, uses comb; funaa-gaňḍu, pennant on a boat; plume: funaagaňḍu duuni, jungle cock [S. panā]

2773 FUNI (funňek) ފުނި n . pile: f. jahanii, piles up (tr.): (met., of people) f. jehenii, pile up (intr.)

2774 FUNOOS ފުނޯސް n. asterism Punarvasu [S. punāvasa]

2775 FUNNA ފުންނަ n. kinds of small fish, blenny or goby

2776 FUNNAABU ފުންނާބު n. heel: f. feḷenii, heel is cracking

2777 -FUFUḶI -ފުފުޅި See vař-

2778 FUFUU (fufulek) ފުފޫ n. ' melon' , benincasa hispida: fufulu murubbaa, melon cake: fufuu haluvaa, a melon sweetmeat [S. puhul, ash-pumpkin]

2779 FUFENII ފުފެނީ v. is puffed up (caus. fuppanii): riyaa vayaa fufifai, riyaluge bañḍu fufifai, the sail is full of wind [S. pipenne, P. pupphati]

2780 FUFEE (fufe-ek) ފުފޭ n. shallow earthen pot (for heating spices)

2781 FUPPANII ފުއްފަނީ v. blows up (tr.); boils up (sugar): fuppi bat, rice beaten up with sugar: fuppi hakuru, beaten up sugar: fuppaafai huri, fuppum laafai huri, convex: koo fuppi, mumps; koo fuppi jehunu, got mumps: aḷugañḍuge mee fuppaa, I have indigestion: fuppaa mee, lungs: fuppaa ham, balloon (caus. of fufenii)

2782 - FUPPILAA -ފުއްފިލާ See hudu-

2783 FUMENII ފުމެނީ v. 1. blows (abs. fume): onugañḍu f., blows pipe: tuñbun f., whistles: siluñbař f., blows into hookah [S. piñbinne]

2. jumps [cf.S. pimma, a leap: paninne, leaps]

2784 FUMMANII ފުންމަނީ v. jumps, jumps down (hon. fummavanii : v.n. fummevum): Kaḷuoř -fummi, 'the fish leapt' , name of Boḍu Takurufaanu's speedy ship

2785 FURA ފުރަ n. asterism Pūrvaphalgunī [S. puvapal]

2786 FURAUTTA VANII ފުރައުއްޓަ ވަނީ v. dies (hon., anc.)

2787 FURAGAS (-gahu) ފުރަގަސް n. the back: furagas kibaa doru, furagas faraatu doru, rectum: furagas faraatu bali, piles; eenaagee furagahugaa, behind him; f. denii, turns the back (on..,..-ař), also used metaphorically

2788 FURATAMA ފުރަތަމަ adj. first; firstly: ekme furatama-ař, at the very beginning: furatama-ař, for the first time: (ekme) furatamain, firstly [Skt. prathama, cf.S. paḷamu]

2789 FURADAANA(pl., furadaanain) ފުރަދާނަ n. (obs.) under-secretary of state [Skt. pradhāna]

2790 FURANII 1. ފުރަނީ v. departs: daturař f., daturař daan f., sets off on a voyage; furaa duvvaa eccehi, seagoing vessels: caus., furuvanii, sees someone off: furuvan danii, goes to see someone off

2791 FURANII 2. ފުރަނީ v. fills (tr.): with dat., fuḷiyař fen f., fills bottle with water: bolař fen f., pours water on the head; with instr., fuḷi fenun f., fills bottle with water; with loc., eñdugai roonu f., puts extra strings on bedstead: goñḍiigai etteyo f.,

canes the chair; kusagaňḍek f., ties a loop: see also furenii
[S. puranne, Skt. pūrayati]

2792 FURABADURUVA ފުރަބަދުރުވަ n. asterism Pūrvabhadrapadā

2793 FURA MAALE ފުރަމާލެ n. Male city [S. & Skt. -pura]

2794 FURA-MEE ފުރަމޭ n. chest (of men)

2795 FURASSAARA ފުރައްސާރަ n. mocking: in phrase aaḍa- furassaara kuranii, mocks

2796 FURAHANI ފުރަހަނި n. kind of pudding

2797 FURAHAḶA ފުރަހަޅަ n. asterism Pūrvāṣāḍhā

2798 FURAA ފުރާ 1. n. period of life: zuvaan furaige anhenun, women of young age: ḷa-furaa, adolescence

2. v. abs. or imp. or 3s.pres. of furanii

2799 FURAATA KURANII ފުރާތަ ކުރަނީ v. (obs.) moves (tr.)

2800 FURAANA ފުރާނަ n. vital breath, life: f. hiňgajje, life has departed: f. aḷanii, gives life (e.g. to an image): g. aḷuvvanii, (of God) gives life [Skt. prāṇa, cf. S. paṇa]

2801 FURAANANII ފުރާނަނީ v. strains, sieves, filters (v.n. fureenum) [cf. S. peranne]

2802 FURAA-VARU ފުރާވަރު n. puberty, esp. of girls: furaavaru vanii, furaavarař aranii, reaches puberty: aňbi-furaavaru vanii, has first period: mas furaavaru, good fishing chance [furaa 1 + varu]

2803 FURAAḶU ފުރާޅު n. roof: f. lanii, f. aḷanii, fixes roof on [S. parāḷa]

2804 FURI ފުރި v. being filled (abs. of furenii): furi baaru vanii, is packed tight: furi sikaara vefaa, being full [S. pirī]

2805 FURI-TAN ފުރިތަން n. the place you set out from: furitan jehenii, gets back to where you started from, (naut.) keeps where one is: furitan ves nujehunu, being lost, (met.) goes bankrupt [furanii 1]

2806 FURI-HAMA ފުރިހަމަ adj. complete (adv., furihama-ař, furihamain, completely); f. kuranii, fulfils [furi + hama]

2807 FURUGAANU ފުރުގާނު n. name used for the text of the Quran [U. furqān, 'separator' (of good and evil)]

2808 FURUVANII ފުރުވަނީ v. sees someone off [caus. of furanii 1]

2809 FURETIKAALU (pl., Furetikaalun) / (FUŘETIKAALU) ފުރެތިކާލު (ފުރެތިކާލު) n. Portuguese (anc.) : furetikaalu aňbu oř, a medicinal seed, cashew, anacardium occidentale [old S. Pratikāl, Portugal]

2810 FUREDENII ފުރެދެނީ v. goes out of line: furedumuge magun kehi, giving up the wrong path

2811 FUREDDE ފުރެއްދެ adj. foreign-going: f. oḍi, foreign-going vessel; f. oḍii kaaři, small cheap coconut: f. mirus, black pepper: f. lonu, imported salt: f. lava, foreign song, lovesong

2812 FURENII ފުރެނީ v. is filled: aharu furee duvas, anniversary: ufalun hit furi araa fada manzarek, a scene at which the heart overflows with joy (invol.of furanii 2, S. pirenne)

2813 FUREETA ފުރޭތަ n. a sea dragon: iruvaa f., kite with long tail: faidař f., faidořu f., squib [Skt. prēta, departed spirit]

2814 FUREENI ފުރޭނި n. strainer [S. penēra, Port. peneira]

2815 FUREENUM ފުރޭނުން v. straining (v.n. of furaananii) [cf. S. perum]

2816 FUROḶANII ފުރޮޅަނީ v. turns over, rolls over (tr.): ulun furoḷaa varu vefai, being lazy enough to need a poke; furoḷenii (invol.), turns over (intr.) [S. peraḷanne, cf. Skt. parivartate, T. puraḷ-]

2817 FUROḶU ފުރޮޅު n. wheel [furoḷanii]

2818 FUROO (furoek) ފުރޯ n. hatchet: furoo-daṇḍi, handle of hatchet; furoodaṇḍi-duuni , kind of dragonfly [S. porō, Skt. paraśu]

2819 FURSATU ފުރުޞަތު n. chance, opportunity [U. furṣat]

2820 FUL- ފުލު- n. See fuu: fulu-goř, bottom knot (of fish-stringing line); (met.) foundation, chief brain: fulugoř neṭṭuniimaa, hurihaa kamek bossum laane, when the bottom knot goes, everything will go wrong: fulugoř jehijjeyyaa, amunaa ḥaa eccek haru laanee, if the bottom knot stays firm, everything on the line will stay firm [fuu]

2821 FULUS (pl., fuluhun) ފުލުސް n. police: fuluhek, a policeman; nut of a bolt: iskurař fulus kurum, screwing the nut on the bolt [E. police]

2822 FULUUNIYAA ފުލޫނިޔާ n. a plant, holarrhena antidysenterica

2823 FULOOKU ފުލޯކު adj. fulooku vaahaka, fable

2824 FULLAA (fullaek) ފުއްލާ n. deer (not found in Maldives)

2825 FUVAK ފުވައް n. See fook

2826 FUVVANII ފުއްވަނީ v. impresses shapes or patterns (on to jewellery, or artificial flowers); makes furious faces

2827 FUS ފުސް 1. adj. cloudy, smoky, opaque; opaqueness: fus keyo, smoky kind of banana: fus-koḷu, bit of cloud, showery period; fuskoḷek eba hadaee, it is a showery time: fus-gaňḍu, big raincloud: fus- tuḷaa, kind of plant, sophora tomentosa (also fus-ruvaa): fus duvahek, fus hadaa duvahek, a cloudy day: fus billuuri, opaque glass; loo fus vejje, has become shortsighted [S. & Skt. puṣpa]

2. n. asterism Puṣyā [S. pusa]

2828 FUSKARU BADDANII ފުސްކަރު ބައްދަނީ v. gets (someone) in a stranglehold

2829 FUSSANII (FOSSANII) ފުއްސަނީ (ފޮއްސަނީ) v. causes to wipe (hon. fussuvvanii) (caus.of fuhenii)

2830 FUHI (fussek) ފުހި n. duster: tan-fuhi, duster: tun-fuhi, handtowel: fai-fuhi, doormat

2831 FUHENII (FOHENII) ފުހެނީ (ފޮހެނީ) v. wipes (off); rubs out (abs. fohe : caus. fussanii): fuhee rabaru, india rubber; mi rabarakun deyyek nufoheveene-eve, this rubber will not rub out ink (invol.): fuhee baaliis, thick duster: buuṭ fohen, to clean shoes [S. pihinne, Skt. prōñchati]

2832 FUŘ ފުށް n. 1. flour; powder; paper fuse: fuř-tak, lumps of flour: fuř boḍu hakuru, thick sugar; fuř-kafa, kapok: fuř-gaňḍu, dough: fuř-guḍi, flying fluff (childish, for

duuni-fuř): fuř-ţaki (-ţatkek) jahanii, snaps the fingers: fuř-fureeni, flour- strainer: fuř-bat, fried flour balls: fuř-maa, fuř jahaa maa, kind of powder-puff: binbi fuř, black flour: maa fuř, millet pudding; fuř-vaļun danii, backfires, (met.) goes flop
[S. piṭi, Skt. pṛṣṭa]

2. back side; side: etere fuř, inside: beeru fuř, outside: nubai fuř, wrong side: fati fuř, wrong side(of cloth), (met.) the full story: bańḍu fuř, palm of the hand, belly of a fish: rař fuřu, not from Male; anek fuřun jahanii, turns upside down, turns inside out: fuř- fuřař jahanii, turns over (tr.); defuř degoi miihek, a two faced man: defuř keheri, a two-faced man; fuřat, back of the hand (at-tilaige fuřat), back of a leaf; fuřatař, in the opposite direction: fuřoļi, back (unsharpened) side of knife-blade: fuř-kiba, back (of the head, boluge fuřkiba): fuřţaru (fuţţaru), exposed side of an island: fuřţaru faraatu, on the rocky side: fuřḍan, fuřḍunu, back burner of cooking fire: fuř-buru, curve (technical term in boatbuilding): fuřu tilooři, outer mooring post: fuřu feeli, a special kind of striped cloth: fuřu vaa, anchor rope at landward end: fuřu hiyaa, temporary boat shed; fuřu erum, overlapping ; (instr.) fuřun, on the part of, from the part of: eenaage fuřun faidaek nuvi, there was nothing to be got from him: eenaage fuřun mi kamtak kurevunii, this got done on his part [S. piṭa, Skt. pṛṣṭha]

2833 FUŘI (fuţţek) ފުރި n. used ifc. in names of islands, e.g. Vihamanaa-fuři (Kurumba Village) [S. piṭi, open space]

2834 FUŘUŇGU ފުރުނގު n. side-tuck (used as a holster) [fuřu uňgu]

2835 FUŘETIKAALU (FURETIKAALU) ފުރެތިކާލު (ފުރެތިކާލު) n. Portuguese (anc.): fuřetikaalu aňbu oř madu, cashew nut [old S. Pratikāl, Portugal]

2836 FUĻA ފުޅަ n. maggot: f. aļanii, maggots appear; (met.) kamnet kamun fuļa aļaafai, becoming lazy [T. puḷu]

2837 FUĻAU ފުޅައު See fuļaa

2838 FUĻAŇGI (fuļangek, fuļatňgek) ފުޅަނގި n. flying fish, exocoetus: goř f., locust: roo fan f., grasshopper [S. paļaňga]

2839 FUĻAFI ފުޅަފި n. outer covering of coconut flower (used as kindling)

2840 FUĻAFU- -ފުޅަފު See fuļař

2841 FUĻALI ފުޅަލި n. cadjan gate or fence: bakari f., gate to stop goats

2842 FUĻAŘ (fuļafek) ފުޅަރް n. fence: gee f., fence round a house; f. aļanii, constructs a fence [S. koļapu, spathe]

2843 FUḶAA / FUḶAU (fuḷal-) ފުޅައު / ފުޅާ adj. wide; width (fuḷaa min): liyaa etigañḍuge fuḷaa, irregularities in turned wood; adv., fuḷaa koř, widely: fasbai fuḷaa koř meḷum, turning up a wide hem [S. paḷal, Skt. pṛthula]

2844 FUḶI ފުޅި n. bottle; tube of toothpaste, dynamo of bicycle: bai fuḷi, half bottle: baaga fuḷi, bottle containing half an aḍubaa:: laahi f., half-pint bottle: fuḷi bai, group of bottles: fuḷimadu uñguri, bottle cork, (met.) one who turns up everywhere; fuḷi toři jahanii, applies broken glass (to kite strings)

2845 FUḶU (with initial doubling, -PUḶU) ފުޅު (-ފުޅު) n. ifc., honorific suffix used after nouns and adjectives (cf. also -koḷu 2), e.g. basfuḷu-tak, honorable words: tuñbuḷifuḷu, nobleman's beard: hitpuḷu heyo, kindly (of noblemen): amillafuḷu, nobleman's own ; occasionally non-honorific, dari-fuḷu, child; e fuḷu, girl friend; used as a proper name for people of the third degree, e.g. Mu<u>h</u>ammad Fuḷu

2846 FUU (fulek) ފޫ n. 1. bottom, outer bottom (as v. aḍi) : occasionally of people, fuu-koḷu, buttocks (= fiñdumasgañḍu), but usually of things : fuu-kiba, fuu-naaři, the half of a coconut without the holes: fuu li taři, stemmed glass (wine glass): fuu hama teli, flat-bottomed pan: fuu haru laa, unshakably based: fuu eñburi, a type of cowrie: fuu-goḷi, sanitary towel; fuugoḷi jahanii, uses sanitary towel: munḍun fuu gaḷanii, tucks up sarong fuu danii, leaks; fulek nudee, does not leak: fuu duvvanii, makes a hole in (tr.): fuu baddanii, mends hole; ties loose ends, makes up deficiencies, (met.) covers things up ; kamuge fuu baddanii, justifies changes: varař fuu nubedee, very nonsensical: ruñbaage fuu veṭṭijje, the jar has a hole, leaks

2. white mould (as v. fii , which is black): mi mastakugai fuu jahajje-ee, mould has appeared on these fish: fuu aḷaa fani vum, the appearing of mould and worms

2847 FUUṬU ފޫޓު n. foot, twelve inches: fuuṭu-fati, footrule: fuuṭu-fiitaa, tape measure [E. foot]

2848 FUUḌU ފޫޑު adj. In don-fuuḍu, see don

2849 FUUDENII ފޫދެނި v. 1. gets wrinkled in the water; gets properly soaked
2. fuudum, fuudee diyavaru, high tide
3. fuudigen, (of mobs) swaying around

2850 FUUDDANII ފޫއްދަނި v. soaks (tr.) (caus. of fuudenii)

2851 FUURUBBA(fuurubbaek) ފޫރުއްބަ n. east [Skt. pūrva]

2852 FUUHI (fuussek) ފޫހި adj. bored; fed up: (of people) dull, uninteresting: aharen mitaa iñdeiñde fuuhi vejje-ee, I'm bored with sitting here: eaa medu aharen fuuhi karuvaa, I'm bored with that: eii aharen fuuhi karuvaa eccek, that bores me: fuuhi filuvanii, whiles away the time

2853 FUUḶU ފޫޅު n. navel; navelstring: fuuḷu-daňḍi, navelstring: kuḍa fuuḷu, kind of djinn: fuuḷu-mai, fuuḷumai-daita, fuuḷu-maama, midwife (often just called 'maama'): fuuḷu digu hanḍi, a mythical spirit with a long navelstring; kanfatu f., lobe of ear

2854 FEIBUM ފެއިބުން v. descending [for feebum,. v.n. of faibanii]

2855 FETTEVUM ފެއްޓެވުން v. beginning (hon.) (v.n. of faṭṭavanii)

2856 FETUM ފެތުން v. swimming: sinking (v.n. of fatanii or of fetenii)

2857 FETURI ފެތުރި n. kinds of rash, such as ringworm

2858 FETURENII ފެތުރެނީ v. spreads (intr.): bali feturenii, disease spreads (invol. of faturanii) [S. pätirenne]

2859 FETENII ފެތެނީ v. sinks (intr.), of things (not of people in this sense): oḍi fetigen, the odi having sunk: (met.) fits : mařakař nufetunu, didn't fit me: bolakun nufetunu, doesn't fit round the neck: mitanakař nufeteene-ee, won't fit in here: vazanař fetenii, fits the style: boḍu goňḍiyakař fetifai eba in, he is fitted into a big chair, i.e. is proud (invol. of fatanii)

2860 FETTUM ފެއްތުން v. causing to sink; causing to fit (v.n. of fattanii)

2861 FEN ފެން n. water (usually fresh); wateriness (of curries) : fen-tak fuhum, wiping off drops of water: bees fenek, a drop of medicinal water: fen eti, pot of water (esp. for the aged): fen-mati, water surface: nuvaree fen, nine-night watersports (formerly practised after a birth) : fenu tereen, out of the water: fenuge taahiru(-kam), (rules for) religious ablutions; (met.) watery, i.e. unsuccessful: fen natiijaa, unsuccessful results: fenař hiňgajje, got cancelled, flopped, went for nothing; fen boḍu, flooded; fen boḍu vejje, got flooded: fen kakkaa boli, very large type of cowrie: fenfodu aruvanii, offers water (e.g. to wash hands before meals): fen jahanii, sprinkles or splashes water (on, dat..); fenu jahanii, tempers; fenu jehifai, splashed with water: fenu kakkanii, cooks in water: fen faibanii, fen niiranii, there is a leak: fenu baaru hifanii, floats, is seaworthy, (met.) can manage by oneself : fen vanii, is not a success: fen varanii, takes a bath; fen varaa beru, drum for bathing formerly beaten at 9.0 a.m. on Fridays: fen aḷanii, takes first bath after circumcision; saaḷiihař fen aḷanii, takes bath on 40th day after death or childbirth; maa fen aḷanii, keeps flower petals in water to preserve the scent: fen mati vanii, rises (above the water-surface), of constellations etc.: fen kiyavanii, fen maturanii, mutters charms over a dish of water; fen- ala, kind of yam (also called goboḷi ala): fen kaḷi vanii, is in tears: fen-kuňburu vaani, a plant, fleabane, vernonia cinerea: f.- kuḷi, water-games (formerly practised at Id, or after a birth (nuva-ree fen): f.- koři, a baby chair for bathing; fen koři aranii, chokes with water: fen-gaňḍu, an amount of water (in a container); a pool, puddle: fengaňḍu boḍakas, reerek birek nugannaane-eve, though the water be deep, the duck will not fear (prov.), i.e. it is all right if you know; (cf. fen gaňḍu-kuranii, freezes water): f.- gas, a

succulent tree: f.- gaagaňḍu, water container on a boat (not of stone):
f.- taři, glass of water: f.-fař, portion of a boat below the waterline: f.- filaa(gaňḍu), platform in the bows whence water is scattered to attract the fish: fen fihi lanii, just exists, is no good (lit. 'brushes water'): f.- foḷi, pancake of eggs and flour: f.- fook, growing arecanut; fenfook duuni, kind of bird, pipit: fen- bat, rice without oil or salt; fen-batpen, hot porridge: fen baru kanii, is soaked with water: fen miiru mas, kind of fish which scavenges in wells: fen-varu, amount, level(depth); (met.) level in general (e.g. of strength, education, wealth): fen-vaḷu, well (of water) : fen-siru, a measure of water;
(met.) insatiable person; Fensiru kaleefaanu, an old Maldivian title: fen-ham, leather waterbottle (anc.): fen-ḷeeňbuu, variety of ḷeeňbuu tree [S. pän, Skt. pānīya]

2862 FENI ފެނި v. having appeared; feniyek deniyek nuve, not to be seen (doublet) (abs. of fennanii) [S. penī]

2863 FENUM ފެނުން v. appearing (v.n. of fennanii) [S. penīm]

2864 FENḌAA (fenḍaaek) ފެންޑާ n. veranda (fenḍaa-mati) [cf. H. baraṇḍā]

2865 FENNANII ފެންނަނީ v. appears; appears good (3 s. fenee : v.n. fenum:: abs. feni : hon. fenuvvanii, feni vaḍaigannanii): lolař fenum, sight: raňgaḷu kamugai fenee, appears good: aḷugaňḍař fenee, it seems right to me, I decide: vaajibu nuvaane kamař kamugai fenigen, it appearing not to be obligatory: kurin fenunu miihakař, to the man who saw (it) first: fennan netenii, disappears from sight: fenevi, being caused to see (invol.): vaḍaigannavanii koř fenijje, he (hon.) was seen going [S. penenne, Skt. prajñāyate]

2866 FENNAA MANIKUFAANU ފެންނާ މަނިކުފާނު n. an old Maldivian title

2867 FENFIYAAZU ފެންފިޔާޒު n. a precious stone

2868 FEFUU ފެފޫ n. a kind of melon, more watery than fufuu [cf. fufuu]

2869 FEMUNU ފެމުނު n. whale: f. miyaru, small kind of shark, tiger shark, galeocerdo

2870 FELANII ފެލަނީ v. squeezes out (only used after diya or kiru) : bakari(n) kiru felanii, milks goats: naariňgu diya felanii, squeezes oranges: ukdaňḍiin diya felanii, squeezes sugarcane

2871 FELIDU ATOḶU ފެލިދު އަތޮޅު n. name of V (W) atoll

2872 FELENII ފެލެނީ v. makes bellowing noise (of animals, or vulg. of people)

2873 FEVUM ފެވުން v. touching up (v.n. of favanii)

2874 FES ފެސް n. box for storing bait-fish [S. päs, P. pacchi]

2875 FESKOO ފެސްކޫ n. fescue plant, tephrosia purpurea [E. fescue]

2876 FESSUM ފެއްސުން v. 1. driving away 2. causing to sew (v.n. of fassanii)

2877 FESSENII ފެއްސެނީ v. 'drives oneself': mitanun fessigen daařee, drive yourself away, get lost! mihaaru anekkaa ves eenaa fessiganegen uḷee irekeve, he is still persisting in coming here (invol. of fassanii 1)

2878 FEHI (fessek) ފެހި adj. green : don f., light green: fatu f., dark green: vaḷu f., dirty green (colour of moss in wells): vilu f.,bright green; (met.) bright: fehi mustaqbal, bright future: fehi bagiicaa, a plant: fehi mugu, green gram; as noun, moss: vaḷugai fehi jahajje, moss has grown in the well

2879 FEHUM ފެހުން v. chasing; sewing (v.n. of fahanii)

2880 FEHURIHI ފެހުރިހި n. kind of shark, whale shark

2881 FEHURU ފެހުރު n. (anc.) cadjan sail

2882 FEŘENII ފެށެނީ v. begins (intr.): bolun feřigen, beginning from the head (invol. of fařanii)

2883 FEḶENII ފެޅެނީ v. is chopped; (of skin) cracks: bañḍu feḷi gamiis, shirt opening right down the front: bañḍu feḷi haa, penultimate letter of the Arabic alphabet: rabaru feḷijje, the tyre is punctured: aḍu feḷijje, his) voice has broken: funnaabu feḷee, the heel is cracking (invol. of faḷanii)

2884 FEE KURANII ފޭ ކުރަނީ v. keeps apart (tr.): at fee kořgen, keeping arms well apart (supposed to show pride when walking): fuḷali fee kuranii, opens the gate: fee vanii, grows away, grows apart

2885 FEEḌI ފޭޑި n. skill, tastefulness: feeḍiek net miihek, a tasteless man: eeḍi-feeḍi nuhunna, heeḍi-feeḍi nuhunna, unskilful (doublets)

2886 FEEDENII ފޭދެނީ v. percolates; is absorbed: deli feedijje karudaahař, the ink was absorbed by the blotting paper: fen feedigen hiñgajje, the water oozed away: (met.) gastakuge tereen hañduvaruge alikam feedigen aisfai vanii, the moonlight filtered through the trees (invol. of faaddanii)
[? cf.S. pähädenne, becomes clear]

2887 FEEBUM (FEIBUM) ފޭބުން (ފައިބުން) v. descending; settling (hon. feebennevum) (v.n. of faibanii)

2888 FEERAA (feeraaek) ފީރާ n. wooden spike for husking coconuts: digging instrument used in latrines; feeraa dat, canine teeth

2889 FEERAAM ފީރާން n. cloth, textiles; quality of weave [S. peherakam, Skt. pēśakārakarma]

2890 FEERU ފީރު n. 1. guava pear (varieties: hudu f., rangu f.) [S. pēra, Port. pera]

2. feeru- kaleege, weaver [S. peherā, Skt. pēśakāra]

2891 FEERENII ފޭރެނީ v. steals with violence (tr.) : miihunge atun mudau feerigenfi, stole goods from people: kañḍu feeree miihun, pirates: magu feerum, highway robbery ; (met.) cheats [S. pähära-ganne]

2892 FEELI (feeyyek) ފޭލި n. 1. old-fashioned unstitched striped and edged skirt (for both sexes: ceremonial wear for men): doḷi feeli, short veil: bolu feeli, kerchief (anc.): feeli-ge, temporary tent

2. ifc., bale of cloth (foti f., riyaa f., kafun f.): doḷu feeyyek haa, the amount of one and a half bales [cf. S. piyali, rag , Helmer Smith, P.pilōtikā]

2893 FEELU (FEEL) VANII ފޭލު (ފޭލް) ވަނީ v. fails (at.., instr.): vaadayakař kuri kamakun feel vum, failure at a competitive activity [E. fail]

2894 FEESTAAŘI ފީސްތާރި n. top portion of mast

2895 FEESSANII ފީއްސަނީ v. sharpens to a point (e.g.pencil) (caus. of feehanii)

2896 FEEHENII ފީހެނީ v. sharpens, pares: kalee feehunu ilořigañḍu herunii kaleege lolař taa-ee, the eakel you sharpened is stuck in your own eye! (prov.), i.e. you are hoist with your own petard. Causative form feessanii is commonly used in the same sense

2897 FOI ފޮއި n. (pron. foe) 1.grinding stone (for use on board)

2. lunar fortnight (foi duvas): de-foi, lunar month: foi- mati (foomati) duvas, spring tides: faru foi diya(varu), neap tides: tinfoi rooda, fasting on the 13th, 14th and 15th of every lunar month: mahakaa foiduvas, six weeks; see also foo [S. pōya, Skt. upōsatha]

2898 FOK ފޮކް 1. n. fok-gas, baobab, adansonia digitata : fok-toři, skin of its fruit

2. adj. unathletic, clumsy

2899 FOṬOGIRAAFU ފޮޓޯގިރާފު n. photograph [E. photograph]

2900 FOṬOO ފޮޓޯ n. picture, illustration: foṭoo(ge) loogaňḍu, glass of a framed picture: foṭoo naganii, takes photo [E. photo]

2901 FOḌI ފޮޑި n. fart : f. jahanii, farts: f. taḷanii, farts at some length [S. paḍa, Skt. √pard]

2902 FOT ފޮތް n. book (esp., one of the 30 books of the Qur'an): fot nerenii, issues a book; fot-kaali, rack for a book (esp. for the Qur'an): fot-gaňḍu, (pej.) old book: fot-goňḍi, book-rest: gotek fotek net(doublet), without manners; fot-foři kiyavanii, recites sections of the Qur'an for the dead: fot-teri, booklover [S. pota, Skt. puṣṭa(ka)]

2903 FOTI (foccek) ފޮތި n. 1. slice: foti kuranii, slices up; disc of metal or plastic, e.g. on hookah: boḍu foti, central pendant of a necklace; 'jack' in game of carrom: laarifoti, an old coin [S. peti, ?Skt. patrikā]

2. cloth: anna foti, male under-garment: eňdu foti, bed sheet; bed curtain: damaa foti, curtain: bolu foti-koḷu, woman's headdress introduced by Amin Didi: riyaa kaňḍaa foti, sailcloth; foti- karudaas, tissue paper: foti-gaňḍu, piece of cloth, esp. curtain, tablecloth: foti faivaan, canvas shoes: foti feeli, bale of cloth : foti-huvaňdu, a small aromatic plant, kaempferia galanga;

foti aḷanii, patches: foti jahanii, folds (for fat jahanii) [S. potu]

2904 FO<u>TT</u>AALI ފޮއްޓާލި n. In fo<u>tt</u>aali taḷ(uv)anii, drags by hand

2905 FODU ފޮދު n. small quantity of liquid: fen fodek, some water [S. poda]

2906 FONI ފޮނި adj. sweet: mila-foni, slightly sweet; foni gada taketi, sweet things, sweets; foni kuratpek, a green sugar cockroach: foni-tuḷaa, a medicinal plant, ocimum gratissimum: foni-toři, cinnamon, cinnamomum zeylanicum: fonitoři kaafuurutoḷi lanii, exaggerates: foni bisgaňḍu, meringue: foni-maa, a scented medicinal plant, valeriana wallichii: foni-roři, sweet pancake: foni-luňboo, orange: foni-looli, a medicinal plant; as n.., sweetness: foni-kam, (met.) boastfulness, self-importance: foni kaňḍanii, boasts [? variant of fani 2]

2907 FONU ފޮނު n. foam , froth [S. peṇa, Skt. phēṇa]

2908 FONUMAT / FONUVAT ފޮނުމަތް / ފޮނުވަތް n. Maldivian carpenter's drill (turned by two men with ropes)

2909 FONUVANII ފޮނުވަނީ v. sends (imp. fonuvaa ! hon. fonuvvavanii): fonuvaa-lanii, sending away from Male (non-judicially , as v. aruvaa-lanii) : fonuvvee too bellevum, expecting to be sent (invol., hon.); fonuvvevum, revelation (of religion) [perhaps Skt. praṇayati]

2910 FOFARU VANII ފޮފަރު ވަނީ v. shows a crumpled or sleepy face

2911 FOFAḶI ފޮފަޅި n. a red-coloured mineral

2912 FORI ފޮރި n. worms which eat dried fish: mastakugai f. aḷajje-ee, worms have infested the fish

2913 FORIKE ފޮރިކެ n . a small black migratory bird, martin

2914 FORUPPANII (HORUPPANII) ފޮރުއްޕަނީ (ހޮރުއްޕަނީ) v. gets on with: nuforuppaa miihek, an impossible person: miina-aa hedi foruppaakař net, it is impossible to get on with him

2915 FORUVANII ފޮރުވަނީ v. (lit.) covers, hides; frustrates [?S.poravanne, wraps round, P. pārupati]

2916 FOL- ފޮލް- See foo

2917 FOLAA (folaek) ފޮލާ n. a rice dish cooked in ghee and spice

2918 FOLAALIINU ފޮލާލީނު n. flannel [E. flannel]

2919 FOSSANII ފޮއްސަނީ v. See fussanii (caus. of fohenii)

2920 FOHENII ފޮހެނީ v. See fuhenii (some speakers distinguish fohenii, sweep, from fuhenii, erase): buuṭ fohen, to clean shoes

2921 FOŘAA (fořaek) ފޮށާ n . cloth for males to wear, usually white; (mod.) turban: laa fořaa, anna fořaa, twin garments esp. worn for Hajj [?S. poṭa, a fold, P. paṭṭa, cloth]

2922 FOŘI (foṭṭek) ފޮށި n. box: aḍu f., loud-speaker: koṭṭaa f., Indian banjo: daturu f., travelling trunk: fahaa f., sewing machine: lava f., record-player; makunu f., white eggs of spiders; fot-foři kiyevum, reciting from the Qur'an for the dead; foři-tanmati, luggage (box and mattress) [S. peṭṭi, T.]

2923 FOŘENII ފޮރެނީ v. pesters, worries (with -aa of the person): mařaa nufořeeře, don't bother me! fořunu kam, the bloody thing (disaster)

2924 FOĻANII ފޮޅަނީ v. opens up, viz.-

1. sifts, winnows: hañḍuu f., winnows rice
2. dusts (with a tanfuhi): arimati f., dusts the seat
3. shakes out: aridafus f., neefat f., blows nose: (enlarged)fen foļaa-lanii, shakes out water: hari f., shakes himself (of an animal); (met., of people) mikamun hari foļaa-lum, shaking off this burden: taļaa foļanii, quarrels (doublet); caus., causes to open, spreads: riya f., spreads out sail ; dida f., unfurls flag: (met.) maa foļuvanii, uses flowery language (esp.to girls) [S. poļanne, Skt. sphuṭati, sphōṭayati]

2925 FOĻI ފޮޅި n. a kind of roll or pancake; velaa f. (made of turtle's eggs), haalu f. (made of hen's eggs): boo foļi, thick unrolled pancakes, eaten on certain religious festivals (boofoļi duvas): foļi-dañḍi(-gañḍu), thin scoop for turning pancakes over while cooking

2926 FOĻU ފޮޅު n. transparent round boil: kura f., hard boil: fen f., watery boil: foļu koṭṭaalanii, pricks a boil [S. poļa, Skt. sphōṭa(ka)]

2927 FOĻU-VAT ފޮޅުވަތް n. line of writing; lines for writing on: foļuvat demi ot, ruled exercise book: foļuvat nudamaa fot, unruled exercise book [S. piṭapata, copy]

2928 FOĻENII ފޮޅެނީ v. blossoms: maa foļenii, flowers blossom: (met., of people) foļifai hunna, looking cheerful, charming; ham foļenii, skin flakes off (invol. of foļanii)

2929 FOO ފޯ n. 1. kind of sweet, eaten on foi duvas, esp. kařikeelu foo (made from screwpine): foo kekkum, a full moon festivity in former time ('cooking sweets'): foo-mati duvas, see foi 2. [For foi 2]
2. In goñḍi-foo (goñḍi-foi), tinder-box

2930 FOO (folek) ފޯ adj. sodden: mi faarořitak foo vaakař nuuļe-ee / folek nuvee, these rolls are still not softened; foo kuranii, makes sodden: (met.) asarun hit foo kurum, saddening the heart with emotion

2931 FOOK (FUVAK) ފޯކް (ފުވަކް) n. arecanuts, areca catechu: fook-kiba, single arecanut: fook-foti, sliced arecanut: fook-vaļi, areca cutter : fook-himeri, sword bean, canavelia ensiformis; kairi meři fook, fas fiyamalař koři f., roo f., hanaa f., various kinds of chew; fen fook, undried arecanuts, nuts on the tree: fook koři erum, choking on arecanuts: Fook Mulaku (Fua Mulaku), name of Ñ atoll; (met.) testicle [S. puvak, P. pūgapakka]

2932 FOOḌARU ފޯޑަރު n. baking powder [E. powder]

2933 FOODENII ފޫދެނީ v. matures (intr.), of inanimates, esp. trees (ara-foodi of animates) [S. pūdinne]

2934 FOONU ފޯނު n. telephone : f. kuranii, telephones [E. phone]

2935 FOONCU ފޯންޗު n. china teapot [S. pōcciya, D. potje]

2936 FOOM ފޯމް n. form (to fill in), esp. school report [E. form]

2937 FOORANII ފޯރަނީ v. reaches (to.., dat.); affects : fiitaa telař nufooranii, the wick doesn't reach the oil: etanař at fooraa ta? can you reach it? manavaraai hama-ař aļugańḍumennař nufooraigen uļeni koř, before we could reach the man-of-war: (met.) is rich: fooraa miihek, a prosperous man; Caus., provides: ehii fooruvum, providing help: enlarged, mage atař fooruvaalii, delivered to me

2938 FOORI (FOORII) ފޯރި (ފޯރީ) n. 1. zest : fooriaa eku hurum, fooriigai hurum, being enthusiastic: fooriigai kuļum, playing eagerly; foori gada, energetic: foorigada duvahek, a pleasurable day; foori-gańḍu, enthusiasm: foori hifanii, is enthusiastic; shows pressure: gunbaage ham feļigen fooriek nuhifaeve, the tyre is punctured and shows no pressure: ebai miihun tibii varugada-ař foori hifaafaeve, they showed great enthusiasm 2. watch-tour, turn of duty: fooriař danii, goes on duty: iraa fooriigai hurum, being on early watch: foori maranii, does turn of duty

2939 FOOLI(fooyyek) ފޯޅި n. a 'twist' of something: roonu f., one twelfth of a bońḍi of coir: mila f., bits of dust and sweat ; esp. the 'ballstick' in games of manḍi or kulli (manḍi fooli), or bobbin for twisting yarn (sarakaige fooli, gataa faige fooli); liyaa fooli, slate pencil : ramanraman fooli, a children's game

2940 FOOVAHI ފޯވަހި n. fishing season; season (in general)

2941 FOOĻAVAHI ފޯޅަވަހި n. the Chagos islands

ޕ PAVIYANI, the 22nd letter of the Maldivian alphabet

In modern Maldivian words this letter occurs as a doubling of f : otherwise only in loanwords

2942 PACIS / PACAS(FACIS) ޕަޗިސް / ޕަޗަސް (ފަޗިސް) n. a game played on a board or cloth [H. pacīsī, from pacīs, 25]

2943 PARII ޕަރީ n. fairy, peri (in stories) [U. parī]

2944 PARUVAANAA (-naek) ޕަރުވާނާ n. moth [U. parvāna]

2945 PA-VIYANI ޕަވިޔަނި n. the letter P in the Maldivian alphabet

2946 PAS ޕަސް onom. pas lanii, makes a popping or banging noise. pas laa veṭṭijje, fell down with a bang (usually of people)

2947 PAAṬII ޕާޓީ n. party: sai paaṭii, tea party [E. party]

2948 PAAN ޕާން n . bread [S. pān, Port. pão]

2949 PAAPAR(U) ޕާޕަރު n. pappadam
[H. pāpaṙ, Skt. parpaṭa, cf. Malayalam pappaṭam]

2950 PAAR(U)SAL ޕާރުސަލް n. parcel: paarusal karudaas, brown paper
[E. parcel]

2951 PAAS ޕާސް onom. paas lanii, makes splashing sound: paas laifai roigenfi, wept noisily: paas laafaa baḍi faḷaigen hiṅgajje, burst into noisy laughter (cf. also poos, hoos)

2952 PAASPOOṬ ޕާސްޕޯޓް n. sideboard [E. sideboard x E. passport]

2953 PINPON ޕިންޕޮން n. pingpong: p. kuḷenii, plays table tennis
[E. pingpong]

2954 PIYAANA ޕިޔާނަ n. piano [E. piano]

2955 PIYOONU ޕިޔޯނު n. peon, official messenger [S. piyun, Port. peão, pawn]

2956 PIRINII ޕިރިނީ n. kind of rice poudding [U. firnī]

2957 PISTAA (-aaek) ޕިސްތާ n. pistachio nut [U. pista]

2958 PUDIINAA ޕުދީނާ n. mint (Also kudiinaa) [U. pudīna]

2959 -PUḶU (-POḶU) -ޕުޅު (-ޕޮޅު) suffix, for -fuḷu after a consonant: Faadippoḷu (Faadiffuḷu), name of Ḷ atoll: atpuḷu, hand (hon.), naseehatpuḷu, advice (hon.), hitpuḷu, heart (hon.)

2960 PUULKOPII ޕޫލްކޮޕީ n. cauliflower [H. phūlgobhī]

2961 PEKEṬU ޕެކެޓު n. packet [E. packet]

2962 PEKIN ޕެކިން n. packing material [E. packing]

2963 PEṬROOLU ޕެޓްރޯލު n. petrol [E. petrol]

2964 PISHOORIN (pl.) ޕިޝޯރިން n. Pathan merecenaries who invaded the Maldives in 1909 [U. Pēshaurī]

2965 POPPO(K) ޕޮޕްޕޮކް onom. p. lanii, makes gentle popping sound (as of drips, or a lamp going out)

2966 POORU ޕޯރު n. fertilizer [S. pōra]

2967 POOS ޕޯސް onom . poos lanii, makes splashing sound (cf. also paas, hoos)

2968 POOSṬU ޕޯސްޓު n.. post, post office: p. kuranii, posts (= poosṭař lanii) [E. post]

ބ BAA, the 5th letter of the Maldivian alphabet

Baa atoḷu, Maaḷosmaḍulu atoll South, the 5th atoll from the north

2969 BAI ބައި n. part, area, share; group, team ; ibc., half; ifc., series, set, 'and a half';

e bai miihun, they: tiya bai miihun, (in sermons) ye: as-bai, double knot: kunbaḷa-bai, group of k. fish: Kulii-bai, Rent Department: kuḷi-bai, set of chessmen: keoḷu-bai, tax on skippers: taas-bai, pack of cards: daa-bai, tax on nets: duuni-bai, flock of birds: mas-bai (obs.), a fish tax: heturu-bai, set of ropes; bai bayař, in groups; bai-lakka, half a lakh, 50,000: bai-laahi, half a laahi, one eighth of a 'measure: bai-gaa, one eighth of a pound weight, two ounces: tinfuuṭu bai, three and a half feet: hat aharaa bai, seven and a half years (coll., hatek bai aharu): tingadi bai, 3.30;

bai-gaňḍu, crowd, mob: bai-mati, width of shoulder: bai- manu, half dumb: bai-medu, distributable property: bai-varu, very many; baivaru miihuntakek, lots of people: baivaru fot-takek, lots of books; bai-haru, (obs.) taxable unit of man and wife; ba(y)ek, some: bayek kamtak, some activities: bayek, some people; bai bahanii, deals out (cards): bai aḷanii, gives out shares: tin iru iraku baek, (take) one three times daily; bai bai kuranii, divides up; bai-veriyaa, partner [S. bā, bā̆ya, Skt. bhāga]

2970 BAI-TIBBANII (BEETIBBANII) ބައިތިއްބަނި (ބޭތިއްބަނި) v. detains more than one person, keeps waiting [cf. baindanii]

2971 BAITU ބައިތު n. verse couplet or stanza (ḷem baitu): baitu baazii, poetical contest [U. bait]

2972 BAIN / BAAN ބައިން / ބާން n. loop of cloth: eli b., hanging loop (to hold during childbirth, or for the aged); looped line to hang things on: b. jahanii, fixes loop; bainugai eccek aḷuvanii, fixes something on the loop or line; sling (med.): atugai b. jahanii, puts arm in a sling; loops to fix strings to a kite

2973 BAINDANII (BEENDANII) ބައިންދަނި (ބޭންދަނި) v. detains a single person (cf. baitibbanii): circumcizes: lee boo fani faigai baindanii, applies leeches to the leg

2974 BAIBALAA ބައިބަލާ n. a kind of game

2975 BAILANII ބައިލަނި v. See baalanii

2976 BAISAA (BAASAA) (baisaek) ބައިސާ (ބާސާ) n. king (at cards): b. kaňḍanii, boasts, chatters [for U. bādśāh]

2977 BAISKAL ބައިސްކަލް n. bicycle [E. bicycle]

2978 BAISKIILI ބައިސްކީލި See baaskiili

2979 BAISKOOFU / BAISKOOPU ބައިސްކޫފު / ބައިސްކޫޕު n. film show; b. dakkanii, shows films: b.- ge, cinema: baiskoofař diyum, going to the pictures [E. bioscope]

2980 BAU ބައު See baa

2981 BAK VANII ބައް ވަނި v. (of ears) is blocked, buzzes

2982 BAKA TAḶANII ބަކަ ތަޅަނީ v. splashes in the water [?onom.]

2983 BAKAMUUNU ބަކަމޫނު n. owl [S. bakamūnā, 'big-faced']

2984 BAKARI (usu. bakaṭṭek, as from bakaři) ބަކަރި n. goat: b. govi (-kaleege), goatherd: b. fuḷali, a low gate in front of the main gate of a house [H. bakrī]

2985 BAKKU ބައްކު n. twine (usu. ibc., bakku-vaa)

2986 BAGALAA (BAŇGALAA) ބަގަލާ (ބަނގަލާ) n. buggalow (bagalaa booṭ), Borah boat: bagalaa- faharu (collective plural), buggalows [Marathi, from Port. baxel?]

2987 BAGIYAA ބަގިޔާ n. lace-making: b. jahanii, makes lace; lacemaking machine: bagiyaek gatanii, uses the machine

2988 BAGIICAA(-aaek) ބަގީޗާ n. 1. garden: bagiicaa onnanii riitikoř gas indaafaee, the garden is beautifully planted with shrubs
2. kinds of plant, usu. ifc.: e.g. kanfat bagiicaa, donfat bagiicaa, farudaa b., fehi b. [U. bag<u>h</u>īcā]

2989 BAGUḌI LANII ބަގުޑި ލަނީ v. clings to (with -gai)

2990 BAŇGALAA (-aek) ބަނގަލާ n. 1. for bagalaa, buggalow
2. baňgalaa-tere, part of the old royal palace [H. banglā, bungalow]

2991 BAŇGU-FILAA ބަނގުފިލާ n. an intoxicating leaf , hemp [H. bhāng, Skt. bhangā]

2992 BAŇGU-RAA (sometimes baňguralek) ބަނގުރާ n. intoxicating liquor [S. baňgahara]

2993 BAŇGURUUṬU ބަނގުރޫޓު adj. bankrupt [D. bankroet]

2994 BACANII ބަޗަނީ v. escapes (v.n.becum) [H. bacnā]

2995 BACCU ބައްޗު n. a nickname

2996 BAJIYAA(-aek) ބަޖިޔާ n. a three-cornered pastry

2997 BAṬEELI (baṭeeyyek) ބަޓޭލި n. a carpenter's instrument

2998 BAṬṬAM ބަޓްޓަމް n.. shape

2999 BAḌI ބަޑި n. 1. gun : boḍu b., cannon; nukaa b., gun fired at the beginning of the daily fast in Ramzan: koo donna b., rooda viillaa b., gun fired at the end of the daily fast; baḍi jahanii, fires gun, shoots : eenaa(ge) gayař b. jahaalaifi, he was shot at: baḍiige unḍa jehunii fatgaňḍugaeve, the shot hit the target: baḍi bahaṭṭaafai huṭṭeve, b. duddaafai oteve, guns were set up: b. halanii, tests guns: (met.) paas laafaa baḍi faḷaigen hiňgajje, exploded into loud laughter (usu. of children): munḍun baḍi hadanii, makes a noise with a fold of cloth (as with lavatory paper);

baḍi-kuḷi, fireworks (mod., alifaanuge kuḷivaru); baḍikuḷi aruvanii, lets off fireworks: baḍikuḷi-maa, showers of fireworks: baḍi-daňḍi aḷanii, exerts controlling force: baḍi-doru, gunports (in ships or on ramparts); baḍidoru kaňḍanii, makes gunports: baḍi-fan, extra piece of thatching on fences: baḍi-beru, drum beaten after the cannon at new moon on certain occasions: baḍi-bees, gunpowder (made with ruvaa charcoal): baḍi-haru, gun site or limber

2. amulet case, locket: huni b., tin for lime

3000 BAḌU ބަޑު n. In aḍu-baḍu, noise (doublet)

3001 BAŇḌAI-DUU ބަނޑައިދޫ n . layer of flesh on abdomen of fishes

3002 BAŇḌAVARU ބަނޑަވަރު n. crossed ropes, esp. to secure thatch: b. aḷanii, fixes such ropes: baňḍavarař duu kuraařee, loosen the securing rope!

3003 BAŇḌAHA (baňḍahalek) ބަނޑަހަ n. stores : b. jahanii, sets up temporary fishing stores: baňḍaha-ge, larder [Skt. bhāṇḍaśālā]

3004 BAŇḌI VANII ބަނޑި ވަނީ v. gets dented

3005 BAŇḌI BAŇḌI LAVVANII ބަނޑި ބަނޑި ލަވްވަނީ v. waggles the hips

3006 BAŇḌIYAA (baňḍiyalek) ބަނޑިޔާ n. waterpot; hanging lamp in mosque, with pot-shaped bowl: kulakulaige b., coloured lamps formerly used at hiti celebrations; b. jahanii, plays musically with finger-rings on brass pots (usu. of women) [H. bhāňřā, Skt. bhāṇḍaka]

3007 BAŇḌU ބަނޑު n. 1. belly, upper belly: dař-baňḍu, belly below the navel; baňḍu boḍee, is pregnant: baňḍař fas mas, five months pregnant : baňḍugai rissanii, has labour pains; riyaluge baňḍu hiňdijje, the billowing of the sail is deflated; baňḍař denii, gives as food allowance: baňḍař maru vanii, dies of hunger: baňḍař jehifai, starving (hon., baňḍufuḷař onnavai); baňḍař jahaigen duvaa, crawling (as a reptile); baňḍu aḷanii, swallows; baňḍu hiki, constipated: b. hindanii, tones down the stomach: baňḍu feḷi gamiis, shirt opening at the front: baňḍu feḷi haa, the penultimate Arabic letter H;

bañḍu-gini, hunger (non-Male usage); aharen b. lajje, I am hungry: bañḍugini araigen, b. vefai, being hungry [S. baḍagini]: bañḍu-dura, bulging or overhanging portion; bañḍudura lum, digging underneath so as to create an overhang: bañḍu-fai, hunger, hungry; ma bañḍufai vejje, I am hungry: bañḍufai vegen, b. genfaa, being hungry: bañḍu-filaa, an underwater plank of a boat: bañḍu-furaana mutti kurum, living from hand to mouth: bañḍu-fuř, reverse side; palm of the hand: bañḍu-musaara-ař beddum, kind of traditional wrestling: bañḍu-riyaa, billowing of a sail; riyaa-bañḍu dařu viyas, kanaku atdařu nuvaařee, even if you can breathe under the sail, you mustn't be in the power of a blind man (prov.): bañḍu-vak, one of the thwarts on a boat: bañḍu vaa akuru, second or rhyming letter in ḷem poetry : bañḍu-veen, diarrhoea; bañḍuveen jehifai, b. aḷaafai, struck with diarrhoea: bañḍu-hai, hunger, hungry (anc., mod. bañḍu-fai); bañḍuhai gen, being hungry: bañḍu-hañḍuu, payment in kind formerly granted to lower grades (cf. boḍu hañḍuu)

2. barge (bañḍu oḍi, also called booṭu batteli)

[S. baḍa, Skt. bhāṇḍa]

3008 BAŇḌEERI ބަނޑޭރި n. storekeeper (kaaḍuge b.); butler: Boḍu B., Treasurer, Finance Minister: Maa B., the King's Clerk: bañḍeeri-gañḍu, thick cover of a book (cf. beerugañḍu): Bañḍeeri-ge, Treasury, Ministry of Finance [S. bañḍäri,Skt. bhāṇḍāgārika]

3009 BAT ބަތް n. cooked rice (as v. hañḍuu): batek, a dish of rice: bat kakkanii, cooks rice: donkeyo-bat, fen-bat, boñḍi-bat, mas-bat, various rice dishes; eenaage bataa kaigen uḷum, living at his expense; bataa noonna, without food, i.e. unpaid: ree huri bat, cold (overnight) rice: bat kañdi, rice pudding: bat-tařiige ekfaḷi kaan, to share a husband: batpen, kind of porridge: batpoḷi, basket for sifting rice [S. bat, Skt. bhakta]

3010 BATAANA ބަތާނަ n.. lining of clothes: b. lanii, puts a lining on: b. foti, lining cloth [A. biṯāna]

3011 BATAAVI ބަތާވި adj. Javanese: in B. kara, Java: bataavi-gaa, pumice stone [Batavia (Jakarta)]

3012 BATKEE ބަތްކޭ n. kind of small boat

3013 BATTI ބައްތި n. lamp (in general): lighthouse; at b., kitchen lamp: fasleenu b., lamp with detachable chimney: fuḷi b., bottle lamp [H. battī, Skt. vartī]

3014 BATTIRIIS ބައްތިރީސް num. thirty-two (= tiriis deek) [cf. H. battīs]

3015 BATTELI (batteyyek) ބައްތެލި n. larger type of sailing craft (for transport): naukoḷu b., official dinghy: naalu b., transport ship: batteli-koḷu, former official boat of an avař : batteli-dooni, Male fishing boat [S. battal, Port. batelão]

3016 BADA ބަދަ n. knuckle (iñgiliige b.): vertebra (maikařiige b., maibada): joint of bamboo (onu bada) or sugarcane (ukdañḍi b.)

3017 BADAN ބަދަން n. (in dressmaking) de-badan, the two sections of a libaas

3018 BADAM ބަދަން n. any small edible nut; almond: siina b., ground nut, arachis hypogaea [H. bādām, Skt. vātāmra]

3019 BADALU ބަދަލު n. change: b. kuranii, changes (tr.), transfers; mi badalu koř diifaanan ta, can you exchange this? b. gennanii, brings about a change: b. denii, pays compensation, recompenses: b. hifanii, gives a return; b. hifan kuḷee kuḷivaru, a return match: kamtakaa medu (badalař) badalu hifum, taking revenge for (his) activities [U. badal]

3020 BADAHI ބަދަހި adj. strong, firm (met.): b. guḷum, firm ties: b. kuranii, consolidates [cf. H., Skt. baddha]

3021 BADI (bajjek) ބަޑި n. 1.set of coconut-shell toddy-cups bound together: badi-hadu, toddy tapper's equipment

2. rocks in the shallows (badi-gaňḍu)

3022 BADIGE ބަދިގެ n. kitchen: badige doř, kitchen area, back of house; badigeař lanii, (met.)treats disrespectfully

3023 BADIYAA ބަދިޔާ n. In hadiyaa-badiyaa, gifts (doublet)

3024 BADII ބަދީ v. (anc.)polite imp. ending: gos badii! go!

3025 BADU- ބަދު- prefix (lit.) un- ; badu-akhlaagii kam, immorality: bad-nasiib, unlucky: badunaamu kuranii, blames (for.., -gai, -ař, -aa medu): mikamun badunaamu vejje, was blamed for this [U. bad-, bad]

3026 BADURUVA ބަދުރުވަ n. asterism Bhadrapadā : b. laigatum, coming of Baduruva (a time of thunder); Fura B., seventh asterism of iruvai season: Fas B., eighth asterism of iruvai [cf. S. -puṭupa]

3027 BADDANII ބައްދަނީ v. grasps, encloses, hugs (v.n. beddum): fuskaru b., gets a stranglehold (in wrestling); fixes, solders: baddaa rankaru, soldering mixture; ties knot (tatun b.); patches up: fuu b., ties loose ends; mends hole in bottom; (met.) covers up; kuri-baddanii, obstructs: mas b., traps fish : see also bedenii [S. badanne, Skt. bādhate]

3028 BADDALU KURANII ބައްދަލު ކުރަނީ v. meets (with.., ..-aa); also baddalu vanii of unplanned meetings or of the inferior: eenaa mařaa b. vaanii kon irakun baavaee, when shall I meet him? eenaa-aai b. vedaane ta? may I see him? aḷugaňḍu maadamaa ves eenaayaai b. kuraanameve, I will meet him again tomorrow : aḷugaňḍu eenaayaai b. kuraan eenaage geař nugos uḷeni koř magumatin iyye b. vejje-eve, while I didn't go to his house to see him, I met with him on the street yesterday: baddalu-vum-tak baavvanii, arranges meetings

3029 BAŇDARU ބަނޑަރު n. harbour, lagoon: b. maṭii rařek, a coastal town (outside the Maldives): b. matii magu, harbour drive; bañdaru jahanii, enters harbour [U. bandar]

3030 BAŇDAA KOPII ބަނޑާކޮޕި n. kind of cabbage

3031 BAŇDI (bañjek) ބަނޑި n. a long rhyming incantation

3032 BAŇDE (BEŇDE) ބަނޑެ (ބެނޑެ) v. having bound (abs. of bannanii) [S. bäňda]

3033 BAŇDELI ބަނޑެލި n. kind of poultice : b. lai denii, puts a poultice on someone [bannanii]

3034 BAN (pron. batn, bän) ބަން v. tied, constructed (p.p. of bannanii) [S. ban]

3035 BANA ބަނަ adj. overcast (of weather)

3036 BANAFSAA ބަނަފްސާ n. a plant, violet [U. banafśā]

3037 BANAS (banahek) ބަނަސް 1. n. bun: banas heyo ta, do you like buns? [S. banis, E. buns]

3038 BANAS ބަނަސް 2. v. though one ties [bannanii]

3039 BANAATU ބަނާތު n. kind of thick cloth, broad cloth [H. banāt]

3040 BANIYAADAN ބަނިޔާދަން adj. (lit.) charming, well-behaved (esp. of girls)

3041 BANII ބަނި v. tied (3s. past of bannanii)

3042 BANUM ބަނުން v. tying (v.n. of bannanii) [S. bäňdum]

3043 BANGAAḶU ބަންގާޅު n. Bengal

3044 BANGI ބަންގި n. prayer call : b. govanii, calls to prayer [U. bāng]

3045 BANḌAARA ބަންޑާރަ adj. ibc., of the Government, state: b. gooccek, Government property: b. gaňḍuvaru, the royal palace: b. naibu, the Attorney General; n. pl.., banḍaarain, the King [T . paṇṭāram, treasury, cf. S. Banḍaara, prince]

3046 BANḌUN ބަންޑުން adv. face downwards: dimaa b., quite upside down: banḍun otum, lying prone: b. jahanii, turns over (tr.); banḍun jehee (of a baby), able to turn over

3047 BANḌELI, BANḌALI ބަންޑެލި - ބަންޑަލި n. bundle (esp. of paper) [E. bundle]

3048 BANDU ބަންދު 1. n. hoop: b. duvvanii, rolls a hoop; metal band, strap: fořiigai b. aḷanii, puts a strap round the box:kuḍadorekgai aḷaafai vaa bandu, fitted window bars [H. bandh, Skt. bandha]

2. adj. closed: b. duvas, bank holidays: b. kuranii, keeps under house arrest; blocks a street; packs up; seals [H. bandh, Skt. baddha]

3049 BANNANII ބަންނަނީ v. binds; constructs (v.n.banum : p.p. ban : past tensebanii : abs.baňde, beňde : 3s. pres. baňdee : hon. bannavanii): at b., ties the hands: dooni b., builds a boat: dau b., makes nets: vadu b., makes or ties fishing fly [S. baňdinne, P. bandhati]

3050 BANBUḌI ބަންބުޑި n. pricker for testing bags of rice etc.: b. jahanii, applies the pricker

3051 BAFAA ބަފާ n. father (low class or obs.): bafaa kaleege, father- in- law (in reference; addressed as bappa or beebe): de-bafaain, father and child: debafaakalun (debafaikalun), father and child (hon.) [old S. bapa, H. bāp]

3052 BAPPA ބައްޕަ n. father: don b., stepfather: bappa-men, father and friends: bappaa-fuḷu, hon. used in Shahi families : miinaage b., the child's father, my husband [Pkt. bappa, cf. S. bāppā, uncle]

3053 BABURU (pl., baburun) ބަބުރު n. negro: b. tin hama, kind of draughts: b. lava, negro songs (part of boḍuberu jehum, improper for children); baburu lava-ař neřum, dancing to such songs: rat baburu kelaa, aloes: b. loofiňdu, kind of dragonfly; (met.) smelly: b.vas, body odour, sweatiness: b. kihilifati, smelly armpit [S. baňburu, cf. U.barbarī, Berber]

3054 BABUḶANII ބަބުޅަނީ v. glitters (v.n. bebuḷum), usu. preceded by vidaa [S. babaḷanne]

3055 BAŇBARA ބަނބަރަ n. kind of creeper (b. veyo)

3056 BAŇBUKEYO (bañbukeelek) ބަނބުކެޔޮ n. breadfruit, artocarpus: b. kañḍanii, picks breadfruit: bañbukeelu hiti, a very good curry

3057 BAŇBUĻABOS ބަނބުޅަބޮސް n. pomelo or shaddock (grapefruit) [T.?]

3058 BAMA ބަމަ See boma

3059 BAYAAN ބަޔާން n. mention: b. kuranii, states, mentions (that.., ..kamugai): b. denii, provides contribution to a publication [U. bayān]

3060 BAYAANAVAI ބަޔާނަވައި num. 92 (= nuvadiha deek) [H. bayānvē]

3061 BAYAANAA (-aaek) ބަޔާނާ n. an advance or deposit: b. denii, pays deposit [U. bayānā]

3062 BAYAAHI ބަޔާހި num. 82 (= aŕḍiha deek) [H. bayāsī]

3063 BAYAAĻIIS ބަޔާޅީސް num. 42 (= saaḷiis deek) [H. bayālīs]

3064 BARAKAAT-TERI ބަރަކާތްތެރި adj. sacred, auspicious [U. barkat, pl.]

3065 BARANI ބަރަނި n. line of cotton thread : tin uḷi b., three-stranded cotton (used for kites): boñḍi b., ball of thread: nanu b., ball of twine: dañḍi b., reel of cotton: barani dañḍi, (empty) cotton reel [Persian, barnūn]

3066 BARAFOOS, BARUFOOS ބަރަފޫސް - ބަރުފޫސް n. projecting ledge or platform, podium [Persian, barfōs]

3067 BARABOO (barabolek)' ބަރަބޯ n. pumpkin, cucurbita maxima: b. haluvaa, sweetmeat made of pumpkins

3068 BARAVELI ބަރަވެލި n. hermit crab, land crab

3069 BARAHANAA ބަރަހަނާ adj. naked: b. kuranii, makes someone naked: barahanain hurum, being naked: roo b., stark naked [U. barahna]

3070 BARAA ބަރާ 1. adj. overladen: b. kuranii, loads heavily; baraa kam, heavy load: atmati baraa anhenek, a woman with too many children [baru]

3071 BARAA ބަރާ 2. n. canoe outrigger: float of seaplane: b. jahanii, fits outrigger

3072 BARAABARU ބަރާބަރު adj. exact: as excl., wonderful! b. haek jehi, it's exactly 6.0.: b. miihek, a punctual man: adv., baraabarař, exactly: baraabarař gaḍiyař annaati, come punctually! [H. barābar]

3073 BARI ބަރި n. 1. weight on a net or line: bari-koḷu, some weights. bari-gaňḍu, weighted line (to catch turtles); bari aḷanii, makes weights

2. rows, regular piles: ruk-bari, row of coconut trees; baribariař, in rows

3074 BARU ބަރު adj. heavy ; as n.., paperweight; (weight of) pendulum: baru aḍu, gruff or bass voice or sound: baru-kam boḍu,weighty : baru kanii, only in fenbaru k., nidi baru k., is full of (water, sleep): baru-dan, weight of an object: baru-marukaa, loading mark on boat: baru-min, weight of an object: baru-heli, slow and clumsy; heavy (of people) [cf. duru-heli, bura-heli] [S. bara, Skt. bhāra]

3075 BARUGONU ބަރުގޮނު n. horn, klaxon; b. aḷanii, aḷuvanii, sounds horn

3076 BARUTIILA ބަރުތީލަ n. presents formerly given in return for appointment to office; b. kuranii, b. aruvanii, offers such presents [A. birt̲īl]

3077 BARUDAAS KURANII ބަރުދާސް ކުރަނީ v. endures [U. bardāśt]

3078 BARUBAADU VANII ބަރުބާދު ވަނީ v. is wasted, is useless; (of people) is a failure [U. barbād]

3079 BARENḌAA (BERENḌAA) ބަރެންޑާ (ބެރެންޑާ) n. upstair balcony [E. veranda, etym. dub.]

3080 BAROS ބަރޮސް n. 1. kind of disease

2. name of an island in Male atoll

3081 BAROOSAA ބަރޯސާ n. confidence, trust [H. bharōsā, Skt.*bharavaśya]

3082 BAROOSII ބަރޯސީ n. weight for sinking objects in the sea

3083 BAL- ބަލް- See baa: balee, is old

3084 BALA ބަލަ excl. of warning, hi! excuse me! what! (hon., ballavaa!) ifc., as a polite imperative termination, balaa-bala, look! ais-bala, come!So also aḷugaňḍu den gos balanii, may I go?

3085 BALAI (BALAA) ބަލައި (ބަލާ) v. in order to get or fetch: rasiidu balai, to get the receipt: ṭanu balai, to get the registration: balai(gen) diyum, coming / going to fetch (something or someone): balaigatum, acceptance, receiving (neg., balaek nugatum) (abs. of balanii) [S. balā, towards]

3086 BALAGA ބަލަގަ excl. of warning, look out! [S. balaga, old imp.of √bal]

3087 BALADU-VERI(YAA) ބަލަދުވެރި(ޔާ) n. (person) legally responsible or in charge

3088 BALANII ބަލަނީ v. looks (v.n. belum : imp. balaa! hon.ballavanii, q.v.) looks at (things), nikam e tan balaabala! just look there! gaḍiyař balaalamun, looking at the clock; looks after (persons) (' looks at a person' requires -aa dimaa-ař): tiya belum nubalaařee, don't look like that; expects, waits: ma mihirii balan, I am waiting: konme kamek ves kuraakař nubalaane-ee, will not hesitate to do anything: nufenidaane kamař balaigen tiben, to expect that (it) might not appear: tiyaii hilee miihakař nubalamee, I don't regard you as a marriageable woman; (invol.) e miihunař belijje, they happened to see; Caus., baluvanii, ballanii, q.v. [S. balanne, Skt. √bhal]

3089 BALAHAṬṬANII ބަލަހައްޓަނީ v. looks after; sees to (v.n.beleheṭṭum) [Enlargement of balanii]

3090 BALAA (-aaek) 1. ބަލާ n. difficulties, bad times: balaa fořenii, bad luck afflicts one: balaa jassavanii, creates difficulties (hon.): balaa faa kurevvum, (of God) sending us trials [U. balā]

3091 BALAA 2. ބަލާ v. abs. or imp. of balanii

3092 BALI (bayyek) ބަލި adj. weak (usually of things); (of people) ill, illness: eenaa bali, he is ill: bali ve hurum / otum, being ill: bali vum, being ill , being weak, losing out: bali viyyaa, if you get ill: balii viyyaa, since you are ill: bali ve inum, being pregnant: bali kuranii, defeats; bali jehenii, disease strikes: raajje bali, rheumatism; bali-kaři, physically weak (cf. varu-bali)

3093 BALIMAANU ބަލިމާނު n . ugly kind of monkey [Persian, balma]

3094 BALIILAAN ބަލީލާން See aliilaan

3095 BALUN ބަލުން adv. alun balun, all over again (doublet) [alun]

3096 BALLANII ބައްލަނީ v. causes to look (v.n. bellum): raahi ballanii, (of the client) gets the eduru to consult the stars [for baluvanii, caus. of balanii]

3097 BALLAVANII ބައްލަވަނީ v. looks (middle grade) (v.n. bellevum): ballavaa-lavvamaa, doek too, let's see, shall we? eats, drinks (middle grade); accepts: ballavaigatii, bought (hon.): kaavani ballavai-gatum, agreeing to a marriage (high hon.) (hon. of balanii)

3098 BAVATI (bavaccek) ބަވަތި n. omen

3099 BAVANII ބަވަނީ v. scolds (v.n. bevum), with dat. of object

3100 BAVAASII ބަވާސީ n. a disease, piles [U. bavāsīr]

3101 BAS (bahek) ބަސް n. 1. word; language: Divehi bas, Maldivian language: bas huṭṭifai, stuck for words: bas hoodan konum, searching for information: bas vikenii, is obeyed; magee bahek nuvikeenee, I shan't be obeyed: eenaa-akii bas vikee miihekee, he gets obeyed: bas naahaa, disobedient: bas nuvikee oḍiige diruñbaakoḷař naaraařee, don't go to the front of an unmanageable boat (prov.) [S. bas, Skt. bhāṣā]
2. bus : bahugaa, bahun, by bus [E. bus]

3102 BASTAA(BASDAA) (-aaek) ބަސްތާ (ބަސްދާ) n. sackful [U. basta, bale]

3103 BASSANII ބައްސަނީ v. includes, involves (v.n. bessum): eenaa e kamtakaa bessumek nufene-ee, I don't feel he should be involved in that: eenaa bassaane kamek net, there is no reasaon to include him: mařaa nubessii kiikve hee, why have (you) left me out? (caus. of bahanii)

3104 BASSAVANII ބައްސަވަނީ v. distributes (hon.)(v.n. bessevum): havaru/ havarař fatafoḷi bessevum, distribution of (former royal) charity to the people (hon. of bahanii)

3105 BAZABAAZU ބަޒަބާޒު n. mace, myristica fragrans (used as a 'concoction' or matikaraa bees) [U. bazbāz, Skt. vasavāsi]

3106 BAHAṬṬANII ބަހައްޓަނީ v. deposits, leaves standing (of single objects) (v.n. beheṭṭum : imp. bahaṭṭaa!): mi saitaři tabakugai bahaṭṭaa gendaařee,take away this cup on the tray: saitaři tabakugai bahaṭṭaafai daařee, leave this cup on the tray: dooni b., sets ship on a course: dooni vayař nagaafai beheṭṭum, keeping course into the wind; (of emotions) displays: hurmatterikam b., shows respect: ekves rahumek nubahaṭṭavai, showing no mercy; fahař b., postpones: farikkoḷu bahaṭṭaa miihaa, servant who lays aristocrats' tables

3107 BAHANAA(-aaek) ބަހަނާ n. excuse: bahanaaek dakkanii, gives an excuse [U. bahāna]

3108 BAHANII ބަހަނީ v. divides, apportions; deals (cards) (v.n. behum): bahaigen (at football), passing: muddu bahaigen, distributing (to the poor) as a voluntary fine: see also behenii [S. bedanne]

3109 BAHIIŇ / BAŇHII ބަހީ Used colloquially after imperatives, especially to children: damaa bahii, let's go! nikam bahii bala, come in! [cf. badii]

3110 BAHURUVA ބަހުރުވަ n. the language of speech, manner of speech: masveriinge b., fishermen's speech: baazaaru matii(ge) b., bazaar talk [?Skt. bhāṣārūpa]

3111 BAHUS ބަހުސް n. disputing [U. bahuth]

3112 BAHE ބަހެ Word used in proclamations, 'I announce'

3113 BAŘI (baṭṭek) ބަޑި n. 1. brinjals, solanum melongena: bařiigai kakkaa rihaek, a brinjal curry: bařigan, a brinjal curry; vilaatu bari, tomato [S. baṭu, Skt. bhaṇṭakī]

2. a girls' game: the ball of woven coconut leaves used in playing it; b. viyegen, making the ball: bari-kooṭu [E. -court], bari-ge, court for playing bari on

3114 BAĻAABUUĻI KURANII ބަޅާބޫޅި ކުރަނީ v. curls up limbs in a fury (e.g. of wild animals), or in a convulsion (baḷaabuuḷi vanii) [From baḷu, on analogy of malaameli etc.]

3115 BAĻIŇDU ބަޅިނޑު n. kind of bumble bee

3116 BAĻU ބަޅު adj. bent, crooked: naguu baḷu, having a crooked tail, i.e. dog: doglike (as an insult): baḷuvaḷi, sickle; baḷu kuranii, bends (tr.) [S. balu, Skt. bhallūka, dog, would appear to be different]

3117 BAA (BAU) ބާ (ބައު) (bal-) 1. adj. old (of inanimate things) baa ge-ek, a dilapidated house (as v. muskuḷi ge-ek, an antique house): baa vaahakaek, a stale story (muskuḷi vaahakaek, an ancient story): balař kaňḍaa, making a reduction because of age: baa vanii, gets shabby: baa hedifai vaa, (of wood) hollow or rotten, full of holes; baa-gaňḍu, an opening or broken place (in fence, roof, etc.), hollow in wood: baagaňḍugaňḍu, holes

3118 BAA ބާ 2. n. the letter B in the Arabic and Maldivian alphabets : baa kiyanii, (of children) reads Arabic script: baaek nukiyeene, B cannot be pronounced: Baa atoḷu, southern part of Maaḷosmaḍulu atoll

3. particle denoting a query (cf. also baava-ee): kiikve baa, why, I wonder: annaane baaee hitař araa, wondering if (he) will come: das kuri baa, I expect (he) has learnt: mihen nuun baa, isn't that so?

4. ibc. in certain numerals, two: baaviis, 22: baavanna, 52 (= fansaas deek): baahaṭṭi, 62 (= fasdoḷas deek): baahattari, 72 (= hatdiha deek) [cf. H. bāīs, bāvan, bāsaṭh, bahattar]

3119 BAAKII ބާކީ n. remainder: baakii de-ek, two left over, two to carry: baakii laari, (of money) the change; in a proper name, Baakii Ḷatuṯṯu [U. bāqī]

3120 BAAGA ބާގަ n. half of an aḍubai, viz. two laahi or one bottle: baaga fuḷi, bottle containing one baaga

3121 BAAJII ބާޖީ n. In baajii maranii, lays bets [U. bāzī]

3122 BAAJJAVERI ބާއްޖަވެރި adj. prosperous, blessed [S. bhāgya-]

3123 BAAḌI ބާޑި n. parapet for defence of an island: baaḍi-fař, slum area beyond the old city walls of Male; fas baaḍi jahanii, mucks up the ground, makes a mess

3124 BAADALAA ބާދަލާ n. gold or silver thread, for ornamenting clothing, hookahs , kites [U. bādlā]

3125 BAADIRII ބާދިރީ n. pearl millet, pennisetum typhoides

3126 BAAŇDII ބާނދީ n. (obs.) lady-in-waiting

3127 BAAN ބާން n. See bain

3128 BAANANII ބާނަނީ v. 1. puts into (v.n. beenum : hon. baanuvvanii) : at / iňgili baananii, pokes fingers into (with dat.): aňga baananii, butts into a conversation

2. catches (fish) by line and rod (v.n. beenum, anc.beevum): mas beenee too belum, seeing if fish can be caught; kuruňbaa baananii, brings down coconuts (by rope or hook), keyo b., picks bananas : see also beenenii [S. bānne, ?Skt. bhraṃśayati]

3129 BAANI ބާނި n. curling waves: ripples, bubbles of water; old kind of rocket

3130 BAABIL ބާބިލް n. Babylon

3131 BAABILI ބާބިލި n. space under the eaves

3132 BAABU ބާބު n. chapter of a book [U. bāb]

3133 BAAMIYAA ބާމިޔާ n. a vegetable, abelmoschus esculentus: b. toḷi, ladies' fingers

3134 BAAMU ބާމު n. embrocation, balm [E. balm]

3135 BAARA ބާރަ num. twelve (= doḷas): baara duvas, the 12th of Rabii'ul avval (the Prophet's birthday) [old S. bara, H. bārah]

3136 BAARALII ބާރަލީ n. In baaralii fen, barley water [E. barley]

3137 BAARII ބާރީ n. ornamental projecting ledge just above the loading line (b. fař)

3138 BAARU ބާރު n. strength; speed; pressure: duveli baaru, speed of travel: baaru-kam, tightness (of clothes): baaru-gada, strong: baaru-min, pressure: baaru-veriyaa, forceful person: muř baaru, closefisted: adv., baarař taḷanii, beats hard: baarař duvanii, runs quickly: baarun, with difficulty; b. aḷanii, gives encouragement: b. erenii, muscles seize up: b. denii, gives encouragement: b. lanii, exerts strength: b. vanii, is tight; fiti baaru vanii, is squashed together: furi baaru vefai, being packed tight: fen baaru hifanii, floats; (met.) manages by oneself

3139 BAAROOZU ބާރޫޒު n. saltpetre (for cleaning jewellery, or as styptic): b. aavi, smell of saltpetre [U. bārūt, bārūd]

3140 BAALANII (BAILANII) ބާލަނީ (ބައިލަނީ) v. lowers; lifts off (v.n. beelum : caus. baaluvanii : hon. baaluvvanii): oḍi b., launches an odi: : libaas b., takes off a libaas : buuṭ b., takes off boots (as v. faivaanun faibanii, takes off shoes): tuňbuḷi b., shaves beard: boo b., shaves head (as v. boo kořanii, cuts hair): booṭun mudaa b., brings goods ashore [baananii 2 + lanii]

3141 BAALIDII ބާލިދީ n. bucket [S. bāldi, Port. balde]

3142 BAALIIS (baaliihek) ބާލީސް n. pillow: baaliihu ura, pillowcase: fohee b., kind of duster [U. bāliś]

3143 BAAVA ބާވަ (lit.) particle denoting a query, 'I wonder' : e kamtak nimunii kihinek baava-ee, I wonder how it all ended [cf. baa 3]

3144 BAAVAI-LAVVANII ބާވައިލައްވަނި v. See baavaalavvanii

3145 BAAVAT ބާވަތް n. category: baavataku eccek, a kind of thing

3146 BAAVANII ބާވަނި v. 1. For baananii 2
2. = baa + vanii, gets old [baa 1]

3147 BAAVANNA ބާވަންނަ num. 52 [baa 4, H. bāvan]

3148 BAAVAA-LAVVANII (BAAVAI-LAVVANII) ބާވާލައްވަނި (ބާވައިލައްވަނި) v. (of God) reveals

3149 BAAVIIS ބާވީސް num. 22 [baa 4, H. bāīs]

3150 BAAVVANII ބާއްވަނި v. puts down, lays down (v.n. beevvum, imp. baavvaa !) : eňdugai b., lays (a person) on a bed, esp. for circumcision: (of telephones) den baavvanii, I'm ringing off; (met.) fixes: mi hurihaa kamek baavvanii, settles this whole affair: baddaluvumtak b., arranges meetings: rahmatterikam b., preserves friendship [caus. of baananii 2]

3151 BAASALA, BAASALU ބާސަލަ - ބާސަލު n. rotten area in timber (baasala-gaňḍu) [? baa 1]

3152 BAASAA ބާސާ n. See baisaa

3153 BAASKIILI (BAISKIILI) ބާސްކީލި (ބައިސްކީލި) n. In baaskiilin, across one shoulder: debaaskiilin, across both shoulders

3154 BAAZAARU ބާޒާރު n. shopping area, bazaar: b. matii(ge) baharuva, traders' language: b. maccař gos hadaigen, going up to market : b. matin, around the bazaar [U. bāzār]

3155 BAAZII ބާޒީ n. contest: baitu baazii kuranii, participates in poetic contest: b. libum, winning in such a contest [U. bāzī]

3156 BAAZU ބާޒު n. hawk, harrier [U. bāz]

3157 BAAHAṬṬI ބާހަށްޓި num. 62 (= fas doḷas de-) [baa 4, H. bāsaṭh]

3158 BAAHATTARI ބާހައްތަރި num. 72 (=hatdiha de-) [baa 4, cf. H. bahattar]

3159 BIKA ބިކަ adj. wretched: b. haalekgai, in a wretched state; b. vanii, is in a poor way [H. bikhā]

3160 BIKURU ބިކުރު n. hymen; virginity: bikuru-veri, virgin: b. kaňḍanii, deflowers [U. bikr]

3161 BIGARU ބިގަރު n. pressure lamp

3162 BICAARU ބިޗާރު n. In laacaara-bicaara(ya)ř uḷum / hiňgum, living / wandering aimlessly [cf. H. bēcārā, destitute]

3163 BICUU (biculek) ބިޗޫ n. scorpion or centipede [H. bicchū, Skt. vṛścika]

3164 BIJILII ބިޖިލީ n. electricity: b. batti, electric lamp [H. bijlī, S. viduli, cf. Skt. vidyut]

3165 BIJOOḌU ބިޖޯޑު adj. odd-numbered: jooḍu-bijooḍu, a game [H. bējōṛ, without joints]

3166 BIḌI ބިޑި 1. n . handcuffs, leg-irons: b. aḷanii, applies irons: applies clamps on tents or scaffolding [H. bēṛī, Skt. vīṭikā]

2. n. 'beedi' cigarette: karudaahu b., paper-wrapped beedi: fat b., fatu b., rařu b., leaf-wrapped beedi: Kalki b., beedi from Calicut [H. bīṛī]

3167 BIT ބިތް n. partition wall, often of woven leaves (bit-gaňḍu) : raajjeege hataru bitun, in the four corners of the country : bit-doř, the wall side, far side (of furniture, cf. magat): enme bitdořun, in the far background [S. bitti, bit, Skt. bhitti]

3168 BIT KURANII ބިތް ކުރަނީ v. lets a vessel drift: bit vanii, drifts out of the way; oyaa bitvani koř, while drifting with the current : (met.) idles, does nothing; faaḍakař bit vefai eba in, is strangely silent [bit]

3169 BIDEESII (pl., bideesiin) ބިދޭސީ n. foreigner [H. bidēsī, Skt. vidēśī]

3170 BIŇDE ބިނދެ v. having snapped off (tr.) (abs. of binnanii) [S. biňda]

3171 BIŇDENII ބިނޑެނީ v. snaps off (intr.); cracks (intr.) (v.n. biňdum, cf. binum) : maa biňdevee too masakkat kurum (invol.), trying to pick flowers; kaaři biňdenii, coconuts crack: at biňdigen, having a fractured arm (invol. of binnanii) [S. biňdenne]

3172 BINAU, BINAA (binaaek) ބިނާ - ބިނައު n . a building: b. kuranii, builds [U. binā]

3173 BINAAṬU ބިނާޓު n. lacelike ornamentation on Maldivian hookah : b. noḷi, decorative hookah mouthpiece; b. kuranii, applies this decoration

3174 BINUM ބިނުން v. picking, plucking (v.n. of binnanii) [S. biňdum]

3175 BINDANII ބިންދަނީ v. breaks up (sticks, logs); snaps (pencil lead); iňgili bindanii, counts on the fingers (by bending them) (caus. of binnanii)

3176 BINNANII ބިންނަނީ v. picks (flowers, fruits); splits open (coconuts) (abs. biňde : 3s. biňde-ee : p.p. bin : v.n. binum : invol. biňdenii , q.v.) [S. biňdinne, P. bhindati]

3177 BINBI ބިންބި n. kurakkan, finger millet, eleusine coracana: binbi fuř, black flour

3178 BIBII ބިބީ n. queen (at cards); laaluge b., queen of hearts : butterfly fish [U. bībī, lady]

3179 BIM ބިން n. ground: kuḷivaru kuḷee bimek, a playground: bimu aḍiigai, below ground; bimař lanii, ceremonially puts a seven-day child on the ground: bim-gaňḍu, ground area, foundations: bim-gaa, foundation stone; bimgaa aḷanii, lays foundation stone: bim-garaas, cellar: bim-mati, the floor: bim-vaḷu, carving in relief; bimvaḷu naganii, carves, inscribes : (met.) hitugai bimvaḷu negum, inscribing on one's heart: bim-maguu, a plant, hedyotis biflora: bim-hima, a medicinal plant, euphorbia thymifolia , also desmodium triflorum [S. bim, Skt. bhūmi]

3180 BIMU-DAABBA ބިމުދާއްބަ n. a mythical spirit

3181 BIYA ބިޔަ adj. huge

3182 BIYARU ބިޔަރު n. beer [E. beer]

3183 BIRIYAANI ބިރިޔާނި n. dish of meat and rice [H. biryānī]

3184 BIRU ބިރު n. fear : biru kuḍa, tame (of animals), shameless (of people); aharen biru ganee, I am afraid (of him, eenaa deke); biru-veri, apprehensive: bom aḷaafaane kamuge biruverikam, fear that bombs might be dropped : biru-veti, meticulous, respectful; maat Kalaañge kibayař biruveti vum, fearing God [S. biri, biru, Skt. bhīru]

3185 BILAADARU ބިލާދަރު n. a certain size of rope

3186 BILIGAA (-aaek) ބިލިގާ n. washtub

3187 BILIMAGU / BILAMAGU ބިލިމަގު - ބިލަމަގު n. a sour-tasting fruit, country gooseberry, averrhoa bilimbi (used with sugar to remove rust stains) [S. bilim̩]

3188 BILISSA ބިލިއްސަ n. In nika-bilissa, a kind of nika tree

3189 BILU ބިލު n. bill (for payment) [E. bill]

3190 BILET ބިލެތް n. betel leaf, piper betle (Divehi b., veyo b.): bilet ari, betel trellis: bilet-kaṭṭala, kind of yam, dioscorea alata: bilet- kuri, the betel creeper shoots: bilet-gañḍu, sheaf of betel leaves : biletmaa loofiñdu, kind of dragonfly: bilet-huni, betel and lime: biletu haki, betel tendrils: biletu hui, kind of grass which grows uunder betel trellises; bilet (-gañḍu) aḷanii, makes up bundles of betel: bilet hadanii, trims edges of betel-sheaf [S. bulat, Skt. tāmbūla]

3191 BILLAḌII ބިއްލަޑީ n. bill of lading [E. bill lading]

3192 BILLI ބިއްލި n. stick turning a cogwheel

3193 BILLUURI ބިއްލޫރި n. glass: b. karudaas, cellophane: b.tari, tumbler: kori b., frosted glass [U. billōr]

3194 BIS (bihek) ބިސް n. egg(s): fish roe (don b., hard roe: kiru b., soft roe); kidney of cocks: bihu goboḷi, yolk: bis-gañḍu, pancake; omelette (kuḷi bisgañḍu); meringue (foni b.); kukuḷu bihugai aḷaa b., omelette made of eggs: bis-maḷi, string attached to leg of hen for tracking purposes: bis-vari, egg-laying season: bis-vaḷu, hole where turtles lay their eggs: bis-hini, kind of ant [S. biju, Skt. bīja]

3195 BISII ބިސީ n. picnic group: bisii keum, bisii bisiiař keum, eating in a picnic group

3196 BISKOODU ބިސްކޯދު n. biscuit: biskoodu-gañḍu, (pej.) rotten old biscuit [S. biskōtu, Port. biscouto]

3197 BISTAANA ބިސްތާނަ n. enclosed burial area [U. bustān, flower garden]

3198 BIHI ބިހި n. pimple: kas bihi-tak, a rash; bihi naganii, pimples erupt

3199 BIHU ބިހު n. See bis

3200 BII VANII ބީ ވަނީ v. slips away: magee atun mifot bii viyaka nudeenameve, I won't let go of this book: vaziifat biivedaane, (one) might lose the job: aňbimiihaa biivanii, the woman slopes off

3201 BIITAA ބީތާ adj. dazed, inattentive: b. vanii, is dazed

3202 BIIDA ބީދަ n. kind, sort (of habits and tastes): kon biidaekge miihek hee, what sort of man? [S. vidiha, H. vidhā]

3203 BII-FAANU ބީފާނު n. name of a respectable woman (cf. Kalaa-faanu)

3204 BIIMAHIIMA ބީމަހީމަ n. valuable product of a marine animal, used for scent

3205 BIIRAṬṬEHI ބީރައްޓެހި adj. not of one's own island: (pej.) strange, not genuine [bii + rař]

3206 BIIRU ބީރު adj. deaf [S. bīru, Skt. badhira]

3207 BIISSANII ބީއްސަނީ v. gets vessel to run aground in the sand (caus. of biihenii)

3208 BIISSAVANII ބީއްސަވަނީ v. In fainpuḷu biissavanii, goes, comes (of the Prophet) (hon. from biihenii)

3209 BIIHENII ބީހެނީ v. touches (usu. accidentally): temifaa onna kuttaaekgai biihum, touching a wet dog: Divehi raajjeege farufarař biihe-eve, runs aground on Maldivian reefs: ham hurakaa nulai biihum, directly touching the skin: nubiihenñaa kaňḍaa hamaee, if you are not aground, it is as good as the open sea, i.e. it'll be o.k. if you don't get caught (prov.)

3210 BUI ބުއި v. See boi

3211 BUIM ބުއިން v. drinking (v.n. of bonii); a drink (buimek) [S. bīm]

3212 BUII ބުއީ v. See bonii

3213 BUK ބުކް n. breast (childish) (med., uramati), also used of men: breast-milk (coll., kiru): buk-koḷu, some milk [? S. boku, intestines]

3214 BUKUŇḌI ބުކުނޑި n . See ukuňḍi-

3215 BUCAA ބުޗާ n. A proper name

3216 BUJAA ބުޖާ n. An imported food made with roasted rice [H. bhujiyā]

3217 BUḌU ބުޑު n. base, esp. of trees (buḍu-gaňḍu) or of buildings (bitu b., faaru b., base of a wall): (slang) buttocks; buḍu-vak, base thwart in a doni [H. būṃḍ]

3218 BUḌḌAA ބުޑްޑާ n. old man (vulg.) [H. buḍḍhā, Skt. vṛddhaka]

3219 BUDA ބުދަ n. Wednesday [S. badā(dā), Skt. Budha-]

3220 BUDU ބުދު n. idol, statue; doll: budu-koolu, Hindu or Buddhist temple [S. Budu, Skt. Buddha, the Buddha]

3221 BUDDI ބުއްދި n. intelligence, judgment: b. goos vanii, is 'backward': b. hama-aǐ hurum, being of sound mind: eenaa b. fas vegen uḷenii, he has lost his head, lost his temper: b. kuranii, uses the brain, is sensible: buddi haluvaa, deceptive: kuḷa buddi, clever ideas; boḍu buddi-veriyek, a very clever chap [Skt. buddhi]

3222 BUN ބުން n. unground coffee bean: bun gas, coffee bush: gahuvaa hadaa bun, bean from which coffee is made [U. bunn]

3223 BUNANII ބުނަނީ v. speaks (basic level word; abs. bune : imp. bunee! 3s.bune-ee : past tense bunñeve, buneppe : hon. bunuvvanii, cf. vidaaḷu vanii): speaks to.., loc. (not dat.), e.g. ..gaatugai, ..kairiigai: tells to do, nubunuvvaa kamek, something you didn't tell me to do; boḍu bunanii, boasts; (invol.) aḷugaňḍaǐ bunevuneve, I burst out with.. [S. baṇinne, Skt. bhaṇati]

3224 BUNBAA ބުންބާ n. Bombay: b. miihun, Borahs (resident in Male until 1965)

3225 BUNVARU ބުންވަރު n. stamina: b. gada, indefatigable; b. dera, easily tired

3226 BUM 1. ބުން n. boom (of sailing ship), goosii bum [E. boom]

2. ބުން adj. sullen (angry and quiet); low (of sounds), as v. ziila : b. vanii, is sullen [S. bummanne]; b. beru, a small double-ended drum, or its music: bum beru jahanii, plays the low drum: b. koḷu, the bass end (as v. toi koḷu)

3227 BUMA ބުމަ n. eyebrow [S. bäma, P. bhamu(ka)]

3228 BUMARU ބުމަރު n.. spinning top: b. jahanii, spins a top [S. bañbara, Skt. bhramara]

3229 BURA ބުރަ adj. heavy (esp. met.): bura masakkatek, a hard job: tiya haa bura kamekgai hifum, taking charge in such a weighty matter: maa bura koř uḷuvvum, doing too much: buraagai inna, pregnant [cf. baru]

3230 BURAKAŘI ބުރަކަޅި n. For burikaři

3231 BURAKI (buratkek) ބުރަކި n. 1. brake (also burek): b. jassanii, applies brake [E. break]

2. a bait fish, anthias or lepidozygus (a damselfish) (also bureki) : Buraki Rani, an infamous 16th century queen of the Maldives

3232 BURAŇDA ބުރަނޑަ n. a creeper, boerhavia repens: b. goňḍi, root of b.

3233 BURAŇDU ބުރަނޑު n. a troublesome small damselfish, sergeantfish (gui-burañdu)

3234 BURANII ބުރަނީ v. flies out in clouds (as of dust or scent); explodes; splashes up; spreads around: kudikudi ve buraigen diyum, buraburaigen diyum, explosion; fen buraifi, water splashes up; gayař tiki buraane-ee, the drops will splash (your) body; kalee muunugai eherii kuvaa buraafa-ee, there are discolorations on your face; kunamehi burum, flies buzzing about: Caus., causes to circulate: dum buruvum, vas buruvum, applying smoke (for fumigation, e.g. of wardrobes); enlarged (met.), buraa-lanii, shows up briefly: buraalaafai hiňgajje-ee, looked in briefly: buraalaafai avahař daa, which quickly moves on: buraa ves nulai, without appearing at all

3235 BURAFATI ބުރަފަތި n. propeller: vai b., toy windmill

3236 BURA-HELI ބުރަހެލި adj. unwell, slack, seedy [cf. baru-heli]

3237 BURAASFATI ބުރާސްފަތި n. Thursday [S. brahaspatin(dā)]

3238 BURI ބުރި 1. n. stump, short part (usu. ifc.): at-buri gamiis, bush shirt: iňgili b., stump of finger : dańḍi b., bits of stick: noḷi b., mouthpiece of hookah: faṭluunu b., shorts: hoḷi buri, striplight: matii buri, upper floor of building; de-buri ge, two-storeyed house (deburiař hadaafai huri ge); buri kuranii, cuts off sections: buri buri kuranii, chops into bits: buriek nuve-ee, is not (properly) cut off;
buri-fan, repair sections of cadjan: buri-varu, part, section (often pej.); fan burivaru, poor section of cadjan: buri- hańḍuu, middle-sized grains of rice (used for cakes): buri-ham naganii, flays prostrate with canes (buriin ham naganii);
buri faibanii, piles erupt on rectum (buri faibaa bali, disease of piles)

3239 BURI ބުރި 2. v. splashed up (past tense of buranii)

3240 BURI-KAŘI (BURAKAŘI) ބުރިކަށި (ބުރަކަށި) n. backbone, back

3241 BURU ބުރު n. circle ; heat or round (of a competition); circular route (for procession); circular frame (for mosquito net): buru-gańḍu, winding wheel; buru jahanii, circles (of an aeroplane): buru aňburaalanii, (slang) makes quick work of it

3242 BURUGAA ބުރުގާ n. woman's headdress: boḍu b., Arabian long headdress : b. aḷanii, wears this headdress [U. burqa']

3243 BURUDAA(-aaek) ބުރުދާ n. b. kiyanii, delivers an all-night recital ; b. gaimu kuranii, checks a fact

3244 BURUNU ބުރުނު n. asterism Bharaṇī [S. beraṇa]

3245 BURUMAA (-aaek) ބުރުމާ n. carpenter's drill : b. kaři, drill bit : saraka b., hand-drill (with wheel): faalu b., geared drill : karanṭu b., electric drill
[S. buruma, Port. verruma]

3246 BURUS ބުރުސް n. brush [E. brush]

3247 BURU-SUURA ބުރުސޫރަ n. human features [U. s̱ūra, form]

3248 BURUSSANII ބުރުއްސަނީ v. scatters, sprinkles: fenfodek b., sprinkles water: (enlarged) vayař burussaa-laafai, having scattered to the winds (caus. of buruhenii)

3249 BURUZU ބުރުޒު n. bastion [U. burj]

3250 BURUHENII ބުރުހެނީ n. is scattered, sprinkled (invol. of burussanii)

3251 BURUU (burulek) ބުރޫ n. knots and snags that form in a slack rope: b. aranii, b. jehenii, knots form: b. baalanii, gets rid of knots [S. burul, slack]

3252 BUREK ބުރެކް n. 1. brake (see buraki 1)
2. a circle (indef. of buru)

3253 BUREKI ބުރެކި n. See buraki 2

3254 BUREVI ބުރެވި n. an aquatic tree

3255 BUROḶI ބުރޮޅި n. a medicinal nut, ‘beleric myrobalan’, terminalia belerica: kaři buroḷi, gallnut, quercus infectoria [S. bulu]

3256 BURRAAS ބުއްރާސް n. (of hens) giving a squawk and running (b. jahanii): (of old women) furious shouting

3257 BULIBULI (bulibuyyek) ބުލިބުލި n. small glass bowl with lid

3258 BULUUKIYAA ބުލޫކިޔާ n. a herb, corchorus capsularis [A. mulūkhiya]

3259 BULUUNI ބުލޫނި n. chemical ‘blue’

3260 BUHUTAAN ބުހުތާން n. deliberate lies (buhutaan dogu) [U. buhtān]

3261 BUḶAA, BUḶAU (buḷalek) ބުޅައު - ބުޅާ n. cat: b. naguu, a flower, acalypha sp.: zabaadu b., civet cat [S. baḷalā, Skt. biḍāla]

3262 BUḶI ބުޅި n. hook : mas baanaa b., fish-hook: buḷi-goř, hook and eye : b. aḷanii, inserts hook: b. jahanii, makes hook; as adj., curly : buḷi bolek, curly hair : b. vanii, is curly ; buḷi-gaňḍu, hook for lifting objects [S. bili, P. baḷisa]

3263 BUḶI-TUŇBI (buḷituňtbek) ބުޅިތުނބި n. curlew [‘hook-mouth’]

3264 BUUGANVILAA ބޫގަންވިލާ n. bougainvillea (also called daa<u>kh</u>iliyyaa maa) [E. bougainvillea]

3265 BUUṬU ބޫޓު n. shoes : b. faivaan, leather shoes; b. lanii, puts on shoes: buuṭu baaluvvaa, (hon.) take off your shoes! [E. boot]

3266 BUUTU ބޫތު n. craving: viyafaariaai b. ganegen, greedy for trade: b. kanii, craves

3267 BUUM ބޫމް n. booming sound (buum aḍu): b. govvanii, booms (of insects); in childish language, aeroplane [E. boom]

3268 BEI (bein) ބެއި See bee

3269 BEINUM ބެއިނުމް See beenum

3270 BEINDANII ބެއިންދަނީ See beendanii

3271 BEIRU ބެއިރު See beeru

3272 BECUM ބެޗުމް v. escaping (v.n. of bacanii)

3273 BEJU ބެޖު n. badge: b. jahaigen, wearing the badge [E. badge]

3274 BEṬ ބެޓް n. cricket bat [E. bat]

3275 BEṬERII ބެޓެރީ n. electric battery [E. battery]

3276 BEDENII ބެދެނީ v. is stuck ; is solidified: masgaňḍu b., shoal is caught in net: abunaa bedigen, pipe is clogged: (met.) miihun kuřekgai b., people are caught in offences: aharen aḍu bedijje, I lost my voice; eenaa uḷenii aḍu bedigen, he has lost his voice: baagaňḍu bedenii, broken fence is joined up, repaired: kaňḍaai faḷaai bedee tan, where the deep sea joins the shallows; (of jelly) sets (invol. of baddanii)

3277 BEDDUM ބެއްދުމް v. grasping (v.n. of baddanii) [S. bädīm]

3278 BEŇDE ބެނދެ v. having bound (abs. of bannanii) [S. bäňda]

3279 BENKU (BEENKU) ބެންކު (ބޭންކު) n. financial bank [E. bank]

3280 BENNEVUM ބެންނެވުމް v. binding (hon. v.n. of bannanii)

3281 BENBOḶU ބެންބޮޅު n. kind of tarafana cake

3282 BEBUḶUM ބެބުޅުން n. glittering (v.n. of babuḷanii) [S. bäbaḷīm]

3283 BEYAS ބެޔަސް v. though one catch (for beeniyas) [baananii]

3284 BEYYAA ބެއްޔާ n. a proper name (non-Male)

3285 BEYYEVE ބެއްޔެވެ v. looked (for beli-eve, past tense of balanii)

3286 BERI ބެރި n. cross timbers, esp. on roofs or on fishing vessels: b. aḷanii, fixes these timbers

3287 BERU ބެރު n. drum: b. jahanii, plays drum; beru-oni, drum frame:beru-daňḍi(-gaňḍu), drumstick: daňḍiberu, drumming with a stick: bum beru, bass drum: boḍu beru jehum, a kind of drumming for dances:beru-dummaari-taaḷafili, the threefold royal band: fen varaa b., drum for bathing at 9 a.m. on Fridays: beru-veriyaa, drummer (anc., beru-kaleefaanu) [S. bera, Skt. bhēri]

3288 BEREKI ބެރެކި n. erotic ballads (bereki raivaru)

3289 BERENḌAA ބެރެންޑާ n. See barenḍaa

3290 BEREBEDI ބެރެބެދި n. kind of tree with red flowers, erythrina variegata, coral tree [S. erabadu]

3291 BELUM ބެލުން v. looking (v.n. of balanii) : belum-terikam, solicitousness; beyyeve, looked (3rd s. past, for beli-eve) [S. bälīm]

3292 BELUUN(U) ބެލޫނު - ބެލޫން n. big balloon, usu. of paper, raised by heat (as v. fuppaa ham): b. aruvanii, sends up balloon [E. balloon]

3293 BELENI-VERI(YAA) ބެލެނިވެރި(ޔާ) n. temporary guardian (cf. baladuveriyaa)

3294 BELEHEṬṬUM ބެލެހެއްޓުން v. supervision (v.n. of balahaṭṭanii): beleheṭṭumuge dařugai / matiigai, under supervision

3295 BELLEVUM ބެއްލެވުން v. looking (hon.) (v.n. of ballavanii)

3296 BEVUM ބެވުން v. scolding (v.n. of bavanii)

3297 BESSUM ބެއްސުން v. involving (v.n. of bassanii)

3298 BESSEVUM ބެއްސެވުން v. distributing (hon.) (v.n. of bassavanii)

3299 BEHENII ބެހެނީ v. 1. drifts, gets lost (of ships) (abs. behe); oḍi behigen Siloonař hiňgajje-eve, the odi drifted to Ceylon: 2. meddles, concerns oneself with: mi-ii aḷugaňḍumennaa behee kamek nuuneve, this is nothing to do with us: ehen miihunnaa nubehee! don't interfere with others: aharumen kuraa kamtakaa kalee nubeheeřeve, don't you meddle with what we are doing! nubehee kamtak, things which don't concern (you); behum-teri, a good passer (at football) (invol. of bahanii)

3300 BEE (BEI) (pl., been, bein) ބޭ (ބެއި) n. brother; older man: bee-kalek (beikalek), a respectable or senior person of at least middle grade (pl., beekalun): muskuḷi beekalun, former royal functionaries: fas mudim beekalun, functionaries of five principal mosques: bee-kaňbalun (pl.) middle-grade ladies: bee-fuḷaa (beifuḷaa), nobleman or noblewoman (pl., beefuḷun), i.e. those of royal or sayyid descent: beebeefuḷun,various noblemen; tiya beefuḷaa, you (to a nobleman, usually female); e-beefuḷaa, my husband; used also of noblemen's children, beefuḷek, a son: anhen beefuḷek, a daughter; raaveri bee, toddy-tapper: bee-keňbi(-daita), midwife: de-bein, deben, two brothers: viyaafaariveriyekge debeekalaku, two people from the traders [S. beiyā, H. bhāī, Skt. bhrātṛka]

3301 BEE- ބޭ- negative prefix appearing in loanwords, e.g. bee-adabii, uncivilized: bee-insaafu, injustice: bee-ikhtiyaaru-gai, involuntarily: bee-kaaru, useless: bee-caara, helpless: bee-vafaateri, faithless [U.bē-, Skt. vi-]

3302 BEEŇGU ބޭނގު n. kind of shallow sea fish, easily adaptable to fresh water

3303 BEEŇḌU ބޭނޑު n. sooty tern

3304 BEETIBBANII ބޭތިއްބަނީ v. See baitibbanii

3305 BEEDANAA ބޭދަނާ n. kind of edible seed, quince [U. bih-dāna]

3306 BEEN ބޭން n. 1. brothers (pl. of bee)
2. band, i.e.music or instruments: b. jahanii, makes music; been-paaṭii, professional band [E. band (party)]

3307 BEENUM (BEINUM) ބޭނުން (ބެއިނުން) 1. n. need; needful: sababutakek beenumek nuun, no excuses needed: kooccek beenumii, what would you like? aharen beenumii tinrufiyaage donkeyo, I should like three rupees' worth of bananas: bappa ruḷi duruvaanee gotek aḷugaňḍu beenumek net, I don't want father to get annoyed: aḷugaňḍu mihaaru beenumii / (beenum vanii) avahař migein daan, I want to get out of this house now: varar boḍu beenumek ovegen, for a very special occasion: kalee beenumiyyaa, if you like: beenum boḍukam, the necessity: beenum-teri, needful, useful; beenum kuranii, makes use (of): visnumuge beinum kořfi miihek, a man who uses (some) thought: beenum hifanii, uses, can use [T. vēṇ(ṭ)um, cf. S. ōnä]

2. v. bringing down, catching; poking in (v.n. of baananii)

3308 BEENENII ބޭނެނީ v. interferes, pokes in: mitanař nubeeneeřee, don't interfere! kaleakii abadu ves nubehee kamtakař tiyahen beeniganna miihakiimu hee, you are always poking your nose into what doesn't concern you (invol. of baananii)

3309 BEENKU (BENKU) ބޭންކު (ބެންކު) n. financial bank [E. bank]

3310 BEENDANII (BEINDANII) ބޭންދަނީ (ބެއިންދަނީ) v. detains (a single person): sets, keeps; circumcizes [cf. baindanii , baitibbanii]

3311 BEE-FUḶU (pl., beefuḷun, beebeefuḷun) ބޭފުޅު n. See bee

3312 BEEBE ބޭބެ n. elder brother (voc., beebeeve !): aḷugaňḍuge beebe-ek eba hunnevi, I have an elder brother : boḍu beebe, uncle; hakuru dee miihekee boḍu beebe, uncle is the man who gives juggery, i.e. you are under an obligation to him (prov.) [bee]

3313 BEERI ބޭރި n. an evil spirit from the sea

3314 BEERU (BEIRU) ބޭރު (ބެއިރު) n. outside : eenaa vii beerugai, he is out (-side): beerař jassaalanii, goes outside: beerař lum, ceremony of taking a baby outside on the seventh day: beeru vanii, resigns (slang): beerař hiňgaa roogaa, dysentery; ifc., part outside the centre: Maalee- beerugai fanaa jassaigen, having anchored off Male: em-beeru, bait area: rař-beeru, area off an island; beeru oi, seaward current: beeru-gaňḍu, cover of a book (cf. baňḍeerigaňḍu): beeru-ge (beeru-getere), sitting room of a house; beerugee ba$\underline{tt}$i, sittingroom lamp: beeru-fuř, the outside of something: beeru rabaru, tyre outer
[S. bähära, Skt. bāhira]

3315 BEERUHULI ބޭރުހުލި n. See veeru-huli

3316 BEELAA (-aek) ބޭލާ n. violin: b. jahanii, plays violin [cf. S. bayila, kind of dance, Port. baile]

3317 BEELI (beeyyek) ބޭލި 1. n. bale (of cloth): bail (at cricket) [E. bale: bail]
2. v. lowered: alař beeli, newly launched (p.p. of baalanii)

3318 BEELUM ބޭލުން v. lowering (v.n. of baalanii) [S. bahālum]

3319 BEEVUM ބޭވުން v. catching (fish) (anc. v.n. of baananii 2, mod. beenum): mas nubeevee, fish are not being caught: faanaek beevunee, a faana fish was caught

3320 BEEVVUM ބޭއްވުން v. placing; circumcising (v.n. of baavvanii) [baananii 2]

3321 BEES (beehek) ބޭސް n. 1. medicine, medicinal treatment: bees-koḷu, some medicine; b. jahanii, applies medicaments: b. aḷanii, applies with a dressing and bandage: b. kuranii, gives medical treatment: b. hadanii, prescribes medicine, prepares medicine: b. vařanii, rubs medicines on to the body; dat uňguḷaa b., toothpaste; medicines are classified as minaa bees, measurable medicines: matikaraa b., concoctions: askanu b.: huvaňdu b., scented medicine: oř bees, nutty medicine: yuunaani b.,western medicine: hakiim b., eastern medicine; bees teyo, special medicinal oil for rheumatism: bees uř, medicinal wax; lak filuvaa b., bleach; bees-veri(yaa), herbal doctor [S. bēt, Skt. bhaiṣajya]

2. (military) base [E. base]

3322 BEEZAARU KURANII ބޭޒާރު ކުރަނީ v. betrays, gets someone involved; lets cat out of bag [U. bēzār, disgusted]

3323 BOI (pron. boe) ބޮއި 1. v. having drunk (abs. of bonii: also boo, bui) [S.bī]

2. n. buoy (also boyaa) [E. buoy]

3324 BOI-GAS ބޮއިގަސް n.. bo tree, ficus religiosa ; also used in proper names, Boi Don Maniku [S. bō, Skt. bōdhi]

3325 BOK ބޮކް n. frog, toad: bok-fati, frog-spawn: bok-mas, frogfish [old S. bek, Skt. bhēka]

3326 BOKARU ބޮކަރު n. a scented medicinal wood

3327 BOKARU-MAA(-malek) ބޮކަރުމާ n. a yellow plant, tecoma stans (smells like bokaru)

3328 BOKI (botkek) ބޮކި n. glass ball; electric bulb; float; bubble: b. dillanii, turns on the light: b. aňdaifi, the bulb has gone: boki- daňḍi, lamppost ; b. jahanii, bubbles; boki hadanii, makes noise with cloth (cf. baḍi hadanii) [S. boku, cavity: Skt. bukkā, innards]

3329 BO<u>KH</u>USAA(-aaek) ބޮޚުސާ n. wrapped bundle of clothes [U. buqca]

3330 BOKKURAA (-aek) ބޮއްކުރާ n. boat: bokkura-ař aranii, gets into a boat

3331 BOKSIN TAḶANII ބޮކްސިން ތަޅަނީ v. boxes (obs.) [E. boxing]

3332 BOŇGARA ބޮނގަރަ n. a thick mild curry

3333 BO(Ň)GO BO(Ň)GO ބޮ(ނ)ގޮ ބޮ(ނ)ގޮ onom. b. lanii, makes a gurgling sound

3334 BOḌATI ބޮޑަޓި See boḍeti

3335 BOḌAVAKI ބޮޑަވަކި n. kind of timber

3336 BOḌAA (boḍalek) ބޮޑާ n. pride, proud (pej., as v. fakhuru) : eenaa boḍaa aranii, he gets sulky

3337 BOḌU ބޮޑު adj. big (of single objects); serious (condition) : boḍu miihek, important person (pl., boḍeti miihun): boḍek, a star (at athletics): boḍuvai (boḍuvaa) iňgili, thumb; adv. , boḍař: enme boḍař, most particularly: boḍař huḷuvum, opening wide; boḍu vanii, grows bigger (e.g. of children): haalu danii boḍu vamunnee, (his) condition is deteriorating: b. kuranii, exaggerates something: b. taḷanii, b. hadanii, boasts; b. ař̌i, big seat (on left of entrance): b. aavi, eucalyptus: boḍu-kam, importance, extent (rihee-lek boḍukamun, by the extent of the pain); nuisance, bother (esp. in women's speech), boḍukamek jehigen, being in trouble: defecation (boḍukamu danii, goes to defecate: boḍukamu daa ecceti, turds: boḍukamu nudevum, being constipated): boḍu kunnaaru, stoneapple: boḍu gas, kind of tree, samanea saman: boḍu guḷa, kind of fishcake: boḍu gifili kurum, defecation: b. daita, aunt (non-Male usage): b. dati, mousetrap: b. diri, fennel (=daviggaňdu): b. duňburi, kind of tree, cerbera odollam: boḍu (gaa) duuni, large crested tern: boḍu beru, kind of dance performance: b. boli, kind of cowrie: b. mirihi, a plant, tithonia diversifolia: b. beebe, uncle or great-uncle (addressed as beebe): boḍu boo, bishop (at chess): b. massaagu, a curry leaf, amaranthus tricolor: b. roonu, thick quality rope (e.g. for trellises): boḍu luňboo, grapefruit or citrus medica: boḍu singaa, very big: boḍu siinu, palatal letter ś : boḍu haňḍuu, former allowance of 30 naaḷi of rice given to government servants, now paid in money; boḍun (pl.), important people [H. baṛā, Skt. √vṛddh]

3338 BOḌETI (BOḌATI) ބޮޑެޓި (ބޮޑަޓި) adj. big (of more than one): b. akuru, big letters: b. miihun, adults: b. veriin, political leaders [boḍu + eti]

3339 BOŇḌAN(boňḍanaek) ބޮނޑަން n. kind of bird; boňḍana kaloo appears in stories

3340 BOŇḌI ބޮނޑި n. 1. bundle (esp. 12 fooli of coir): daru b., bundle of firewood: bilet b., 50 leaves of betel: maa b., bouquet: rihaakuru b., fish balls kept in rihaakuru (not in Male): hilaa b., sweetmeat which needs stirring: huunu b., poultice: boňḍi -kaňdoḷu, kind of plant: boňḍi-kopii, cabbage, brassica oleracea: boňḍi-gaňḍu, a long form of boňḍihaluvaa:: b.- taan kuranii, massages with cloth in warm water, gives fomentation: boňḍi-bat, rice porridge: b. barani, thread in a ball-- square ball of cloth formerly used in game of bař̌i : boňḍi kuḷum, playing bař̌i, or children's game of 'Touch': boṇḍi-varu, bundle, heap: boňḍi-haluvaa, a sweetmeat esp. made in Aḍḍu and Huvadu and formerly sold in bundles:

boňḍi vanii, gets crowded: mitanař miihun gaňḍu boňḍi vejje, there's a great squash here: boňḍi boňḍi vefai, crushed (of pages of a book). In certain phrases, a blow: b. aḷanii, gives blows: b. jahanii, gives blows: b. baalanii, takes it out on someone (with dat.): boňḍiek boon, to get into trouble: b. denii, tricks someone (dat.); boňḍiek diifi, tricked: b. libenii, gets cheated, hurt, looses out

2. ifc. eyelid (matii boňḍi: tirii boňḍi, part below the eye

3341 BOŇḌU ބޮނޑު n. lizard: b. naguu, lizard tail; (met.) boňḍunagulař diyum, proving a failure [S. bohoňḍā, chameleon]

3342 BOŇDANII ބޮނދަނީ v. ducks aside, hides (usu. of animals)

3343 BOŇDU ބޮނދު n. 1. king (at chess): chief marble (at marbles)

2. kind of seabird: boňdu duuni, little tern

3344 BONII ބޮނީ v. drinks; of tobacco, smokes (abs. bui, boi:: inf. boon : v.n. buim : past tensebuii, boifi : invol. bovenii): eenaa buiikii nuunii, keyye, he didn't drink but he ate: inṭaval bonii, drinks in the interval [S. bonne, cf. Skt. pibati]

3345 BONTI ބޮންޓި n. unfolded tree-top of coconut or banana: b. ratkeyo, a common kind of banana: bonti-gaňḍu, wand, sceptre; bonti jahanii, b. jahaafaa fumenii, uses stick for the ancient pole- vault

3346 BONBAA ބޮންބާ n. pump (also gunbaa) [cf. S. pōmpē, E. pump]

3347 BOŇBI (boňtbek, bonbek) ބޮނބި n. coconut fibre in husk: b. kaaři, complete coconut: boňbi-gaňḍu, lump of fibre used as a brush: b. naru, individual fibres: b. taḷanii, separates fibres from the husk; boňbi-faḷi, part between the shoulderblades, upper back

3348 BOŇM ބޮނމު n. bomb: boňm eḷiyee, dropped bombs [E. bomb]

3349 BOMA (BAMA) ބޮމަ (ބަމަ) n. fathom [S. baňba, P. byāma]

3350 BOMAKAŇDU ބޮމަކަނދު n. vice of turner's lathe

3351 BOMAŘI ބޮމަޅި n. hilt of knife: b. fili, band round the hilt

3352 BOYAA ބޮޔާ n. (anc.) buoy (mod. boi): boyaagai hifanii, ties up at buoy [E. buoy]

3353 BORI ބޮރި adj. In ori- bori, lopsided (doublet)

3354 BOLAAKIIN(I) ބޮލާކީން - ބޮލާކީނި n. creosote [E. blacking?]

3355 BOLI (boyyek) ބޮލި n. cowrie: vaaru b., common small cowrie: boḍu b., larger kind: fen kakkaa b., large cowrie (used as doorstop): rihaakuru b., dark shiny cowrie: kafihi b., small striped cowrie; boli-gaňḍu, kind of game played with small cowries: boli-ke(e), kind of reef fish: boli-rava, baby's rattle with small cowrie inside; bolirava taḷuvanii, shakes rattle [S. bolu]

3356 BOLIHI (bolissek) ބޮލިހި n. a liquid measure, quarter of an aḍubaa, two doḷahagi

3357 BOLU- ބޮލު- n. See boo: bolu-feeli, ancient type of kerchief: bolu-fotikoḷu, woman's cap: bolu-rumaa, kerchief: bolu-huḷi, hair bun

3358 BOVANII ބޮވަނީ v. wishes to drink: fen bovaagatum, thirstiness: aharen fen bovaa, I am thirsty: enmen fen bovaa ta, are you all thirsty? [bonii]

3359 BOVENII ބޮވެނީ v. swallows, drinks accidentally: kalee boo haa ginaek koř mařakař noboveene-eve, I can't drink as much as you can (invol. of bonii)

3360 BOS ބޮސް n. formal kiss : bos denii, kisses, worships; atpuḷugai bos d., kisses the hand: filaagai bos dinum, kissing the Qur'an slate [U. bōsa]

3361 BOSSUN LANII ބޮއްސުން ލަނީ v. goes wrong, gets out of hand, falls away: reevum bossun laafaane, the plans may go agley

3362 BOH ބޮހ excl. of pained surprise, what a mess! I told you so!

3363 BOHOLAA (pl., boholaain) ބޮހޮލާ n. (anc.) idiot

3364 BOḶU ބޮޅު n. link of chain: ui boḷu, skein of yarn : boḷu-fati, chain; a game played with interlocking rings; boḷufati (aḷuvaa) neṭṭum, (doing up and) undoing the rings, playing the game of b.

3365 BOḶUM ބޮޅުން n. in oḷum-boḷum vejje, got all confused (doublet) [oḷum]

3366 BOO (bolek) ބޯ 1. n. head; hair of head: fan bolek, straight hair: buḷi bolek, curly hair: boo laa koḷu, head of bed; bappage boo laa koḷugai, beside father's (sick) bed: boo matiigai, overhead; boo aňburanii, (my) head is swimming: boo kořanii, cuts hair: boo baalanii, shaves head (often ceremonial): boo jahaalum / boo jehum, nodding head: boo laňbaalum, surrendering: boo diidiifai uḷe-ee, head is peeping out: boo negum, raising head (from pillow, as v. is negum, met.): boo heevanii, hair goes awry; boo haru, headstrong, obstinate: boo himenum, census; plain betel leaf of an ornamental pair: boo-(kaři)keyo, kind of small screwpine, pandanus odoratissimus [S. ōkē]: boo-gaňḍu, tip of penis: boo-maḷi, trap for birds; boomali jahanii, sets trap: boo-vaḷu, smocking round the neck; libaahugai boovaḷu aḷaifi, applied smocking to libaas : foti boovaḷu, detachable collar: kasabu boovaḷu, earlier type of fixed collar: boovalu fotigaňḍu, fixed collar of digu libaas : see also bolu- [S. olu]

2. adj. thick: boo-kam,boo-min thickness: adv. boo koř, thickly: boo karudaas, cardboard: boo-kibaa (-kibalek), a thick fishcake; foni bookibaa, coconut cakes: bookibaa aḷanii, makes cakes: boo kiru, thick coconut milk: boo fotfot, thick volumes: boo foḷi, kind of pancake; boofoḷi duvas, festival days when pancakes are traditionally eaten: boo vilaa-takek, thick clouds: boo- huni, a coconut pudding; boohuni hiḷanii, prepares the pudding; Boohuni Ali Bee, a mythical saint to whom vows are made for lost objects; boo kuranii, makes thicker, viz.1. (of rain or cloud) increases (intr.): vaaree boo kuranii, the rain is increasing: 2. cooks in sugar : faḷoo boo kuranii, cooks papaw [old S. bol, ? Skt. bahula]

3. v. drinking (part. or 3s. pres. of bonii): hama boo hit nuvanii, just don't want to drink : boo-laa, for boyilaa, having drunk: boo taři, serving bowl (in shape of cup) for porridge, etc. [S. bona]

3367 BOOKU ބޫކު n. archway [S. bōkku, culvert; Dutch boog, bow]

3368 BOOGA ބޫގަ n. endowment land formerly belonging to a mosque (miskitu b.) [Skt. bhōga]

3369 BOOṬU ބޫޓު n. 'boat', usu. with engine; collective pl., booṭu-faharu: kaaḍu b., ration food- supply ship: booṭu-deli, coal : matin daa b., aeroplane [E. boat]

3370 BOOḌU ބޫޑު n. board (for notices: also of a business) [E. board]

3371 BOODAA ބޫދާ adj. old- style (of people or things): boodaa bas, proverbs

3372 BOODI ބޫދި n. a bait fish, cardinal fish, apogon: b. naganii, collects b.

3373 BOON ބޫން v. to drink (inf. of bonii)

3374 BOOBOO VANII ބޫބޫ ވަނީ v. is finished (children's language)

3375 BOOVA ބޫވަ n. a small polypod: boovaa dila mas, cuttle fish:b. naganii, collects b.

3376 BOOS GOVVANII ބޫސް ގޮއްވަނީ v. makes discouraging noises, says boo [onom.]

3377 BOOSAA ބޫސާ n. adjustable ropes for tying up vessels: b. jahanii, fixes ropes

3378 BOOŘI (booṭṭek) ބޫށި n. 1. banana flower (keelu b.): kuri-booři, decorative spire

2. kind of tree, messerschmidia argentea (sometimes used for chewing)

3379 BOOḶA ބޫޅަ n. ball: b. kuḷenii, plays at ball; booḷa- dańḍu, playing field: booḷa- ge, athletic pavilion or store: booḷa kufuraa, whole or best copra [E. ball]

މ MIIMU, the 10th letter of the Maldivian alphabet

Miimu atoḷu, Mulaku atoll, the 10th atoll from the north

3380 MA މަ pr. me, I (emph. mařakii, gen. magee, dat. mařař, pl. (non-Male usage) mamen): ma gendaanu hee, will you take me? ma gellan dannamee, I can do division: mařek nudaanam, I will not go: mařakař nudeveene, I cannot give: mařaa eku, with me: kaleaa mařaa, you and I: mařee bunaa taagai, instead of saying 'me': ma-futu, son! ma-saahibu, Your Majesty! Enlarged form: ma-vaa, I for my part [S. mam, Skt. mām]

3381 MAI މައި n. 1. mother (pl., main): de-main, mother and child: de-mafirin, husband and wife: enme main, mother and all children: mai-miihaa, mother: mai(n)bafain, parents; maibafaa kiyanii / govanii, insults one's parentage (by saying 'Kalee amaa!'): mayakaa nulaa, without a mother: mayaa eku,with the mother: mai net kujjek, a motherless child: hataru main, mother and triplets: mainnař fen nudee, who won't (even) give his mother water: dari-mai ve-eve, mothers and children exist, i.e. children get born: mai-daita, mother-in-law (in reference): mai-fuř, the mother's side; maifuřuge boḍu beebe, uncle on the mother's side (see also maa) [S. mav, Skt. mātṛ]

2. ifc. main, principal: mai-kańḍinma, main harbour entrance; mai-kaři, spine, backbone: mai-gańḍu, principal thing or person; fas maigańḍu viya, five main arithmetical processes (see viya): adv., maigańḍakař, principally: mai-doru, main door: mai-naaru, heel-strings; ankle tendons: mai-farumaanu, principal yardarm: mai-faaru, former town wall of Male mai-bada, vertebra: mai-soobu, main cogwheel (see also maa-) [S. mā, Skt. mahā]

3382 MAITIRI މައިތިރި adj. calm (maḍu maitiri); maitiriek nuve-ee, (of illnesses) is cured [? Skt. maitrī]

3383 MAIDA (-aek) މައިދަ n. stomach (medical term, cf. bańḍu) [U. ma'ida]

3384 MAIDAAN މައިދާން n. battlefield [U. maidān]

3385 MAINAA މައިނާ n. mynah bird, gracula [H. mainā, ?Skt. madanā]

3386 MAIMELI (MAIMEELI) މައިމެލި (މައިމޭލި) n. In maimeli daita, witch

3387 MAIZAAN މައިޒާން n. 1. maizaan-ge, former headquarters of the four wards of Male: maizaan doř, area round the maizaange : maizaandoř hadanii, decorates the area of the maizaange for Hiti festival [U. mauẕa']
2. for mauzan

3388 MAU މައު n. See maa 1.

3389 MAUMUUMU މައުމޫމު n. ordinary member of the congregation

3390 MAUMUULU (MAAMUULU) މައުމޫލު (މާމޫލު) n. export or import duty: m. naganii, charges the duty [U. ma'mūl, custom]

3391 MAULUUDU (MAALUUDU) މައުލޫދު (މާލޫދު) n. religious chanting sung on birthdays (now discouraged): boḍu m., general festivities held on provincial islands: gaňḍu m., held on llth Rajab in Male [U. maulūd]

3392 MAULUUMAATU މައުލޫމާތު n. factual information [U. ma'lūmāt]

3393 MAUZAN (MAIZAAN) މައުޒަން (މައިޒާން) n. thread of screw

3394 MAK މަކް adj. ordinary; undistinguished (of people)

3395 MAKANA މަކަނަ n. a way of wearing the turban: makana-ař fořaa laigen, with the turban covering the head [U. maknūn, covered]

3396 MAKARA މަކަރަ n. the sign Capricornus [Skt. makara]

3397 MAKARU މަކަރު n. deceit; deceiver: makaru hadanii, acts deceitfully; kamakař m. hadanii / jahanii, shirks something: makaru-veri, deceitful [U. makr]

3398 MAKUḌI މަކުޑި n. door wedge

3399 MAKUNU މަކުނު n. 1. bug (tan-makunu, bed bug) [S. makuṇu, Skt. matkuṇa]
2. spider: fai digu m., ordinary house spider: vaa m.,

spider in web: ran m., spiders out of doors: makunu-vaa, spider's web; makunuvalek furanii, constructs a web: makunu-filaa, a creeper, portulaca quadrifida: makunu-fořī, spider's white egg [S. makuḷu, Skt. markaṭa]

3. monkey (raamaa makunu, 'Rama's spider' - not found in Maldives); makunu-kuḷi, makunu-bali, buggery

3400 MAKKAARU މައްކާރު n. cunning man [U. makkār]

3401 MAGAT މަގަތް n. nearside (as v. bitdoř): enme magatugai, on the very (nearside) edge [magu + at]

3402 MAGAAMU މަގާމު n. position, status [U. maqām]

3403 MAGU މަގު n. road, way (literal and met.): siidaa m., direct road: tedu m., path of virtue: magu matiigai, on the road: magun laafai, along the street; (instr.) at the rate of: fas rufiyaage magun, at the rate of Rs.5: fasdoḷas rufiyaa-ař ge-ek magun, at the rate of one house for Rs.60 [S. maga, Skt. mārga]

3404 MAG͟H͟URIBU މަޣުރިބު n. West [U. mag͟hrib]

3405 MAGULAS (magulahek) މަގުލަސް n. kind of slipknot, sheepshank (sometimes opposed to goř): m. baddanii, m. jahanii, ties such a knot [maguu + as 2?]

3406 MAGUU (magulek) މަގޫ n. a plant, scaevola taccada: maguu- fat, (edible) m. leaves: m.- dañḍi, m. stalks: m.- madu, white pulp of m .(used as packing, or as a children's toy): kudi maguu, a different plant: bim maguu, hedyotis sp.

3407 MAGEE މަގޭ pr. my (gen. of ma) [S. magē]

3408 MAG(U)BUUL މަގުބޫލް adj. acceptable, popular; amiable [U. maqbūl]

3409 MAGSADU މަގްސަދު n. purpose [U. maqsad]

3410 MACCANGOḶI މައްޗަންގޮޅި n. name of one of the four wards of Male: Maccangoḷii miihun, men from M.

3411 MACCAŘ މައްޗަށް See mati

3412 MAJALLAA މަޖައްލާ n. literary magazine [U. mujallā, illustrated]

3413 MAJAA (majalek) މަޖާ n. 1. fun: enme majalii.., the funniest is..: majaa hevvaa, funny: majaa vagutukoḷek, an enjoyable time: m. kuranii, enjoys oneself

2. a hot mixed salad or punch: añbu m., mango

punch: faḷolugai hedi m., salad made with papaw [U. majā, maza, savour, fun]

3414 MAJ(U)BUURU މަޖްބޫރު (މަޖުބޫރު) n. compulsion: mi-ii majbuurek, bappage majbuurek, this is forced, forced by father: majbuuru kaaveni, forced marriage: m. kuranii, exerts compulsion [U. majbūr, forced]

3415 MAJ(I)LI(I)S (majliihek) މަޖިލިސް - މަޖިލީސް - މަޖްލިސް n. assembly, parliament: majiliihar̃ araa beekalun, former officials of the royal assembly: majlihun nimigen, when the assembly was over: keumuge majliihek, a lunch party [U. majlis]

3416 MAJUURII (pl., -iin) މަޖޫރީ n. labourer, porter [U. majūrī]

3417 MAḌA މަޑަ n. harpoon with wooden handle: gaff

3418 MAḌI މަޑި n. 1.kind of kite (aruvaa m.): m. ellanii, flies kite : 2. saddle of bicycle: 3. stingray (e.g.veli-maḍi, em (boo) m., kar̃i-m.): m. miyaru, kind of shark [S. maḍu]: 4. kinds of beetle (ṭaki kañḍaa m., ruku m.)

3419 MAḌI މަޑި adj. gently sloping: m. furaaḷu, sloping roof: m. vas(koḷu), splayed apex : maḍi-kam, slope (of roof)

3420 MAḌIPPANII މަޑިއްޕަނީ v. fastens on tightly

3421 MAḌISIILA މަޑިސީލަ n. betel- bag [S. maḍis(s)ala, string-bag]

3422 MAḌII މަޑީ for maḍu vii: see maḍu

3423 MAḌU މަޑު 1. adj. calm, quiet, soft (of sound): vai maḍiyyaa, if the wind is gentle: raha-tak maḍii too, is the taste too bland? maḍun huree! be quiet: maḍumaḍun e ove-ee, it is keeping quiet: maḍu nuul kula, light blue colour ; adv., maḍun, quietly; maḍu (maitiri) kujjek, a quiet lad: maḍu tanmaccek,a soft bed: miinaa hiñgaa-lek haada maḍee, he walks very slowly: maḍumaḍun inna, always stopping; maḍu kuranii, slows down (tr.); waits: maḍu kor̃laa, wait! maḍu vanii, becomes calmer: (of food) gets soft: maḍu jassaalanii, maḍu jehilanii, hesitates: maḍu miyaru, 'soft shark' , hexanchus griseus [cf. S. moḷok; Skt. mṛdu]

3424 MAḌU މަޑު 2. n. dirty deposits: kanfatu m., neefatu m., wax in ears, nose: teyo m., sludge: bolugai hedee m., dandruff [S. maḍa, mud]

3425 MAḌUU (maḍulek) މަޑޫ n. main plank of a fishing vessel: ifc. in names of atolls Maaḷos-maḍulu (R and B) and Miladun-maḍulu (Ř and N); arithmetical factor

3426 MATA KURANII މަތަ ކުރަނީ v. controls (person or thing): eenaa mařakař mataek nuviee, he was not under my control [U. māt karnā]

3427 MATA-RAS , MATA-RES ދަތަރަސް - މަތަރެސް n . top section of fence: matares maa, kind of flower [res]

3428 MATAA (-aaek) މަތާ n. lever : m. jahanii, applies large lever: m. lanii, applies smaller lever

3429 MATI (maccek) މަތި n. top; lid; superstructure : maccaai hama-ař, up to the top, quite full: mati-kiba, the windward side: maccař aranii, rises (of prices): maccař danii, gets promotion; kaleege kamtak mihaaru tiya danii maa-maccař, things are going too far with you, you are overdoing it:

mati aḷuvanii, puts the blame on; aharen nuves kuraa kamakař eenaa mati aḷuvaifieve, he blamed me for something I didn't do at all: mati kañḍanii, levels off the top: mati kuranii, unloads on to, puts on top of: mati jahanii, covers up, puts lid on: mati balanii, looks up: mati vanii, takes on oneself; aharen eenaage maraa mati vum, my responsibility for his death; aharen mi kamaa mati van jehunii, I had to take on this responsibility: mati-matin, on the surface only; matimatin kiyanii, skims through: matin-bai, onesidedness; aharen matinbai nujeheenam, I won't make the first move (met.); matinbain jehigen, of one's own volition (usu. of girls); used ifc. with little meaning: at-mati, ari-mati, uḍu-mati, tan-mati, duniye-mati, etc.

Much used postpositionally: doru matiigai, in front of the door: faru matin danii, gets past (over) the reef: rař matin, on windward side of island: vai maccař, with following wind: (met., of a variety of relationships) lafaafuḷuge matiin, on (his) advice (hon.): khaassa amuruge matin, in accordance with special orders: śara'ii hamatakekge matin, legally: aḷugañḍumen mi tibii kiyamanterikam adaa kuḷaum matiigaee, we are engaged in obedient compliance: mi gotuge matin, in this fashion: defaharekge matiin, twice: mahekge maccař, per month: naseehat devvum matiigai demi hunnevi, who continued to give advice: ehiiterikam maccař taariifu kurum, praise for the help: eenaage maccař hitugai ufedifai vaa lootbaai iḥtiraamu, love and respect for him: duu kořlaan jehunii kaakuge at maccakař too ee, must hand over to whom? deduvas matin, during two successive days; mati-kan, top edge of gunwale: mati-karaa bees, 'concoctions', a class of medicines: mati-kiba, higher side of sail: mati-koḷu, family descent; matikoḷu kiyum, recites one's family history: mati-gañḍu, top bract of coconut or fruits:lid of pan or jar; matigañḍu nujehee, the lid doesn't fit: mati-ge, central hall of former royal palace: matin daa booṭu, aeroplane ('boat which travels aloft', anc. matin duvvaa booṭu): mati-fuř, side of the family (mai matifuř, bafaa matifuř): mati-mas, moustache (matimas bahaṭṭanii, matimas lanii, grows a moustache: matimas baalanii, cuts it off) [Skt. śmaśru]: mati-vak, fruit of a kind of creeper, dioscorea globosa: mati-varu, coconut shoots: mati-veri, important ; mativeriyaa, important person; mativeri daraja-akař, to a considerable extent: mati-hañi naganii, puffs out the chest

matii (used adjectivally), upper: enme matii daraja-ař, to the greatest extent: varař matii harufatekgai, on a very high rung: matii tali, upper palate: matii tañi, saucer used as a lid: matii bai, highest part: matii buri, upper floor: matii res, horizon: enme matii veriyaa, the highest authority; also used postpositionally for matiige, matiigai: atmatii fot, handbook: kaiveni matii tin gañḍek, three pieces (of clothing) for weddings: rař matii kujjek, a lad owned by the island: baazaaru matii baharuva, huckster's language: furaaḷu matii bañḍavaru eḷum, fixing ropes over the roof: fuřṭaru matii ainu, a shoal on the rocky side: (met.) khidmatek kurum matii demi hurum, remaining at his post : taahirukam matii hurevee too balaařee, see if you can remain clean ('in cleanliness') [S. matu, Skt. mastaka]

3430 MATURANII މަތުރަނި v. utters charms (v.n. meturum): fen (tañi) m., charms a cup of water (against sickness): maa nidi maturaafai, having charmed people to sleep: liyunu tañi m., charms an inscribed dish whose contents the eduru-bee's patient then drinks (for illness, or to bless dhonies) [S. maturanne, cf. Skt. mantra]

3431 MADADU މަދަދު n. help, encouragement: madadu-veri, encouraging (adj.) [U. madad]

3432 MADAN މަދަން n. local caulking putty: m. aḷanii, applies putty: (met.) kanfatař madan eḷii kaaku ta, who blocked your ears?

3433 MADIRI މަދިރި n. mosquito : m. hifanii, mosquitoes are attacking,biting: madiri-ge, mosquito net: m. fani, mosquito larvae: fai digu m., daddy longlegs [S. maduru, ? Skt. mandira]

3434 MADU 1. މަދު n. pith (vakaruge m.): core (ořuge m.): marrow (kařiige m.); fuḷi-madu, cork of bottle: maguu- madu, pith of maguu stalks (used as packing): madu uḷi (for medu uḷi), centre strand [S. mada, Skt. majjan]

3435 MADU 2. މަދު adj. few, rare: madu kamtak, rare occurrences: hañḍuu libee-lek madu-kam, shortage of rice: geegeař miihun vanum madukam, scarcity of visitors; adv., madun, madumadun, seldom: madek kоř nuun, not rarely: enme madu vegen, at the very least [S. madi, mañda]

3436 MAD(U)RASAA މަދުރަސާ n. school [U. madrasa]

3437 MADOŘI (madoṭṭek) މަދޮށި n. berries of adenanthera pavonina, ‘red saunders’, used for weighing, or in games such as tinhama, ořvaḷu [S. madaṭa, T. mañjādi]

3438 MADDU މައްދު n. sign of prolongation, extra-long sign (for tajvīd recitation): maddu jahaafai, marking a prolongation [U. madd]

3439 MANAVARU މަނަވަރު n. man-of-war, warship [E. man of war]

3440 MANAA 1. މަނާ n. pawn (at chess)

3441 MANAA (manaek) 2. މަނާ adj. forbidden: kurum manaa kamtak, forbidden activities: lee manaa kuranii, staunches blood [U. mana‘]

3442 MANI މަނި n. semen [U. manī]

3443 MANIKAAROOJJAA މަނިކާރޫއްޖާ excl. well I never! dear me!

3444 MANIKU މަނިކު n. a name marking upper class men [S. mäṇikā]

3445 MANIKU-FAANU މަނިކުފާނު n. a title of honour, esp. for the Faňḍiyaaru (Chief Justice); you (in writing to beefuḷu noblemen); used as a proper name in the South, and in Sikkage [Maniku + -faanu]

3446 MANIKE މަނިކެ n female equivalent of Maniku [S. mäṇike]

3447 MANIPPUḶU މަނިއްޕުޅު n. prince of royal blood [Maniku + fuḷu]

3448 MANU މަނު n. a measure, 'maund', 40 seers (about 80 lbs.): teo manek, a case of two large tins of oil: bai manu ḍabiyaa, a large biscuit tin (containing half a maund) [H. man]

3449 MANJE މަންޖެ n. girl (in Male seldom used, except in jest): manje kon-taakař, where are you going, girl?

3450 MANJOOḶI JEHENII މަންޖޫޅި ޖެހެނީ v. gets over-excited, usu. at somewhat trivial things (dat.); esp. of infatuations (not generally used in Male): manjooḷi jehee varuge kujjek, a girl worth bothering about [?S. mana-doḷa]

3451 MANḌI މަންޑި n. a game, played with sticks (daňḍi(-gaňḍu)) and a wooden ball (fooli), often on evenings in Ramzan

3452 MANTARU މަންތަރު n. bad charm [H. mantar, Skt. mantra]

3453 MANTIRI މަންތިރި n. queen (at chess) [Skt. mantrī, counsellor]

3454 MANNA މަންނަ n. ace (at cards)

3455 MANFAA (-aaek) މަންފާ n. profit; efficacy [U. manfa']

3456 MANMANU (pl., manmanun) މަންމަނު n . deaf and dumb person (cf. bai-manu) [H. maun]

3457 MANSAFA މަންސަފަ n. inner pocket of libaas

3458 MANZARU މަންޒަރު n. scene [U. manẕar]

3459 MABUSTAAN މަބުސްތާން n. mangosteen, garcinia mangostana

3460 MAMMA މަންމަ n. mother (also used to mother-in-law, cf. mai-daita): (voc., mammaa!) de-mammain, mother and child [higher class usage]

3461 MAYAA-INU މަޔާއިނު excl. of disgust (vulgar) [mayaa in = mother-fucker, see mai 1]

3462 MAYAA-HOKI (-hotkek) މަޔާހޮކި n. 'dreadful fellow!' [= mayaa-inu]

3463 MAYYAA (mayyalek) މަްޔާ n. base edgings of hull : m. lanii, lays down the edgings

3464 MAYYITAA މައްޔިތާ n. corpse [U. maiyit]

3465 MARAKII މަރަކީ adj. (anc.) American [E. America]

3466 MARANII މަރަނީ v. kills (v.n. merum : impv. maraa !) ; also met., filmuge kuri numaraa, don't spoil the story (of the film): loo maranii, shuts the eyes: foori maranii, does turn of duty: see also merenii [S. maranne, Skt. mārayati]

3467 MARAVAḶI މަރަވަޅި n. wooden sandals, sabots (for indoor use); uř jehi m. (um jehi m.), sandals with knobs (the original kind): vadu jehi m., sandals with straps [S. maraväḍi]

3468 MARAA މަރާ 1. v. imp. or abs. of maranii
2. n. maru + -aa: maraa vidifai, close to death

3469 MARAAMAATU KURANII މަރާމާތު ކުރަނީ v. repairs, patches up [U. marammat]

3470 MARIYAÑBU މަރިޔަނބު n. Divehi form of the feminine name Mariyam (voc., Mariyañbaa !): m. goř, granny knot: Santi M., a character in children's mythology

3471 MARIYAADU މަރިޔާދު adj. decorous: mariyaadu-kam matii, gracefully (of women): mariyaadu-ge, pavilion adjacent to a house [U. maryād, decorum]

3472 MARU މަރު n. 1. death: m. kuḍatan vanii, death is near: maraa vidigen, near to death: maru vanii, dies; (of skin) flakes off: ham marek nuve-ee, the skin is not flaking off ; kamakaa maru vanii, wants something desperately (cf. E. 'is dying for'); ibc., very large: maru-kaři kañḍaigen, after a struggle, somehow or other: maru-kohu, very foolish; marukohek, a great fool; marukos vanii, is very foolish: maru-goos, quite useless; marugoos hadanii, makes stupid mistakes; marugoos govanii, speaks nonsense: maru-tabaan, a large jar

(usu. buried in the earth): maru-dogu, big lie: maru-doḷi, 'big mouth', one who stupidly offends others: maru-moolu, great fool (= boḍu moolek) [S. maru, Skt. māra]
2. slot in the head of a screw
3. kind of tree, xylocarpus moluccensis (maru gas): maru raavanii, does a jigsaw made of nuts from the maru tree

3473 MARUKAA (-kaaek) މަރުކާ n. mark, trademark: shipping mark (on baggage): baru m., loading line: m. jahanii, makes the mark [H. mārkā, E. mark]

3474 MARUKEEṬU (MAARUKEEṬU) މަރުކޭޓު (މާރުކޭޓު) n. open-air market [E. market]

3475 MARUJAANU މަރުޖާނު n. a jewel [cf. U. marjān, coral]

3476 MARUTABAAN މަރުތަބާން n. large jar [U. martabān]

3477 MARUTEYO, MARUTEELA މަރުތެޔޮ - މަރުތޭލަ n. iron hammer: kaňburu m., smith's hammer [H. mārtōl, Port. martello]

3478 MAR(U)HABAA މަރުހަބާ n. congratulations! welcome! [U. marhabā]

3479 MARHUUMU މަރްހޫމު adj. the late.. (al- m...) [U. marhūm]

3480 MALA މަލަ n. outline, shape (of things) ; rařekge m., the distant outline of an island: mala-mati, general appearance (of people); malamati riiti, of handsome appearance

3481 MALAM މަލަމް n. sticky ointment; sticking plaster (rool m.) [U. malam (marham)]

3482 MALARU މަލަރު n. rivet : malaru kuranii, hammers home a rivet : kabiilaa m. kuranii, hammers home a large rivet: (met.) puts a stop (to something, ...-gai): m. aranii, gets a scolding (eenaa / eenaa-ař m. araifi, he got a scolding): mařař m. annanii, I get a scolding, reprimand

3483 MALAAIKATUN މަލާއިކަތުން n. (pl.) angels [U. malāika, pl. of malak]

3484 MALAAFAT މަލާފަތް n. kinds of container: lacquered wooden box for food, usu. round; brass tray for betel (with lid): ař-kan m., octagonal container; digu m., oblong container; vař m., circular container

3485 MALAABAARIIN މަލާބާރީން n. (pl.) Malabars, people of south-west India (who occupied Male in 1752)

3486 MALAAMAAT މަލާމާތް n. mocking laughter: m. kuranii, mocks (at, dat.) [U. malāmat]

3487 MALIKU މަލިކު n. the island of Minicoy (part of the Laccadives, but inhabited by Maldivian people): M. boḍu-maa, a plant, jasminum pubescens: M. ruvaa, 'Madagascar periwinkle', catharanthus roseus

3488 MALIMA މަލިމަ n. long bead at the ends of a rosary

3489 MALIMU މަލިމު n. former title of the mudims of Hukuru and Eterekoilu mosques in Male, in charge of the kiyevenin (kiyeveninge veriyaa); one of the duaaverin: : Malim-ge, house where they lived

3490 MALU- މަލު- See maa

3491 MALMAL މަލްމަލް n. malmal foti, a very fine cotton, Indian 'mull cloth' (used for turban of a khatib, or praying veil for women) [H. malmal, muslin]

3492 MA-VAA މަވާ pr. strengthened form of ma (cf. ma-ves), I for my part: ma-vaa gat birun, through the fear I personally felt [vaa 7]

3493 MAS (mahek) މަސް n. 1. fish, esp. bonito (kaňḍu- mas) : mahař danii, goes deepsea fishing by day (as v. keoḷu kamu diyum): hiki mas, dried fish: roo mas, fresh fish: faru-mas, lagoon fish ('white fish'): kiraa mas, dried fish weighed for export: mas kořanii, chops fish: mas baddanii, traps fish: mas baananii, catches fish by rod: mas hifanii, catches by net or harpoon: mas liyanii, slices fish: mas dila jassanii, smokes fish; mastakugai dila jehee, fish is smoked: mas-ari, half-fish (two gaňḍu s): mas-oḍi, ordinary fishing dhoni (non-Male usage): mas-kaňḍu, deep sea: mas-kaňdu, kind of tree, hernandia nymphaeifolia (cf. varukaňdu); maskaňdu-gaňḍu, wooden post on dhoni for stunning fish when caught: mas-kaři, fishbone: mas-kaaři, a dish of pounded hard dry fish and coconut (hut-maskaaři); maskaaři-duuni, a kind of grasshopper found in graveyards: mas-kuroḷi, a kind of sambol of pounded fish, eaten with batpen in Ramzan: mas-kotan, kind of herb, anisomeles malabarica: mas-gaňḍu 1., quarter section of fish; shoal of small fish in lagoon: mas-goňḍi, low board for chopping fish on: mas- daňḍigaňḍu, large spatula for straining off cooking water: mas-dat, fish tooth; powdered fish tooth (used as antiseptic after childbirth); masdat vaḷi / fiyohi, sheath knife: mas-dooni, fishing dhoni: mas- fatafoḷi, kind of fishcake: mas-fati, bunch of caught fish; fish on a spit: mas-fen, cold milky fish soup: mas-fuu, the useless bottom end of a fish: mas-bai, (anc.), fish tax: mas-bat, a savoury dish: mas-mati 1., top end of fish: mas-mahaa-mehi, all kinds of fish: mas-vaḷi, fish chopper: mas-veri (pl.,-verin), fisherman; masveri-kamař kiyevum, summoning to a recitation of fish-catching charms: mas-hibaru, a kind of sword- fish, marlin, makaira: mas-huni (huňňek), fish chutney; (met.) mas-huni vanii, is mixed together (with..,.. -aai); mahek gannan, (met.) to catch a girl
[S. mas, Skt. matsya]

2. meat, flesh (ekgamu mas): mas tura vanii, the afterbirth comes away (baňḍugai jahaa mas): mas-gaňḍu 2., lump of flesh; fiňdu masgaňḍu, buttock; fala masgaňḍu, thigh: mas-guḷa, muscles; masguḷa kanii, gets stiffened muscles after exercise: swelling; mas roo vanii, diseased growth appears in the eye (cataract): mas lanii, (of seeds in water), swells up: maa mas-haru, with very firm flesh [S. mas, Skt. māṃsa]

3. month: mi mahu, in this month: mahař hańdu fenigen, when the (new) moon is visible: mahu eccetikoḷu, (anc.) monthly allowances: mas-mati 2., monthly observances; masmati balahaṭṭanii, keeps monthly observances after death: mas-varu, massaru, months (pl.): woman's period; massaru laigannanii, has her period; massaru jehenii, the period occurs

[S. mas, Skt. māsa]

4) ifc. in mati-mas, moustache [Skt. śmaśru]

3494 MASAKKAT މަސައްކަތް n. (hon., masakkatpuḷu) work . bura m., heavy work: masakkatu miihun, hired labourers: masakkatu danii, goes to work: masakkatu govanii, summons to work: masakkat kuranii,works [U. maśaqqat]

3495 MASALAS KURANII މަސަލަސް ކުރަނީ v. soothes (a child, tr.) (the Male equivalent of lossum; masalas vum = lohum) [U. ma<u>s</u>la<u>h</u>, reconciliation]

3496 MASAARII މަސާރީ n. bed-curtain: m. kuranii, closes the bed-curtains: m. naganii, opens the bed-curtains [H. masahrī, Skt. maśahara]

3497 MASAALA މަސާލަ n. spicy sauce (masaala-gańḍu): m. fat, a particular curry leaf [U. ma<u>s</u>āla<u>h</u>]

3498 MASUUL-VERI މަސްއޫލުވެރި n. trustee [mas-ūl, responsible]

3499 MASTAKAA (-kaaek) މަސްތަކާ n. a kind of incense, 'gum-mastic' : mastakaa lakuḍi, timber with incense-bearing sap [U. ma<u>s</u>takā, Gk. masti<u>kh</u>ē]

3500 MASTU VANII މަސްތު ވަނީ v. gets drunk [U. mast, Skt. matta]

3501 MASDARU މަސްދަރު n. verbal noun (considered the verbal root) [U. ma<u>s</u>dar]

3502 MAŚVARAA މަޝްވަރާ n. debate [U. maśvara]

3503 MASSALA(-aek) މައްސަލަ n. question, problem: massalaek oḷum filuvanii, solves a problem: vaahakaige a<u>s</u>lu massala, the main story [U. mas'ala]

3504 MASSAAGU މައްސާގު n. a curry leaf, amaranthus sp. (varieties: boḍu m., rat m., hudu m.)

3505 MAŚHUURU މަޝްހޫރު adj. well-known [U. maśhūr]

3506 MAZMUUNU މަޒްމޫނު n . article for publication [U. maźmūn]

3507 MAHANII މަހަނީ v. puts through; (of shirts or bangles) puts on (v.n. mehum, see also mehenii) [cf. S. mahanne, sews]

3508 MAHAA މަހާ n. fish and.. (mas + -aa)

3509 MAHAANA މަހާނަ n. tomb: mahaana-gaa, tombstone (set up on 40th day): mahaana-filaa, tomb board (set up temporarily before the stone): mahaana-harimma, low wall round grave [Skt. śmaśāna]

3510 MAHAA-RADUN މަހާރަދުން n. King [S. maharaja, Skt. mahārājan]

3511 MAHI މަހި n. clasp of a necklace; m. naganii, makes ripples

3512 MAHUJANU މަހުޖަނު n. (anc.) rich man, rich trader [H. mahājan, Skt. mahājana]

3513 MAHUMAA މަހުމާ n. velvet (m. foti) [U. makhmal]

3514 MAHULAŇBOO, MAHULUŇBOO މަހުލަނބޫ - މަހުލުނބޫ n. a plant: m. oř, seeds thereof, a scented medicament

3515 MAHUŚARU މަހުޝަރު n. in mahuśaru duvas, the hereafter [U. mahśar]

3516 MAŘ- މަޅ- See ma

3517 MAŘAN މަޅަން n. rake : mařan aḷanii, uses rake: mařan-dati, rake

3518 MAŘANII މަޅަނީ v. scrapes, rubs (v.n. meřum): grazes (parts of the body): lakuḍi m., planes wood: peels (with an instrument, as v. noḷanii): iloři m., cuts out broom from an eakel [cf. vařanii 2, Skt. mrakṣayati]

3519 MAŘI (maṭṭek) މަޅި n. clay (used for whitening slateboards): m. teo, kerosene: saafu mařiteo, clear kerosene [S. mäṭi, Skt. mṛttikā]

3520 MAḶANII މަޅަނީ v. turns up, folds over (v.n. meḷum, enlarged maḷaa-lum): atukuri m., turns up the cuff: fasbai m., turns up the hem: (of paper) fotuge gaňḍutak meḷi, the pages of the book being dogeared (invol.); maḷaa datgaňḍu, attachment for hemming on a sewing machine; at maḷanii, kaṇḍi maḷanii, draws arm / sword back threateningly [S. moḷavanne, clenches (the fist)]

3521 MAḶI މަޅި n. loop : tun-maḷi, ring in bull's nose: fuḷaliige maḷi essum, tying up the gate-loop, fastening the gate; maḷi-fati, trap (composed of a series of loops): maḷifati jahanii, sets trap

3522 MAḶU މަޅު n.. 1. fitted slat, shaped plank (as in aři, or boat thwarts): dař-maḷu, lower central thwart: maḷu-mati, decking of small boats
2. resin (rugun-maḷu): maḷu kuranii, causes to set or jell (of food)

3523 MAA, MAU(malok) މާ - މަލް n. 1. flower : maa jassanii, heats grain till it pops: maa lanii, (of grain) opens (intr.): maa jehi, decorated with flowers; maa-kurańḍi, flower bowl: maa-gańḍu, budded flowers; also used of corals; maagańḍu-mas, maagańḍaa kuḷee mas, kind of lagoon fish, anemone fish, amphiprion; pointer of compass; shower head, rose of watering-can: maa-teyo, a medicinal flower-oil: maa-fati, garland; maafati aḷanii, puts on a garland: maa-faaḷa, kind of beautiful creeper: maa-fuř, millet pudding: maa-bońḍi, bunch of flowers, bouquet; officer's 'pip' : maa-mui, bee's honey: maa-muřigańḍu, vase, flowerpot: maa-malun (instr.), with various flowers: maa-melaa-meli (-meyyek), all kinds of flowers: maa-ḷeeńbuu, kind of tree, stachytarpheta sp. [S. mal, Skt. mālā]

3524 MAA, MAI މާ - މައި n. mother: mai net kujjek, a child with no mother: mai-fuř, the mother's side : maa-bańḍu, mother's womb; maabańḍun firukenii, is being born; maabańḍu anhenek, a pregnant woman [S. mava, mā-, Skt. mātṛ]

3525 MAA- މާ- adj. (with neg., maaka): ibc., much, great: maa- harek kooř, rather quickly: maaka faseeha kamakař nuviee, was not a very easy thing: ekani maa-ekani, quite alone: maa- loobin, with great love: maa- ginain masakkat kurevunii, work was constantly done: maa-boḍař bolugai rissanii, has a severe headache: nanu maa-ḷaee, the thread is too soft; maa-ala, a large yam, alocasia indica: maa-uniya, kind of fish: maa-kańḍu, deep sea: maa-kařikeyo, large kind of screwpine, pandanus leram: maa-kaḷuvaa (-mas), thigh: maa-gifili kuranii, defecates (formal): maa-toḷi, kind of fish: maa-daa, 1. large fishing net; maadaa aḷanii, casts net [S.mādäl]; 2.hook and eye for attaching rudder: maa-diri, fennel (see s.v.): maa-duuni, kind of seabird; gini kaa maaduuni, ostrich: maa-nidi maturanii, charms into a deep sleep: maa-nifaa, a medicinal creeper, canavalia cathartica: maa-niya mas, kind of fish, elagatis: maa-neevaa lanii / levenii, pants (vb.): maa-filaa, kind of creeping grass: Maa-Bańḍeeri, Lord Chamberlain (obs.): maa-buru, a booming blue-coloured wood-eating insect: maa-buḷaa, a medicinal plant, abutilon indicum (used as an aperient): maa-muguru, sledge- hammer: maa-muguu (-mugulu-), captain of team for tug of war (obs.):maa-mudim, principal mudim (obs.): maa-muřimas, adult or large sardine: maa-rińda, sea serpent: maa-vaḍi, chief carpenter (maavaḍi- kaleege, maavaḍi- bee): maa-varu, kind of dangerous jellyfish: maa-vina, tall kind of grass, tridax procumbens: maa-viha, a disease: maa-singaa, huge (e.g.of fish or trees); maasingaa kańḍu, the high seas: maa-hiti, large kind of margosa tree: maa-hui, a grassy plant, dactyloctenium aegyptium: maa-heńdunaa, soon after dawn: maa hefum, a special meal eaten before the beginning of Ramzan ; see also mai [S. mā, maha, Skt. mahā]

3526 -MAA, -MAI -މާ / މައި suffix , temporal verbal ending used with past stem: viimaa, viimai, that being so: feřiimaa, when (it) began [S. -(ā)ma, -ahama]

3527 MAA މާ n. 2. asterism Maghā , Māgha [S. mā]

3528 MAA-KANAA މާކަނާ n. heron: m. taḷudańḍi, m. fořі, kinds of drifting coral [kanaa]

3529 MȦAṬṬAŘ AḶANII މާއްޓަރ އަޅަނީ v. (anc.) does a pole-jumping exercise (in old games)

3530 MAAḌU މާޑު n. spit where weed is exposed at low tide

3531 MAAT މާތް adj. honourable (religious or secular); great, holy, respectable; nice: maat bas, honorific language: maat miihaa, gentleman: maat sifaek, a gentlemanly quality: maat veriyaa, head of state: maat (ras)kalaañge, God: maat saahibaa, the Prophet: maat mamma, mother (hon.): maat koř hitanii, respects (with dat.) [Skt. mahat]

3532 MAATURA މާތުރަ conj. however (anc.)

3533 MAADAM, MAADAMAA މާދަމް / މާދަމާ n. to-morrow: maadamaayakii, tomorrow is..: maadamain, by tomorrow: maadamaa-ař, for tomorrow: maadannee, it is tomorrow: maadam nuun anek duvahu, the day after tomorrow

3534 MAADARII މާދަރީ adj. In maadarii bas, original tongue [U. mādarī]

3535 MAADIRI މާދިރި n. 1. (anc.) model (mod., namuunaa): m. jahanii, m. naganii, makes a model (of carpenters) [S. mādiri, mādili, U. mādrī]

3536 MAA-DIRI މާދިރި n. 2. fennel [S. mā-duru]

3537 MAADDAA މާއްދާ n. subject of discussion: article: section; maaddii gotun, materially [U. mādda]

3538 MAANA މާނަ n. meaning : m. kuranii, interprets [U. ma'nā]

3539 MAAFA މާފަ n. maternal grandfather (Southern usage)

3540 MAAFAT މާފަތް n. a Maldivian title (maafat kaleefaanu) [? for Maafahat]

3541 MAAFANNU މާފަންނު n. name of one of the four wards of Male

3542 MAAFU މާފު n. pardon; maafu kuree! I'm sorry: maafu kořfim, that's all right [U. māf, mu'āf]

3543 MAAMA މާމަ n. grandmother: fuuḷu m., midwife: de-maama-kañbalun, grandmother and granddaughter (hon.) [U. māmā, old lady]

3544 MAAMAA VANII މާމާ ވަނީ v. goes stale, goes off (of rihaakuru or pickle)

[cf. kaafaamaamaa vum, raamaa vum]

3545 MAAMUULU (MAUMUULU) މާމޫލު (މައުމޫލު) n. export or import duty: m. naganii, charges the duty [U. ma'mūl, custom]

3546 MAARAŇGA މާރަނގަ n. a black sea-bird, noddy: maarañga-ař danii, goes to catch m.

3547 MAARAAMAARII މާރާމާރީ n. physical assault

[H. mārāmārī, affray, Skt. √māraya, kill]

3548 MAARU މާރު n. 1. exchange : m. kuranii, exchanges; mi faisaa maaru koř diifaanan ta, can you change this money for me? [T. māṟu]

2. thick rope: maaru-gañḍu, piece of thick rope: maaru aḷanii, plaits a thick rope

3. yard length, for measuring circumference of bundles of firewood: fansaas maaru kuredi daru, 50 yards of kuredi wood: daru-maaru, bundle of firewood: dañḍi-maaru, bundle of logs

3549 MAARU VANII މާރު ވަނީ v. dozes: mendurař maaru vanii, takes siesta

3550 MAARUKEEṬU (MARUKEEṬU) މާރުކޭޓު (މަރުކޭޓު) n. open-air market [E. market]

3551 MAALI (maayyek) މާލި n. disguise : m. hadanii, m. bannanii, dresses up in disguise; man in disguise, ghost: m. annaane, the ghost is coming: m. genee!, bring on the ghost (to frighten or amuse children)

3552 MAALIMII މާލިމީ n. navigator; captain or pilot of foreign-going ships (cf. nevi) [U. mālim, mu'allim]

3553 MAALIYYATU މާލިއްޔަތު n. finance: mahkamat ul maaliyyatu, Department of Finance [U. māliyat, cf. māl]

3554 MAALU މާލު n. property: maalu-veri, man of property [U. māl]

3555 MAALUUDU މާލޫދު n. See mauluudu

3556 MAALE މާލެ n. name of the island which forms the capital of the

Maldives: Maalee Hukuru Miskit, the Male Friday mosque

3557 MAAVAHARU މާވަހަރު n. ambergris (=goma)

3558 MAAZII މާޒީ n. the past [U. māẕī]

3559 MAAḶAÑBU-GE މާޅަނބުގެ n. enclosure for travelling carpenters

3560 MAAḶAS- މާޅަސް- See maaḷos

3561 MAAḶIKA މާޅިކަ n. heavenly palace [?Skt. mālikā]

3562 MAAḶOS (MAAḶAS-) މާޅޮސް (މާޅަސް-) n. m.keyo, ash plantain (for cooking)

3563 MAAḶOS-MAḌULU މާޅޮސްމަޑުލު n. name of R and B atolls

3564 MI މި adj. (as n.., gen. miige) this (before nouns); here (before verbs); mi gas, these trees: mi annanii, is coming this way: mi kihaa riiti ta, how pretty this is! mi-ii..., this is.. (also mii.., mi-iikii..): mi-adu, today: mi-ok, look here (cf. eok, tiok); fot miok fennanii taa! here is the book; miok haa iru, all this time; miok fada, of this kind: mioomen, these people… : mi-kalakař ais, hitherto (anc.): mi-kahala, of this sort : mi-koi, this my son: mi-koḷař, this way! mikoḷakař nudeveene, no entry! mi-tak, this much, so many (mitakek); used in dates, 17.1.64 mitak vii taarii<u>kh</u>u, on the indicated date: mi-taa, here (mitaaku, mitaañgai): mi-daa(kař) duvahu, recently: mi-nuun, other, not this: miyoo, ah,what is this? anekkaa miyoo,what's all this? mi-langalan, see elangalan: mi-vaa .., now this.. [vaa 7]: mi-veni, this particular (followed by indef. ending); vaki miveni gotek neti, without any particular system: mi-saahitu, quite soon (cf. isaahitu): mi-haa (mihai), this much; mihaa boḍu, so big; mihaa tanař (ais), hitherto; mihaa hisaabun, at this juncture: mi-haaru (miha-iru), now; mihaaruge zamaan, the present; mihaarakař ais, nowadays: mi-hira, this here (also of person addressed); also mihiragen (cf. eokgen etc.) : mihirii, here stands (for mi -hurii): mi-hen, like this, thus: mihen annaařee, come this way! mihen danii, (I'm) just going (answer to greeting 'kon taakař?'): mihenii, the reason is.. (cf. e-henii): mihennaa, if so [S. mē]

3565 MIAKAN މިއަކަން See miyakan

3566 MIARU މިއަރު See miyaru

3567 MIAHELIA މިއަހެލިއަ See miyaheliya

3568 MITURU މިތުރު n. close friend (formal or poetic) (pl., miturun: voc., mituraa ! [S. mituru, Skt. mitra]

3569 MIDILI މިދިލި n. 'country almond' tree, terminalia catappa (of which the fruits are called kana-madu) [S. mideli]

3570 MIN މިން n. measure, amount; label on medicine bottle: min-tak, measurements: min net, limitless: min-gañḍu, measuring line: baru min, weight: ..-ge min balanii, surveys the boundaries of..: ...-gai min aḷanii, takes measurements of..: min jahanii, makes carpenter's or tailor's marks: min-varu, size, limit, amount; minvarař iimaan vanii, is content with what one has; (Kalaañge) minvaru-fuḷu, the will of God; minvaru kuravvanii (of God), wills something [cf. minanii]

3571 MINANII މިނަނީ v. measures out (abs. mine : p.p. mini) minaa bees, a class of (measurable) medicines [S. maninne, Skt. minăti]

3572 MINAA މިނާ 1. n. beads: minaa-fati, bead necklace; minaafati aḷanii, wears necklace

2. v. measuring (pres. part. of minanii) [S. manina]

3573 MINI މިނި 1. n. mankind; usu. ibc. mini-kiru, breast milk: mini maraa miihaa, executioner: mini-rañgaḷu, healthy and prosperous (minirañgaḷu rařek); minirañgaḷu kuraa jammiyyat, Human Improvement Society (a former official body for encouraging goat-farming etc.): mini-heyo, habitable, inhabited [S. minī, Skt. manuṣya]

2. v. measured (p.p. of minanii) [S. mäni]

3574 MINIVAN މިނިވަން adj. free: as n. (pl.) minivanun , free men; minivanakař vaa nama, if (one is) a free man

3575 MINEṬ (MINIṬ) މިނެޓް (މިނިޓް) n. minute (of time) [E. minute]

3576 MINJU KURANII މިންޖު ކުރަނީ v. saves, protects: masakkatun minju vanii, is freed from labour

3577 MINNAT މިންނަތް n. perseverance [U. minnat]

3578 MINBARU މިންބަރު n. preaching platform in a mosque [U. minbar]

3579 MIYA މިޔަ n. blade, cutting edge (as v. fuřoḷi): miya danii, blade wears down (m. hiñgajje, as v. koři vejje): m. aḷanii, resets blade

3580 MIYA-KAN (MIAKAN) މިޔަކަން (މިއަކަން) n. corners of mouth (de-miyakan) [S. muva-, Skt. mukha-]

3581 MIYARU (MIARU) މިޔަރު (މިއަރު) n. shark (Varieties: ainu m. or aanmatii m., kaři -m., kaaligaňḍu- m.(hammerhead), tungaňḍu- m., nidan-m. (basking), femunu m.(tiger), maḍi- m., maḍu m., vořimas-m.): maḍu miyarař danii, hunts 'soft' sharks: nidanmiyarekee ekgotee, is half asleep [S. muvaru, mōru, Skt. makara]

3582 MIYAREM މިޔަރެމް n. kind of baitfish (shaped like a shark), stolephorus [miyaru + em]

3583 MIYALANI މިޔަލަނި n. kind of steel: name of a mosque in Male; miyalani mas, kind of fish

3584 MIYAVAALI (miyavaayyek) މިޔަވާލި n. end of fishing line, where hook is attached: (met.) m. digu miihek, a slow man

3585 MIYAHELIYA (MIAHELIA) މިޔަހެލިޔަ (މިއަހެލިއަ) n. asterism Mřgaśiras [S. muvasiriya]

3586 MIYAAŇGU މިޔާނގު n. buffalo horn (used for handles, or medicinally) [S. mī + aňga, horn]

3587 MIYUZIK މިޔުޒިކް n. music [E. music]

3588 MIRI މިރި n. young coconut (bigger than goboḷi ; used for chutneys; produces fani heva syrup)

3589 MIRIHI މިރިހި n. a plant, melanthera biflora: boḍu m., tithonia diversifolia: mirihi vaa, kind of creeping grass

3590 MIRIYAAS މިރިޔާސް n. a medicinal plant

3591 MIRUS (miruhek) މިރުސް n. chillies, capsicum annuum: miruhu lanii, cooks with chillies: miruhu li diya, curry- water; asee m., pepper: giteu m., capsicum frutescens: lonu m., a chutney of chillies: roo m., green chillies: vi-fuku m., very small hot chillies: hiki m., dried chillies [S. miris, Skt. marica]

3592 MILA މިލަ n. dirt: mila-fooli, bits of dust and sweat on the body: mila-foni, slightly sweet: da-mila, tarnish: m. jahaafai, m. araa, m. vefaa, turned brown in cooking: mila filaa varař, enough to get rid of the dirt; in doublet with dila, ekves dilaek milaek naaraa, without any trouble [S. mala, Skt. mala]

3593 MILADUN-MAḌULU މިލަދުންމަޑުލު n. name of Ř and N atolls

3594 MILANII މިލަނީ v. withers; is scorched or toasted; (of human faces) loses colour: caus., miluvanii, softens by fire, singes [S. mälavenne, Skt. mlāyati]

3595 MILKU KURANII މިލްކު ކުރަނީ v. claims ownership: milku vanii, belongs [U. milk, possessions]

3596 MISAALU މިސާލު n. example (of..,..-ge) [U. mi$\underline{th}$āl]

3597 MISURU މިސުރު n. Egypt: Misurek nudaane, will not go to Egypt; m. gaňdakooḷi, angelonia salicariifolia [U. Mi$\underline{s}$r]

3598 MISKIT މިސްކިތް n. mosque: miskitař aranii, enters mosque; miskit-tere, inside of mosque: miskit-daara, wall of mosque yard: Iidu miskitu laage, dome of Id mosque(in Male): miskitu vakaru, mosque timber (which should not be reused); (met.) rejected wives in noble families [A. masjid]

3599 MISKIINU މިސްކީނު n. lowly person [U. miskīn]

3600 MISRAABU މިސްރާބު n. course (of boat), direction: Koḷuňbaa misraabu jehiiee, set course for Colombo [mi$\underline{s}$rāb]

3601 MIZAAJU މިޒާޖު n. temperament: kaleaa mařaa ek misaajek nuunee, you and I have different temperaments [U. mizāj]

3602 MIHURAABU މިހުރާބު n. the niche or apse in a mosque : mihuraabu-ge, special place of prayer [U. mi$\underline{h}$rāb]

3603 MII މީ for mi-ii, emphatic of mi, this; also miikii: mii beefuḷek nuun, I'm not a nobleman: mii baa aḷugaňḍuge galam, is this my pen? tiya hoodaa aňgoṭiyakii mii ta, is this the ring you are looking for? mii taa magee fot! look, here is my book! miiti (miiccek), this thing: miicceti varař agu heyo, these are very cheap: miin (instr.), of this; miin suruvaafodek, a drop of this soup (= mi suruvain etifodek): miinaa, this person, he; miinaa kaa varek taa! what a lot he eats: miinaa mii Fonaduu kujjek, this is someone from Fonadu: miiňda, for mi + iňda, this sitting (cf. eeňda): miinii, this is..(for mi-inii)

3604 MIIGONU މީގޮނު n. water buffalo [S. mī(vā), Skt.mahiṣā + gon, P. gōṇā]

3605 MIIDAA (MIIDAU) (miidalek) މީދާ (މީދައު) n. rat : miidaa horu, rat-hole: Japanu m., mouse: mugoři m., squirrel; miidalek hadanii, winds rope into a 'bun' [S. mī(yā), Skt. mūṣika]

3606 MIIBA މީބަ n. an old royal title (ran- miiba), of uncertain meaning

3607 MII-MAS (-hek) މީމަސް n. kind of lagoon fish

3608 MIIMU މީމު n. the letter M in the Arabic and Maldivian alphabets: Miimu atoḷu, Mulaku atoll

3609 MIIRAN މީރަން n. graphite [S. miniran]

3610 MII-RAA މީރާ n. evening toddy (the best of the three tappings) [miiru-raa]

3611 MIIRU މީރު adj. tasty (as v. nubai) : raha miiru, nice-tasting: hiti miiru, nicely bitter: boňḍibat miiru, tasty in porridge: miirii.., it is tasty..
[S. miyuru, mihiri, sweet, Skt. madhura; in Maldivian, 'sweet' is foni]

3612 MIIRUBAHURU-GE މީރުބަހުރުގެ n. 'harbourmaster's house', name of a house in Male where the former functionary lived (now holding a reference library) [U. mīr-bahr]

3613 MIILAADII މީލާދީ n. prefix for Christian era dates: Iidu m., the Prophet's birthday

3614 MIIS (miihek) މީސް n. men and women (stemform): miis-tak(un), humanity, people (religious and formal: voc., miistakunnee(ve) !): miis-koḷek, some people: miis-gaňḍu, people : miiis-miihun vaki nuvaa / neeňgee, miis numiis vaki nuvaa / neeňgee, who doesn't know what's what [S. minis, Skt. manuṣya]

3615 MIIHAA (miihaayek; pl., miihun) މީހާ n. human being: miihun-tak, a lot of people; miihun gaňḍu, a group of people : e miihaa / e miihaku, whoever it may be: aňbi-miihaa, wife: aadaige m., 'ordinary man' (grade 3) : khatiib m., the khatib : e miihaage kamtak fennanii varař nubai kořee, he is not shaping up well; he is dangerously ill
[S. minihā, Skt. manuṣya]

3616 MUI މުއި n. sap

3617 MUIRU, MUIRI މުއިރު - މުއިރި n. banana fibre (used as a bow)

3618 MUKABBA މުކައްބަ n. wicker food cover: m. jahanii, places foodcover (over.., ...-gai) [A. muqabbab, domed]

3619 MUKOḶU މުކޮޅު n. wood to cover screw holes; rawlplug: m. jahanii, applies m.

3620 MUGU މުގު n. lentils, lens esculenta; gram: kaḷu m.,black gram, phaseolus radiatus: nuu m., green dhal, phaseolus aureus: fehi m., green gram, phaseolus mungo: maśuuru m., masoor dhal, lens culinaris: rat mugu, red gram: sanaa mugu, chickpea, cicer arietinum [S. muṃ, Skt. mudga]

3621 MUGUDARU މުގުދަރު n. club (for exercise) [H. mugdar, Skt. mudgara]

3622 MUGURANII މުގުރަނީ v. crushes: grinds (dry, with mortar or grindstones, as v. fuňḍanii): haňḍuu muguraa dati, ricemill: muguraa dati, mincer: fuř mugurum, grinding flour: at mugurunii, (invol.)the arm was crushed; (met.) gavaaidutak mugurum, breaking the rules

3623 MUGURAAM މުގުރާމް n. kind of baitfish, fusilier, caesio [cf. S. maguru]

3624 -MUGURI -މުގުރި n. jahaa -muguri, wood apple, feronia elephantum

3625 MUGURIIN މުގުރީން n. (pl.) reciters of the Qur'aan [U. muqrī]

3626 MUGURU މުގުރު n. large mallet or club: police baton (used to split coconuts) [S. muguru, Skt. mudgara]

3627 MUGUU (mugulek) މުގޫ n. end of rope in tug-of-war: controlling section of rope in felling trees; captain of a team, e.g. in baibalaa : fas maamugulu fas vagun, the five captains of the teams; (met.) controlling power (verikamuge m., kamekge m.)

3628 MUGOŘI މުގޮޅި n. mongoose: m. miidaa, squirrel [S. mugaṭi, P. mungusa]

3629 MUGOOLI މުގޯލި n. circular pit in the sand used in game of tin-mugooli : mugooli aḷanii, makes the pits

3630 MUŇGUḶI މުނގުޅި n. in suňguḷi-muňguḷi , jumble, junk (doublet)

3631 MUJIIB-VANTA މުޖީބްވަންތަ adj. (hon.) responsive (usu. of God) [U. mujīb, answering]

3632 MUJUMARAA (-aaek) މުޖުމަރާ n. fireholder, censer [U. mijmar]

3633 MUṬIYAA މުޓިޔާ n. yoke (in dressmaking)

3634 MUḌA-HAŇDI (-hañjek) މުޑަހަނޑި n. kind of fish (resembling fani-haňdi), trevally, caranx

3635 MUḌI މުޑި n. 1.fence post; prop: m. bari, row of supports; m. jahanii, fixes supports: m. naganii, stands on hind legs, (met.) hiyanñař m. naganii, is frightened at nothing [old S. muḍa]

2. fluffy cake inside seed coconut: muḍi-kaaři, seed coconut [S. muḍu]

3636 MUḌUKAA(-aaek) މުޑުކާ n. kind of food container

3637 MUḌU-GAA(-galek) މުޑުގާ n. kind of hard stone

3638 MUḌUTU މުޑުތު n. sounding lead, plumbline: m. lanii, casts the lead

3639 MUḌU-DAARU މުޑުދާރު adj. filthy [U. murdār, but cf. tat-muḍu]

3640 MUḌUDAAS މުޑުދާސް n. a class of medical minerals (Varieties: at m., ali m., rihi m.)

3641 MUḌU-VAK މުޑުވަކް n. cutting, stock; sample: muḍuvakař, for breeding purposes: m. kuranii, breeds: (met.) rañgaḷu muḍuvakekge kujjek, a child of a good stock

3642 MUḌU-HAA (-haalek) މުޑުހާ n. breeding poultry (imported large variety)

3643 MUT މުތް n. pearl (itaa m.): mut-toři, mother of pearl : ran mut, golden pearl [S. mutu, Skt. muktā]

3644 MUTAAMA, MUTAAMU މުތާމަ - މުތާމު n. In phrase m. jehee den , fully loaded (of ship's cargo)

3645 MUTII މުތީ n. pearls [mut]

3646 MUTUNI މުތުނި n. shoots of a yam

3647 MU<u>TT</u>I VANII މުއްތި ވަނީ v. escapes: bañḍu furaana m. vanii, lives from hand to mouth [Skt. mukti, release]

3648 MUDAA, MUDAU (mudalek) މުދާ - މުދައު n. goods (esp. as cargo): mudaa koḷu, some goods: haru m., fixed property: firuaunge mudaa, jelly fish [H. mudal; cf. S. mudal, money]

3649 MUDI (muñjek) މުދި n. ring : kanfatu m., ear-ring: hat- mudi, baby's necklace with seven circular pendents: rectum (of animals; (slang), of men)

[S. mudu, Skt. mudrā]

3650 MUDIMU މުދިމު n. official in charge of a mosque (formerly also in charge of an avař) (mudim-kaleege): fas mudim beekalun, five former royal mosque officials [U. mu'azzin]

3651 MUDUNAŘ ARUVANII މުދުނަށް އަރުވަނީ v. opens (the eyes) wide (in horror) [S. mudun, Skt. mūrdhan, head]

3652 MUDDATU މުއްދަތު n. period of time (esp. of jail sentence) [U. muddat]

3653 MUDDU މުއްދު n. an optional fine or penance: m. bahanii, distributing such fine (to the poor: in order to marry the same woman for the seventh time) [U. muddu, an amount]

3654 MUNAAJAA މުނާޖާ n. prayers in the middle of the night [U. munājāt]

3655 MUNAASABATU މުނާސަބަތު n. auspicious occasion [U. munāsabat, suitability]

3656 MUNI މުނި n. 'he' in game of elangalan:: muni-dańḍi, 'home' in the game

3657 MUNI-AVAS މުނިއަވަސް n. discontent

3658 MUNI-KAAFA މުނިކާފަ n. great-grandfather

3659 MUNI-FUUHI މުނިފޫހި n. boredom: m. filuvanii, avoids boredom: m. filanii, boredom is avoided

3660 MUNI-MAAMA މުނިމާމަ n. great-grandmother

3661 MUNIIFAAS މުނީފާސް n. ship's manifest [E. manifest]

3662 MUNḌAAM މުންޑާމް n. bollard, post to tie up to

3663 MUNḌU މުންޑު n. man's sarong: m. annanii, puts on sarong: munḍun aruvaa jahanii, partially tucks up sarong: munḍun fuu gaḷanii, fully tucks up sarong; kanbaa m., one-piece sarong (ekfatii m.): hatarufatii m., sarong woven in two pieces: fatigańḍu nagaa m., old type of sarong with pleat in front [S. munḍu, T. muṇṭu]

3664 MUNNAARU މުންނާރު n. minaret (esp. the one by the Friday mosque in Male) [U. mīnār]

3665 MUNÑOOI މުންނޫއި excl. uttered by the 'he' in game of elangalan [muni+oot]

3666 MUBAARAATU މުބާރާތު n. competition [A.]

3667 MURAKA މުރަކަ n. coral fern (used as akiri for flooring): m. naganii brings up m.: m. (ekgamař) aruvanii, brings m. ashore; ekgamu muraka, 'milk-hedge', euphorbia tirucalli

3668 MURAÑGA މުރަނގަ n. 'drumsticks', moringa oleifera : katuru m., feeru m., sesbania grandiflora : valu m., indigo; m. kiru, sap of m. (used as glue): m. toḷi, pod of m. [S. murumgā, T. murunkai, 'horseradish tree']

3669 MURANA މުރަނަ adj. crisp, brittle (usu. of food): murana-kam keňḍi, having lost its crispness

3670 MURAAKI (muraatkek) މުރާކި n. kind of intoxicating berry, physalis minima

3671 MURAADU މުރާދު n. objective, aim [U. murād]

3672 MURAALI (muraayyee) މުރާލި adj. industrious : muraalifuḷu-kam, industriousness (hon.)

3673 MURIŇGU މުރިނގު n. direction: araa m., east: ossee m., west

3674 MURIIDU މުރީދު n. leader of secular choir or musicians (muriidu-kaleege) [U. murīd, proselyte]

3675 MURUBBAA(-aaek) މުރުއްބާ n. jam, coonserve: m. aḷanii, makes jam [U. murabbā]

3676 MURUMURU މުރުމުރު onom. murumuru lanii, crackles (as of fire, or eating rusks [H. murmur]

3677 MURRU މުއްރު n. myrrh [U. murr]

3678 MULA މުލަ n. asterism Mūla: m. nakatu, during the asterism M. (the first of iruvaa season, when guns used to be tested)

3679 MULAK މުލައް See mulok

3680 MULAKU މުލަކު n. name of M atoll: Boḍu M., the atoll Fook Mulaku

3681 MULAK-DAŇḌI މުލައްދަނޑި n. upper arm

3682 MULAARI(-GAŇḌU) މުލާރި(ގަނޑު) n. top (best) section of fish (cf. kaři-ari) [mula + ari]

3683 MULI (muyyek) މުލި n. 1. transverse spit from a reef [S. mulu, nook]
2. name of an island in M atoll

3684 MULIHI (mulissek) މުލިހި n. big boils (cf. bihi) or blisters: m. (gaigai) jahaigen, having developed boils (on the body)

3685 MULU- މުލު- See muu

3686 MULU-VAGU މުލުވަގު n. chief thief (in stories) [for mugulu-]

3687 MULOK (MULAK) މުލޮއް (މުލައް) n. curved bows of fishing dhonis (mulok-gaňḍu, mulak-gaňḍu)

3688 MUSANMAA މުސަންމާ n. a dry curry

3689 MUSALLAA މުސައްލާ n. prayer-mat [U. muṣallā]

3690 MUSAḶU މުސަޅު n. hare (as a joke, used for the name Muusaa Fuḷu) [T. mucal]

3691 MUSAARA މުސާރަ n. salary : m. nangavanii, receives salary

3692 MUSINBI (musinbek) މުސިންބި n. kind of poisonous turtle, leatherback

3693 MUSINBII މުސިންބީ n. Mozambique

3694 MUSIIBAT މުސީބަތް n. calamity [U. muṣībat]

3695 MUSKUḶI މުސްކުޅި adj. old (of people; muskuḷiyaa, old man); antique (of houses, as v. baa , dilapidated): muskuḷi aada-tak, ancient customs: muskuḷi gas, aged trees: m. bas, old sayings: m. vaahaka, old stories: m. rahmat-teriyek, an old friend: muskuḷi takuru, former chief virger of the Friday mosque: muskuḷi beekalun, former members of the Majlis;
m. vanii, grows old: m. kuravvanii, gives pension

3696 MUSTAGBALU މުސްތަޤްބަލު n. the future [U. mustaqbil]

3697 MUSSATI މުއްސަތި adj. ancient form of mussaňdi

3698 MUSSAŇDI (mussañjek) މުއްސަނދި adj. rich : as n. (pl.) mussaňdin rich men [U. mus 'ad]

3699 MUZAAHIRAA މުޒާހިރާ n. demonstrations [U. muẕāhir]

3700 MUKHAATIBU KURANII މުޚާޠިބު ކުރަނީ v. addresses (with - aa of person addressed) [U. mukhāṯib]

3701 MUHIMMU މުހިންމު adj. important [U. muhim]

3702 MUHUTAADU މުހުތާދު n. needs: muhutaadu fuddanii, supplies one's needs [U. muhtāj]

3703 MUŘ މުށް 1. n. fist (goř-muř): muř-baaru, tightfisted, miserly: (goř)muř kavanii, closes fists; graspable handle (usu. detachable), e.g. of umbrellas, axes, pans, brushes, knives (muř-gaňḍu): muř-varu, handful; tin muř(varu) veli, three handfuls of sand: muř-vaḷu, notch for grasping a stick [S. miṭa, miṭi, Skt. muṣṭi]

2. n. 2 spans, 18 inches: kitak muř foti, how many m. of cloth?

3704 MUŘI (muṭṭek) މުށި n. 1. earthenware: m. kula, brownish colour: muři-gaňḍu, vase (nowadays often made of cement); maa-muřigaňḍu, flowerpot : muři-tař, earthenware plate: tař-muři, crockery in general: m. daḷu, tin for ointment (nowadays of plastic); muřidaḷu bees, ointment (esp. for ringworm): muři-foti, kind of washer in hookah (nowadays of iron, dagaňḍu-foti): gas-muři, flowerpot: ruňbaa muři, earthenware [S. mäṭi, Skt. mṛttikā]

2. smith's hammer : ham-muři, horsewhip [S. miṭi, Skt. muṣṭikā]

3. a children's game (muři kuḷen, to play m.)

3705 MUŘI-MAS (-mahek) މުށިމަސް n. kind of sardine or scad, selar (maa-m., larger variety: medu-m., smaller variety)

3706 MUḶA މުޅަ adj. rotten (of food, esp. rice, or dead animals): (met.) kannetkamun muḷa aḷaafai / vefai hunna, half-dead with laziness: muḷa devi, a dead spirit made use of in fanḍita magic [S. maḷa, dead, Skt. mṛta]

3707 MUḶAA މުޅާ n. a medicinal leaf (muḷaa fat), eaten raw for stomach complaints

3708 MUḶI މުޅި n. 1. coop or basket : kukuḷu m., for hens: uva m., for transporting lime
2. 50 naaḷis of rice

3709 MUḶI މުޅި adj. 3. whole: muḷi duvahu, the whole day; adv., muḷin (muḷiin), completely: muḷin diyaii, gone for ever; always (muḷinme, muḷinves, hama muḷin: muḷiin hen, almost entirely: with neg., muḷiakun) [S. muḷu, T. mu<u>l</u>u]

3710 MUḶOO (muḷolek) މުޅޯ n.. large axe

3711 MUḶOOŘI މުޅޯރި n . wicker waste basket, dustbin (with handle)

3712 MUU (mulek) މޫ n. root: muu lanii, takes root (also met.); mulun laigen veṭṭijje/ mulun laifi, uprooted itself, fell root and all [S. mul, Skt. mūla]

3713 MUUḌU މޫޑު n. large container

3714 MUUDU މޫދު n. shallow sea, lagoon: muudař danii, goes into the lagoon: muudař erenii, goes into the sea to defecate: muudu aḷanii, dips (timber) into the sea (to season it): muudu- nai, kind of prawn, 'sea worm' : muudu- vina, a maritime grass, thalassia hemprichii [S. muhudu, Skt. samudra]

3715 MUUNI-MAA(malek) މޫނިމާ n. large scented flower, or the tree on which it grows, mimusops elengi

3716 MUUNU މޫނު n. face: m. aḷanii, covers the face of the dead: m. dekum, paying last respects to the dead: m. hadanii, frowns: muunu donna tiři, washbasin: muunu-aňdiri-kam, twilight; muunu-mati, the face (of a person, hon., muunufuḷu-mati), face of a watch, mask, goggles; eenaage muunumatiigai mořum, answering back to him [S. muhunu, ?Skt. mukha-]

3717 MUUMIYAA (-aaek) މޫމިޔާ n. a medicament (red powder) [U. mōmiyā]

3718 MUURITI މޫރިތި adj. graceful and beautiful [U. & Skt. mūrti, figure, form]

3719 MUUSADARU މޫސަދަރު n. ammonium chloride, used in soldering [U. nausādar]

3720 MUUSUM މޫސުމް n. season (monsoon); period of weather
[U. mausam]

3721 -ME -މެ emphatic enclitic particle, often alternating with ves : kon-me ra̋ekgai-me (kon-me ves ra̋ekgai), in some island or other : defot-me (defot ves), both the books: ek-me, a single (with indef. nouns), ekme miihek, a single person; the most (with adjectives), ekme riiti, the most beautiful: kon-me duvahaku (ves), every day: kon-me-akas, anyway: gos-me ekamek nuve, having gone but not completed the task: budu hadaa-me budakař nuve, having tried to make an image but not succeeded. (See menuvii: the usage of this particle is somewhat different from the corresponding use of -ma in Sinhalese)
[S. -ma, Skt. evameva]

3722 MEI މެއި See mee

3723 MEKUNU މެކުނު n. kind of jumping mullet: mekunu fumunas, gaa-haka-akař nufumeveene-ee, though the fish may jump, the clam cannot (prov.)

3724 MEKENII މެކެނީ v. touches, is smeared on (+ ..-gai): anc. or non-Male, except in the proverb atugai mekeñaa (or heekeñaa), datugai mekeene / heekee, what you touch, you eat (of food) [S. mäkenne, väkenne, Skt. mrakṣyatē]

3725 MEKKU މެކްކު n. wooden thole pin: mekkutak jahai, having fixed the tholepins

3726 MEC މެޗް n. match, contest [E. match]

3727 MEṬAA (-aek) މެޓާ n. imported sweetmeats, and esp. a large Maldivian sweet eaten at Boḍu Mauluud : meṭaa-gañḍu, a single such sweet; m.hilanii, cooks or stirs m.: m. hilaa dabu, stirrer for cooking such sweets: rabaru m., chewing gum [H. mīṭhā, Skt. miṣṭaka]

3728 METURUM މެތުރުމް v. uttering charms (v.n. of maturanii)
[S. mätirīm]

3729 MEDU މެދު n. middle: eige medugai, in the middle of it: eige meden haa taagai / eige medakaa hisaabun, about in the middle of it: medutere, middle part; hañguraamaage medutereegai, in the middle of the war: demedu, the part between; degeege demedugai, between the two houses; medu- kañḍanii, interrupts: iru medu-jehenii, the sun is at the zenith: medař huri kujjaa, the middle child: medun bindum, breaking in the middle: medu lanii, attaches the centre rope in cadjan thatching: medař huṭṭum, half-time; medu-kani, kingpost , window post: medu-keyo, kind of ever-bearing screwpine: medu-ge, central living area of house: medu- gooti(-tere), central courtyard: medu-firi, (anc.) middleman to break a series of marriages (fař keñḍum): medu-min, average, mean: medu- muřimas, kind of sardine: Medu Raajje(-tere), central and northern Maldives: medu-roonu, middle-sized rope: rař medu kudiin, fatherless (bastard) children: ek-medu mudaa, property which must be shared: medu-veri(yaa), intermediating (person); meduveriyakař vii, acting as intermediary: meduveri kuranii, allows to occur; Naadiyaa-ař śakku vaa got meduveri nukuraati, don't let N. suspect:

meduveri vanii, occurs: hurelaan deveene got meduveri ve, getting the chance to stay; adv., miaa medu (in neg., medakaa), concerning this [S. mäda, Skt. madhya]

3730 MEDURI މެދުރި n. carrying mat, with two sticks for carting away rubbish (kuni ukaa m.) or covering cricket pitch

3731 -MEN -މެން plural personal suffix : dariful̩u-men, children: soru-men, chaps: Yahya-men, Y. and others: bappa-men, father and friends

3732 MENUVII މެނުވީ v. except (lit.), used postpositionally like fiyavai : rañgal̩u kamek menuvii nukuraaře, don't do anything except good: mihen vegen menuvii, except in this way, otherwise: aharenge atun diniyyaa menuvii batek nukaane-ee, he won't eat rice unless I give it with my hand (he won't eat food unless I feed him) [-me + nu-vii]

3733 MEN-KAFAAḶA މެންކަފާޅަ n. soft head of small children [for medu-kafaal̩a]

3734 MENṬEL, MENṬELI (menṭeyyek) މެންޓެލް - މެންޓެލި n. incandescent mantle [E. mantle]

3735 MENDAM މެންދަމް n. period after midnight, the small hours: mendamun ali ve, very early when it was getting light [for medu-dam]

3736 MENDURU މެންދުރު n. midday: menduru haa iru, at about midday: menduru dam, 12.0 - 3. 0: mendurun añburaa / menduru eñburi tanaa, in the afternoon: menduru-fas, afternoon: menduru fahun, in the afternoon [? for medu-duhu]

3737 MEMBARU މެންބަރު - މެމްބަރު n. member (personal) (pl., membarun) [E. member]

3738 MERUM މެރުން v. killing ; meriyas, though one should kill: closing the eye (v.n. of maranii) [S. märum]

3739 MERENII މެރެނީ v. (of the eyes) is closing: eenaa otii loo merifai, he was resting, dozing (invol. of maranii, but not used in the sense of 'dying' (maru vum))

3740 -MELAA-MELI -މެލާމެލި n. flora , in maa-melaameli, all kinds of flowers [S. malāmäli]

3741 MELLA މެއްލަ n. short roof-post, kingpost: m. jahanii, fixes the post

3742 MEŚIN މެޝިން n.. machine [E. machine]

3743 MESEJ މެސެޖް n. cabled message: mesej jahanii, sends cable [E. message]

3744 MEHI (messek) މެހި n. fly (insect) [S. mäsi, Skt. makṣikā]

3745 MEHITARU މެހިތަރު n. (anc.) sergeant gunmaster on the bastions [U. mihtar, headman]

3746 MEH(U)MAANU (pl., mehumaanun) މެހުމާނު n. guest: mehmaan-daarii beheṭṭum, showing hospitality [U. mihmān]

3747 MEHENII މެހެނީ v. gets stuck, gets involved: dalař boo mehifai, with head stuck in the net (invol. of mahanii)

3748 MEŘUM މެރުން v. scraping, grazing (v.n. of mařanii])

3749 MEḶUM މެޅުން v. turning up clothing (v.n. of maḷanii)

3750 MEE, MEI މެއި - މޭ n. 1. liver (of animals): mee-gaňḍu, human liver
2. chest (mee-mati): fuppaa mee, lung: aharenge mee fuppaa, I feel indigestion: aḷugaňḍu(ge) mee nubai kuranii, it makes me feel sick: mee heyo kuranii, makes one feel all right: mee endum, heartburn: mee-kařigaňḍu, ribs: (met.) mee dera, timid: mee gada, bold [Skt. mēdas, fat]

3751 MEENAA މޭނާ n. an old Maldivian kangati title: eenaa-ař meenaakamař koli laifi, he has had the title of M. officially conferred

3752 MEEBIS-KADURU މޭބިސްކަދުރު n. grapes, currants etc. : hiki m., raisins

3753 MEE-BIS-KURAŇḌI މޭބިސްކުރަނޑި n. entrails of animals

3754 MEEYYA BONII މޭއްޔަ ބޮނީ v. becomes wrinkled through water [meeli]

3755 MEERUM KURANII މޭރުން ކުރަނީ v. makes intelligible: meerum vanii, becomes intelligible

3756 MEELA މޭލަ n. in heela-meela vanii, enjoys oneself (doublet) [H. mēlā, a fair]

3757 MEELI މޭލި adj. wrinkled: m. vanii, becomes wrinkled: m. bonii, becomes wrinkled through water

3758 MEELU މޭލު n. mile [E. mile]

3759 MEEVAA (-aaek) މޭވާ n. fruit (in general), esp. kaḷuhuttu meevaa (anona glabra) [U. mēva]

3760 MEESA މޭސަ n. the sign Aries [Skt. mēṣa]

3761 MEESTIRI މޭސްތިރި n. expert, esp. architect, building overseer [S. mēstiri, Port. mestre]

3762 MEEZU މޭޒު n. table: m. foti, table-cloth [U. mēz, S. mēsa, Port. mêsa]

3763 MOI މޮއި n. ripples: muudun moi naganii, makes ripples in the sea: hungaanu moi, wake of a vessel: moi-hiru, wake of a vessel

3764 MOK މޮކް 1. adj. with blunted point (as v. koři, with blunted edge) [for moř, S.moṭa, T. moṭṭai]

3765 MOK މޮކް 2. n. knuckles (mok-tak)

3766 MOṬARU މޮޓަރު n. motor car [E. motor]

3767 MOṬOO މޮޓޯ n. (school) motto (such as Nihil difficile labori, motto of Majiidii School, Male)

3768 MOḌENII މޮޑެނީ v. massages (abs. moḍe): gai m., massages the body: fuřgañḍu m., kneads dough: bat m., mixes food: avali m., prepares a sweetmeat: mas m., mixes fish for mas-huni : (invol.) moḍevenii, gets mixed or massaged [S. maḍinne, Skt. mardati]

3769 MOYA މޮޔަ adj. madly foolish: Alii Havvaa-aai moya vegen uḷenii, A. is in love with H.: duniye m., jinni m., of types of madness: moya hadanii, pretends madness: as n..(pl.) moyain, foolish people: moyain temmaa vaaree, drizzle: moyafari (anc.), foolish [?S. mōḍa or Skt. mōha]

3770 MOSSEVUM މޮއްސެވުން v. untying, untangling (hon.) (v.n. of mossavanii) [mohanii]

3771 MOHANII މޮހަނީ v. unties, undoes (hon., mossavanii): goř mohanii, undoes knot: boňḍi mohanii, unties bundle : doru mohaigen, opening curtain-door [S. mudanne, Skt. muñcati]

3772 MOHODEE މޮހޮދޭ For Muhammad Maniku

3773 MOHORII މޮހޮރީ n. gold coin, mohur (in stories) [U. muhrī]

3774 MOHORU މޮހޮރު n. carpentry nails: m. taḷanii, makes nails: m. jahanii, fixes nails: m. naganii, pulls out nails; dos mohoru, an eye disease

3775 MOHOḶA މޮހޮޅަ n. cotton wool for blocking up orifices of corpses: m. lanii, applies the cottonwool

3776 MOŘ މޮށް n. hoof, paw (moř-gaňḍu)

3777 MOŘAVA, MORAVAK މޮށަވަ - މޮރަވަކް n. 1. nonsense, babble [mořenii]

2. root shoot of kuḷḷavak tree

3778 MOŘENII މޮށެނީ v. speaks (obs. in original sense, exc. in mořum-teri(yaa), good speaker); speaks angrily, answers back: magee muunumatii(gai) m., answers back to my face; numořee guraa baarař daigannaane, the parrot who cannot speak will bite fiercely (prov.); miihunnaa m., has sexual intercourse with people [T. moṛi]

3779 MOḶI މޮޅި n. sadness (moḷi-verikam): moḷin in duvahek, a day when one felt sad

3780 MOḶU މޮޅު adj. excellent, noble, proud: moḷu miihun, respectable people: kamtakař moḷu, good at things, practical; m. vanii, wins (at a game). Sometimes also of bad things, roogaa moḷee, the epidemic is fierce. Of plural objects, moḷeti (cf. boḍeti)

3781 MOO (moolek) މޯ n. rice-mill: pestle; (met.) boḍu moolek, maru moolek, a great fool; a homosexual [S. mōla, Skt. musala]

3782 MOOZA މޯޒަ n. socks (anc.) [S. mēs, Port. meias]

3783 MOOHI މޯހި n. woven bag or basket (for collecting cowries: non-Male usage)

3784 MOOḶA-LAŇBOO މޫޅަލަނބޫ n. a wading bird, male counterpart of teeravaa

3785 MOOḶI މޫޅި adj. faded, droopy (of flowers, or of people); m. vanii, becomes lifeless and sleepy: eenaa varař mooḷi duvahek, a day when he was very sleepy: nidi-mooḷi, half-awake: adi mooḷi nufilaa, not properly awake yet: mooḷiař demenii, stretches out sleepily

ޔ YA-VIYANI, the 21st letter of the Maldivian alphabet

3786 YAGIIN ޔަގީން n. certainty: y. kuranii, is certain; (with dat.) assures, yagiin- fuḷu kor aruvanii, assures (hon.) [U. yaqīn]

3787 YATIIMU(pl., yatiimun) ޔަތީމު n. fatherless, orphan [U. yatīm]

3788 YAMANU ޔަމަނު n. the Yemen (Y. kara) [U. Yaman]

3789 YAHUUDII (anc., iyahuudi, iyafuudi) (pl., yahuudin) ޔަހޫދީ n. Jew, cheat: yahuudii-kam, deceitfulness: yahuudii hadanii, cheats [U. yahūdī]

3790 YAA ޔާ n. the last letter of the Arabic alphabet: alifun yaa-ař, from A to Z

3791 YAAGUUTU ޔާގޫތު n. ruby [U. yāqūt]

3792 YAARI ޔާރި n. rope and chain

3793 YAARU (pl., yaarun) ޔާރު n. friend; lover: yaarunaa yaarun, all one's friends [U. yār: ?S. yālu]

3794 YAASIIM ޔާސީން n. part of faatiha : eenaa inii boḍu takuru yaasiimař araa in henee, he sits like Boḍu Takuru reciting on the ařiˌ i.e. in a very lordly way [A. yā sīnu]

3795 YAAZUUMAŘ ޔާޒޫމަށް adv. very quickly (of escapes)

3796 YUUNAANII ޔޫނާނީ adj. Greek; European: y. bees, medical mixtures [U. yūnānī, Ionian]

3797 YOOT ޔޫޓް excl. to attract attention: y. govanii, shouts Hi! ekve-yoot!, assemble ye! [cf. toot!]

3798 YOOLA KURANII ޔޫލަ ކުރަނީ v. speaks doubtfully : yoola nukuraaře, don't haver! [-oola]

ރ RAA, the 4th letter of the Maldivian alphabet

Raa atoḷu, Maaḷosmaḍulu north, the 4th atoll from the north

3799 RAI ރައި n. loosening: dařmaanař rai kuranii, loosens the sail rope

3800 RAIVARU ރައިވަރު n. old ballads in ḷem style: bereki r., erotic ballads: gooti r., nursery rhymes

3801 RAIVERI ރައިވެރި See raa-veri: raiveri-mas, squirrelfish, neoniphron or sargocentron

3802 RAIIS ރައީސް n. President : R. ul jumhuuriyyaa, president of the Republic [U. ra'īs]

3803 RAUḶU ރައުޅު See raaḷu

3804 RAKARAKA ރަކަރަކަ onom. rakaraka lanii, makes a chattering noise (as of birds, children)

3805 RAKI ރަކި n. embarrassment: r. vanii, gets embarrassed: raki-hini, giggles: ladu-raki, shy, modest (of women): raki maa, a plant, stachytarpheta indica

3806 RAKIS-BOŇḌU ރަކިސްބޮންޑު n. large type of male lizard (formerly used in magic)

3807 RAKKAA, RAKKAU (rakkalek) ރައްކާ - ރައްކައު n. protection, safe hiding: r.kuranii, protects ; etifaharun r. vanii, dodges blows: as hon., rakkaa vanii, is born: rakkaa-teri, careful; rakkaateri kamek, an act of prudence: rakkaateri tanek, a safe place: nu-rakkaateri, dangerous [Skt. rakṣā]

3808 RAKVAA ރަކްވާ n. religious prostration in prayer [U. rak'at]

3809 RAGAR / RAGUBII ރަގަރ / ރަގުބީ n. rugger, rugby football (ragubii booḷa - played by the police) [E. rugger, rugby]

3810 RAŇGA ރަނގަ n. suit of cards: kaalaa r., suit of spades; (anc.) colouring [Skt. ranga]

3811 RAŇGABIILU ރަނގަބީލު n. bell: r. jahanii, rings bell

3812 RAŇGA-VAAḶU ރަނގަވާޅު n. long underpants (no longer worn by the young) [cf. haruvaaḷu]

3813 RAŇGAḶU ރަނގަޅު adj. good: rañgaḷař, well (adv.): really? eii rañgaḷař, that's right: rañgaḷař viyyaa, if (I'm) right; no doubt: liyuna(ka)s enme rañgaḷu, no matter if you write, all right if you write: enme ranˇgaḷu, o.k.: varař rañgaḷu, very good: muḷin rañgaḷu, perfectly correct: kaleař rañgaḷii kooccek, which would you prefer? enme rañgaḷii.., the best is... (for rañgaḷu vii); rañgaḷu gotek, what is best to do: rañgaḷu hañḍuu, largest size of rice grain; r. kuranii, adjusts, corrects: makes better: eenaa-ař rañgaḷu, he is better now: rañgaḷiyyaa, if it is all right (for rañgaḷu viyyaa); magee hařigañḍu varař rañgaḷu vejje, I have put on weight

3814 RAJAA(-aek) ރަޖާ n. blanket (to wear): rajaek laigen, wearing a blanket [H. razāī, Skt. rañjikā]

3815 RAJIS ރަޖިސް n. rajis fiyohi, a large folding knife [trade name]

3816 RAṬṬEHI ރައްޓެހި See rař

3817 RAŇḌA ރަނޑަ adj. exaggeratedly shy ; dirty [rañḍu]

3818 RAŇḌAALI ރަނޑާލި adj. womanlike [rañḍu]

3819 RAŇḌU ރަނޑު adj. womanish, shy: miinaa rañḍu-kamun, because of his absurd shyness [cf. H. ranḍī, harlot]

3820 RAŇḌUU ރަނޑޫ n. a marsh plant, rhizophora mucronata

3821 RAT ރަތް adj. red: rat-keyo, kind of banana (bonti ratkeyo): rat-kirutina, kind of grass: rat-gaa, red coral (formerly exported to India): rat-daka avi, intense sunlight: rat-mas, kind of reef fish, snapper, lutjanus: rat hakuru, brown sugar: rat hañḍuu, red rice: rat-hini, ordinary small ant;
ratu-ran, pure gold, red gold [S. ratran]: ratu-ruk, commonest type of coconut tree, with red fruits (raturuku kaaři): ratu-loo, copper [S. ratu, Skt. raktaka]

3822 RATA-FAI ރަތަފައި n. kind of red-footed bird, turnstone [rat]

3823 RATA-BAḌI ރަތަބަޑި n. kind of dragonfly [rat]

3824 RADIIFU ރަދީފު n. alphabetical section (e.g. of dictionary) [U. radīf]

3825 RADUN ރަދުން n. King (nominal rulers of the Maldives until 1968) [S. radu, Skt. rājan]

3826 RADDU ރައްދު n. delivery: raddu kuranii, hands over, delivers; returns (tr.); raddu vaa, (gram.) transitive, volitive: istiufaa raddu kuravvanii, withdraws resignation; raddu-veri, recipient; sakku laa raddek netee, there is no room for doubt [U. radd, return]

3827 RAN ރަން n. gold: ranuge sikkaek, a gold coin: ratu-ran, pure gold: Ibraahiimii ran, an inscribed gold coin: innan ran kiyanii (tin sateeka rufiyaa-ař), agrees to marry a girl for the agreed brideprice (e.g.300 rupees - maximum 500): vihadaňḍi ranakun andanii, burns off poison with heated gold thread; ran-koḷu, an affectionate form of address: ran-makunu, outdoor spiders: ran mut, golden pearls: ranvan (ranman), golden: ranvan kaňdili, a plant, evolvulus alsinoides or turnera ulmifolia: ranvan loo, brass (mixture of copper and zinc) [S. ranvan, Skt. hiraṇyavarṇa]: ran varaňgu, gilt paper [S. ran, Skt. hiraṇya]

3828 RANA-URAA (RANOVARAA) ރަނައުރާ (ރަނޮވަރާ) n. a plant, cassia sp. [S. raṇavarā]

3829 RANAHAMAADI ރަނަހަމާދި n. one of the ancient teams (koři) for ceremonial games

3830 RANI (pl., ranin) ރަނި n. (usu. ibc.) queen (rani-kaňbalek, rani-beekaňbalek) [old S. räjni, Skt. rājñī]

3831 RAN-KARU ރަންކަރު n. soldering mixture (baddaa r.)

3832 RANGU ރަންގު n. purple dye: rangu-kaṭṭala, kind of sweet potato (as v. hudu kaṭṭala): rangu-feeru, kind of pear, guava pear: rangu-veyo, kind of creeper, ? passiflora suberosa [S. raňga, Skt. ranga]

3833 RAN-DIYA ރަންދިޔަ adj. beloved (poet.)

3834 RANNA-BAŇḌEERI ރަންނަބަނޑޭރި n. a high title of honour (rannabaňḍeeri kilegefaanu) [for ratuna-baňḍeeri: Skt. ratnabhāṇḍāgārika]

3835 RANNAMAARI ރަންނަމާރި n. a traditional sea dragon

3836 RANNAA ރަންނާ n. ancient Maldivian kangati title

3837 RANBUSTAANU ރަންބުސްޓާނު n. rambutan fruit [S. rañbutan, from Malay]

3838 RAFIIGU ރަފީގު n. cricket, cicada [?U. rafīq, companion]

3839 RAFUU KURANII ރަފޫ ކުރަނީ v. darns (by hand, as v. rodi aruvanii) [U. rafū]

3840 RABARU ރަބަރު n. rubber : demee r., elastic: fuhee r., indiarubber, eraser: rabaru meṭaa, chewing gum; tyre: etere r., inner tyre: beeru r., outer tyre ; also of rubber soles, rubber sheets etc. [E. rubber]

3841 RAŇBA ރަނބަ n. 1. secret gossip : rañba taḷanii, rañba taḷuvanii, gossips

2. locally used for ranbustaanu

3842 RAMATA KURANII ރަމަޓަ ކުރަނީ v. controls: settles (quarrels): tidies up (rooms) [?U. rām karnā]

3843 RAMAN ރަމަން n. lumps on the head: r. kahanii, removes such lumps: r. naganii, (of cocks) raises coxcomb in fright; (met., of people) shows fear

3844 RAMANRAMANFOOLI ރަމަންރަމަންފޫލި n. a children's game, similar to tinmugooli

3845 RAMALU ރަމަލު n. a science to foretell auspicious times: r. balanii, practises this art [U. ramal, geomancy]

3846 RAYYATUN, RAYYITUN ރައްޔަތުން - ރައްޔިތުން n. (pl.) citizens, the public [U. rai'yat]

3847 RAVA ރަވަ n. lower edge of the eye (where kohl is put): kaḷi-rava, whole shape of the eye

3848 RAVAA ރަވާ n. granules used in cooking [H. ravā, ?Skt. lavaka]

3849 RAVAANAA ރަވާނާ n. port clearance certificate [U. ravāna]

3850 RAVAABIINAA ރަވާބީނާ n. one who casts the evil eye

3851 RAVOO VANII ރަވޯ ވަނީ v. wastes away (esp. of children)

3852 RAS- ރަސް- prefix used ibc., royal: ras-kam, kingship; regime : raskamuge ta<u>kh</u>tu, royal throne: raskam kuravvanii, rules (hon.): raskamfuḷu, God: raskalaa (pl., raskalun), king: raskalaaňge, God (maat raskalaaňge): rasge 1., infidel king (or king in a game): rasgefaanu, Muslim king: ras-daňburuk, old name for don daňburuk, king coconut: ras-boli, cowrie tribute formerly paid from Riňbuduu island: ras-matifuř, royal ancestry: ras-roonu, special coir formerly sent from Riňbuduu island: ras-huvaňdu, rassuvaňdu, an imported sticky medicament [cf. S. raju, Skt. rājā]

3853 RASIIDU ރަސީދު n. receipt, quittance [U. rasīd]

3854 RASUULAA ރަސޫލާ n. the Prophet, the messenger of God [U. rasūl]

3855 RASGE ރަސްގެ n. 2. mark of a cross: r. lanii, puts a cross, cancels

3856 RASMII ރަސްމީ adj. official: rasmii hedum, official dress: rasmii tanek, i.e. open to the public [U. rasmī, customary]

3857 RAHA ރަހަ n. 1. taste (either good or bad): raha-miiru, tasty: raha-tak maḍii too, (of tea) is it too weak? : mi batugai haada lonuraha maḍee, this rice has far too little salt; raha lanii, gives a savour (impers.): rihaigai lonu-rahaek nulaee, the curry lacks salt: raha-akun (kure) rahaek nulaa, altogether tasteless: dumfatugai raha lai too, (of a hookah) has it a taste? raha denii, gives a savour (impers.); rihaagai foni-raha denii, the curry tastes sweet: raha balanii, tastes: raha balaabala, try it! [S. rasa, Skt. rasa]

2. mercury (diree raha): billuuriigai r. lanii, silvers a mirror: r. kahanii, r. filuvanii, removes the silvering: raha-fatigaňḍu, spirit level: r. kuranii, levels: raha-ař (adv.), level: raha-ař meezu bahaṭṭaaře, level the table [S. rasa-diya]

3858 RAHAA ރަހާ n. (anc.) king: (mod.) a male personal name in the South

3859 RAHUMAT-TERIYAA ރަހުމަތްތެރިޔާ n. friend [U. ra<u>h</u>mat, mercy]

3860 RAŘ ރަށް n. island: inhabited centre, town : veri rař, capital city: Mufiidaa kon rařek, where are you from, M.? aḷugaňḍumen rařu Mufiidaa, M. from our island: rařu miihun, people of the island: rař-raru, in various islands: rařutere, interior of an island, the whole island: rař-koḷu, deserted corner of an island: rař-goňḍu, coast of an island; rařgoňḍun danii, rařgoňḍu dařun danii, goes into the lee of an island for shelter: rař-guḍaa, kind of drumbeat for boḍuberu (rařguḍaek jahanii): rař-beeru, water surrounding an island; in stories, uninhabited area surrounding a town: rař-fuřu, islands outside Male (derog., cf. biiraṭṭehi, raajjetere): rařṭehi, raṭṭihi, (anc.) local inhabitants; (mod.) friendly (people): rař-vehi (-vessek), local inhabitants; (met.) civilized, cosmopolitan: rařvehi ge, local resthouse for visitors;

rařaa rařaa, inter-atoll
[S. raṭa, Skt. rāṣṭra, country]

3861 RAA (raaek) ރާ n. 1. toddy: doo raa, morning toddy: haviiru raa, evening toddy: raa aranii, follows toddy-tapping profession; raa araa rukek, a coconut tree which is being tapped: raa baalanii, collects toddy from the tree: raa kakkanii, heats toddy, makes juggery; raa-et, tapped coconut flower: raa-eri, see raaveri (inf): raa-kanigaňḍu, stand for toddy-tapper's equipment: raa-guḍi, toddy tapping cup: raa-foni,top layer of heated toddy: raa-badi, toddy tapper's equipment: raa-bee, toddy tapper: raa-ruk, coconut tree tapped for toddy; raaruku harugaňḍu, ladder fixed up toddy tree: raa-vaḷi 1., toddy tapping knife: raa-veri (raiveri, raa-eri), raaveriyaa, raaveri bee, toddy tapper: raa-hut, toddy vinegar [S. rā, cf. Skt. surā]

3862 RAA ރާ n. 2. the letter R in the Arabic and Maldivian alphabets: Raa atoḷu, Maaḷosmaḍulu atoll north

3863 RAAKANI ރާކަނި n. kind of shellfish

3864 RAAGU ރާގު n . tune, music: raagek fume / kuḷe dii bala, please whistle / play a tune: raagu riiti kujjek, raagi huri kujjek, a musical child (i.e.with a good voice)
[H. rāg, Skt. rāga]

3865 RAAGOŇḌI ރާގޮނޑި n. kind of small fish resembling bonito, frigate tuna, auxis

3866 RAAJAA ރާޖާ n. king (among infidels, cf. radun) [Skt. rājā (nom.)]

3867 RAAJJE ރާއްޖެ n. kingdom: country; raajje-tak, countries: Divehi Raajje, the Maldive Islands: raaje matiigai, in Maldivian waters: raajje-tere, the other islands apart from Male island; raajeteree kujjaku, a country girl: raajjeen beerař, for export: raajje bali, spondylitic rheumatism [Skt. rājya]

3868 RAAḌI VANII ރާޑި ވަނި v. is stymied (at game of ořvaḷu); (met.) gets fed up

3869 RAATAA (raatalek) ރާތާ n. pound weight (lb.), equal to four gaa: haňḍuu raatalek, a pound of rice [U. raṯl, ?Gk. litrā (S. rattal)]

3870 RAATIBU, RAATIIBU ރާތިބު - ރާތީބު n. commemorative recital
[? U. rātib, rations]

3871 RAADA- ASDUUNI ރާދަ އަސްދޫނި n. swan

3872 RAADA-FUS (-fuhek) ރާދަފުސް n. a disease of the eyes resembling cataract

3873 RAANANII ރާނަނީ v. plasters, builds with mortar (hon. raanuvvanii : v.n. reenum) : raanaa miihun, masons: used also of heating a new cooking dish for the first time

3874 RAANII ރާނީ n. Queen (among infidels) [Skt. rājñī]

3875 RAABUḶA ރާބުޅަ n. kind of reef fish, surgeonfish, acanthurus

3876 RAABEBURI ރާބެބުރި n. a medicinal herb, 'wild mustard', polanisia icosandra or cleome viscosa

3877 RAABOŇDI (-boñjek) ރާބޮނޑި n. kinds of bittern or heron

3878 RAAŇBAA ރާނބާ n. a curry-leaf plant (r. fat)

3879 RAAMAA VANII ރާމާ ވަނީ v. (of food)is on the turn, is almost stale (cf. (kaafaa)maamaa vanii)

3880 RAAMAA-MAKUNU ރާމާމަކުނު n. monkey (lit. 'Rama's spider')

3881 RAARAA ރާރާ n. device attached to kites to make them hum: raaraa aḍu gada, (kite) whose r. makes a loud sound [onom.]

3882 RAAROHI ރާރޮހި n. a plant with many seeds, colubrina asiatica

3883 RAAVANII ރާވަނީ v. designs, reassembles; makes plans (hon. raavvavanii: v.n. reevum) : maru raavanii, fits together a jigsaw of nuts from the maru tree: raavaa ge, private temporary house for travellers: eenaa-ař gaḍi raavaakař neeňge-eve, he doesn't know how to put watches together again (opposite of ruuḷum, dismantling)

3884 RAAVAḶI ރާވަޅި n. 2. tail feathers of a cock

3885 RAA-VERI ރާވެރި See raa

3886 RAAS ރާސް onom. ras lanii, makes tearing sound (of cloth), rattling sound (of falling fruit), rustling sound (of leaves): raas raas laafai, rattling: raas ṭas kiyaafai, very quickly : raas aḷanii, makes similar noise; cf. also riis

3887 RAASTAA (raastaaek) ރާސްތާ n. (lit.) way, road [H. rāstā]

3888 RAAZUVAA ރާޒުވާ n. chess: raazuvaa goňḍi, chessboard

3889 RAAHAT ރާހަތް n. effect : mi beehakun eenaa-akař ekves raahatek nukuri, this medicine had no effect at all on him: e kamtakuge raahat libifai, experiencing the results of that [U. rāhat, repose]

3890 RAAHI (raasseek) ރާހި n. sign of the zodiac: Makaru raahin miadu fahekee, today is the fifth day of Capricorn; r. balanii, consults the stars (of the eduru) , r. ballanii, baluvanii, consults the stars (of the client) -- nakat belum is, however, preferred: r. jahanii, casts horoscope [H. & Skt. rāśī]

3891 RAAḶU (RAUḶU) ރާޅު (ރައުޅު) 1. n. wave : raaḷu-fař, line of waves on the sand, or similar design: raaḷu-bis, kind of drifting coral [S. raḷa, räḷi, ?Skt. lahari]

2. adj. rough, not smooth: raaḷu koř (adv.), roughly, not finely: raaḷu koř mugurum, grinding roughly [S. raḷu, ?Skt. dṛḍha]

3892 RIKAABII ރިކާބީ n. (lit.) food container [U. rikābī]

3893 RIKAABU ރިކާބު n. stirrup [U. rikāb]

3894 RIT ރިތް n. punt pole (rit-daňḍi): rit-mas, see rimmas [cf. S. riṭi, Skt. aritra]

3895 RIŇDA ރިނދަ n. scallop

3896 RIŇDALI ރިނދަލި n. scallop shell

3897 RIBAA ރިބާ n. monetary interest (strictly speaking forbidden in Islam, as in Christianity): r. kanii, accepts interest

3898 RIMMAS ރިއްމަސް n. kind of fish, decapterus (also written ritmas)

3899 RIYA ރިޔަ n. 1. rook (at chess) [Skt. ratha]
2. (anc.) 500 cowries (four hiya)

3900 RIYAU ރިޔައު See riyaa

3901 RIYAN ރިޔަން n. 27 inches (three kaivat) [S. ruvan, riyan, P. ratana,

Skt. aratni]

3902 RIYAA (RIYAU) (riyalek) ރިޔާ (ރިޔައު) n. ship's sail: hama r., square sail: kati r., lateen sail; r. kaňḍanii, r. fahanii, makes a sail; riyaa kaňḍaa foti, sailcloth: r. hadanii, repairs sail: riyaa baňḍu, billowing of sail; riyaa-kan vanii, (of ships) has tip of mast showing, is just visible [S. ruval, cf. P. lakāra]

3903 RIYAALA ރިޔާލަ n. an old coin, sometimes found as a pendant [Port. real]

3904 RILEE ރިލޭ n. relay (race) [E. relay]

3905 RIVAA KURANII ރިވާ ކުރަނީ v. repeats a story: accepts a preaching [U. rivāyat, story]

3906 RIVETI ރިވެތި adj. beautiful [rīti]

3907 RIVELI ރިވެލި n. (lit.) reflection, shadow

3908 RIŚVATU ރިޝްވަތު n. bribe: r. denii, gives bribes: r. kanii, takes bribes [U. riśvat]

3909 RISSANII ރިއްސަނީ v. (it) hurts, aches: aharenge karugai rissanii, my neck aches: magee bolugaa rissaa varun, because of my headache [rihenii]

3910 RISSEYO (RISSEU) ރިއްސެޔޮ (ރިއްސެއު) n. a medicament (fařu-risseyo): risseyo lanii, turns yellow in ripening (e.g. papaw)

3911 RIHA ރިހަ n. curry: hiki r., dry curry: diya r., wet curry: kukuḷu riha, chicken curry: riha-miiru, nice for currying

3912 RIHAAKURU ރިހާކުރު n. concentrated fish essence (a Maldivian delicacy): r. boli, a shiny cowrie of the colour of rihaakuru: r. leburu, kind of dragonfly with dark wings

3913 RIHI ރިހި n. silver: rihi mut, a silver pearl: rihi varaňgu, silver paper [S. ridī, Skt. rajata]

3914 RIHENII ރިހެނީ v. (it) hurts, aches: bolugai rihenii, (my) head aches: baňḍugai rihenii, (esp.) has labour pains [S. ridenne, Skt. rujati]

3915 RII ރީ v. having excreted (abs. of renii)

3916 RII AḶANII ރީ އަޅަނީ v. blocks up with a glutinous substance

3917 RIITI (RIVETI) (riiccek) ރީތި (ރިވެތި) adj. beautiful, handsome: riiti gas, albizzia lebbeck or delonia regia (Flamboyant tree): riiti bas, honorific language: riiti hańḍuu, largest size of rice (= rańgaḷu hańḍuu); r. kořlanii, smartens up, adjusts nicely: kudiinař riiti vanii, appeal to the young [cf. Skt. rūpavat]

3918 RIIŇDUU (riińdulek) ރީނދޫ n. turmeric (‘saffron’), curcuma longa: r. kula, pale colour: riińduu- kam, sense of impending woe

3919 RIIMU ރީމު n. ream of paper [E. ream]

3920 RIIS ރީސް onom. riis lanii, makes a sharp tearing noise (of paper or silk, as v . raas of cloth)

3921 RUIM ރުއިމް v. weeping (v.n. of ronii): also 1 s. past tense, wept

3922 RUK ރުކް n. palm, esp. coconut palm, cocos nucifera; Main varieties: Divehi ruk (tall, including nulu ruk and ratu ruk) and Jaafanu ruk (short): dańbu ruk, king coconut: kaduru ruk, date palm: fen- fook ruk, arecanut palm : fankaa ruk, tasbiihu ruk, fan palm (inedible, used for rosaries): kuri ruk, a valuable type of coconut palm; kuriruku et, flowers of the same; ruk-kaaři, coconut: ruk-kuri, indigestible new shoots of coconut: ruk-keńḍiyaa, tree-feller: ruk-gańḍu 1., grove or plantation of coconut trees (rukgańḍu-tere) 2., log of coconut timber: ruk-galu bees, herbal medicine for fractures (general term): ruk-gas, palms and other trees: ruk-guḷi, coconut log; rukguḷi beenum, the art of felling coconuts: ruk-fati, ruku fati, row of coconut trees: ruk-bari, row of coconut trees: ruk-buḍu filaa, a creeper, psilotum nudum: ruku maḍi, rhinoceros beetle, coconut beetle: ruku mui, milky sap of coconut ; ruk faḷuvanii, propagates coconuts: ruku aḷanii, picks nuts from a tree
[S. ruk, rik, Skt. vṛkṣa]

3923 RUKUN ރުކުން n. In fas rukun, the five pillars of Islam [U. rukn]

3924 RUKURANI, RUKURENI ރުކުރަނި - ރުކުރެނި n. a medicinal ground creeper (r. filaa), dipteracanthus; also called kunahańgaali and nitubaḍi

3925 RUKURUVANII ރުކުރުވަނީ v. (lit.) puts in alignment : sifain rukuruvaalaifi, drew up the soldiers (caus. from rukurenii)

3926 RUKURENII ރުކުރެނީ v. is put in line

3927 RUGUN ރުގުން n. rugun- maḷu, a kind of wax, rosin

3928 RUNU ރުނު v. excreted (past t. of renii) [S. runnā]

3929 RUNKURU ރުންކުރު adj. brittle (of things); impulsive, impatient (of people)

3930 RUFIYAA (-aek) ރުފިޔާ n. rupee, Maldivian rupee: tin rufiyaage donkeyo, three rupees worth of bananas [S. rupiyal, H. rupiyā, Skt. rūpyaka]

3931 RUŇBAA (-aek) ރުނބާ n. large jar: ruňbaa muři, clay

3932 RUMAA (rumaalek) ރުމާ n. 1. scarf of cloth, for either sex, usu. red and ornamental: kuḍa rumaa, handkerchief: teo r., stiffened cloth for oily babies: bokhusaa(ge) r., cloth with which washermen tie up bundles of washing: bolu r., woman's side cap: rumaa-faḷi, sidecap when specially folded to half-size [U. rumāl]
2. (in card games) suit of diamonds: rumaalun de-ek, two of diamonds

3933 RUVANII ރުވަނީ v. transplants (binbi r., transplants grain: ruk r., transplants palmtrees): fixes in position, e.g. of arrow on the string, or harpoon on the handle [S. ruvanne, inserts, Skt. rōpayati]

3934 RUVAA ރުވާ n. kind of bush, calotropis gigantea : ruvaa kiru, juice of the r.: r. deli, charcoal of ruvaa (used in gunpowder for fireworks); fus-ruvaa / fus-tuḷaa, a plant, sophora tomentosa; ruvaa gas noḷanii, peels r. (the inner bark is used for fishing lines) [S. varā]

3935 RUSSANII ރުއްސަނީ v. gains approval of a person (hon. russavanii): gos eenaa russaa bala, go and get his approval : (invol.) eenaa russee too balaabala, see if he will approve: kuḍa kudin russan, to please children: maat kalaaňge russeviyyaa, God willing: maat kalaaňge russum levvi, whom God approved (caus. of ruhenii)

3936 RUHENII ރުހެނީ v. approves, is agreeable (to.., ..-aa) (hon., ruhi vaḍaigannanii): mi kamaa kalee nuruhee nama ves, even if you don't agree to this: gina miihun ruhee, approved by many, popular: kaleege ruhum hoodaigen, after asking your approval; ruhi voḍigen (c. dat.), approved (of God: in neg., russek nugati) [Skt. rucyatē]

3937 RUḶI ރުޅި n. anger: aharen eenaa-ař ruḷi, I'm angry with him: ruḷi annanii, r. duruvanii, gets angry (grades 2 and 3); bafaa ruḷi atuvejje, father got angry: bappaa ruḷi duruvaane, father will be angry: ruḷi naadee, don't be angry! ruḷi vanii, are at enmity: eenaa mařaa ruḷi, he and I are not on speaking terms: ruḷi aruvanii, annoys: r. is kuranii, shows anger easily: r. filuvanii, gets rid of anger: ruḷi gada, irritable: ruḷi-verikam, anger [? Skt.

ruṣṭi]

3938 RUU (rulek) ޫރ n . 1. wrinkles (on people), miihaage ruu: crush marks, folds (on cloth); libaahugai ruu jehenii, wrinkles appear on the libaas: ruu jassanii, makes wrinkles, crushes, pleats: ruu kuruvum, ruu keruvum, making wrinkles, crushing: ruu naganii, makes pleat [S. räli]

2. image, picture: ruu kurahanii, draws picture [S. rū, Skt. rūpa]

3939 RUUFA ފަޫރ n. shape, build (of people): ruufa heyo, plump: ruufaek net, is thin: ruufa jehenii, puts on weight [Skt. rūpa]

3940 RUURUU ޫރޫރ onom. r. aḷanii, shivers noisily (as v. turuturu aḷanii)

3941 RUUS ސޫރ onom. ruus lanii, makes flapping sounds (of kites), or hissing sound (of rockets, cf. vuus, vus)

3942 RUUSIHAA- BAT ތަބާހިސޫރ n. ordinary cooked rice with coconut milk and salt (as v. fen-bat)

3943 RUUḶANII ީނަޅޫރ v. dismantles; pulls down (house), unfurls (sail): (invol.) ruuḷenii, disperses (intr.) e. g. of assemblies, clouds: enlarged, ruuḷaa-lanii, hon. ruuḷaa-lavvanii (opposite of reevum, reassembling)

3944 REI ިއެރ See ree

3945 REKENII ީނެކެރ v. 1. protects oneself: shrinks from, shirks (cf. rakkaa) : masakkatun rekum, shirking work [S. räkenne, Skt. rakṣyate]

2. (anc. or local) sifts, winnows, sieves (reki-lanii)

3946 REDAN ްނަދެރ n.. phosphorescence: r. lanii, glows; r. kokaa, kind of moth: r. fani, glowworm

3947 REDALI ިލަދެރ n. reign: redali kuravvanii (hon.), reigns

3948 REDIN ްނިދެރ n. (pl.) prehistoric giants credited with cyclopean building

3949 REŇDU ުޑްނެރ n. crack: reňḍu aḷanii, eḷenii, cracks appear

3950 RENII ީނެރ v. excretes ordure (abs. rii:: p.p. runu : v.n. revum : invol. revenii): eenaa-ař gui revijje, he was taken short [S. renne, Skt. rīyatē]

3951 REFRII ރެފްރީ n. referee (at football) [E. referee]

3952 REVI (revvek) ރެވި n. mustard seed, brassica: boḍu r., brassica nigra: hudu r., sinapis alba [H. rāī, Skt. rājika]

3953 REVENII ރެވެނީ v. See renii [invol.]

3954 RES ރެސް n. 1. top row of thatching 2. small crack (local usage): tar̃iigai res aḷanii, crack appears on the dish

3955 RES VANII ރެސް ވަނީ v. (lit.) assembles (intr.) [S. räs vanne, Skt. rāśī, multitude]

3956 RESSI ރެއްސި n. a spirit, demon: dooniigai ressi aḷaigen, a spirit haunts the boat [cf. S. rāssa, Skt. rākṣasa]

3957 REHA ރެހަ n. relief patterns in basket or mat weaving

3958 REHAN ރެހަން n. a coloured varnish applied to fishing lines: r. jahanii, applies r.

3959 REHI ރެހި n. kind of bait fish, silver sprat, spratelloides gracilis

3960 REHENDI ރެހެންދި n. eldest daughter (obs.)

3961 REE (REI) ރޭ (ރެއި) n. night: ree-re(e), nights: ree(gai), last night: mi ree, to-night: iyye ree, the night before last: ihar̃ ree, two nights ago: ihar̃ reaku, a few nights ago: re-ek duvaalek neti, both day and night: re-ek duvaalek nubalaane, carries on all night: (hama) reaa duvaalu, both day and night: ree hataru damu, the whole night: ree huri, kept overnight (as of batpen, garudiya); nuva-ree fen, sprinkling of new babies with water for nine nights: nuvaree fenun kem̃ḍenii, finishes the nine-day sprinkling; ree-kanu, blind by night, night-blindness: ree kuranii, stays overnight (neg., re-ek nukuree), esp. of sleeping with a woman (am̃bimiihaa gaatugai ree kurum): ree-gam̃ḍu, night time, at night, after dark; reegam̃ḍuge keum, supper: ree-dalaa danii, goes fishing with net by night: ree vilee ree, Sunday or Thursday nights: ree vanii, night falls [S. rā̃, Skt. rātrī]

3962 REEKAA LANII ރޭކާ ލަނީ v. shows understanding or attention (neg., reekaek nulaa)

3963 REEḌIYOO ރޭޑިޔޯ n. radio: reeḍiyooin, on the radio: r. nivaa-lanii, turns off the radio: reeḍiyoo huḷuvaa-lanii, turns on the radio: r. jahaa-lan, to play the radio [E.

radio]

3964 REEŇDAA ރީނދާ n. lace: reeňdaaek, a piece of lace [S. rēnda, Port. renda]

3965 REENUM ރީނުމް v. plastering (v.n. of raananii: : hon. reenuvvum): reenum-gaňḍu, section of building

3966 REEFANAA ARANII ރީފަނާ އަރަނީ v. reaches the capability of understanding: mi kujjaa adi ves reefanaa araakař nuuḷe-ee, this child has not yet reached the age of understanding

3967 REERU ރީރު n. kinds of small duck (ratu r., kaḷu r.): fengaňḍu boḍakas reerek birek nugannaane-ee, though the water be deep the duck will not fear (prov.) [S. rēru]

3968 REERU VANII ރީރު ވަނީ v. is petrified, stunned (as of some ducks which fall if you yell)

3969 REELU ރީލު n. railway train: reelu dagaňḍu, railway lines [E. rail]

3970 REEVA ރީވަ n. asterism Rēvatī (last asterism of the iruvai season)

3971 REEVUM ރީވުމް v. 1. fitting together; plans (v.n. of raavanii): reevum-teriyaa, designer

2. nightfall (ree + vum)

3972 REES (reehek) ރީސް n. race, contest [E. race]

3973 REEZARU ރީޒަރު n. razor [E. razor]

3974 REEZAA (-aek) ރީޒާ n. ‘shot’; ballbearing: r. fuk, single shot or ball: reezaek lanii, puts single shot in gun: r. aḷanii, puts shots (pl.) in gun [U. reza, fragment]

3975 ROI , ROO ރޮއި - ރޯ v. having wept (abs. of ronii; enlarged, roo-laa); also impv. and pres. part.

3976 ROŇGAALI (roňgaayyek) ރޮނގާލި n. loafer, useless chap (roňgaali-gaňḍu)

3977 ROŇGU ރޮނގު n. line: r. damanii, rules lines; roňgu roňgu demi munḍu, sarong with lines on it: r. aḷanii, draws line; (met.) sphere of interest: ek roňgun, in one respect: tiyaii aḷugañḍuge roñgek nuun, that's not my line

3978 ROŇḌU ރޮނޑު n. class of trigger- fish, balistoides (maa-roñḍu)

3979 ROŇḌU VANII ރޮނޑު ވަނީ v. stops growing, gets blighted (of trees)

3980 RODI (rojjek) ރޮދި n. thin thread (cf. nanu): r. aruvanii, darns by machine (cf. rafuu): (met.) vilaa rojjek, a wisp of cloud; rodi-gañḍu, smocking: rodigañḍu gatanii, makes smocking: rodigañḍu alanii, applies smocking; duvaa rojjek, chain-stitch
[S. roda, Skt. rājī, line]

3981 RODU ރޮދު n. trap used to catch fish, buried in the sand: rodu aḷanii, rodu lanii, fishes by this method

3982 RONII ރޮނީ v. weeps (v.n. ruim , cf. rovum, rovvum: inf. roon : abs.and impv., roi (roo)) : tiya ruim nuroi! don't cry like that : roigatum, bursting into tears
[H. rōnā, Skt. rōditi]

3983 RONDAA (-aaek) ރޮންދާ n. carpenter's plane [U. randa]

3984 ROL- ރޮލް- See roo

3985 ROVENII ރޮވެނީ v. bursts into tears: mařař rovunii, I burst into tears (invol. of ronii)

3986 ROVVANII ރޮއްވަނީ v. causes to weep (caus. of ronii)

3987 ROŘI (roṭṭek) ރޮށި n. 'roṭi', flat pancake: foni r., sweet roti: faa roři, wet rusk: tuni r., kind of pappadam: mas r., fish cake: kuḷi r., spicy cake; (vulg.) female pudenda
[S. roṭi, H. rōṭī, Skt. rōṭikā]

3988 ROO ރޯ 1. adj. (rolek) fresh; raw: rolař kanii, rolaa kanii, eats raw: rolun kanii, (of animals) eats alive: rolař hunnanii, is raw: roo filuvanii, cooks; roo fook, kind of 'chew': roo mirus, green chillies: roo barahanaa, stark naked: roo-kam, freshness, greenness: roo- fan fuḷañgi, kind of grasshopper; roo maa duvaalu-me, in broad daylight: aa roo, brand new: roo maru goos, absolute nonsense

2. n. catching alight: roo kuranii, lights (tr.), e.g. of cigarettes, fires, ovens (but dillanii of lamps); roo vanii, catches fire: geegai (alifaan) roo vii, the house caught fire; (met.) gasgas roo vum, bushes shooting again after transplanting or grafting: mas roo vanii, a growth appears (esp. in the eye)

3. v. weeping (part. of ronii); roo, roi, imp. or abs. of ronii : roo-laa, enlarged abs.

3989 ROOGAA ރޯގާ n. epidemic: roogaa moḷu vanii, r. aḷaafaa, epidemic is prevalent [H. & Skt. rōga]

3990 ROODA ރޯދަ n. fasting: r. hifanii, begins the fast; de-rooda hifaifim, I have fasted for two days: r. viillanii, ends the fast: r. duu kořlanii, gives up the fast: rooda-ař hurum, fasting; rooda mas, the month Ramzan: tin foi rooda, supererogatory fasting: ha-rooda, six days of optional fasting after Ramzan [U. rōza]

3991 ROODI ރޯދި n. our daily food (roodi barakaat) [U. rōzī]

3992 ROON ރޯން v. to weep (inf. of ronii)

3993 ROONAA ރޯނާ n. night blindness: r. vanii, is blind at night (esp. of animals): roonaa-ař danii, goes to catch insects by night (which are blinded by light - esp. in cemeteries) [cf. Skt. rātryandha]

3994 ROONU ރޯނު n. 1. coir rope (graded as fala r., medu r., hima r.): r. fař, bit of coir rope: r. fooli, quantity of coir rope, one twelfth of a boňḍi ; r. furanii, makes repairs with coir: eňdugai r. furum, repairing bed: vaa aḷaa r., coir suitable for making rope: r. vařanii, makes rope; roonu eduru, self-styled expert
2. asterism Rōhiṇī [S. reheṇa]

3995 ROOL(U) ރޯލު n. roll of somethimg (esp. as used for a ruler, for weighted windowbars, for a paperweight): roolu malam, roll of sticking plaster: keseṭ roolek, a cassette [E. roll (H. rūl)]

3996 ROOS KURANII ރޯސް ކުރަނީ v. fries (e.g. bread, chicken) [E. roast]

3997 ROOḶI ރޯޅި n. blast of wind (vai- rooḷi, vilaagaňḍuge rooḷi): r. aranii, blast arises: r. faibanii, blast dies down; rooḷi-fař, gentle breeze

ލ LAAMU, the 14th letter of the Maldivian alphabet

Laamu atoḷu, Haddunmati atoll, the l4th atoll from the north

3998 -LA -ލަ politely used ifc. in compound verbs, fonuvaa-la devvum, sending (me) [for laa, abs. of lanii]

3999 LAI (LAA-) ލައި (-ލާ) v. used postpositionally in the south (usu. after - aa), with (in Male, hifaigen); lai-gen, laa-gen, with : laagen kaa eccek, a side dish: muḷin biskoodu laigen, always with biscuits: dumfat laigen dufum, having a chew with tobacco in it: fotek ves laigen genee, bring a book when you come (abs. of lanii)

4000 LAI-GANNANII ލައިގަންނަނީ v. (of time) arrives (v.n. laigatum): namaadu vagutu laigatumuge kuriin, before prayer time arrives: Doř̃a nakat laigenje, the asterism Jyestha has arrived: aḷugañḍař boḍukamek laigenfi, something awful happened to me; (met.) come across someone or something: aharen eenaa-aa laigat, I came across him: aḷugañḍumen sabmeriinakaai laek nugateve, we didn't come across any submarine: deeti laigenfai, the two craft have collided; adv., lai nuganegen, in a hurry: ehen laigen, by that road [lanii 5]

4001 LAU-KAM, LAA-KAM ލައުކަން - ލާކަން n. starchiness, (proper) consistency (e.g. of mortar)

4002 LAK ލައް n. patch, spot (esp. on animals) : lak-gañḍu, a stain; lakgañḍu jehenii, is marked: lakgañḍun lak jehifai vaa, stained: lak filuvaa bees, bleach

4003 LAKI (latkek) ލަކި n. rocking motion: l. jahanii, l. ellanii, (of kites) dances in the air: l. jassanii, rocks (a boat): l. talanii, shakes vigorously (tr.): l. taluvanii, jerks, drags by the hand

4004 LAKUḌI ލަކުޑި n. wood, timber: lakuḍi-gañḍu, piece of wood: sarukaaru l., reserved timber (Government property): lakuḍi-fakuḍi (doublet)
[H. lakṟī, Skt. lakuṭikā, a club]

4005 LAKUNU ލަކުނު n. scar: at keñḍi lakunu, inoculation scar
[S. lakuṇu, mark, Skt. lakṣaṇa]

4006 LAKUVANII ލަކުވަނީ v. stirs up; rocks (v.n. lekuvum : invol. lekuvenii)

4007 LAKKA ލައްކަ num. 100,000, a lakh (ek lakka); very many, lakka gina duvas, a very long time: lakka iru van den, for a very long time [S. lak, Skt. lakṣa]

4008 LAGAN ލަގަން n. reins: as vikkiyas lagan nuvikkaařee, though you sell the horse, don't sell the reins! (viz. don't give away the know-how) (prov.) [U. lagām]

4009 LAGANAA (-aaek) ލަގަނާ n. kind of bird resembling stork

4010 LAGABU ލަގަބު n. title of honour [U. laqab]

4011 LAGARI ލަގަރި n. large box for keeping bait

4012 LAGOŇḌI ލަގޮނޑި n. (of men) Adam's apple; (of fish or poultry) heart: lagoňḍi-vaḷu, depression beneath the Adam's apple; lagoňḍiyař ket vaane too, doesn't it affect you? lagoňḍiigai naaři laafai huri miihek (prov.), a stingy man ('hard- appled'): viha-lagoňḍi, a plant, gloriosa superba

4013 LAGGANII ލައްގަނީ v. (v.n. leggum) 1. drifts ashore : e-rařu goňḍudořař laggaafai ot lakuḍigaňḍek, a piece of timber which drifted ashore on that island [for laňgu vanii, cf. S. laňgā vanne]

2. leans up (tr., of inanimates): mitaa nulaggaa, don't lean things here! (enlarged)faarugai laggaa-laaře, lean (it) against the wall: (invol.) mařař lagganevumun muḷin gamiis haraabu vejje-eve, my shirt was quite spoilt by my leaning (on the wall): see also leňgenii [H. lagānā, Skt. lagyatē]

4014 LAŇGIRI ލަނގިރި n.. a kind of dancing, squatting dance for men (leňgee kuḷivarek, cf. baňḍiyaa jehum for women): laňgiri jahanii, performs this dance

4015 LAŇGOṬI ލަނގޮޓި n. 1. maranii, third stage of tucking up clothes (cf. munḍun aruvaa jehum and fuu geḷum : not done in Maldives): laňgoṭi maraalaa haa fotikoḷek, enough cloth to tuck up [H. langōṭ, spancloth, Skt. lingapaṭṭa]

4016 LAṬI ލަޓި n. club or stick (laṭi-gaňḍu) [H. lāṭhī, Skt. yaṣṭikā]

4017 LAṬṬI ލައްޓި n. kind of fish, 'kawakawa', euthynnus affinis: haada laṭṭiek beeniee, caught many l. fish

4018 LAḌANII ލަޑަނީ v. hits; collides with (v.n. leḍum): gaigai laḍaifi, hit the body: (invol.) ekaku anekaku leḍuniiee, one collided with the other

4019 LAŇḌAA (laňḍaek) ލަނޑާ n. kind of fish, parrot fish (difficult to catch); varieties: nuu l., oḷu l.

4020 LAŇḌU ލަނޑު n. goal, point, run (in games): l. hadanii, l. jahanii, scores a point; (pej.)trick, disaster: l. denii, tricks someone; ahannař laňḍek libijje, I was cheated: laňḍu-daňḍi, goalposts; (met.) laňḍudaňḍiař vaas̲il vum, reaching the goal

4021 LATPE ލަތްޕެ v. for laifieve, past tense of lanii

4022 LADU ލަދު n. shyness, embarrassment; modesty: aharen kalee deke ladu gane-ee, I feel embarrassed in your presence : ladu net, shameless: ladu-kamek, a shameful thing: ladu-raki, shy, modest (of women): ladu-vehi, modest (of men): ladu-veti, shy: ladu hayaat, decency: ladu-maa, ladu-gas, a plant, mimosa pudica [old S. lada, Skt. lajjā]

4023 LANII ލަނީ v. puts (v.n. lum:: abs. laa, lai:: past tense laifi, latpe, lajje, lii : p.p.li : imp. laa! inf. laan : invol. levenii, q.v.: caus. and hon., lavvanii): 1. (basic meaning): aňgayař lum, putting in the mouth: annaunu laa foři, box for keeping clothes in: avii lanii, puts in the sun: uraa bimař lum, sowing millet: navař ecceti laan, to load cargo into ship: goojjař lum, putting in dry dock: nagili lum, dropping anchor: poosṭař lum, putting in the post: bimař lanii, ceremonially places a baby on the ground: beerař lum, putting outside: vaḷu lanii, buries: vooṭ lum, registering vote: kamakař ciṭii lum, depositing a job application: (vulg.) anhenakaa eku lum, has intercourse with a woman;

2. applies, fixes, puts on: ataru l., applies scent: atdoř l., puts on ovencloth: kaḍi l., applies paint (doonii-gai, to boat): koli l., uses ceremonial gong: gamiihek l., puts on a shirt: goř l., 1. fixes button or knot: ṭafu l., uses knotline: timara l., applies lead to: daňḍi l., fixes handle: dumfat l., uses tobacco (in chew): deli l., applies lampblack (doonii-gai, to boat): fehi dorek laafai huri ge, house fitted with a green door: faliitaa l., fits fuse: furaaḷu l., fixes roof: fen fihi lanii, 'brushes water' , i.e. uselessly exists: bataana l., fixes lining: muḍutu l., uses plumb-lead: medu l., affixes centre-rope: rodu l., uses fishingline: salaamati l., uses a rope: sṭeemp l., affixes stamp: haru l., has a foothold, is firm: huni l., uses lime (in chew), applies whitewash (faaru-gai, to the wall): huvaňdu l., puts on scent; caus., hedum lavvanii, dresses somebody

3. makes: kani l., kani kani l., makes sparks, i.e. becomes faintly visible: kaavani lai denii, marries someone (of the official): hitugai garuba l., becomes heavy-hearted: guḍuguḍu l., wobbles: baguḍi l., clings on (gaigai , to the body): baṇḍi baṇḍi lavvanii (caus.), wiggles the hips: baňḍudura laigen, with an overhang: fasdaanu l., makes grave: fařan l., makes keel: faara lanii, keeps a watch (on.., ..-ař): faahi l., makes loop;

4. emits, sends forth: aňga keheni l., gets itchy mouth: goř l., 2. a boil erupts: duli l., forms a skin (of liquids): neevaa l., breathes: faharuva l., pisses: mas l., swells up (of seeds): maa l., opens up (of grains): muu l., sends out roots: mulun laifi, (bimun laifi), uprooted itself: raha l., gives a savour: vas l., gives off a smell: hiis l., pisses; used of making certain sounds: kaakaa lanii, croaks, babbles: gis lanii, sobs;

5. appears (cf. lai-gannanii): fajru lanii, dawn appears: rat vilaa laa iru, at twilight (when red clouds appear); vilaagaňḍu lai maḍu vum, clouds that come getting less threatening; abs. laafai, laigen, with : sai bonii biskoodu laigen, drinks tea with biscuits: mulun laigen veṭṭijje, (of a tree) fell roots and all: ehera siḍiin laafai, by that staircase: magun laafai, along the street: ehen laafai, that way:

Much used ifc. in verbal compounds, esp. in form -la, as a politeness: kiyaala deeře, please tell me: fattaa-la fattaa-la! do sit down; and in the conditional form -liya before dinum, permitting; ali aḷuvaaliya devvaařee, let (me) cast some light (hon.)

[S. lanne, cf. Skt. lāgayati]

4024 LANKAA ލަންކާ n. Ceylon (anc. name, Oḷu-duu): Lankaa-vaalaa, Ceylonese person

4025 LANṬAN ލަންޓަން n. (anc.) street light [E. lantern]

4026 LANBUVANII ލަންބުވަނީ v. attracts: hit-tak lanbuvaalaa, attracting the minds (caus. of laňbanii)

4027 LANSIMU ލަންސިމު n. plant with a scented root, vetiveria zizanioides

4028 LAFANII ލަފަނީ v. brings close (v.n. lefum) - of sailing craft: dooni goňḍudořař lafaifiee / lafajje, brought the dhoni to land: (enlarged) doonñaaigen lafaa-lum, bringing (somebody) to land on the dhony: mammage urutereař darifuḷu lafai-liiee, the mother clasped the child to her bosom; see also lefenii

4029 LAFAA(-aek) ލަފާ n. advice: lafaafuḷu denii, gives recommendations (hon.): lafaa kuranii, estimates, judges; ahannař lafaa kureyee fadain, as I guess (invol.): as adj., reliable, well-behaved: nu-lafaa, unreliable, unpleasant, naughty

4030 LAFU ލަފު n. 1. scruff of the neck (usu. of animals) 2. raised birth mark [S. lapa]

4031 LAFUZU ލަފުޒު n. word [U. lafz]

4032 LAPPANII ލައްޕަނީ v. shuts (v.n. leppum : impv. lappaa!) (caus. of lafanii)

4033 LABARI ލަބަރި n. 1. large box for keeping bait [=lagari]
2. (met.) kaňḍu- labari, copycat

4034 LABBA ލައްބަ excl. yes (mid- grade): yes I can. In repetitions, labbaee: labba-duruvan, forms of address for 'Class 2'

4035 LAŇBANII ލަނބަނީ v. bows, bends (tr.), steers (v.n. leňbum : caus. lanbuvanii): vaatař laňbaa-laa, steer to the left! gas leňbuniyyaa, if the trees bend down (invol.): (met.) boo laňbaa, obeying (as v. is jahaa, bowing the head) [cf. S. laňba, hanging, Skt. lamba]

4036 LAŇBURAAN ލަނބުރާން n. ropes supporting the mast: l. jahanii, fixes these ropes

4037 LAMBARU ލަންބަރު n. (anc.) number : numbered official shop [for nambaru, E. number]

4038 LAVA ލަވަ n. song: l. kiyanii, recites a song: l. jahanii, plays music on record; baburu lava, negro song: lava- fořì, gramophone: lava-hoḷi, gramophone record; lavahoḷiek jahanii, puts a record on: lava aḷaafai vaa keseṭ-roolek, a cassette recording the song

4039 LAVANII ލަވަނީ v. 1. drives (animals somewhere) (v.n. levum): e duuni maḷifaccaa dimaa-ař lavaa-la balaařeve, please drive those birds towards the trap
2. gives food by hand: kaa taketi levum, feeding by hand
[cf. kavanii in both senses]

4040 LAVVANII ލަވްވަނީ v. 1. joins, includes, connects (v.n. levvum): karař maḷi l., applies lasso: diuḷi l., connects driving-belt: tinoohakař rodi l.,threads needle: eenaa nulavvaa kuḷeetii, because they were playing without him: aharen kuḷen lavvaařc, let me join you: darifuḷu mi faharu skuulakař nulevvuneve, the child was not admitted to school this time

2. caus. of lanii: hedum lavvanii, dresses someone (tr.): lavvaa (lavvai), by the agency of (used postpositionally with causative verbs) [S. lavā, lavvā]

3. hon. of lanii: rahmat lavvaařieve, have mercy! laanet lavvanii, (of God) shames, makes accursed

4041 LAV-VANII ލަވްވަނީ v. drifts ashore; floats around (v.n. lav-vuṃ): lav-vefai hun eccissek, piece of flotsam; leans against [for lagganii]

4042 LAS (lahek) ލަސް n. slowness; lateness: lahek nuve, without delay: maa lastakek nuve, without much delay: lahek fahek, delay (doublet): adv., (las) lahun, slowly; las kuranii, postpones (pej., as v. fas kuranii): maadama-ař las kuranii, delays till tomorrow: gaḍi las vejje, the clock is slow: varař las vejje aḷugaňḍař, I have got very late [S. las, alasa, lazy, Skt. alasa]

4043 LASKARU, LAŚKARU (pl. also laśkariin) ލަސްކަރު - ލަޝްކަރު n. army of soldiers: ařvana laśkaru, the Eighth Army [U. laśkar, cf. A. 'askar]

4044 LAHAṬṬAVANII ލަހައްޓަވަނީ v. keeps, maintains (v.n. leheṭṭevum): (invol.) aharen duniyeegaa leheṭṭeviyyaa, if I remain in this world [enlargement of lanii, cf. erahaṭṭanii]

4045 LAHI VANII ލަހި ވަނީ v. gets quite exhausted

4046 LAḶI ލަޅި n. penis

4047 LAA ލާ 1. n. lacquer: laa- daňḍi, sealing wax: laa-fen, liquefied lacquer; laa taḷanii, prepares lac: laa jahanii, applies lac [S. lā(kaḍa), Skt. lākṣā]

2. v. placing (pres. part. or abs.of lanii; also imp.): faaraa laa, against the wall

4048 LAAGUḶA ލާގުޅަ n. seeds of kařikuňburu (caesalpinia bonducella), which get hot when rubbed

4049 LAA-GE ލާގެ n. ornamental domed portion of a large mosque: Maalee Hukuru miskitu laage, one of the 3 domes of the Male Friday mosque [laa]

4050 LAACAARU ލާޗާރު n. In laacaaru-bicaarař hiňgum, wandering aimlessly [H. lā-cār, destitute]

4051 LAATA ލާތަ n. a pre-Muslim god [U. Lāt]

4052 LAADAN ލާދަން n. black resin of cistus creticus, used for incense or medicine, gum mastic [U. lādan, Gk. lādanon]

4053 LAADII GOVANII ލާދީ ގޮވަނީ v. teases for being in love

4054 LAAŇDAA (laaňdalek) ލާނދާ n. circular fishing net, seine net: l. ukanii, l. ellanii, casts net [for ellaa daa or laa daa]

4055 LAAN ލާން v. to place (inf. of lanii)

4056 LAA-NET (LAANAT) ލާނެތް (ލާނަތް) adj. cunning (pej.): as n.., laa netu = laa net miihaku [U. la'nat, curse]

4057 LAANCU ލާންޗު n. launch (vessel) [E. launch]

4058 LAABA ލާބަ n. gain, esp. religious or charitable: laaba huri kamek, a profitable activity: beehakun laabaek nukuri, got no help from medicine [Skt. lābha]

4059 LAA-BOŇDI, LAA-BOŇDU ލާބޮނޑި - ލާބޮނޑު n. tassels, e.g. on towels or lampshades

4060 LAA-MAŘI ލާމަޅި n. a chalky mixture used in fireworks

4061 LAAMI ލާމި n. a medicinal timber, canarium zeylanicum

4062 LAAMU ލާމު n. the letter L in the Arabic and Maldivian alphabets: Laamu atoḷu, Haddunmati atoll

4063 LAA-MEHENII (anc. LAA-MEKENII) ލާމެހެނީ (ލާމެކެނީ) v. gets tangled up, knitted up: deeti deeccař laamehum, two things getting entangled [mehenii]

4064 LAARI ލާރި n. lari coin (l00 to the rupee); money (in gen.): baakii laari, the change: vaki laari, small change: laari-foti, (old) coin ; ekgotakař ves laariyek nulibee, it is impossible to make money: laari-koḷu genguḷee, fairly well off [originally hook-money from Persian district of Lar]

4065 LAALU ލާލު n. hearts (at cards): hukum bunii laalaŕee, declared hearts trumps [U. lāl, red]; ruby or precious stone (diree laalu) [U. la'l]

4066 LAAS DENII ލާސް ދެނީ v. gives a scolding or ticking-off

4067 LAAZIMU ލާޒިމު adj. essential: laazimukamek kamugai vejje, became necessary [U. lāzim]

4068 LAAHI (laassek) ލާހި n. a dry measure, quarter of a naaḷi or 'measure' (approx. one kilo); tin laahi hañḍuu, three quarters of a 'measure' of rice; of liquids, equal to quarter of an aḍubaa: : laahi fuḷi, pint bottle [S. laha, which however is 4 näli]

4069 LAAHIKU ލާހިކު adj. bearable: mikam kuraakaŕ laahikek nuun, (I) dare not do this: laahikek nuun rakkaa vegen daakaŕ, (you) can't escape: bayyakaŕ tankoḷek laahiku duvahek, a day when one feels slightly better: eenaa-aŕ vure laahiku miihek, a more tolerable person than him: nu-laahiku kujjek, a difficult child

4070 LAAŘI ލާޅި n. sap: only in giuḷi laaři, gum arabic [S. lāṭu]

4071 LI ލި v. put (p.p. of lanii) [S. lū]

4072 LIUM ލިއުން v. For liyum, see liyanii; so also liuvvanii [S. līm]

4073 LITOO ލިތޯ n. litho printing (litoo caapu) [E. litho(graph)]

4074 LIBAAS (libaahek) ލިބާސް n. old half-length gown (formerly for both sexes) (hon., libaas-koḷu); Divehi libaas, boḍu libaas (for men): digu libaas (for women, = faas kuri hedum): libaahu goř, button of l. : libaahu fati, seam of l. ; at eñburi l., gown with turned (puffed out) sleeves: atgañḍu kuri l., gown with fitted arm-gusset: bañḍu feḷi l., gown opening down the front; libaas jahanii, takes in, tightens gown: libaas lavvaa umuru, age of puberty in girls (when upper body must be covered) [U. libās]

4075 LIBENII ލިބެނީ v. is received, is got (by, dat.) (hon., libi vaḍaigannanii): libeekaŕ net, is not available: dulun libi-ganevee asaru, impressions received by the tongue (invol.): libi-deene, one can get [S. läbenne, P. labbhati, Skt. labhyatē]

4076 LIBBANII ލިއްބަނީ v. causes to supply (libbai denii) (hon. libbavanii)

4077 LIYANII ލިޔަނީ v. 1. writes (abs. liye : imp. liyee! p.p. liyunu : v.n. lium (lium) : hon. li(y)uvvanii); registers: liyaa filaa, chalkboard: liye deven huri faalabba, land to be leased out: liyuvvaigatum, getting land on lease: liyefai otum, being recorded in writing: liyum, writings: liyum-teri, philologist:

2. slices thinly longwise (of fish, with fook-vaḷi , or of screwpine, with kařikeyo liyaa vaḷi): mas liyaa filaagaňḍu, fish-slicing board:

3. turns, engraves: liye laa jahanii, turns and lacquers: diguharugai liyanii, turns on lathe: liyaa kaři, chisel used with lathe

[S. liyanne, Skt. likhati]

4078 LILII ލިލީ n. lily (lilii maa): rat lilii, hippeastrum puniceum: hudu lilii, hymenocallis [E. lily]

4079 LISṬU ލިސްޓު n. list: lisṭek liyanii, makes a list: lisṭař kiyanii, distributes invitations (refused by writing salaam on the list) [E. list]

4080 LII ލީ 1. n. hair- louse [S. likkā]

2. v. placed (past tense of lanii)

4081 LIILI ލީލި n. short bits of rope (the first stage in plaiting rope): l. aḷanii, twists into strands

4082 LUI ލުއި adj. light; easy (lui faseeha); improved in health (hon., luifuḷu): lui etigaňḍek, a light object: lui kamek, a light task: lui ge-ek, a house which is easy to run : lui koř dee miihek, a helpful man: lui vanii, gets better (in health); adv., maa lui lui koř, very easily [Skt. laghu; cf. S. lihil]

4083 LUGUMA ލުގުމަ n. mouthful (of solids) [U. luqma]

4084 LUCCAA ލުއްޗާ n. cunning villain (usu. in voc., luccaaee !) [H. luccā, villain]

4085 LUNGI ލުންގި n. silk cloth formerly worn by noblemen: lungi-koḷu, royal cloth [U. lungī, 'Muslim dhoti']

4086 LUŇBOO (-oek) ލުނބޯ n. lime fruit, citrus aurantifolia: boḍu l., lemon, citrus media: kudi l., 'citron', citrus limonum: kaaḷu l., phyllanthus maderaspatensis [H. līmbū, Skt. nimbuka]

4087 LUM ލުން v. putting (v.n. of lanii) [S. līm]

4088 LUSSANII ލުއްސަނީ v. pulls up, pulls out : gas lussum, pulling up plants [Skt. luñcati]

4089 LUHENII ލުހެނީ v. pulls out an artificial insert: (intr.) comes out (abs. luhe, luhigen):bat l., strains water off rice: mas l., takes fish out of water [back formation from lussanii]

4090 LUUṬU ލޫޓު n. In luuṭu karudaas, coloured cellophane (used for large kites) [E. lutestring]

4091 LUUṬUVANII ލޫޓުވަނީ v. robs; loots (tr.) [H. lūṭnā, Skt. luṇṭati]

4092 LUUDIYAANAA FOTI ލޫޑިޔާނާ ފޮތި n. Louisiana cloth [E.]

4093 LUUDENII ލޫދެނީ v. mischievously disarranges things: drags oneself about, crawls: loafs about; (of seams) comes away; Luudaḷee-Baadaḷee hifaigen faihalee (referring to a character in a children's story), come down (the tree) with (the mischievous) L-B.!

4094 LUUVA ލޫވަ n. louvre window [E. (French) louvre]

4095 LUUḶAAFATI ލޫޅާފަތި adj. slim, elegant, nimble (of women)

4096 LUUḶU ލޫޅު n. luuḷu gaa, a kind of very hard coral

4097 LEI ލެއި See lee

4098 LEK ލެއް n. a game, of Indian origin (lek kuḷenii, plays l.)

4099 -LEK -ލެއް suffix required after participles in certain contexts: a) to indicate manner, as subject of a clause: miinaa uḷee-lek varař nubaee, the way he behaves is very bad: natiijaa fennamun diya-lek varař ves laheve, the way the results appeared was very slow; b) before abstract nouns ending in -kam : agu boḍu vamun daa-lek boḍukamun, because of the prevalence of price rises

4100 LEKUVUM ލެކުވުން v. rocking (v.n. of lakuvanii)

4101 LEGGUM ލެއްގުން v. drifting ashore: leaning against (tr.) (v.n. of lagganii)

4102 LEŇGENII ލެނގެނީ v. sways from side to side; leans (against, ..-gai): leňgevifai hurum (invol.), being thrown against (your neighbour) [lagganii]

4103 LEḌUM ލެޑުން v. colliding (v.n. of laḍanii)

4104 LEFENII ލެފެނީ v. approaches (on land - not of mechanical ships or aircraft, cf. lafanii): aharemennař lefijje, we managed to arrive: mitanaa nulefee, don't approach! (invol. of lafanii)

4105 LEPPUM ލެއްޕުން v. shutting (v.n. of lappanii): leppenii, can be shut (invol.)

4106 LEBURU ލެބުރު n. kind of dragonfly: rihaakuru l., a dragonfly with dark-coloured wings

4107 LEŇBUM ލެނބުން v. bending (v.n. of laňbanii)

4108 LEVENII ލެވެނި v. invol. of lavanii or of lanii : ataru levenii, scent is applied: sarudaarek levuneve, an officer was appointed: duuni bai levum, driving birds: leveen ot, applicable: kudinnař kaa taketi levum, feeding children

4109 LEVVUM ލެއްވުން v. including; placing (v.n. of lavvanii)

4110 LEHEṬṬUM ލެހެއްޓުން v. maintaining (v.n. of lahaṭṭanii)

4111 LEE, LEI ލެއި - ލޭ n. blood: lee aḷanii, gives blood transfusion: lee kekenii, the blood is stirred, inspiration comes: haada lee kekee kuḷumek, a very thrilling game: lee kakkuvaalum, stirring the blood: lee lanii, spurts blood; lee-karuna, 'bloody' tears: lee-kokaa, kind of reddish butterfly: lee boo fani, leech: lee-naaru, blood vessels, esp. redness of the eyes: lee-hoḷi, vein [S. lē, lōhita]

4112 LEENU ލީން n. fishing line in the sea; electric cable [U. lain, E. line]

4113 LEENDEEN ލީން ދީން n. credit, credit account: aḷugaňḍuge leendeen e fihaarugai onnaane, my account is at that shop: l. kuranii, gives credit [H. lēn dēn, taking & receiving]

4114 LEEFA ލީފަ n. love (Southern dialect) (cf. loobi)

4115 LOI ލޮއި See loo

4116 LOKI ލޮކި adj. very fat and flabby (fala loki)

4117 LOḌU ލޮޑު adj. tired, sluggish: aharen loḍu vejje-ee, I became exhausted; as n. (pl.) loḍun, slow workers [S. leḍa, ill]

4118 LOTAARI ލޮތާރި n. small five-pronged anchor: l. lanii, casts anchor

4119 LOŇDI ލޮނޑި adj. slippery

4120 LONU ލޮނު n. salt; saltwater : lonu gada, salty: kaňḍuge lonu-gaňḍu, sea-water ; lonugaňḍu kafanii, makes a wake in the sea: lonu-fuk, lump of salt: lonu-mas, whole (uncooked) salt fish : lonu-mirus, a chillie chutney: lonu-hakuru, salt and sugar: hiňdi lonu, a medicinal salt [S. luṇu, Skt. lavaṇa]

4121 LONU-MIDILI n. a timber tree, melia

4122 LONUMEDU ލޮނުމެދު n. garlic, allium sativum: lonumedek, a segment of garlic: lonumedu boňḍi, bunch of garlic segments: lonumedu teyo, a medicinal oil: lonumedu faṭaas, a 'cracker' (in segments like garlic); lonumedu sarubatu, a medicinal liquid [S. lūnu, Skt. laśuna]

4123 LONDAA-LANII ލޮނޑާލަނީ v. skids (on slippery surfaces) [loňdi]

4124 LONNANII ލޮންނަނީ v. licks (abs. love : v.n. lovum : caus. lovvanii) [S. lovinne, cf. Skt. lihati]

4125 LONSI ލޮންސި n. lance: lonsi hevikam, lance practice: lonsiyař diyum, spear-diving [cf. S. lansē, Port. lânça]

4126 LOBUVETI ލޮބުވެތި adj. beloved

4127 LOLII ލޮލީ n. lollypop [E. lolly]

4128 LOLU- ލޮލު- See loo 1

4129 LOVUM ލޮވުން v. licking (v.n. of lonnanii) [S. levīm]

4130 LOVVANII ލޮއްވަނީ v. gives to lick (caus. of lonnanii)

4131 LOS ލޮސް excl. used in Tuḷusduu, dear me! [ḷos]

4132 LOSSANII ލޮއްސަނީ v. appeases, lulls (non-Male usage) (caus. from lohenii)

4133 LOHENII ލޮހެނީ v. is appeased, is lulled (non-Male usage, cf. masalas)

4134 LOḶANII ލޮޅަނީ v. shakes(intr.), quivers: loḷum araee, vibrations arise, we feel vibrations: eege loḷum araane sarukaarek, a government that would be affected by it [S. leḷenne, Skt. lōḍati]

4135 LOḶUVANII ލޮޅުވަނީ v. causes to shake: (slang) gulps down (caus. of loḷanii)

4136 LOO (lolek) ލޯ n. 1. eye: lolař neeňgee, lolař nufenna, blind: lolař fenum, sight: lolař govanii, 'insults the eyes', calls blind (pej.): loo maranii, shuts the eyes: loo hinganii, directs the eye: loo boḍu koř, enlarging the eyes, i.e. in anger; loo aňdiri, shortsighted: loo kanu, blind (pej.); lolu-bees, eye-salve: lolu-boňḍi, eyelid: loo-kiba, loo-naaři, half- coconut shells with the 'eyes' in them (as v. fuukiba, fuunaaři): loofan, born blind [loo + ufan]: loo-boo koři vanii, faculties of sight and mind are failing: loo-vaḷu, small hole; loovaḷu aḷanii, bores small holes

4137 LOO (LOI) (looin) ލޯ (ލޮއި) n. 2. brass or other metal alloy (not approved of for waistchains): ratu loo, copper: ranvan loo, brass: kafu loo, an alloy used for trumpets; loo-gaňḍu, 1. large fishkettle (kakkaa loogaňḍu), small bowl (koo donna loogaňḍu:) 2. mirror : foṭoo(ge) loogaňḍu, glass of a picture 3. gong in tne old damu-aři ; ceremonial gong (koli loogaňḍu): loo taři, metal tray (with high rim; for servants): loo faaru, wall of the universe (a metal wall said to bound the universe): loo-fiňdu, kind of dragonfly (varieties: baburu l., biletmaa l.): loo-maafaanu, ancient copperplate documents; tiya vaahakaek loomaafaanaku netee (prov.), such a tale cannot be found even in old copperplates (i.e. must be untrue): loo-vaři, kind of wide low metal cup (esp. for servants) [S. lō, Skt. lōha]

4138 LOOBI (lootbek) ލޯބި n. love (towards..,.. deke): loobi vanii, feels loving (usu. with deke, of animates): loobi kuranii, loves, respects; makes love; qaanuunař loobi kuraa baek, people who respect the laws: loobi jehenii, falls in love; loobi-veri, loobi-veti, loving [Skt. lōbha]

4139 LOORI ލޯރި n. lorry [E. lorry]

4140 LOOLI ލޯލި n. body hair [cf. Skt. lōma]

ވ VAAVU, the 9th letter of the Maldivian alphabet

Vaavu atoḷu, Felide atoll, the 9th atoll from the north

4141 VA-AT (VAAT) ވައަތް (ވާތް) n. left hand [S. vam, Skt. vāma + Mald. at]

4142 VAI ވައި n. wind: (met.) atmosphere: vai gada, windy: vayař naganii, turns (craft) into the wind: vayař bahaṭṭanii, keeps into the wind: telaňga vaigai hifaifi, the kite has caught the wind (has gone up), (met.) vai hifanii, gets rheumatic swellings:

vai beeru kuranii, farts: vai jehenii, wind blows: vai jassailanii, takes the air, enjoys the breeze: vai lanii, belches vai aḷuvanii, (met.)wins the favours (of..,..-ař), flatters; vai eḷenii, has to do with; eenaa-aa vaek neeḷeenam, I won't have anything to do with him; mitanař vai eḷigen ves nuvaane, you mustn't come here at all; bańḍuge vai, wind in the stomach: vai dař,the leeward: vai-guguu (-gugulek), kind of imported medicinal incense: vai- guraabu, toy ship on wheels: vai-noḷi, windpipe (of animates): vai-filaa, a creeper, gynandropsis gynandra: vai-mati, the weather; vaimati faraat, windward side: vai-rooḷi, blast of wind; vairooḷi jehenii, blast of wind arises: vai-vani, deformed and cracked coconut: vai- varu kuranii, gets ready to go about; aims at (Maaleař vaivaru kořfai, aiming for Male): vai-vilaa(-gańḍu), windcloud without rain (as v. koḷigańḍu): vai-ham, 'bag of wind', a fart [S. vā, Skt. vāta, vāyu]

4143 VAIRU (VAYIRU) ވައިރު (ވަޔިރު) n. steel cable: vairu naru, strand of wire [E. wire]

4144 VAIRLES (vairlehu) ވައިރލެސް n. See vayarlehu-

4145 VAISARI ވައިސަރި excl. bravo! [U. vācharā]

4146 VAU ވައު See vaa (vau-gańḍu, vau-fař)

4147 VAUDU ވައުދު n. promise : v. kuranii, promises [U. va'da]

4148 VAK ވައް n. 1. single fruit of certain trees (ahi v., kańḍuu v., keyo v.) [S. pak, Skt. pakva] 2. stems of young coconut fruit (goboḷi) or coconut flowers (etu-maa), used as toothbrushes; ihaa-vak damanii, removes stems from nuts: twigs on betel; bilet vak jahanii, betel puts forth twigs (when ready for use): vakvakař kańḍanii, cuts (betel) by shoots, not by leaves 3. timbers of a boat: buḍu-vak, base thwarts; fai-vak, cross timbers

4149 VAK-GAŇDU ވައްގަނޑު n. 1. stems on coconut (ihaa-v.); twigs on betel (bilet-v.) 2. projecting spout ; kuraa vakgańḍu, spout of kettle: nipple, teat

4150 VAK-VAK JAHANII ވައްވައް ޖަހަނީ v. barks and snaps: hifaane vagek vakvakek nujahanane-ee, (prov.) the active thief will not shout [onom., of dogs]

4151 VAKA ވަކަ n. fibrous inner bark of certain trees: vaka valek aḷanii, makes a rope of bark fibre; (met.) vaka vanii, becomes flabby [Skt. valkalā]

4152 VAKARU ވަކަރު n. coconut wood (vakaru-gańḍu): gas vakaru, timber other than coconut: vakarugańḍu maavaḍiyaa hitekee (prov.), the wood is for the carpenter to use as he will; fatfoři v., centre beam: siisan vakaru, an imported timber, dalbergia sisu; hai v., teak; vakarugee kudin, distressed orphans (formerly accommodated in government woodstore)

4153 VAKAALAATU KURANII ވަކާލާތު ކުރަނީ v. acts as advocate [U. vakālat]

4154 VAKI (vatkek) ވަކި 1. adj. separate; special: vaki gotek, a certain manner: vaki miveni gotek neti, without any special plan: vaki faraatakař jehunu, bent towards one side: vaki laari, small change: vaki hisaabek, a particular place: adv., vakin, vakiin, separately; else: vakin innaanii kaakaa hee, who else will (you) live with? vakiin boḍař, especially much: vaki-vakiin, separately, apart; often used after vure, more: ..vure vakin, any more; vaki kuranii, separates (tr.), identifies: samaalukam vaki kor̃ levenii, attention is diverted: tandoru vaki kor̃ datum, age of responsibility: aḷugañḍu vaki kurevvunu too, can you identify me (hon.)? (intr.) aharen kaleaa vaki viiee, I am separated from you: mi vagutu vaki ve lanii iñgee, I am leaving you now, I'm going

2. n. claws; hooks, folding handles (vaki-gañḍu); suckers of a creeper: buḷaa magee gaigaa vaki aḷaifiee, the cat has fixed its claws on my body: vaki-fuu (-fulek), kinds of creeper, piper longum and scindapsus officinalis (classed as matikaraa bees)

4155 VAKIILU ވަކީލު n. Government Secretary, head of department: v. kuranii, entrusts (the responsibility) , Maatkalaañge kibafuḷař vakiil koř, entrusting the matter to God [U. vakīl]

4156 VAKKAM ވައްކަން n. theft [vagu + kam]

4157 VAK-KAḶI ވައްކަޅި n. covert glance [vař + kaḷi]

4158 VAGU ވަގު n. thief : vagu-kaleege, thief: vagu-firi, paramour: vagu mudaa, stolen goods: vagu tinhama, kind of game (as v. baburu tinhama): fas vagun, captains of teams in ancient games: vagu baazu,wild hawk: vagu buḷaa, wild cat, ownerless cat : mini kaa vagu, tiger; (adv.,) vagař, dishonestly ; vagu vanii, becomes wild, becomes unfriendly: mi geaa vagu vegen, unfriendly to, i.e. avoiding, this house
[S. vaga, Skt. vyāghra, tiger (not found in the Maldives)]

4159 VAGUTU ވަގުތު n. time: mi vagutu, now: vagutu(n) vagutař, at regular times: hama vagutař, in time, on time: vagutek net, there is no time: vagutu-gaa (galek), sundial;
v. jehenii, the time comes; adj., vagutii, temporary [U. vaqt]

4160 VA-GOŘ ވަގޮށް n . reef knot : v. jahanii, ties a reefknot [va-, left]

4161 VAJIDU, VAJJIDU ވައްޖިދު - ވަޖިދު n. ecstatic practices: v. vanii, practises ecstasy (now discouraged): vajji taara, music to accompany ecstasies
[U. vajd]

4162 VAJJU ވައްޖު n . in hajju-vajju, pilgrimages (doublet) [hajju]

4163 VAṬALAPPAN ވަޓަލައްޕަން n. a sweet dish

4164 VAṬṬANII ވަށްޓަނީ v. fells (trees); drops (v.n. veṭṭum) : dorufoti v., draws curtains: nagili v., drops anchor: (enlarged) vaṭṭaa-lanii, knocks down; ge vaṭṭaa kakuni, a burrowing land crab [S. vaṭṭanne, Skt. vartayati; tr. of veṭṭenii ₁ q.v.]

4165 VAṬṬAFAAḶI ވަށްޓަފާޅި n. art, skill: vaṭṭafaaḷi huri, skilful: vaṭṭafaaḷi boḍu, fussy

4166 VAṬṬARU ވަށްޓަރު n. name of an island in N atoll

4167 VAṬṬEK ވަށްޓެއް See vaři

4168 VAḌAI-GANNA(VA)NII ވަޑައި ގަންނަ(ވަ)ނީ v. goes, comes (class 1 honorific; neg. abs. vaḍai nugen). Also used honorifically after various other verbs, e.g. deke v., jehi v., libi v., eňgi v., feni v., visni v., ivi v., faibaa v., araa v., keri v., furaa v., edi v., (in compound verbs) ..ve v. (e.g. baddalu ve v., meets) and ..kuravvamun vaḍaigat, continuing to be done (cf. kuramun diya): e-kam varař feni vaḍai nugannavaeve, they didn't much care for that idea; (invol.) eenaa-ař Koḷuňbař vaḍaigenneveene taa, since he will have reached Colombo [S. vaḍinne]

4169 VAḌAAM ވަޑާމް n. carpentry (classified as kissaru v. (for boatbuilding), tedui v. (for housebuilding), himun v. (fine joints)): v. kaři, chisel: v. saamaan, carpenter's tools; (met.) kon vaḍaamek, what are you doing, what have you come for? fen aruvaa vaḍaam, fountain [S. vaḍukam, Skt. vardhakikarma]

4170 VAḌI (pl., vaḍin) ވަޑި n. carpenter: vaḍi fatigaňḍu, set-square [S. vaḍu, Skt. vardhaka]

4171 VAḌUVANII ވަޑުވަނީ v. places honourable animates (cf. baavvavanii, of placing objects): radun ta<u>kh</u>tugai vaḍuvaifiimu, placed the king on the throne (cf. uru- vaḍuvanii, of carrying children): hinifuḷu v., laughs (hon.) [S. vaḍanne]

4172 VAT ވަތް n. internal bottom, esp. of boats or pans: fořiige vatugai, in the bottom of the box: enme vatugai, at the very bottom; bat (tavaa-) vatugai hifaifi, the rice has stuck to the bottom (of the pan); em-vat, hee-vat, compartment for bait on a dhony; vatu oḍi, lower spool of sewing machine: vatu tаři, saucer under cup; billuuriige vatař laa taři, saucer under tumbler; vatař, on to (aňga vatař, on to the tummy: baňḍufuř vatař, on to the palm: uňguru vatař, on to the back); vat kuranii, (hon.) serves food, lays table: salavaatař v. kuranii, serves the imam's special dish; vat-gaňḍu, drawer; shelf; drawer space: vatař vatgaňḍu varu kuranii, (of carpenter) fits the drawer into the space: nimmaa vatgaňḍu, out-tray; vataku too jahanii, makes a complete mess of things: vataku too jehenii, is a complete failure

4173 VATANIYYAT ވަތަނިއްޔަތް n. patriotism [U. vaṯanī, cf. vazan 4]

4174 VATTARU ވައްތަރު n. kind, sort : gina vattaruge saamaanu, many kinds of goods: vattarekge fotek, a kind of book; (adv.) vattarakař, after a fashion; of the same sort as , like (followed by -aa): miinaa enme vattarii bappa-aa, he most resembles his father: miinaa bappa-aa varař vattaru, he is very like his father; vattaru jassanii, makes faces or gestures (at.., .. dimaa): vattaru dakkanii, makes excuses

4175 VATTIINI ވައްތީނި n. figs (not grown in Maldives) [A. wa al tīni]

4176 VADAA (anc. VADAI) ވަޑާ (ވަޑައި) See vadu

4177 VADU ވަޑު n. 1. strap, thong (of shoe or sandal): v. jehi maravaḷi, thong sandals (as v. um jehi maravaḷi): kati v., diagonal straps: huras v., crosswise straps [S. vada, Skt. vardhra]

2. fishing fly, spinner (vadu- fat): v. bannanii, makes a fly: vadaa danii, goes fly-fishing; vadu-dooni, small fishing boat: vadu-nanu, spinner line: vadu-fat, fine tail feathers of a cock (used for fly-fishing): vadu-mas, fish caught by fly

4178 VADE ވަދެ v. having entered (abs. of vannanii: also 3s. pres.) [S. väda, Skt.√vraj]

4179 VADDANII ވައްދަނީ v. pushes in; admits (to school) (v.n. veddum): (met.) biruverikam vaddai dee too belum, seeing if (it) could frighten (them): tiyahen hitař nuvaddaati, don't imagine that! (caus. of vannanii) [S. vaddanne]

4180 VAŇDU ވަނޑު adj. (of fruits which fall early) undeveloped, yellowish: faa vaňdu baňbukeelek, a soft yellowing breadfruit; vaňdu vanii, gets shrivelled [S. vaňda, Skt. vandhya]

4181 VAN ވަން 1. n. pounding mortar (haňḍuu kaňḍaa van): vanař aḷaa, having put in the mortar [S. van(geḍiya)]

4182 VAN ވަން 2. v. entered (p.p. of vannanii, pron. vãt) [S. van]

3. v. to become (for vaan, inf. of vanii) [cf. S. vanna]

4183 -VANA -ވަނަ adj. ordinal ending, e.g. de-vana, second: vihi-vana, 20th; as n.., vana-tak, 'places', i.e. 1st, 2nd or 3rd: abtaalunge vanain, from among the heroes [S. -veni]

4184 VANA-EK ވަނައެއް num. Used for nuvaek, nine (which might mean 'let it not be') in auspicious counting

4185 VANAM ވަނަން n. nickname

4186 VANARA ވަނަރަ In fanara-vanarakař, about fifteen [doublet]

4187 VANAVARU ވަނަވަރު n. information; a saga

4188 VANAA ވަނާ n. curved ornamental shape

4189 VANI ވަނި n. (of the sea) sheltered corner

4190 VANII ވަނީ v. 1. becomes; happens (abs. ve : p.p. vi : v.n. vum : imp. vee ! 3s. pres. ve-eve : past vii, vejje : invol. vevenii , q.v.) : kaleař vii gotek bune balaařee, tell me what's happened to you ; with dat. or loc. complement:: vakiilakař vum, becoming a Secretary: natiijaaek kamař vii, happened as a result : nukoř nuvaanee kamek kamugai vejje-ee, became unavoidable;

is possible (to do): mi-in vaane ta, can you manage with this? tiya kamek mařakař nuvaane, I shan't be able to do that: haaḍu nulaek nuvaane, not possible without making a loop; hence serves as invol. or pass. counterpart of kuranii : nubunuvvaa kamek aḷugañḍař vii too, did I happen to do something I wasn't told to? adi ves e kamtak vee too balaařee, try again to see if you can do it: kaleař vanñaa, if you can : and commonly with compd. verbs , e.g.baddalu kuranii / vanii;

with inf., can, should: aharen huṭṭaalaakař nuvee, I don't have to stop: hedumek eccek fahaaa-deekař nuvee ta, shouldn't you make me a garment? dañḍugai dañḍubuḷi aḷaakař nuvee hee, shouldn't one scythe the field? mikam kuran vii nu, please do this: with ellipsis : adu too maadam too vefai in miihek, someone who might die any time (sc. maru vaan): budu hadaa-me budakař nuve, having unsuccessfully tried to make a statue: gos-me ekamař / ekamek nuve, going but not completing my task;

vaa nuvaa, every possible: vaa nuvaa got, general conditions: as n.. (sc. kamtak), what will happen: vaa nuvaa mařakař neeñge, I don't know what will happen; vanñaa nuunii, unless (one) is : viimaa, when it happens; (initially) therefore: vee-vee huri kam, (gram.) incomplete present tense, e.g. kuranii, duvanii . See also ve [S. vanne, Skt. bhavati]

2. entered (past tense of vannanii)

4191 VANUM ވަނުން v. entering (v.n. of vannanii)

4192 -VANTA -ވަންތަ adj. adjectival suffix, e.g. mujiibvanta, responsive: rahiimvanta, merciful: anhenvanta, feminine

4193 -VANNA -ވަންނަ num. suffix for 'and 50' in old numerals (baavanna, 52, etc.)

4194 VANNANII ވަންނަނީ v. enters (abs. vade, vede : v.n. vanum : p.p. van, pron. vãt: 3s. vade : imp. vadee ! hon. vannavanii (v.n.vennevum): caus. vaddanii (v.n.veddum): invol. vadevenii): with dat., geař vanum, entering the house: vanna! entrance: vannanñaa, if you enter : (enlarged) vade-lavvanii, enters, visits

[S. vadinne, Skt. vrajati]

4195 VANNI ވަންނި n. shades of resemblance: vanni vanni jassanii, makes excuses: vanni vanni lavvanii, makes fun of somebody's appearance

4196 VANHA ވަންހަ n. clan [Skt. vaṃśa]

4197 VANHANAA ވަންހަނާ adj. hidden : v. kuranii, hides (tr.); mařař e kamtak vanhanaa kuranii, hides this from me: ekves vanhanaa kamek net, there is nothing to hide: vanhanaa vegenek nuvaane-ee, it will not be hidden

4198 VAFAA-TERI ވަފާތެރި adj. faithful [U. vafā]

4199 VABAA (vabaaek) ވަބާ n. plagues, epidemics [U. vabā]

4200 VAYARLEHU- (VAIRULEHU-) ވަޔަރލެހު- (ވައިރުލެހު-) n. radio, telegraph : vayarlehuge zarii'aain, by wireless telegraphy [E. wireless]

4201 VAYIRU ވަޔިރު See vairu

4202 VARA ވަރަ n. bowstring: wing; vara-fat, (strongest) wing-feathers

4203 VARAŇGU ވަރަނގު n. silvered or gilt paper (varaňgu karuadaas) [U. varaq]

4204 VARANII ވަރަނީ v. pours; spills (v.n. verum : hon. varuvanii : invol. verenii, q.v.): sai tař verijje, the tea was spilt: fen varanii, bathes, has a bath; fen varaa beru, drum formerly beaten at bath time [Skt. avarīyate, Turner 814]

4205 VARAŘ ވަރަށް adv. very; very much (often followed by ves): varař raňgaḷu, very good! tiya varař, so much: varař durugai, very far away; varař maguu gas ginaee, m. trees are very numerous; also used with verbs : mi kořiigai varař mirus hede-ee, chillies grow well in this plot: aharen varař kukuḷu genguḷee hit ve-ee, I much like keeping poultry: varař edunu, asked pressingly (dat. of varu, amount)

4206 VARAA-VERIKAM ވަރާވެރިކަން n . influence of spirits

4207 VARI ވަރި n. 1. vari-variař, at various times:

2. of fruits, solidity: vari boo kaaři, coconut with much solidity, viz. little hollow space (as v. vari tuni kaaři)

3. divorce: vari kuranii, divorces (of the man): vari vanii, is divorced (of the woman): vari-toḷi, charms to seduce married women; istiri varitoḷi hadanii, uses such charms

4208 VARI-HAMA ވަރިހަމަ n. all the same: mařař varihama(ee), it's all the same to me: konme eccekves vařihama, I don't mind which

4209 VARU ވަރު n. amount; level; size: varuvaruge doonitak, various sizes of fishing vessels: miinaa kaa varek taa, what a lot he eats! konme ves varakař, to a certain extent: ti-varu, your price: kihaa varakař ta, at what price? kaleař devunu varek, whatever you like to give: heyo varek nuun, it doesn't fit; ifc. after numerals, appproximately: fas-varakař, about five: ha-varakař, about six; varař varun uḷegen, slowly, with difficulty: eenaa-ař varař varu vejje, is too much for him: kobai adi ves vaa varek nuvee? isn't that enough?

strength: hařigaňḍugai varu huri, strong in body (of people): (met.) eegai huri varu, its effectiveness; varu-gada, strong: varugada daturek, a good journey: varugada-ař (adv.), strongly: varu-dera, weak (of people): varu-bali, weak, ill, tired; kon varubayyek, why so het up? aharen varubali vejje, I got tired: varubali filuvaalanii, rests:

varu kuranii, fits (tr.), e.g. at carpentry, or of clothes: varu vanii, fits (intr.), is of right consistency; dufumgaňḍu varu vanii, the chew is nicely mixed: meṭaagaňḍu varek nuviee, the sweet has not come out right : varu aranii, reaches a climax (of anger, or of a career): v. aruvanii, shows anger (by shouting): kaigen varu jessum, gaining strength by eating: varu naganii, marks show on the body; essi-lek baarukamun mihirii varu nagaafaee, by the tight tying my body has got marks: varu faibanii, calms down: varu balanii, tests: varu lanii, gets calm (of the sea): maa varař varu hunnanii, takes much interest (in.., -ař or inf.); varu-hunna, interested:

competence, esp. after participles: kuran vaa varu kamek nuunee, is not a thing which could be done: miihaku jadalu kuraa varu miihek, a man worth arguing with: tedu vaan keree varek nuunee, (I) can't get up: aḷugaňḍu adi miihakaa inna varek nuvee, I'm not yet ready for marriage: aḷugaňḍar vii vareve, it's the best I could do: vevunu varakun, as much as (he) could: saabas dee varu vee, (he) is worthy of praise;

varun is used with part. in sense 'because of (the amount)': burikařiigai rihee varun, because of pain in the back: madiri hifaa varun, because of numerous mosquito attacks:

varu- ağri, a part of the old royal palace: varu-kaňdu, kind of tree, hernandia peltata: varu-hagu, a class of ancient functionaries

4210 VARUNIIS ވަރުނީސް n. varnish: v. kuranii, applies varnish with pad: v. lanii, applies varnish with a brush [E. varnish]

4211 VARUVAA (-aaek) ވަރުވާ n. rental payment for islands or trees [T. varuvāy]

4212 VALAVERI ވަލަވެރި n. all ropes and tackle (= vaa-velaaveli)

4213 VALII ވަލީ n. official consent : valii denii, gives official consent (amuru) to a marriage; valii komiṭii, Regency Committee set up in the time of Abdul Majid in the 1940s; valii-veri, entitled to give such consent (valiiveriyaa): valiiveriin (pl.), minor (present-day) saints [U. valī]

4214 VALU- ވަލު- n. jungle: valu-tere, wooded or jungle area; outside the Home base in game of gaňḍufillaa : valu-muraňga, indigo plant, indigofera tinctoria: valu-suufi, wild beast [vaa 3]

4215 VALLA ވައްލަ n. a tuneful sea bird, roseate tern

4216 VAVOI ވަވޮއި n. westward current [va-, left]

4217 VAS (vahek) ވަސް n. 1. smell: duvaa vahek! what a smell! nubai kuraa vahek, a smell that makes you vomit: maa-takun vas duvanii, scent comes from flowers: neefatun vas duvanii, smell comes through the nose; vas duvvanii, gives off scent, uses scent, scents (tr., e.g clothes): vas buruvanii, applies scent (to wardrobes): malugai vas gannanii, sniffs flowers: muunugai vas gannanii, kisses the face (vas gen, kissing): vas lanii, diffuses scent; vas-kaři, ridge of the nose (neefatu vaskaři) [S. vas, Skt. vāsa]

2. crossbar of swing

4218 VASARU ވަސަރު n. washer [E. washer]

4219 VASVAAS (vasvaahek) ވަސްވާސް n. disbelief, doubt: śakkek vasvaahek netee, there is no doubt: miihunař vasvaas lai denii, implants doubts, gives bad advice, exerts an evil influence: ibuliihuge vasvaahař nuhelleeřee, don't succumb to the promptings of the devil (prov.): vasvaas bali jehifai, suffering mental breakdown [U. vasvās]

4220 VAZAN ވަޒަން n. 1. weight: v. kuranii, weighs

2. ammunition: baḍiyař v. lanii, loads gun

3. style, rhythm: vazanař fetenii, suits the style [U. vazan]

4221 VAZAN ވަޒަން n. 4. homeland: vazanveri vanii, settles down (hon., vazanveri ve- vaḍaigannanii) [U. vaṯan]

4222 VAZIIFAA ވަޒީފާ n. job: v. adaa kuranii, does a job: v. naganii, undertakes a job [U. vaẕīfa]

4223 VAZIIRU ވަޒީރު n. minister of state (pl., vaziirun): vaziir ul auzam, (anc.) prime minister [U. vazīr]

4224 VAHUTAAN ވަހުތާން n. revolving charm tied to trees: rukekgai v. jahanii, fixes the charm to a palmtree

4225 VAHUMU ވަހުމު n. unreasoning doubts (vahumu-tak) [U. vahm]

4226 VAHULU ވަހުލު in ahulu -vahulu, persons [doublet]

4227 VAHUSII ވަހުސީ adj. vulgar, lascivious (of words, people) [U. vaẖśī, barbarous]

4228 VAŘ ވަށް adj. circular: vař-tiyara, an edible plant, cassia tora: vař-fufuḷi, a plant, acalypha indica: vař-bas, deceptive words; vařbahun vaahaka dekkum, beating about the bush: vař-buru, circle; vařburu hama kořr, making an exact circle; ufaaveri vařburu, merrygoround: vař-hañdu, full moon; vař kuranii, makes circular; shapes the head of babies (no longer practised); fai vařkoř, sitting crosslegged [S. vaṭa, Skt. vṛtta]

4229 VAŘAŇGULI (vařañguyyek) ވަށަނގުލި n. a herb, belonging to askanu bees

4230 VAŘANII ވަށަނީ v. 1. twists (v.n. veřum): ul v., twists a thread: guḷa v., rolls into balls; vařaa-lanii (vařailanii), vař kořlanii, places around, surrounds (tr.): vařaa (abs.) used postpositionally : gee vařaa, around the house: booḷabimuge vařaigen, around the sports ground [S. vaṭanne, Skt. vartayati]
2. smears on , brushes on : bees v., brushes medicaments on (with poultry leg) [for mařanii, q.v.; cf. mekenii]

4231 VAŘI (vaṭṭek) ވަށި n. wicker basket: em-vaři, basket for baitfish: vaři-gañḍu, wastepaper basket

4232 VAḶI ވަޅި n. knife: kati v., pruning sickle: kořaa v., knife for woodwork: kařikeyo liyaa v., knife with long handle for use with screwpines: niyafati kañḍaa vaḷi / dati, nail trimmers: fook v., knife for slicing areca: baḷu v., sickle: mas v., fish knife: mas liyaa v., long-handled knife: masdat v., sheathknife (of shark's tooth); vaḷi-buri, short knife: vaḷii muřgañḍu, handle of knife; vaḷi riiti tuuniyyaa, a knife is good when sharp (prov.); v. aḷanii, uses knife with violence (with dat. or gaigai): v. jahanii, makes knife; uses e.g. tin-opener: gayař vaḷi haranii, stabs [?T. vāḷ, sword]

4233 VAḶI-FAN ވަޅިފަން n. wayside decorations of cut palmleaves

4234 VAḶU ވަޅު n. dug hole: well: hole in game of ořvaḷu : oř-vaḷu, kind of game ('seed-pit'): kař-vaḷu, grave: tin vaḷu, kind of game: dorumati vaḷu, outside or front well (for drinking and cooking): vaḷu jahanii, digs oneself into the ground; (met.) goes to ground; vaḷu lanii, buries (hon., vaḷufuḷu lanii); vaḷu Iid, the day following each Eid: vaḷu-kaafa, kind of jumping insect found in wells: vaḷu kotari, bathroom: vaḷudoř, well area: vaḷu fehi, dirty green: vaḷu-bari, row of holes: vaḷu-buri, one of the three sections of a concrete well; dañḍi-vaḷu, moment [S. vaḷa, P. āvāṭa]

4235 VAḶOO ވަޅޯ adj. faded and limp: v. vanii, becomes limp; of fish, smoked: vaḷoo kuranii, smokes (fish): vaḷoo duuni, a bird, whiskered tern

4236 VAA, VAU (vaalek) ވާ - ވައު 1. n. bat (animal), flying fox: kind of bat-shaped kite [cf. S. vavul, T. vauvāl]

4237 VAA , VAU (valek) ވާ - ވައު 2. n. rope, string : makunu vaa, spider's web: vaa-koḷu, bit of string: vaa-gañḍu noḷi, coiled mouthpiece of hookah: vaa-fař (vaufař), strap : vaa-makunu, spider: vaa-mankaa, hooks for mast-ropes: vaa-velaa-veli, ropes and tackle: vaa-voři, kind of seaweed, also small kind of turtle that lives in it ; vaa aḷanii, makes rope (oḍi aḷaa vaa, rope to tie up dhony); vaa damanii, holds tug-of-war ; (met.) e demiihunge vaahakain mihaaru vaa demeene, those two are now deep in chat: hakuru vaa demum, making coils of treacle

4238 VAA (valek) ވާ 3. n. jungle (valu-tere: see valu-) : vaa vannanii, gets lost (in the jungle) [S. vala, cf. Skt. vana]

4239 VAA ވާ 4. adj. disabled (vaa miihek), paralyzed: vaa vanii, becomes disabled: at vaa vefai, with thin arms (or branches): vaa- kam, sagginess: aňga vaa kořgen vaahaka dakkanii, speaks laxly, mumbles: vaa bat, rice burnt on the bottom: vaa bali, polio; vaa bali jehigen, suffering paralysis

4240 VAA ވާ 5. n. ifc. for vai: nee-vaa, breath

4241 VAA ވާ 6. v. becoming (part. of vanii) ; also used as noun : vaa nuvaa oḷumek nufiliee, nothing was clear ('what was and what was not'): vaa nuvaaek mařakař nee5ge, I don't understand anything: tanaka3 bayaku vaaek, an occurrence of people at a place, assembly: vaa kam (gram.), present tense verb [S. vana, vena]

4242 VAA ވާ 7. emphasizing particle, not used initially: aḷugaňḍumen vaa nuves dena huriimu, now <u>we</u> didn't even know: e duvasvaru e otii vaa majaakamek, well, it was rather fascinating: bappaek vaa net, oh, father is absent: haada haa vaa, very much indeed: ma vaa vi ufalun, because of <u>my</u> happiness [S. vanāhi]

4243 VAAGI (vaatgek) ވާގި n. strength (hon., vaagi-fuḷu): vaagi gada, strong: maat raskalaaňge vaagifuḷu laigen, with God's help: hii vaagi, hardworking: vaagi-veriyaa, helper: aňga- vaagi netunu iru ves, even after losing one's strength ; v. aranii, gets fits (on dehydration): v. duu vanii, strength is lost: v. netenii, gets tired; vaagi netee bali, paralysis: v. jahanii, shows strength

4244 VAAJIBU ވާޖިބު adj. obligatory: enme us vaajibu kamugai vejje-ee, became the most important duty [U. vājib]

4245 VAAT ވާތް n. left hand: vaatu fai, left foot: vaat-teriyaa, lefthanded person [va + at]

4246 VAATAA VANII ވާތާ ވަނީ v. is starving: aḷugaňḍu vaataa vejje, I was starving

4247 VAADA ވާދަ n. debate; rivalry: v. kiyanii, argues, debates: v. kuranii, competes (with..., ..-aai): dedooni vaada duvvanii, enters two dhonies for the race: v. jahanii, races, competes; vaada raivaru, competitive poetic couplets; vaada-ař, (adv.) in emulation, competitively [Skt. vāda]

4248 VAAN (VAAM) ވާން adj. taut: v. kuranii, makes tension; pulls hard (of a strong kite): bali guḍi vaanek nukuraane, a weak kite will not pull: tightens (of rope, or drum): ek vaamakař vaan, to be taut

4249 VAAN ވާން 1. n. vaan gaa (galek), a hanging stone weight serving as a partial anchor; vaan jassanii, drops this anchor: a trap for mice etc.; vaan jassanii, sets trap

4250 VAAN ވާން 2. v. to become (inf. of vanii) [S. vanna]

4251 VAARU ވާރު n. 1. an ancient tax: v. koḷḍenii, tax is abolished. v. boli, the ordinary cowrie: vaaru-ge (anc.), administrative centre for an atoll (mod., atoḷuge);
2. in vaarun iyaarun (pl.), helpers (doublet)

4252 VAARUTA ވާރުތަ n. succession, inheritance: vaaruta-ař libenii, is inherited: v. mudaa, heritable property; v. kuranii, bequeaths : eenage faraatun v. kořfai vaa, inherited from him : vaaruta-veri, inheritor [cf. U. vāri<u>th</u>, heir]

4253 VAAREE ވާރޭ n. rain : v. tiki, raindrops: v. vilaagaňḍu, raincloud: himafodu-vaaree, drizzle: moyain temmaa vaaree, drizzle [S. vāre, Skt. varṣa]

4254 VAALAA ވާލާ n. vaa 1 + -aa, the bat and..

4255 VAALI ވާލި n. 1. kind of sea-bird, brindled tern
2. kind of fish, scomberoides or trachinotus
3. for vaalu

4256 VAALU ވާލު n. 1. cross-members (also vaali) : v. aḷanii, fixes cross members
2. in vaalek iyaarek netee, there is none to help (doublet)

4257 VAAVU ވާވު n. the letter V (W) in the Arabic and Maldivian alphabets: Vaavu atoḷu, Felide atoll

4258 VAAHAKA ވާހަކަ n. speech; story: v. dakkanii, speaks (to.., ..-aa): v. kiyanii, tells a story, reads a story: vaahakaek bunan vejje, I have something to say : bunefaane vaahakaek! what things you say! after past part., the fact that : aharen ai vaahaka bune! say that I've come [T. & Skt. vācaka]

4259 VAAHVAA ވާހްވާ excl . well done! [U. vāh vā]

4260 VAAḶU VANII ވާޅު ވަނީ v. gets tired: masakkat kořkoř vaaḷu vejje, (I) got tired by going on working

4261 VI ވި 1. n. paddy husks: hañḍuluge viin hadaa, making (it) from paddy husks: vi-fuku mirus, small and hot kind of chilly [S. vī, Skt. vrīhi]

4262 VI ވި 2. v. become, became (p.p. and past tense of vanii, see also vii) [S. vū, Skt. bhūta]

4263 VIAFAARI ވިއަފާރި See viyafaari

4264 VIAVATI ވިއަވަތި See viyavati

4265 VIKANII ވިކަނީ v. pinches (with -gai): atugai v., pinches the arm [cf. S. vikanne, chews, Skt. vikhādati]

4266 VIKUM ވިކުން v. pinching: being sold (v.n. of vikanii and of vikenii)

4267 VIKEṬ ވިކެޓް n. wicket (at cricket) [E. wicket]

4268 VIKKANII ވިއްކަނީ v. sells (imp. vikkaa ! hon. vikkavanii , vikkaa- lavvanii : v.n. vikum : invol.vikenii); (met.) magee bahek nuvikeenee, I shan't be obeyed [S. vikuṇanne, P. vikkiṇāti]

4269 VIGANI ވިގަނި n. a ghost: vigani duni, the halo of light which surrounds this ghost

4270 VITURI ވިތުރި n. a short prayer said (vituri kuranii) after the last prayer of the day

4271 VIDANII ވިދަނީ v. sparkles; (impers.) it lightens [cf. Skt. vidyōtatē]

4272 VIDAAḶU-VANII ވިދާޅު ވަނީ v. speaks (hon. 1st class): reads, recites (vidaaḷu ve-lavvanii); kiyavaa vidaaḷu vum, getting education (hon.): das vidaaḷu vum, completing the Quran test (hon.) [cf. S. vadāranne (p.p. vadāḷa), Skt. vacas + √kṛ]

4273 VIDIGEN ވިދިގެން v. (met.) following (upon, ...-aai): vidividigen, successively; also vidifai: maraa vidifai, close to death (abs. of videnii)

4274 VIDU ވިދު n. small aperture, artificial hole: v. aḷanii, makes such holes [Skt. viddha; S. vidinne, pierces]

4275 VIDUM ވިދުން v. 1. glittering; lightning: vidum keňḍenii, lightning ceases (v.n. of vidanii)

2. being hit, hurt, pierced (v.n. of videnii)

4276 VIDUVANII ވިދުވަނީ v. See viddanii

4277 VIDU-VARU ވިދުވަރު n. lightning rays: kulli v., flash of lightning: viduvarakaai gen, with lightning as well [S. vidu, Skt. vidyut]

4278 VIDENII ވިދެނީ v. is struck, is pierced: ingili videnii, toe is stubbed (on..,..-gai): arikařiigai videnii, (my) side is hurting: iru-vidifai, struck motionless; (of mats) is woven, cf. vinnanii [S. videnne, P. vijjhati (p.p. viddha), Skt. vidhyatē]

4279 VIDDANII (VIDUVANII) ވިއްދަނީ (ވިދުވަނީ) v. rests against (tr., caus. viddavanii): faarugai at viddaigen, resting hand on wall: at viddaafai tedu vum, standing up with the support of the hand (usu. on the ground), pushing ineself up: bolugai at viddum, (lazily) propping up one's head: dat-doḷiigai at viddum, resting one's hand on one's chin (as a sign of sadness); abs. viddaigen, referring to, next to: e vaahakayaa viddaigen, following that utterance [videnii]

4280 VINA ވިނަ n. grass : vina gas, clumps of grass: maa vina, kind of grass, tridax procumbens [cf. tina]

4281 VINAVAA-LANII ވިނަވާލަނީ v. clips off: tuňbuḷi v., clips beard

4282 VINDU ވިންދު n. pulse (med.): v. balanii, takes pulse rate; avas v., racing pulse: dera v., weak pulse

4283 VINNANII ވިންނަނީ v. weaves thatch (v.n. vinum): fangi vinum, also fangaňḍu vidum, threads cadjan [P. vināti; cf. viyanii]

4284 VIYA ވިޔަ 1. n. mathematical problems: v.kuranii, solves problems: v. jahanii, solves problems: fas maigaňḍu viya (fas qavaaidu), five principal arithmetical operations (addition, subtraction, multiplication, division, fractions): viya-filaagaňḍu, slate for doing arithmetic

4285 VIYA ވިޔަ 2. v. form of vanii used with dinum , allowing: viyaka nudii, not allowing to go (conditional)

4286 VIYANI (viyaňňek) ވިޔަނި n. suffix used for the names of non-Arabic Maldivian letters of the alphabet, e.g. ṭa-viyani, pa-viyani [cf. S. -yanna: ṭa-yanna, pa-yanna]

4287 VIYANII ވިޔަނީ v. weaves (abs. viye : v.n. viyum : invol. viyevenii): viyaa dati, loom: feeli viyeveekař netee, skirts could not be woven ; viyavaa kaři, knitting needle [S. viyanne, Skt. vayati; cf. also vinnanii]

4288 VIYAFAARI (VIAFAARI) ވިޔަފާރި (ވިއަފާރި) n. business: viyafaari-verin (pl.), businessmen [cf. H. baipārī, trader, Skt. vyāpāri]

4289 VIYA-MAS ވިޔަމަސް n. kind of fish

4290 VIYAVATI (VIAVATI) ވިޔަވަތި (ވިއަވަތި) adj. (anc.) comfortably off

4291 VIYAS ވިޔަސް v. though it be; even (concessive form of vanii; see -as) [S. vuvat]

4292 VIYAA-DAA ވިޔާދާ adj. desirable (literary form, viyaa vaa: viyaa nuvaa, no good)

4293 VIYAAGI ވިޔާގި n. a disease, swelling of the fingers

4294 VIYYA ވިއްޔަ particle equivalent to 'you know': aḷugaňḍař eňgee viyya, I realize of course..: ramata kuranii Yahya viyya, it's Y. who tidies up, you know

4295 VIYYAA ވިއްޔާ 1. v. if it be (conditional form of vanii): ehen viyyaa, if so

2. used as an emphasizing particle : mi batugai denii garu raha viyyaa-ee, the taste of this rice is scummy: Mufiidaa ves annaakař nuuḷuunu viyyaa doo, I suppose M. didn't mean to return

4296 VIYYEVE ވިއްޔެވެ v. For vi-eve, past tense of vanii

4297 VIRUVANII ވިރުވަނީ v. melts (tr.): viruvaa baddanii, solders: viruvaa aḷanii, makes a mould; viruvaa aḷaafai hunna hen, like a perfect copy (caus. of virenii)

4298 VIRENII ވިރެނީ v. melts (intr.): (met.) birun virenii, melts with fear: viri kekenii, melts in the fire [S. virenne, Skt. vi-rīyatē]

4299 VILAA ވިލާ n. 1. cloud (vilaa-gaňḍu); vilaa-tak, clouds [S. valā(-kuḷu), Skt. valāhaka]

2. villa, house (in proper names, e.g. Maanduu vilaa) [E. villa]

4300 VILAAT ވިލާތް n. a foreign country, usu. European: Iňgireesi vilaat, England: Turukii v., Turkey: vilaatu miihun, westerners (as v. karaa miihun): vilaatu ata, kind

of custard-apple: v. alui, potato: v. kunnaaru, kind of stone-apple: v. bař̃i, tomato
[U. vilāyat]

4301 VILU ވިލު n. marine pool: vilu nuu, vilu fehi, blue and turquoise colour of such pools: vilu doḷi, edge of such pools [S. vil, Skt. vila]

4302 VILENII ވިލެނީ v. dawns (only used with ali, or as part.): vilee ree, the evening before: Hukuru vilee ree, Thursday evening

4303 VISAA ވިސާ n passport visa [E. visa]

4304 VISNANII ވިސްނަނީ v. thinks, supposes (imp. visnaa ! invol. visnenii, hon. visnavanii (v.n. visnevum), visnavaa-lavvanii): mi vaahaka-ař visnavaa, pondering on these words: e vaa got-takakař visnevum, thinking of what was happening : visnumuge beinum kořfi miihek, a man who uses thought, a sensible man; visnum-teriin (pl.), wise people

4305 VISSANII ވިއްސަނީ v. 1. sprinkles: gayař fen vissaalan, to sprinkle water on the body: vaaree vissenii, spray comes in (invol.): vissi- vihaali vanii, (met.) are scattered, disappear [S. isinne, Skt. siñcati]
2. causes to be born or hatch (caus. of vihanii)

4306 VISSAARA ވިއްސާރަ n. storm rains: vissaara-gañḍu, storm: vissaara-kooṭu, raincoat: vissara-duni, rainbow: vissaara duvahek, a stormy day: vissaara-kam, storminess; vissaara hadatpee, stormclouds have formed [Mal. viśaru or A. i'sār]

4307 VIHA ވިހަ n. poison (usually mild): vihaek kaigen, eating something poisonous : vihaige bees, antiseptic, antidote: (met.) samaasaa viha vegen gos, the joke turning sour: viha-giguni, a plant, crotolaria: viha-dañḍi, area of blood-poisoning; faigai vihadañḍiek jahaigen, having contracted poisoning of the leg: viha-lagoñḍi, a plant, gloriosa superba [S. viha, vaha, Skt. viṣa]

4308 VIHANII ވިހަނީ v. gives birth; hatches (eggs) (v.n. viheum, vihum : caus. vissanii): aharu dekoḷu vihaa miihun, girls who give birth twice in a year
[S. vadanne, Skt. vijāyatē]

4309 VIHAA ވިހާ 1. n. asterism Viśākhā [S. visā]
2. v. bringing forth (pres. part. of vihanii)

4310 VIHAARAKA ވިހާރަކަ n. kind of medicament

4311 VIHAALI ވިހާލި v. In vissi-vihaali vanii, disappears

4312 VIHI (vissek) ވިހި num. 20 : vissakař kudiin, about twenty children; (ifc. - viis , q.v.) [S. visi, Skt. viṃśati]

4313 VIHURUVANII ވިހުރުވަނީ v. scatters, unfurls (flags) (invol. vihuruvenii, vihurenii : v.n. vihuru(vu)m) [S. visuruvanne, Skt. visārayati]

4314 VIHEUM ވިހެއުން v. bringing forth (v.n. of vihanii, as if from form vihavanii)

4315 VIHENII ވިހެނީ v. 1. is born: vihee-ge, a birth (invol. of vihanii, q.v.)

2. fans (abs. vihe): fankaain gayař vihe deeřee, fan (my) body: taṭṭař vihelaa, fanning the saucer ; vihee fař, tasselled fringe on fan or canopy [Skt. vījati]

4316 VII ވީ v. became (p.p. and past tense of vanii; see also vi): ..vii taa, since it was: tiya vii kiik hee, what happened to you? vii nuviiek neeňgi, without any explanation: viimaa, therefore (when it was so)
[S. vū, Skt. bhūta]

4317 VIIDANII ވީދަނީ v. tears, destroys; breaks off (branch) (invol. viidenii) [Skt. vijjhāyati]

4318 VIIRAANAA KURANII ވީރާނާ ކުރަނީ v. causes to crumble away (lit. and met.) [U. vīrāna, a desolation]

4319 VIIRU (pl. viirun) ވީރު n. (lit.) strong man : ekkaři v., strong man without individual bones [Skt. vīra]

4320 VIILLANII ވީއްލަނީ v. sets free, lets go: doroořin at viillanii, lets go of the gate: at viillaa ukaa ecceti, things thrown away: rooda v., breaks the fast: keeta viillaifi, the eclipse ended: (invol.) duuni viillenii, birds fly away : vaziifaain viillenii, is relieved of his post: atun viillijje, slipped out of one's hand

4321 VIIS ވީސް 1. n. ifc. for vihi : ekaaviis, 21:baaviis, 22 etc.
2. v. would have been (vii + -s)

4322 VUM ވުން v. becoming (v.n. of vanii) [S. vīm]

4323 VURE, VUREN ވުރެ - ވުރެން adv. more (than, dat.): eař vure, more than that [cf. S. vaḍā]

4324 VUS ވުސް onom. vus lanii, makes a whizzing sound (cf. vuus, ruus)

4325 VUZAARAA (vuzaaratu) ވުޒާރާ n. Ministry : Vuzaarat ud Daakhiliyyaa, Ministry of Home Affairs (now Minisṭrii of Hoom Efeyarz) [U. vizārat]

4326 VUUS ވޫސް onom. vuus aḷanii, makes a whizzing sound (cf. vus)

4327 VE ވެ v. having become (abs. of vanii); enlarged, ve-gen, ve-fai, ve-lai: aḷugaňḍař ve-daane kamek, a thing I could do: vegen (vaan) vaane gotek, something inevitable: ve-diya tan, the past: kiik ve, kiik vegen, why? ehu ve-denu, gives help in action: with dat. complement, vaziirař vii, became Minister: budakař nuve, not becoming a statue; vegen after inf. represents 'about to', 'trying to', 'because': furan vegen, (because I am) about to sail; ve-eve, becomes (pres. tense); see also vee [S. vī]

4328 VEATU , VEITU ވެއަތު - ވެއިތު See veeti

4329 VEU ވެއު See veyo

4330 VEJJE ވެއްޖެ v. became (See vanii) [S. vecci]

4331 VEṬṬENII ވެއްޓެނީ v. falls down, falls off (of single objects, cf. verenii) [S. väṭenne, ?Skt. vartyatē; see also vaṭṭanii]

4332 VEḌUVUM ވެޑުވުން v. placing (v.n. of vaḍuvanii) [S. väḍīm]

4333 VEDUM ވެދުން n. present to a nobleman: vedum oḍi, the former tribute ship to Colombo: v. kuranii, presents: vedumař aruvanii, offers as a present (hon.) [S. väňdīm, salutation]

4334 VEDE ވެދެ v. having entered (abs. of vannanii: also vade) [S. väda]

4335 VEDDUM ވެއްދުން v. admitting (v.n. of vaddanii) [vannanii; S. väddīm]

4336 VEN ވެން n. conger eel (kaḷu v., black; gaḷi keňḍi v., striped): ven boḷu, kind of bait: van haru, eel hole

4337 VENILAA ވެނިލާ (ވެނީލާ) n. vanilla (also veniilaa) [E. vanilla]

4338 VENNEVUM ވެންނެވުން v. entering (hon.) (v.n. of vannavanii) [vannanii]

4339 VEYO, VEU,VEVU (vevek, veyoge, vevuge) ވެޔޮ - ވެއު - ވެވު n.
'tank', reservoir [S. väv, Skt. vāpi]

4340 VEYO (velek) ވެޔޮ n. creeper (veyo-gaňḍu): veyogaňḍu eḷum, drawing arabesques: veyo-faḷoo, kind of papaw: veyo-bilet, Ceylon betel (with black leaf, as v. Divehi bilet) [S. väl, Skt. vallī]

4341 VERI (pl., verin) ވެރި n. possessor, person in charge (veri miihaa): geege veri, owner of house: atoḷu-veri, atoll chief: veri-kam, regime: veri kujjaa, starter of a game: veri-rař, capital island, capital city; veri kuranii, puts in charge: hitař veri vefai, obsessive: veri ve-gatum, becoming a ruler; veriin kuravvaanii raňgaḷařee, what our rulers do is right (prov.); much used as an adjectival suffix, e.g. ilmu-veri, ufaa-veri, kuř-veri, diin-veri, dekoḷu-veri, nuus-veri, milku-veri, śukru-veri (cf. also -vehi)

4342 VERI ވެރި v. fallen (abs. of verenii)

4343 VERENII ވެރެނި v. spills over (intr.)(caus. veruvanii): fen verenii, water spills: miihunař verenii, males ejaculate; falls (of numbers of things together, cf. veṭṭenii): baňbukeyo v., breadfruits fall: fii fan v., rotted leaves fall (invol. of varanii)

4344 VELAŇBULI (velaňbuyyek, velaňbuliyek) ވެލަނބުލި n.
a medicament, cassytha filiformis

4345 VELAA (-aek) ވެލާ n. edible turtle (as v. kahaňbu)

4346 VELAANAA ވެލާނާ n. a former royal official

4347 VELI (veyyek) ވެލި n. sand: veyyař vamun danii, turns to rubble, crumbles: veli lanii, applies fresh sand: v. bannanii, ties sand round cuttings; veli-gaňḍu, sandy area: veli-fař, sandy shore; develi-(fen)fař,where white and black sand adjoin: veli-foti, kind of coral sand, sequins made in that shape: veli-maḍi, kind of stingray, pleuronectiformes: veli-ran, gold dust: kaři veli, coarse sand [S. väli, Skt. vālukā]

4348 VEVU ވެވު See veyo

4349 VEVENII ވެވެނި v. is able to be done (by.., dat.): aharemennař vevee konmne <u>kh</u>idmatakii, any service we can render: fiyavaḷek naaḷaa veveekař net kam, inability to avoid taking steps: baiveri veveen tibi hurihaa firihenun, all the males who could participate: boḍu veveen ot enme boḍu minvaru, the highest possible amount : vevunum, possible occurrence (invol. of vanii)

4350 VES ވެސް enclitic particle, sometimes alternating with -me: also, even; ma-ves, I too: adi oḷu ves kukuḷekeve, it's a tame hen too: nu-ves nidee, can't even sleep;

konme hen ves, konmes, somehow or other; used also with verbs, nai nama ves, even if (he) doesn't come

4351 VES-NUU ވެސްނޫ n. washing 'blue' [E. wash + Maldivian]

4352 VESSANII ވެއްސަނި v. makes to rain (caus. of vehenii)

4353 VEHANII ވެހަނި v. knits around: ruňbaa roonun vehanii, surrounds jar with casing of rope

4354 VEHAALI ވެހާލި n. embryonic stem in coconut flower

4355 -VEHI -ވެހި adjectival suffix : kam- vehi, practical: ge-vehi, domestic: rař-vehi, local (cf. also -veri)

4356 VEHI-MAS ވެހިމަސް n. a class of lagoon fish

4357 VEHUM-GAŇḌU ވެހުންގަނޑު n. rope casing round glass buoy or jar: kind of fried cake wrapped in leaves (v.n. of vehanii)

4358 VEHENII ވެހެނި v. (it) rains (caus. vessanii): vaare vehenii, it is raining: vissaara vehenii, there's a rainstorm [S. vahinne, Skt. varṣati]

4359 VEŘUM ވެރުން v. twisting (v.n. of vařanii)

4360 VEE ވޭ v. pres. tense (ve-eve) or imp. of vanii: adi-ves e kamtak vee too balaařee, try again and see if you still can; vee-ve(e), while being: veeve huri kam, (gram.) incomplete verbal tense form, e.g. danii, annanii [S. vē, ve-vī, cf. P. hōti]

4361 VEETI (VEATU, VEITU) KURANII ވޭތި (ވެއަތު - ވެއިތު) ކުރަނި v. spends, passes (time): v. vanii, (time) passes. Also in form faaitu kuranii [U. faut]

4362 VEEN ވޭން n. great pain (esp. of labour pains): veen-varu, wave of pain; veenvaru naganii, pains come [?Skt. vēdanā]

4363 VEE-MUI (veemuyek) ވޭމުއި n. a minty medicinal root, liquorice, glycyrrhiza glabra: veemui sarubatu, cough syrup [S. välmī]

4364 VEERU-HULI (BEERU-HULI) ވޭރުހުލި (ބޭރުހުލި) n. a slow-flying burrowing insect

4365 VEELAA ވޭލާ n. time, usu. in form e-veelaa, (of) ancient times [S. velā, Skt. vēlā]

4366 VOṬṬEK ވޮއްޓެއް See voři

4367 VOḌIGEN ވޮޑިގެން v. abs. used in highest honorifics: voḍigen-vanii, exists (of God): voḍigatum, sitting, being: used also as second member in compound verbs, ruhi-voḍigen, approving: assavaa-voḍigen, listening:kutt̲an ve-voḍigen vaa, immanent (of God)

4368 VOḌENII ވޮޑެނީ v. gets deposited (of sand)

4369 VOḌ-ḌUNI (voḍḍunñek) ވޮއްޑުނި n. bow (to shoot)

4370 VOŘ ވޮށް n . large hanging metal oil-lamp, usu. with many wicks, now obsolete: ibc., general word for 'lighting': vořu teyo, lighting fuel: voř añdiri, pitch dark [old S. väṭa]

4371 VOŘI (voṭṭek) ވޮށި n. circular frame or rim, esp. of the ear (voři-fař); also of tambourines, or of frames for embroidery (maa jahaa voři); ifc. in kamu-voři, important (of people)

4372 VOŘI-FILAA (VOŘU-FILAA) ވޮށިފިލާ (ވޮށުފިލާ) n. sandboard (for infants' schooling) [cf. S. väli-piḷa]

4373 VOŘI-MAS ވޮށިމަސް n. kind of fish, dogtooth tuna, gymnosarda unicolor : vořimas-miyaru, kind of shark, isurus oxyrhinchus

4374 VOOṬU ވޯޓު n. vote: v. denii, votes (by hand): v. lanii, votes (by ballot) [E. vote]

4375 VOORAA ވޯރާ n. Borah, Gujarati merchants formerly prominent in Male [H. bōhrā, Skt. vyavahāraka]

ސ SIINU, the 17th letter of the Maldivian alphabet

Siinu atoḷu, Aḍḍu atoll, the 17th atoll from the north

4376 -S -ސް suffix used of potentiality after past-tense verbs: viis (lit., viiheve), would have been; or of temporal priority after negated incomplete forms, nu-daniis, before going, iru noossuniis, before sunset

4377 SA- ސަ- num. (anc., mod. ha-) six (used ibc.): satiriis, 36 (= tiriis haek): sayaaḷiis, 46 (= hataḷis haek): savanna, 56 (=fansaas haek): sahaṭṭi, 66 (= fasdoḷas haek): sahattari, 76 (=hatdiha haek): sayaahi, 86 (= ar̃ḍiha haek): sayaanavai, 96 (= nuvadiha haek) [S. sa-, Skt. ṣaṭ; cf. H. chattīs, chiyālīs, chappan, chiyāsaṭh, chihattar, chiyāsī, chiyānvē]

4378 SAI ސައި 1. n. tea: brewed tea, with sugar: sai-fat, tea leaf; saifatu fen, tea without sugar: kiru-sai, tea with milk: sai-eti (usu. pej.), cup of tea: sai-fodu, cup of tea (hon.): sai-kuraa, kettle (i.e. teapot); Saikuraa- ge, ancient name of Husnuu-ge: sai-jooḍu, cup and saucer: varugada sai-paaṭii, big tea-party: sai-maa, shoeflower, hibiscus rosa-sinensis; sai hadanii, makes tea: sai aḷanii, pours tea: saikuraa kakkaalum, boiling the kettle [U. cā]

4379 SAI ސައި 2. excl. used in chess: sai kiyanii, calls 'Check!' (pron.. sssai!) [U. śāh]

4380 SAITAANU ސައިތާނު n. Satan [U. śaiṯān]

4381 SAIPOOṬ ސައިޕޯޓް n. sideboard [E. sideboard]

4382 SAIBOONI ސައިބޯނި n. soap, cake of soap [U. s̲ābūn, Port. sabao]

4383 ŚAUGUVERI-KAM ޝައުގުވެރިކަން n. eagerness [U. śauq-]

4384 SAUTUVERI-KAM ސައުތުވެރިކަން n. rivalry [H. saut, co-wife, Skt. sapatnī]

4385 SAUDA ސައުދަ See saada [H. caudah, cf. old S. tudus]

4386 SAURA- ސައުރަ- num. ibc. plus four (in compound numbers): sauratiriis, 34 (= tiriis hatarek): saurayaaḷiis, 44 (= hataḷis hatarek): sauravanna, 54 (= fansaas hatarek): saurahaṭṭi, 64 (= fasdoḷas hatarek): saurahattari, 74 (= hatdiha hatarek): saurayaahi, 84 (= ar̃ḍiha hatarek): saurayaanavai, 94 (= nuvadiha hatarek)
[S. hataru-, Skt. catur-; cf. H.cauṃtīs, cavālīs, cauvan, cauṃsaṭh, cauhattar, caurāsī, caurānve]

4387 SAUVIIS ސައުވީސް 1. num. 24 [H. caubīs, Skt. caturviṃśati]

4388 SAUVIIS ސައުވީސް 2. n. In sauviis kuranii, serves (in games) [E. service]

4389 SAKA ސަކަ n. joke : jocular (saka miihek): s. kuranii, makes jokes: s. kuruvanii, makes to laugh: s. jahanii, larks about (esp. of children)

4390 SAKARAAT ސަކަރާތް n. making jokes (pej. of adults): s. jahanii, jokes; flirts: s. gannanii, jokes; sakaraat nugen, without larking about [?U. sakarāt, fainting]

4391 SAKUMAKU ސަކުމަކު n. locking wedge

4392 ŚAKUVAA ޝަކުވާ n. complaint, grumble: ś. kuranii, complains [U. śakvā]

4393 SAKKU ސައްކު n. doubt : sakku laa raddek net, there is no room for doubt: Naadiyaa-ař sakku vaa got meduveri nukuraati, don't let N. suspect (anything) [U. śak]

4394 SAK-KEYO (sakkeelek) ސައްކެޔޮ n. jakfruit, artocarpus heterophyllus [T. cakkai]

4395 SAŇGALAA JEHENII ސަންގަލާ ޖެހެނީ v. gets twisted up, coiled up

4396 SAJIDA JAHANII ސަޖިދަ ޖަހަނީ v. touching all requisite parts in religious prostration [U. sijda]

4397 SAṬANI ސަޓަނި n. chutney [H. caṭnī]

4398 SAḌU ސަޑު n. tail of a rocket; wavy hair of women: s. hadanii, adopts such hairstyle

4399 SATARI ސަތަރި n. awning, tarpaulin [U. satrī]

4400 SATARU ސަތަރު n. very large royal kite (sataru-koḷu): s. ellavanii, (hon.) flies such kite

4401 SATAA- ސަތާ- num. ibc., plus seven (in compound numbers): sataaviis (mod. hataaviis) 27: sataaḷiis, 47 (=hataḷis hatek): sataahi, 87 (= ařḍiha hatek): sataanavai, 97 (= nuvadiha hatek) [cf. H.sattāīs, saiṃtālīs, sattāsī, sattānavē]

4402 SATAARA ސަތާރަ num. seventeen [cf. H. satrah, P. sattarasa, old S. sataḷos]

4403 SATAAVARII, SATAAVARU ސަތާވަރީ - ސަތާވަރު n. kind of creeper [H. satāvar]

4404 SATU- ސަތު- num. ibc., plus seven (in compouind numbers): satutiriis, 37 (= tiriis hatek): satuvanna, 57 (= fansaas hatek): satuhaṭṭi, 67 (= fasdoḷas hatek): satuhattari, 77 (= hatdiha hatek) [cf. H. saiṃtīs, sattāvan, sarsaṭh, sat-hattar]

4405 SATEEKA ސަތޭކަ num. one hundred: sateekain sateeka-ař, 100 % : sateekaekka, about 100 [cf. Skt. śatam]

4406 SATTA ސައްތަ num. (anc.) one hundred: (mod.) ifc. in ona-satta, 99: dui-satta, 200

4407 SADAGAAT ސަދަގާތް n. alms [U. sadqa]

4408 SADABU ސަދަބު n. 1. lead holder for burner of hookah
2. in adabu-sadabu, manner (doublet)

4409 SAŇDARA-BOLI ސަނދަރަބޮލި n. kind of sea snail

4410 SAŇDU-BARAKA ސަނދުބަރަކަ n. flower resembling a marigold, tagetes erecta

4411 SAŇDUVAA ސަނދުވާ n. canopy suspended from the ceiling over bed or aři ; s. damanii, spreads the canopy

4412 SANADU ސަނަދު n . certificate (non-medical) [U. sanad]

4413 SANAA-MUGU ސަނާމުގު n. chickpea, cicer arietinum [H. canā , Skt. caṇaka + mugu]

4414 SANGU ސަންގު n. conchshell: s. govvanii, s. fumenii, blows conch [S. sak, Skt. śaṃkha]

4415 SANTI-MARIYAŇBU ސަންތި މަރިޔަނބު n. name of a mythical female who comes with a lame child and fixes adult teeth

4416 SANDARUUS ސަންދަރޫސް n. sandarach resin [U. sandarōs]

4417 SANDOOK ސަންދޯކް n. coffin : s. jahanii, makes coffin: sandooku aḷanii, puts in coffin (hon., sandookpuḷu) ; cf. also sunduuk [U. sandūq]

4418 SANNEṬI (SANNAṬI) ސަންނެޓި (ސަންނަޓި) n. a breadfruit curry

4419 SANFAA, SANPAA ސަންފާ - ސަންޕާ n. kind of banana (sanpaa-keyo, gor̃-sanpaa); gul sanpaa, a fragrant tree, michelia campaka or frangipani, plumeria: SANPA is also used as a female nickname [H. campa, Skt. campaka]

4420 SANBOOSAA (-aaek) ސަންބޫސާ n. a savoury pastry [U. sambūsa]

4421 SAFARI ސަފަރި n. kind of citrus fruit [U. safarī]

4422 SAFARU ސަފަރު n. third sail of a schooner: Safaru Katda, a mythical female being who grants capricious favours

4423 SAFIIRU ސަފީރު n. ambassador [U. safīr]

4424 SAFU ސަފު n. row, line: s. hadanii, (of soldiers) falls in; safugai tibi, in parade order: safu safar̃, in lines ; safun (lit.), at all [U. s̱af]

4425 SAFEEDU ސަފޭދު n. whitewash, whiting [U. safēd]

4426 SAPPU ސަޕްޕު n. the thirteenth blow in games such as bon̈ḍi, bar̃i, manḍi, played facing the players : s. jahanii, gives the 13th blow (used also for a kick in football)

4427 SAPLAI / SAPLAA ސަޕްލައި / ސަޕްލާ n. supply (usu. of electricity): s. lanii, s.kuranii, supplies (electricity) [E. supply]

4428 SABABU ސަބަބު n. reason: sababek ovegen, for some reason: eenaage sababun, because of him [U. sabab]

4429 SABUDELI ސަބުދެލި n. woodapple, achras sapota [E. sapodilla]

4430 SABBIIS ސަބްބީސް num. 26 [H. chabbīs, Skt. ṣaḍviṃśati]

4431 SABBU ސަބްބު n. a chemical imported in waxy lumps, used for cleaning metal or for gluing, alum: sabbu fenu kakkaalum, dipping in solution of s.: sabbu or̃, cleaning material; (met.) a hairless man [U. śabb]

4432 SAMAT̲T̲ARU ސަމަތްތަރު n. shape

4433 SAMAA(-aek) ސަމާ n. (obs.) extraordinary royal festival: s. annanii, festival arrives: s. kuḷenii, celebrates festival: s. gennanii, announces festival [? U. samāẖat, benevolence]

4434 SAMAALU ސަމާލު n. attention, alertness: samaalugai hunnanii, keeps alert: samaalu-kam denii, pays attention (to.., dat.): samaalu vanii, is attentive

4435 SAMAAVARU ސަމާވަރު n. water urn, samovar [Russian, samovar]

4436 SAMAASAA (-aek) ސަމާސާ n. practical joke: s. kuranii, plays practical jokes: samaasa-veri, joker: samaasaa viha danii, the joke turns sour [?U. tamāśā]

4437 SAMUGAA ސަމުގާ n. mariner's compass : s. maagaňḍu, north mark on compass: samugaage dekunu daňḍi, south mark on compass

4438 SAMUSAA (samusalek) ސަމުސާ n. spoon: nai-boli s., serving spoon for sweets or batpen, made from nautilus or in that shape: batař laa s., serving spoon for rice: riha-ař laa s., curry spoon: sai (boo) s., teaspoon [H. camcā]

4439 SAMEEDAAN ސަމީދާން n. candlestick [U. śama'dān]

4440 SAYAAHI ސަޔާހި num. 86 (= ařdiha haek) [H. chāyāsī, Skt. ṣaḍaśīti]

4441 SARAKA ސަރަކަ n. winding wheel (bigger than firooři): arimatii saraka buruma, drill with side-wheel [Skt. cakra]

4442 SARAŇGU ސަރަނގު n. bosun, man in charge of welfare of crew on foreign-going vessels [U. sar-hang]

4443 SARANFII ސަރަންފީ n. long easy chair (s. goňḍi)

4444 SARAFOOS ސަރަފޯސް n. metal lid of cooking pot [U. sarpōs]

4445 ŚARAHA ޝަރަހަ n. commentary: ś. kuranii, gives commentary [U. śaraẖ]

4446 SARAHADDU ސަރަހައްދު n. frontier , boundary [U. sarẖad]

4447 SARAASARU ސަރާސަރު adj. vast; as adv., unobstructedly [U. sarāsar]

4448 SARIKU ސަރިކު num. times four (in Navata multiplication tables: sa sariku sauviis, 6 x 4= 24)

4449 SARIDAALEES ސަރިދާލީސް n. royal throne

4450 SARIYAT ސަރިޔަތް n. legal trial: maaraamaariige s. kuranii, holds trial for assault: s. hinganii, brings a case [U. śar'īat]

4451 ŚARIIK ޝަރީކު n. partner with God, 'mediator' [U. śarīk]

4452 SARUKAARU ސަރުކާރު n. Government : sarukaaru lakuḍi, reserved timber (such as funa, kaani, heleňbeli) [U. sarkār]

4453 SARUJANU ސަރުޖަނު n. sergeant of Customs [E. serjeant]

4454 SARUDAARU (pl., sarudaarun) ސަރުދާރު n. foreman, headman (formerly in each avař below the avařuveri; nowadays in the army, sifainge sarudaaru): sarudaaru-kam, office of foreman; sarudaaraa (obs.) female headwoman in the royal palace; boḍu s., a very large ant [U. sardār]

4455 SARUBATU ސަރުބަތު n. sherbet, syrup; cool drink [U. śarbat]

4456 SARUBII ސަރުބީ n. fat (usu. of animals) [U. carbī]

4457 ŚARTU ޝަރުތު n. condition; stipulation [U. śarṯ]

4458 SALAVAAT ސަލަވާތް n. benedictions: salavaatu tař, large serving dish : salavaatař vat kuranii, serves a special dish to the imam ofthe feast [U. s̱alvāt]

4459 SALAA MISRII ސަލާ މިސްރީ n. See saalaa Misurii

4460 SALAAM ސަލާމް n. greetings; regards: s. kuranii, greets: s. fonuvanii, declines an invitation (aḷugaňḍu salaam, I don't wish to): ofiihař s. bunum, sending a sick note to the office: ma-vaa salaam, not me! salaam jahaa miihun, beggars (more politely, salaam dee miihun): salaam levvi, Blessed; gaumii s., national anthem [U. salām]

4461 SALAAMAT ސަލާމަތް n. safety, protection: s. kuranii, protects: s. vanii, escapes safely; salaamat kam, safety: s. haalu, condition of security [U. salāmat]

4462 SALAAMATI (salaamaccek) ސަލާމަތި n. 1.kind of thick rope: s. lanii, uses a thick hawser: s. aḷanii, plaits a thick rope 2. a kind of royal music

4463 SALIIBU ސަލީބު n. Christian cross [U. s̲alīb]

4464 SALLAA KURANII ސައްލާ ކުރަނީ v. holds discussions: kamakaa sallaaek koř̌fai, having discussed a point; makes plots

4465 SALLI ސައްލި n. in salli damanii, passes something in a chain: salli bahaṭṭanii, works a rota

4466 SAVANNA ސަވަންނަ num. 56 (= fansaas haek)
[cf. H. chappan, Skt. ṣaṭpañcāśat]

4467 SAVAA (savalek) ސަވާ n. rope which holds the mast

4468 SAVAABU ސަވާބު n. blessings of God [U.t̲h̲avāb]

4469 SAVAARII ސަވާރީ n. beast of burden [U. savārī]

4470 SAVAARU ސަވާރު n. sitting on, riding: koňḍu maccař s. kuranii, gives a pickaback ride: as maccař s. vanii, rides a horse [U. savār]

4471 SAZAA ސަޒާ n. just rewards, punishment [U. sazā]

4472 SAHAṬṬI ސަހައްޓި num. 66 (= fasdoḷas haek) [cf. H. chayāsaṭh, Skt. ṣaṭśaṣṭi]

4473 SAHARAA ސަހަރާ n. cemetery [U. s̲ah̲rā, desert]

4474 SAHARU ސަހަރު n. small town [U. śahr]

4475 SAHAROO ސަހަރޯ excl. of distress or astonishment: aňhaa saharoo, oh alas! kobaa, saharoo hiive? are you surprised ? (= I told you so)

4476 SAHALU ސަހަލު adj. reliable, affable (of people); pleasant (of places): sahalu rařek, a pleasant island: nu-sahalu, intolerable [U. sahl, easy]

4477 ŚAHAADAT ޝަހާދަތް n. witnessing to Islam: ś. kiyanii, declares There is no God but God & c. : śahaadat iňgili, forefinger; second toe [U. śahādat]

4478 ŚAHIIDU ޝަހީދު n. martyr: s. marek, sudden accidental death; s. vanii, sacrifices oneself [U. śahīd]

4479 SAḶI ސަޅި adj. boastful: s. kaňḍanii, boasts

4480 SAAGU ސާގު n. sago: saagu fani, a kind of soft drink: saagu boňḍibat, sago pudding [H. sāgū, from Malay]

4481 SAAṬANU ސާޓަނު n. satin [E. satin]

4482 SAATU ސާތު num. seven (in Navata tables: saatu tiin das, 7 + 3=10)

4483 SAADA (SAUDA) ސާދަ (ސައުދަ) num. fourteen: saada vilee ree, the evening of the 13th day [cf. H. caudah, Skt. caturdaśa]

4484 SAADAA ސާދާ adj. simple, plain: teyoguḷaa saadaa kuranii, builds castles in the air : (adv.) saadaa koř, clearly [U. sāda]

4485 ŚAADII ޝާދީ n. (lit.) wedding : ś. kuranii, weds [U. śādī]

4486 SAANIYAA (-aek) ސާނިޔާ n. second of latitude [U. thāniya]

4487 SAANTI (saancek) ސާންތި n. woven mat without pattern (thick cross-weave, esp. from Bileffahi island)

4488 SAAFU ސާފު adj. clean; clear (of skies): s. kuranii, cleans; (of yards) weeds: khabaru s. kuranii, checks the news; saafu teo, s. mařiteo, kerosene, 'clear' (colourless) oil: muunu saafu, with smooth face [U.sāf]

4489 SAABAS (saabahek) ސާބަސް n. praise: saabahuge bas, words of praise: kaleař saabas! oh well done (sometimes sarcastic), bless you (referring to accidents): saabasfuḷu, (to a nobleman) well done! saabas denii, gives praise [U. śābāś]

4490 SAABITU ސާބިތު adj. proved: saabitu miihek, a trustworthy or dedicated man: saabitu-kam, proof; reason; perseverance; s. kuranii, proves, shows forth [U. thābit]

4491 SAAMARAA ސާމަރާ n. 1. 'chamara' fan: s. duuni, peacock [S. cāmara]

2. heavy club for stunning sharks

4492 SAAMAANU ސާމާނު n. goods, chattels : vaḍaam saamaan, carpenter's tools [U. sāmān]

4493 ŚAAMU ޝާމު n. Syria [U. Śām]

4494 SAAMOORU ސާމޫރު n. pulley block on mast

4495 SAARI ސާރި num. four (in Navata tables: tiin eeku saari, 3 + 1 = 4)

4496 SAARIDOOḶU ސާރިދޫޅު n. bear (not found in Maldives)

4497 SAALAA MISURII (SALAAMISRII) ސާލާ މިސުރީ (ސަލާމިސްރީ) n. a plant, orchis latifolia [U. tha'lab Misrī]

4498 SAALU ސާލު n. thin embroidered blanket, 'shawl' (suspended from the ceiling after circumcisions): uduhee s., flying carpet [U. śāl, cf. E. shawl]

4499 SAALLAA ސާއްލާ n. rogue: eii boḍu saallaaek, he is a great rogue [?H. sālā, brother-in-law]

4500 SAAS-KAFU ސާސްކަފު n. 1000 years, millennium [saas = haas; S. kap, epoch , Skt. kalpa]

4501 SAAHIBU ސާހިބު n. master : saahibu miihaa, the boss: ma-saahibu, your Majesty (way to address the king): maat saahibaa, the Prophet: saahib ul rif'at, title taken by Ibrahim Ali Didi in the 1950s [U. sāhib]

4502 SAAḶAŇGA ސާޅަނގަ n. catapult or sling

4503 SAAḶI ސާޅި n. saree [H. sāṛī, Skt. śāṭī]

4504 SAAḶIIS (saaḷiihek) ސާޅީސް num. 40: eenaa-aṙ saaḷiis vejje, it is the 40th day after his death (or after her delivery): saaḷiihaṙ fen aḷanii, washes ceremonially on the 40th day after childbirth [H. cālīs, cf. Skt. catvāriṃśat]

4505 SIKANTI ސިކަންތި n. former ceremonial javelin

4506 SIKAARA ސިކާރަ n. hunting: the quarry: s. kuranii, hunts (high hon., s. hippavanii) [U. śikār]

4507 SIKAARA KURANII / SIKAARU KURANII ސިކާރަ ކުރަނީ -

ސިކާރަ ކުރަނީ v. fills up: baňḍu s. koř̌gen, having filled the belly: furi sikaara vefaa, being full

4508 SIKUŇḌI ސިކުނޑި n. brain : s. hikifai, sikuňḍiigai tetkamek net, the brain is dried up, one is not thinking properly

4509 SIKUNTU (SUKUNTU) ސިކުންތު (ސުކުންތު) n. second (of time) [Port. secundo]

4510 SIKKA ސިއްކަ n. seal: stamped coin or medal; Sikkage, the old mint: Kaḷu Sikka, 'Black Label' (an old kind of thread); sikka jahanii, applies a state seal (as v. takgaňḍu); coins money [U. sikka]

4511 SIGIREṬ, SIGEREṬ, SIŇGIREṬ, SIGIREEṬU ސިގިރެޓް - ސިގެރެޓް - ސިނގިރެޓް - ސިގިރީޓު n. cigarette [E. cigarette]

4512 SIŇGU ސިނގު adj. emaciated and swollen-bellied: siňgu- baňḍu , with swollen belly (usu.of sick children) [S. siňgu, thin]

4513 SIṬII ސިޓީ n. letter, epistle: kuḍa s., a wartime government IOU: lakuḍi s., a coupon to serve as official IOU; s. duu kuranii, issues such coupon; kamakař s. lanii, applies in writing for a post [H. ciṭṭhī]

4514 SIḌII ސިޑީ n. stairs; gangway: siḍiin laafai, by the stairway [H. siṛhī]

4515 SITTI ސިއްތި n. feminine equivalent of Siidi (sayyid)

4516 SIDURIYAA (-aaek) ސިދުރިޔާ n. (anc.) Turkish waistcoat or cloak [U. sadrī]

4517 SINA- ސިނަ adj. Chinese: sina asduuni, kind of duck: sina fat, cigarette tobacco; as n. (pl.) Sinain , (anc.)the Chinese (mod., Cainaa miihun) [Skt. Cīna; cf. also siinu]

4518 SINA-FAT ސިނަފަތް n. cigarette tobacco

4519 SINGALU ސިންގަލު adj. single: singalu foti, single-thickness cloth [E. single]

4520 SINGAḶA ސިންގަޅަ n. Sinhalese [S. Siṇhaḷa]

4521 SINGAA (-aaek) ސިންގާ n. lion (not found in Maldives); ifc. huge: boḍu-singaa, maa-singaa, huge [S. siṇha]

4522 SINGAASANAA(-aek) ސިންގާސަނާ n. royal throne [S. & Skt., siṇhāsana]

4523 SIFA ސިފަ n. shape; characteristic quality; eige sifa bayaan kuranii, describes it: eige sifa jassanii, makes model of it, copies it: eař sifa genaum, providing a model for it [U. sifat]

4524 SIFAIN ސިފައިން n. (pl.) soldiers: enme sifainnekme, every soldier [U. sipāhī]

4525 SIMAAGU ސިމާގު n. name of two compass directions: s. astamaan, W.N.W.: s. iiraan, E.N.E. [U. simāk, Arcturus]

4526 SIMENTI ސިމެންތި n. imported cement: faarugai s. jahanii, applies cement with a trowel, renders: s. lanii, applies cement with a brush: ṭinugai simenti lum, covering the rust marks on corrugated iron: simentin / simenti laigen reenum, bricklaying (in coral stone) [S. simenti, cf. E. cement]

4527 SIYARATU ސިޔަރަތު n. stories about the Prophet [U.sīrat]

4528 SIYAASA ސިޔާސަ adj. naughty: siyaasa kujjek, a naughty boy: siyaasayas, though (he) be naughty

4529 SIYAASATU ސިޔާސަތު n. politics; policy: siyaasataa behenii, meddles in politics, plots against or criticizes the Government ; adj. siyaasii: siyaasii guḷum, diplomatic relations [U. siyāsat]

4530 SIRUVALU ސިރުވަޅު n. a square in the game of pacis : in carrom, the part behind the line

4531 SIRRU ސިއްރު n. secret; real cause: sababaai sirrek kamugai, as the reason and real cause: Naadiyaa-ař sirrun, unknown to N.: sirraai fauḷugai, privately and publicly: Kaatib-us-Sirru, the King's private secretary; bas sirru kuranii, conceals what was said; sirru-veri, confidential [U. sirr]

4532 SILAVARU ސިލަވަރު n. See silvaru

4533 SILIŇBU ސިލިނބު n. See siluňbu

4534 SILU ސިލު n. seal: s. jahanii, seals up, applies seal (to, ..-gai) [E. seal]

4535 SILUŇBU, SILIŇBU ސިލުނބު (ސިލިނބު) n. burner of hookah [U. cilam]

4536 SILUVARU ސިލުވަރު n. See silvaru

4537 SILUVAANU ސިލުވާނު n. punishment formerly given for pestering other men's wives: s. kuranii, gives such punishment

4538 SILEEHA ސިލޭހަ n. lance [U. silāh]

4539 SILLI ސިއްލި n. a direction (l5th from the north)

4540 SILVARU (SILUVARU, SILAVARU) ސިލްވަރު (ސިލުވަރު - ސިލަވަރު) n. silver-plating [E. silver]

4541 SILSILAA ސިލްސިލާ n. series [U. silsila, and cf. hilihilaa]

4542 SISSANII ސިއްސަނީ v. startles : (enlarged) sissuvaa-li kamtakgaňḍu, a disturbing incident, hullabaloo (caus. of sihenii)

4543 SIHURU ސިހުރު n. bad magic: s. hadanii, employs black magic [U. sihr]

4544 SIHENII ސިހެނީ v. is timid; has nightmares : sihum huri, timid: kulli sihumek, a sudden start or shiver; caus., sissanii, q.v.

4545 SIHHATU ސިއްހަތު n. health: mahkamat us sihhaa, Department of Health [U. sihhat]

4546 SII ސީ n. stools (childish, acci): s. lanii, defecates (= boḍu-kamu dani); s. levijje, automatic loose motion occurred: sii lavaigatiimaa,when one feels the urge to defecate: hama s. lanii, has permanent loose motions; s.- tafaa, lump of excrement : sii-valu, a nickname

4547 SIIṬU- FOTI ސީޓު ފޮޓި n. striped or multicoloured cloth for chairs etc. : siiṭu-maa, flowers of differing colours as a result of grafting [? E. seat]

4548 SIIDAA (siidalek) ސީދާ adj. straight; vertical; parallel: siidaa magu, straight path (also met., in religious sense): huvafen siidaa vanii, dream comes true; adv., siidalař diyum, going straight [H. sīdhā, Skt. siddhaka]

4549 SIIDI ސީދި n. a name, Sayyid (fem.Sitti): siidi firihenek, a womanlike man

4550 SIIN ސީން n. (childish) pancake ('sizzler'): siin lanii, makes sizzling noise [onom.]

4551 SIINA BADAM ސީނަ ބަދަން n. ground nut

4552 SIINU ސީނު n. 1. the letter S in the Arabic and Maldivian alphabets: Siinu atoḷu, Addu atoll; boḍu siinu, the letter Ś: siinu dati, mousetrap
2. ibc., Chinese: Siinu kara, China: siinu taři, china dish [cf. sina]

4553 SIIRAA KURANII ސީރާ ކުރަނީ v. preserves (fish or food): siiraa aḷanii, dips in preservative; siiraa eḷi mas, canned fish [? U. sīrā, cold]

4554 SIIRI(Y)AS ސީރިއަސް - ސީރިޔަސް adj. (of diseases) grave [E. serious]

4555 SIISAN ސީސަން n. an imported hard white timber (s.vakaru), dalbergia sisu [H. sīsoṃ]

4556 SIISI (HIISI) ސީސި (ހީސި) n. (childish) penis

4557 SUKUNTU (SIKUNTU) ސުކުންތު (ސިކުންތު) n. second (of time) [Port. secundo]

4558 SUKUN ސުކުން n. virāma sign used over consonants: used over alifu to double the following consonant; taa sukun, the letter t̲ with sukun, i.e. without a vowel [U. sukūn, cessation]

4559 ŚUKURIYYAA ޝުކުރިއްޔާ excl. thanks! [U. śukrīya, gratitude]

4560 ŚUKURU ޝުކުރު n. thanks; śukuru-veri, grateful: śukuruveri vanii, is grateful (used in writing): śukuru dannavanii (resp.), gives verbal thanks: ś. kuranii, gives thanks; libee minvarař śukuru kuraařee (prov.), be content with what you have [U. śukr]

4561 SUŇGUḶI- MUŇGUḶI ސުނގުޅި މުނގުޅި n. jumble of objects, junk (doublet)

4562 SUJJAADU-KOḶU ސުއްޖާދުކޮޅު n. (anc.) the royal prayer mat [U. sajjāda]

4563 SUṬṬAA (-aaek) ސުއްޓާ n. cigar [S. suruṭṭu, T. curuṭṭu]

4564 SUTULI ސުތުލި n. jute fibre (for sacking): s. barani, twine: s. foti, inferior kind of silk [H. sutlī, cf. Skt. sūtra]

4565 SUDDAANU ސުއްދާނު n. excrement from a corpse: s. hifanii, stops discharging excrement: s. nuhifenii, continues to discharge

4566 SUNAARU (pl., sunaarun) ސުނާރު n. goldsmith (anc.): s.- kaleege, goldsmith [H. sunār, Skt. svarṇakāra]

4567 SUNDUUK ސުންދޫކް n. chest: in amiin us sunduuq, former lost property office ; cf. also sandook [U. s̱undūq]

4568 SUNNAT ސުންނަތް n. correct religious observances [U. sunnat]

4569 SUNNAAFATI KURANII ސުންނާފަތި ކުރަނީ v. destroys [H. sanāpat, massacre]

4570 SUNPAA ސުންޕާ adj. unlucky, ill-omened (of people or things, s. miihun, s. kamtak)

4571 SUNBULI (sunbuyyek) ސުންބުލި n. bag, esp. Umaru s., invisible cornucopia (in Hamza story)

4572 SUFURAA ސުފުރާ n. cloth for dinner table [U. sufra]

4573 SUŇBE ސުނބެ v. in uňbe suňbe, kissing amorously (doublet) [see uňbunanii]

4574 SUM ސުން n. zero [H. sun, Skt. śūnya]

4575 SURUKAA HUT ސުރުކާ ހުތް n. imported vinegar [U. sirka]

4576 SURUMUTI ސުރުމުޓި n. small hawk, kestrel

4577 SURUVAA (-vaaek) ސުރުވާ n. thin soup [U. suruvā]

4578 SURUHII ސުރުހީ n. title, headline [U. sur<u>kh</u>ī, red ink]

4579 SULUUKU ސުލޫކު n. conduct [U. sulūk]

4580 SULEIMAANII ސުލެއިމާނީ n. onyx [U. sulaimānī]

4581 SULHA ސުލްހަ n. peaceableness: s. vanii, is peaceable; s. vegen uḷenii, lives peaceably [U. <u>s</u>ul<u>h</u>]

4582 SUVARU ސުވަރު n. swine (not found in Maldives: used metaphorically as an insult) [cf. S. ūru: H. sūar, Skt. sūkara]

4583 SUVARUGE ސުވަރުގެ n. heaven [H. svarg, Skt. svarga]

4584 SUVAA (suvalek) ސުވާ n. 1. handful of food, mouthful: bat s., mouthful of rice
2. an old game for boys, kicking bags of sand (s. kuḷum)

4585 SUVAALU ސުވާލު n. question: s. kuraniii, asks (of..., ... kure or .. -aai) ; biiraṭṭehiinnaai kurevunu suvaalu-tak, questions asked of islanders [U. suvāl]

4586 SUVAASAA (-aaek) ސުވާސާ n. rolled gold, alloy of gold and copper

4587 SUHAILU ސުހައިލު n. south point of the compass [U. suhail, Canopus]

4588 SUU (sulek) ސޫ n. penis (slang)

4589 SUUJII ސޫޖީ n. sweet dessert porridge (imported for Ramzan) [H. sūjī, semolina]

4590 SUUTU ސޫތު n. one eighth of an inch [H. sūt, one sixteenth of an inch, Skt. sūtra]

4591 SUUDU ސޫދު n. monetary interest (see ribaa): s. kanii, accepts interest [U. sūd]

4592 SUUFI (suutpek) ސޫފި n. small animal(s); insect: valu s., wild animals: suufaasuufi, all kinds of small creatures [S. siv-pā, Skt. catuṣpāda]

4593 SUURA ސޫރަ n. shape; image, portrait. s. rīti, prettily shaped [U. s̱ūrat]

4594 SUURAT ސޫރަތް n. chapter of the Qur'ān [U. sūra]

4595 SUURI KAŇḌANII ސޫރި ކަނޑަނީ v. walks up and down

4596 SEṬIGAMU ސެޓިގަމު n. Chittagong

4597 SEṬU ސެޓު n. set of objects: goňḍi s., set of chairs: teli s., set of pans [E. set]

4598 SEṬFIKEṬ ސެޓްފިކެޓް n. medical certificate [E. certificate]

4599 SENṬ (SEENṬ) ސެންޓް (ސޭންޓް) n. scent, perfume : s. levifai vanii, scent is wafted [E. scent]

4600 SENṬARU ސެންޓަރު n. an official of the Health Department, or his office [E. centre]

4601 SEŇBUREMUN ސެނބުރެމުން v. in eňburemun seňburemun, twisting (doublet) [eňburenii]

4602 SERU ސެރު n. two lbs.weight (in tables) [H. sēr, 'seer']

4603 SEVUU-NARU ސެވޫނަރު n. vermicelli [H. sev + T. nār]

4604 SEḶḶI ސެއްޅި n. kind of tick or flea, sandfly: s. hafanii, sandflies are biting [T. seḷḷu]

4605 SEEKU ސޭކު adj. silly: s. hedenii, plays the fool

4606 SEEṬU ސޭޓު n. proprietor of an Indian shop [H. sēṭh, Skt. śrēṣṭha]

4607 SEENṬ ސީންޓް n. For senṭ

4608 SEEBUU (seebulek, seebuuek) ސީބޫ n. (anc.) apple (mod., aafalu) [H. sēb]

4609 SEELA ސީލަ n. crane, hoist

4610 SEEVAA(-aaek) ސީވާ n. fool, madman

4611 -SEESARU -ސީސަރު n. In naguu-seesaru, sea-dragon: (met.) unreliable or bad person

4612 SOI ސޮއި n. signature: siṭiigai soi kuranii, signs letter [H. svī-]

4613 SOK ސޮކް onom. shooing sound: kukuḷaai dimaa-ař s. govanii, shoos hen away

4614 SOKAŘ DANII ސޮކަށް ދަނީ v. goes for nothing, ends in smoke [sok?]

4615 SOṬAA-GAŇḌU ސޮޓާގަނޑު n. club, stick [H. soṇṭā]

4616 SOḌAA ސޮޑާ n. flavoured sodawater (as v. ḍonḍon) [E. soda]

4617 SONI ސޮނި n . dribbling saliva [? S. soṭu]

4618 SOFAA (SOOFAA) ސޮފާ (ސޯފާ) n. sofa, couch (sofaa-goňḍi) [E. sofa]

4619 SORU (pl., sorumen) ސޮރު n. chap, male person : mi-gee ḷa-soru, our young son; also used of animals

4620 SOSSANII ސޮއްސަނީ v. glides (down): dekoḷu dekoḷař sossaalaee, glides up and down; mooches about [sohenii]

4621 SOHENII ސޮހެނީ v. slips down (esp. of clothing)

4622 SOHOLU ސޮހޮލު n. fool

4623 SOONAA ސޯނާ n. In soonaa gaḍi, alarm clock [H. sōnā, to sleep]

4624 SOOFAA ސޯފާ n. For sofaa

4625 SOOBU ސޯބު n. cogwheel: mai s., chief cogwheel; mai soobu nuhiñganñaa kudi soobek nuhiñgaane-ee, if the chief cogwheel doesn't work, the small wheels won't either (prov.)

4626 SOORU KURANII ސޯރު ކުރަނީ v. prolongs the end of a verse

4627 SOORUFOTI-KOḶU ސޯރުފޮޓި-ކޮޅު n. ornamental sarong string (as v. dagañḍu), popularized by Hasan Farid (who used a tie)

4628 SOOSAN ސޯސަން n. a flowering creeper: S. magu, name of a principal street in Male [U. sōsan, lily or iris]

4629 SOOHU ސޯހު adj. interested in (with dat.); lava-ař varař soohu hunna miihek, a man devoted to song [U. śō<u>kh</u>, playful]

4630 SOOḶA ސޯޅަ num. sixteen [S. soḷos, H. sōlah, Skt. ṣōḍaśa]

4631 SOOḶIYAA ސޯޅިޔާ n. a class of Indian Muslim from Calicut: s.-kaleege, s. soru, member of this class: Sooḷiyaa huni, a Soli dish of ground coconut [? Chola dynasty; cf. Hoḷi 2]

4632 SṬEEMP, SṬEEM ސްޓޭމްޕް - ސްޓޭމް n. postage stamp: s. nerenii, issues stamps [E. stamp]

4633 -(S)SURE(N) -ްސުރެ(ން) temporal enclitic since... Used after nouns : fatihussure, since early morning: hatek jehiissure feřigen, since 7 o'clock: iyyeessure, since yesterday: maa kuriissure, since very long ago;
or after participles : viissure, since (it)was: feřiissure, feřuniissure, since it began: fajru liissure, since dawn appeared [also written -nsure]

ޒ ZA-VIYANI, the 19th letter of the Maldivian alphabet

4634 ZAITUUNI ޒައިތޫނި n. olive [U. zaitūn]

4635 ZAIIMU ޒައީމު n. political leader [A. za'īm]

4636 ZAKARU ޒަކަރު n. penis (coll., firihen hař̌i) [U. zakar]

4637 ZAKAAT ޒަކާތް n. prescribed almsgiving: zakaatař deene eccek, something to give as alms [U. zakāt]

4638 ZAGGUUMU ޒައްގޫމު n. a plant, argemone mexicana [U. zaqqūm]

4639 ZANGIN ޒަންގިން n. (pl.) masked dancers, clowns [U. zangī, Ethiopians]

4640 ZANBIILU ޒަންބީލު n. ancient kind of basket [U. zanbīl]

4641 ZABAADU ޒަބާދު n. civet (used medicinally) [U. zabād]

4642 ZAMAAN ޒަމާން n. times, epoch: ihu z., former times: mi z., mihaaruge z., modern times: mi zamaanuge, up- to- date: zamaanii (adj.), modern [U. zamān]

4643 ZAVI ޒަވި adj. In zavi raha, a nasty fizzy taste

4644 ZA-VIYANI ޒަވިޔަނި n. the Maldivian letter Z

4645 ZAHARU ޒަހަރު n. poison [U. zahr]

4646 ZAA ޒާ n. the Arabic letter Z

4647 ZAAT ޒާތް n. type; peculiar character (hon., zaatu-fuḷu): zaatekge miihek, an odd chap: zaatekge gotek vegen, an unusual thing happened: zaat-koḷu boḍu, fussy: zaat zaat nukuree, don't give excuses; adv., zaatakař, oddly : zaatii kam, grudge, bias [U. zāt, or Skt. jāti]

4648 ZINEE ޒިނޭ n. adultery; fornication: z. kuranii, commits adultery or fornication (mostly used of women) [U. zinā]

4649 ZINKU ޒިންކު n. aluminium: z. karudaas, silver paper [E. zinc]

4650 ZIBU ޒިބު n. zip fastener [E. zip]

4651 ZIYAARAT ޒިޔާރަތް n. tomb, shrine: z. kuranii, visits (with dat. of place): z. raddu kuranii, returns a visit [U. ziyārat]

4652 ZILEEBI ޒިލޭބި n. a sweetmeat (also jilaabi) [U. jalēbī]

4653 ZIIN ޒީން onom. z. lanii, makes a zinging sound (as of kites, or arrows)

4654 ZIINAT ޒީނަތް n. embellishment, elegance: ziinat-terikamuge feeramtak, ceremonial dress; (adv.) ziinat-teri kořfaa, decoratively [U. zīnat]

4655 ZIINAARU ޒީނާރު n. kind of crumpet (dipped in kiru-hakuru)

4656 ZIILA ޒީލަ adj. (of sounds) loud and high, shrill [U. zīl]

4657 ZUMARRADU ޒުމަރްރަދު n. emerald [U. zumurrad]

4658 ZUVAAN ޒުވާން adj. young; zuvaan-veriyaa, young person (pl., zuvaanun (-tak)): ihař zuvaanek, one who was young once [H. juvān, Skt. yuvān]

4659 ZUVAABU ޒުވާބު n. answer; answering back; z. kuraniii, ařgues (as v. javaabu denii)

4660 ZUVAARI ޒުވާރި n. maize, zea mays or andropogon sorghum : zuvaari bat, cooked maize [H. juvārī]

4661 ZUU (zulek) ޒޫ n. zoo [E. zoo]

4662 ZUUN ޒޫން onom. z. lanii, makes a zooming noise: hama z. laafai, (viz.) very fast

4663 -ZOOŇGU -ޒޯނގު n. collective plural ending, ifc. in nau-zooňgu, sailing ships

ހ HAA, the first letter of the Maldivian alphabet

Haa atoḷu, Tiladunmati, the first atoll from the north (including Ihavandippoḷu)

4664 HA (haek) ހަ num. six : haekka, a few, half a dozen [haĕk haa]: ha-sateeka rufiyaa, 600 rupees: ha-faraat, the six directions (three dimensions): ha-rooda, six days of optional fasting after Ramzan: ha-varu, the six groups of the population, the public, the mob (led by the nagaa kiyaa miihaa); havarař govanii, calls the people to assemble; havaru beru, the drum beaten to assemble the people; havaru boḍu fatafoḷi, havaru tunfuhi, notorious courtesans: ha-vana, sixth [S. sa-, Skt. ṣaṭ]

4665 HAI ހައި n. 1. kind of grass, used for weaving in the south, fimbristylis ferruginea: remainder of grass left after weaving it (hai-gaňḍu) [cf. haa-gooři]

2. hunger; baňḍu-hai, hunger (in Male, baňḍu-fai); baňḍuhai ve hurum, being hungry: hai-baňḍu, hunger; haibaňḍaa / haibaňḍař hurum, being hungry: hai-huunu, great hunger; haihuunugai jehijje, (I) am very hungry [S. hā-mata]

ހައި - ހާ 3. hai aḷanii , hai vanii, see haa

ހައި - ހާ 4. hai, haa: amount, when used after participles or nouns : vii haa raňgaḷakař, as well as possible: vii haa durekgai hunnan, to keep as far away as possible: hii nukuraa hai avahař, unthinkably quickly: masakkat kuraa hai vee, it's worth a try: koḷek net haa faidaatak, limitless advantages: net hai eccek, what (we) don't have: huri-haa, all: hurihaa haa enmen, everybody: doḷugaḍiyek haa iru, about an hour and a half: mi ot haa iru, all this time: degaḍibaek haa irun, within two and a half hours: kuran jeheene haa ves kamakii, all you have to do is..: lugmaek haa etikoḷu ves, even as much as a mouthful: naaḷiek hai haňḍuu, one measure of rice: kitanme haa ves boḍee, it's very big

4666 HAIBA ހައިބަ n. grandeur (usu. of people): h. huri, h. boḍu, grand: haiba-vanta, grand [haibatu]

4667 HAIBATU ހައިބަތު n. grandeur : h. huri vagutu, important time [U. haibat]

4668 HAIRAAN ހައިރާން n. amazement: h. vanii, is surprised, is puzzled (at.., -aa) [U. hairān]

4669 HAI-VAKARU ހައިވަކަރު n. teak, tectona grandis

4670 HAIVAANU ހައިވާނު n. member of the animal kingdom [U. haivān]

4671 HAU ހައު See haa

4672 HAUDA ހައުދަ For haada

4673 HAURU (HAARU) ހައުރު (ހާރު) n. meal eaten before breakfast time in Ramzan, supper

4674 HAEḶU VANII ހައެޅު ވަނީ v. menstruates [U. ẖaiz, 'period']

4675 HAK ހައް n. 1. pulley for raising kites: h. jahanii, fixes such pulley (on tree)
2. (anc.) conch (mod. sangu): h. govvanii, sounds the conch
[S. sak, Skt. śankha]

4676 HAKA ހަކަ n. idle gossip: h. taḷanii, gossips

4677 HAKATA ހަކަތަ n. stamina, energy [H. sakat]

4678 HAKI (hatkek) ހަކި n. suckers of a creeper

4679 HAKIIMU ހަކީމު n. ayurvedic doctor [U. ẖakīm]

4680 HAKURAA ހަކުރާ n. a royal functionary (h. beekalek, h. manikufaanu)

4681 HAKURU ހަކުރު n. juggery, palm syrup ; (mod.) white sugar : uk-sakuru, ussakuru, unprocessed juggery, molasses: kani-hakuru, spoilt juggery: karu-hakuru, thick white juggery: guuḍu hakuru, unrefined juggery: diyaa-hakuru, liquid juggery honey (hakuru buim, drinking this): Divehi h., juggery from Maldivian cocopalms: dooburaali h., white sugar: nabaazu h., medicinal barleysugar: fuppi hakuru, beaten-up sugar: rat- h., Divehi brown sugar; kiru hakuru, curds with sugar: lonu hakuru, salt and sugar; sai hakurugai hadanii, makes (cup of) tea with sugar ; hakuru dee miihekee boḍu beebe, uncle is the man who gives juggery, i.e. you are under an obligation to him (prov.) [S. hakuru, Skt. śarkarā, cf. E. sugar]

4682 HAGIIGATU ހަގީގަތު n. truth; hagiigatakii e-ek nuunee, that is not the truth; adj., hagiigii, true [U. ẖaqīqat]

4683 HAGU ހަގު adj. younger [S. saga]

4684 HAGGU ހައްގު n. a right: Mufiidaage haggugai bunaa saafu tedu, a truth you, Mufida, have a right to know: Mufiidaage haggugai saabitu vevee too uḷunim, I tried to be straight for your sake, M. : haggu-veriyaa, rightful owner [U. ẖaqq]

4685 HAÑGAA KURANII ހަނގާ ކުރަނީ v. brings disturbance, annoyance

(to.., ..-aa)

4686 HAŇGU-BEEKALUN ހަނގުބޭކަލުން n..(pl.) royal guards (in the old palace): hañgu- hañḍuu, their allowances of food

4687 HAŇGURAAMA ހަނގުރާމަ n. war : hañguraama-veriyaa, soldier [Skt. saṃgrāma]

4688 HAJAMU ހަޖަމު n. digestion: h. kuranii, chews the cud: h. vanii, is digested: h. nubai vanii, has indigestion [U. haẕm]

4689 HAJJAAMU ހައްޖާމު n. barber (anc.), hajaamu- kaleege: h. kuranii, shaves and cuts nails (to be done on certain days) [U. ẖajjām]

4690 HAJJU ހައްޖު n. pilgrimage (to Mecca): h. kuranii, h. vanii, hajjař danii, goes on the pilgrimage: Hajju duvas, 9th and l0th of Zūlhijja: hajju-vajju, pilgrimages (doublet) [U. ẖajj]

4691 HAṬṬI ހައްޓި num. 60 (anc.: mod. fas-doḷas) [S. häṭa, Skt. ṣaṣṭi]

4692 HAḌI ހަޑި adj. dirty (of people or things): h. hañḍuu, red rice [S. häḍi]

4693 HAŇḌANII ހަނޑަނީ v. pisses (vulg.) (v.n. heñḍum): goru h., pisses (of animals)

4694 HAŇḌAS (hañḍahek) ހަނޑަސް n. 1. pair of tongs or pliers
2. latrine area (also hañḍas- buri)

4695 HAŇḌUU (hañḍulek) ހަނޑޫ n. uncooked rice, oryza sativa: hañḍuu-tak, grains of rice: ali h., white rice: rat h., red rice: nii h., buri h., rañgaḷu or riiti h., three sizes of rice grain (for fodder, cakes and curries respectively): boḍu h., bañḍu h., hañgu h., rice rations given by way of life pension; h. kañḍanii, husks rice: h. foḷanii, sifts rice: h. hovanii, cleans rice (but bat kakkanii, cooks rice) [S. hāl, cf. P. taṇḍula]

4696 HAT ހަތް 1. num. seven: hat a̱ttavaaḷi, seven pits (kind of game): hat duvas, week; dehatduvas, fortnight (anc. or ceremonious): Hukuru hatduvas, week up to Friday: hat-mudi, child's gold necklace with seven pendants: hataaviis, 27: hat-tari (anc.), 70 (mod. hat-diha): hat-taan, times seven (in Navata multiplication tables: tin hattaan, 3 x 7): hat-diha, 70: hat-vana, seventh [S. sat, hat, Skt. sapta]

4697 HAT ހަތް 2. n. royal umbrella (hat-koḷu): hañḍi-hat, kind of mushroom [S. sat, Skt. chatra]

4698 HATARU ހަތަރު num. four: hataragi (for hataru agi), four measures (of shells): hataru-guna, fourfold: hataru-fotii munḍu, a sarong woven as two pieces, top and bottom: hataru-vana, fourth: hatares-kam, a square; hatareskam meezu, square table: hatares-fai, four limbs; four-footed [S. hatara, Skt. catur-]

4699 HATAA (-aek) ހަތާ n. 1. beehive: honeycomb: swarm of bees; kind of flat-ended coral, shaped like a beehive (hataa-gaa), hanḍi-hataa, kind of mushroom (= hanḍihat) 2. for hatoo

4700 HATI ހަތި n. fungus: mushroom-shaped cloud [S. hatu, Skt. chatrikā]

4701 HATIYAARU ހަތިޔާރު n. weapon, weapons: (jastu) baddaa h., soldering iron: vaḍaamuge h., tools: karenṭ hatiyaarek, a power tool [H. hathiyār, Skt. hastakāra]

4702 HATURU ހަތުރު n. (anc.) enemy: haturu-verikam, hostility [S. haturu, Skt. śatru]

4703 HATEELI (hateeyyek) ހަތޭޅި n. cover for the palm when using bodkin: hateeli-kaři, large bodkin [H. hathēlī, palm, Skt. hastatalikā]

4704 HATOO (HATAA) ހަތޯ (ހަތާ) n. error, in balaa-hatoo, difficulties and errors (see taaniyaa) [U. khaṯā]

4705 HAT̲T̲AA ހައްތާ adv. altogether, always: hat̲taa diyaii boḍu kuramun, was constantly increasing: hat̲taa ves Ingireesiinge eccesseve, all were English vessels: hat̲taa mi-hirii nubai kaaṭṭee, all here are bad coconuts [P. samantā]

4706 HAT̲T̲IYAA ހައްތިޔާ n. for fat̲tiyaa (non-Male usage)

4707 HADANII ހަދަނީ v. makes; mends (v.n. hedum : p.p. hedi : hon. haddavanii): dogu h., tells lies: bilet-dafi h., arranges betel in pan: fus hadaa duvahek, a cloudy day: muunu h., frowns, makes angry faces: muunumati h., washes face;with predicate, e-fada nurakkau eccek kamugai hedum, making (them) a less dangerous thing; used after abs. of most verbs with no additional meaning: hee lai hadaigen, having woken up (= hee lai): jahaalaa hadaa, having hit; hadaigen (abs.) may represent 'because': hurihaa kamek goos vii kalee angada kuraan hadaigeneve, everything went wrong because of your chatter: caus., haddanii, gets done; nourishes a plant (v.n. heddum): bagiicaa hadanii, plants a garden: seeku haddanii, makes a fool of ; see also hedenii
[S. hadanne, Skt. sajjayati]

4708 HADIYAA (hadiyaaek) ހަދިޔާ n. present : hadiyaa kuranii, presents (tr.): hadiyaa-ař denii, gives as a present: hadiyaa denii, hadiyaa hadanii, gives food, prepares food, for long journeys [U. hadiya]

4709 HADU ހަދު n. earthenware pot

4710 HADDU ހައްދު n. limit (met.): haddun naṭṭanii, goes out of control: haddu fahanaḷai, having gone beyond (all) limits: haddu jahanii, gives official legal beating with durra : aňga-haddu, punishment for blasphemy etc. ('prescribed amount')
[U. h̲add]

4711 HADDUNMATI (Haddunmacc-) ހައްދުންމަތި n. name of L atoll

4712 HAŇDAAN ހަނދާން n. memory: h. kuranii, remembers: hañdaanek nuvanii / netenii, forgets ; aḷugaňḍu hañdaan kuran uḷeuḷe hañdaanek nuviee, I can't remember even when I try; demiihek h. eba huṭṭeve, I remember two men; aḷugaňḍu mihirii h. netifaee, I have forgotten: aḷugaňḍu Mufiidaage matin hañdaan na<u>tt</u>aek nulaanameve, I won't forget you, Mufida; hañdaan na<u>tt</u>aalaigen vaanee kamkamek nuunee, are not things one can forget ; teli donnan ot hañdaanek nuvee, forgetting how you sat down to wash dishes; badige tereegai uḷunu hañdaanek nuḥuree, forgetting how you used to be in the kitchen: h. koř denii, reminds [S. saňdahan, ?Skt. sandhāna]

4713 HAŇDI (hañjek) ހަނދި n. mason's trowel; used ifc. in names of flat fish (fani-haṇdi, muḍa-hañdi) [S. häňdi, spoons]

4714 HAŇDU ހަނދު n. moon: hañdaa-hañdu, moons: Muharram mahař hañdu balaifi, the moon of M. was seen, i.e. the Muslim month M. began: tiya rařař roodayař hañdu fenunu hee, did you see the Ramzan moon from your island? hañdu balaa mas, the moon you are looking for, i.e. the following month: h. fenunu mas, 29-day month: h. nufenunu mas, 30-day month; hañdu-ge, circle round the moon (sign of rain): hañdu-baḍi, small cannon; shot formerly fired thereon at the beginning of certain months: hañdu-mas, lunar month; hañdumahun, by the lunar calendar : hañdu-varu, moonlight
[S. haňda, Skt. candra]

4715 HAŇDUMA ހަނދުމަ n. memory: h. kuranii, remembers; tiya beefuḷun hañdumafuḷu hunnaanee fadain, as you gentlemen will remember: h. koř denii , reminds (hon., hañdumafuḷu koř aruvanii) [hañdaan]

4716 HAŇDUVANII ހަނދުވަނީ v. (anc.) is loving (v.n. heňduvum)

4717 HAŇDUVARII ހަނދުވަރީ n. a plant, duranta repens

4718 HAŇDEEGIRI (pl., hañdeegirin) ހަނދޭގިރި n. a former royal official; protocol officer

4719 HANA-FAS ހަނަފަސް n. loose dry earth or sand

4720 HANAA (hanalek) AḶANII ހަނާ އަޅަނީ v. beckons: anhenunnař hanaa eḷumakii ladu kamek, it is shameful to beckon to women

4721 HANAA-KAFA ހަނާކަފަ n. a kind of cotton; tree which supplies it

4722 HANAA KURANII ހަނާ ކުރަނީ v. bakes: h. kuri mas, a dish of fish baked in spice: h. kuri fook, a kind of chew baked in sand; (met.) h. kořlanii, beats up: beats in a game: h. vanii, perishes tragically

4723 HANI (hanñek) ހަނި adj. narrow, thin (of things, cf. hima, hiki of people): e hanihani deetereegai, in that very narrow place; (adv.) hanikoř meḷum, making a narrow turn-up

4724 HANU ހަނު n. 1. grindstone: aňdun h., kohl grinder: oḍi h., medicine grinder: teo h., hone: h. taḷanii, constructs a grindstone: h. lanii, sharpens (tr.) [S. haṇa, Skt. śāṇa]

2. quietness (mod. hanu-himeen): hanun (mod. hanuhimeenun) hurum, keeping quiet and still

4725 HANJARU ހަންޖަރު n. kris, dagger [U. <u>kh</u>anjar]

4726 HANJAA(hanjalek) ހަންޖާ n. halliard for raising sail : h. kavanii, fixes this rope [?H. hāṃjā]

4727 HANḌI ހަނޑި n. a female spirit: eenaa h. hellaifi, he had a wet dream (<u>lit</u>. 'a spirit shook him'); aḷugaňḍu h. fillaifi, I lost the way; hanḍi-kuḍa, h.- hat, h.- hataa, kind of inedible fungus

4728 HANDA ހަނދަ n. sea snail

4729 HANDARU ހަނދަރު n. hundredweight. [cf. S. hoṇḍarē, ? Dutch]

4730 HANHAARA ހަންހާރަ n. (poet.) love: hanhaara-veti, amorous [?Skt. śṛngāra]

4731 HAFANII ހަފަނީ v. chews up, gnaws (v.n.hefum); of insects, bites, stings: gaigaa hefum, biting the body; maa hefum, a special meal eaten before the beginning of Ramzan [S. hapanne, P. cappēti, cf. Skt. carvati]

4732 HAFU ހަފު n. kind of insect [S. sapu, insect, Skt. ṣaṭpāda]

4733 HAFUTAA ހަފުތާ n. week [U. hafta, cf. Skt. saptāha]

4734 HAFUS KURANII ހަފުސް ކުރަނީ v. ties up tight [cf. habees]

4735 HAFOḶU ހަފޮޅު n. reinforcing timbers at sides of dhoni

4736 HAPPANII ހައްޕަނީ v. feeds (v.n. heppum): bakari hui happaa kaleege, goatherd (caus. of hafanii)

4737 HAPPU ހައްޕު interj. quiet! hush! h. kiyanii, says one will keep quiet

4738 HAPPUŇḌU ހައްޕުނޑު n. end of a chew : h. ukum, h. eḷum, spitting out a chew [hafanii]

4739 HABA ހަބަ n. mouth full of chew : h. aḷanii, takes full mouthful of chew

4740 HABARU ހަބަރު n. aloes, an askanu medicament, aloe vera

4741 KHABARU ޚަބަރު n. news: khabaru-dabaru, news (doublet): khabaru hus vum, being unconscious: khabardaar , beware! [U. khabar]

4742 HABEES (KURANII) (ކުރަނީ) ހަބޭސް v. tightens: habees kiyaafai, very fast, very hard; h. kiyaafai jahanii, hits very hard [cf. hafus]

4743 HABBA ހައްބަ n. a minimum: eenaa atugai habba ves netee, he hasn't a bean [U. habba, grain]

4744 HAM ހަމް n. skin ; leather; jerrycan; balloon: hamek, a plastic bag: bakaraige ham damanii, skins the goat: h. fuppanii, blows up balloon: ham jahanii, gives S.O.S. signal: ham-ṭooṭoo, old and wrinkled: ham-fiiru, a rasp; dorufatugai hamfiiru lanii, applies rasp to door: ham-muři, (horse-)whip; hammuři aḷanii, applies whip [S. ham, Skt. carma]

4745 HAMA ހަމަ n., adj. & adv. order, rhythm, principles; true, exact; just, simply: bahuge hama(tak), rules of speech: hamatakuge matiin, according to the rules: hama na-hama, pros and cons: hamain neṭṭigen, irregularly: hamain naṭṭaalaafai, beyond the limit: hama-ař adaa kořfieve, has paid in full: reegai hama-ař nuves nidunu, didn't sleep at all either: aharemen e miihunakaa hamahamaek nuunee, we are not on a level with those people; Aḍḍuvaa hama-ař, up to Addu atoll: Kaařiduaai hamain, in the K. area: adaa hama-ař, up till today: debai kuḷa ekbayaa ves hamaek nuve-ee, is not as much as a half: meyaa hamaagai, at the same time as this;
hama nuun, unfair: hama bim(tan), level ground : hama riyaa, square sail: hama neevaa,

ordinary breathing; hama-neevaa lanii, recovers one's breath : tin hama, 'three in a row', a kind of game: hama aḷanii, gets three in a row at this game: hama jassanii, arranges: gaḍi hama vanii, the time is up; gaḍi varař hama-ař hiňgaee, the clock keeps very good time: kamakaa medu hama dakkanii, shows cause or proof for something, justifies: hama kuranii, puts in order; hama gabuul kuraa, impartial: hama roonu naganii, employs the final levelling rope (for building): hama-ař defaḷi kuranii, divides exactly in half : furaa hama kuranii, fills right up: hama rodi jahanii, does loose stitching or tacking: adi hama-rooḷi nu-nukunnanii (nu-libijje), normal breeze hasn't yet restarted: hama-vai jehee hisaabu, where the normal breeze is blowing, (met.) out of the storm; hama jehenii, works properly : eenaa-akař hamaek nujessuneve, could not be settled by him : hama hee huṭṭeve, was fully conscious;
hama gaimu, most certainly: hama denme, just now: hama vaḍaigat aagubooṭun, on the same steamer that he arrived on (hon.): hama kiriyaa, only just: hama tedek too, is that really so? hama fisaari tedek mii, it is really so: mi geař hama aiiee, just came to this house (for no particular reason): miadu hama boo hit nuvanii, I just don't feel like drinking today: mi geegai maamui fodek hama netiiee, there simply isn't any honey in this house : hama hadaane gotek netifai, without knowing just what to do: hama ekani, one and only: hama ekme membarek, one single member: hama- hilaa nudaanamee, I most certainly won't go: hama muḷin, altogether: hama varař ves boḍu, really very big: kharadu hama boḍu kamun, because of the huge expense : hama mihen damun vadelii, I just popped in here: hama vagutun mihaaru, just now: hama hum annanii, keeps getting fever [Skt. sama, equal]

4746 HAMALA ހަމަލާ n. attack: h. denii, attacks [U. hamla]

4747 HAMDARDII ހަމްދަރްދީ n. sympathy [U. hamdardī]

4748 HAMMATA KURANII ހަންމަތަ ކުރަނީ v. controls (usu. applied to troublesome children) [mata]

4749 HAMMAALAA ހަންމާލާ n. square lighter, barge

4750 HAMLU ހަމްލު n. the first sign of the zodiac, Aries [U. hamal]

4751 HAYAAT ހަޔާތް n. 1. life (hon., hayaatpuḷu) [U. hayāt]
2. decency (ladu hayaat): h. kuḍa, shameless [U. hayā]

4752 HAYYARU ހައްޔަރު n. 1. obstruction: hayyarek neti, without obstruction: h. kuranii, arrests [U. hāyal]
2. pregnancy: hayyarugai inum, being pregnant (kaakař hee, by whom?): hayyarun neṭṭenii, suffers miscarriage

4753 HARAKAAT ހަރަކާތް n. activity; adj., harakaat-teri(-yaa), active (person): harakaatterikam hiňgamun daalek avas min, the speed of activity [U. harakāt]

4754 KHARADU ޚަރަދު n. expenditure [U. kharc]

4755 HARANII ހަރަނީ v. pierces, pricks; pokes into (v.n. herum): gayař vaḷi haranii, stabs the body ; see also herenii

4756 HARAADU KIYANII ހަރާދު ކިޔަނީ v. lays bets

4757 HARAABU VANII ހަރާބު ވަނީ v. is spoilt, ruined [U. kharāb]

4758 HARAAM ހަރާމް adj. religiously forbidden: haraam ekaccek ves nukam, I won't eat anything forbidden: kalee hadaa sai haraam, I mustn't drink your tea: kaiveni haraam kudin, those whom it is illegal to marry: haraamun haraam e kiyaa eccek, whatever is said: haraam (fada) toocce, it is unthinkable (used in strong denials); haraam toocce eňgee nama, I certainly don't know [U. harām]

4759 HARAAMU-JAADAA ހަރާމުޖާދާ n. scoundrel [U. harāmzāda]

4760 HARI JAHANII ހަރި ޖަހަނީ v. argues (Southern usage)

4761 HARINMA ހަރިންމަ n. mosque 'compound' (harinma-tere): mahaana harinma, low wall round a grave [U. harīma]

4762 HARISA ހަރިސަ n. a spicy pudding [U. harīsa]

4763 HARU ހަރު 1. adj. firm; hard, loud ; (of people) mature, stable; (of fruit) full-grown: h. kuranii, fixes; hungaanugai maadaa haru kuraařee, fix the net on the rudder: h. lanii, gets settled; dooni matiigai fai haru nulaa miihek, a man who didn't get firm foothold on the boat: amunaa haa eccek haru laane-ee, everything on the line will stay firm; (adv.) haru koř, quickly: maa harek koř, quite firmly; haru vanii, solidifies: (of fruits) sets firm; haru-kaři, stiff, strict; harukaři vum, rigor mortis; maa harukaři javaabu, impolite rejoinders: haru-dańḍi kořlanii, makes unable to move (by beating): harudanaa, reliable, stable (of people); harudanaa aḍu, confident voice; harudanaa fiyavaḷek, a bold step; harudanaa naslakun, of an honourable ancestry: haru-bihi (-gańḍu), a rash of hard patches: haru-bas, proverb: haru-bees, solid medicines as a tonic (esp. for new mothers, see also hili bees): haru-mudaa(-tak), moveable property [S. hara, Skt. sāra]

4764 HARU ހަރު 2. n. burrow of animal or bird (nai-haru, kakuni-haru, hini-haru, burrows of nautilus, crab, ant): bai-haru, (obs.) married couple as taxable unit:

3. domestic machine, for carving (liyaa haru, lathe) or weaving (viyaa haru, loom)

4. haru, haru-gańḍu: rack, set of shelves, dresser ; ladder: raaruku harugańḍu, fixed ladder on toddy-tapping trees; harufat (-gańḍu), steps (to climb); harufatu keim (keem), food offered on the steps of the haruge for Mauluud [S. hära]

4765 HARU-GE ހަރުގެ n. temporary shed, esp. boatshed or carpenter's shop: structure to accommodate the overflow from a mosque (The Male haruge is a permanent structure)

4766 HARUFA ހަރުފަ n. snake (not found in Maldives) [Skt. sarpa]

4767 HARUBII ހަރުބީ n. kind of royal music: h. jahanii, plays this music: harubiiař hingavanii, (of the King) walks in time with the music [U. harubī, warlike]

4768 HARUMANIYA ހަރުމަނިޔަ n. portable harmonium [E. harmonium]

4769 HARUVAAḶU ހަރުވާޅު n. loose underpants: h. lanii, puts them on [S. saruvāla, U. sarvāl]

4770 -HARE -ހަރެ imperative suffix, often in repetitions: nukahare, (I repeat) don't eat!

4771 HAROŘI ހަރޮށި adj. fully mature (of people) [haru-kaři ?]

4772 HAROOŘI ހަރޯށި n. 1. ladder [haru + aři]
2. rack for yarn [cf. firooři]

4773 HALAKA ހަލަކަ n. handle for lifting boxes

4774 HALANI ހަލަނި n. sieve [halanii]

4775 HALANI ހަލަނި adj. fidgety [halanii]

4776 HALANII ހަލަނީ v. shakes up; stirs (v.n. helum): aňga h., moves the mouth: baḍi h., tests guns (formerly done at Iruvai before the invasion season); caus., gas haluvanii, shakes trees: buddi haluvaa, deceptive; see also helenii [S. halanne, Skt. calati]

4777 HALA-BOLI ހަލަބޮލި adj. fidgety (esp. of children): rough (of the sea); (adv.) halaboli koř uḷum, being fidgety [halanii]

4778 HALAVELI ހަލަވެލި n. kind of scented bush, suriana marittima

4779 HALAAKU ހަލާކު n. damage, destruction: duniyeege halaakakii anhenunnaai faisaa, women and money are the ruination of the world: h. kuranii, breaks, damages: godankoḷu nubaive halaaku vamun daa tii ve, because the grain was going bad; (met.) birun halaaku vefai, petrified with fear; ma halaaku, I was doubled up with laughter: halaaku vaa varu vegen, heartbroken: diriuḷum halaaku, my life is spoilt: Divehin halaaku ve hiňgajje, Maldivians were destroyed (died) [U. halāk, death]

4780 HALAALU ހަލާލު adj. ritually correct (of slaughter etc., opposite of haraam): na-halaalař bali ve iňde, becoming illegally pregnant [U. halāl]

4781 HALI ހަލި adj. swift [haluvi]

4782 HALUI ހަލުއި See haluvi

4783 HALUVAA ހަލުވާ 1. n. kind of sweetmeat (baraboo h., fufuu h.); boňḍi haluvaa, a south Maldivian sweetmeat [U. h̲alvā]

2. v. deceiving (caus. part. of halanii): buddi haluvaa, deceptive

4784 HALUVI (HALUI) ހަލުވި (ހަލުއި) adj. speedy, agile: (adv.) halui koř, speedily

4785 HALUVIDAA / HALUUDAA ހަލުވިދާ - ހަލޫދާ n. 'Chinese moss', an imported jelly

4786 HALLANII ހައްލަނީ v. tries to persuade [for haluvanii, caus. of halanii]

4787 HAVAA ހަވާ n. atmosphere, space; rocket: havaek aruvanii, lets off a rocket: havaa(ge) rasgefaanu, a fairy king: havaa boḍu eduru kaleegefaanu, fairy king's royal tutor [U. havā]

4788 HAVAADU ހަވާދު n. curry stuff, spices: havaadu li bis, spiced eggs: havaadu raha gada, 'hot' (of curries); h. naganii, prepares curry stuffs

4789 HAVAALU ހަވާލު n. the care of, the charge of: kaleaa havaalu, up to you: Mufiidaage havaalugai aii kaaku, who is in charge of you, M.? h. kuranii, entrusts (to.., -aa): ehen miihakaai h. kuraařee, entrust (it) to someone else: kamaa h. vegen huri miihaa, the man who is in charge of the matter [U. h̲avāla]

4790 HAVAASAA ހަވާސާ n. margin, border [U. h̲avāṣī]

4791 HAVIIRU ހަވީރު n. late afternoon; in the late afternoon (evening), approx. from 3 till 6: haviirař foḷee, blooming in the evening: h. kuranii, holds a poetry appreciation or criticism [? cf. S. havasa]

4792 HAVEELI ހަވޭލި n. palace, palace balcony [U. havēlī]

4793 HAS ހަސް n. strength: has huri, strong: has net, weak, poor: has-fas (doublet) netum, lack of basic necessities; hasfas netifai, (of clothes) threadbare

4794 HASADA ހަސަދަ n. envy, jealousy: ḥ. vanii, is jealous (of.., -ge maccař): hasada-veri (adj.), grudging [U. ḫasad]

4795 HASKAA (-aek) ހަސްކާ n. flatness: haskaa jehenii, goes flat (of sails when the wind drops): (met.) haskaa denii, scolds: haskaa dee/ haskaa huri/ haskaa kuri duvahek, a punishing (tiresome) day (e.g. when the boss is around)

4796 HASTII ހަސްތީ n. (lit.) the environment, the world [U. hastī]

4797 HASFATAALU ހަސްފަތާލު n. (anc.) hospital (mod. ḍokṭaruge) [?Dutch]

4798 HASSA ހައްސަ n. 576 (6 x 96), in the ancient system of counting fish [ha + hiya]

4799 HAHARU ހަހަރު n. (poet.) love: haharuveti, loving

4800 HAŘA-BAS ހަށަބަސް n. speaking with changed letters, as in children's riddles (Lullu Fiifii, Fuuḍaa Dubu, for Tuṯṯu Diidii, Muusaa Fuḷu)

4801 HAŘAN BANNANII ހަށަން ބަންނަނީ v. crosses arms over stomach to pray

4802 HAŘANARA ހަށަނަރަ n. the Divehi or Maldivian alphabet [first 4 letters of same]

4803 HAŘAVAADA KIYANII ހަށަވާދަ ކިޔަނީ v. utters flirtatious remarks

4804 HAŘI (haṭṭek) ހަށި n. body, esp. of animals: hai eňgee hisaabař, (of fish) close enough for the silhouette to be visible; firihen hai, membrum virile: hai-gaňḍu, human body

4805 HAḶA ހަޅަ n . period of steady wind at the beginning of the north-east monsoon (iruvai): de-haḷa, the asterisms Fura-haḷa and Uturu-haḷa; dehaḷa jehenii, the 'haḷa' winds are blowing strongly [cf. Skt. āṣāḍha]

4806 HAḶAŇGU ހަޅަނގު n. soft coconut fibre for caulking

4807 HAḶUTAALU ހަޅުތާލު n. hartal, commercial strike [H. haṛtāl]

4808 HAḶEEK ހަޅޭކް n. shout: haḷeekek nulavaa, don’t shout! haḷeel-lanii (haḷeil-lanii), see haḷeelanii

4809 HAḶEE-FAŘ , HAḶEE FAḶEE (doublet) ހަޅޭފަޅް - ހަޅޭފަޅޭ n. confused shouting

4810 HAḶEE-LANII (HAḶEILLANII) ހަޅޭލަނި (ހަޅެއިއްލަނި) v. shouts: haḷeela-haḷeelaa in miihaa, the man who was shouting

4811 HAA ހާ n. the letters H in the Arabic and Maldivian alphabets: Haa atoḷu, Tiladunmati atoll, including Ihavandippoḷu

4812 HAA (HAI) ހާ (ހައި) n. amount [hai 4]

4813 HAA (HAI) AḶANII ހާ (ހައި) އަޅަނި v. is transparent: mi gastakun haa aḷaa, visible through these bushes

4814 HAA (HAI) KURANII ހާ (ހައި) ކުރަނި v. makes an opening, opens wide (vulg.): disperses (a crowd): hai nukoř, one after another, continuously: (invol.) haa vefai ot tanek, an opened up space, bare space: haa-viyaa kuranii, disperses (a crowd): (doublet) haa-saa kuranii, opens up

4815 HAA (HAU)(halek) ހާ (ހައު) n. very shallow place, sandbank

4816 HAA (HAU) (haalek) ހާ (ހައު) n. cock: Divehi h. (medium size), Japanu h. (small), muḍu haa (large): haa fiyok, young cock

4817 HAA- - ހާ n. ibc., small bits: haa- naru, useless bits of fibre: haa-mas, subsidiary portions of fish (not masgañḍu or arimas): haa-rihi, silver filings

4818 HAAKANII ހާކަނި v. rubs off (on) (v.n.heekum): mitaagai at nuhaakaa, don’t rub your hands along it! kufiirugañḍu haakaa, rub (it) with a stiff brush! karudaasgañḍekgaa fansuru haakaalum, scribbling on a piece of paper; see also heekenii

4819 HAAKIMU ހާކިމު n. judge [U. ḫākim]

4820 HAAKIS LANII / GOVANII ހާކިސް ލަނި - ހާކިސް ގޮވަނި v. sneezes [onom.]

4821 HAA-GOOŘI ހާގޯރި n.. a medicinal plant, ? fimbristylis ferruginea [cf. hai 1]

4822 HAAJIT ހާޖިތް n. In haajitař danii, goes to excrete or piss: (invol.) de-kamu haajitař devunas, though I both excrete and piss [U. h̲ājat, needfulness]

4823 HAAJII ހާޖީ n. one who has performed the Hajj pilgrimage [U. h̲ājī]

4824 HAAḌU ހާޑު n. loop for holding yardarm to mast for lowering: h. lanii, applies loop

4825 HAADA (HAUDA) ހާދަ adj. many a (with indef. nouns): very much (with added surprise): haada eccek goviee, spoke many insults: haada duvahek vejje, it is many a day (since..): haada iraku iniimee, I waited a long time: haada laṭṭiek beeniee, caught many laṭṭi fish : mi geegai haada tasviiru ginaee, there are many pictures in this house : Yahyage haada buddi rañgaḷee doo, you are quite sensible, Y., aren't you? magee bolugai haada varakař eba rihe-ee, I have a bad headache: haada varakař rehi arajje-ee, bait came up in great numbers: haada hii ve-ee, I am strongly of the opinion..

4826 HAADA-HAA (HAADAHAI, HAUDAHAI) ހާދަހާ (ހާދަހައި – ހައުދަހައި) adv. very: haadahaa hedumek istiri kuraa reyek! you're doing a lot of ironing this evening: haadahaa hit faseeha rařek, a very comfortable island: haadahaa varubali ve-lavvaifai, being very tired; haadahaa vaa riicceve, is very pretty

4827 HAADISAA ހާދިސާ n. sudden occurrence, accident [U. hādit̲h̲a, cf. S. hadisi]

4828 HAANANII ހާނަނީ v. 1. trains (tr.) (v.n. heenum : hon. haanuvvanii, v.n. heenuvvum): miihun kamkamař heenum, training people at activities; shapes (wood etc.); arikaři heenum, massaging the ribs; see also heenenii

2. makes oil by boiling (teo heenum) [cf. S. tel hiňdīm]

4829 HAA-NIDI GOVANII v. talks in one's sleep

4830 HAANIIKKA ހާނީއްކަ n. painful damage: h. libee kamek, a painful activity: h. kuranii, harms (with dat.) [? cf. S., Skt. hāni]

4831 HAANTI VANII ހާންތި ވަނީ v. is exhausted with hunger

4832 HAA-FUS n. non-rainy clouds

4833 HAABOŇGA LEVENII ހާބޮންގަ ލެވެނީ v. useless racket or uproar arises

4834 HAAMA ހާމަ adj. opened up: haama-ař huri ge-ek, an exposed house: haama-ař beheṭṭi bat, rice left exposed: boo haama-ař laigen, bareheaded: fai haama-ař laigen, barefooted; haama kuranii, reveals, discloses

4835 HAA-MUNḌI ހާމުންޑި n. kind of goblin which appears as poultry

4836 HAARU ހާރު n. 1. necklace (of modern type) [S.& Skt. hāra]
2. See hauru
3. ifc., time : mi-haaru (mihaaru), now. e-haaru, then [mihaa-iru]

4837 HAALI (haayyek) ހާލި n. nest (haali-gaňḍu)

4838 HAALI-FOḶI / HAALU-FOḶI ހާލިފޮޅި - ހާލުފޮޅި n. kind of preservable thin pancake, esp. made in Kuḷaduffuři

4839 HAALU ހާލު n. condition, state: nubai h., lack of prosperity; state of health: dera haalu, poor health: boḍu haalu , serious state of health (hon., haalu-koḷu); goos h., bad condition (in health or finance): haalugai jehigen, in a poor way economically: haalu-ahuvaalu, general condition (doublet): haalu balan, to see how people are, to visit; also used of time : edee haalu, while asking: haalu-haalun, seldom [U. h̲āl]

4840 HAALU- ހާލު- n. See haa (haalek)

4841 HAAVANII ހާވަނީ v. 1. disarranges, messes up, scratches about (of poultry); combs aside (v.n. heevum): tiya heevum den na-haavai, having stopped making such a mess of things: uňgu haavaa-laafai, having opened up the sarong: boo heevifai (invol.), with dishevelled hair
2. haa vanii, see haa kuranii

4842 HAAS (haahek) ހާސް 1. num. thousand: ek haas, one thousand: haahaa duisat̲t̲a, twelve hundred: haas baigen, catching 1000 fish: haas-fai, millipede [S. dahas, cf. Skt. sahasra; see also saas-kafu]

4843 HAAS (haahek) ހާސް 2. n. difficulties: haahek nuvee, no difficulties: h. araafai, difficulties having arisen: haas-kam, difficulties: haas vanii, is worried, pressed, choked

4844 HAA-SARU ހާސަރު n. rubbishy nonsense

4845 HAASILU ހާސިލު n. (anc.) customs dues: h. naganii, charges the dues (mod. ma'muul); haasil kuranii, wins, achieves, acquires [U. h̲āṣil]

4846 HAAZIRU ހާޒިރު n. presence, present (adj.): h. kuranii, brings a person to appear: h. vanii, duly appears : haazirii, attendance register [U. h̲āz̲ir]

4847 HAAHAA LANII ހާހާ ލަނީ v. makes confused noises [onom.]

4848 HAAHUURA ހާހޫރަ n. magic curse: h. jehifai, struck by magic

4849 HAAḶALA ހާޅަލަ n. a medicinal plant

4850 HIKA ހިކަ n. a children's game, 'touch on the head'

4851 HIKAŇDI ހިކަނޑި n. 1. a kind of shrew [cf. S. hik-mīyā, Skt. cikkā]

2. a shrub, murraya koenigii (hikaňdi gas): h. fat, 'curry leaves'

4852 HIKAA(-aek) ހިކާ n. a baitfish, wrasse (also called huḷi-hikaa)

4853 HIKI (hikkek) ހިކި adj. dry : hiki mas, dried fish; dryness: hikiige ekoḷukoḷu, the opposite of 'dry'; constipated (baňḍu hiki): (met.) sikuňḍi hiki, unintelligent: hiki-bali jehenii, gets dehydrated (of people); (of people) thin, skinny (hařigaňḍu hiki): hiki-kaři koř hurum, being thin; ebbing tide (diyavaru hiki): enme hiki diyaagai, at low water [S. hiku (lex.), Skt. śuṣka]

4854 HIK(U)MAT ހިކުމަތް n. cleverness, smartness (sometimes pej.); hikumat-teri(yaa), clever (person): hikmat-teri kuḷivarek, an intellectual game: (of God) hikmat-vanta, omniscient [U. h̲ikmat]

4855 HIKENII ހިކެނީ v. gets dry: gets constipated: gets thin: diya hiken jehenii, tide is starting to go down [hiki]

4856 HIKKANII ހިއްކަނީ v. dries (tr.): fen boo vaḷu diya h., bales out water from the drinking well: aḷugaňḍu karu hikkaa, I am thirsty; karu hikkaa duvahek, a thirstmaking day (caus. of hikenii)

4857 HIGAHALI (higahayyek) ހިގަހަލި n. needle for net-making

4858 HIŇGANII ހިނގަނީ v. walks (impv. hiňgaa! hon. hingavanii : caus. hinganii , q.v.) : of clocks, is going: of ships, sets sail (furaigen hiňgajje): of laws, is valid: e deetereegaa hiňgii aḷugaňḍee, it was me who walked in the middle, i.e. I arranged it all: hiňgaa-lanii, walks: hiňgaafai, on foot: (invol.) aharen mi uḷenii nuhiňgigennee, I can't walk just now: naibukamaa hiňgum, an old ceremony of judges processing on 6th Rajab: hiňgaa koři, walking pen for children: hiňgum, (as a street name) avenue.

Used as exhortative after another verb: damaa hiňgaa, let's go! adaa kuramaa hingavaařee, let's pay! (hon.) [S. hiňganne, walks round for alms]

4859 HIJRA KURANII ހިޖުރަ ކުރަނީ v. migrates (of birds) [U. hijra]

4860 HIT ހިތް n. mind, (met.)heart (hon., hitpuḷu): magee hitun, I think, in my opinion: kalee hitun, as far as you know: hitu huri got, one's heart's desire: hitu tereegai,within one's heart: hitař gennanii, imagines: hit denii, gives one's heart: kaleege hit, your darling: hit hitakař denii, gives gifts without strings: hit hama jassanii, satisfies oneself (that.., .. kamugai): hitař aranii, (impersonal) comes to mind, is thought of, is wished for; hit kiyanii, discloses one's desire, 'fancies' (someone): vakarugaňḍu maavaḍiyaa hitekee, the wood is for the carpenter to use as he will (prov.): niyaa faňḍiyaaraa hitekee, the decision is up to the judge: hit vanii after part., wants to; varař kaa hit ve-ee, much wants to eat: godan kaa hitek nuvee, doesn't want to eat wheat: aḷugaňḍu adi miihakaa iňna hitek net, I don't want to get married yet; hit ali, intelligent, quick to learn: hit koři, mentally dull: hit-gaimu, pleasing, comforting: hit gada, strong-minded, unemotional: hit gaa, mentally dull (of people): hit-taru, thought processes: hit- tiri, humble (hon., hitpuḷu tiri), modest, practical: hit tuunu, intelligent: hit dati, discontented, distressed: hit- dahi lavvanii, provokes: hit faseeha, comfortable, convenient: hit fahi, mentally contented: magee maccař hit baru kuranii, has a grudge against me: hit bali, weepy, squeamish: hit biru gannanii, shows timidity: hit moḷu, proud (pej.),vain, demanding: hit-varu, perseverance; hitvaru gada, brave: hitvaru dera, fainthearted: hitvaru jassanii, builds up strength: hitvaru denii, encourages: hitvaru kuranii, perseveres: hitvaru elenii, confidence is lost; hit saafu, open-hearted: hit haru, hard-hearted: hit-haři hama vum, being contented in mind and body: hit heyo, kind, affable; hitu gini, feeling of annoyance: hitu das, knowing by heart; Guruvaan h. beekalun, those who know the Quran by heart: masverikam hitudas, knowledgeable on fishing: Koḷuňbu hitudas, well acquainted with Colombo: hitu(n) das kuranii, learns by heart: hitu lafaa, estimate, idea of; magee hitulafaa-ař, according to my lights: hitu loobi, goodness of one's heart, lovingkindness: hitu viya, mental arithmetic [S. hit, Skt. citta]

4861 HITA ހިތަ n. asterism Citrā [S. Sita]

4862 HITANII ހިތަނީ v. thinks carefully (hon. hiṯṯavanii): kalee hitanii kiikee ta, what do you think you're doing? often used with adverbs : nubai koř h., thinks ill of, treats badly: hurmat-teri koř hitaigen, with respectful feelings: raňgaḷu koř h., heyo koř h., respects: kamee hitanii, respects [S. hitanne, cf. Skt. cintayati]

4863 HITAA (HITAI) VANII ހިތާ ވަނީ - ހިތައި ވަނީ v. falls in love (with.., ..-aa): hitai nuvum, hitakaa nuvum, disapproving, disliking; aḷugaňḍu mi fotakaa hitakaa nuvee, I don't care for this book: eii aḷugaňḍu hitaa nuvaa kamek, that's a thing I don't care for [hit]

4864 HITAAMA ހިތާމަ n. sadness; sad (hitaama-veri): tiya kamaa h. kuranii, is sad about that: hitaamain hurum, being sad, mourning: hitaama huṭṭeve, alas! (referring to the past)

4865 HITI (hiccek) ހިތި adj. bitter : hiti-miiru, pleasantly bitter: h. kekuri, bitter gourd: h. damui, bitter parsley, ptychotis ajowan: hiti teyo, a medicinal oil: hiti daňḍi, a medicinal stick; hitidaňḍii fen, hitifatu fen, kinds of medicinal water: hiti boo(bolek), kind of baitfish, silverside, atherinoides [S. tit, Skt. tikta]

4866 HITI (hiccek) ހިތި n. 1. kind of tree, margosa, neem, azadirachta indica: kudi hiti, a medicinal tree, phyllanthus sp.

2. an important festival formerly held on 22, 24, 26 and 28 Ramzan: boḍu de-Hiti, the two important festival days: hiti-ge, ceremonial tent for hiti celebrations, used for the King to stay the night in: Hitii keem, a feast for Hiti: Hitii booṭu, a carnival 'boat' for Hiti

4867 HITUN ހިތުން n. in the opinion of: aḷugan̆ḍu hitun, I think (instr. of hit)

4868 HITUM ހިތުން v. thinking (v.n. of hitanii) [S. hitīm]

4869 HI<u>TT</u>AN ހިއްތަން n. a medicament, nail of a sea creature: h. dorooři , the chief (northern) gate of the old Royal Palace at Male

4870 HITTANII ހިތްތަނީ v. tantalizes

4871 HI<u>TT</u>ALA ހިއްތަލަ n. kind of yam, 'Indian arrowroot', tacca leontopetaloides: hi<u>tt</u>ala boo, bald head [S. hiritala]

4872 HI<u>TT</u>EVUM ހިއްތެވުން v. thinking carefully (hon.) (v.n. of hi<u>tt</u>avanii) [hitanii]

4873 <u>KH</u>IDUMAT ހިދުމަތް n. service (usu. political) [U. <u>kh</u>idmat]

4874 HIN̆DI - LONU ހިނދިލޮނު n. a medicinal salt [hin̆denii]

4875 HIN̆DU ހިނދު n. space of time: hin̆duhin̆du-koḷun, now and again: hin̆du-koḷakař, for a short moment : ehin̆du-ehin̆dun, at that very moment [S. san̆da, Skt. sandhi]

4876 HIN̆DURI ހިނދުރި n. nostril [? S. sidura, hole, Skt. chidra]

4877 HIN̆DENII ހިނދެނީ v. evaporates (intr.)(caus. hindanii, q.v.); (of balloons, tyres, sails) is deflated; (of the wind) drops; is choked (with sobs, laughter, ticklishness); (at game of ořvaḷu) ends one's turn opposite an empty hole: ma hin̆dijje, my turn has ended thus [S. hin̆denne]

4878 HIN ހިން n. waist : only in hin damaalanii / demilanii, straightens the back, relaxes: hin diruvanii, makes swallowing movements; see also gabuḷa

4879 HINANII ހިނަނީ v. ritually bathes (hinai-gatum); caus., hinavanii (v.n. hine(v)um), washes a corpse, embalms : hinaa jahanii / hinee jahanii, (of animals) takes a sandbath, churns up the sand

4880 HINI ހިނި n. 1. ant (Varieties: rat h. (aadaige h.), kiňbi h., avas h., bis h., kaḷu h. (kaňḍaa) : boḍu sarudaaru, very large ant): hakuru-koḷař hini araa, ants have got into the sugar [S. hini]

2. laughter: hini annanii, laughs (hon., hinifuḷu vaḍuvanii: of the Prophet, hini varuna kuravvanii): hini-gaňḍu, guffaw: hini-tun vanii, smiles [S. hinā]

4881 HINE(V)UM ހިނެވުން - ހިނެއުން v. washing a corpse (v.n. of hinavanii)

4882 HINEVENI ހިނެވެނި n. (anc.) lady-in-waiting

4883 HINEE JAHANII ހިނީ ޖަހަނީ v. See hinanii

4884 HINGANII ހިންގަނީ v. makes to go: runs(tr.), administers; nazaru h., casts a glance: eenaage maccař śariyat h., brings him to trial: (invol.) hingee varuge veriyaku, an official competent to administer: kamek qavaaidař hingee fada miihek nuunee, is not a man who could administer efficiently: ‘adl insaaf hingiya nudevvai, (hon.) not permitting the administration of justice: (enlarged) aḷugaňḍuge nufuus hingaa-levee varař vure, more than I could control : hingaa faraat, those in charge: hingum matii hure, remaining in control: hingum-teri, executive (caus. of hiňganii)

4885 HINCI ހިންޗި n. inch [E. inch]

4886 HINTAA (-aaek) ހިންޓާ n. tricks: h. hadanii, is cunning, is a cheat

4887 HINDANII ހިންދަނީ v. makes to evaporate; boils dry: baňḍu h.,tones down the stomach (caus. of hiňdenii)

4888 HINDUURA ހިންދޫރަ n. red lead [Skt. sindūra]

4889 HINNA ހިންނަ n. privately dedicated land: hinna onnanii miskit maccařee, the land is dedicated to the mosque

4890 HINMANII ހިންމަނީ v. solders, mends cooking pots

4891 HINMI ހިންމި n. joint, thin gap

4892 HINHURA ހިންހުރަ n. shallow sea round an island

4893 HIFANII ހިފަނީ v. catches; embraces; grasps: catches fish by net or harpoon (not by hook & line); hungaanugai hifum, holding the tiller: biletkuriige haki hifaakař nuuḷee hee, aren't the betel suckers going to stick? bat vatugai hifaifi, the rice has stuck to the bottom (of the pan): gada-ař hifaa terahek, a strong glue: da<u>tt</u>age atugai hifaigen, holding sister's hand: (enlarged) valugai hifaa-lan aade, come and hold the rope: (met.) eenaage meegai fini hifanii, he is catching a chest cold: deetin ekaccař hifum, adopting one of two courses: huḷu hifanii, bursts into flame: wrestles, fights: dekudin hifaa-lek gadakamun, by the fury of the youths' fight: guḷamati hifanii, performs ancient ceremonial wrestling: hifaa genguḷee takeccek, a domestic utensil: badalu h., gives a return, exacts vengeance: beenum h., uses, can use: fen baaru h., floats, can float: keeta hifaifi, the eclipse began: rooda hifanii, begins fasting; mihaaru derooda hifaifim, I have fasted two days now: abs. hifaigen is often used in the sense 'bringing with one', 'with..' [S. sipanne]

4894 HIFAHAṬṬANII (HIFAAṬṬANII) ހިފަހައްޓަނީ (ހިފާއްޓަނީ) v. holds, retains; maintains (a habit) (v.n. hifeheṭṭum): hataru avař hifahaṭṭavan, to control four wards: (enlarged) nubune hifahaṭṭaa-liimeve, I kept quiet: intizaam hifeheṭṭi, arrangements being made: hifeheṭṭum, mental reservations: hifeheṭṭum-teriyek, a patient man [enlargement of hifanii, cf. obahaṭṭanii]

4895 HIPPANII ހިއްޕަނީ v. sticks on (tr.), makes to hold: duli h., applies a poultice: kavaa fuḷi h., applies a cupping bottle: hippaala denii, helps to pull up a boat to shore: guḍi hippaa karudaas, tissue- paper used in making smaller kites: (invol.) atoḷuveriinnař valugai hippidaane-ee, baarek nulevveene-ee, an atoll chief can be made to hold the rope, but not to pull (prov.) (caus. of hifanii)

4896 HIPPAVANII ހިއްޕަވަނީ v. takes (hon.), esp. in sense drinks (hon. of hifanii)

4897 HIBA ހިބަ n. 1. kind of poisonous reef fish
2. hiba koř dinum, hiba-ař dinum, giving unconditionally [U. hiba]

4898 HIBARU ހިބަރު n. swordfish (Varieties: tungaňḍu h., xiphias; fan(-gaňḍu) h., sailfish, istiophorus; mas h., marlin, makaira)

4899 HIMA ހިމަ adj. (of things) thin and round: fine (thread, needle): hima-toḷi, (of people) slim: hima fodu, drizzle: hima bihi, measles; h. aḷaigen, having caught measles [S. sihin, siyum, Skt. sūkṣma]

4900 HIMANANII ހިމަނަނީ v. includes: enumerates (v.n. himenum : hon., himanuvvanii): boo himenum, census

4901 HIMAAYAT ހިމާޔަތް n. protection: h. kuranii, protects: h. denii, gives protection: himaayat-terikam, protection [U. <u>h</u>imāyat]

4902 HIMAARU ހިމާރު n. donkey [U. <u>h</u>imār]

4903 HIMUN ހިމުން adj. finely ground (of powder, sugar, salt, sand etc.): (in carpentry) fine: h. vaḍaam, fine carpentry work: h. kuranii, grinds fine, sets fine

4904 HIMENUM ހިމެނުން v. inclusion (v.n. of himananii)

4905 HIMERI ހިމެރި n. bean, lablab (himeri-toḷi): fookvaḷi h., swordbean: h. duuni, for nimeri duuni, q.v. ; duu himeri, a straggling plant

4906 HIMEEN ހިމޭން adj. quiet, quietness (himeen-kam): himeenun hurum, keeping quiet: hanu-himeen, quiet

4907 HIMMAT ހިންމަތް n. effort: himmat-terikam, effort [U. himmat]

4908 HIMMANII ހިންމަނީ v. See hinmanii

4909 HIYA ހިޔަ num. (anc.) 96: hiya doḷissa, 144 : hiya-rakaat duvas, a festival, 15th day of Shaubaan (when 100 rakvaa s are prescribed) [cf. S. siya-, 100]

4910 HIYAU ހިޔައު See hiyaa

4911 HIYANI ހިޔަނި n. shadow, image, outline: h. aḷanii, casts shadow : eenaage hiyaniigai karuna aḷa-aḷaa, weeping for him [S. hevana]

4912 HIYAMA ހިޔަމަ n. sea- urchin

4913 HIYARI ހިޔަރި n. sledgehammer

4914 HIYALA ހިޔަލަ n. a girl's name

4915 HIYAVIHAA ހިޔަވިހާ n. asterism Śatabhiṣak [S. siyāvasa]

4916 HIYAḶU ހިޔަޅު n. jackal [S. hival, Skt. śṛgāla]

4917 HIYAA, HIYAU (hiyalek) ހިޔައު - ހިޔާ n. shade; temporary cadjan shelter on a boat

4918 KHIYAALU ޚިޔާލު n. opinion, idea: khiyaalii (adj.), imaginary [U. khiyāl]

4919 HIYAAVAHI (hiyaavassek) ހިޔާވަހި n. hut or shelter [hiyaa]

4920 HIRAFUS ހިރަފުސް n. dust

4921 HIRI ހިރި n. coral limestone: hiri gaa, lump of coral limestone [S. hiri-gal]

4922 HIRI ހިރި v. having moved (intr.) (abs. of hirenii)

4923 HIRI-KUḶḶA ހިރިކުއްޅަ n. a plant, emilia sonchifolia

4924 HIRI-DATI ހިރިދަތި n. kind of grass, eclipta alba ; also for hunigoňḍi-filaa, phyla nodiflora

4925 HIRI-FAAḶA ހިރިފާޅަ n. a herb

4926 HIRI-MAGUU (-magulek) ހިރިމަގޫ n. a herb, thecagonum biflorum (hedyotis biflora)

4927 HIRIMI ހިރިމި n. water-pot

4928 HIRIYAA ހިރިޔާ adj. (anc. honorific descriptive): radunge hiriyaa faaturaage dařař, to the King's presence [P. sirī]

4929 HIRIHAAMAADI / HIRIHAAMAANTI ހިރިހާމާންތި - ހިރިހާމާދި n. an old kangati title (h. kaleegefaanu)

4930 HIRU ހިރު n. 1. ornamental stripe on feeli: : hiru aḷanii, applies such stripes; moi h., wake of ship;
2. gums (hiru-gaňḍu)

4931 HIRUDDA ހިރުއްދަ n. inner sill of window or door

4932 HIRUŇDU ހިރުނދު n. kind of tuliptree, thespesia populnea: Efrikaa h., spathodea campanulata: h. duuni, kind of ladybird found on h. trees [cf. S. sūriya]

4933 HIRUVANII ހިރުވަނީ v. itches (intr.): fai eba hiruvaee, (my) leg itches [cf.S. hori, itching]

4934 HIRENII ހިރެނީ v. moves gently (intr.), usu. of animates or of boats; enlarged, hiri-lanii

4935 HILA ހިލަ n. stone (not from the sea, cf. gaa): h. karudaas, sandpaper: h. caap, litho: h. bim, land where stone is quarried: hila-toři, hard outrer skin of certain trees (such as bamboo): hila-veli, non-coral sand (imported, hard and black): hila-vaḷu, pit of sand; fai hilavaḷu obenii, all sounds die away; hila vanii, becomes hard, petrified [old S. sala, Skt. śilā]

4936 HILANII ހިލަނީ v. stirs up in cooking, thickens food (e.g. boohuni, furahani, harisa, hakuru, haluvaa, meṭaa, fuřgaňḍu): messes up, spoils (of cooking bookibaa, batpen), usu. hilaa-lanii in this sense; also of doing a job badly: collects cowries (boli h., faru h.); caus., hiluvanii, stirs up (trouble, revolt), brings up a subject; (invol .) is spoilt: is stirred up: appears on the surface: muudu matiigai teo hilenii, oil appears on the surface of the sea: diya hilijje, water has seeped in: bali hilijje, the disease (re)appeared: (met.) gets excited, [illegible] hiligen uḷee duvahek, a day when he got excited

4937 HILAM ހިލަމް n. appearance, indication of (esp. used in neg. sentences): miihekge hilamek ves nuve-ee, there is no sign of anyone [U. hilm, dream]

4938 HILAA ހިލާ adv. at all (in neg. sentences): tiya kamtak hilaa kuriaka nudeenamee, I will not allow that to be done at all: hilaa nuves aii, didn't come at all: hilaa naee, just wouldn't come: hama hilaa nudaanamee, I certainly will not go

4939 KHILAAFU ހިލާފު n. contrary: eaai khilaafař, contrary to that (adv.) [U. khilāf]

4940 HILI-KUSA ހިލިކުސަ n. a sweetmeat [hilenii]

4941 HILI-BEES ހިލިބީސް n. medicinal pastilles (esp. for new mothers)

4942 HILIHILAA(-aaek) ހިލިހިލާ n. large chain (e.g. for anchor) [silsilaa]

4943 HILI-HUNI ހިލިހުނި n. a sweetmeat [hilenii]

4944 HILEI, HILEE ހިލޭ - ހިލެއި adj. gratis, free and for nothing: hilee miihaa, woman who is not related to you

4945 HILLANII ހިއްލަނީ v. brings to the surface; exudes (caus. hilluvanii): daa hillanii, sweats; aharen daa hillaa, I am sweating: neevaaa hillanii, pants asthmatically [hilanii]

4946 HIS ހިސް excl. his his! shoo! his govanii, makes shooing noises [onom.]

4947 HISAABU ހިސާބު n. 1. number: account, amount: h. kuranii, does accounts; takes stock, audits: h. hama jassanii, prepares accounts: h. jahanii, does sums; hisaabu-tak, figures, statistics: h. akuru, figures, digits; hisaabugai nulai, not taking into account: hisaabuge tereař laigen, taking into account [U. hisāb]

2. point, place: mi hisaabakař huṭṭaalaafai, having stopped at such a point: h. hifanii, makes course for; hisaabu-gaňḍu, area: ein hisaabekgai ves, anywhere near there

4948 HISSAA ހިއްސާ n. shares: kamekgai hissaa kuranii, contributes a share, takes part: kunfuniin h. gatum, taking shares in the company [U. hissa]

4949 HIHUU (hihulek) ހިހޫ 1. n. 'Spanish windlass': h. aňburanii, applies this

2. adj. cooled down: hihuu kořlanii, cools down(tr.): h. vanii, cools down (intr.) [S. sihil, Skt. śītala]

4950 HII ހީ n. 1. imagination: hii kuranii, imagines (hopes, suspects); thinks of: eccek hii nukuraaře, think nothing of it: nufenna kamugai hii vamun, thinking (it) wouldn't appear: huunu hen hiivee ta, do you feel hot? ahannař hiivanii hum annanii hen, I think (you) are getting feverish: hii vaa got, how it looks, the effect it has: hii nukoř tibbaa, while not thinking, i.e. unexpectedly [S. sihi, P. sati, Skt. smṛti]

2. shivering: hii karuvanii, shivers (v.n. hii keruvum ; non-Male usage, hii kerum): hii gatum, shivering (non-Male usage) ; hii bihi, gooseflesh: aharen mi inii hii-bihi nagaafaee, I have got goosepimples: hii-hum, ague; mikoi hiihum annanii, the child is getting feverish [old S. sī, Skt. śīta]

4951 HIIŇ ހީނ v. having laughed (abs., or imp., of henii): hiiň hii(ň), by laughing: h. gatum, laughing: h. lum, laughing; hiiň laa aḍu, sound of laughter: hii samaasa, jokes and laughter [old S. sī]

4952 HII-EVETIGEN ހީއެވެތިގެން v. (anc.) diligently [abs. form]

4953 HIINARU ހީނަރު adj. moribund (of trees, or businesses)

4954 HIINAA ހީނާ n. henna, lawsonia inermis (used for cracks on the feet): husnu h., queen of the night, cestrum nocturnum [U. hinnā]

4955 HII-VAAGI (-vaatgek) ހީވާގި adj. hardworking

4956 HIIRAS ހީރަސް n. binding of a book; stapling: h. dati, stapler

4957 HIIRAA ހީރާ n. diamond [H. hīrā]

4958 HIIRAAFOOS ހީރާފޯސް n. green medicinal wax

4959 HIIRI ހީރި n. kind of worm

4960 HIILAT ހީލަތް n. trickery, deceit; deceptive (hiilat-teri) [U. ẖīla]

4961 HIILI ހީލި n. ticklishness: h. hunna, ticklish: h. gada, very ticklish: h. maḍu, not very ticklish: h. neti, not ticklish; hiili kar̃igaňḍu, funnybone; hiili karuvanii, makes to squirm: ma hiili karuvaa, it makes me feel ticklish: h. koṭṭanii, tickles (tr.)

4962 HIIS ހީސް n. urine (esp. childish): h. lanii, urinates; aharen hiis lavaa, I want to urinate

4963 HIISI ހީސި n. (childish) penis [siisi]

4964 HUI ހުއި n. maritime grass (varieties: onu h., panicum maximum: tuňbuḷi h., eragrostis tenella: maa h., dactyloctenium aegyptium: biletu h.)

4965 HUI-FILAŇḌAA ހުއިފިލަނޑާ n. sea cucumber

4966 HUIVANI ހުއިވަނި n. kind of jellyfish

4967 HUISUM ހުއިސުމް n. an aromatic medicine, costus speciosus

4968 HUKUM ހުކުމް n. 1. verdict, judgment: h. kuranii, delivers judgment: h. kaňḍa aḷanii, decides verdict [U. ẖukm]

2. trumps: hukum bunii laalar̃ee, declared hearts trumps

4969 HUKURU ހުކުރު n. Friday: h. kuranii, attends Friday prayers: h. faibanii, comes out of Friday prayers: h. kuravvanii, leads Friday prayers; hukuru hat duvas, week beginning from Friday: Hukuru miskit, Friday mosque [S. sikurā-dā, Skt. śukra, Venus]

4970 HUKUREDI, HUKURADI (hukurejjek) ހުކުރެދި - ހުކުރަދި n. a plant

4971 HUŇGU ހުނގު n. a medicinal lotion, assafoetida (ferula foetida), used against colds and for worms [S. hiṃgu, Skt. hinku]

4972 HUŇGULI ހުނގުލި n. edge of thatching strip: h. kaňḍanii, trims bottom of a thatching strip: h. kor̃anii, trims thatching strips (pl.)

4973 HUŇGUU (huňgulek) ހުނގޫ n. tip of leaf

4974 HUJJAT ހުއްޖަތް n. excuses: h. dakkanii, h. hadanii, proffers excuses [U. h̲ujjat]

4975 HUṬṬANII ހުއްޓަނީ v. stops (tr. and intr.); finishes (imp. huṭṭee ! caus. huṭṭuvanii): vaare huṭṭaifi, the rain stopped: aḷugaňḍař huṭṭaek nulevuneve, I didn't stop at that: huṭṭum aranii, puts a stop (to, dat.): medař huṭṭum, half-time (at games): huṭṭaa (huṭṭai), while one was, while there was; baara jahaan fanara huṭṭaa, at 11.45; iru huṭṭaa, before sunset: huṭṭaa nulaa, ceaselessly (adv.): (invol.), kuḷi huṭṭi ree, on the last night of the games: mi fot mi huṭṭunii, I got to the end of (reading) this book: huṭṭi dee, looks like stopping (e.g. of pendulum): huṭṭum erenii, gets stuck, gets held up, stops short
[S. hiṭinne, cf. Skt. tiṣṭhati]

4976 HUŇḌALI ހުނޑަލި See hoňḍali

4977 HUT ހުތް n. sour juice: raa hut, toddy vinegar: surukaa hut, imported vinegar: luňboo hut fitum, squeezing a lime: 'pig' of an orange: hut teyo, a medicinal oil: as adj., sour: hut maskaaři , a sour fish dish: h. gada, very sour: hut-foni, sweet but slightly sour (e.g. grapefruit); hut denii, constrains, brainwashes [Skt. śukta]

4978 HUTURU ހުތުރު adj. ugly

4979 - HUT̲T̲U -ހުއްތު adj. ifc., younger (childish, or in proper names): Kuḍa-hut̲t̲uaa ekugai, with Kuḍahut̲t̲u: kaḷuhut̲t̲u meevaa, kind of fruit, anona glabra [=Tut̲t̲u]

4980 HUDU ހުދު adj. white : hudu kaakii, an indeterminate pale colour: hudu kaaḷu, white crow, i.e. a great rarity: hudu faḷu, a sandy shallow: hudu-fuř, white-bellied (of fish): hudu fuřpilaa, a plant, aerva lanata: hudu feeli, bale of white cloth: hudu bali, a skin disease: hudu loo, white brass: huduhudaa, kind of bird, hoopoe: hudem, a bait fish
[S. sudu, Skt. śuddha]

4981 HUDDA ހުއްދަ n. permission [? U. huddā]

4982 HUN ހުން See gabuḷa

4983 HUNARU ހުނަރު n. skill : hunaruveri, skilful [H. hunar]

4984 HUNI ހުނި n. 1. lime: h. lanii, uses lime for a chew; faarugai h. lanii, whitewashes the wall; bilet huni, betel and lime: huni-koḷu, lump of lime (for a chew): huni-guraabu, case for lime: huni-fat, tip of betel leaf where lime is put: huni-fen, medicinal lime water: huni-baḍi, lime tin: hunu-boli, (anc.) bowl for lime
2. ground white of coconut: huni gaananii, scrapes coconut; huni-goňḍi, coconut-scraper: hunigoňḍi-filaa, a ground creeper, phyla nodiflora (also called hiridati) [S. hunu, Skt. cūrṇa]

4985 HUNUM ހުނުން v. laughing (v.n. of henii)

4986 HUNGAANU ހުންގާނު n. rudder: steeringwheel: handlebars; h. aḷanii, fixes rudder: h. hifanii, steers: hungaanugai hunnanii, acts as steersman; hungaanu-ge, bridge of steamer: hungaanu duuni, ornamental tiller [cf. S. suṃgāḍam]

4987 HUNGUḶA ހުންގުޅަ n. lamp (literary)

4988 HUNNANII ހުންނަނީ v. stands; is; waits (abs. hure : imp. huree ! v.n. hurum : past tense huṭṭe(ve), huri, hurejje : hon. hunnavanii): bappa annan den nukal hunnam, I will wait till father comes before eating: fansurutak hunnanii nuu kulaigaa, the pencils are blue ones: baḍi duddaafai huṭṭee, the gun is ready primed: ree huri, which has stood overnight (i.e.stale): galamek eba huri ta, have you a pen? hurii istiri kuraařeve, is ironing; with verbal infinitives : fennan eba huri, is to be seen: deven hunna eccek, what could be given: aḷugaňḍu dakkan huri vaahaka, what I have to say [cf. S. hiṭinne, Skt. tiṣṭhati]

4989 HUŇBUḶU ހުނބުޅު n. kind of flying insect

4990 HUM ހުން n. fever : humaa (uḷee), feverish: aharen hum aisfai, I have a fever: Faatumatu hum annanii, Fatima is getting a fever: hum faaḍu kuranii, looks feverish; hum-koři, swollen stomach: hum-bees, quinine [S. uṇa, Skt. uṣṇa]

4991 HURA-GE ހުރަގެ n. prison-house, jail [S. hira-ge]

4992 HURAS (hurahek) ހުރަސް n. obstruction: crossbeam: hurahakaa nulai, without anything in between: (ařii) huras kunaa, the imam's mat; h. aḷanii, places obstructions (also met.), places crossbeams: magu huras kuranii, crosses the street: (invol.) dedoonňař haras kurevunii, the two boats crossed [S. haras, across]

4993 HURAHAḶANII ހުރަހަޅަނީ See huřahaḷanii

4994 HURAA ހުރާ n. rocky island (huraa-gaňḍu); name of a particular island

4995 HURI-HAA, HURI-HAI ހުރިހާ - ހުރިހައި adj. all (of them), used with pl. or -ek : hurihai dorugai, in every doorway: hurihaa kamek, everything: mi-hira hai.., all these.. [hurum + hai 4]

4996 HURUM ހުރުން v. standing, being (v.n. of hunnanii): p.p. huri: mi-ii mařař huri got, this is my natural bad luck: e-hera (for e huri), that there; (invol.) aḷugaňḍař hurevunii, I found myself to be.. [cf. S. hiṭīm]

4997 HURE ހުރެ v. having stood (abs. of hunnanii):geegai huregen, staying at home: kalee aadee too hure hure, waiting for you to come; after -aa, about, because of: tiya kamaa hure, because of that [cf. S. hiṭa]

4998 HURMAT ހުރުމަތް n. respect: hurmat-teri, respectful: (adv.) hurmatteri koř, respectfully [U. hurmat]

4999 HULI ހުލި adj. stunted (of fruit: children: rockets): huli vanii, (of people) gets thinner, weaker (hulijje = huli vejje): (of fire, hookahs) dies down, gets low: (of fruit) is undeveloped: (of rockets) fails to go off: (met.) foorii h. vanii, enthusiasm dies down; huli-huli koř hunna, remaining thin (of children): huli koř levvum, burning down low(tr.); ifc. in names of certain beetles : gaa-huli, veeru-huli

5000 HUVAI ހުވައި See huvaa

5001 HUVAGOŘ ހުވަގޮށް n. a medicinal seed plant, acorus calamus, sweet flag

5002 HUVADUU ހުވަދޫ n. name of G atoll, north and south [anc., Suvaduu]

5003 HUVAŇDU ހުވަނދު n. scent: h. lanii, applies scent (on clothing or on face, esp. for mauluud ceremnies, or after dinner parties): h. kelaa, sweet sandalwood: h. maa, a scented jasmine, jasminum grandiflorum: h. kotan, a herb [S. suvaňda, Skt. sugandha]

5004 HUVAN ހުވަން n . asterism Śravaṇa [S. suvana]

5005 HUVANI ހުވަނި n. kind of (irritating) tree spider

5006 HUVAFAT ހުވަފަތް n. widow: h. vanii, becomes widowed

5007 HUVAFEN ހުވަފެން n. dream: h. fennanii, sees a dream: h. siidaa vanii, dream comes true [Skt. svapna]

5008 HUVA-RODI ހުވަރޮދި n. baby's charm-chain: (met.) h. ves netee, hasn't a bean, is broke

5009 HUVAA (HUVAI) ހުވާ (ހުވައި) n. oath: h. kuranii, takes an oath: h. laa denii, swears (someone) in [Skt. śapatha]

5010 HUVAAS ހުވާސް n. pulse: h. netijje, (his) pulse has stopped [Skt. śvāsa]

5011 HUS (huh-) ހުސް adj. empty: finished: huhař hurum, being empty: meesa raahi hus vejje, Aries is over; hussi mahu, last month (for hus vi): vayař h. vanii, evaporates: khabaru hus vum, being unconscious: jahaigen h. kořfi, snatched away: kai h. kořfi, gobbled up: hus haṭṭař huri, being unmarried (see hussari-): e vaḷugaňḍu foruvaalii hus kilaafahunneve, that hole was just filled with dirt; adv. , hus ekani, only [S. his, Skt. tucchya]

5012 HUŚIYAARU ހުށިޔާރު adj. vigilant, alert [U. huśiyār]

5013 HUSNU HIINAA ހުސްނުހީނާ n. queen of the night, cestrum nocturnum ['beautiful henna']

5014 HUSSARI-BAI ހުއްސަރިބައި n. unmarried person [hus- hař̌i-]

5015 HUHI ހުހި n. undeveloped coconut fruit: boňḍihuhi-vak, such a coconut, wrapped in cloth and used as a sponge for slates

5016 HUŘA-HAḶANII, HUŘA-HOḶANII (HURA-HAḶANII) ހުށަހަޅަނީ - ހުށަހޮޅަނީ (ހުރަހަޅަނީ) v. proposes:brings forward (a document), adduces (hon. huřahaḷuvvanii); huřanaaḷai, not having adduced

5017 HUŘI ހުށި v. which was [literary variant of huri]

5018 HUḶAŇGU ހުޅަނގު n. west: April-December monsoon [S. huḷaňga, wind]

5019 HUḶI ހުޅި n. crest : bolu h., hair bun: haalu h., feathers behind a coxcomb, (of horses, lions) mane: raaḷu h., crest of wave: kan h., sideburns: huḷi-hikaa, a bait fish (hikaa) [S. siḷu, Skt. cūḍā]

5020 HUḶU ހުޅު n. 1. joint: hinge: kuḍa huḷu, wrist: ankle

2. flame: geegai h. jahanii, sets fire to house: geegai h. hifanii, house catches fire: huḷu-gaňḍu, flame; huḷugaňḍu jahanii, lights bonfire: baṯṯiige huḷugaňḍu kuḍa kořlaařee, turn down the flame of the lamp: huḷu-daan kuranii, lights up brightly (tr.): huḷu-fan, torch of coconut leaves: huḷufan jahanii, lights torch: huḷufanaa danii, goes fishing with lights: huḷu lanii, lights up flame for the first time; Boḍu Huḷu, the Great Fire of Male (in 1887) [S. huḷu]

5021 HUḶUŇBU ހުޅުނބު n. fish-scale

5022 HUḶUVANII ހުޅުވަނީ v. opens (tr.), turns on (radio) (imp. huḷuvaa ! hon. huḷuvvavanii): boḍař huḷuvanii, opens wide

5023 HUUŇ ހޫން excl. particle of assent, I agree, yes I see (quoted, in repetitions, huunėkee)

5024 HUUKU ހޫކު n. 'hook' used as keyrimg, or to join fishhook to line [E. hook]

5025 HUUNU ހޫނު adj. hot; heat : koṭari huunee, the room is hot: ahannař huunee/ huunu vee, I feel hot. huunu min, the temperature: attilaige huunuge sababun, because of the heat of one's palm: (met.) huunu-finñař balaigen, judging the situation; huunu uḷaa, 'hot bracelet', mild discipline for children, or attempt to please a disgruntled wife (huunu uḷalek aḷai dinum): huunu boňḍi, warm poultice, esp. for the eyes (huunuboňḍi aḷailum) [S. huṇu, Skt. uṣṇa]

5026 HUUNEKEE ހޫނެކޭ excl . [repetition of huuň]

5027 HUURANII ހޫރަނީ v. wave: dida huuranii / huuruvanii, waves flags, semaphores: fankaa huuranii, waves fan: at h., waves (to someone): fai h., swings the leg (a bad habit); (invol.) kuňbu huuruna nudinumař, so as not to let the mast swing about

5028 HUURALAIIN ހޫރަލައިން n. (pl.) houris [U. ẖūr]

5029 HUURU-KAAFA ހޫރުކާފަ n. great-great grandfather

5030 HUURU-MAAMA ހޫރުމާމަ n. great-great grandmother

5031 HEI ހެއި n. asterism Svāti (Arcturus)

5032 HEI, HEIVARI ހެއިވަރި - ހެއި See hee, heevari

5033 HEU ހެއު See heyo

5034 HEKI (hekkek) ހެކި n. a witness: heki gennanii, produces a witness; evidence: heki denii, gives evidence: heki dakkanii, proves one's witness; de-hekin, two witnesses, as required for weddings: heki-veriyaa, representative of the bride: heki-bas, evidence

5035 HEṬṬI ހެއްޓި n. a sail knot: h. jahanii, applies this knot

5036 HEŇḌUM ހެނޑުން v. pissing (v.n. of haňḍanii)

5037 HETURU ހެތުރު n. strong fishing rope: h. bai, set of rope

5038 HEDUM ހެދުން n. 1. sewn clothing: faas kurı hedum, nambaru hedum, official long women's clothing: karaa h., foreign clothes; h. aḷanii, gets dressed (hon., hedum aḷuvvanii): h. aḷuvanii, h. lavvanii, dresses someone else [S. äňdum]
2. making (v.n. of hadanii) [S. hädīm]

5039 HEDENII ހެދެނީ v. grows; is made: gahek hedenii, a tree grows (not usu. used of diseases): imitates, pretends to be: seeku hedenii, plays the fool: miihakař h., pretends to be a person: ruḷi anna kamař h., pretends to be angry: hiňgi kamek nuhiňgaa kamakař hedee too , pretending that what happened didn't happen; hedi ran, jewellery: hedi- kaa (hedikaaek), 'short eats', snacks; hedi after -aa may represent 'because': e-gee Nafiisayaa hedi, because of N. of that address (invol. of hadanii) [S. hädenne]

5040 HEDDUM ހެއްދުން v. causing to make, do, nourish (v.n. of haddavanii) [hadanii]

5041 HEŇDI-VAĻU ހެނދިވަޅު n. places for applying ointment: hurihaa heňdi-heňdivaḷugai, in all the right places for ointment [? Skt. sandhi, joint]

5042 HEŇDUN ހެނދުން n. morning: h. sai, breakfast: heňdunaa, very early in the morning: tankoḷek heňdunu, heňdun-koḷu, rather early; earlier

5043 HEŇDUVUM ހެނދުވުން v. making love (v.n. of haňduvanii)

5044 HEN ހެން adv. in the manner; like: as if (after a participle): tiya hen, like that, in that way: anek hen, the other way: aḷugaňḍu hen, like myself, as I do: muḷin hen, almost entirely: konme hen (ves), anyway: tiya henñaa, if so: e bunaa hen! it's just as (she) says [? cf. S. sē]

5045 HENII ހެނީ v. laughs (abs. hiiň : past hunu : imp. hiiň! heeře ! v.n. hunum: : fut. heenii: : invol. hevenii (v.n. hevum): caus. hevvanii): baarař hunum, laughing loudly [S. (hinaa)-henne]

5046 HENḌELI ހެންޑެލި n. handle: (slang) penis [E. handle]

5047 HEFUM ހެފުން v. chewing, crushing (v.n. of hafanii) [S. häpīm]

5048 HEPPUM ހެއްޕުން v. feeding, grazing (tr.) : hui heppum, feeding on hay (v.n. of happanii) [hafanii]

5049 HEMUN ހެމުން v. laughing : hemun hemun, while laughing (pres. abs. of henii) [S. (sinā)semin]

5050 HEYO / HEU (heveve, hevee) ހެޔޮ - ހެއު adj. good; kind : heyo kamtak kurum, doing right: agu heyo, cheap: den heyo, that's enough: mařař heyo, it's all right with me; often with concessive verb : nayas heyo, never mind if (you) don't come: heyo viyas nuviyas, never mind whether or not; come what may: mi geyař nuvanakas hevee, I don't mind if you don't come here; heyo kuranii, cures, heals:; mee heyo kuranii, cures vomiting or indigestion: heyo kor (adv.) well: heyo koř hitanii, is kind (to), shows generosity: heyo koř viyyaa, if I'm right; no doubt: heyo vanii, is cured; is kind: has a male orgasm; heyo-varu, right amount, right size: riha etiige lonu heyovaru too belum, seeing if there is enough salt in the curry: hurihaa taakař ves heyovaru miihek, someone equally affable to all: (konme gotek) heyovaru miihek, an adaptable person, easy-going: libaas gayař heyovaru too belum, seeing if the garment fits: heyovaru kuranii, fits (tr.), alters to fit

5051 HEYYEE ހެއްޔޭ particle emphasized form of hee

5052 HERENII ހެރެނީ v. is pierced, stabbed:pierces (invol.): kaṭṭakař at herijje, hand was pricked by a thorn: iňgiyyař tinoos herijje, finger was pricked by a needle: gayař vaḷi herijje, the knife pierced the body: neezaaek heri, wounded by a dagger: idikiili heree mitanař, the grain of the wood catches here (invol. of haranii)

5053 HELENII ހެލެނީ v. is shaken up: shakes (intr.): helee ḍat, loose teeth: bim helum, earthquake: gaḍiige baaru helum, swinging of the pendulum: heli-feli vanii (doublet), moves, is mobile: (enlarged) heli-laan ves nukerifaa, unable to move: (met.) Divehi Raajje heligat heligatum, the instability which afflicted the Maldives (invol. of halanii)

5054 HELEŇBELI ހެލެނބެލި n. tamarind tree, tamarindus indica [S. siyaňbalā]

5055 HELLANII ހެއްލަނީ v. swings (tr.); rocks (tr.); (invol.) swings (intr.): (met.) is deceived: kula-akař hellum, being deceived by appearances: hellum-terikam, machinations [helenii, halanii]

5056 HEVAT ހެވަތް n. kindness [heyo]

5057 HEVAA (hevalek) ހެވާ n. developed white of coconut : h. foni kuruňbaek, a coconut with a sweet kernel: fani h., white of undeveloped miri coconut; (met.)hevaa ves nulaa kujjek, an immature lad

5058 HEVI-KAM ހެވިކަން n. old formal military exercises (e.g. lonsi hevikam)

5059 HEVENII ހެވެނީ v. bursts into laughter (invol. of henii)

5060 -HEVE -ހެވެ v. literary form of potential suffix -s : viiheve, would have been

5061 HEVEE ހެވީ See heyo

5062 HEVVAA ހެއްވާ v. (used adjectivally) amusing, odd (caus.part. of henii)

5063 HES ހެސް n. excessiveness: only in hes kiyaafaa, very strongly (of actions); hes kiyaafai masakkat kuranii, works like a trojan: and in hes gatum: tiya hen hes ganegeṇ uḷee varu kamek nuun, is not something worth getting excited about; esp. of lovers: e-gee Jamiila-aai hes genfaa, deeply in love with that Jamila

5064 HESA-AŘ ހެސައަރ adv. fast: fisaari hesa-ař duvefai, moving very fast [hes]

5065 HEHENII ހެހެނި v. husks (tr.): kaaři hehum, husking coconuts [S. sahinne]

5066 HEE ހީ 1. particle of formal query (emphatic, heyyee): mi-ii kihaa riiti bagiicaaek heyyeve, what a beautiful garden! kon javaabek heyyee too ee, do you say 'What answer'?

2. v. laughing (pres. part. of henii)

5067 HEE / HEI ހީ / ހެއި n. consciousness: h. jehenii, is sensible: hee jehee rañgaḷu vaahaka dakkaa, speak sense! hame hee jehi bala, be sensible! hei nujehum, foolishness: hee aranii, revives; he-ek naaraa, unconscious: hee netigen, being unconscious; hysterically: hee na<u>tt</u>anii, anaesthetizes: hee lanii, wakes up, opens eyes; nuheelavvaa, not awake: is visible clearly; hee nulavvaa, unaware; vat hee laa hisaabu, where thebottom (of the sea) is visible; diinii heelum-terikam, awareness of religious duties: hee balanii, is wary: hee boo aranii, gives undivided attention; hee boo naaraa, without a pause; hee-fař, shallow sea where the bottom is visible: hee-vat, frontmost compartment of hull of fishing boat: heevari (heivari), sensibility: heevari(kam) vanii, comes to one's senses [Skt. cētas]

5068 HEEKENII ހީކެނި v. rubbing off (intr.): muunugai gedabuḷi heekeene-ee, (your) face will get smeared with soot; (met.) kam kuran kamař heekenii, gives outward signs of doing something (invol. of haakanii)

5069 HEEḌI-FEEḌI ހީޑިފީޑި n. skill : h. hunna, skilled: h. nuhunna, clumsy (doublet, cf. eeḍi, feeḍi)

5070 HEEDA KURANII ހީދަ ކުރަނި v. finishes; accomplishes: spends (time, money)

5071 HEENA ހީނަ n. large cold chisel (cf. fuk-kaři)

5072 HEENII ހީނި v. will laugh (future of henii)

5073 HEENENII ހީނެނީ v. is trained, trains (intr.); (of wood) is shaped; (of oil) is expressed (heeni teo, expressed oil) (invol. of haananii)

5074 HEE-MAS ހީމަސް n. artificial baitfish

5075 HEERIYAA KURANII ހީރިޔާ ކުރަނީ v. tacks (naut.)

5076 HEERENII ހީރެނީ v. makes an animal noise (e.g. brays): (slang , of people) weeps ; Caus., heeruvanii , makes to cry or to feel resentment; (slang) defeats crushingly, takes the micky

5077 HEELA- MEELA VANII ހީލަމީލަ ވަނީ v. enjoys oneself (doublet) [H. mēlā, a fair]

5078 HEEVALLAA ހީވައްލާ excl. 'ready!' [U. hū + Allah]

5079 HEEVUM ހީވުން v. disarranging, raking up (v.n. of haavanii)

5080 HEEḶI ހީޅި n. bushy edge of an island: heeḷiyaa jehigen, adjacent to the coast

5081 HOI ހޮއި n. hollow portion (e.g. inside of bamboo stalk)

5082 HOKII ހޮކީ n. hockey: hokii mec, hockey match [E. hockey]

5083 HOKENII ހޮކެނީ v. copulates (esp. of animals) [S. hukanne]

5084 -HOKKO -ހޮއްކޮ n. (anc.) ifc. for kokko, younger sibling

5085 HOṬAA (hoṭalek) ހޮޓާ n. hotel, restaurant : hoṭaa-hoṭalugai, in hotels [E. hotel]

5086 HOḌU ހޮޑު n. vomit: h. lanii, vomits (hon., hoḍufuḷu lanii)

5087 HOŇḌALI ހޮނޑަލި n. kind of bait fish, blue sprat, spratelloides delicatulus

5088 HOŇḌU ހޮނޑު n. proboscis (elephant's trunk, insect's antenna) [S. hoňḍa, Skt. śuṇḍā]

5089 HOTVE ހޮތްވެ v. chose (for hovi-eve]

5090 HOŇDI ހޮނޑި n. 'porridge' [S. hodi, 'gravy']

5091 HOŇDU ހޮނޑު n . grooves made by a hatchet

5092 HONIHIRU ހޮނިހިރު n. Saturday [S. senasurā(dā), Skt.saṇicara]

5093 HONINMA ހޮނިންމަ n. northeast

5094 HONU ހޮނު n. thunderbolt : rukakař h. aḷaifi, the lightning struck a coconut tree: honu dagaňḍu, lightning conductor [S. hena, Skt. aśani]

5095 HORU ހޮރު n. hole, burrow (for animals): horuhoru, holes in the ground; ifc. also -haru (kakuni-haru, crab-holes) [?S. hila - but cf. anc. form dura]

5096 HORUPPANII ހޮރުއްޕަނީ See foruppanii

5097 HOVANII ހޮވަނީ v. chooses, sorts out: finds lying around: haňḍuu hovum, winnowing rice (past hovi, hotve : caus. hovvanii : hon. hovvavanii)

5098 HOHAḶU / HOHAḶA (HOHOḶU) ހޮހަޅު - ހޮހަޅަ (ހޮހޮޅު) n. cave

5099 HOḶAAŘI ހޮޅާރި See hoḷu-ař̌i

5100 HOḶI ހޮޅި n. 1. hollow rod, pipe: (kitchen) chimney; hoḷi jahanii, fits chimney: drinking straw; disc, record; hoḷi lum, (of waves) arching; hoḷi-gaňḍu, record, disc: hoḷigaňḍu jahanii, plays record; blowpipe for the fire (uˇdunař fumee h.): hoḷi-buri, striplight tube; hoḷi-raaḷu naganii, arching waves arise

2. Malabari (pl., Hoḷiin) (cf. Sooḷiyaa)

5101 HOḶU ހޮޅު n. trunk of screwpine: hoḷu-ař̌i (hoḷaař̌i), public bench of screwpine (usu. on the shore): hoḷu-gaňḍu, screwpine trunk, (met.) aged man

5102 HOOK GOVANII ހޫކް ގޮވަނީ v. says high-pitched 'ho!' as warning (if climbing trees overlooking latrines): hook govaa kessum, whooping cough [excl., cf. hoo-hoo]

5103 HOOGUḶAA (-aaek) ހޫގުޅާ n. a black seabird, shearwater

5104 HOOJAA KURANII ހޯޖާ ކުރަނީ v. castrates [U. khoja]

5105 HOODANII ހޯދަނީ v. searches for, seeks; procures, earns (hon. hooddavanii): hoodaigatum, searching hurriedly: (invol.) hoodeen annanii, will be procurable [S. hoyanne, ? Skt. śōdhayati or T. sōti-]

5106 IIOODDUM ހޯއްދުން n. good appearance, good countenance : h. huri, well seeming: h. nubai, evil-looking (hooduvum, caus. v.n. of hoodanii)

5107 HOODDEVUM ހޯއްދެވުން v. seeking (hon.) (v.n. of hooddavanii) [hoodanii]

5108 HOONASSAA GAA ހޯނައްސާ ގާ n. stone shelf outside a mosque for depositing things

5109 HOONU ހޯނު n. gecko [S. hūnā, ?Skt. śiśunāga]

5110 HOO-BOO ހޯބޯ n. noise of a large crowd: hooboo lanii, makes such a noise [onom.]

5111 HOOMA ހޯމަ n. Monday [H. sōm, Skt. sōma, moon]

5112 HOORA ހޯރަ n. frigate bird: hoora-fiya, wings of frigatebird; smocking made in the shape of the wingspan

5113 HOOLI ހޯލި n. useless twigs [for fooli]

5114 HOOS ހޯސް onom. sound of splashing or pouring: hoos laafaa, makes sound of splashing or pouring (as of rain): also of sniffing or smelling

5115 HOO HOO ހޯހޯ excl. stop! hoohoo govanii, calls 'stop!'

ރ ŘA-VIYANI, the 2nd letter of the Maldivian alphabet

Řaviyani atoḷu, Miladunmaḍulu atoll North, the second atoll from the north

5116 ŘA-VIYANI ރަވިޔަނި n. the letter Ř in the Maldivian alphabet

5117 -ŘE -ރެ (v.) imperative ending: kuraaře, do! deeře, give! [cf. S. -ṭa as imp.]

ޅ ĻA-VIYANI, the 6th letter of the Maldivian alphabet

Ļaviyani atoļu, Faadippoļu (Faadiffuļu) atoll, the sixth atoll from the north. The people of Tuļusduu are said to have lost the distinction between ļaviyani and laamu

5118 ĻA ޅަ adj. younger; childish; weak: ļa aňbu, unripe mangoes: ļa iru, infancy: ļa uňḍali, undeveloped layer round coconut: ļa kujjaa, young child: ļa gas, sapling: ļa dari, young child: ļa duvasvaru, childhood: ļa fat, tender leaves: ļa fan, green palmfronds: ļa fangi, green thatch: ļa furaa, adolescence: ļa bees, tonic medicines: ļa maa, tender flowers: ļa ruk, young coconut trees: ļa soru, young chap: ļa haňḍuu, unripe 'porridge rice': ļa hit, foolish heart; used in proper names : Ļa-tuttu, younger male: Ļatuttiidi (m.) for Ļatuttu Diidii: Ļa-diidii (f.), younger Didi lady: Ļa-siidii, young sayyid: ļa-kam, childishness: ļa-baala, young and plump (healthy): ļaňdoļu, young and plump (of children, or trees); maa ļa-ee, (of thread) is very soft: umurun ehaa ļa nama ves, though so young in age; ļa aļanii, ļa fangi aļanii, puts green matting below cargo: ļa fangi jahanii, puts matting at side of cargo: ļa eccek aļanii, picks poor quality fruit, i.e.does something badly
[S. ļā, ?Skt. *ṛdu, soft]

5119 ĻAI KURANII ޅައި ކުރަނީ v. softens up the body, makes it receptive (e.g. with boňḍibat): ļaivanii, (of weather) clouds over [ļa]

5120 ĻAIMAGU ޅައިމަގު n. name of an island in Řaviyani atoll

5121 ĻA-VIYANI ޅަވިޔަނި n. the letter Ļ in the Maldivian alphabet

5122 ĻAAŇBU ޅާނބު n. ring or thong for toddy tappers to climb, or to fasten oars to tholepins

5123 ĻIŇDU ޅިނދު n. small of the back, back of hips (ļiňdu-mati): junction of blade and handle (of knife or oar)

5124 ĻIYA ޅިޔަ n. strips (of fish, or bark), a 'cut': ļ. jahanii, cuts in strips to the bone each side of a fish: ļ. aļanii, cuts strips of bark

5125 ĻIYANU ޅިޔަނު n. brother- in -law, sister-in -law (ļiyan bee, ļiyan kokko) [Malayaalam, aļiyan]

5126 ḶIS ޅިސް n. dowelling : ḷis lanii, inserts dowelling: (met.) ḷis jehenii, overeats

5127 ḶII ޅީ n. ḷii- goyye, daughter- in -law: ḷii- darifuḷu (hon., ḷii- darikaňbalun), daughter-in-law [ḷiyanu, ? cf.S. lēli]

5128 ḶEM ޅެމް n. learned poetry, poetry in general: ḷem-veri, writer of learned poetry

5129 ḶEEŇBUU (ḷeeňbulek) ޅޭނބޫ n. kind of tree, stachytarpheta sp. (varieties: maa ḷ., trichodesma zeylanicum ; kaři l., achyranthes aspera; fen ḷ.)

5130 ḶOS (ḷohek) ޅޮސް n. a tall weak timber tree, pisonia grandis: (met.) a stupid man: ḷos uňdooli, a weak position: ḷohaaru, an antiseptic made from this tree